NON-COMPETITION INTERESTS IN EU ANTITRUST LAW

This book is the first to empirically examine the role of non-competition interests (public policy) in the enforcement of the EU's prohibition on anti-competitive agreements. Based on an original quantitative and qualitative database of more than 3,100 cases, this book records all of the public enforcement actions of Article 101 TFEU taken by the European Commission, EU Courts, and the national competition authorities and courts of five representative member states (France, Germany, Hungary, the Netherlands, and the United Kingdom). The book not only exposes explicit tools in which non-competition interests played a role but also sheds light on the 'dark matter' of balancing, namely invisible forms of balancing triggered by the institutional and procedural setup of the competition enforcers. Moreover, it contributes to the empirical-legal study of various other aspects of EU competition law enforcement, such as its objectives, the more economic approach, decentralised enforcement, and the functioning and success of Regulation 1/2003.

Or Brook is Lecturer of Competition Law and Deputy Director of the Center for Business Law and Practice (CBLP) at the University of Leeds. She is also the Director of the UK branch of the International Association of Competition Law Scholars (ASCOLA). She holds bachelor's degrees in economics and law, both from the Hebrew University of Jerusalem (Honors), a master's degree in EU competition law and regulation (Honors), and a PhD in law from the University of Amsterdam.

GLOBAL COMPETITION LAW AND ECONOMICS POLICY

This series publishes monographs highlighting the interdisciplinary and multijurisdictional nature of competition law, economics, and policy. Global in coverage, the series should appeal to competition and antitrust specialists working as scholars, practitioners, and judges.

Non-Competition Interests in EU Antitrust Law

AN EMPIRICAL STUDY OF ARTICLE 101 TFEU

OR BROOK
University of Leeds

CAMBRIDGE
UNIVERSITY PRESS

CAMBRIDGE
UNIVERSITY PRESS

University Printing House, Cambridge CB2 8BS, United Kingdom

One Liberty Plaza, 20th Floor, New York, NY 10006, USA

477 Williamstown Road, Port Melbourne, VIC 3207, Australia

314–321, 3rd Floor, Plot 3, Splendor Forum, Jasola District Centre, New Delhi – 110025, India

103 Penang Road, #05–06/07, Visioncrest Commercial, Singapore 238467

Cambridge University Press is part of the University of Cambridge.

It furthers the University's mission by disseminating knowledge in the pursuit of education, learning, and research at the highest international levels of excellence.

www.cambridge.org
Information on this title: www.cambridge.org/9781108837606
DOI: 10.1017/9781108946674

First published 2022

A catalogue record for this publication is available from the British Library.

Library of Congress Cataloging-in-Publication Data
NAMES: Brook, Or, 1985- author.
TITLE: Non-competition interests in EU antitrust law : an empirical study of Article 101 TFEU / Or Brook, University of Leeds.
OTHER TITLES: Non-competition interests in European Union antitrust law
DESCRIPTION: Cambridge, United Kingdom ; New York, NY : Cambridge University Press, 2022. | Series: Global competition law and economics policy | Based on author's thesis (doctoral - Universiteit van Amsterdam, 2019) issued under title: Coding non-competition interests under Article 101 TFEU. | Includes bibliographical references and index.
IDENTIFIERS: LCCN 2021037848 (print) | LCCN 2021037849 (ebook) | ISBN 9781108837606 (hardback) | ISBN 9781108931229 (paperback) | ISBN 9781108946674 (epub)
SUBJECTS: LCSH: Antitrust law–European Union countries. | Treaty Establishing the European Economic Community (1957 March 25). Article 101.
CLASSIFICATION: LCC KJE6456 .B766 2022 (print) | LCC KJE6456 (ebook) | DDC 343.2407/21–dc23
LC record available at https://lccn.loc.gov/2021037848
LC ebook record available at https://lccn.loc.gov/2021037849

ISBN 978-1-108-83760-6 Hardback

Contents

Figures

Tables

Acknowledgements

Destiny, as Carlos Ruiz Zafón once said, does not usually do home visits. You just have to go for it. The writing of this book certainly involved a number of just-go-for-it moments. Beyond the obvious geographical move(s), it also entailed going back to academia, diving into the mysteries of EU law and culture, and moving away from my natural comfort zones. Just going for it has, undoubtedly, led me through some of the most exciting years of my life, largely due to the amazing community and environment accompanying it.

During the writing of my PhD thesis at the University of Amsterdam, which led to this book, I was blessed with the invaluable supervision and encouragement of two true role models, Kati Cseres and Christina Eckes. I cannot thank you enough for making me feel like I knew what I was doing, even when I didn't, and for your continuous guidance. I am also incredibly thankful to the members of my reading committee – Alessio Pacces, Giorgio Monti, Ioannis Lianos, Jonathan Zeitlin, Rein Wesseling, and Suzanne Kingston – for their detailed and generous comments, their ongoing support, and making the defence of the thesis an unforgettable event.

My PhD years turned out to be actually enjoyable(!) due to the supportive intellectual environment at the Law Faculty in Amsterdam, and my inspiring and diverse colleagues at the Amsterdam Centre for European Law and Governance (ACELG). Candida Leone, Karoline Haug, Anna van Duin, Elina Demertzi, and Teresa Cabrita, I am especially grateful for your academic, emotional, and gastronomic support, as well as for being my (often not metaphorical) home. I could not imagine a more incredible group of friends.

This book also reflects the subsequent development of my research, developed during my time as a lecturer of competition law at the Centre for Business Law and Practice (CBLP) at the University of Leeds. I am grateful to Pinar Akman, Peter Whelan, and Konstantinos Stylianou for their guidance and thoughtful advice and for making Leeds my new academic home. Special thanks are due to Andreas Stephan, Christopher Townley, Francisco Costa-Cabral, Magali Eben, and Oles

Andriychuk for their illuminating conversations and comments in various stages of this research.

This book is dedicated to my parents, Alan and Irit, and to my grandmother, Bracha, for inspiring me, by way of example, to take chances and not be afraid to just go for it. And to Alon, for his continued support through space and time, notwithstanding his continuous protests that I should become a City lawyer.

Definitions

	The definition is further elaborated in	Chapter	Section
Article 101 TFEU	Articles 101 TFEU (ex 81 EC 85 EEC) and 53 EEA	1	1.3.2.1
Article 101 TFEU enforcement actions	Public enforcement of Article 101 TFEU in EU, mixed, and purely national cases	1	1.3.2.1
Balancing	The process of reconciling between competition and non-competition interests	1	1.2.2
Competition enforcer(s)	NCAs, the Commission, and EU and national Courts	1	1.3.2.2
Competition interests	The protection of the competitive process and structure	1	1.2.1
Database	The database of cases forming the basis of the empirical findings of this study	1	1.3.2
Direct economic benefits	Cost and qualitative efficiencies that occur to direct or indirect users of the product or service covered by the agreement	2	2.2.3.1
Enforcement periods	(i) Foundation period (1962–1977); (ii) workable competition period (1978–1987); (iii) economic social and political EU era (1988–April 2004); (iv) post-modernisation era (May 2004–2017)	2	2.5
EU cases	Enforcement actions of Article 101 TFEU alone, without the national equivalent provision	1	1.3.2.1
EU Courts	The GC and CJEU	1	1.3.2
Explicit-substantive balancing tools	Accounting for non-competition interests by applying Article 101(3) TFEU individual exemptions/exceptions, BERs, Article 101(1) exceptions, and some of the national balancing tools	1	1.1.2
Five NCAs	The NCAs of France, Germany, Hungary, the Netherlands, and the UK	1	1.3.2.2

(continued)

(continued)

	The definition is further elaborated in	*Chapter*	*Section*
Implicit-procedural balancing tools	Accounting for non-competition interests by exercising the competition enforcers' detection, target, instrument, or outcome discretion (priority setting choices)	1	1.1.2
Indirect economic benefits	Cost and qualitative efficiencies that do not occur in the market in which the agreement takes place or has direct impact	2	2.2.3.1
Mixed cases	National enforcement actions of Article 101 TFEU and the national equivalent provision	1	1.3.2.1
Modernisation	The substantive, procedural, and institutional pillars of modernisation of EU competition law	1	1.1.1
National balancing tools	Unique national laws of Member States that account for non-competition interests	1	1.1.2
National courts	Relevant national court exercising judicial review over Article 101 TFEU enforcement actions	1	1.3.2.2
Non-competition interests	All interests, except competition interests (as defined above)	1	1.2.1
Non-economic benefits	Benefits that are not directly related to the characteristics of the product or service of the agreement in question	2	2.2.3.1
Objectives of EU competition policy	Maintenance of economic freedom, market integration, and economic efficiency	2	2.2.1
Policy-linking clauses	EU Treaty clauses requiring the EU institutions to consider public policy interests	2	2.5.3.2
Purely national cases	Enforcement actions of the national equivalent provision of Article 101 TFEU alone	1	1.3.2.1

Abbreviations

ACM	Autoriteit Consument & Markt (NL)
AG	advocate general
BER	block exemption regulation
CAT	Competition Appeals Tribunal (UK)
CFI	Court of First Instance
CJEU	Court of Justice of the European Union
CMA	Competition and Markets Authority (UK)
Commission	European Commission
DG COMP	Directorate-General for Competition
ECN	European Competition Network
ECSC	European Coal and Steel Committee
EEC	European Economic Community
EU	The European Union
GC	General Court
GVH	Gazdasági Versenyhivatal (HU)
ICN	International Competition Network
IPRs	intellectual property rights
MFN	most favoured nation clause
MIF	multilateral interchange fee
NCA	National Competition Authority
NMa	Nederlandse Mededingingsautoriteit (NL)
OECD	Organisation for Economic Co-operation and Development
OFT	Office of Fair Trading (UK)
RPM	resale price maintenance
SGEI	Services of General Economic Interest
TEU	Treaty on the European Union

TFEU	Treaty on the Functioning of the European Union
Treaty(ies)	The Treaty on the European Union and the Treaty on the Functioning of the European Union, as amended by the Lisbon Treaty
UNCTAD	United Nation Conference on Trade and Development

1

Introduction and Methodology

1.1 INTRODUCTION

1.1.1 *Research Question*

'I have never known much good done by those who affected to trade for the public good', stated Adam Smith in his 1776 *Wealth of Nations*; 'it is an affectation, indeed, not very common among merchants, *and very few words need be employed* in dissuading them from it'.[1] While Smith's work has fundamentally inspired the economic theory underlying (European Union – EU) competition law, this statement does not reflect the EU state of affairs. On the contrary, much ink has been spilled over the question of whether – and, if so, how – non-competition interests should or could be taken into account to justify an otherwise anti-competitive agreement prohibited by Article 101 TFEU (Treaty on the Functioning of the European Union). For lack of a better term, this process is referred to in this book as the *balancing* of competition and non-competition interests ('balancing').[2]

The story behind Article 101 TFEU balancing is, to a large extent, the tale of the development of EU competition law and policy itself.[3] It can be traced as far back as 1957, when Article 101 TFEU (formerly Article 85 EEC - The Treaty establishing the European Economic Community was first included in the Rome Treaty establishing the European Community. The vague wording of the Article suggests that there is room for consideration of non-competition interests, but it details neither the precise extent of such balancing nor the test guiding it. Over the years, the Council, Commission, EU Courts, and European Parliament have repeatedly endorsed consideration of non-competition interests – such as employment, environment, and culture – within the enforcement of Article 101 TFEU. They have emphasised

[1] Emphasis added (Smith, 1937, 572).

[2] On the different meanings of balancing in EU competition law, see Section 1.2.2.

[3] See Chapter 2.

that EU competition law is not an end unto itself, but rather an instrument for achieving the EU Treaty's economic and social goals.[4] Despite this, the rationale, method, and limits for considering non-competition interests remain persistently subject to political discussion. Favouring consensus over clarity, the EU institutions and the Member States have never codified the Article's goals or defined a comprehensive balancing framework in EU primary or secondary law.

At the same time, in the past, this practice had rather limited consequences. Article 101 TFEU was mostly applied to purely private situations and was not fully enforced in regulated and liberalised sectors that have traditionally been considered to be part of the public realm. This had resulted in narrow areas of conflict between competition and non-competition interests.[5] Moreover, the enforcement structure was well suited to address those conflicts. Under the old enforcement regime of Regulation 17/62, all agreements were notified to the Commission prior to their implementation for the purpose of receiving an exemption. The Commission balanced competition and non-competition interests in a centralised and *ex-ante* manner. Although the Commission did not develop a set of balancing principles, undertakings across the EU learned about the compatibility of their agreements with Article 101 TFEU prior to their implementation.

Therefore, the debate over the role of non-competition interests was only revived around the turn of the millennium, when the Commission advocated a comprehensive three-pillared reform to the enforcement of EU competition law (the 'modernisation'). As elaborated below, each of the three pillars raised fundamental questions as to the role of non-competition interests in the enforcement of Article 101 TFEU.[6]

Under the first *substantive pillar of modernisation*, the Commission adopted a set of guidelines and notices introducing more stringent economic thinking to EU competition law and policy. Those policy papers offered a new interpretation of Article 101 TFEU, which considerably reduced the role of non-competition interests under the Article. According to this new approach, Article 101 TFEU must be understood as directed at the protection of competition as a means of enhancing consumer welfare. Subsequently, many non-competition interests that had previously been taken into account under Article 101 TFEU were no longer applicable in the Commission's view, at least to the extent they could not be expressed in efficiency or monetary terms.

The Commission's new approach encountered a two-front opposition: First, from a constitutional perspective, the compatibility of the Commission's new approach with EU law is, at the very least, questionable. The limited role of non-competition interests cannot be squared with the EU Courts' earlier case law on balancing.

4 For example, former Competition Commissioner Karel van Miert (1993, 1). See also *Ibid.*

5 See Section 2.5.3.1.

6 The three pillars of modernisation and their effects on balancing are elaborated in Section 2.5.4.

Legally and hierarchically, the Commission is not competent to alter the substantive scope of the EU competition provisions by means of soft-law policy papers.

Second, from a political perspective, the development of the EU has created new areas of conflict between competition and non-competition interests. In particular, as more and more traditional public sectors of the economy become subject to EU competition law, the Commission has to balance the protection of competition against the Member States' sovereignty as a reflection of their national public interests. The tension between competition and non-competition interests was pronounced following economic and societal upheavals brought about by the economic crisis of 2008, the rise of populist movements from the beginning of the 2010s, Brexit, and the coronavirus pandemic. Questions on how to strike the right balance have been raised in the context of regulating online platforms and Big Tech, the growing demand to consider sustainability considerations in market regulation, and the development of the EU's industrial policy to compete with foreign competition supported by national subsidies. All of those challenges bring to the forefront new questions about the desirable boundaries of EU competition law.

To make matters even more complicated, the balancing also transformed in the wake of the procedural and institutional pillars of modernisation. In parallel with the substantive modernisation, Regulation 1/2003, which entered into force in May 2004, swept away the old centralised notification regime in favour of radical institutional and procedural reform. Under the *institutional pillar of modernisation*, the enforcement of Article 101 TFEU became decentralised; national competition authorities (NCAs) and courts were entrusted with powers allowing them to fully apply Article 101 TFEU. To this end, NCAs exercise discretionary powers to balance competition and non-competition interests. Since the Commission's notices and guidelines are binding on the Commission alone, NCAs may adopt diverging interpretations where EU primary and secondary laws and the EU Courts' case law do not prescribe otherwise and subject to the duty of sincere cooperation anchored Article 4(3) TEU (Treaty on the European Union).[7] NCAs enjoy a wide margin of discretion to shape their national approaches to balancing based on their respective legal, economic, and social traditions. Accordingly, this decentralisation, coupled with the lack of a clear balancing framework, bears the serious risk that Article 101 TFEU is not enforced in a uniform manner across the EU.[8]

The *procedural pillar of modernisation* further aggravates this risk. Under the realm of Regulation 1/2003, undertakings no longer give notification of their

[7] The impact of Article 4(3) TEU on the Member States' and national enforcers' discretion to adopt diverging balancing interpretations is further discussed in Sections 3.6.3.1 and 5.2.2.

[8] Section 2.5.4.2 argues that one of the motivations for introducing the substantive modernisation was to combat this risk. The more economic approach attempted to rebrand Article 101(3) TFEU as an objective tool facilitating economic assessment that is devoid of national political considerations.

agreements prior to implementation. Rather, the Regulation has transformed Article 101(3) TFEU into a directly applicable provision. Undertakings must self-assess the compatibility of their agreements with Article 101 TFEU, and particularly, they must evaluate whether non-competition interests can justify an otherwise anti-competitive agreement. This self-assessment regime is based on the assumption that the principles governing the enforcement of Article 101 TFEU are sufficiently clear, precise, and unconditional. In such circumstances, the lack of a coherent and uniform framework to guide balancing runs counter to the very premise of the self-assessment regime, thereby raising serious concerns about legal uncertainty and fragmentation.

Against this background, this book addresses the following research questions: *How have the rationale, method, and limits for balancing competition and non-competition interests in the enforcement of Article 101 TFEU evolved in the first sixty years of its existence? How has this process of evolution affected the objectives of Regulation 1/2003, namely effectiveness, uniformity, and legal certainty? And what role should non-competition interests play in order to conform to such objectives?*

1.1.2 *Novel Approach*

An impressive array of legal scholarship has already explored the role of non-competition interests under Article 101 TFEU and the shift in the Commission's approach from doctrinal, historical, constitutional, and economic perspectives.[9] Yet, thus far, only limited attention has been given to the manner in which the EU and national competition enforcers have actually administered this balancing in practice.

Studying balancing as applied in practice is vital for understanding the factual and analytical richness of questions that come before competition authorities and courts, how undertakings structure their arguments, and how the authorities reason their decisions. It is especially important in the context of the EU, where – in the lack of a designated balancing framework in primary and secondary laws – the balancing rules are developed in the decisions of the competition authorities and the judgements of EU and national courts.

9 For example, see Frazer (1990), Gyselen (1994, 2002), Wesseling (1999, 77–113), Ehlermann (2000), Mortelmans (2001), Schmidt (2001), Monti (2002, 2007, 88–123), Odudu (2006, 160–174), Sufrin (2006, 933–936), Schweitzer (2007), Semmelmann (2008a), Townley (2009, 2018, 141–176), Parret (2009), Petit (2009, 6–9), Vedder (2009), Lavrijssen (2010), Prosser (2010), Kingston (2011, 97–194), Ginsburg and Haar (2014), Witt (2012, 2016b, 160–174), Gerber (2012), Van Rompuy (2012), Kieran (2013), Lianos (2013), Maziarz (2014), Gerbrandy (2015), Sauter (2016, 64–75), Bailey (2016), Claassen and Gerbrandy (2016), Talbot (2016), Schinkel and Spiegel (2016), Kloosterhuis (2017), Monti and Mulder (2017), Loozen (2019), and Dunne (2020).

Against this backdrop, this study takes a novel combination of empirical, evaluative, and normative approaches. It contributes to the existing scholarship on the role of non-competition interests under Article 101 TFEU in four ways.

First, this study examines the role of non-competition interests on the basis of an *original large quantitative and qualitative database*. Comprising more than 3,100 enforcement actions, the database was composed by applying systematic content analysis ('coding') on *all* Article 101 TFEU public enforcement actions taken by the Commission, the EU Courts, and the NCAs and courts of five representative Member States[10] (the 'competition enforcers') from the creation of the EEC in 1957 through 2017. Using a bottom-up approach, it lays down a comprehensive description of the development of the principles, rules, and concepts governing balancing in practice over the years and across the Member States.[11]

With this first contribution, this study establishes a robust empirically based point of reference for reflection on the existing balancing practices. The empirical findings are used to identify previously unnoticed balancing patterns, to verify and refute previous theories on balancing that have been based on case studies, and to draw innovative policy recommendations.

Second, the bottom-up approach applied by this study has identified *new balancing tools* used by competition enforcers to account for non-competition interests, which were not yet explored. Traditionally, Article 101(3) TFEU has been seen as the main Treaty provision for balancing non-competition interests within Article 101 TFEU and was the focus of most scholarship. Most scholars argue that since Article 101(3) TFEU defence was not accepted by the Commission following modernisation, non-competition interests no longer play a role in the enforcement of Article 101 TFEU or at least in the Commission's practice.

This conclusion, however, is *not* supported by the empirical findings presented in this book. This study reveals that Article 101(3) TFEU is certainly not the only legal tool to take account of non-competition interests. In fact, far from being the primary balancing tool, Article 101(3) TFEU can be classified as one of the following five types of balancing tools:[12]

(1) Article 101(3) TFEU individual exemptions/exceptions
(2) Block exemption regulations (BERs)
(3) Article 101(1) TFEU exceptions

[10] The five Member States are France, Germany, Hungary, the Netherlands, and the UK. On the jurisdiction selection, see Section 1.3.2.2.

[11] On the methodology and database, see Section 1.3.

[12] Monti (2007, 113–117) and Van Rompuy (2012, 229–281) have identified various methods to integrate non-competition interests via Article 101(1) and (3) TFEU and commitments. By systematically mapping the enforcement practices, this study builds on their observations and points to additional balancing tools and methods.

(4) Unique national balancing tools originating from rules adopted by NCAs and Member States
(5) Enforcement discretion and priority setting choices of the competition enforcers

In addition to the above, the Treaties exclude certain sectors from the scope of EU competition rules. This includes trade in nuclear materials, arms, ammunition, war materials, and, prior to the expiration of the ECSC Treaty in July 2002, also coal and steel agreements. The Treaties also enact special rules for the agriculture sector.[13] Those types of exceptions are not discussed in this study.

With this second contribution, the empirical approach followed by this study not only assists in identifying *explicit-substantive* forms of balancing in which competition enforcers have overtly considered non-competition interests (i.e. the balancing tools of Article 101(1) and (3), BERs, and some national balancing tools) but also shows that balancing has taken place in an *implicit-procedural* manner, in the competition enforcers' choices *not to apply* the Article to agreements that promote non-competition interests, or by settling such cases by means of alternative enforcement mechanisms (e.g. negotiated remedies, informal opinions, or sector regulation). As such, the book is the first to shed light on the *dark matter of balancing*, namely invisible forms of balancing triggered by the institutional set-up and the specific enforcement procedures of the Commission and various NCAs.

The book demonstrates that the choice between the various balancing tools is not neutral. Each tool assigns a different weight and function to non-competition interests. The book points to a great divergence in the frequency with which the Commission, NCAs, and EU and national courts have invoked and accepted the various balancing tools, as well as in the legal and economic tests that guided their application. Those differences, the book submits, impacted the rationale, method, and limits for balancing and the manner in which balancing has conformed to the objectives of the enforcement.

Third, the book studies *national balancing practices*. The study of national balancing is particularly significant following the entry into force of Regulation 1/2003, by which the vast majority of the public enforcement of Article 101 TFEU – and, consequently, of balancing – takes place in front of NCAs.[14] Nevertheless, to date, national enforcement practices have gone predominantly unnoticed. Most of the scholarship has been confined to the balancing prescribed at the EU level, as applied by the Commission and EU Courts.[15]

This study points to two parallel trends in the context of national balancing. In the first place, the book shows that given the lack of a clear and binding EU framework for balancing, national enforcers devised distinctive interpretations on how to apply the balancing tools of Article 101(1) and (3) TFEU and the BERs. They differed in

[13] See, for example, Goyder (2009, 126–137) and Bailey and Whish (2015, 1017–1021).
[14] See Section 2.5.4.1.
[15] See note 9 and Gerber (2012, 89–91).

their interpretations of the objectives of Article 101 TFEU, the types of economic or non-economic benefits that can be taken into account, the balancing method, the intensity of control, and the frequency in which they applied the different types of balancing tools.

In the second place, the national approaches have also led to the creation of unique national balancing tools. Some Member States have shielded certain agreements from the prohibition of Article 101 TFEU by adopting rules that explicitly or implicitly limit the enforcement of EU competition law in favour of promoting non-competition interests. Consequently, the decentralisation of the enforcement has afforded the Member States a new opportunity to introduce national balancing principles that supplement the EU balancing framework.

With this third contribution, the book provides a unique perspective on the enforcement challenges in the era of decentralised enforcement and discusses the compatibility and limits of the national balancing practices and tools. Relying on a functional comparative law approach, it acknowledges that EU competition law is applied by different enforcers, which vary in their legal and political structures, competencies, and interpretations of the law. As such, it is sensitive to the implication of such diversity in the decentralised enforcement regime of EU competition law.

Fourth, in addition to the focus on the role of non-competition interests, the book advances the very *limited empirical study of EU law in general, and of EU competition law in particular*. In fact, this is one of the first studies to present a complete qualitative and quantitative analysis of Article 101 TFEU formal and informal enforcement actions and the development of the enforcement practices throughout the years.[16] Hence, in addition to the study of balancing, the empirical findings may contribute to the legal and empirical study of the more economic approach, decentralised enforcement, EU multilevel governance, the objectives of EU competition law, and the functioning and success of EU competition law following the entry into force of Regulation 1/2003's reform.

With the combination of the above four contributions, the book establishes a fundamental point of reference for reflecting on or reforming existing balancing practices.

1.1.3 *Structure and Argument*

The book is structured as follows. Chapter 1 introduces the research topic and context and sets out the definitions and the methodology guiding the study.

[16] There is some quantitative empirical research on the enforcement of Article 101 TFEU. For example, Carree, Günster, and Schinkel (2010) surveyed Commission decisions, and Massadeh (2015) examined the practices of UK, French, and German NCAs. In addition, Ibáñez Colomo (2018) and Ibáñez Colomo and Kalintiri (2020) undertook a comprehensive study of the Commission and EU Courts' formal enforcement practices.

Chapter 2 provides a historical overview of the development of Article 101 TFEU balancing to frame and identify the uncertainties surrounding it. The chapter begins with the EU primary and secondary law provisions, illustrating that they do not prescribe a clear balancing framework. Against this backdrop, the chapter shows that the balancing principles have been greatly shaped by the practices of the Commission and EU Courts. It affirms that the development of the balancing principles is best understood by sorting the practices into four enforcement periods, which are then explored throughout the empirical chapters of the book. In addition to the developments at the EU level, the chapter devotes special attention to the competition law set-up and balancing approaches of each of the five Member States examined in the study.

Chapters 3–7 present and evaluate the empirical findings. Each chapter first provides an empirical and legal overview of one of the five types of balancing tools presented above, mapping the quantitative and qualitative aspects of balancing as applied in practice. They highlight the frequency of invoking and accepting the balancing tool, the types of benefits that were taken into account, the balancing method, and the intensity of control. Moreover, each chapter examines the role of EU and national courts in scrutinising the application of the balancing tools. They illustrate that the courts have adopted diverse approaches to balancing, which have in turn left the Commission and NCAs with different levels of discretion. Finally, each chapter evaluates how the balancing tool has evolved over the years.

Chapters 3–5 first detail the application of the explicit-substantive balancing tools. Chapter 3 studies the balancing function of Article 101(3) TFEU individual exemptions/exceptions. It reveals a great divergence in the frequency with which the Commission, NCAs, and EU and national courts have invoked and accepted Article 101(3) TFEU, as well as their interpretations of the types of relevant benefits, the balancing process, and the intensity of control. Moreover, it uncovers the 'death' of Article 101(3) TFEU defence in the Commission's practice following modernisation.

Chapter 4 focuses on the balancing embedded in BERs. This balancing tool has received limited attention in scholarship, especially following modernisation. The chapter demonstrates that BERs were initially introduced to EU competition law to accommodate the enormous number of notifications that resulted from the set-up of the old enforcement regime. Although this workload-reducing function perished following the entry into force of Regulation 1/2003, the special BER instrument still remains in force. This chapter concludes that this may be related to the fact that BERs play, and have played in the past, an important role in addition to their administrative function. BERs, like Article 101(3) TFEU individual exemptions, may also reflect a form of balancing between competition and non-competition interests. They offer a pre-determined, clear balancing rule. This chapter shows that balancing under BERs takes place in both the adoption and the application of a BER. It discusses different types of BERs and the effects of modernisation of BERs in the late 1990s.

Chapter 5 is dedicated to Article 101(1) TFEU balancing tools. It examines tools aimed at balancing competition with state or public interests, such as the state action defence, the notion of undertakings, the Article 106(2) TFEU exception for services of general economic interests, the exception for collective bargaining agreements between employers and employees, and the inherent restriction doctrine. The chapter also studies tools for balancing competition and commercial interests, such as the rule of reason, objectively necessary agreements, ancillary restraints, and the *de minimis* doctrine.

The chapter shows that unlike most of the explicit-substantive balancing tools that are based on EU primary or secondary law and which were largely developed by the Commission, the wording of Article 101(1) TFEU does not explicitly refer to a balancing function. Rather, the balancing tools of Article 101(1) TFEU are predominantly derived from the CJEU's (Court of Justice of the European Union) case law. It reveals that the CJEU introduced those tools to counterbalance the Commission's broad interpretation of what constitutes a restriction of competition falling within the ambit of Article 101(1) TFEU. The Court has held that agreements restricting the commercial freedom of parties might escape the prohibition of Article 101(1) TFEU if they are necessary for attaining social or efficiency-related goals.

In short, Chapters 3–5 demonstrate that prior to the modernisation, the Commission and EU Courts accounted for non-competition interests by reference to the explicit-substantive balancing tools of Article 101(1) and (3) TFEU. They have interpreted those balancing tools as entailing a flexible legal proportionality test, leaving ample room for consideration of non-competition interests on a case-by-case basis. The Commission and Courts did not limit the types of benefits that could justify an exemption and set a low evidential threshold for proving the existence of those overriding benefits.

This has changed upon the modernisation of EU competition law. In line with the Commission's attempts to limit the room for non-competition interests as part of modernisation, the explicit-substantive balancing tools were seldom accepted, or even invoked, after May 2004. These findings could initially be viewed as confirmation of the commonly held view that non-competition interests no longer play a role in the enforcement of Article 101 TFEU.

Nevertheless, Chapters 6 and 7 argue that the consideration of non-competition interests has only *shifted* to national and implicit-procedural balancing tools. Accordingly, Chapter 6 studies the balancing entrenched in unique national rules of the Member States. Those national balancing tools bear significantly on balancing in the decentralised enforcement era, during which almost 90% of Article 101 TFEU enforcement actions have taken place in front of NCAs. This chapter highlights the doubts about the compatibility of those national tools with EU competition law, a topic that has been largely overlooked by legal scholarship.

Chapter 7 examines the implicit-procedural balancing tools, embedded in the exercise of the competition enforcers' enforcement discretion and priority setting powers. Setting enforcement priorities is an inherent feature of any administrative action. It is a necessary precondition for allowing the Commission and NCAs to make effective use of their scarce resources to ensure effective enforcement of Article 101 TFEU. At the same time, enforcement choices are not just about achieving compliance with Article 101 TFEU but are also for determining the scope and boundaries of the Article. To this extent, this chapter shows that the modernisation has entrusted the Commission and NCAs with a new balancing tool in the form of their discretional enforcement powers.

More specifically, the chapter maintains that under the old notification regime, when the Commission had limited discretion to set its enforcement priorities, it was compelled to actively apply the designated balancing tools of Article 101(1) and (3) TFEU. This has prompted an abundance of decisions explaining how and in which circumstances non-competition interests may justify a restriction of competition.

Yet, following the entry into force of Regulation 1/2003, two contradicting effects of modernisation have incentivised the Commission and NCAs to direct their enforcement efforts towards clear-cut infringements of Article 101 TFEU, which are unlikely to be justified by overriding non-competition interests: On the one hand, the more economic approach (substantive pillar of modernisation) has narrowed down the room for the consideration of non-competition interests under the explicit-substantive balancing tools. In parallel, on the other hand, the shift to the decentralised self-assessment enforcement regime (procedural and institutional pillars of modernisation) have incentivised the competition enforcers to focus their enforcement efforts on hard-core restrictions of competition. Those types of restrictions, which were often handled by means of leniency applications and settlements, are unlikely to be justified. The competition enforcers have used their detection, target, instrument, and outcome discretion to decide *not to* enforce Article 101 TFEU against other types of agreements even when they do not meet the conditions for an exception under Article 101(1) and (3) TFEU. As a result, investigations into agreements that raised balancing questions were often settled with negotiated remedies or terminated by closing the probe into the case altogether.

Finally, Chapter 8 reflects on the empirical findings presented in the previous chapters and offers policy recommendations. It points to a remarkable three-fold shift in the role of non-competition interests in the post-modernisation era and concludes that those three shifts have hindered the attainment of the very objectives of Regulation 1/2003, namely, the effectiveness, uniformity, and legal certainty of the enforcement.[17]

First, the chapter points to a shift in the *types of balancing tools* employed in practice, reflecting a transition from explicit-substantive to implicit-procedural

[17] Regulation 1/2003, Preamble 1, 3, 22; Modernisation White Paper (1999), para 43–51. Those objectives also guided the old enforcement regime governed by Regulation 17/62 (see in the Preamble).

balancing tools. It submits that in contrast to the balancing tools of Article 101(1) and (3) TFEU, competition enforcers have a *carte blanche* to account for non-competition interests when applying their enforcement discretion. There is neither a limit on the types of benefits they can take into account nor a legal or economic test that guides the assessment. Consequently, competition enforcers may take into account non-competition interests beyond what would be deemed permissible under the explicit-substantive balancing tools, even in their broad interpretation prior to modernisation. There is no guarantee that the competition and non-competition interests are being balanced and weighed against each other or that the harm to competition will be limited to what is necessary for respecting the non-competition interests.

Second, the chapter uncovers a shift in the *locus of the balancing tools*, transitioning from EU-based to Member States-based balancing. Given the lack of a clear and binding EU framework, national enforcers devised distinctive interpretations on how to apply the explicit-substantive balancing tools and were subject to different national rules when exercising enforcement discretion. Moreover, as described in Chapter 6, the national approaches have also led to the creation of unique national balancing tools. As a result, non-competition interests did not have a uniform role across the EU.

Third, the chapter affirms a shift from an *active to a passive role of the EU Courts* in shaping the balancing principles. It shows that the EU Courts, and especially the CJEU, had an active and leading role in shaping the balancing principles prior to modernisation. In a series of landmark cases, the Courts have laid out the fundamental balancing principles. They shaped the types of benefits that can be recognised under Article 101 TFEU, introduced the balancing standard, interpreted the scope of the BERs, and devised new balancing tools to account for state involvement and commercial interests under Article 101(1) TFEU.

This changed following modernisation. When the Commission embarked on the substantive modernisation in the early 2000s, it also took the reins on the development of the balancing principles. The Commission's new balancing approach, which is clearly incompatible with the CJEU's old case law, had created an urgent need for judgements clarifying the scope of balancing in the post-modernisation era.

This gap, however, was not filled by the EU Courts. On the one hand, the EU Courts did not embrace the Commission's new approach to balancing, at least in part. On the other hand, the Courts have not staked out a clear position on the applicable balancing principles. Departing from their active role in the past, the Courts have missed the opportunity to shape the balancing framework following modernisation.

Combining the above three transitions in balancing, Chapter 8 highlights the great ambiguity surrounding the role of non-competition interests following modernisation and concludes that while the modernisation of EU competition law might have been successful in general, its effect on balancing has been counterproductive.

After identifying the three transitions in balancing and analysing their impacts, the chapter moves to make policy recommendations. It advocates re-shifting the balancing towards the ambit of the explicit-substantive balancing tools and limiting balancing practices by exercising enforcement discretion. An active and transparent application of the explicit-substantive balancing tools, the book maintains, will oblige competition enforcers to clarify many of the open questions surrounding balancing and will facilitate public debate on political issues related to the objectives of Article 101 TFEU, the types of benefits that can be taken into account, the balancing method, and the limits of the implicit and national balancing tools.

1.2 DEFINITIONS

The mystery surrounding the role of non-competition interests is manifested by the lack of consensus over the basic terminology guiding this debate. There are no universally accepted definitions of 'balancing', 'competition', and 'non-competition interests'. Therefore, to structure the debate and set the scene for this study, this section defines those terms for the purposes of this book.

1.2.1 *Competition and Non-Competition Interests*

1.2.1.1 A Narrow Definition

The term *competition interests* is used in this book in a narrow sense. It refers to the *protection of the competitive process and structure as such.*[18] Competition interests thus reflect an objective and independent economic value.

All other interests are referred to as *non-competition interests*. These interests include economic and non-economic values such as consumer welfare, economic efficiency, industrial policy, growth, market and social stability, market integration, environment, and culture. Hence, as further elaborated in Section 2.2.3.1, non-competition interests include both economic benefits (cost and qualitative efficiencies that either affect prices or provide additional non-price value for consumers) and non-economic benefits (non-market driven public policy interests).[19]

In particular, interests that are often attributed to the *objectives of EU competition policy*, namely economic freedom, market integration, and economic welfare, are classified as non-competition interests. Section 2.2.1 shows that those three objectives

[18] Competitive process relates to the dynamic interaction of firms during a specified time frame. Competitive structure refers to a static state of a market during a specific period in time. See Nazzini (2011, 15).

[19] That section demonstrates that this definition matches the classification of benefits drawn up by a group of experts and summarised by the OFT Roundtable on Narrow versus Broad Definition of Benefits (2010). A similar definition is also followed by UNCTAD Coherence Between Competition and Government Policies (2011), 3, which defines competition as 'the pressure exerted in the market by different players in search of market shares and profits. It is a game of outdoing one another in winning customers, so that customers will purchase a given company's goods or services'.

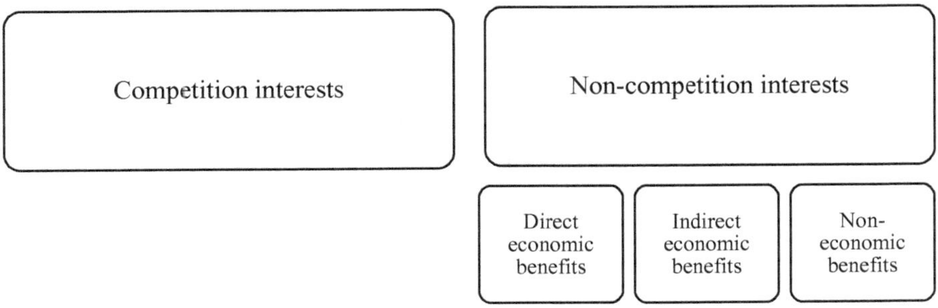

FIGURE 1.1. Competition and non-competition interests

encompass various political-societal values, none of which are directly related to the competitive process or structure as such. The protection of competition interests is an instrument to achieve these outcomes or objectives, which might need to be balanced against other (economic and non-economic) non-competition interests.

This narrow definition of competition interests is represented in Figure 1.1.

The narrow definition of competition interests followed in this book is *not normative*. It represents an agnostic view of the normative question of the role of non-competition interests. It does *not* entail that protecting the competitive structure and process is an end in itself. It does *not* deny that the three objectives of EU competition policy (i.e. consumer welfare, economic freedom, and market integration), or any other interest for that matter, are or should be the overarching aims of EU competition policy, of Article 101 TFEU, or enjoy primacy over competition interests in a specific case.

Put differently, the narrow definition of non-competition interests is not the end of the process of balancing, but only the beginning. It is perfectly acceptable that after acknowledging the harm to the competitive structure and process, a competition enforcer may decide to give preference to the promotion of welfare, economic freedom, market integration, or to the protection of other non-competition interests. As elaborated below, this definition merely recognises from a theoretical and empirical-methodological point of view that the objectives might not be entirely consistent with the promotion of competition or with one another.

This approach is of value to those who believe that the protection of the competitive process and structure should be the main aim of Article 101 TFEU.[20] It also serves those who advocate a consumer welfare centric or a polycentric competition policy, because it allows the various elements that constitute EU competition law and policy to be captured and evaluated. In particular, as will be demonstrated in Chapter 7, the narrow definition of competition interests is well-suited for questioning whether consumer welfare centric or polycentric competition

[20] For an interesting discussion on the benefits of this approach in the context of US antitrust law, see Wu (2018).

policies truly achieve their declared aims and how the institutional set-up and specific enforcement procedures trigger the invisible forms of balancing that derive from the implicit-procedural tools.

In order to reflect the different types of non-competition interests, however, the empirical findings distinguish between economic and non-economic benefits. The narrow approach to the definition of non-competition interests, therefore, does not preclude including or excluding them from further analyses or by scholars who subscribe to a different definition of competition and non-competition interests.

1.2.1.2 Dialectic Approach

The narrow definition of competition interests adhered to in this book reflects the *dialectic approach* to competition law, advocated by and detailed in the work of *Andriychuk*.[21] Dialectics is a method of legal reasoning in which controversy between norms is considered inevitable and productive. Instead of searching for a definition of competition interests that reconciles the various objectives of Article 101 TFEU and EU competition policy as a whole, the dialectic approach focuses on the discourse between the different objectives. Inconsistency between those social and economic objectives is regarded, in and by itself, as an engine that stimulates the development of competition law.[22] The manner in which competition interests interact with non-competition interests is used to reflect on the internal conflicts within the law and to understand the scope of Article 101 TFEU.

Notably, the dialectic approach to the definition of competition interests used in this book departs from those used in previous scholarship on the role of non-competition interests in Article 101 TFEU. Many studies have incorporated into the notion of competition interests, or comparable terms, not only the protection of the competitive process and structure but also some of the objectives of EU competition policy and, particularly, welfare. Those definitions centre on the *outcomes or effects* of competition, and not on the competitive *structure and process* as an independent value. For instance, *Semmelmann*, *Townley*, *Van Rompuy*, and *Dunne* classify efficiency-related considerations as competition interests.[23]

[21] Andriychuk (2010, 2012).

[22] Andriychuk (2010, 156–157) and Lianos (2013, 30).

[23] Semmelmann (2008b, 17) defines 'non-competition goals' as those characterised by an absence of a cost–benefit analysis as their driving force; Townley (2009, 1) defines the term 'public policy objectives' by means of a particular negation to encompass all public policy objectives with the exception of economic efficiency; Van Rompuy (2012, 8) defines 'non-efficiency considerations' as a catchall concept covering any consideration that cannot be strictly confined to economic efficiency; Dunne (2020, 3) uses the term 'public interest concerns' to encompass any application of the competition rules that embraces values that extend beyond the conventional (if disputed) wisdom that competition law aims, in the final analysis, to enhance efficiency.

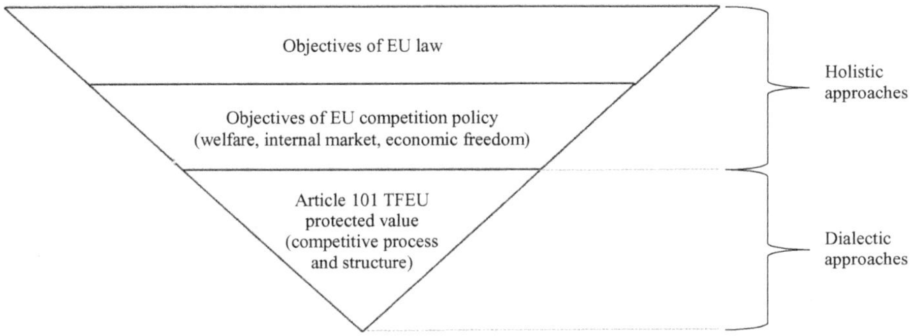

FIGURE 1.2. Dialectic and holistic approaches
The objectives of EU competition policy are detailed in Section 2.2.1, and the protected value of Article 101 TFEU is described in Section 2.2.2.

Monti opts for an even broader definition that includes, in addition to efficiency, economic freedom and market integration.[24]

These broad definitions represent a *holistic approach*. They do not focus on the core value protected by Article 101 TFEU, namely the promotion of competition process and structure. Instead, they define competition interests in light of the overarching objectives of the EU in general and EU competition policy in particular.[25] As elaborated below, under a holistic approach, the definition of competition interests reflects an internal balance between the various economic and social objectives of EU competition policy. Unlike the dialectical approach, such a holistic definition entails a policy choice. It seeks to establish a harmonious homogeneous hierarchy between the competing objectives. Agreements are classified as promoting competition interests to the extent they help attain certain *outcomes*, e.g. enhancing welfare, promoting the single market, and protecting individual freedoms.

The differences between the dialectic and holistic approaches are illustrated in Figure 1.2, which shows that a dialectic approach defines competition interests and assesses balancing in light of the narrow value protected by Article 101 TFEU, i.e. the protection of the competition process and structure itself. In comparison, holistic approaches are result-oriented and focus on the general function the Article serves in the EU legal order.

The following sub-sections maintain that a dialectic approach offers an array of theoretical and methodological advantages for the purpose of the study documented in this book.

1.2.1.3 Theoretical Justifications: The Example of Consumer Welfare

EU primary and secondary laws have not come up with a clear economic or legal theory that fully delimitates the competition interests protected by Article 101 TFEU

[24] Monti (2002, 1064).
[25] Andriychuk (2012, 359).

or which serve to explain the balancing practices. Article 101 TFEU prohibits agreements having as their 'object or effect the prevention, restriction or distortion of *competition* within the internal market', and Regulation 1/2003 declares that the objective of the Article is the 'protection of *competition* on the market'.[26] Yet, the Treaty and Regulation do not explain what competition is.

The EU Courts have also not developed a clear definition. In some cases, the CJEU has alluded to a holistic definition, which ties the protection of competition to its *outcomes*. In a series of cases, the Court declared that the function of the EU competition rules is to 'prevent competition from being distorted *to the detriment of the public interest, individual undertakings and consumers*, thereby *ensuring the well-being of the European Union*'.[27] However, in other cases, the Court has invoked an independent-dialectic *value* of competition, holding that Article 101 TFEU aims to protect 'competition as such'.[28] It should be noted that even when the Court has taken a holistic approach, it has referred to a host of uncommerciable values and not provided a clear standard to define competition interests.

Furthermore, the empirical findings presented in this book show that the interpretations ascribed to the term competition also cannot be fully explained by the economic, legal, or political objectives of the EU's competition policy. Rather, those objectives are widely defined policy preferences that shift over time.[29] The meaning of restriction of competition under Article 101(1) TFEU, the justification for such restriction under Article 101(3) TFEU, and the exercise of enforcement discretion when adopting remedies and setting priorities are constantly evolving and cannot be ascribed to one legal or economic theory of competition. A holistic definition of competition and non-competition interests, therefore, may lead to loss of information, as it does not fully illuminate how the clashing interests are reconciled over time and between jurisdictions.

The theoretical difficulties of using a holistic approach to define competition can be illustrated by the attempt to equate the protection of competition with the maximisation of consumer welfare.[30] The concept of consumer welfare was imported to EU competition law from US antitrust law. It had emerged from the writings of Bork in the mid-1970s and was further developed by the Chicago

[26] Emphasis added. Regulation 1/2003, Preamble 9. See also Section 2.2.1.

[27] Emphasis added. C-52/09 TeliaSonera (2011), para 22, quoting C-46/87 C-227/88 Hoechst (1989), para 25. This was repeated by the GC, for example, in T-458/09 T-171/10 Slovak Telekom (2012), para 38; T-357/06 Bitumen (Netherlands) (2012), para 230; T-325/16 Falcon (2018), para 173; T-705/14 Perindopril (2018), para 306; T-701/14 Perindopril (2018), para 236; T-691/14 Perindopril (2018), para 238; T-682/14 Perindopril (2018), para 167; T-680/14 Perindopril (2018), para 88; T-679/14 Perindopril (2018), para 200.

[28] C-8/08 T-Mobile (2009), para 38; C-501/06P C-513/06P C-515/06P C-519/06P GlaxoSmithKline (2009), para 63; C-68/12 Slovak Banks (2012), para 18. The CJEU's approach is elaborated in Section 2.5.3.2.

[29] Lianos (2013, 3), Talbot (2016, 264).

[30] This will be elaborated in Sections 2.5.4.4 and 3.4.4.1.

School.[31] While this concept has become the cornerstone of both the EU and US systems, it does not have a clear definition. In fact, consumer welfare has been dubbed 'the most abused term in modern antitrust analysis'.[32] It is often used loosely, without the credence of a robust standard economic definition. Nevertheless, there are two main approaches to the definition of consumer welfare:

The first definition equates consumer welfare with the economic concept of *consumer surplus*. This definition refers to the price consumers would be willing to pay for a good or service, less what they actually had to pay. The second definition, which was advocated by Bork, links consumer welfare to the economic concept of *total welfare*.[33] According to this definition, consumer welfare amounts to the aggregate of the consumer and the producer surplus produced by a certain agreement. In addition to benefits for consumers, this definition takes into account the value of the product that was produced less the cost of producing it.

Equating competition interests with either of those definitions of consumer welfare ties the notion of competition to the notion of economic efficiency. It shifts the analysis away from focusing on the protection of the competition process and structure as an independent *value* to seeking to maximise economic welfare as an *outcome*.[34] Other benefits that may result from protecting the competition process and structure – such as the promotion of unquantifiable social objectives – will not be taken into account to the extent they are not reflected in the creation of economic welfare.

The choice between the two definitions of consumer welfare entails a policy preference. The first definition, which focuses on the wealth created for consumers, is sensitive to wealth transfer effects between different members of society – i.e. between consumers and sellers The second definition, which measures the aggregated wealth created for the society, does not take into account distributional concerns and does not distinguish between the effects of an agreement on various types of members of society. An agreement that increases total welfare may nevertheless harm the economic welfare of many other groups in society, such as (vulnerable) consumers or SMEs.[35]

[31] Bork (1978, 107–115). On the development of the consumer welfare standard in the US, see also Brodley (1987), Orbach (2011), Fox (2013), and Melamed and Petit (2019).

[32] Brodley (1987, 1032). See also Motta (2004, 19–22), Geradin (2006, 313), Cseres (2007b, 122), ICN Competition Enforcement and Consumer Welfare (2011, 7–9), Orbach (2011, 134, 137), Keyte (2017), Foer and Durst (2018, 497–499), Townley (2018, 37–40), and European Court of Auditors, Special Report on the Commission's EU Merger Control and Antitrust Proceedings (2020, para 6).

[33] Bork (1978, 90) argued that consumer welfare 'is merely another term for the wealth of the nation'. In the second edition of the book, he continued to defend the position that wealth transfer should not be taken into account, noting that '[t]he distribution of that wealth or the accomplishment of noneconomic goals are the proper subjects of other laws' Bork (1993, 427). See also Orbach (2011, 148–149).

[34] Wu (2018, 2).

[35] Hovenkamp (1982, 5), Farrell and Katz (2006, 6), Foer (2006, 566), Cseres (2007b, 125), ICN Competition Enforcement and Consumer Welfare (2011, 27), and Fox (2013, 2159).

Hence, a mere reference to consumer welfare does not offer a clear and decisive theoretical definition of competition interests, which can be used to explain the limits of competition and how it is balanced against other interests. Rather, it already reflects an internal balance between different economic, social, and political preferences.[36] By equating competition interests with consumer welfare, one may run the risk of overlooking how different competition enforcers have interpreted the notion of consumer welfare when applying Article 101 TFEU and how they have weighted and reconciled tensions between the competing economic, social, and political considerations.

A holistic definition based on a concept of consumer welfare may also distort the study of balancing since the calculation of consumer welfare is not a straightforward task. Measuring the effect of an agreement on consumer welfare can merely provide an 'illusion of certainty'.[37] It merits sophisticated calculations and predictions about past and future consumer behaviour. Rather than a purely mathematical exercise, it necessitates making some assumptions and simplifications. As a result, in many cases, different economic experts present conflicting opinions.[38]

In particular, the definition of consumer welfare under either approach requires determining the relevant period of time in which the consumer or total welfare should materialise and the relevant type of benefit that can be considered in the analysis. In terms of time, some competition enforcers follow a *short-term consumer welfare standard*, which focuses on measuring static efficiency, namely, the optimal distribution of resources among alternative production targets at a certain point in time (typically, between 1 and 3 years). Others observe a *long-term consumer welfare standard* and also take into account dynamic efficiency, namely the increase of welfare over time in light of the incentive to innovate and renew processes and products.[39]

In terms of the relevant types of benefits, competition enforcers that follow a *narrow consumer welfare standard* are limited to calculating parameters related to price, output (quantity, quality, or range), and innovation. A *broad consumer welfare standard* is more flexible, allowing other non-economic benefits that improve living quality to be taken into account within the efficiency framework, such as health and safety, environmental protection, or culture.[40]

36 Section 1.2.2.1 defines this as an economic balancing process.

37 Pitofsky (1979, 1065).

38 Cseres (2007b, 122–123) and ICN Competition Enforcement and Consumer Welfare (2011, 17–36). This was also extensively discussed in the context of US antitrust law. Foer and Durst (2018, 497), for example, have warned that consumer welfare 'is nowhere near as scientific as it sounds'. Wu (2018, 2) added '[e]conomics does not yield answers, but arguments'. Orbach (2011, 136) noted that it can be used to promote ideas that have questionable economic merit, while dismissing the genuine economic objections to those ideas.

39 Cseres (2007b, 125), ICN Competition Enforcement and Consumer Welfare (2011, 31–33), and Vision Document on Competition and Sustainability (2014, para 2.6).

40 Cseres (2007b, 134–135), ICN Competition Enforcement and Consumer Welfare (2011, 31–33), and Claassen and Gerbrandy (2016, 3).

Finally, equating competition with consumer welfare is also problematic for the purposes of this study because no definition of consumer welfare has been able to fully seize the scope of the prohibition contained in Article 101 TFEU. An agreement is only prohibited under that Article if it harms the competitive process or structure. The Article cannot be applied to an agreement that does not harm competition in this narrow sense, even if it has negatively affected total or consumer surplus. In other words, even if one adheres to a holistic definition that links competition interests to consumer welfare, an agreement can only be prohibited if there is: (i) harm to the competitive structure or process (i.e. competition interests in their narrow definition) and (ii) harm to consumer welfare.[41] Collapsing those two stages into a single holistic definition would mean that the term competition interests already reflects a complex balance between harm to the competitive structure or process and various types of efficiencies. This too could distort the study of balancing by overlooking the relationship between the harm to competitive structure and process, creation of efficiencies, and the promotion of other non-economic benefits.

Defining competition interests as a form of consumer welfare, therefore, does not produce a precise legal or economic yardstick that can be used to investigate the role of non-competition interests in the enforcement of Article 101 TFEU. The application of the consumer welfare standard inherently entails explicit or implicit policy choices, involving an internal balancing between conflicting interests.[42] Indeed, the empirical findings presented in this book reveal that even those competition enforcers that have chosen to rely on consumer welfare in the application of Article 101 TFEU have relied on different theories and tests. Similar theoretical problems are likely to arise if competition interests are equated with the other two objectives of EU competition policy, namely market integration and economic freedom.[43]

Admittedly, the dialectic definition of competition interests also fails to provide a balancing formula that can be precisely calculated. Yet, unlike the holistic definitions, it does not attempt to do so. Instead of trying to *resolve* conflicts between competition and non-competition interests, the proposed dialectic approach aims to *understand* how competition is balanced vis-à-vis other interests.[44] Therefore, from a theoretical perspective, the narrow definition of competition interests is beneficial to avoid integrating incommensurable economic and political-societal values into a single reference framework.

1.2.1.4 Methodological Justifications

A dialectical approach also comes with methodological advantages as it corresponds to the systematic content analysis methodology deployed in this study and detailed

[41] Evans (1985, 104), Farrell and Katz (2006, 10), and Melamed and Petit (2019, 746).
[42] Cseres (2007b, 122).
[43] Lianos (2013, 30–31).
[44] Andriychuk (2010, 156–157) and Lianos (2013, 30).

in Section 1.3. A dialectical approach deconstructs the legal and economic notions guiding balancing into basic building blocks, which can be recorded empirically. Because a dialectical approach defines competition interests as a self-standing value, competition and non-competition interests can be accurately identified. A holistic approach, on the other hand, is unsuitable for systematic content analysis. Since the objectives of EU competition policy are broad and vague, a holistic definition requires discretion in deciding how to classify an agreement.

Moreover, a holistic approach cannot empirically capture situations of conflict amongst the three objectives of EU competition policy themselves (i.e. between economic freedom, market integration, and economic welfare). In most cases, such conflicts do not arise. Competition law usually serves multiple economic and political goals. Protecting the process and structure of competition is expected to promote economic efficiency, remove barriers to the single market, and reduce the undue concentration of economic power. Yet, in some instances, the protection of the competitive process and structure may be at odds with one or more of the objectives of EU competition policy.[45] For instance, a price-fixing agreement between manufacturers from several Member States might be classified as anti-competitive because it increases prices and impedes consumer welfare (the welfare objective) but also pro-competitive because it makes it easier to trade across borders (the market integration objective). Therefore, a holistic approach is unsuitable for pinpointing and categorising balancing between the three objectives.

A dialectical approach to competition interests is also better suited to capture the differences between the balancing practices of the EU and national enforcers. There is no consensus among the Member States that the three objectives of EU competition policy should guide the enforcement practices of their NCAs.[46] One prominent example is Germany, which declares that it focuses on the competitive process rather than on the consumer welfare standard advanced by the Commission.[47] The Member States that have embraced the consumer welfare standard ascribe different meanings to it, and they differ considerably in the scope and degree to which they protect other values and public policies beyond competition.[48] Therefore, a holistic definition that classifies the three objectives as competition interests may be inconsistent with national interpretations. A narrow definition of competition interests allows a more nuanced analysis of national practices.

[45] Such situations are examined, for example, in Sections 2.5.1, 2.5.3.3, 3.4, and 3.6.2.
For a similar discussion with respect to US antitrust law, see Elzinga (1977, 1192–1194), Pitofsky (1979, 1066), and Brodley (1987, 1033–10334).

[46] ICN Report on Interface between Competition Policy and Other Public Policies (2010). See Sections 2.2.1 and 2.6.

[47] Heitzer (2008, 3).

[48] Dunne (2020, 6).

1.2.2 *Balancing*

This book studies whether non-competition interests should or could be taken into account to justify an otherwise anti-competitive agreement prohibited by Article 101 TFEU. This process is referred to as the *balancing* of competition and non-competition interests.

This term is not without its flaws. In constitutional law, balancing often refers to theories of constitutional interpretation based on the identification, valuation, and comparison of competing interests. Each interest must be recognised on its own and directly compared with competing interests.[49] The meaning of balancing in this study is broader in scope. It includes not only the weighing of competition interests against non-competition interests but also other techniques in which non-competition interests play a role in the enforcement – such as excluding one interest in favour of another or measuring the impact of the interests on a consumer welfare standard.

The various techniques of balancing confer varying roles to non-competition interests, which will be elaborated throughout the empirical chapters of the book. To capture those differences, the following sub-sections identify various aspects of balancing, which will be used throughout the book to explore the balancing practices. Such aspects relate to the balancing process, the remedy pursued by balancing, and the level of discretion.

1.2.2.1 Process: Legal Balancing, Economic Balancing, and Exclusion

There are several possible processes, or mechanisms, to balance competition and non-competition interests. The definition of the balancing process, as set out below, is based on the classification offered by *Townley*, who distinguishes three types of balancing processes:[50]

First, an *economic balancing process* uses economic principles to compare the quantifiable impact of an agreement on competition against its quantifiable effect on non-competition interests. This balancing is based on an economic cost–benefit analysis. It aims to ensure the maximisation of consumer welfare (under either of the definitions presented in Section 1.2.1.3), or of an alternative economic concept. Therefore, applying economic balancing to a specific case does not require the prioritisation of one type of interest over another. Rather, the effects of both competition and non-competition interests on consumer welfare are expressed in monetary terms. If the welfare generated by non-competition interests offsets the

49 Aleinikoff (1986, 945).

50 Townley (2009, 6–7, 28–29). Townley uses slightly different terminology, referring to market balancing, mere balancing, and exclusion.

harm caused by an anti-competitive agreement, the agreement will be permitted, and *vice versa*.

Second, a *legal balancing process* is not linked to an economic welfare assessment. Competition and non-competition interests are balanced by means of a legal proportionality analysis. The competition enforcers examine whether an anti-competitive agreement has gone beyond what is required to attain a legitimate non-competition interest and whether the claimed benefits exceed the harm to competition interests. A legal balancing process introduces a degree of subjectivity to competition law enforcement. Both the decision to recognise a non-competition interest as legitimate and the weighing of competing interests are at the competition enforcer's discretion. Consequently, legal balancing provides a more abstract analysis compared to the economic balancing process.

Third, balancing can take place by way of *exclusion*. The two balancing processes described above are based on a compromise, reconciling competition and non-competition interests. Exclusion, on the other hand, resolves clashes between competition and non-competition interests by promoting one interest and ignoring the other. For example, Chapter 4 shows that certain practices or sectors were excluded from the application of Article 101 TFEU altogether by means of BERs, irrespective of the agreement's actual impact on competition.

1.2.2.2 Remedy: Corrective and Regulatory Balancing

The possibilities for taking non-competition interests into account under Article 101 TFEU also depend on the type of remedy pursued by balancing. In this regard, a distinction is made between balancing within corrective versus regulatory enforcement:[51]

Corrective balancing aims to restore the situation that would have occurred in the absence of the anti-competitive agreement. Accordingly, balancing within corrective enforcement takes non-competition interests into account only to the extent required to ensure that the rights of consumers, undertakings, and third parties are not adversely affected by the enforcement of Article 101 TFEU. A corrective tool does not promote non-competition interests any more than is required to remedy a specific competitive harm.

Regulatory balancing, on the other hand, uses the enforcement of Article 101 TFEU as a means to regulate markets and promote interests that are not directly related to the anti-competitive behaviour of the undertakings concerned.[52] A regulatory tool might protect non-competition interests even where no harm has been inflicted on competition interests, or at any rate not disproportionately; it could

[51] Townley (2009, 42–43), Lavrijssen (2010, 655), Ibáñez Colomo (2010, 263), and Gerard (2013, 18–22).

[52] The regulatory function of Article 101 TFEU is also elaborated in Sections 2.5.2.1 and 2.5.3.1.

utilise the enforcement of Article 101 TFEU to prevent an agreement harming other public policies. For instance, a competition enforcer might invoke Article 101 TFEU to prohibit an agreement that impedes market integration or public health even if such an agreement *does not* have a significant negative impact on competition.

1.2.2.3 Level of Discretion

Finally, the leeway to account for non-competition interests is also dependent on the level of discretion left to the competition enforcer when administrating each balancing tool. A competition enforcer, like any other administrative authority, can be said to have discretion whenever the law leaves it a certain amount of freedom to choose among various possible courses of action.[53] There is room for discretion when the applicable legislative, constitutional, and case law has not laid down rules that fully specify which course of action the enforcer must take.

Discretion is a matter of degree. An enforcer will have narrower or wider discretion according to the extent to which the law circumscribes the range of possible choices. The law can limit the range of choices, for instance, by excluding certain courses of action, prescribing the objectives to be pursued, or requiring that certain elements be considered during the decision-making process.[54] This study differentiates between balancing tools having a high versus a low level of discretion.

Balancing tools that are characterised by *a low level of discretion* are the most constraining on the competition enforcer's courses of action. Once the facts of the case have been identified and it has been determined that a certain agreement lies within a relevant category, a pre-determined categorical rule applies that requires a rigid set of balancing principles. Hence, such balancing tools apply equally and consistently to all types of agreements.

Balancing tools that are characterised by *a high level of discretion*, in comparison, employ indeterminate terms by referring, for example, to the purpose of a regulation, a proportionality test, or to a vague consumer welfare standard. The outcome of balancing in a specific case is essentially based on the discretion of the competition enforcer and is, therefore, less certain.

1.3 SYSTEMATIC CONTENT ANALYSIS

Systematic content analysis of legal texts can be described as a hybrid of traditional legal methodologies and empirical research, or as a unique legal empirical methodology.[55] It consists of recording features of legal documents – in this study: decisions of the Commission and NCAs and judgements of EU and national courts – and

[53] On administrative discretion, see Galligan (1990, 1–2), Wils (2011, 354), and Mendes (2014, 7).
[54] Galligan (1990, 6–7) and Wils (2011, 354).
[55] Hall and Wright (2008, 64).

drawing inferences about their use and meaning. This technique is also labelled as *coding*.[56]

Because systematic content analysis is a technique rarely used in European legal scholarship, it may be worth dedicating a few words to the methodology guiding the coding and the design of this study. Before moving to present the case selection and coding protocol, therefore, this section begins by discussing the benefits and risks of systematic content analysis.

1.3.1 *Promises and Pitfalls of Systematic Content Analysis*

This study applies systematic content analysis to identify the modalities of balancing competition and non-competition interests in public enforcement actions of Article 101 TFEU. One of the unique characteristics of content analysis, which distinguishes it from other more qualitative or interpretative methodologies, is its attempt to meet the standards of scientific research methods. Systematic content analysis offers a scientific understanding of the balancing practices themselves by way of generating falsifiable and reproducible knowledge about the competition enforcers' practices.[57] It provides a tool for testing hypotheses on the basis of theory, ensuring the reliability, validity, and generalisability of the results. In this book, it assists in identifying previously unnoticed balancing patterns, which are further interpreted using doctrinal and normative methodologies. Moreover, it is used to verify or refute theories on balancing that have been based on anecdotal or subjective studies.

Systematic content analysis provides an analytical method for understanding large numbers of public enforcement actions. It is based on the assumption that each of the enforcement actions has roughly the same value. It therefore represents a departure from traditional legal analysis, which tends to focus on leading cases or precedent. This methodology views the decisional practices of competition enforcers as not only a reflection of the law *but rather as the law itself*.[58] This book asserts that this is predominantly true with respect to the enforcement of EU competition law. As detailed in Chapter 2, the wording of the Treaty tells us little about the particularities of balancing, and the EU Courts have not yet supplied an overall balancing framework. Similarly, the non-binding Commission's guidelines and notices outline only a general normative perspective. In the absence of a designated balancing framework, the balancing rules are substantially reflected by case law. Especially under Regulation 1/2003's self-assessment regime, undertakings evaluate their compliance with EU competition rules essentially pursuant to Commission, NCA, and court practices.[59]

[56] Kort (1963, 134), Tyree (1981), and Hall and Wright (2008, 64). More generally on the method of systematic content analysis, see Neuendorf (2017).

[57] Hall and Wright (2008, 64) and Neuendorf (2017, 16–17).

[58] Hall and Wright (2008, 78, 84–86).

[59] GCLC Annual Conference (2010, 19, 58–76).

At the same time, it is important to acknowledge the limitations inherent to content analysis and hence of this study. First, content analysis is not designed to predict or explain the outcomes of proceedings. It does not study causality. It uses the details gleaned from decisional practices to *understand* the body of case law.[60] This research method is also known as *descriptive statistics*.[61]

Second, content analysis is restricted to the endogenic information extracted from the examined proceedings, without reference to exogenous data. In other words, the empirical findings do not contain considerations that are not reflected within the wording of the cases. Admittedly, this is an important limitation of this study. Yet, as already mentioned, analysis of the cases merits an important study; they represent the law in practice and are the main source of information directing undertakings' conduct. The cases demonstrate the factual and analytical richness of questions that come before competition enforcers and courts, how undertakings structure their arguments, and how the enforcers reason their decisions.[62]

Third, another limitation of any content analysis of case law relates to the fact that not all infringements result in a reasoned administrative act. While the database of cases purports to cover all public enforcement of Article 101 TFEU,[63] aspiring to encompass all consideration of non-competition interests, it cannot fully code infringements that did not end with a reasoned decision.[64] There are several types of Article 101 TFEU infringement that have not been recorded in the database: The database does not include information on undetected infringements, which are estimated to be the vast majority of anti-competitive agreements;[65] the database does not record detected infringements if no administrative procedure was initiated or if the investigation was dropped without publication; finally, the database holds only partial information on cases in which competition enforcers did not issue an Article 101 TFEU decision on the merits. Balancing by alternative instruments (e.g. sector regulation, markets-work) or implicit-procedural balancing tools (e.g. priority setting and commitments) is not fully reflected in the database.[66]

Consequently, it must be acknowledged that there is a large body of unidentified 'dark matter' of Article 101 TFEU infringements. This caveat applies to the use of the database and what can be learned from it.[67] This dark matter, referred to by Davies and Ormosi as the 'known unknowns'[68] and summarised in Figure 1.3, may certainly

60 Hall (2011, 12). For a critique of the use of content analysis to predict outcomes, see Tyree (1981).
61 Neuendorf (2017, 244–245).
62 Lawlor (1968, 107) and Hall (2011, 3–4).
63 The composition of the database of cases is elaborated in Section 1.3.2.
64 Davies and Ormosi (2010, 34–35).
65 For example, Combe, Monnier, and Legal (2008) estimated detection chance between 12.9% and 13.2%. See also Davies and Ormosi (2010, 43) and Davies and Ormosi (2013).
66 Those balancing tools are discussed in Chapter 2.
67 Carree et al. (2010, 98).
68 Davies and Ormosi (2013, 4).

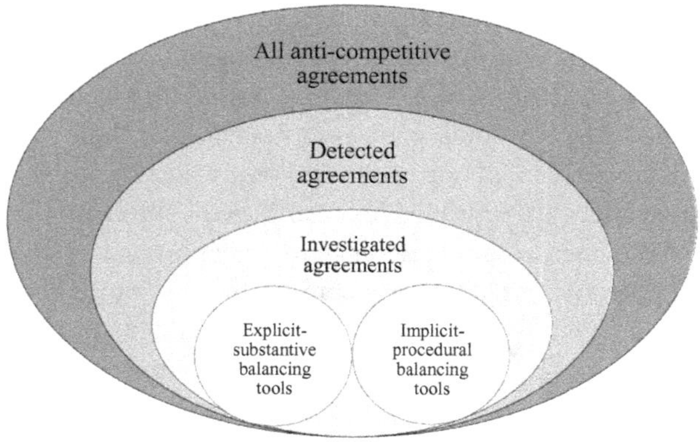

FIGURE 1.3. The 'dark matter' of balancing[69]

involve balancing. Of the totality of anti-competitive agreements in the EU market, only agreements handled by the explicit-substantive balancing tools in reasoned and published decisions are fully represented in the database.

Despite this limitation, the dark matter is a noteworthy subject of study in itself. As demonstrated in Chapter 7, the choices competition enforcers make, when devising detection policies, setting enforcement targets, choosing which legal instrument to apply to a case, and shaping the outcomes, are an independent form of balancing. This type of balancing tool is particularly significant since it is often implicit and overlooked.

Like the dark matter in the universe, the dark matter of enforcement cannot be directly observed. Yet, by identifying the entire scope of enforcement activities, the empirical exercise in this study yields important conclusions also on the areas that have remained untouched by EU competition enforcement and in which anti-competitive agreements are *de facto* tolerated. The database thus allows evaluation of the balancing practices not only on the basis of observed cases but also on the basis of unobserved cases.[70]

1.3.2 *The Database: Case Selection and Definitions*

The empirical study is based on a unique database including all public enforcement actions of Article 101 TFEU rendered by

(i) The Commission, since the establishment of the EEC in 1957 until 2017.

[69] Figure 1.3 was originally published in Brook (2020). Reproduced by permission of Oxford University Press. The proportions depicted for the various types of agreements are merely for purposes of illustration.

[70] Davies and Ormosi (2013, 4).

(ii) The CJEU and GC, since the establishment of the EEC in 1957 until 2017 (the 'EU Courts'). It includes appeals on the Commission's decisions as well as the CJEU's preliminary rulings.
(iii) The Five NCAs, since the entry into force of Regulation 1/2003 decentralising the enforcement in May 2004 until 2017. In addition to Article 101 TFEU, the database includes the public enforcement of the national equivalent provisions.
(iv) The national courts of the five representative Member States, since the entry into force of Regulation 1/2003 decentralising the enforcement in May 2004 and until 2017 in appeals on the abovementioned NCAs' proceedings.

The cut-off date of this database is 31 May 2018. Therefore, it includes only decisions that were rendered before 31 December 2017 and published by 31 May 2018.

The cases in the database reflect the entire population of published Article 101 TFEU public enforcement actions in the relevant jurisdictions, yielding a sufficiently large and representative sample of over 3,100 cases. As demonstrated below, the proceedings are essentially homogeneous; they involve the public enforcement of Article 101 TFEU or closely related national equivalents. Differences that potentially impede uniformity are controlled (e.g. between the Commission's and NCAs' institutional and procedural set-up; differences in enforcement before and after entry into force of Regulation 1/2003; differences between by-object and by-effect infringements).

The following sub-sections outline these selection criteria and clarify some of the definitions used throughout the study. The latter are also summarised in the Table of Definitions found at the beginning of this book.

1.3.2.1 Legal Provisions

The database comprises all public enforcement actions involving Article 101 TFEU. It also covers the identical versions of the Article in previous European Treaties (Articles 81 EC and 85 EEC) and in the Agreement on European Economic Area (Article 53 EEA). Unless explicitly stated otherwise, references to Article 101 TFEU should be understood as references to those other identical provisions. Proceedings involving the enforcement of Article 101 TFEU and those identical provisions are labelled collectively as *EU cases*.

In addition, the database encompasses public enforcement actions of the national prohibitions equivalent to Article 101 TFEU.[71] It includes cases in which both

[71] French Commercial Code, Articles L420–1, L420–3, L420–4; German Competition Act, Sections 1–3; Hungarian Competition Act, Articles 11–13; Dutch Competition Act, Articles 6–10; UK Competition Act, Sections 2–4.

Article 101 TFEU and the national equivalent were applied and cases where only the national provision was applied. Those proceedings are referred to as *mixed cases* and *purely national cases*, respectively.

EU cases, mixed cases, and purely national cases are labelled collectively as *Article 101 TFEU enforcement actions*. This terminology is used as shorthand to refer to the enforcement of both the EU and the national equivalent provisions.

The inclusion of purely national cases in the database has a three-fold aim. First, NCAs and EU and national courts have mostly ascribed virtually identical meaning to the EU and national prohibitions. They apply them interchangeably or without clearly distinguishing between the two, even when the wording of a national prohibition differs from its EU counterpart.[72] This has led the CJEU to declare that it is competent to issue preliminary rulings on the interpretation of the national equivalent prohibitions even in purely national cases.[73] Therefore, the balancing principles that have been developed in national cases also inform the balancing applicable to Article 101 TFEU. Second, the inclusion of purely national cases is required to account for cases that gave no indication of whether they were based on the EU or the national provisions.[74] Finally, as elaborated in Section 7.5.4, purely national cases provide insight into the application of the effect on trade criterion and the extent to which it has been used for balancing purposes.

1.3.2.2 Jurisdiction Selection

The database comprises all of the enforcement actions taken by the Commission and the NCAs of France, Germany, Hungary, the Netherlands, and the UK. In addition, it includes the decisions of the EU Courts in actions for annulment of the Commission's decisions, preliminary rulings of the CJEU, and national courts in appeals. The Commission, NCAs, and EU and national courts are collectively referred to in this book as the *competition enforcers*.

The five Member States studied were chosen from among the EU twenty-eight Member States by employing a purposive-heterogeneous selection method. In other words, the selection aimed to capture a wide range of approaches to the balancing of competition and non-competition interests.[75] The five Member States represent a wide spectrum of legal and economic structures, traditions, and approaches to competition policy and balancing. The heterogeneous sample demonstrates how the consideration of non-competition interests differs across jurisdictions and highlights the difficulties of balancing in the EU multi-governance enforcement system.

72 This is further discussed in Sections 2.6 and 3.6.4.

73 C-32/11 Allianz (2013, para 20–23) and C-413/13 FNV Kunsten Informatie en Media (2014, para 17–20).

74 See Table 1.1 and Section 2.5.4.

75 Ritchie et al. (2013, 113–114).

France, Germany,[76] and the UK[77] were selected since they are the Member States that have exercised the greatest influence on the substantive and procedural development of EU competition law and balancing. As detailed in Chapter 2, each of those Member States has advocated for a distinct balancing regime stemming from their domestic competition law traditions. To a large extent, EU competition law could be understood as representing a compromise between those varying approaches.[78]

It should be noted that at the time of finalising this study, there is not yet a clear prediction on the future of UK competition law following Brexit or its relationship with EU competition law. Nevertheless, since the study focuses on past practice, the UK is simply regarded as one of the EU Member States in this context. Moreover, studying the UK's approach to balancing may help predict the future of EU competition law balancing following the diminish of the UK's influence.

The Netherlands was chosen in light of its vibrant national debate on the role of non-competition interests under EU and national competition laws. The Netherlands generally supports the consideration of broad, non-economic benefits in competition law enforcement, especially in the field of sustainability. The Dutch legislator has specifically acknowledged that non-competition interests should play a role in EU and national competition law enforcement.[79]

Hungary was selected to include the balancing challenges encountered by the eastern and central European Member States that have joined the EU since 2004. As elaborated in Section 2.6.5, upon accession to the EU, those new Member States had to transform from centrally planned to market economies and, within a short period of time, enact new competition laws and develop new cultures.[80] Moreover, as transitional economies, they had to overcome structural weaknesses to ensure effective competition law enforcement.[81] Particularly due to the fact that those significant legal and economic changes were a result of external forces rather than organic-internal competition culture, they raised questions about the appropriate balance of competition and other public policy considerations and the treatment of

[76] In Germany, only federal cases handled by the Bundeskartellamt are included in the database. Cases of the Supreme Land Authorities dealing with cartels in which the effect of the restrictive conduct does not extend beyond the territory of a Land (in the meaning of Article 48 of the German Competition Act) are not included.

[77] The UK follows a concurrency model, which prescribes different authorities and procedural and substantive rules according to the sector examined (UK Competition Act, Section 54(1)). Therefore, in addition to the OFT/CMA cases, the database includes Article 101 TFEU enforcement actions of the Office of Communications, the Gas and Electricity Markets Authority, the Water Services Regulation Authority, the Office of Rail Regulation, the Northern Ireland Authority for Utility Regulation, the Civil Aviation Authority, and the health care sector regulator for England (NHS Improvement, formerly Monitor). On the UK concurrency model, see Section 2.6.4.3.

[78] Van Rompuy (2012, 134), Kuenzler and Warlouzet (2013, 91), and Talbot (2016, 269).

[79] See Section 2.6.2.2.

[80] Geradin and Henry (2004, 2) and Pittman (2004).

[81] Geradin and Henry (2004, 25) and Tóth (2004).

newly liberalised sectors.[82] Finally, Hungary provides an example of balancing against a backdrop of strong, politically inflected government influence over the administrative discretion of the NCA. This trend became evident following the 2010 national elections, at which time the newly elected right-wing government passed a series of laws that have been criticised as undermining the rule of law, at both the domestic and EU levels.[83]

1.3.2.3 Sources of Information

The database includes all public enforcement actions of Article 101 TFEU, published in the form of a decision, formal or informal opinion, press release available on the competition enforcers' websites, or reference in an annual report. Both formal and informal proceedings are included. The database covers proceedings related to infringements,[84] findings of inapplicability,[85] settlements,[86] formal or informal commitments,[87] decisions not to investigate or to terminate investigations,[88] and *ex-ante* informal opinions on the conduct of a specific undertaking (as opposed to general or sectoral guidelines or advocacy).[89]

The database also includes limited, aggregate data on the Commission's comfort letters.[90] While comfort letters go largely unpublished, aggregate data indicating the date, name of the case, and the result of the Commission's preliminary assessment is available going back to 1990.[91]

The inclusion of all types of Article 101 TFEU public enforcement actions is warranted by the functional approach of comparative law.[92] This is based on the assumption that rules that have the same function or effect may take different forms in various jurisdictions. In the context of EU competition law, it must be considered that EU and national competition enforcers are subject to different procedural rules and follow different practices (different forms) when enforcing the same legal provision of Article 101 TFEU (same function).[93] A comparative overview of

[82] Cseres (2007a, 465–467) and Kovács and Reindl (2013, 38).
[83] Ziegler and Horváthy (2017, 33–37).
[84] Regulation 1/2003, Article 7; Regulation 17/62, Article 3.
[85] Regulation 1/2003, Article 10; Regulation 17/62, Article 2. See Section 2.6.3.
[86] Commission's Settlement Notice (2008). See Section 2.3.3.
[87] Formal commitments refer to proceedings pursuant to Article 9 of Regulation 1/2003. Informal commitments refer to cases in which after undertakings have agreed to voluntarily end the infringement, the competition enforcer decided that there were no grounds to continue the proceedings. See Section 2.6.2.1.
[88] See Section 2.4.
[89] See Section 2.5.3.
[90] On comfort letters, see Sections 2.3.2 and 7.5.3.
[91] The data are available on the Commission's website: http://ec.europa.eu/competition/antitrust/cases/comfort_letter.html.
[92] Zweigert and Kötz (1992, 32–47).
[93] On the functional comparative law approach in EU competition law, see Larouche (2013, 158) and Cseres (2014, 41).

Article 101 TFEU enforcement, therefore, must take into account all the forms in which public enforcement actions have been issued.

1.3.2.4 Types of Proceedings

The database includes public enforcement actions, as well as appeals and actions for annulment of those decisions. In addition, it covers CJEU preliminary rulings that specify Article 101 TFEU in the questions referred to the Court. Criminal, civil, procedural, and interim procedures are excluded from the database. Those proceedings are governed by procedural rules that significantly vary across the Member States. In those cases, differences in balancing may be associated with procedural aspects rather than disparate enforcement of Article 101 TFEU.

Table 1.1 summarises the number of Article 101 TFEU enforcement actions included in the database, according to their enforcement period,[94] competition enforcer, and legal provision.

1.3.3 *Coding Book*

The study employs classic content analysis[95] to record both the quantitative and qualitative aspects of the cases included in the database. The coding is based on a designated *coding book* developed for the purpose of this study on the basis of an extensive literature review.[96] The coding book offers a systematic and reproducible method for reducing the text of the cases to pre-determined codes representing the various balancing aspects.

The coding book defines 41 variables. Each variable describes a feature of the case or of the balancing. The variables include details of case identification (date, case number, competition enforcer), the undertakings, substantive aspects of balancing (the non-competition interest examined, its normative legal source, the types of benefits, and the balancing method), the proceeding (leniency, settlement, commitments), and on the outcome and remedy imposed. Each variable has been assigned with a pre-determined closed list of value labels that represent possible variations of each variable. As is customary in legal systematic content analysis, the coding has been restricted to the legal assessment part of the proceedings. Consequently, in the event a competition enforcer failed to address an argument presented by an undertaking, it was not recorded.

The coding book ensures the validity of the coding as a reliable basis for drawing normative conclusions about the enforcement of EU competition law. The validity and reliability of the coding are inherently linked to the type of content that has been coded. Most of the variables defined by the coding book provide a quantitative

94 As mentioned, the four enforcement periods are defined in Section 2.5.

95 Webley (2010, 12).

96 The coding book is available upon request from the author.

TABLE 1.1. *Database of cases*

Enforcement period/ competition enforcer	Total	Commission/NCA: EU and mixed cases	Commission/NCA: Purely national cases	Commission/NCA: Legal provision not mentioned	Courts
		EU level			
First enforcement period (1962–1977)	108				49
Second enforcement period (1978–1987)	127				75
Third enforcement period (1988–April 2004)	331				306
Fourth enforcement period (May 2004–2017)	170				570
		National level			
France	357	156	177	24	185
Germany	170	57	19	94	40
Hungary	174	56	117	1	134
The Netherlands	192[a,b]	67	88	37	102
UK	70	33	30	7	24

[a] This figure includes reassessment proceedings of the Dutch NCA's decisions by an advisory committee. This procedure is detailed in Section 2.6.3.3.
[b] For methodological reasons, a special coding protocol was applied to coding the so-called Dutch construction cartel cases. In 2001, following numerous complaints, the Dutch NCA investigated anti-competitive agreements in various sectors of the Dutch construction industry. These investigations were supported by over 480 leniency applications, which in 2005 led to the imposition of fines on about 1,400 firms. Given the immense magnitude of those cases, the NCA instigated a special fast-lane procedure in which undertakings agreed to waive their right to contest the legal and factual claims of the NCA in favour of a 15% fine reduction. This procedure and its interesting legal implications are explored by Gerbrandy and Lachnit (2013). Coding all of those proceedings separately would have created distortions in the data, especially since they are significantly higher in number than all of the other NCAs' enforcement activities combined. Therefore, the Dutch construction cartel cases were aggregated and coded as eleven independent cases. This categorisation was based on the case identification number allocated by the Dutch NCA, which identified eleven sectors in the construction industry in which the infringements took place.

description of *manifest content*,[97] namely of content that is on the surface, and hence is easily observable and countable without need for interpretation (e.g. the number of cases that invoked Article 101(3) TFEU, or the number of cases that were concluded by way of settlement). Because this type of coding essentially comprises clerical recording, it is the most reliable and valid type of content analysis.

[97] Potter and Levine-Donnerstein (1999, 259–261) and Neuendorf (2017, 31–33, 170–171).

A smaller number of variables involve *latent pattern content*.[98] These variables are more qualitative in nature, focusing on patterns identified in the text itself. As such, this coding left some room for the coders' judgement. The coding of the application of certain legal doctrines, such as the proportionality tests of Article 101(1) and (3) TFEU, merited such a value judgement. Yet, the coding book has strived to limit the value judgement inherent to such interpretations, and hence to increase the reliability of the coding, by providing detailed and unequivocal criteria for coding on the basis of a detailed literature overview.

The validity and reliability of the coding were also ensured by the use of *overlapping coding*. Accordingly, two independent coders separately and simultaneously coded 10% of the cases in the database to ensure the coding replicability.[99]

Before moving ahead to discuss the empirical findings and their implications, the next chapter places the debate on balancing in an appropriate historical EU context by providing a historical overview of the development of balancing under Article 101 TFEU.

98 *Ibid.*

99 On overlapping coding as a measure for ensuring the validity and reliability of content analysis, see Neuendorf (2017, 41–42).

2

History of Article 101 TFEU Balancing

2.1 INTRODUCTION

The possibility of considering non-competition interests under Article 101 TFEU and the manner in which that would occur are intrinsically linked with the objectives pursued by the Article. To paraphrase Bork, the enforcement of Article 101 TFEU and the balancing principles cannot be made rational until one determines what the objectives of the Article are.[1] This chapter explains why, more than sixty years after the drafting of Article 101 TFEU, there is still no simple answer to this question. It illustrates that the content of competition law and the balancing principles are policy choices. Favouring consensus over clarity, the EU institutions and the Member States have never identified the Article's objectives or created a defined balancing framework.[2]

The chapter tackles this question from a historical perspective. It examines five aspects. First, Section 2.2 details the historical development of the balancing principles embedded in *EU primary law*. It shows that the Member States have not agreed on the objectives of the Article and the room, scope, or method for balancing. Next, Section 2.3 focuses on *EU secondary law*. It explores how the Council and the Commission have shaped the procedural rules governing the application of Article 101 TFEU in general and balancing in particular. Section 2.4 investigates the *EU Courts'* role in filling the gaps in the law and interpreting the balancing rules. Finally, the chapter offers a historical overview of how balancing has been *applied in practice by the Commission and NCAs*. For this purpose, Section 2.5 discusses the development of the Commission's balancing practices. Section 2.6 examines the

1 Bork (1978, 50); see also Frazer (1990, 623), Townley (2009, 11, 46), and Witt (2016b, 77–79).

2 Questions surrounding the objectives of competition law and the limits of balancing are also subject to a parallel debate in the United States. See, for example, Bork and Bowman (1965), Blake and Jones (1965), Elzinga (1977), Pitofsky (1979), Easterbrook (1986), Stucke (2012), and Wu (2018).

approaches of the five Member States examined in this study, which have not always converged to the Commission's practice.

It should be pointed out that many of these topics have already been extensively discussed elsewhere. This chapter merely lays out the necessary background for discussing the empirical findings that are presented in Chapters 3–7.

2.2 BALANCING IN EU PRIMARY LAW: MORE QUESTIONS THAN ANSWERS

2.2.1 *Normative Value of Competition in the EU Treaties*

The search for the objectives of Article 101 TFEU must begin by identifying the role of *competition policy* in the EU Treaties. There is no straightforward answer to this question. Although Article 3 TEU defines a list of broad and inter-related economic and social objectives for the EU, the promotion of competition is *not* one of those objectives. Until the Lisbon Treaty of 2009, the EU Treaties referred to 'a system ensuring that competition in the internal market is not distorted' as one of the EU 'activities'.[3] Nevertheless, they did not detail the relationship between the various objectives and activities, nor how to resolve conflicts among them.

The vague wording of the Treaties has sparked a long discussion on the objectives of EU competition policy.[4] That debate goes beyond the scope of this study. For the purpose of this book, it is sufficient to note that EU Courts and legal scholarship often point to three possible constituent objectives, which have been accorded varying weights throughout the years.

The first objective of EU competition policy is the maintenance of economic freedom, which is drawn from an Ordoliberalism concept of competition policy. According to this objective, competition policy is a means for preserving a free society.[5] This objective is to be achieved by eliminating private economic power concentrations, and more specifically, by establishing and enforcing complete competition on markets. This theory runs counter to the neo-classical concept of competition, which is embedded in *laissez-faire* economic philosophy and limits intervention in markets. Ordoliberalism advocates for governmental intervention

3 Article 3(1)(g) EC.

4 For example, see Wesseling (2000, 77–113), Motta (2004, 17–30), Odudu (2006, 13), Monti (2007, 23), Parret (2009, 11), Lavrijssen (2010), Van Rompuy (2012, 52), Maier-Rigaud (2012, 132), Parret (2012, 65–68), Lianos (2013), Heide-Jorgensen (2013, 96–100), Pérez and Scheur (2013), Witt (2016b, 77–109), and Sauter (2016, 64–75).

5 The objectives of protecting economic freedom and safeguarding against concentrated economic power have also characterised US antitrust law, at least in its early years. See Pitofsky (1979, 1052–1060) and Blake and Jones (1965, 382–384).

imposing obligations of fair conduct and suppressing economic power to safeguard economic freedom in the marketplace.[6]

The second objective of EU competition policy is market integration. Unlike other jurisdictions' competition policies, EU competition law is a mechanism for integrating EU markets. Competition policy is a complementary measure to the EU free movement rules, ensuring that private firms will not re-establish national market divisions that were previously put in place by Member States' protectionist measures.[7]

The third objective of EU competition policy is the promotion of economic welfare. According to this objective, EU competition policy is designed to ensure an efficient allocation of resources throughout the EU. As elaborated in Section 2.5, the objectives of economic freedom and market integration have played a significant role in directing the enforcement of EU competition policy in the past. Since the mid-1990s, however, EU competition policy has taken a turn, now focusing on economic welfare. There are various views as to the type of economic welfare EU competition policy should promote. Some argue that EU competition policy is or should be directed at the advancement of the total, aggregated welfare of all groups of citizens in the economy. Others maintain that it advances, or should advance, consumer welfare only.[8]

The three above objectives of EU competition policy encompass various political–societal values, none of which is directly related to the competitive process or structure as such. In other words, the protection of competition interests is only an instrument to achieve those three objectives,[9] which must be balanced against other economic and political non-competition interests. In fact, the three objectives reflect various theories of markets and societies and manifest different preferences towards the balancing of the economic, social, and political objectives of the EU.[10]

The debate about the objectives of EU competition policy was revived in the mid-2000s. In 2004, the (discarded) draft of the Treaty establishing a Constitution for Europe advocated enhancing the normative value of competition. It proposed to declare, for the first time, that 'an internal market where competition is free and

6 On the Ordoliberalism objective of EU competition policy, see Monti (2007, 22–24), Maier-Rigaud (2012, 136), Parret (2012, 66–68), Lianos (2013, 24–28), Pérez and Scheur (2013, 21–31), and Talbot (2016). On the German origins of Ordoliberalism, see Section 2.6.2.1.

7 On the market integration objective of EU competition policy, see Gerber (1998, 334–391), Monti (2007, 39–44), Parret (2012, 65–66), Lianos (2013, 14–15), and Pérez and Scheur (2013, 22, 26, 40–52).

8 The welfare standards and their origin in US antitrust law are discussed in Section 1.2.1.3. On the economic welfare objective of EU competition policy, see Kjolbye (2004, 566), Nazzini (2006, 504), Gerber (2008, 1247), Parret (2012, 14–16), and Witt (2016b, 80–83).

9 This approach dates back to Smith's economic theory detailed in an Inquiry into the Nature and Causes of the Wealth of Nations (1776). Accordingly, competitive markets are seen as a desirable framework for fostering welfare and growth. See also Pera (2008, 129–130).

10 Townley (2009, 48). See also Sufrin (2006, 953). Section 1.2.1 asserts that this justifies the narrow definition of competition interests used in this study.

undistorted' is a stand-alone EU objective and not merely an 'activity' aimed at achieving the other aims.[11] Yet, France opposed this change when the Lisbon Treaty was adopted in 2009. French President Sarkozy argued that competition should not be a means and an end unto itself, but rather a mechanism for the realisation of EU industrial policy.[12] Accordingly, not only was competition *not* included as an objective of the Lisbon Treaty, but it was also no longer even mentioned as an 'activity'. At the same time, the substantive reference to competition is still part of EU primary law. The Protocol on the Internal Market and Competition annexed to the Lisbon Treaty provides that the internal market 'includes a system ensuring that competition is not distorted'.[13] Moreover, Article 119 TFEU specifies that EU economic policy follows 'the principles of an open market economy with free competition'.

As a consequence, the normative implications of the change concerning competition in the Lisbon Treaty are disputed. On the one hand, some scholars have listed several factors indicating that the change has no real impact, but is at most symbolic. They have stressed that the Protocol is an integral part of the Treaties and that the Treaties do not form a clear hierarchy between the various EU policies. The fact that competition is listed as neither an objective nor an activity has, therefore, not reduced its importance.[14] They have also cited the CJEU, which has reaffirmed the legal value of competition policy by emphasising that the Protocol is an essential part of the objectives of the Treaty.[15] Finally, those scholars have noted that neither the competition law provisions of the Treaties nor secondary regulations were modified following the Lisbon Treaty.[16] As confirmed by *Kroes*, the European Commissioner for Competition at the time, the Lisbon Treaty upholds the existing status of competition.[17]

On the other hand, others have maintained that the change could be understood as a political declaration that competition policy has less weight compared to other EU policies. This position may affect the weight the competition enforcers ascribe to competition vis-à-vis other non-competition interests.[18]

This approach has seemed to gain support from various Member States as a response to the Commission's decision to block the *Siemens/Alstom merger*

[11] Draft Treaty Establishing a Constitution for Europe (2004), Article 3(2).

[12] Quoted in Drexl (2010, 663) and Van Rompuy (2011, 2). See also Schweitzer (2007, 1).

[13] Protocol 27 on the Internal Market and Competition. See also Article 51 TEU.

[14] Semmelmann (2008b, 32), Lavrijssen (2010, 637), Drexl (2010, 662–667), and Seidel and Federico Pace (2013, 4–5).

[15] C-52/09 TeliaSonera (2011), para 20; C-496/09 Commission v Italy (2011), para 60; T-456/10 Animal feed phosphates (2015), para 212.

[16] Mestmäcker (2000, 7–8), Seidel and Federico Pace (2013, 637), and Kuenzler and Warlouzet (2013, 38–43).

[17] MEMO/07/250 Statement by European Commissioner for Competition Kroes on results of June 21–22 European Council – Protocol on Internal Market and Competition (2007).

[18] Schweitzer (2007, 5), Riley (2007, 2), Graupner (2007, 96–97), Townley (2009, 50), Parret (2009, 8), and Prosser (2010, 318).

(2019).[19] In this case, the Commission prohibited the merger, noting that the proposed acquisition of Alstom by Siemens would deprive European rail operators of a choice of suppliers and innovative products. Some Member States have argued that despite the expected harm to competition and consumer welfare, EU competition policy should allow for the creation of European champions to compete with foreign competitors that receive subsidies from their national governments. Accordingly, they called to revise the EU competition rules to allow them 'to adequately take into account industrial policy considerations in order to enable European companies to successfully compete on the world stage'.[20] This statement reflects an approach that views competition only as a mechanism for the realisation of EU industrial policy.

For the purpose of this study, it is not necessary to subscribe to a single objective of EU competition policy. It is sufficient to note that the EU Treaties do not clearly define the objectives of EU competition policy. Those objectives are still contentious and subject to ongoing political and legal debate.

2.2.2 *Article 101 TFEU Wording and Structure: Member States Agree to Disagree*

A separate yet linked question relates to the *objectives of Article 101 TFEU*. This question moves away from examining the objectives of EU competition policy as a whole and towards rationalising the objectives behind the EU's prohibition on anticompetitive agreements. The wording and structure of Article 101 TFEU are the results of lengthy negotiations preceding the adoption of the Rome Treaty of 1957.[21] It was settled upon by the national delegations attending the Messina conference of 1955.[22]

The drafting of the Article was strongly influenced by French competition law. Being the only Member State having comprehensive competition rules at the time,

[19] 8677 Siemens/Alstom (2019).

[20] A Franco-German Manifesto for a European Industrial Policy Fit for the 21st Century, of 19 February 2019, 3, available here: www.gouvernement.fr/en/a-franco-german-manifesto-for-a-european-industrial-policy-fit-for-the-21st-century. A few months later, the French and German governments have once again supported this position, this time with another joint policy paper with the Polish government, titled Modernising EU Competition Policy, of July 7 2019, available here: www.bmwi.de/Redaktion/DE/Downloads/M-O/modernising-eu-competition-policy.pdf?__blob=publicationFile&v=4. Those joint calls followed up on a prior initiative of nineteen EU governments in December 2018, asking the Commission to update the EU competition rules to foster the emergence of European champions and compete with US and Chinese companies. See CPI (2019). See also Lianos (2019).

[21] On those negotiations, see Forrester (2001, 30–39), Sufrin (2006, 538–540), Goyder (2009, 919–920), and Seidel and Federico Pace (2013, 78–94).

[22] The Messina conference was a meeting of European foreign ministers aimed at setting up the intergovernmental committee. In 1956, the committee produced the Spaak Report, which laid the foundation for establishing the EEC in the Rome Treaty.

French law served as a prominent model for Article 101 TFEU.[23] As elaborated below, the French law was based on a *principle of abuse* and thus did not unequivocally prohibit all anti-competitive agreements. Instead, it used an *ex-post, case-by-case* analysis to determine if positive effects on economic development or on society could counterbalance an agreement's negative effect on prices. Thus, non-competition interests inherently influenced the scope of the French prohibition.[24]

During the negotiations of the Rome Treaty, Germany was in the process of adopting its own competition law. Although the issue was subject to heated political debate, the German delegation advocated an EU law provision based on a *principle of prohibition*, that is to say, a *total prohibition* on any (horizontal) anti-competitive agreement, leaving no room for balancing.[25]

The Netherlands proposed a third, intermediate model. It offered a compulsory notification system with provisional validity, analogous to its domestic competition regime at the time. According to this suggestion, all agreements should have been notified to the Commission. Yet, if an agreement was found abusive, its lack of validity would only be effective prospectively.[26]

The clash between the Member States' approaches was resolved by means of a compromise between the French and German suggestions: The wording of Article 101 TFEU closely followed the French proposal. Like the French law, Article 101 TFEU has a bifurcated structure that leaves room for balancing: Article 101(1) TFEU imposes a general ban prohibiting any anti-competitive agreement affecting trade between Member States,[27] and Article 101(3) TFEU provides a structured framework for balancing. The latter limits the general prohibition by stating 'the provisions of paragraph 1 *may, however, be declared inapplicable*' if an agreement 'contributes to improving the production or distribution of goods or to promoting technical or economic progress, while allowing consumers a fair share of the resulting benefit, and which does not: (a) impose on the undertakings concerned restrictions which are not indispensable to the attainment of these objectives; (b) afford such undertakings the possibility of eliminating competition in respect of a substantial part of the products in question'.

At the same time, Article 101 TFEU was also inspired by the German approach. Based on the principle of prohibition, it declares that an anti-competitive agreement is prohibited (Article 101(1) TFEU) and is automatically void (Article 101(2) TFEU).

[23] Seidel and Federico Pace (2013, 59, 62).

[24] On the French law and principle of abuse, see Section 2.6.1.1. See also Mestmäcker (2000, 223–224), Seidel and Federico Pace (2013, 59, 62), and Kuenzler and Warlouzet (2013, 100, 103–104).

[25] On the German law and the principle of prohibition, see Section 2.6.2.1. See also Mestmäcker (2000, 223–224), Seidel and Federico Pace (2013, 60–61), and Pace (2007, 65–66).

[26] Forrester (2001, 78).

[27] 'All agreements between undertakings, decisions by associations of undertakings and concerted practices which may affect trade between Member States and which have as their object or effect the prevention, restriction or distortion of competition within the internal market'.

Article 101(3) TFEU sets an exception to the general prohibition, rather than defining the scope of the prohibition itself, as suggested by the principle of abuse advocated by the French.

Still, the wording of Article 101 TFEU has left many issues unresolved. In particular, the Member States have avoided taking controversial decisions on how to balance competition and non-competition interests: At a substantive level, the Article does not define the *types of relevant benefits, method of balancing, or intensity of control*; at a procedural level, although Article 101(3) TFEU states that the prohibition 'may, however, be declared inapplicable', it does not specify *whom* should make such a declaration, or *when*. The substantive aspects are detailed in the next section, and the procedural aspects are elaborated in Section 2.3.

2.2.3 *Substantive Aspects: The Four Conditions of Article 101(3) TFEU*

The wording of Article 101(3) TFEU lays out the Treaty's framework for balancing under Article 101 TFEU. An anti-competitive agreement that is otherwise prohibited by Article 101(1) TFEU can only be accepted if all four conditions of Article 101(3) TFEU have been met. Hence, an agreement (i) must produce benefits; (ii) must allow consumers a fair share of those benefits; (iii) must be limited to restrictions that are indispensable for attaining such objectives; and (iv) must not eliminate competition in the relevant market. The four conditions are cumulative and exhaustive. That is, all of them must be fulfilled for an exemption to be applicable, and once they have been met, an exception may not be made dependent on any other condition.[28]

Chapters 3 and 4 will examine the balancing function and practices of Article 101 (3) TFEU in detail. For the purpose of this chapter, this section demonstrates that each of the four conditions was drafted in ambiguous terms, leaving the competition enforcers wide discretion to balance in a specific case.

2.2.3.1 First Condition: Benefit[29]

The first condition of Article 101(3) TFEU stipulates that an agreement must contribute 'to improving the production or distribution of goods or to promoting technical or economic progress'. This is known as the *benefit* resulting from an agreement. From the early days of EU competition law, scholars, regulators, and

[28] See C-43/82 C-63/82 VBVB/VBBB (1984), para 61; T-185/00 Eurovision (2002), para 86; T-17/93 Ford-Volkswagen (1994), para 85; T-213/00 Far East Trade Tariff Charges and Surcharges Agreement (FETTCSA) (2003), para 226. See also Commission Article 101(3) Guidelines (2004), para 42.

[29] I have previously discussed questions related to the first benefit condition of Article 101(3) TFEU in Brook (2019, 125–129).

practitioners have alluded to the uncertainty surrounding this condition.[30] In particular, it raises two important sets of questions.

First, the Article does not clearly define the *nature* of benefits that fall within the scope of the first condition. Some types of benefits are clearly covered by the Article. This includes cost-efficiencies related to production and distribution chains ('improving the production or distribution'), development of new technologies and products ('technical progress'), and economic growth ('economic progress'). Yet, the consideration of less quantifiable non-competition interests is more equivocal. Article 101(3) TFEU does not indicate if industrial policies (e.g. protection of the national or the common market, development of industries, employment) or political policies (e.g. culture, preservation of traditional forms of trade) may also constitute a relevant benefit.

Second, the Article does not define the relevant *beneficiaries*. It does not specify, for instance, whether only direct benefits to direct consumers should be considered or whether indirect benefits to consumers in other markets or to society as a whole should also play a role.

The answer to these questions bears a significant impact on balancing. Accepting broad types of benefits for a wide group of beneficiaries reserves a greater role for non-competition interests and *vice versa*. To structure the discussion, this study follows the categorisation of benefits offered by a group of experts and summarised by the Office of Fair Trade (OFT). Combining the above two questions, it differentiates between three categories of benefits:[31]

Direct economic benefits are cost and qualitative efficiencies that occur to direct or indirect users of the product or service covered by the agreement. These benefits either directly affect prices or directly provide additional non-price value for consumers, such as new products, better quality, or greater product variety.

Indirect economic benefits are cost and qualitative efficiencies that do not occur in the market in which the agreement takes place or has a direct impact. Such benefits typically arise in two-sided markets, where an agreement concluded on one side of the market produces indirect benefits for consumers on the other side of the market.

Finally, *non-economic benefits* are non-pecuniary benefits that are not directly related to the characteristics of the relevant product or service. Often more subjective than direct or indirect economic benefits, they include cultural interests, environmental benefits (that are not directly valued by consumers within the relevant market), financial stability, or the promotion of national or international interests.

The distinction between the three categories of benefits is not always clear cut. Rather, they can be placed on a scale depending on the degree of remoteness.

[30] For example, see Ehlermann (2000, 549), Wesseling (2000, 77–113), Monti (2002, 1064–1066), Sufrin (2006, 933–936), Odudu (2006, 160–174), Monti (2007, 88–123), Townley (2009, 141–176), Petit (2009, 6–9), Van Rompuy (2012, 253–266), Witt (2016b, 160–174), and Sauter (2016, 64–75).

[31] OFT Roundtable on Narrow versus Broad Definition of Benefits (2010), para 3.2–3.17.

Benefits enjoyed by remote beneficiaries are more likely to be characterised as an indirect economic benefit than as a direct economic benefit. Moreover, a high degree of remoteness makes a benefit more intangible, and hence more similar to a non-economic benefit.[32]

On a side note, it should be observed that the term 'benefits' is not identical to the notion of 'non-competition interests' as defined in this study.[33] Non-competition interests describe the type of *policy* promoted by an agreement (e.g. environmental or employment). The notion of benefits refers to the *case-specific* improvement resulting from an agreement. The promotion of a single non-competition interest might produce various types of benefits. For example, an agreement that stimulates environmental policy might create direct economic benefits (e.g. quality improvements in the form of green credentials), while another agreement might produce non-economic environmental benefits enjoyed by society as a whole (e.g. reducing pollution).

2.2.3.2 Second Condition: Fair Share

The second condition of Article 101(3) TFEU states that an agreement must allow 'consumers a fair share of the resulting benefit'. This condition also raises two sets of questions.

The first set of questions relates to what constitutes a *fair share*. The Article does not specify a quantitative definition of fair share. It is unclear if consumers can only be compensated for the anti-competitive harms or if the overall effects of an agreement should be positive. Should consumers receive a fair share of each type of benefit?[34] Article 101(3) TFEU, likewise, does not stipulate how different types of benefits should be weighted. For example, can an increase in prices be compensated by improved quality? And if so, what degree of improvement is sufficient?[35]

The answers to those questions outline the limits of balancing. A broad definition of fair share, which allows offsetting benefits and competitive harm across groups of consumers and between different types of benefits, broadens the discretion of competition enforcers to balance competition and non-competition interests.

The second set of questions centres on the definition of *consumers*. The meaning of this term is especially ambiguous as some of the linguistics versions of the Treaty state the term 'users' rather than 'consumers'. Some have argued that the term 'users' is limited to the ultimate buyers of the product or service in question, entailing that benefits to indirect consumers and consumers in downstream markets should not be

[32] *Ibid*, para 3.13.

[33] For a definition of non-competition interests, see Section 1.2.1.

[34] Van Rompuy (2012, 264).

[35] Nicolaides (2005, 137).

taken into account for the purpose of Article 101(3) TFEU.[36] Yet, in practice, this term was interpreted more broadly. The Commission and EU Courts have typically understood it as referring to all users of the product or service in question. In some cases, the competition enforcers have interpreted this condition even broader, as including the benefits brought by the agreement to the society as a whole.[37]

Even if one limits the second condition of Article 101(3) TFEU to direct and indirect consumers, the Article does not specify if each consumer must be individually compensated or whether benefits to a group of consumers can compensate for the harm caused to another group.[38] Similarly, the Article does not explain if the benefits and costs within each affected relevant market should be considered separately (i.e. for each group of consumers) or aggregated across all affected markets. If two separate geographic markets are affected by an agreement and the gains in one market significantly outweigh the harm done in the other, should one aggregate the two sets of costs and benefits in order to examine the agreement (i.e. cross-subsidisation of consumers groups)?[39]

The definition of consumer also relates to the issue of future consumers. For instance, can the calculation of the fair share incorporate gains enjoyed by future consumers? Are inter-generational benefits sufficient to compensate anti-competitive harm inflicted on present consumers? And if so, how should a discount rate be applied to future benefits?[40]

Constructing the notion of relevant consumers broadly increases the likelihood that non-competition interests could offset anti-competitive harm. Instead of compensating each consumer for the specific harm caused to him or her, the harm could be countered by benefits to other consumers, consumers in other markets, future consumers, or society as a whole.

2.2.3.3 Third Condition: Indispensability

The third condition of Article 101(3) TFEU states that an agreement must not 'impose on the undertakings concerned restrictions which are not indispensable to the attainment of these objectives'. This means that the restrictions of competition must be indispensable to the attainment of the benefits (i.e. to the improvement of production or distribution or to the technical and economic progress).

36 The French version, for example, refers to 'utilisateurs', and the Italian to 'utilizzatori'. Other versions, like the German ('Verbraucher'), Dutch ('gebruikers'), and Danish ('forbrugere'), refer to similar terms as the English version. See also Evans (1985, 101) and Goyder (2009, 151). Cseres (2007b, 131–133), moreover, notes that this narrow interpretation also guides consumer protection law.

37 See Section 3.6.2.2.

38 Van Rompuy (2012, 262).

39 OFT Roundtable on Narrow versus Broad Definition of Benefits (2010), para 4.1.

40 *Ibid*, para 5.1.

The Article does not explain which features of indispensability are required. As early as *Grundig/Consten (1966)*, the CJEU pointed to two aspects of this condition:[41] First, the Court maintained that there should be a *causal link* between the restriction on competition and the benefit. The restriction must contribute to the realisation of the benefit. Second, the Court clarified that indispensability entails *balancing*. An agreement may be exempted only if it generates benefits large enough to compensate the distortion of competition. This also means that the applicability of Article 101(3) TFEU might be limited in time. An agreement is exempted only as long as the restriction is necessary to realise the benefits. The third condition of Article 101(3) TFEU, therefore, contains a proportionality test.[42] Accordingly, strict application of the indispensability condition makes it difficult to accept any anti-competitive measure, and *vice versa*.

2.2.3.4 Fourth Condition: Elimination of Competition

The final condition of Article 101(3) TFEU stipulates that an agreement must not afford undertakings 'the possibility of eliminating competition in respect of a substantial part of the products in question'. The interpretation of the fourth condition is particularly ambiguous and has changed over the years. In the past, the prevailing view was that the condition was closely linked to the concept of dominance. According to this interpretation, undertakings having a large market share were automatically in breach of the fourth condition and could never be exempted under Article 101(3) TFEU.[43] Hence, non-competition interests could not be examined under Article 101 TFEU if they were included in an agreement involving dominant undertakings.[44]

Towards the 2000s, the interpretation shifted to a more economic-based analysis.[45] The fourth condition of Article 101(3) TFEU was seen as *ascribing weights* to

[41] C-56/64 C-58/64 Grundig/Consten (1966), 348.

[42] Goyder (2009, 152–152) and Sauter (2014, 329).

[43] In 30979 31394 Decca Navigator System (1988), para 122, the Commission held that an agreement that arises from abuse of a dominant position could not benefit from an Article 101(3) TFEU exemption. This seemed to apply regardless of the four conditions, which were analysed separately. See also Nicolaides (2005, 140).

[44] In some cases, nevertheless, non-competition interests may still play a role under Article 102 TFEU. A behaviour may be justified under the Article where a dominant undertaking proves that its behaviour is objectively necessary – for example, for health or safety reasons – or produces substantial efficiencies that outweigh any anti-competitive effects. See, for example, C-27/76 United Brands (1978), para 184; T-30/89 Hilti (1991), para 115–119; C-333/94P Tetra Pak II (1996), para 37. On the role of non-competition interests in Article 102 TFEU, see also Vijver (2012) and the many sources there.

[45] The old interpretation was explicitly rejected by the GC in T-191/98 Atlantic Container Line (2003), para 937–939. The Court explained that such an interpretation was inconsistent with EU competition theory and Article 102 TFEU, in which being dominant is not regarded as harmful to competition in itself. The Court stated that an agreement between undertakings having a dominant position could be exempted, as 'the prohibition on eliminating competition

the balance between competition and non-competition interests. Namely, the condition was understood as a declaration that the protection of rivalry and the competitive process are prioritised over other benefits. Short-term benefits arising from an anti-competitive agreement cannot prevail over a long-term harm to the competitive process.[46] This reading allows dominant undertakings to also benefit from Article 101(3) TFEU.

The above demonstrates that, although the four conditions of Article 101(3) TFEU establish the substantive framework for balancing under Article 101 TFEU, they do not provide a detailed substantive balancing regime. The four conditions were drafted in broad terms, leaving each competition enforcer a wide margin of discretion to decide *whether* to take non-competition interests into account, *what types of benefits* to consider, and *how*. As the next section shows, in the past, these gaps were primarily filled by the practices of the Commission and EU Courts. Since May 2004, however, NCAs and national courts have also influenced the balancing exercise.

2.3 BALANCING IN EU SECONDARY LAW: BETWEEN NOTIFICATIONS AND SELF-ASSESSMENT

The vague wording of Article 101 TFEU leaves not only the substantive elements of the Article open to interpretation but also the applicable procedural framework.[47] This section shows that the Treaties have entrusted the Council with a choice between an *ex-ante* authorisation system and a directly applicable *ex-post* exception enforcement system and between centralised and decentralised regime.[48] As will be elaborated in Section 2.5 and throughout this book, those procedural choices have had a tremendous influence on the application of the explicit-substantive balancing tools and have given rise to new invisible forms of implicit-procedural balancing tools.

is a narrower concept than that of the existence or acquisition of a dominant position'. The Commission Article 101(3) Guidelines (2004), para 106, which were adopted shortly after the judgement, follow an effects-based approach to the fourth condition. They explain that it is possible to exempt a restrictive agreement involving a dominant undertaking if it has little effect on competition and therefore does not lead to substantial elimination of competition, provided that it does not constitute an abuse under Article 102 TFEU. See also Section 3.4.4.1.

46 Commission Article 101(3) Guidelines (2004), para 105.

47 Modernisation White Paper (1999), para 12–13, 18; Wils (2004, 10), Goyder (2009, 4041), Seidel and Federico Pace (2013, 63), and Kuenzler and Warlouzet (2013, 110–111).

48 Article 103 TFEU. See also Modernisation White Paper (1999), para 12–13. Notably, the wording of Article 101 TFEU is significantly different from the equivalent Article 65(4) ECSC Treaty, specifying 'the High Authority shall have sole jurisdiction [. . .] to rule whether any such agreement [. . .] is compatible with this Article'.

2.3.1 *Notification-Centralised Regime of Regulation 17/62*

The procedural framework for applying Article 101(3) TFEU balancing was first clarified in 1962 with the adoption of Regulation 17/62. As with the adoption of Article 101 TFEU itself, this too was the product of 'extremely tense' negotiation between the French and German delegations.[49] Whilst France was prominent in the drafting of Article 101 TFEU itself, this time around, the German approach prevailed.

France (supported by Luxemburg) had proposed that a declaration of inapplicability under Article 101(3) TFEU should be based on self-assessment with *ex-post* control, corresponding with the principle of abuse that guided its domestic law.[50] This was not only inspired by competition concerns but was also motivated by the political aim of avoiding a 'too rigid' supervision of cartels.[51]

The German delegation (supported by the Netherlands, Belgium, and the Commission) pursued a different approach. After its proposal for a total prohibition on cartels in Article 101 TFEU had been rejected, Germany strove to ensure a strict *ex-ante* application of EU competition rules similar to its own national system.[52] Moreover, the German delegation rejected the French proposal as incompatible with the wording of Article 101 TFEU. It noted that the phrase 'may, however, be declared inapplicable' required a constitutive decision for exemption.[53]

Regulation 17/62 reflected a notification and authorisation system based on the German proposal. The Regulation introduced a centralised system by which all agreements need to have been notified to the Commission prior to their implementation.[54] Under this procedural arrangement, the Commission had exclusive competence for balancing under Article 101(3) TFEU.

The Member States also debated the level of involvement they would retain in enforcement. On the one hand, France aimed to safeguard the role of national governments. It demanded that the Commission and the affected Member States take infringement decisions jointly and that the Member States have veto powers via an Advisory Committee. Similarly, France objected to granting the Commission independent investigation and fining powers.[55] On the other hand, the German

49 As described by von der Groeben, the first Competition Commissioner. See der Groeben (1987, 108).

50 Seidel and Federico Pace (2013, 70), der Groeben (1987, 109), Wesseling (2000, 20), Wilks (2005, 434), and Sufrin (2006, 923).

51 der Groeben (1987, 109).

52 Wesseling (2000, 20) and Pace (2007, 71).

53 Sufrin (2006, 923) and Seidel and Federico Pace (2013, 70). This criticism was repeated with the adoption of Regulation 1/2003, as detailed in Section 2.3.3.1.

54 Articles 4(1) and (2) of Regulation 17/62 set a very limited exception to bilateral agreements on distribution of goods and licensing of technology.

55 der Groeben (1987, 109), Wesseling (2000, 20), and Seidel and Federico Pace (2013, 70–71, 78–83).

proposal, which had been adopted by the Regulation, granted the Commission complete independence. An Advisory Committee, an *ad hoc* body composed of officials appointed by the Member States, had only advisory, non-binding powers.[56]

Notably, the Commission's independence and monopoly to apply Article 101(3) TFEU were based on the assumption that it was the only actor capable of employing the discretionary balancing powers in a coherent and uniform manner. Other enforcers, it was feared, would incorporate domestic non-competition interests into their decisions.[57] This position was summarised in the Commission's policy report in 1993, noting 'the grant of a derogation from the ban on restrictive agreements requires assessment of *complex economic situation and the exercise of considerable discretionary* power, particularly where *different objectives of the EC Treaty are involved*. This task *can only be performed by the Commission*'.[58] The strength of this assumption should not be underestimated. *Ehlermann*, the Director-General of DG COMP until 1995, described the Commission's monopoly as 'natural' and 'almost a religious belief'.[59]

2.3.2 *Blessing and Curse: Consequences of Regulation 17/62*

The consequences of Regulation 17/62 are well documented.[60] Shortly after it was issued, the Commission was flooded with an unmanageably large number of notifications. The Commission had to process more than 34,500 notifications requesting a negative clearance (i.e. declaring that Article 101(1) TFEU did not apply) or an individual exemption under Article 101(3) TFEU.[61] As will be elaborated in Chapters 3–5, many of those notifications involved balancing questions. The large number of notifications was reinforced by the Commission's and CJEU's broad interpretation of Article 101(1) TFEU. They constructed the notions of 'restriction of competition' and 'trade between Member States' so broadly that they included almost any restriction imposed on the commercial freedom of undertakings.[62]

Faced with the enormous number of notifications, the Commission quickly developed several tools to avoid having to apply a full competition analysis in each

56 Regulation 17/62, Article 10 as replaced by Regulation 1/2003, Article 14.

57 Modernisation White Paper (1999), para 17. See also Temple Lang (1998, 3), Ehlermann (2000, 537–538), Wils (2004, 14–17; 2005, 6–7), Gerber (2008, 1239), Jones (2010, 787–788), and Sauter (2016, 41–42).

58 Emphasis added. Policy report 1993, para 190.

59 Ehlermann (2000, 537–538).

60 In particular, see Van Bael (1986, 62–63), Temple Lang (1998, 3, 4–5), Ehlermann (2000, 541), Riley (2003a, 614), Wils (2005, 5–7), Sufrin (2006, 917–918), Gippini-Fournier (2008, 5–8), Goyder (2009, 52–53, 613–615), Jones (2010, 789–790), and Temple Lang (2014, 3).

61 Green Paper on Vertical Restraints (1997), iv; Modernisation White Paper (1999), para 25; Korah (1981a, 15), Ehlermann (2000, 541), Goyder (2009, 40), and Temple Lang (2014, 3).

62 See Sections 5.1.1 and 7.5.4, respectively.

case: First, as early as 1967, the Commission had introduced the first Block Exemption Regulation (BER) on distribution agreements.[63] The BER exempted categories of agreements *en bloc*, depending on their form (i.e. if they contained certain provisions and omitted others). The BER relieved the Commission from the duty of undertaking case-by-case analysis and significantly reduced its backlog of cases.[64] In fact, out of the 40,000 notifications received by the Commission during the first years of Regulation 17/62, 25,000 were settled by the BER.[65] Chapter 4 maintains that in addition to this workload reduction function, BERs also constitute a tool to balance competition and non-competition interests.

Second, the Commission had issued notices indicating that certain agreements were not prohibited under Article 101(1) TFEU. Some of those notices, such as those on patent licensing, cooperation between undertakings, and the *de minimis* rule, too, have expressed a form of balancing.[66]

Third, from the early 1970s, the Commission had developed an informal instrument in the form of comfort letters. A comfort letter is an administrative letter signed by a Commission official stating that no action will be taken with respect to a particular agreement. Following the issuance of such a letter, the Commission terminates the proceedings without adopting a formal decision. The Commission has used comfort letters to deal with agreements that 'at first sight raise no problems with respect to the rules of competition and do not require a formal decision'.[67] Initially, comfort letters were only employed for negative clearance, but since the mid-1980s, they have been extended to Article 101(3) TFEU exemptions.[68]

Although comfort letters are not binding on national courts, NCAs, or third parties,[69] since the 1980s, in an effort to increase their legal authority, the Commission has begun to publish the essential contents of the notified agreements in the official journal and invited comments from third parties.[70] Moreover, from 1990 onwards, the Commission has circulated general information specifying the reasons for closing a case by means of a comfort letter. Chapter 7 submits that comfort letters offer the competition enforcer a flexible tool to explicitly and implicitly account for non-competition interests.

63 Regulation 67/67 on Distribution Agreements.

64 Policy report 1968, 43; policy report 1971, 41.

65 Policy report 1979, 16.

66 Policy report 1971, 101. See also Sections 5.3.5, 5.3.4, and 5.3.6, respectively.

67 Policy report 1981, para 15. On comfort letters, see also Van Bael (1986, 63), Temple Lang (1994, 566–567), and Norberg (2007, 525).

68 Policy report 1983, 13.

69 This was clarified by the CJEU, see C-253/79 C-3/79 Procureur de la République (1980), para 13; C-31/80 L'Oréal (1980), para 11–12.

70 Policy report 1981, para 15; see also Van Bael (1986, 78–79).

Fourth, the Commission closed proceedings by accepting voluntary commitments.[71] For this purpose, the Commission has employed its exclusive power to apply Article 101(3) TFEU to invite undertakings to modify their agreements. Those modifications have been incorporated into both formal and informal decisions to secure a practical solution to a competition problem. The empirical findings presented in Chapters 3 and 7 will show that voluntary commitments were often used to strike a case-by-case balance between competition and non-competition interests.

By virtue of combining the four above measures, more than 95% of Article 101 and 102 TFEU proceedings under Regulation 17/62 have been resolved by means of informal measures.[72] Those cases have often gone unpublished. *Van Bael* has estimated that only 4% of the informal proceedings have been mentioned, even briefly, in the Commission's policy reports or press releases.[73] This has led the enforcement regime of Regulation 17/62 to be perceived as being 'both a blessing and a curse':[74]

On the one hand, the centralised-enforcement regime has facilitated an EU culture of competition. At a time when most Member States did not have robust competition laws, it empowered the Commission to apply uniform rules throughout the EU.[75] Moreover, the combination of BERs, notices, comfort letters, and voluntary commitments had empowered the Commission to monitor the development of competition policy and the EU markets. The Commission had not only enforced competition law to correct specific infringements but had also regulated the activities of undertakings and the functioning of markets.[76]

On the other hand, the enforcement regime suffered from serious procedural and substantive flaws. At the procedural level, the Commission was never able to totally eliminate its backlog of cases, especially as it gradually began to assess more complicated infringements.[77] Most decisions were informal in nature, lacking sufficient transparency and fully binding effect.[78] Chapters 3–5 illustrate that in particular, in the context of balancing, this had created great uncertainty as to the role of non-competition interests in the enforcement. Reform also became pressing in light of the gradual enlargement of the EU and particularly the significant accession of ten

[71] Policy report 1982, 59. On voluntary commitments, see also Korah (1981a, 15), Van Bael (1986, 63), Bailey (2016, 115), and Section 7.6.2.

[72] The statistical information extracted from the Commission's policy reports on competition policy is reproduced in Van Bael (1986, 61). See also Policy report 1971, 24; policy report 1976, 11; policy report 1999, 26; Forrester (1994, 469); and Wesseling (2000, 22–23).

[73] Van Bael (1986, 64–65).

[74] In the words of Wilks (2005, 434).

[75] Modernisation White Paper (1999), para 4.

[76] Van Bael (1986, 62), Wils (2005, 5–7), and Bailey (2016, 114). See also Sections 2.5.2.1 and 3.4.3.

[77] Policy report 1996, 24; policy report 1999, 20.

[78] Policy report 1981, 27–28; policy report 1982, 38; policy report 1983; 61–62; policy report 1984, 13; Ehlermann (2000, 541, 554); Wilks (2005, 436); and Norberg (2007, 525).

Central and European Member States in 2004.[79] Under those circumstances, the notification system of Regulation 17/62 had simply become unmanageable.

At the substantive level, the Commission's scarce resources were used to manage notifications rather than investigate complaints or pursue *ex officio* procedures. In fact, by the late 1990s, only 0.5% of the agreements notified to the Commission ended in a prohibition decision.[80] In the more than 40 years of application of Regulation 17/62, there have been only 9 decisions in which a notified agreement was prohibited without a complaint having been lodged against it.[81] At the Member States level, the NCAs have rarely dealt with infringement of Article 101 TFEU. Although around half of the NCAs were formally competent under their national laws to apply Article 101(1) TFEU, the Commission's monopoly to apply Article 101 (3) TFEU had discouraged them from doing so.[82] Reform was vital to allow the Commission to refocus its enforcement priorities to combat the most serious restrictions on competition.[83] In parallel, the justification for the Commission's monopoly for granting Article 101(3) TFEU exemptions weakened. Over the years, the Commission developed EU competition policy, and Member States adopted national competition laws and set up specialised authorities to implement them.[84]

To conclude, the procedural regime of Regulation 17/62 has had mixed effects for balancing. It has allowed the Commission to resolve conflicts between competition and non-competition interests in an *ex-ante* and centralised manner. Meanwhile, this enforcement system has not had the effect of pressuring the Commission to adopt a clear and comprehensive balancing framework. Those effects on the balancing are examined in Section 2.5.

2.3.3 *Modernisation of Competition Law*

2.3.3.1 Origin and Reactions to the White Paper

By the mid-1990s, there was a clear need for a reform to increase the effectiveness of Article 101 TFEU enforcement.[85] The establishment of the Modernisation Group in 1997 marked the first step towards reform. Consisting of approximately a dozen

[79] Modernisation White Paper (1999), para 40–42. See also policy report, 1994, 18; policy report 1995, 7, 45; policy report 1996, 24; policy report 1997, 7, 89; policy report 2000, 11; policy report 2001, 4.

[80] Policy report 1999, 9. See also Modernisation White Paper (1999), para 43–44.

[81] Modernisation White Paper (1999), footnote 53.

[82] Wils (2004, 24) and Blanco (2006, 44).

[83] Commission Staff Working Paper accompanying the Report on Functioning of Regulation 1/2003 (2009), para 3.

[84] Temple Lang (1998, 4) and Ehlermann (2000, 554).

[85] See also policy report 1999, 25–26; policy report 2000, 30; policy report 2003, 4, 20.

Commission officials, the Group's work was kept secret, even within the Commission itself.[86]

The Group's recommendations were presented in the Modernisation White Paper of 1999. It advocated a radical, and largely unforeseen, three-pronged reform.[87] The *procedural* pillar of modernisation proposed a shift towards a self-assessment system, in which Article 101(3) TFEU is reviewed *ex-post* by the competition enforcers. Under the *institutional* pillar of modernisation, the Commission gave up its monopoly to apply Article 101(3) TFEU in favour of decentralised enforcement. Finally, the *substantive* pillar of modernisation introduced economic thinking to EU competition law. The effects of those three pillars on balancing are detailed in Section 2.5.4.

While the Modernisation White Paper had generally received positive reactions,[88] it did encounter some opposition. Germany, in particular, expressed strong disagreement with the White Paper. While acknowledging that procedural reform was necessary, the German Monopolies Commission[89] submitted that such a reform required a Treaty amendment. It argued that the positive wording of Article 101(3) TFEU ('may, however, be declared inapplicable') does not support a self-assessment system. Similarly, it maintained that a decentralised self-assessment system contradicts the CJEU's case law declaring that Article 101(1) TFEU has direct effect. According to the Monopolies Commission, the proposed enforcement regime granted the Member States discretion to apply Article 101(3) TFEU in a manner that denies the conditions for direct effect.[90] It also believed that the shift – from a notification to a self-assessment system – was unnecessary to deal with the Commission's excessive workload. Rather, this could have been resolved by a more efficient allocation of resources or modification of the existing system (e.g. a decentralised notification system).[91]

The German Monopolies Commission further highlighted that the Commission's sole power to grant Article 101(3) TFEU exemptions served an important balancing aim. It ensured uniform application of the exemption criteria 'in view of the great differences between the national competition laws and the legal

[86] Norberg (2007, 527–528) and Wils (2013, 294).
[87] Sufrin (2006, 918) and Wils (2013, 294). For example, the German government and German NCA requested that the Commission share its monopoly to grant exceptions. The more radical solution of shifting to a self-assessment system, however, was rarely suggested or discussed. See Ehlermann (1996, 90; 2000, 541–542).
[88] Wils (2013, 295). On the process and Member States' reactions to the proposal, see Kassim and Wright (2009, 746–749).
[89] The German Monopolies Commission was established by the Second Amendment of the German Competition Act of 1973 to oversee and report on competitive conditions and to play an occasional role in merger review. The Monopolies Commission is an independent expert committee that advises the German government and legislature in areas of competition policy-making, competition law, and regulation. See German Competition Act, Sections 44–47.
[90] German Monopolies Commission (2000, 16–21).
[91] Ibid, 45–47 and Bdge (2001, 68). See also Ehlermann and Atanasiu (2001, 18).

and economic policy ideas of Member States'.[92] The Monopolies Commission submitted that only the Commission had both the mandate and the ability to reconcile the conflicts of interest, holding that 'this is essentially a political act, whose subject matter is the weighing up of incommensurable factors'.[93] In fact, the Monopolies Commission was concerned that the new priority setting powers granted to the Commission pursuant to the regime would give rise to political considerations. For instance, opening or withdrawing procedures could be guided by industrial policy rather than by pure competition interests.[94]

A designated Committee of the UK House of Lords raised similar concerns, although the UK government was more supportive of the Commission's proposal.[95]

Nevertheless, given the overall positive reactions to the Modernisation White Paper, in 2000 the Commission submitted to the Council a legislative proposal for the reform.[96] The proposal was worded similarly to the version finally adopted by virtue of Regulation 1/2003. Yet, as the next sub-section reveals, it was different in one important respect: the relationship between EU and national competition laws.

2.3.3.2 Point of Contention: EU and National Competition Laws

The decentralisation of enforcement has generated new questions as to the relationship between EU and national competition laws. The Commission, Council, European Parliament, and industry representatives were concerned that decentralised enforcement would lead to the re-nationalisation of EU competition policy.[97] They highlighted that the enforcement system must ensure that Article 101 TFEU is applied in a uniform manner throughout the EU, despite differences in national competition laws and traditions.[98]

To accommodate such concerns, the legislative proposal for Regulation 1/2003 originally suggested that national competition laws would not apply to agreements that fall within the scope of Article 101 TFEU.[99] In other words, EU and national

92 German Monopolies Commission (2000, 37).

93 *Ibid.*

94 *Ibid*, 40. This is discussed in Section 7.4.

95 Select Committee on European Union (2000), para 11, 150; and Byers (2000).

96 Proposal for a Council Modernisation Regulation (2000). See also policy report 1999, 8.

97 Council's Progress Report on Proposal for Modernisation (2001), para 10; Commission's Staff Working Paper on Proposal for Modernisation (2001), para 11; Committee on Economic and Monterey Affairs Report on Proposal for Modernisation (2000), 22. See also Temple Lang (1998, 13–15) and Wils (2013, 295).

98 Those differences are presented and discussed in Section 2.6.

99 Proposal for a Council Modernisation Regulation (2000), Preamble 8 and Article 3. The Article states 'where an agreement, a decision by an association of undertakings or a concerted practice within the meaning of Article [101 TFEU] or the abuse of a dominant position within the meaning of Article [102 TFEU] may affect trade between Member States, Community competition law shall apply to the exclusion of national competition laws'. This provision was not reproduced in Regulation 1/2003.

competition laws would not be applied in parallel. Nevertheless, this provision drew significant opposition from a number of Member States. In fact, it proved to be the most contentious point in the Council's deliberations.[100]

A compromise was ultimately found in the form of Article 3 of Regulation 1/2003. The Article introduced a duty for the *parallel application* of EU and national laws. It has obliged NCAs and national courts to apply EU competition law when applying national competition law to agreements falling within the scope of application of Article 101 TFEU that is, agreements having an effect on trade between Member States (the primacy rule of Article 3(1)). It further establishes the primacy of EU law by holding that the application of national competition law may not lead to the prohibition of an agreement that is not prohibited under Article 101 TFEU (the convergence rule of Article 3(2)).[101] The implications and limitations of this parallel application on balancing are examined in Chapters 6 and 7.

2.3.3.3 Commission's and NCAs' Role under Regulation 1/2003

Regulation 1/2003 empowers the Member States to apply Article 101(3) TFEU directly. Although it entrusted the NCAs with the power to *apply* EU competition rules, the development of competition *policy* still remains the Commission's prerogative. This is reflected by various provisions of the Regulation.[102]

First, only the Commission can adopt a *positive decision*, that is, a formal decision explaining why an agreement is not in breach of Article 101(1) TFEU or fulfils the conditions of Article 101(3) TFEU.[103] The NCAs can only find that there are *no grounds for action* on their part when, on the basis of the information in their possession, the conditions for Article 101 TFEU have not been met.[104] As confirmed by the CJEU in *Tele2Polska (2011)*, the NCAs do not have the power to formally declare that Article 101 TFEU is inapplicable. The difference between positive decisions and 'no grounds for action' findings is vindicated by the need to ensure uniformity in the decentralised enforcement system:[105] Only the Commission can reach a binding conclusion on the application of Article 101 TFEU, and thus on balancing. NCAs can simply explain why an investigation was discontinued, while the Commission or another NCA may reach a different decision in the future.[106] Nevertheless, decisions including 'no grounds for action' findings are noteworthy. As

[100] Staff Working Paper on Article 3 – The Relationship between EU and National Law (2001). See also Kassim and Wright (2009, 746–749) and Wils (2013, 295).

[101] See also policy report 1971, 105–106; and Faull and Nikpay (2014, 101–112).

[102] Kingston (2001, 334) and Sauter (2016, 173–174).

[103] Regulation 1/2003, Article 10. The Commission will adopt those decisions of its own initiative where the EU public interest requires.

[104] Regulation 1/2003, Article 5.

[105] C-375/09 Tele2Polska (2011), para 27–28.

[106] Such conflicts are discussed in Section 3.6.

demonstrated by the empirical findings presented throughout this book, NCAs have used those decisions to shape and clarify Article 101 TFEU balancing principles.[107]

Second, Regulation 1/2003 safeguards the Commission's role in ensuring the consistent application of EU competition law. The Regulation set the ground for the European Competition Network (ECN), a forum for informal contact and consultation between the Commission and NCAs on enforcement policy aimed at avoiding divergent application.[108] The Commission has a central role to play in this network. In particular, Articles 11(3) and (4) of the Regulation obliges NCAs to inform the Commission before commencing a first formal investigative measure, adopting a decision requiring an infringement brought to an end, accepting commitments, or withdrawing a benefit conferred by a BER.[109] Subsequent to those notifications, the Commission may initiate its own proceeding while relieving the NCA of its competence to apply Article 101 TFEU to such a case.[110] According to the Commission's and Council's declaration, the Commission will only do so in exceptional cases, if NCAs are about to issue conflicting decisions in a single case, when a decision 'is obviously in conflict with consolidated case law' or when a decision has 'significant divergence' with respect to the facts. The Commission may also initiate proceedings when its decision is necessary for the development of EU competition policy.[111] In practice, however, the Commission has not formally initiated such proceedings.[112]

Third, in a similar vein, Article 15(3) of Regulation 1/2003 entrusts the Commission with the submission of *amicus curiae* briefs on its own initiative in proceedings taking place before national courts when the coherent application of Article 101 TFEU so requires.[113]

In conclusion, this section has demonstrated that EU secondary law indirectly affects balancing by dictating the actors that may do so and the relevant point in time. Yet, EU secondary law has not established any substantive criteria for balancing. It has not defined what types of benefits can be taken into account, the

[107] See also Section 7.6.3.

[108] Regulation 1/2003, Preamble 15–18 and Article 11; Council and the Commission ECN Statement (2004), para 3. On the purpose and functioning of the ECN, see also Wils (2005, 62–67), Goyder (2009, 528–530), Cengiz (2010b), Monti (2014), and Sauter (2016, 146–158).

[109] This applies only to agreements affecting trade between Member States.

[110] Regulation 1/2003, Article 11(6). The Commission shall initiate proceedings where an NCA is already acting on a case following prior consultation with the relevant NCA.

[111] Council and the Commission ECN Statement (2004), para 21.

[112] Commission Staff Working Paper Accompanying the policy report 2010, 107; Commission Staff Working Paper accompanying the Report on Functioning of Regulation 1/2003 (2009), para 256.

[113] On the application of Article 15(3) of Regulation 1/2003, see Modernisation White Paper (1999), para 107; Commission Staff Working Paper accompanying the Report on Functioning of Regulation 1/2003 (2009), para 283–290; Report on the functioning of Regulation 1/2003 (2014), para 22; Wright (2008, 16–17) GCLC Annual Conference (2010, 358–376), and Sauter (2016, 178–187).

balancing method, or the intensity of control. The next section shows that the EU Courts have played an important role in filling some of these gaps, especially prior to modernisation.

2.4 EU COURTS' ROLE IN SHAPING BALANCING

Over the years, the EU Courts have played an important role in developing certain balancing principles. As elaborated throughout the book, the EU Courts have shaped balancing in two types of proceedings:

First, CJEU preliminary rulings have interpreted various aspects of balancing.[114] To this end, preliminary rulings have facilitated a dialogue between the CJEU and national courts seeking guidance on the appropriate scope of balancing. The CJEU has advised national courts in matters such as the objectives of Article 101 TFEU, the types of benefits that can be taken into account when applying the various balancing tools, and the balancing method. By comparison, NCAs are not considered to be a 'court or tribunal' in the meaning of Article 267 TFEU and therefore cannot refer questions for preliminary rulings.[115]

Second, the CJEU - and since 1988 also the GC - have examined actions for annulment against the Commission's balancing decisions.[116] The Commission's decisions have been reviewed by the GC on points of fact and law and, subsequently, by the CJEU on points of law. The EU Courts apply two standards of judicial review. A full merit review guides the assessment of fines imposed by the Commission for an Article 101 TFEU infringement.[117] A marginal review is used to assess the application of the Article itself. This entails that the Courts only examine the relevance of the facts, and the legal consequences the Commission deduces therefrom.[118] The marginal review standard also demands that if a court annuls the Commission's decision, the case is referred back to the Commission. Unlike many other national administrative courts, the EU Courts do not substitute their appreciation of the facts for that of the Commission. They do not decide whether to grant an exemption.[119]

114 Article 267 TFEU. On the role of preliminary rulings in competition law, see Rodger (2008), Semmelmann (2008b, 44), Sauter (2016, 171–194), Kalintiri (2016, 44), and Toader (2017).

115 As confirmed by the CJEU in C-462/19 Asociación Nacional de Empresas Estibadoras y Consignatarios de Buques (Anesco) (2020), para 35–51.

116 Article 263 TFEU. On judicial review on the Commission's application of Article 101 TFEU, see also Bailey (2004), Meij (2009), Schweitzer (2013), Paz (2014), Prek and Lefèvre (2016), Sauter (2016, 188–191), and Kalintiri (2016, 188–191).

117 Article 261 TFEU in combination with Regulation 1/2003, Article 31.

118 C-56/64 C-58/64 Grundig/Consten (1966), 347. See also C-17/74 Transocean Marine Paint Association (1974), para 16; C-71/74 Frubo (1975), para 42–43; T-9/93 Langnese/Iglo (1995), para 140; Evans (1981, 435), Bailey (2004, 1327–1328, 1347), Sauter (2016, 188–191), and da Cruz (2018, 2–3).

119 See also Witt (2016b, 75–76) and Sauter (2016, 188).

The marginal review standard of the Commission's decisions (excluding the imposition of fines) has a number of justifications. It has been linked to the Commission's central role in developing competition policy and ensuring compliance with competition rules.[120] It was also explained by the complex evaluation of economic matters involved in applying Article 101 TFEU, which necessarily implies a degree of discretion. Finally, it has also been vindicated by the need to maintain the uniform application of Article 101(3) TFEU.

Despite the marginal standard of review, the empirical findings show that, prior to modernisation, the EU Courts, and especially the CJEU, held the reins in the development of balancing principles. In a series of landmark cases, the CJEU filled certain gaps in EU primary and secondary law concerning balancing. The Courts engaged in complex evaluations to influence the types of benefits that could be taken into account under the Article, the balancing method, and the development of new balancing tools. The GC played a similar role in influencing balancing, especially with respect to Article 101(1) TFEU balancing tools, albeit to a lesser extent than the CJEU.

As elaborated in the following chapters, the CJEU and GC have differed in their approaches to balancing. Historically, the CJEU has facilitated the consideration of a wide array of economic and non-economic benefits under Article 101 TFEU. As early as the 1960s, it promoted a more case-specific application of Article 101 TFEU, which took into account the effects of an agreement on other non-competition interests. The Court annulled a number of the Commission's decisions, finding that it had failed to adequately reflect the specific circumstances of the case. The GC, however, was generally more positive towards the Commission's approach. It called for a more market-based analysis in applying Article 101 TFEU and had typically accepted the Commission's balancing decisions.

The next section illustrates that while the EU Courts have not produced a detailed balancing framework, their case law has had an immense influence on the scope of Article 101 TFEU balancing, to a degree by which it is difficult to separate the EU Courts' approach to balancing from the development of the Commission's approach. The next section also reveals that the modernisation has marked a change in the EU Courts' role. Following modernisation, the EU Courts have played only a marginal role in shaping balancing principles, mostly in reaction to the Commission's practice. Although the Courts, and especially the CJEU, have not fully endorsed the Commission's more economic approach and its attempts to introduce a consumer welfare-based interpretation of Article 101 TFEU, neither have they taken a clear stand on those matters.

[120] T-29/92 Building and Construction Industry in the Netherlands (1995), para 288.

2.5 BALANCING IN PRACTICE I: THE COMMISSION'S APPROACH

This section provides a historical overview of the Commission's approach to Article 101 TFEU balancing as applied in practice. It details the development of the objectives and focus of enforcement.[121] An orderly review of such developments calls for distinguishing between different enforcement periods. This study roughly follows the periodisation established by previous scholars:[122] (i) the foundation period (1962–1977), from the entry into force of Regulation 17/62 to the *Metro I* judgement; (ii) the workable competition period (1978–1987), from *Metro I* to the signing of the SEA; (iii) the economic social and political EU era (1988–April 2004), from the SEA up until the entry into force of Regulation 1/2003; and (iv) the post-modernisation era (May 2004–2017).

It should be emphasised that this periodisation has been used to provide a sense of time structure and should not be taken too strictly. It offers an analytical guide for understanding changes in the modalities of balancing. It is also supported by the empirical findings, which point to changes in balancing patterns and are elaborated throughout the book.

2.5.1 *First Enforcement Period (1962–1977): The Foundation Period*

2.5.1.1 Balancing Guided by Keynesian Theories

The Commission began enforcing Article 101 TFEU with the adoption of Regulation 17/62, with its first decisions being handed down two years later, in 1964. During the first enforcement period, the Commission applied Article 101 TFEU very carefully. It focused on minor cases centred on jurisdictional and procedural issues. It refrained from imposing fines for infringements, only levying its first fine in 1969.[123]

Nevertheless, the Commission's practice during those first years should not be undervalued. It set the theoretical basis for enforcement, which guided its decisions for decades to come.[124] In particular, the Commission was openly and increasingly inspired by Keynesian economic theories. According to the Keynesian theory of competition, free market forces are not the only source of economic development. Market forces should be limited to promote other public interest values, such as industrial and social policy. Thus, Keynesian theories advocate the use of planning (*planification*) and neo-corporatism in the market.[125]

[121] On this development, see also Gerber (1998, 2008), Wesseling (2000), Van Rompuy (2012, 137–203), Patel and Schweitzer (2013), Witt (2016b), and Sauter (2016, 27–60).
[122] Gerber (1998, 335–369), Wesseling (2000, 9), Van Rompuy (2012, 122), and Pérez (2013).
[123] Policy report 1969, 59.
[124] Gerber (1998, 353) and Goyder (2009, 65–66).
[125] Buch-Hansen and Wigger (2010, 29) and Pérez and Scheur (2013, 21).

Based on this theory, from its inception and until the late 1970s, EU competition policy chiefly served as a mechanism for completing the internal market and developing EU industrial policy. As observed by various scholars and affirmed by the empirical findings presented in Chapter 3, the balancing under Article 101(3) TFEU exemplified strong neo-mercantilist and protectionist traits. The Commission tolerated significant distortions of competition in favour of promoting industrial and social policy in general and market integration in particular.[126]

Maan Sassen, the second European Commissioner for Competition, who took office in 1967, led this approach.[127] He asserted that protection of the competitive process should not enjoy priority over political considerations linked to the prominence of EU firms. Along those lines, the Commission's policy report stated: 'the Commission's policy necessarily consisted in preserving effective competition in the common market while at the same time encouraging schemes for cooperation, reorganisation and combination calculated to render Community enterprises as competitive as possible both inside and outside the Common Market. A competition policy on these lines is a first essential to the success of the industrial policy'.[128] The three successors of Sassen, who were consecutively in office until 1985, followed a similar approach.[129] They envisioned a 'modified' free market system in which economic values are not the sole criteria guiding competition policy.[130] They expressly acknowledged that social interests often demand different results than those prescribed by purely market forces.[131]

2.5.1.2 Market Integration as the Primary Aim

Based on the above, market integration was the main objective of EU competition policy during the first enforcement period. As observed by *Hawk*, market integration played a double role in the enforcement of Article 101 TFEU:[132]

On the one hand, the Commission overtly declared that it would direct its enforcement efforts to fighting agreements that had the most negative impact on cross-border trade rather than on competition as such.[133] Accordingly, it

[126] Hawk (1972, 232), Frazer (1990, 611–612), Sauter (1997), Gerber (1998, 347–348, 354), Wesseling (2000, 32), Buch-Hansen and Wigger (2010, 28–32), Van Rompuy (2012, 142–144), Pérez and Scheur (2013, 28–29), and Pérez (2013, 19).

[127] Pérez and Scheur (2013, 32).

[128] Policy report 1970, 17.

[129] Pérez and Scheur (2013, 33–37).

[130] Policy report 1971, 12-13; policy report 1972, 11. See also Hawk (1972, 232), Buch-Hansen and Wigger (2010, 29), and Witt (2016b, 93–102).

[131] Policy report 1971, 17.

[132] Hawk (1972, 231).

[133] Policy report 1971, 15-16. der Groeben (1961, 25), the first European Commissioner for Competition, explicitly noted that 'priority will have to be given to the abolition of those types of cartels whose effects resemble those of customs duties and quotas, that is to-say those which prevent or impede the establishment of common markets. They include in particular

concentrated the enforcement on vertical restraints that separated or protected national markets. This stood in contrast with the practices of most other competition law jurisdictions that targeted horizontal agreements, which are perceived as a serious form of distortion of competition. The US and German competition laws at the time, for instance, did not prohibit vertical agreements at all.[134]

The Commission paid considerably less attention to horizontal agreements.[135] The few horizontal agreements examined were prohibited only when they impeded market integration in addition to competition (e.g. geographic market-sharing).[136] The focus on market integration was also evident from the remedies imposed for infringements. Agreements involving serious restrictions of competition (e.g. price and quotas fixing or export bans) were settled by accepting voluntary commitments or attaching conditions without imposing fines if they did not impede market integration.[137]

On the other hand, the Commission exempted agreements that did not hinder cross-border activity or promote EU industrial policy, even when they considerably restricted competition. In fact, the empirical findings demonstrate that all of the horizontal cooperation agreements examined by the Commission during the first enforcement period were either found to fall outside the scope of Article 101(1) TFEU or were exempted under Article 101(3) TFEU if they did not impede market integration.[138] Informed by Keynesian theory, the Commission took into account industrial policy interests aimed at growth, regional cohesion, and employment.[139] Those decisions reflected a political choice. They promoted strategic economic sectors and the use of 'fair' business practices over the promotion of competition as such.

2.5.2 *Second Enforcement Period (1978–1987): Workable Competition*

2.5.2.1 Workable Competition Standard and Regulatory Balancing

The emphasis on market integration guided the application of Article 101 TFEU well into the 1990s. During the second enforcement period, however, the

international price, quota and cartels dividing the Common market as well as export and import cartels regulating trade between Member States'. See also policy report 1969, 26–27; policy report 1974, 29; Wesseling (2000, 23); and Van Rompuy (2012, 151).

134 Gerber (1998, 354) and Hawk (1995, 973).

135 Gerber (1998, 354), Hawk (1995, 981), Goyder (2009, 69), and Witt (2016b, 118).

136 Policy report 1971, 25, 28. See also Annex A, Section 2.1.

137 642 Papier mince (1972); 26825 PRYM-BEKA (1973); 26603 Rank/Sopelem (1974); 27073 Bayer/Gist-Brocades (1975); 27093 De Laval/Stork (1977).

138 See Section 3.4.2.

139 Sauter (1997, 1–2).

Commission shifted its reasoning from *establishing* the single market towards *regulating* it.[140]

This trend was marked by the CJEU's judgement in Metro I (1977). As detailed in Section 3.3.3.1, the Court declared that Article 101 TFEU is not necessarily guided by a standard of *perfect* competition. Instead, it introduced the notion of *workable* competition, that is to say, a degree of competition 'necessary to ensure the observance of the basic requirements and the attainment of the objectives of the Treaty'.[141] According to the Court, a lower degree of competition may be optimal where an agreement is necessary for the pursuit of an economic or social objective.[142] The workable competition standard does not have the same solid economic-theoretical foundation as the perfect competition theory. Applying it necessitates a value judgement to strike a balance between competition, economic, and social objectives.[143]

This standard was inspired by the workable competition school of thought, which had dominated US antitrust policy in the 1950s.[144] The term workable competition was first coined by the economist John M. Clark as a second-best, realistic standard of competition. The standard aims to allow enforcers to consider the differences between the economic model of perfect competition and the more limited degree of competition that exists in the real world.[145] Competition is considered to be workable to the extent that it is likely to result in socially beneficial outcomes. It was dubbed as the 'economists' attempt to identify the conditions which could provide appropriate leads for policy in assuring society the substance of the advantages which competition should provide. It is a kind of economist's 'Rule of Reason' – not, of course, to be confused with the legal rule of reason, but analogous to it in the sense that it is also an acknowledgment of the inevitability of the exercise of human judgment and discretion in classifying different forms of economic behavior'.[146]

The workable competition school of thought had gradually lost its influence in the United States towards the late 1970s and was replaced by the growing influence of Chicago School.[147] During the same period of time, however, the CJEU has

[140] Frazer (1990, 612) and Wesseling (2000, 33).

[141] C-26/76 Metro I (1977), para 20–21.

[142] See also policy report 1979, 10; policy report 1981, 11; policy report 1982, 9. Section 3.3.3.2 shows that despite the CJEU's phrasing, linking the workable competition standard to the 'attainment of the objectives of the Treaty', the Commission and Courts have applied the workable competition standard without distinction to all types of non-competition interests, including to interests lacking a formal EU law basis.

[143] Jacquemin (1999, 18).

[144] Hovenkamp (1985, 221–222). On the US workable competition school of thought, see also Clark (1940), Markham (1950), Stocking (1956), Sosnick (1958), Easterbrook (1986), The Attorney General's National Committee to Study the Antitrust Laws (1955, 315–339), and Budzinski (2003, 6–7).

[145] Clark (1940).

[146] The Attorney General's National Committee to Study the Antitrust Laws (1955, 320).

[147] Hovenkamp (1985, 217).

borrowed this term to explain the standard of applying Article 101(3) TFEU balancing.

Because the workable competition standard does not offer a formula that can be precisely calculated, it inherently requires employing a degree of policy value judgement.[148] Hence, applying the workable competition standard under Article 101(3) TFEU had resulted in incoherent balancing, deviating from its original meaning under US antitrust law. Instead of following a uniform set of balancing principles, such principles were modified according to the desired degree of competition in each market.[149]

Those differences were particularly visible during the 1980s, as the Commission began to apply Article 101 TFEU to agreements subject to specific sector regulation, such as banking and insurance.[150] The workable competition standard also guided the BERs adopted during that period, which applied to specific sectors rather than to types of restrictions.[151] The flexibility and discretion embedded in the workable competition standard vested the Commission with powers to apply Article 101 TFEU as a market-building tool. The Commission used the Article not only to correct infringements of Article 101 TFEU but also as a means to regulate and promote EU industry.[152]

This regulatory role of Article 101 TFEU, in turn, encouraged the European Parliament to join the debate on balancing.[153] The Parliament advocated a broader role for non-competition interests under Article 101(3) TFEU. In VBVB/VBBB (1981), for example, the Commission prohibited a price-fixing agreement between Dutch and Flemish book associations.[154] Prior to the adoption of the decision, the Parliament had stated that 'exclusively economic criteria *should not apply* to the book industry and trade because of the specific nature of books as products which directly affect *the interests of the citizen in the cultural, educational and information field*'. According to the Parliament, Article 101(3) TFEU should be interpreted 'in the light of the cultural and educational aspects of books'.[155] In recognition of the Parliament's resolution, the Commission gave the associations an extension to bring the anti-competitive agreement to an end. It wished to resolve the matter informally by asking the associations to submit proposals for a system compatible with the rules of competition.[156]

148 Markham (1950, 349) and The Attorney General's National Committee to Study the Antitrust Laws (1955, 337).
149 Gerber (1998, 356) and Wesseling (2000, 36–37).
150 Policy report 1983, 59; policy report 1984, 13. See also Section 3.4.3.
151 See Section 4.3.1.2.
152 See Section 3.4.3.1.
153 Policy report 1981, 102; policy report 1982, 16–20.
154 428 VBBB/NBVB (1981), para 49–51.
155 Emphasis added. Resolution of 13.2.1981 on book prices, OJ C 50,9.3.1981, 103–104, para 1, 5.
156 Policy report 1981, 56.

As the room for balancing within the application of EU competition law expanded, other stakeholders also asked to be involved. Since 1981, the Economic and Social Committee, for instance, has been involved in inter-institutional discussions regarding competition policy in terms of both general policy and specific matters.[157] The Committee had emphasised that 'competition policy must pay due regard to other sectoral policies in the economic field, e.g. social and employment policies, industrial policy, foreign trade policy, regional policy and structural policy in general'.[158]

2.5.2.2 Balancing in Times of Economic Crisis

The workable competition standard was also prominent in applying Article 101 TFEU to agreements affected by the EU economic crisis of the mid-1970s. The crisis profoundly changed the economic and political context of EU competition policy. Against the backdrop of a decrease in economic activity and an increase in unemployment, market integration was no longer seen as the sole aim of EU economic policy. The Commission faced political pressure to take active measures for the protection of the Member State economies and to strengthen the competitiveness of European firms.[159]

The Commission advocated a 'flexible' application of competition rules in times of crisis.[160] It mostly refused to exempt agreements that directly set prices or quotas or hindered market integration. Yet, it exempted, under Article 101(3) TFEU, other agreements that protected national industries against foreign competition or the national economy. The empirical findings presented in the following chapters illustrate that the effects of the financial crisis were also taken into account in the balancing tools of Article 101(1) TFEU and at the remedy stage.[161]

The workable competition standard empowered the Commission to regulate the markets and adjust competition policy to different, changing situations. For the very same reasons, however, it also impeded the development of a consistent balancing regime for application of Article 101 TFEU.[162] The balancing principles greatly remained case-specific.

[157] Policy report 1982, 19–20. The Committee is an advisory body to the Commission, Council and Parliament, representing workers' and employers' organisations and other interest groups. See www.eesc.europa.eu/en/about#downloads.

[158] The Economic and Social Committee Opinion on Competition Policy (1982), para 1.2.

[159] Policy report 1977, 10; policy report 1979, 9; policy report 1980, 9; policy report 1981, 12–13; policy report 1983, 11; policy report 1984, 12; policy report 1985, 11; policy report 1988, 13; Van Houtte (1982, 497–498), Gerber (1998, 356), Wesseling (2000, 34), and Van Rompuy (2012, 148).

[160] Policy report 1985, 12; Wesseling (2000, 36–37), Motta (2004, 27), and Van Rompuy (2012, 152–153).

[161] See Section 5.3.6 and Section 7.6.1.3, respectively.

[162] As admitted by the Commission itself in policy report 1984, 16.

2.5.3 *Third Enforcement Period (1988–April 2004): Economic, Social, and Political EU*

2.5.3.1 Sectoral Approach

The third enforcement period was embarked upon with the entry into force of the Single European Act (SEA) in 1987, followed by the Maastricht Treaty on the European Union of 1992. The SEA represented a political commitment of the Member States to comply with various actions intended to complete the internal market by 1992. The two Treaties involved regulation of new sectors (e.g. banking), in combination with delegation, self-regulation, and privatisation (e.g. in the transport, telecommunications, energy markets). The combination of those measures subjected new sectors and policies to in the EU to market forces. During the first two enforcement periods, Article 101 TFEU was enforced only against agreements between purely private undertakings. The Member States, consequently, remained competent to pursue public policies at the expense of competition. Yet, the new Treaties blurred the dividing line between private and state conduct. They increased the competencies and the objectives of the EU beyond economic integration towards social and political integration.[163]

Subsequently, from the third enforcement period, the Commission expanded the reach of Article 101 TFEU enforcement to regulated and liberalised markets in which 'a competitive environment is not yet fully established'.[164] Moreover, competition had a role in ensuring that liberalisation and deregulation would realise their expected economic and social advantages.[165] Hence, although the Commission continued to refer to competition as a means for economic integration, it highlighted its social and political implications.[166]

This promoted the adoption of a *sectoral approach* to Article 101 TFEU. The workable competition premise of the second enforcement period was utilised during the third enforcement period to alter the application of Article 101 TFEU balancing tools depending on the sector concerned. In turn, the shift from market integration to a broader economic, social, and political EU agenda required modifying the way balancing took place. Chapters 3 and 5 show that the Commission and CJEU took two different approaches to do so. The Commission broadened the types of benefits that could be taken into account in the enforcement of Article 101(3) TFEU to include a wide variety of social and political policies. The CJEU also balanced under Article 101(1) TFEU. It gradually created new balancing tools, which are not

163 Gerber (1994b, 137–138), Wesseling (2000, 41–42), Semmelmann (2008b, 32), Van Rompuy (2012, 160–161), and Sauter (2016, 78).

164 Policy report, 2000, 21.

165 Wesseling (2000, 41), Geradin (2000, 9–12), Bellamy and Child (2013, 885–886), and Eckert (2018, 1).

166 Wesseling (2000, 48) and Van Rompuy (2012, 161).

explicitly pronounced in the Treaties, to weigh interests related to state or public powers and efficient market outcomes.

2.5.3.2 Policy-Linking Clauses

The SEA and the Maastricht Treaties introduced so-called *policy-linking* or *cross-sectional* clauses to EU law. Those clauses require EU institutions to consider certain public policies when enforcing EU policies. The first three policy-linking clauses in the SEA concerned industrial, cohesion, and environmental policies.[167] The Maastricht Treaty also added health, culture, consumer protection, development cooperation, education, employment, and equality between men and women.[168] The policy-linking clauses granted a formal status to the above non-competition interests and formalised the obligation to balance them against competition interests.[169] They instruct the Commission and EU Courts (as EU institutions) to consider certain social policies within the application of Article 101 TFEU (as an EU policy).

Nonetheless, the clauses do not explain *how* such balancing should take place. They do not form a clear hierarchy or provide mechanisms to solve conflicts between the various policies.[170] Moreover, the empirical findings presented throughout this book show that the competition enforcers have rarely relied on the policy-linking clauses as a normative source guiding balancing. Similarly, they did not give priority to interests protected by the policy-linking clauses over competition or other non-competition interests.[171] Accordingly, the empirical findings demonstrate that the introduction of the policy-linking clauses during the third enforcement period did not impact balancing in practice.

2.5.3.3 First Seeds of the More Economic Approach

Until the mid-1990s, the Commission's overall approach to Article 101 TFEU was form-based. The competition analysis hinged on identifying certain *forms* of restrictions imposed on the commercial freedom of undertakings rather than on their

[167] Articles 130, 130a, 130r EC.

[168] Articles 3, 126–130 EC. See also Agreement on Social Policy (1992), Article 2.

[169] Policy report 1993, 51, 87; Gerber (1998, 371), and Semmelmann (2008b, 32).

[170] For instance, Kingston (2010, 789) points to three possible interpretations: first, a 'weak' obligation to consider the policies protected by the policy-linking clauses. As a result, the competition enforcer has a wide discretion to decide whether to adjust the application of Article 101 TFEU to fulfil such policy; second, an obligation to pursue the protected policy in a systematic way – this obliges the competition enforcer to choose from the available friendlier options for attaining the protected policy; and third, a 'strong' obligation that always gives priority to protected policy over conflicting competition interests. See also Semmelmann (2008a, 141) and Lavrijssen (2010, 637).

[171] See Section 3.3.3.2.

actual effects. Over the years, this policy has encountered growing criticism.[172] This was especially highlighted when the Commission's decisions clashed with its US counterpart in cases with an international dimension, such as in the (in)famous *GE/Honeywell* merger.[173] It became evident that EU and US law did not adhere to the same substantive principles.

By the mid-1990s, the Commission responded to this criticism with an increasing use of economic theory and tools for applying Article 101 TFEU. As elaborated below, the more economic approach informed the analysis of what amounts to a restriction of competition under Article 101(1) TFEU, the investigation of what type of non-competition interests may justify an exemption under Article 101(3) TFEU, and the setting of the Commission's enforcement priorities. The driving force behind this more economic approach was Commissioner *Mario Monti*. Being the first Competition Commissioner with an economic rather than a legal background, he introduced new procedural and substantive changes, earning him the epithet 'great reformer'.[174]

The shift to a more economic approach was first marked by the adoption of the new vertical BER in 1999. The BER and most of the BERs adopted since centred on the market power held by the undertakings and on economic principles.[175] This approach was extended to individual exemptions in the Commission's Vertical Guidelines of 2000. The Guidelines declared that only benefits that 'can improve economic efficiency' or produce 'efficiency-enhancing effects' can be examined under Article 101(3) TFEU.[176] Section 2.5.4.2 shows that the Modernisation White Paper (1999) took a similar approach. Similarly, the Commission Horizontal Guidelines adopted two years later affirmed that Article 101(3) TFEU relates to 'economic benefits'[177] and 'efficiency gains',[178] calling for greater emphasis on 'economic criteria'.[179]

Nevertheless, the Commission did not articulate an exact method for applying the more economic approach or its implications. In 1999, at the beginning of his period in office, Monti referred to the more economic approach essentially as the use of

[172] For instance, Hawk (1988; 1995), Gerard (2012, 20–22), Peeperkorn (2016, 393–395), and Witt (2016b, 10–25).

[173] In 2001, both the US and EU competition enforcers investigated a proposed merger between two US undertakings. While the merger was cleared in the United States, subject to modifications, the Commission prohibited it. The Commission's decision was heavily criticised as based on outdated economic theory and protectionist motives. It was claimed that EU competition law protected competitors, rather than competition. See, for instance, Morgan and McGuire (2004), Gerber (2008, 1254), and Witt (2016b, 14, 18).

[174] Witt (2016b, 35).

[175] See Section 4.3.3.

[176] Commission Vertical Guidelines (2000), para 6–7.

[177] Commission Horizontal Guidelines (2001), para 3, 4, 12, 32, 34.

[178] *Ibid*, para 10.

[179] *Ibid*, para 6.

economic tools in competition assessment.[180] Accordingly, the Commission placed more emphasis on the generic benefits of competition policy such as economic efficiency and consumer welfare rather than on market integration.[181] It used economic norms and methods to interpret the data it encountered and to decide cases.[182] Towards the end of the third enforcement period, the Commission also appointed a Chief Economist to provide economic advice on all competition matters.[183]

The more economic approach also guided setting the Commission's enforcement priorities. Whilst during the first two enforcement periods it had focused on practices hampering market integration, starting in the mid-1990s the Commission identified the fight against cartels as an enforcement priority. It declared that cartels were the most harmful agreements to consumers and the European economy in general.[184] The Commission explained that by focusing its enforcement efforts on the fight against cartels, it 'gives priority to the important sectors of the European economy and in particular to sectors where its action is directly capable of enhancing *consumer welfare*'.[185]

For this purpose, in 1996 the Commission also issued its first leniency notice aimed at incentivising undertakings to reveal secret cartels. Modelled on similar US and Canadian policies, the notice allows fines imposed for participation in cartels to be reduced or waived.[186]

Remarkably, during the third enforcement period, the more economic approach did not prevent the Commission from continuing to examine broader types of benefits under Article 101(3) TFEU. This was evident from the Commission's decisions, its policy papers, and Commissioner Monti's public statements: First, as shown in Section 3.3.3, until the end of the third enforcement period, the Commission took into account a broad array of economic and non-economic benefits in its enforcement practices. In fact, the empirical findings show that they were more prominent in the Commission's decisions than ever before.

Second, while referring to the benefits of the first condition of Article 101(3) TFEU as 'efficiencies', the Vertical and Horizontal Guidelines explicitly left room for consideration of non-economic benefits. The Commission Vertical Guidelines

[180] Monti (2000b, 2), Witt (2016b, 55–57), and the many sources referred to there.
[181] Policy report 2000, 21; policy report 2002, 20; and Van Rompuy (2012, 171).
[182] As elaborated in Chapter 3. See also Gerber (2008; 2009, 27), Witt (2016b, 7–39), and policy report 2010, 4–7.
[183] Policy report 2003, 5, 20; policy report 2004, 16.
[184] Policy report 1996, 27; policy report 1999, 31; policy report 2000, 35; policy report 2001, 24, 30.
[185] Policy report 2002, 32. See also policy report 2003, 5; policy report 2004, 14.
[186] Commissions Leniency Notice (1996). The notice was amended in 2002 and 2006 to increase the transparency and certainty of the conditions for fines reduction. See also policy report 2001, 24, 30; policy report 2002, 26, 27; policy report 2003, 24; Commission Staff Working Paper accompanying the policy report 2013, 19; Kovacic (2015a), and Wils (2016).

(2000) mention market integration as one of the objectives of Article 101 TFEU,[187] and the Commission Horizontal Guidelines (2001) specifically accepted environmental agreements benefiting society as a whole.[188]

Third, in public statements, Monti emphasised the need to balance competition and non-competition interests. He rejected *laissez-faire* capitalism as the standard for EU competition law in favour of a social market economy in which social standards and other objectives of society are respected.[189] Monti compared Article 101(3) TFEU to the public interest defence in the area of free movement of goods, in which broad policy considerations are relevant.[190] He affirmed that non-economic benefits to future consumers were compatible with EU competition law. In particular, he stated, 'that environmental concerns *are in no way contradictory with competition policy* [...] provided that restrictions of competition are proportionate and necessary to achieving the environmental objectives aimed at, *to the benefit of current and future generations*'.[191]

In 2004, towards the end of his time in office, Monti first suggested that the more economic approach went beyond the introduction of economic instruments. He pointed to a substantive shift according to which competition policy focuses on *consumer welfare*.[192] As described in the next section, this considerably limited the scope for balancing under Article 101(3) TFEU.

This section, however, has suggested that this was perhaps not the original intention when introducing the more economic approach.[193] The more economic approach did not initially aim to limit the scope for consideration of non-competition interests under Article 101 TFEU but, rather, was confined to introducing new economic thinking and tools for competition analysis.

2.5.4 *Fourth Enforcement Period (May 2004–2017): Post-Modernisation Era*

The previous sections have demonstrated that up until the third enforcement period, the Commission and EU Courts followed a case-by-case approach to balancing. While they regularly emphasised the possibility, and even the duty, to balance competition against a variety of social and political interests, they did not establish a clear balancing framework under Article 101(3) TFEU. Nevertheless, the lack of a set of well-defined legal or economic balancing tools had rather limited

[187] Commission Vertical Guidelines (2000), para 7 states that 'market integration is an additional goal of EC competition policy. Market integration enhances levels of trade in the Community. Companies should not be allowed to recreate private barriers between Member States where State barriers have been successfully abolished'.

[188] Commission Horizontal Guidelines (2001), para 10.

[189] Monti (2000a).

[190] Monti (2000c).

[191] Emphasis added. Commission Press Release IP/00/148 of 11.2.2000.

[192] Monti (2004).

[193] Witt (2016b, 55–57).

consequences prior to May 2004. Under the realm of Regulation 17/62, conflicts between competition and non-competition interests were balanced *ex-ante* and resolved in a centralised and fairly independent manner by the Commission. This dramatically changed with the introduction of Regulation 1/2003. As elaborated below, each of the three aspects of modernisation altered the balancing principles and created a pressing need for a clearly defined regime.

2.5.4.1 Institutional Pillar of Modernisation (Decentralisation)

Regulation 1/2003 entrusted the NCAs, for the first time, with the power to apply Article 101(3) TFEU directly. While only the Commission can adopt a positive decision, NCAs may declare that there are no grounds for action on their part, where on the basis of the information in their possession the conditions for establishing an Article 101 TFEU infringement are not met.[194]

The motivation for decentralisation, as mentioned, was essentially a pragmatic one. In the enlarged EU, the Commission could not effectively enforce Article 101 TFEU alone.[195] Indeed, from May 2004 to 2017, 89% of the investigations for infringements of Article 101 and 102 TFEU were carried out by NCAs.[196]

In addition to this pragmatic motive, the Modernisation White Paper also ascribed a substantive aim to decentralisation. The Commission stressed a *political* objective in the form of 'bringing the decision-making process closer to citizens [. . .] to ensure that that the citizens of Europe view competition policy in a positive manner and recognise it as playing an important role in their daily lives'.[197] Allowing consumers to address NCAs and national courts was perceived as a step towards improving EU citizens' perception of competition policy. Decentralisation was essential to provide the Commission with 'strong political support' for its competition policy.[198]

Bringing the decision-making process closer to citizens, however, carried an inherent risk. As the NCAs and national courts became the mediators of the economic and political forces that shape EU competition policy, they influenced the way in which the policy was applied.[199] Faced with the lack of a clear framework, balancing became subject to the discretion of each national enforcer, to its institutional, procedural, and political characteristics and competition culture. The empirical findings presented throughout this book reveal that in such settings, the unclear role of non-competition interests has endangered the effectiveness,

[194] Regulation 1/2003, Article 5. See also Section 2.3.3.3.
[195] See Section 2.3.2.
[196] This calculation is based on the ECN data, available at: http://ec.europa.eu/competition/ecn/statistics.html.
[197] Policy report 1999, 10.
[198] *Ibid*, 21.
[199] Maher (2002, 224) and Simonsson (2010, 111).

uniformity, and legal certainty of balancing under the new enforcement regime. Section 2.3.3 has already shown that the Commission had attempted to respond to this risk by enacting a set of information and cooperation mechanisms to resolve conflicts arising between the competition enforcers.[200] The following sections further illustrate that the Commission had also altered the substantive competition rules to limit the discretion of the competition enforcers to account for non-competition interests under Article 101 TFEU.

2.5.4.2 Substantive Pillar of Modernisation (1): White Paper

From the very inception of the Modernisation White Paper, the Commission was concerned that decentralised enforcement would result in the incorporation of politically induced national non-competition interests into the application of Article 101(3) TFEU. While DG COMP is generally free from political interference in the enforcement of individual cases, not all NCAs are equally independent. Some NCAs are institutionally and politically independent of their governments, whilst others are considerably less so.[201]

To avoid undue national influence, the Modernisation White Paper has reframed Article 101(3) TFEU into an 'objective' tool facilitating economic assessment that is devoid of political considerations.[202] It explained that Article 101(3) TFEU was intended 'to provide a legal framework for the *economic assessment* of restrictive practices and *not to allow* application of the competition rules to be set aside *because of political considerations*'.[203]

Commentators quickly pointed out that the new interpretation of Article 101(3) TFEU was incompatible with the Commission's and the CJEU's previous case law, which reserved significant room for non-competition interests under that provision.[204] *Ehlermann*, the former Director-General of DG Competition, suggested a restricted interpretation of the Modernisation White Paper, explaining: 'It would probably be an exaggeration to assume that, according to the Commission, non-economic considerations are to be totally excluded from the balancing test required by Article [101(3) TFEU]. Such an interpretation *would hardly be compatible with the Treaty*, the Court of Justice's case law, and the Commission's own practice.

[200] Modernisation White Paper (1999), para 103; Council and the Commission ECN Statement (2004), para 1. See also Regulation 1/2003, Preamble 9.

[201] ECN+ Directive (2019), para 17; Temple Lang (1998), Riley (2003b, 659), and Guidi (2016, 93–136). See also Section 7.7.

[202] Monti (2002, 1092), Komninos (2005, 17), Sufrin (2006, 964), Monti (2007, 21), Cseres (2007b, 169), Petit (2009, 6), Townley (2009, 80), GCLC Annual Conference (2010, 82), and Van Rompuy (2012, 257).

[203] Emphasis added. Modernisation White Paper (1999), para 57. See also para 72.

[204] Schweitzer (2007, 9), Townley (2009, 178–181), Jones (2010, 791), Townley (2011, 448), Van Rompuy (2012, 255–256), Gerard (2012, 36–38), Baarsma and Rosenboom (2015, 404), and Witt (2016b, 261–295).

However, the passage quoted is a clear indication that non-competition-oriented political considerations should not determine the assessment under Article [101(3) TFEU]'.[205]

Similarly, while the German Monopolies Commission seemed to agree with the White Paper's substantive merits, it considered it to be incompatible with EU law. It stated: 'in the White Paper the Commission attempts to *tone down the significance of a discretionary process* of weighing up in the frame of exemption decisions [...] No matter how much such a viewpoint should be welcomed the Commission is neither empowered nor able to issue a binding interpretation of the EC Treaty'.[206]

2.5.4.3 Substantive Pillar of Modernisation (2): Commission's Guidelines

Despite the above criticism, the Commission took yet another step to limit the scope of Article 101(3) TFEU balancing in the guidelines it adopted from May 2004 onwards. Up until that time, the Commission had stipulated that the first condition of Article 101(3) TFEU was fulfilled when an agreement produced 'benefits'.[207] Although the Commission's policy papers from the end of the 1990s onwards introduced elements of economic efficiency and consumer welfare to the application of Article 101(3) TFEU, they explicitly left room for non-economic benefits.[208] During the fourth enforcement period, however, the Commission's policy papers no longer referred to Article 101(3) TFEU as involving 'benefits'. Instead, Article 101(3) Guidelines (2004) first rebranded the Article as limited to 'objective economic efficiencies'[209] and then increased the evidential requirement necessary to prove such efficiencies.[210]

Article 101(3) Guidelines were also the first to introduce the notion of *consumer welfare* as the primary aim of EU competition policy in general and Article 101(3) TFEU in particular. They declared that the aim of EU competition rules was to protect competition 'as a *means of enhancing consumer welfare* and of ensuring an efficient allocation of resources'.[211] In parallel, they discarded market integration as an objective of EU competition policy.[212]

[205] Emphasis added. Ehlermann (2000, 54).

[206] Emphasis added. German Monopolies Commission (2000), para 52.

[207] Commission Vertical Guidelines (2000), para 5, 62, 136; Commission Horizontal Guidelines (2001), para 3, 4, 12, 32–35, 68, 102, 132, 151, 169, 192.

[208] See Section 2.5.3.3.

[209] Commission Article 101(3) Guidelines (2004), para 59. See also para 33, 43, 48–72.

[210] See Section 3.3.4.1.

[211] Emphasis added. Commission Article 101(3) Guidelines (2004), para 33. See also Technology Transfer Guidelines (2004), para 5; Technology Transfer Guidelines (2014), para 5.

[212] Market integration is portrayed in the Commission Article 101(3) Guidelines (2004), para 13 as a parallel policy to competition law. On the other hand, in 40023 Cross-border access to pay-TV (2016), para 38, the Commission referred to market integration noting that 'an agreement which might tend to restore the divisions between national markets is liable to frustrate the

The Guidelines, together with the Modernisation White Paper, clearly deviate from the Commission's and EU Courts' previous case law. Many non-economic benefits that had been taken into account until the third enforcement period – such as social benefits, industrial policy, or environmental protection – were no longer applicable, in the Commission's view.

Although this is often attributed to the more economic approach, scholars have also explained the change in the guidelines as prompted by the fear that the decentralisation of enforcement would induce national enforcers to tolerate unlawful agreements on national public policy grounds.[213] As *Sufrin* put it, 'this exclusion of public interest considerations from Article [101(3) TFEU] *is partly a matter of principle but largely a matter of pragmatism*'.[214] The narrow definition of relevant non-competition interests serves as a safeguard against national protectionism. By transforming Article 101(3) TFEU into a purely economic efficiency norm, the Commission had limited the discretion of national competition enforcers to incorporate non-competition interests.

Other scholars have linked the Commission's narrow approach to the direct applicability of Article 101(3) TFEU in the new regime.[215] Direct applicability, as a concept of EU law, requires that the legal provision be clear, precise, and unconditional.[216] According to this interpretation, the narrow approach to Article 101(3) TFEU was warranted by the need to reduce the margin of discretion in the application of the provision to allow it to be applied under the realm of Regulation 1/2003. It could be argued that in this context, narrowing down the room for non-competition interests was necessary for adapting the application of Article 101(3) TFEU to the new self-assessment regime.

While not admitting as much explicitly, the Commission acknowledged that Article 101(3) Guidelines entailed a new interpretation of the Article. The Guidelines declare that 'with regard to a number of issues, the present guidelines outline the current state of the case law of the Court of Justice. However, the Commission also intends to explain its policy with regard to issues that have not been dealt with in the case law, or that are subject to interpretation'.[217]

To align the Commission's new interpretation with the Commission's and EU Courts' previous case law, Article 101(3) Guidelines left some room for the consideration of non-economic benefits by concluding in paragraph 42 that 'goals pursued by

Treaty's objective of achieving the integration of those markets through the establishment of a single market'.

[213] Sufrin (2006, 964), Cseres (2007b, 169), Semmelmann (2008b, 39), Petit (2009, 6), and Van Rompuy (2012, 257).

[214] Emphasis added. Sufrin (2006, 964).

[215] Wesseling (1999, 425, 432–433), Schweitzer (2007, 5, 8–9), and Semmelmann (2008b, 196–198).

[216] C-26/62 Van Gend en Loos (1963), 12, 13.

[217] Article 101(3) Guidelines (2004), para 7.

other Treaty provisions can be taken into account to the extent that they can be subsumed under the four conditions of Article [101(3) TFEU]'.

This paragraph, in fact, imposes two additional cumulative conditions for granting an Article 101(3) TFEU exception on the basis of non-economic benefits. First, only interests that can be ascribed to the 'goals pursued by other Treaty provisions' could be relevant. Second, these interests can only be taken into account to the extent they can be 'subsumed' by the four conditions of Article 101(3) TFEU. This, in conjunction with the general spirit of the Guidelines, suggests that non-competition interests could only be taken into account under Article 101(3) TFEU if they could be reckoned as economic efficiency gains. The legal and normative difficulties of the shift in the Commission's approach and the two conditions added to Article 101(3) Guidelines are further discussed in Section 3.3.4.1.

2.5.4.4 Substantive Pillar of Modernisation (3): Consumer Welfare

As mentioned above, the Commission's Article 101(3) Guidelines and policy papers have introduced the notion of consumer welfare as the main objective of Article 101 TFEU.[218] While up until the third enforcement period the enforcement focused on the protection of economic freedom and market integration, since 2004 the Commission stated that Article 101 TFEU is aimed 'to protect competition on the market as a means of enhancing consumer welfare'[219] and that the 'main thrust of competition policy should be on maximizing consumer welfare'.[220] From the fourth enforcement period onwards, consumer welfare was advanced by the Commission to guide the theory of harm of an Article 101(1) TFEU infringement, the balancing standard for an Article 101(3) TFEU exemption, and the setting of the enforcement priorities.

The adoption of the consumer welfare standard has promised to offer 'an effects-based approach, grounded in solid economics'.[221] This was praised as a genius from a public relations perspective. It presents a 'seemingly objective, logical, scientific alternative' to the other political goals of competition law, while averting opposition to the minimising of the role of non-competition interests in the enforcement.[222] After all, who would oppose protecting the interests of consumers? In practice, however, as was demonstrated in Section 1.2.1.3, the consumer welfare standard is not as objective and robust as it might seem. Both its definition and its calculation

[218] On the various objectives of EU competition policy, see Section 2.2.1.
[219] Article 101(3) Guidelines (2004), para 13 and 33.
[220] Policy report 2008, 27.
[221] Kroes (2005, 2).
[222] Kovacic, in Keyte (2017, 20). See also Easterbrook (1986, 1703–1704), Wu (2018, 1), and Foer and Durst (2018, 497–498, 502–503).

reflect complex political choices and striking a balance between various legal, economic, and social public policies.

This is especially true since the Commission's Guidelines have not adopted a clear definition of consumer welfare but have merely declared that Article 101 TFEU is based on such standard. In particular, like the policy papers and decisional practices preceding them, the Commission's Guidelines have once again refrained from laying down a detailed standard to govern Article 101(3) TFEU balancing. They did not explain a method to account for non-competition interests under the Article. In fact, the Commission had consciously left this question open, proclaiming that it was case-specific.[223] As *Daskalova* proficiently observes, it is ironic that the meaning of consumer welfare remains unclear when one of the reasons for its introduction was to bring legal certainty and uniformity to the decentralised regime.[224]

The EU Courts, too, have not clarified this issue. They did not issue detailed judgements explaining whether they had accepted the Commission's notion of consumer welfare as a standard for applying Article 101 TFEU, and if so, how it ought to be applied. In fact, in *T-Mobile (2009)* and *GlaxoSmithKline (2009)*, the CJEU actually left open the question of whether consumer welfare was at all the legal standard for Article 101 TFEU.[225] Passing on a valuable opportunity to clarify the matter, the Court ambiguously stated that the Article 'like the other competition rules of the Treaty, is designed to protect not only the immediate interests of individual competitors or consumers but also *to protect the structure of the market and thus competition as such*'.[226]

The unclear role and scope of the consumer welfare standard created much uncertainty about balancing in the post-modernisation era. This uncertainty was amplified because the standard is mostly absent from the Commission's decisional practice. Section 2.3.4.2 shows that despite the importance of the standard in the Commission's policy papers, consumer welfare is rarely mentioned in the

[223] Commission's position in ICN Competition Enforcement and Consumer Welfare (2011), 27. See also Kalbfleisch (2011, 111–112), Lianos (2013, 16), Daskalova (2015, 144–151), and Gerbrandy (2015, 771–772).

[224] Daskalova (2015, 133). See also Cseres (2007b, 152).

[225] C-8/08 T-Mobile (2009); C-501/06P C-513/06P C-515/06P C-519/06P GlaxoSmithKline (2009); see Sections 3.5.3.2 and 3.6.2 for the approach of the EU Courts and NCAs, respectively.

[226] C-8/08 T-Mobile (2009), para 38. Notably, the Court deviated somewhat from the opinion of AG Kokott who stated that competition interests are the primary aim of the competition rules: 'Article [101 TFEU], like the other competition rules of the Treaty, is not designed only or primarily to protect the immediate interests of individual competitors or consumers, but to protect the structure of the market and thus competition as such (as an institution)' (AG Kokott opinion in C-8/08 T-Mobile (2009), para 58). Unlike the AG's opinion, the Court left some room to account for the interests of individual competitors and consumers (efficiency interests).

Commission's decisions and is almost never defined.[227] It is unsurprising, therefore, that national enforcers have adopted divergent interpretations in this regard.[228]

Finally, the uncertainty surrounding the consumer welfare standard has increased because Article 101(3) TFEU nearly disappeared from the decisional practice of the Commission after May 2004. The empirical findings presented in Section 3.2 reveal that the Article was never accepted and seldom discussed by the Commission following modernisation.

2.5.4.5 Procedural Pillar of Modernisation: Self-Assessment and Enforcement Discretion

The disappearance of Article 101(3) TFEU from the Commission's decisional practice might initially be seen as proof that non-competition interests no longer play a role in the enforcement of Article 101 TFEU, or at least in the Commission's practice. This conclusion, nevertheless, is *not* supported by the empirical findings presented in this book. In its place, the empirical findings indicate that during the fourth enforcement period, the consideration of non-competition interests shifted from the *explicit-substantive balancing tools* of Article 101 (1) and (3) TFEU to various *implicit-procedural and national balancing tools*.

First, the empirical findings uncover that non-competition interests are embedded in the exercise of the competition enforcers' detection, target, instrument, and outcome enforcement discretion. The procedural pillar of modernisation enhanced the competition enforcers' powers to set their own enforcement priorities.[229] Whereas under the old notification regime the Commission examined all notified agreements, under the new self-assessment regime of Regulation 1/2003 the competition enforcers could allocate their own enforcement efforts. Chapter 7 illustrates that the competition enforcers have made use of their new discretional enforcement powers to explicitly and implicitly account for non-competition interests. They have directed their enforcement efforts to clear-cut infringements of Article 101 TFEU, often by use of leniency applications and/or settlements,[230] which are unlikely to be justified by overriding non-competition interests. The competition enforcers have

[227] In addition, the Commission's staff working paper accompanying its 2017 policy report does not mention consumer welfare in the context of Article 101(3) TFEU at all. Rather, it maintains that a restrictive agreement might be allowed under Article 101(3) TFEU 'if it ultimately *fosters competition*' (page 3, emphasis added).

[228] See Section 2.6.

[229] Modernisation White Paper (1999), para 45.

[230] The settlement procedure first came into force in July 2008. Undertakings may choose to acknowledge their involvement in the cartel, the precise nature of their infringement, and their liability for the infringement in favour of a 10% fine reduction. Settlements aim to simplify the administrative proceedings and allow the Commission to devote its resources to other cases. See Regulation 622/2008 on Settlement Procedure; Commission Settlement Notice (2008); policy report 2008, 6.

rarely adopted positive decisions or given individual informal guidance.[231] Rather, agreements that raise balancing questions have mostly been resolved by accepting negotiated remedies or by closing the investigation into a case altogether. The selection of enforcement priorities, therefore, has rendered the balancing to be invisible and left very limited room for the use of the explicit-substantive balancing tools following modernisation.

Second, the NCAs and national courts have often made use of national balancing tools instead of the exceptions of Article 101(1) and (3) TFEU. Those unique national exceptions are considerably different from the EU-based balancing tools. They might indeed result in the fragmentation of applicable competition rules across the EU. These unique national balancing tools are elaborated in Chapter 6.

The shifts in balancing brought about by the three pillars of modernisation have created many ambiguities concerning the role of non-competition interests in the enforcement of Article 101 TFEU in the post-modernisation era. As a result, and as will be demonstrated in the next chapters, many aspects of balancing remain unclear today, more than fifteen years after the adoption of Regulation 1/2003.

2.6 BALANCING IN PRACTICE II: THE FIVE MEMBER STATES

This section provides a short summary of the historical development of the approaches taken to balancing by the five Member States examined in this study. Those national approaches are significant in light of the mutually determinative connection between national and EU-level balancing. The Member States *are affected* by EU balancing rules when NCAs and national courts implement the balancing rules in practice. In parallel, the Member States *affect* balancing in two ways. First, they take an active part in shaping the balancing rules contained in EU primary and secondary law. As discussed above, the role of non-competition interests under Article 101 TFEU is the result of ongoing negotiations between the Member States and the EU institutions. Second, national approaches affect the application of balancing. The empirical findings presented in Chapters 3–7 illustrate that the NCAs have followed divergent interpretations of the Article 101 TFEU balancing tools and adopted unique national balancing rules that influence the way balancing is administered by national enforcers.

This section, therefore, provides background information for understanding both the development of the balancing tools and their implementation in practice. Each section describes the origins of the national competition legislation, the national provision equivalent to Article 101 TFEU, the standard for balancing (e.g. type of

[231] A formal positive decision was described in Section 2.3.3.3. An informal guidance letter can be issued at the request of undertakings in cases posing novel legal questions. The letter is not binding and has the same legal effect as negative clearance decisions under the old notification regime. See Modernisation White Paper (1999), para 89; Commission Informal Guidance Notice (2004). See also policy report 2004, 22; and Gippini-Fournier (2008, 53–56).

consumer welfare standard), and the institutional and procedural structure of the national enforcement system. In addition, each section details the appeals procedure against the NCA's decisions. They show that national appeals systems differ in the characteristics of the relevant appellate body (i.e. civil/administrative court or a specialised tribunal) and its competence (i.e. full/limited review of legal/factual elements).[232]

2.6.1 *France*

2.6.1.1 Origins of National Competition Law

The roots of French competition law can be traced back to the French revolution.[233] At the beginning of the nineteenth century, competition rules were entrenched in human-rights thinking rather than based on economic motives. They prohibited forms of horizontal price fixing, which were viewed as hindering equal access to commercial life and a violation of the right to equality among men.[234] Those early laws enacted a competition system based on the *abuse principle*, which guided French competition law for many decades to come.[235]

During the Second World War, France progressively became a controlled economy, characterised by extensive governmental control and cartelisation. New laws fostered and imposed forms of mandatory cartelisation.[236] Even when France formally ceased to be an authoritarian corporative state in 1946, the government's pivotal role in the economy persisted. The French competition regime adopted in the mid-1950s, correspondingly, focused on price control and the limitation of practices negatively affecting prices.[237]

Since the 1980s, France has gradually transformed into a more market-based economy. The government has opened markets up to competition and privatised many state-owned companies while retaining control over certain companies and industries.[238] In 1986, the Ordinance on Competition and Freedom of Prices established modern French competition policy[239] and was later codified in Book IV of the Commercial Code.

[232] On the standards of judicial review of NCA decisions, see Graham (2009), Essens, Gerbrandy and Lavrijssen (2009), and ECN Decision Making Powers Report (2012), 19-28.
[233] Riesenfeld (1960, 578) and Kuenzler and Warlouzet (2013, 93).
[234] See French Chapelier Law of 1791, Article 1; French Penal Code of 1810, Article 419.
[235] Riesenfeld (1960, 577) and Kuenzler and Warlouzet (2013, 93, 105). On the abuse principle, see also Section 2.2.2.
[236] French Law on the Organisation of the Nation in Time of War of 1938 and French Law on Provisional Organisation of Industrial Production of 1940.
[237] French Price Decree 53-704 of 1953; French Price Ordinance 45-1483 of 1954, Articles 37, 59. See also Kuenzler and Warlouzet (2013, 99–101).
[238] Jenny (1990, 317), Souam (1998, 207), and Souty (2006, 378).
[239] French Ordinance 86-1243 of 1986 on competition and freedom of prices.

2.6.1.2 National Equivalent of Article 101 TFEU and Consumer Welfare Standard

As mentioned, 1950s French competition law served as the model for Article 101 TFEU.[240] In its present version, Article L. 420-1 of the French Commercial Code contains an absolute cartel ban. Like Article 101(1) TFEU, it prohibits any agreement having the aim or effect of preventing, restricting, or distorting the free play of competition in a market. Article L. 420-4 lays down three exceptions to the general prohibition: a regulated-conduct defence, the possibility of issuing BERs, and a provision similar to Article 101(3) TFEU.[241] The latter is broader in scope than Article 101(3) TFEU. Its wording covers wide-ranging policy considerations including those that benefit society as a whole. Notably, the French exceptions are not drafted in the form of exemptions but rather detail the scope of the prohibition itself. As such, they reflect the distinction between 'good' and 'bad' cartels recognised under the principle of abuse.

The French NCA declares that it enforces Article 101 TFEU on the basis of a long-term consumer welfare standard, which is broadly construed. It assumes that intermediate objectives (such as enhancing the competitive process, stimulating efficient allocation of resources, and preventing unchecked market power) foster consumer welfare in the long run. Competition is therefore not an end unto itself but a means to safeguard the market economy alongside other public policies.[242]

2.6.1.3 National Enforcement System

Like the EU system following modernisation, the post–Second World War French system was based on a self-assessment system that did not require prior authorisation. Unlike many other Member States, France maintained its self-assessment regime even after Regulation 17/62 opted for an EU notification and exemption system. Regulation 1/2003 thus drew the EU enforcement system closer to the French one.

The French enforcement system of the mid-1950s was highly susceptible to political interference. It was based on a two-tier review: The competition assessment was performed by the *Commission technique des ententes*, an independent specialist body with merely advisory powers; at a second stage, the decisions were adopted by the Ministry of Economic Affairs.[243] In 1977, as part of the general trend towards a more market-based economy, the system transformed into a single-stage examination, which no longer involved the Ministry. The *Conseil de la concurrence* was established, a quasi-judicial independent body having powers to initiate

[240] See Section 2.2.2. The 1954 Ordinance focused on practices having effect on prices. The 1986 Ordinance expanded this prohibition also to other forms of restriction of competition.

[241] Those exceptions are elaborated in Sections 5.4.1, 4.4.1.3, and 3.6, respectively.

[242] See Section 3.6.2.2.

[243] French Ordinance 45-1483 of 1954, Article 59 quater.

proceedings, issue orders, and impose fines.[244] This enforcement system is less susceptible to political influence.

In 2004, the *Conseil* was endowed with additional powers, bringing it into line with other NCAs.[245] In 2008, those powers were extended to include self-referral and investigation powers, and the Conseil was renamed *Autorité de la concurrence*.[246] Yet, the Ministry still holds some powers. It may review certain anti-competitive practices considered to be less significant and has the right to appeal the decisions of the *Autorité de la concurrence*.[247]

Decisions of the French NCA can be appealed to civil law courts. The Paris Court of Appeal examines the factual and legal grounds of the decision. If it declares that the NCA's decision is void, it may replace it with its own decision. A second appeal on points of law may be submitted to the Supreme Court (the Court of Cassation).[248]

2.6.2 *Germany*

2.6.2.1 Origins of National Competition Law

Germany was the European pioneer in terms of introducing legislation specifically intended to protect the competitive process itself, and not merely to control prices. Its Regulation Against Abuse of Economic Power Position of 1923 was part of the emergency measures adopted by the Weimar Republic following the First World War. It aimed to ensure market freedom, increase production, and reduce inflation. Yet, during the years of Nazi control (1933–1945), Germany transformed into a fully planned, state-controlled economy.[249]

Following the Second World War, the occupying forces adopted the Decartelisation Laws of 1947. The Laws represented the belief that excessive concentration of economic power was one of the causes of German military aggression and the Nazis' rise to power. Suppression of economic power was seen as a precondition for social justice.[250] The competition provisions in those laws were heavily influenced by the American occupation and the American Sherman Act.[251]

[244] French Competition Law of 1977; see also Souam (1998, 207).

[245] French Ordinance 2004-1173 adapting French Competition Law to EU Competition Law; French NCA annual report, 2004.

[246] French Ordinance 2008-1161 on Modernisation of Competition Regulation.

[247] French Commercial Code, Article L 464-8; French NCA annual report (2012), 2–7.

[248] French Code of Civil Procedure, Article 561.

[249] Kuhn (1997, 116–117), OECD Regulatory Reform in Germany (2004, 8), Motta (2004, 9–10), and Pace (2007, 17).

[250] Gerber (1994a, 25), Kuhn (1997, 117–118), Pace (2007, 65), and Kuenzler and Warlouzet (2013, 94).

[251] In the American Zone, Law No. 56, Military Government Gazette, Germany, United States Area of Control, issue C, at z (1947); In the British Zone, Ordinance No. 78, 16 Military Government Gazette, Germany, British Zone of Control 412 (1947); In the French Zone,

The laws in the American and British Zones were similar, including a detailed prohibition against horizontal and vertical practices. The law in the French Zone was less comprehensive, reflecting France's more lenient approach towards cartels at the time, which was discussed above.

When occupation ended, the adoption of a new competition regime was subject to rigorous debate: On the one hand, representatives of the German industry supported an abuse-based self-assessment regime, similar to the French system. They argued that a strict prohibition on cartels would impede the reconstruction of national industry.[252] On the other hand, supporters of Ordoliberalism, including the German Minister of the Economy, advocated for a *principle of prohibition and control*. Namely, that anti-competitive agreements should have no legal force unless notified and approved by a regulatory body. They aimed to establish an order-based competition policy as the cornerstone for a democratic order protecting citizens against an authoritarian threat.[253] As the next sub-section shows, the German Competition Act of 1957 represented a compromise between those two approaches.

2.6.2.2 National Equivalent of Article 101 TFEU and Consumer Welfare Standard

The German Competition Act of 1957 was based on an authorisation system enacting an absolute cartel ban subject to many sectoral and individual exceptions. The Act is still in force today, although with subsequent significant revisions. The prohibition on anti-competitive agreements is laid down in Section 2.1. The original provision provided that an agreement concluded between enterprises is ineffective insofar as it is likely to influence production or market conditions by restraining competition. In 1998, the Sixth Amendment of the Act changed the wording to follow the formulation of Article 101(1) TFEU. At the same time, up until 2005, the prohibition did not generally apply to vertical restraints. Certain forms of vertical restraint were regulated, bound to different prohibition and exception rules.[254]

Over the years, the Act has included four types of exemptions: First, individual exemptions were granted to certain business practices.[255] Second, sectoral

Military Government Ordinance No. 96, 9 June 1947, 2 Journal officiel du Commandement en chef français en Allemagne 784 (1947). See also Kuenzler and Warlouzet (2013, 94).

252 OECD Regulatory Reform in Germany (2004, 10), Motta (2004, 10–11), Pace (2007, 66), and Kuenzler and Warlouzet (2013, 98).

253 Pace (2007, 66) and Kuenzler and Warlouzet (2013, 98). On the principle of prohibition, see Section 2.2.2.

254 For instance, RPM, exclusive dealing, license agreements, and certain agreements concerning prices or terms of business.

255 The individual exemptions were set forth in Sections 2.2–2.6. These include standardisation agreements; specialisation agreements; efficiency-promoting agreements between SMEs (added by the Second Amendment of the German Competition Act of 1973); rationalisation agreements (following the Second Amendment of the German Competition Act of 1973; this exemption applied only to agreements improving SMEs' competitiveness); structural crisis

exceptions shielded various industries from the cartel prohibition.[256] The number of industries protected by the Act has been gradually reduced since the late 1980s, yet some still exist today.[257] Third, a political exemption was granted by the Minister of the Economy, confined to narrowly defined circumstances relating to an agreement 'necessary for prevailing reasons concerning the economy as a whole and the public interest' or upon an 'immediate danger to the existence of a majority of the undertakings in a sector'.[258] Fourth, in 1998, the law first introduced an exemption based on the effects of an agreement, similar to Article 101(3) TFEU.[259]

The German exemptions drastically changed following the modernisation of EU competition law. The seventh amendment of 2005 aimed at harmonising national law with EU competition law. The amendment was adopted at the end of a long and controversial debate, including a mediation procedure between the *Bundestag* and the *Bundesrat* (the Lower and Upper Houses of the Federal Parliament).[260] The amendment abolished both the specific and ministerial exemptions. Instead, Section 2(1) of the revised Act included a general exception, identical to Article 101(3) TFEU. Despite the abolishment of most specific exemptions, Section 3 of the Act still provides that the general exception of Section 2(1) has been fulfilled when an agreement rationalises an economic activity and serves to improve the competitiveness of SMEs. This only applies to purely national agreements that do not affect trade between the Member States.[261]

In addition, the amendment provides that Regulations of the European Council and the Commission on the application of Article 101(3) TFEU apply *mutatis mutandis* to purely national cases.[262] Remarkably, the draft of the amendment initially also referenced EU guidelines and principles as a source of interpretation. However, this was removed before the legislation was finalised, noting that such guidelines and principles were binding on neither the German administration nor the German judiciary.[263]

The German NCA has rejected consumer welfare as a standard for balancing. It has declared that it bases its exemption decisions solely on competition criteria: 'it is undisputed that there are other important economic and socio-political goals than

agreements; and rebate cartels, export and import cartels (cancelled by the Sixth Amendment of the German Competition Act of 1988). See also Drahos (2001, 260).

256 For instance, transportation and postal (Section 99), agriculture and forestry (Section 100), banking and insurance (Sections 101–102), copyright associations (Section 102a), supply of public utilities including electricity, gas and water (Section 103).

257 The Fifth Amendment of the German Competition Act of 1989 cancelled the exceptions. The exceptions that remained in force following May 2004 are discussed in Section 6.3.3.

258 German Competition Act, Section 8. This authorisation has almost never been used in practice. See Drahos (2001, 96) and Wilks and Bartle (2002, 163).

259 German Competition Act following the Sixth Amendment of 1998, Section 7.

260 Klees (2006, 399).

261 This exception is discussed in Section 6.3.2.

262 German Competition Act following the Sixth Amendment of 1998, Section 2(2).

263 Ashurst (2005, 1).

ensuring competition. However, it is not the Bundeskartellamt's responsibility to realise these interests'.[264] According to the NCA, the purpose of its competition law 'is to serve the same purpose in the economic sector as the purpose served by our democratic order in the political arena, i.e. to ensure that not too much power lies in the hands of only a few'.[265]

2.6.2.3 National Enforcement System

The Competition Act of 1957 established the Federal Cartel Office, the *Bundeskartellamt*. It is an independent higher federal authority assigned to the Federal Ministry of Economic Affairs and Energy. The procedural regime followed EU practice and was originally based on a notification and authorisation system. Since the 2005 amendment, it has transformed into a self-assessment system.[266]

Decisions of the German NCA can be appealed to civil courts. At first instance, the Düsseldorf Higher Regional Court (OLG Düsseldorf) investigates both factual and legal aspects of the decisions and has full jurisdiction over fines. A second appeal on points of law can be submitted to the Federal Court of Justice.[267]

2.6.3 *The Netherlands*

2.6.3.1 Origins of National Competition Law

Dutch competition policy has been famously ineffective for many years.[268] The Law Regulating Economic Competition of 1956 introduced a compulsory notification system with provisional validity, representing a mix of the German and French approaches: Similar to the German approach, it established a notification system, and similar to the French approach, it was based on the *abuse principle*. Accordingly, the Dutch Minister of Economic Affairs would examine the effect of an agreement on the 'public interest'.

The term public interest remained undefined. It mandated a case-by-case evaluation and involved consultation with other ministries and the Economic Competition Commission.[269] Following the assessment, the Minister could issue a 'declaration of general application', expanding the effect of an agreement that was

[264] www.bundeskartellamt.de/EN/AboutUs/Bundeskartellamt/bundeskartellamt_node.html. See also German NCA annual report 2008, 5; and Section 3.6.2.3.
[265] German NCA annual report 2018, 4.
[266] German Competition Act following the Seventh Amendment of 2005, Sections 9–10.
[267] German Competition Act, Sections 63 and 70.
[268] Russe and Griffiths (1998, 15) and Kuenzler and Warlouzet (2013, 91).
[269] OECD Regulatory Reform in the Netherlands (1998), 9.

deemed positive for the common good to a whole sector. Alternatively, it could grant a 'declaration of invalidity' to an agreement with negative effects.[270]

Although it was frequently amended, up until the mid-1990s, the law had little use in practice, and the Netherlands remained a 'cartel heaven'.[271] At the same time, Dutch firms were increasingly subject to Article 101 TFEU infringement procedures at the EU level. In fact, the Commission condemned some agreements even after the Dutch government approved them.[272]

This phenomenon reached its peak in the Commission's *Dutch construction cartel* (1992) decision.[273] In addition to imposing fines on the undertakings, the Commission initiated an infringement procedure against the Dutch government, claiming that the Dutch law and enforcement practices have hindered the proper functioning of EU competition rules. The Commission terminated the proceedings after the government agreed to enact a more modern domestic competition policy.[274] Initially, the Dutch government only enforced its existing competition laws more rigorously. Yet, the adoption of the Dutch Competition Act of 1997, which is still in force today, modelled the national law closely after its EU counterpart.

2.6.3.2 National Equivalent of Article 101 TFEU and Consumer Welfare Standard

Since the late 1990s, two opposing forces have shaped the Dutch approach to balancing. On the one hand, subsequent to the adoption of Regulation 1/2003, the Dutch government called for the 'Europeanisation' of the Dutch law, bringing it 'as far as possible into line with the [EU] regime'.[275] Hence, Article 6(1) and (3) of the Dutch Competition Act repeat the wording of Article 101(1) and (3) TFEU, respectively.

On the other hand, the Dutch government has consistently pushed for the consideration of broad non-competition interests. In particular, in addition to Article 6(3), the Act includes a broad *de minimis* exception, exceptions for undertakings entrusted with the provision of services in the public economic interest, BERs, and sectoral exceptions for collective labour agreements and agreements on pensions.[276] Those exceptions were criticised as being overly broad, still

[270] Kuenzler and Warlouzet (2013, 102–104).
[271] *Ibid*, 115.
[272] Drahos (2001, 366).
[273] 31572 and 32571 Building and construction industry in the Netherlands (1992).
[274] Drahos (2001, 214).
[275] Dutch NCA Annual report 2003, 16.
[276] Those exceptions are detailed in Sections 6.3.1, 4.4.1.3, and 5.4.1, respectively.

encompassing most of the exemptions that could be considered under the old Dutch public interest test.[277]

In a similar vein, in 2003, the Social and Economic Council of the Netherlands (SER)[278] critiqued the manner in which the Dutch NCA examined non-competition interests, noting that Dutch competition policy was a means to boost the prosperity of Dutch society, rather than an end unto itself. Such prosperity was defined broadly, including economic progress (income and productivity growth), social progress (well-being and social cohesion), and good quality of life (in both a spatial and environmental sense).[279] The SER condemned the Dutch NCA for following the Commission's approach to balancing. It noted that the Commission had not provided a clear and transparent criterion and confined balancing to benefits having economic effects.[280] The SER thus recommended that the Commission and NCA take broader types of benefits into account.

The SER proposal for an EU Treaty amendment was not accepted. The Dutch Competition Act, however, was amended to order the Dutch NCA 'to include *other interests besides economic interests* in its considerations for purposes of Article 6(3)'.[281] Following this amendment, the Dutch government demanded that the Dutch NCA consider a broad array of non-economic benefits in the application of Article 101 TFEU. In particular, a 2007 Dutch Court of Audit report concluded that the NCA should balance in a clearer manner and include broader interests.[282] Following this critique, the Dutch NCA has regularly dedicated special attention to balancing in its annual reports.[283]

In 2014, the Dutch NCA took a significant stand in favour of including non-economic benefits by adopting a Vision Document on Competition and Sustainability. Interpreting both Dutch and EU competition laws, the Vision Document claimed that sustainability interests could play an important role in the enforcement of agreements on sustainable initiatives.[284] The Vision Document is remarkable on account of offering a broad interpretation of the role of

277 OECD Regulatory Reform in the Netherlands (1998), 10.

278 The SER advises the Dutch government and parliament on key points of social and economic policy.

279 SER (2003, 2).

280 *Ibid*, 9.

281 Emphasis added. Dutch Competition Act, Article 5d.

282 Algemene Rekenkamer (2007, 65–68). The Netherlands Court of Audit is a central government body created to ensure the functioning of the democratic system. It monitors the central government's revenues and expenditures and whether the central government's policies are implemented as intended.

283 Dutch NCA annual report 2008, 10; Dutch NCA annual report 2009, 42; Dutch NCA annual report 2010, 12; Dutch NCA annual report 2011, 4, 15; Dutch NCA annual report 2012, 4; Dutch NCA annual report 2013, 10; Dutch NCA annual report 2014, para 4.1.5; Dutch NCA annual report 2016, para 3.14-3.1.5; Dutch NCA annual report 2019, 8.

284 Vision Document on Competition and Sustainability (2014), 6.

non-competition interests under both EU and Dutch law and is further elaborated in Section 3.6.2.2.

2.6.3.3 National Enforcement System

The Competition Law of 1998 established the *Nederlandse Mededingingsautoriteit* (NMa). At first, the NMa was part of the Ministry of Economic Affairs, which retained decision-making powers. In 2004, it was transformed into an autonomous administrative authority.[285] Yet, the Minister has remained responsible for competition policy and has the power to issue general directives.

The enforcement system underwent reform in 2013. First, the NMa, consumer, and post and telecommunication authorities were consolidated into the *Authority for Consumers and Markets* (ACM). Second, the Minister of Economic Affairs and the Minister of Infrastructure and the Environment were vested with the power to overturn an 'order of general application' issued by the Dutch NCA if the NCA was 'not competent to take one'.[286] While the wording of the provision is rather vague, it could be seen as allowing the Minister to annul a decision due to public policy considerations.

When the Dutch NCA decides to impose sanctions, the undertakings concerned may ask the NCA to reassess the case. This administrative review is based on the opinion of an advisory committee, which is independent of the NCA. Following review, the parties may appeal to the District Court of Rotterdam and then to the Trade and Industry Appeals Tribunal. Both courts are competent to examine the legality of the decision, with a full review of sanctions.[287]

2.6.4 *UK*

UK competition law and policy are likely to undergo significant reform upon the departure of the UK from the EU (Brexit). At the time of finalising this study, there is still great uncertainty about the modalities of exiting the EU and the impact it might have on EU and UK competition law. Scholars have already explored various alternatives, including their impact on balancing.[288] Nevertheless, Brexit has no direct bearing on this study. Since the study focuses on past practice, the UK is simply regarded as one of the EU Member States in this context.

[285] The Dutch Competition (Independent Administrative Authority) Amendment Act of 2005.
[286] Dutch Act Establishing the Authority for Consumers and Markets of 2013, Article 10.
[287] Dutch Competition Act, Articles 92–93. On the standard of judicial review, see Lavrijssen (2009, 182). On the reassessment procedure, see Frese (2014, 146).
[288] See, for example, Lianos *et al.* (2017), Vickers (2017), Jones (2017), Fingleton *et al.* (2017), and Monti (2017). This matter was also mentioned in the Commission's policy report 2017, 24.

2.6.4.1 Origins of National Competition Law

The roots of UK competition policy are grounded in the private-law *restraints of trade* doctrine. Developed in the fifteenth century and valid to the present day, the doctrine holds that an agreement that leads to unreasonable restraints on the freedom of economic activity is unenforceable by its parties. The doctrine is based on a two-stage assessment. The plaintiff must first prove the existence of a restraint on trade. If such restraint can be established, the burden of proof shifts to the defendant. The defendant must show that its behaviour was not unreasonable and that it gave due consideration to the interests of other parties.[289] This public interest test implies that courts will refuse to enforce a contract only if it impinges on both competition rules and the public interest.

The UK's early public-law competition policy was adopted following the Second World War in pursuit of recovery of industries and full employment. Accordingly, it was not based on solid economic theory but rather on the public interest test.[290] Moreover, between the 1940s and 1960s, the substantive, procedural, and institutional rules were regularly revised to respond to immediate concerns and developments:[291]

The Monopolies and Restrictive Practices (Inquiry and Control) Act of 1948 created an informal enforcement procedure. Any governmental department with an interest in an agreement could apply the public interest test to determine whether to take action. The Act also created the Monopolies and Restrictive Practices Commission (MRPC) – the first administrative European competition agency. While the MRPC had no decision-making capabilities, it investigated monopolies and restrictive practices following references from the Board of Trade.[292] This informal procedure was criticised as being too vague, unpredictable, and political. As a response, the Restrictive Trade Practices Act of 1956 enacted a more formal notification system. It created the Registrar of Restrictive Trading Agreements and imposed the duty to give notification of all agreements involving the production or supply of goods that determined prices, supply terms or quantities, or imposed sale restrictions. The powers of investigation and decision were transferred to the Restrictive Practices Court (RPC), a newly established judicial body.[293] Unlike the MRPC, the RPC was independent of political and economic pressure.[294] It examined all agreements of which it had been notified by using a rebuttable

[289] Kuenzler and Warlouzet (2013, 93).
[290] Policy Studies Institute (1989, 154) and Kuenzler and Warlouzet (2013, 93).
[291] Motta (2004, 11) and Kuenzler and Warlouzet (2013, 93).
[292] Wilks and Bartle (2002, 158).
[293] Scott (2012, 196).
[294] Restrictive Trade Practices Act of 1956. See also Kuenzler and Warlouzet (2013, 110).

presumption that they had contradicted the public interest.[295] Because the 1956 Act significantly reduced the MRPC's role, it was renamed the Monopolies Commission (MC). In 1965, The Monopolies and Mergers Act granted the MC a role in merger review and renamed it the Monopolies and Mergers Commission (MMC).

The novelty of the 1956 regime was significant, yet still unsatisfactory: Although it prompted more rigid competition assessment, it did not specify *how* to apply the public interest test. In addition, it did not apply to agreements that were not subject to obligatory registration, which continued to be examined under the 1948 Act. During the 1960s and 1970s, the registration requirements were expanded to include other types of agreements.[296]

The Fair Trading Act of 1973 was adopted in parallel to the UK's accession to the EU. It marked the first step away from the public interest test by referring for the first time to competition as a public aim unto itself.[297] Yet, it still recognised other aims such as the promotion of consumer interests, reduction of costs, efficiency, employment, and UK competitiveness. The 1973 Act once again changed the institutional structure of enforcement. It created the office of Director General of Fair Trading (DGFT). Agreements subject to registration were notified to the DGFT, which had inherited the Registrar's duties. Restrictive agreements not subject to registration could have been referred by the DGFT (subject to the veto power of the Secretary of State[298]), the Secretary of State, or a Minister acting in concert with the Secretary of State.[299] Referred agreements were investigated by the MMC and decided by the Minister. In practice, those enforcement efforts were limited. The high inflation rates of the 1970s focused most of the enforcement on price control.[300]

The UK's economic governance underwent significant reform after the election of Margaret Thatcher in 1979. The Competition Act of 1980 was adopted as part of the new administration's neoliberal market-oriented philosophy. It abolished the price control regime and attempted to reduce prices and fight inflation by means of competition.[301] It replaced the UK's former form-based approach (i.e. examining the type of the agreement) with an assessment of the agreement's effect on competition, like the EU regime. The 1980 Act extended the DGFT's powers, allowing it to

[295] According to the Restrictive Trade Practices Act of 1956, Section 12, the Board of Trade could, upon the representation of the Registrar, remove from the Registrar and not refer to the RPC agreements having no substantial economic significance.

[296] The UK Resale Price Act of 1964, UK Restrictive Trade Practices Act of 1968, and UK Fair Trading Act of 1973, which broaden the registration requirements to other forms of agreements, including collective RPM, information exchange, and agreements in the services sector.

[297] The UK Fair Trading Act of 1973, Section 84.

[298] In 1969, the monopolies functions were transferred from the Board of Trade to the Secretary of State. See Korah (1982, 20).

[299] The UK Fair Trading Act of 1973, Sections 40, 50–51, and 94.

[300] Kuenzler and Warlouzet (2013, 120).

[301] The UK Competition Act of 1980, Section 1. See also Merkin and Williams (1980, 429).

initiate and conduct investigations. Yet, if the DGFT did find a restriction, it filed a reference with the MMC, which then examined whether there was a restriction, and if that was the case, assessed it using the public interest test.

A more fundamental modernisation of UK competition policy took place only two decades later with the Competition Act of 1998 and the Enterprise Act of 2002, which are still in effect today. The reform aimed to align the UK regime as closely as possible with its EU equivalent.[302] The Enterprise Act of 2002 replaced the DGFT with the *Office of Fair Trade* (OFT). While decisions of the DGFT were executed in the name of the individual appointed to that position by the Secretary of State, OFT decisions were actually taken by a Board appointed by the Secretary of State.[303] The reform revised that institutional structure. The DGFT's powers were significantly increased at the expense of powers previously reserved to the judiciary and the executive. The DGFT was assigned the tasks of assessing infringements, granting exemptions, issuing directions, and imposing remedies. The MMC was renamed the Competition Commission (CC). Its powers were reduced and were bound to a DGFT referral but still included investigation of markets, mergers, and economic regulation.

The Enterprise and Regulatory Reform Act of 2013 merged the CC and the OFT to create the Competition and Markets Authority (CMA).[304]

2.6.4.2 National Equivalent of Article 101 TFEU and Consumer Welfare Standard

Modelled on the design of EU competition law, Chapter 1 of the UK Competition Act of 1998 includes a cartel prohibition similar to Article 101(1) TFEU. The Chapter I prohibition is subject to three types of exception: an exception similar to Article 101(3) TFEU, BERs, and a regulated conduct defence.[305] The first exception imposes conditions almost identical to those of Article 101(3) TFEU and abolished the public interest test. The Other Enactments (Amendment) Regulations of 2004 accommodated the UK regime to changes introduced by Regulation 1/2003. Most importantly, it abandoned the notification regime in favour of legal exceptions.

The UK has not explicitly adopted a consumer welfare standard. Yet, Section 3.6.2.1 shows that, in practice, it had opted for a short-term, narrow consumer welfare standard similar to the one advocated by the Commission following modernisation.

[302] Scott (2012, 195).

[303] Bailey and Whish (2015, 63–64).

[304] Enterprise and Regulatory Reform Act, Sections 25–26.

[305] Those exceptions are detailed in Sections 3.6, 4.4.1.3, and 5.4.1, respectively.

2.6.4.3 National Enforcement System

In addition to the OFT and the CMA described above, British sector regulators are also empowered to apply Article 101 TFEU and the national equivalent provision. Sector regulators were created in the UK starting in the 1980s in conjunction with the national privatisation initiatives. The regulators were gradually required to promote competition and sometimes also had to make references to the competition authorities (the MC/MMC).[306]

The powers of the sector regulators were reinforced by the Competition Act of 1998, which introduced a formal concurrent enforcement model.[307] It entrusted the Office of Communications, the Gas and Electricity Markets Authority, the Water Services Regulation Authority, the Office of Rail Regulation, the Northern Ireland Authority for Utility Regulation, the Civil Aviation Authority, and the healthcare sector regulator for England (NHS Improvement, formerly Monitor) with reference powers to the CC. Later, following the entry into force of Regulation 1/2003, these powers were extended to the enforcement of EU competition rules.

The empirical findings presented in this study demonstrate that, in practice, only a very few competition decisions were adopted by means of the concurrency model. Sector regulators have mostly chosen to rely on their specific sector regulation rather than enforce EU or national competition rules.[308] The Enterprise and Regulatory Reform Act of 2013 was designed to remedy this shortcoming. The Act obliges sector regulators to consider using their competition powers in appropriate cases and supports their efforts through greater coordination with the CMA.[309] Failing to apply concurrent competition powers in a sufficiently rigorous manner might elicit losing jurisdiction to the CMA.

The Enterprise Act of 2002 established the Competition Appeal Tribunal (CAT). This is a specialised administrative body serving as an appellate instance for NCA and sector regulator decisions. Unlike many other appeal instances, the CAT can reopen cases, hear new evidence, and is not bound by the NCA's prior decisions. A second appeal on matters of law or fines is submitted to the appropriate court, according to a geographic criterion.[310]

306 Dunne (2014c, 258).

307 The UK competition Act, Section 54 and Schedule 10; CMA Guidance on Concurrent Application (2014).

308 See Section 7.5.1. See also Dunne (2014c, 262).

309 Enterprise and Regulatory Reform Act, Schedule 14.

310 Tribunal proceedings in England and Wales are appealed to the Court of Appeal; in Scotland to the Inner House of the Court of Session; and in Northern Ireland to the Court of Appeal of Northern Ireland. On the UK appeals system, see also Graham (2009) and Frese (2014, 152–153).

2.6.5 *Hungary*

2.6.5.1 Origins of the National Competition Law

Hungary applied some competition rules as early as the 1920s. It had private-law remedies for unfair marketing and practices contrary to morals or business fairness. From the early 1930s, it required notification of large cartels that were potentially subject to private or public enforcement. However, these rules were rarely enforced in practice.[311]

Following the Second World War, Soviet occupation transformed Hungary into a communist state. Consequently, as pronounced by Hungary's Supreme Court in 1952, 'under the socialist economic order the regulation of competition lost its substance'.[312] Yet, Hungary still adhered to certain market-based principles. Subsequent to the Hungarian Revolution and withdrawal from the Warsaw Pact in 1956, the Hungarian Civil Code of 1959 enacted provisions encouraging efficiency and reliance on price mechanisms to improve firms' performance in the planned economy. It prohibited price fixing, foreclosing customers from suppliers, and business activities that gave an unfair advantage to undertakings or harmed consumers. Next, in 1968, the government put an end to the National Planning Office that had previously fixed the types and quantities of goods and products to be produced in the country.[313] Ordinances in opposition to price cartels, certain types of market sharing, and vertical restraints were passed in 1967 and 1975.[314]

The Act on the Prohibition of Unfair Economic Activities of 1984 prohibited unfair market practices, cartels, and abuse of dominance. Since the Act did not include an enforcement mechanism, it, too, had little use in practice.[315] Nevertheless, it had significant symbolic value. Together with similar Yugoslavian and Polish legislation, it was one of the first economic reforms to be passed in the East and Central European socialist countries. Hungarian Justice *Salamon* described the Act as guided 'not by the actually existing market, but by the desire aimed at it'.[316] A decade later, during the 1990s, most of the other (former) socialist countries adopted similar rules.[317]

Following the fall of communism, Hungary gradually opened up its markets to competition. A 1989 amendment to Hungary's constitution acknowledged a

[311] Hungarian Act No. V on Against Unfair Competition of 1923; Hungarian Act No. XX on Agreements Regulating Economic Competition of 1931. See also Várady (1999, 231), OECD Regulatory Reform in Hungary (2000, 6), and Cseres (2005, 348).

[312] As translated by Várady (1999, 231).

[313] Wessman (1991, 17).

[314] Hungarian Ordinance on Price Regulation of 1967 and Hungarian Ordinance on Exchange of Products of 1975.

[315] Várady (1999, 231).

[316] English translation from Várady (1999, 238).

[317] ibid, 246 and Cseres (2005, 351).

market-based economy and the freedom of competition.[318] Simultaneously, the government introduced vast privatisation, particularly in the industry, services, and agricultural sectors.[319] A designated competition policy was adopted quickly after the election of the first post-communist government in 1990. Inspired by the EU and German models, it enacted a general cartel prohibition and a set of exemptions.[320] Those included agreements intended to prevent abuse of economic superiority, *de minimis*, and a defence similar to Article 101(3) TFEU.

Hungary began negotiating EU accession shortly thereafter. It applied for EU membership in 1994, started formal negotiations in 1998, and acceded the EU in May 2004. Consequently, the new Competition Act adopted in 1996 was closely modelled on the EU regime.[321]

2.6.5.2 National Equivalent of Article 101 TFEU and the Consumer Welfare Standard

The wording of the Hungarian law is similar to Article 101 TFEU. Article 11 is almost identical to Article 101(1) TFEU. Article 17 resembles Article 101(3) TFEU. Section 3.6.4 shows that, despite certain differences, the Hungarian NCA has interpreted it as essentially identical to the provision of Article 101(3) TFEU.

The preamble of the Competition Act declares that the Act is not confined to the promotion of competition as such, but rather to the promotion of 'the public interest attached to the maintenance of competition on the market ensuring economic efficiency and social progress, the interests of undertakings complying with the requirements of business fairness and the interests of consumers require the state to protect by law fairness and freedom of economic competition'. By the same token, the Hungarian NCA pronounces that it enforces competition rules for the public interest in a manner that enhances long-term consumer welfare and efficiency. It states that competition should stimulate economic growth and employment, resulting in an increase in the standard of living. In cases of market failure, however, competition does not provide the best result.[322]

2.6.5.3 National Enforcement System

The 1990 competition Act established the Hungarian competition authority, the *Gazdasági Versenyhivatal* (GVH). The GVH is an administrative authority reporting only to parliament. It is vested with investigation and enforcement powers. In the past, enforcement was based on a notification system. Following accession to

[318] Article 9.
[319] OECD Regulatory Reform in Hungary (2000, 9).
[320] Hungarian Act LXXXVI of 1990 on the Prohibition of Unfair Market Practice, Articles 14–17.
[321] Hungarian Act LVII of 1996 on the Prohibition of Unfair and Restrictive Market Practices.
[322] GVH, Fundamental Principles of Competition Policy (2007, 7–8).

the EU and the modernisation of EU competition law, it has shifted to a self-assessment system.[323]

Appeals on decisions of the Hungarian NCA take place at three levels. There are two instances of ordinary review, which examine the legality of the decision on points of law and fact. In exceptional cases, the Supreme Court (Curia) reviews cases on legal matters.[324] In the past, the ordinary instances were the Budapest Metropolitan Court followed by a second appeal to the Budapest Appeal Court. Since 2013, the Metropolitan Administrative and Labour Court of Budapest is the court of first instance, and the Metropolitan Court of Budapest is the court of second instance.

2.7 NON-COMPETITION INTERESTS UNDER ARTICLE 101 TFEU: AN OPEN QUESTION

The possibility of considering non-competition interests under Article 101 TFEU and the manner in which that would occur are intrinsically linked with the objectives pursued by the Article. As was suggested in the opening of this chapter, those objectives inform the scope of the Article and the possibility to limit its application in favour of promoting other policies.

The historical overview presented in this chapter has shown that, over the years, the Member States and the EU institutions have not taken a clear stand on the objectives of EU competition policy in general and Article 101 TFEU in particular. Both the procedural and substantive elements of EU competition law enforcement were the outcome of heated negotiation and compromises among Member States having substantially different economic policies and traditions, which were often influenced by social and historical factors, and in response to entirely different objectives. Favouring consensus over clarity, the EU institutions and the Member States have never identified the Article's objectives in EU primary or secondary laws. Moreover, while the EU Courts have filled some of those gaps, they have too not developed a clear list of objectives that can inform the balancing of competition against non-competition interests.

Consequently, the rules guiding balancing have mostly been developed through the Commission's decisional practices and policy papers. This chapter has demonstrated that the Commission's approach to balancing has changed across the four enforcement periods. It was informed by various legal and economic theories, the surrounding social and political challenges, and the applicable institutional and procedural enforcement structures.

323 Hungarian Act LXVIII of November 2005.

324 Hungarian NCA annual report 2008, 5; Hungarian NCA annual report, 2012, 15. See also Papp (2017, 257–258).

Since modernisation, Member States, NCAs, and national courts also play a decisive role in shaping the role of non-competition interests via the multilevel governance enforcement system. Although the Commission's case law and soft law instruments are an important source of influence for national interpretation, they are self-binding on the Commission alone. Where EU primary and secondary laws or the case law of the EU Courts do not prescribe otherwise, NCAs enjoy a wide margin of discretion to shape their national approaches based on their legal, economic, and social traditions.

As mentioned in the introduction of this book, an impressive array of legal scholarship has already explored the role of non-competition interests under Article 101 TFEU and the shift in the Commission's approach from doctrinal, historical, constitutional, and economic perspectives. Yet, thus far, only limited attention has been given to the manner in which the EU and national competition enforcers have actually administered this balancing in practice.[325] To fill this gap, the following chapters move away from focusing on the *declared* objectives of Article 101 TFEU. Instead, they examine balancing *as applied in practice* by the various competition enforcers and across the four enforcement periods.

[325] See Section 1.1.2.

3

Article 101(3) TFEU

Individual Exemptions

3.1 INTRODUCTION

Article 101(3) TFEU is the 'classic' provision for accepting non-competition interests as a justification for an otherwise anti-competitive agreement that is prohibited by Article 101(1) TFEU. The wording and structure of Article 101 TFEU, as well as the EU Courts' case law[1] and the Commission's decisions and guidelines,[2] suggest that an exclusion from the prohibition on anti-competitive agreements can only be granted to agreements that fulfil the four conditions of Article 101(3) TFEU. As such, Article 101(3) TFEU outlines the substantive scope of non-competition interests that can be taken into account under Article 101 TFEU.[3]

Despite its great importance, the application of Article 101(3) TFEU to an individual case, and hence balancing, is far from unequivocal. Chapter 2 has shown that the wording of the four conditions of Article 101(3) TFEU created a great deal of uncertainty about balancing, leaving each competition enforcer a wide margin of discretion to decide *if* to take non-competition interests into account, *what types of benefits* to take into account, and *how*.[4]

[1] The Courts have stated that non-competition interests arising from an agreement should only be examined within the framework of Article 101(3) TFEU. See the CJEU in C-382/12P MasterCard (2014), para 181 upholding the GC's judgement in T-111/08 MasterCard (2012), para 182. See also C-243/83 Binon (1985), para 43–46; T-112/99 TPS (2001), para 106–107; T-360/09 E.ON/GDF (2012), para 64–65; T-470/13 Lundbeck (2016), para 307; T-208/13 Telefónica/Portugal Telecom (2016), para 102–104.

[2] The Commission Article 101(3) Guidelines (2004), para 42 provide that 'goals pursued by other Treaty provisions can be taken into account to the extent that they can be subsumed under the four conditions of Article [101(3) TFEU]'. See also 38606 Cartes bancaires (2007), para 367–368; 39188 Bananas (2008), para 303; 39839 Telefónica/Portugal Telecom (2013), para 395–396.

[3] See Section 2.2.3.

[4] *Ibid.*

Against this backdrop, this chapter takes an empirical approach to mapping out the competition enforcers' interpretations of balancing under Article 101(3) TFEU. This reveals a substantial divergence in the frequency with which the Commission, NCAs, and EU and national courts have invoked and accepted Article 101(3) TFEU, the types of benefits they have been willing to examine under the Article, the balancing method, and the intensity of control.

The chapter begins by focusing on the Commission's approach. Section 3.2 provides an empirical and legal overview of the Commission's application of the Article. Next, Section 3.3 maps the development of the Commission's approach as to the types of benefits that can be taken into account under the Article. It shows that while in the past the Commission had considered economic and non-economic benefits, following modernisation, it has re-interpreted the Article to cover only economic benefits. Section 3.4 reports a similar trend with respect to the balancing method and intensity of control. It affirms that following modernisation, the Commission has attempted to narrow down the scope of Article 101(3) TFEU by introducing a short-term narrow consumer welfare standard to guide the application of Article 101 TFEU in general, and Article 101(3) TFEU balancing in particular, and has demanded more robust economic evidence.

Section 3.5 goes on to analyse the practice of the EU Courts. Prior to modernisation, the EU Courts were active in shaping Article 101(3) TFEU balancing. This section shows that they had an important role in developing the principles guiding the Commission's assessment of the types of benefits examined under the Article and the balancing method. Yet, the EU Courts have not fully embraced the Commission's narrow approach to Article 101(3) TFEU following modernisation. In fact, Article 101(3) TFEU has become an area of inconsistency between the Commission's and EU Courts' approaches to balancing.

Section 3.6 then points out a similar divergence in the Member States' approaches, which thus far have been greatly underexplored by legal scholarship. It illustrates that NCAs and national courts have reached conflicting decisions with respect to the same or similar agreements and adopted different balancing principles on the types of relevant benefits, balancing method, and intensity of control for applying the Article's four conditions. This fragmentation, the section concludes, impedes the level playing field and legal certainty of economic actors across the EU, exposing undertakings to multiple balancing standards.

Section 3.7 concludes by presenting the transitions in Article 101(3) TFEU balancing brought about by the three pillars of modernisation.

The differences in the competition enforcers' approaches to Article 101(3) TFEU balancing, which are elaborated throughout this chapter, are summarised in Table 3.1.

TABLE 3.1. *Trends in Article 101(3) TFEU balancing*

Enforcement period/ jurisdiction	Types of benefits	Balancing method	Intensity of control	Frequency (%)	
				Invoked	Accepted
		Commission			
First enforcement period (1962–1977)	Industrial policy	Legal balancing, impact on market integration	Focus on 1st condition, flexible application	72	31
Second enforcement period (1978–1987)	Economic and non-economic benefits	Legal balancing, workable competition standard	Focus on 1st and 3rd conditions, sectoral approach	76	31
Third enforcement period (1988–April 2004)	Economic and non-economic benefits	Legal balancing, workable competition standard	Focus on 1st and 3rd conditions, sectoral approach	45	27
Fourth enforcement period (May 2004–2017)	Only narrow economic benefits	Economic balancing, short-term narrow consumer welfare	Focus on 1st condition, strict application	25	0
		EU Courts (following May 2004)			
CJEU and GC	Economic and non-economic benefits	Unclear	Mainly procedural elements		
		NCAs (following May 2004)			
France	Economic and non-economic benefits	Until 2009, long-term broad consumer welfare. Since then, short-term narrow consumer welfare	Focus on 1st and 3rd conditions. Until 2009 flexible, since then strict application	14	1
Germany	Industrial policy or national public interests	Effect on competitive process and structure	Focus on 1st and 3rd conditions, strict application	25	2

(continued)

TABLE 3.1 (*continued*)

Enforcement period/ jurisdiction	Types of benefits	Balancing method	Intensity of control	Frequency (%)	
				Invoked	Accepted
Hungary	Only narrow economic benefits	Until 2006, long-term broad consumer welfare. Since then, short-term narrow consumer welfare	Focus on 1st and 3rd conditions. Until 2006 flexible, since then strict application	34	6
The Netherlands[a]	Economic and non-economic benefits	Long-term broad consumer welfare	Varying control, sectoral approach	23	4
UK	Only narrow economic benefits	Short-term narrow consumer welfare	Focus on 1st and 3rd conditions, strict application	27	0

[a] The frequency of invoking and accepting Article 101(3) TFEU in front of the Dutch NCA does not include reassessment proceedings of the Dutch NCA's decisions by an advisory committee; see note (a) in page 32.

Before presenting the legal and empirical background, a quick note on definitions: Under the old notification regime of Regulation 17/62, Article 101(3) TFEU was applied by way of issuing an *exemption*. Namely, at the request of an undertaking, the Commission would exempt an agreement *ex-ante* from the prohibition imposed by Article 101(1) TFEU. The shift to a self-assessment regime brought about by Regulation 1/2003 transformed Article 101(3) TFEU into a directly applicable *exception*. Therefore, this book uses the terms Article 101(3) TFEU *exemptions* and *exception* according to the applicable enforcement period. For the sake of convenience, general references to the Article use the term *exemption*.

3.2 LEGAL AND EMPIRICAL BACKGROUND

Figure 3.1 outlines the application of Article 101(3) TFEU by the Commission. It presents the number of enforcement actions in which the Article was invoked by undertakings (grey line) in relation to the total number of Article 101 TFEU enforcement actions each year (black line). In addition, the figure indicates the number of individual exemptions granted by the Commission. It differentiates three types of exemption: first, exemptions granted without any conditions or obligations attached (black bars); second, exemptions – in which, initially, one or more of the four conditions of the Article had not been fulfilled – granted only after the Commission attached specific conditions or obligations to bring the agreement

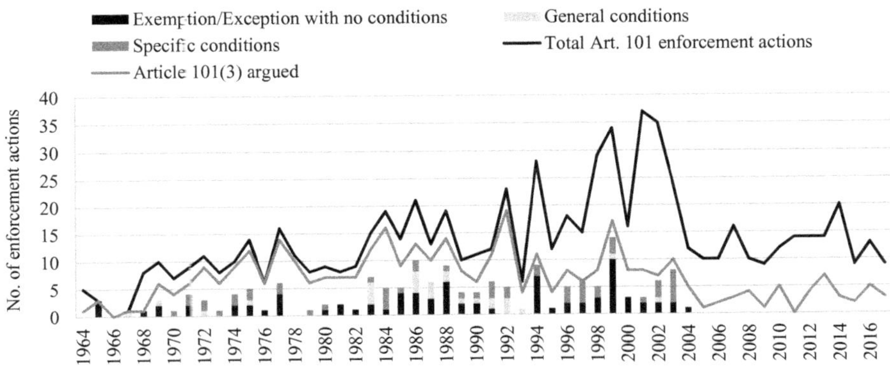

FIGURE 3.1. Article 101(3) TFEU, Commission
All of the Commission's Article 101 TFEU enforcement actions, excluding unpublished comfort letters. In some proceedings, only certain restrictions were exempted

within the scope of Article 101(3) TFEU ('specific conditions', dark grey bars); and third, exemptions subject to other general conditions or obligations ('general conditions', light grey bars).[5]

The figure highlights changes in the enforcement of Article 101 TFEU in general and Article 101(3) TFEU in particular across the four enforcement periods. During the first two enforcement periods (i.e. until 1987), the possibility of granting an Article 101(3) TFEU exemption was central to many Article 101 TFEU enforcement actions. Article 101(3) TFEU was invoked in more than 70% of the proceedings. Exemptions were granted in around 30% of those proceedings, of which approximately half were subject to general or specific conditions.[6]

By comparison, the third enforcement period (1988 to April 2004) was characterised by three interrelated developments. First, the number of Article 101 TFEU enforcement actions had increased significantly. Second, the number of cases in which Article 101(3) TFEU was invoked had experienced a substantial drop (from 76% in the second enforcement period to only 45% in the third period). Despite that, third, the success rate when invoking Article 101(3) TFEU had risen (from 40% during the second enforcement period to 58% of the proceedings in which Article 101(3) TFEU had been invoked during the third enforcement period).

The first development, namely the increase in the total number of Article 101 TFEU enforcement actions, is explained by the geographical enlargement of the EU (i.e. the accession of new Member States) together with the expansion of the substantive scope of EU competition law (i.e. applying Article 101 TFEU to new sectors that had traditionally been considered to be part of the public realm).[7] The

[5] The Commission was empowered to attach conditions or obligations to exemptions pursuant to Regulation 17/62, Article 8(1).

[6] The practice of attaching conditions to exemptions is further elaborated in Section 3.4.3.1.

[7] See Sections 2.3.2 and 2.5.3.1.

latter two developments can be understood in light of the change in the *types of agreements* that the Commission examined during the third enforcement period. By the late-1990s, various agreements that had required individual assessment in the past were assessed by means of the new Vertical and Horizontal BERs[8] or unpublished comfort letters.[9] Those agreements are not fully reflected in the empirical database,[10] which might explain the decline in the invocation rate of Article 101(3) TFEU. On the opposite side of the same coin, the increase in the success rate of Article 101(3) TFEU exemptions could be linked to the growing substantive scope of EU competition law. As elaborated in Section 3.4.3.3, the enforcement of Article 101 TFEU to newly liberalised and regulated markets had expanded the scope of application of Article 101(3) TFEU and required the development of tailored balancing to fit those types of agreement.

Finally, the figure reveals that the Commission has never accepted an Article 101(3) TFEU exception following the entry into force of Regulation 1/2003 in May 2004. Some scholars link this disappearance of Article 101(3) TFEU to the Commission's more economic approach. As elaborated in Sections 3.3.4 and 3.4.4, they maintain that this change is explained by the Commission's attempt to narrow the types of benefit that can be examined under the Article and to increase the evidentiary requirement.

Yet, this explanation does not account for the other trend identified by Figure 3.1, that is, the significant decline in the percentage of enforcement actions in which Article 101(3) TFEU was discussed. During the fourth enforcement period (May 2004–2017), the undertakings invoked Article 101(3) TFEU in only 25% of all of Article 101 TFEU enforcement actions (compared to 45% and 76% of the proceedings in the third and second enforcement periods, respectively).

Chapter 7 argues that this trend is related to the new priority setting powers granted to the Commission and NCAs by virtue of Regulation 1/2003. Whereas under the old notification regime the Commission examined all notified agreements, under the new self-assessment regime the Commission and NCAs set their own enforcement priorities.[11] That chapter shows that the Commission has decided to focus its enforcement efforts on clear-cut restrictions of competition, often supported by leniency applications and settlements, which are unlikely to raise genuine balancing questions. Cases raising balancing questions are likely to be

[8] In some cases, the Commission exempted agreements that later served as a model for future BERs. In 31498 Delta ChemieDDD (1988), for example, it exempted an agreement by which a German firm had granted a know-how license to a British firm for the manufacture and packaging of stain-removal products. The Commission exempted the agreement since it encouraged the manufacturer to make the necessary investments to exploit the licensed know-how, thereby increasing the number of plants manufacturing the products in the EU. Following the adoption of Regulation 556/89 on Know-How Licensing Agreements, similar agreements no longer required an individual decision. See also Chapter 4.

[9] See Section 7.5.3 and Figure 7.5.

[10] See Section 1.3.2.3.

[11] Modernisation White Paper (1999), para 45.

resolved by applying the implicit-procedural balancing tools, such as negotiated remedies, regulatory mechanisms alternative to Article 101 TFEU, or by closing the probe into the case. As a result, that chapter submits, the Commission was no longer required to address the balance of interests under Article 101(3) TFEU.

The following sections demonstrate that the above changes across the four enforcement periods reflect a much more extensive development in Article 101(3) TFEU balancing approaches and practices.

3.3 TYPES OF BENEFITS

The types of benefits that can be examined under Article 101(3) TFEU are one of the great mysteries of EU competition law. Article 101(3) TFEU, as described in Section 2.2.3.1, does not clearly spell out the types of benefits that can be taken into account. The empirical findings presented in this section illustrate that in the absence of a clear balancing framework in EU primary or secondary law, the Commission has developed its own approach in its policy papers and decisional practice. This approach was adapted over the four enforcement periods to match the general political, economic, and social advances of the EU.

3.3.1 *Overview*

3.3.1.1 Improving the Production or Distribution of Goods or Promoting Technical or Economic Progress

The wording of the first condition of Article 101(3) TFEU specifies four alternatives for the types of benefits that can, possibly, justify an exemption. The Commission's and EU Courts' decisional practices indicate that they have not adopted precise definitions for those four alternatives. In many cases, the Commission and EU Courts have referred to all four alternatives jointly, making it difficult to ascertain which part of the benefits should be ascribed to each alternative.[12] The Commission has also maintained that it is possible to take into account other factors than those expressly mentioned in the Article.[13] This trend has increased following modernisation, with the Commission often using the term efficiencies instead of attributing the benefits to a specific alternative.[14]

The first two alternatives, *improving production and improving distribution*, were interpreted broadly to include almost any kind of improvement to the operation of an industry or trade, and they cover both goods and services.[15] As elaborated below,

[12] See Annex A, Section 3.1.
[13] The Commission's position in T-17/93 Ford/Volkswagen (1994), para 96.
[14] See Section 2.5.4.3.
[15] Although Article 101(3) TFEU refers expressly to goods, it was applied by analogy to services. See, for example, C-45/85 Fire insurance (1987), para 54 and Article 101(3) Guidelines (2004), para 48.

the competition enforcers have taken into account not only improvements to the production or distribution of the goods or services subject to the specific agreement but also improvements to the economy as a whole. In *Metro I (1977)*, for example, the conclusion of supply contracts for a period of six months was found to promote the stability of the supply. In addition to the benefits created for consumers, the Court viewed the stabilisation of employment conditions as an improvement to production.[16]

The third alternative, the promotion of *technical progress*, was mostly understood as the advancement of innovation. The Commission used this alternative to exempt a number of joint R&D agreements and licensing agreements that facilitated the development and marketing of technologically advanced products.[17]

The meaning of the fourth alternative, the promotion of *economic progress*, is particularly opaque.[18] In fact, this alternative was used on its own to justify exemptions in only a relatively small number of cases.[19] It was used to vindicate that granting of exemptions to agreements relating to patent and know-how licensing,[20] coordination of international payment systems,[21] cooperation for setting up national-wide communication systems,[22] air alliances,[23] and insurance.[24]

In *Bayer-Gist-Brocades (1975)*, the Commission seemed to link the notion of economic progress to the correction of market failure by noting that 'the question of a contribution to economic progress within the meaning of Article [101(3) TFEU] can only arise in those exceptional cases where the free play of competition is unable to produce the best result economically speaking'.[25] Similarly, in *FIFA rules on*

[16] C-26/76 Metro I (1977), para 43. See also Section 3.3.3.1.

[17] See, for example, T-17/93 Ford/Volkswagen (1994), para 110. See also Annex A, Section 3.2.

[18] Van Houtte (1982, 511). According to Goyder (2009, 148–149), those terms originated in French law, which inspired the wording of Article 101 TFEU. See also Section 2.2.2.

[19] The meaning of economic progress was also unclear when it was invoked together with another of Article 101(3) TFEU's alternatives, as detailed in Annex A, Section 3.2. A reference to technical and economic progress is also found in a number of BERs, such as Regulation 870/95 on Consortia, Preamble 4 ('by facilitating and encouraging greater utilisation of containers and more efficient use of vessel capacity'). See also Regulation 246/2009 on Consortia, Preamble 5; Regulation 4056/86 on Maritime Transport, Article 7(2)(b); Regulation 1217/2010 on Research and Development, Preamble 8–9 ('contribute complementary skills, assets or activities to the cooperation'). See also Regulation 2659/2000 on Research and Development, Preamble 10–11 and Article 3(4); Regulation 418/85 on Research and Development, Preambles 4 and 7 and Article 2(d), and Regulation 2349/84 on Patent Licensing, Preamble 21.

[20] 17545 6964 26858 26890 18673 17448 Davidson Rubber Co. (1972), para 11; 21353 Kabelmetal/Luchaire (1975), para 10; 32736 Moosehead/Whitbread (1990), para 16.

[21] 31291 Uniform Eurocheques (1988), para 45.

[22] 32737 Eirpage (1991), para 15; 35337 Atlas (1996), para 51–52.

[23] 35545 LH/SAS (1996), para 64–73; 37730 AuA/LH (2002), para 85–89.

[24] 30373 37143 P&I Clubs (1999), para 106.

[25] 27073 Bayer/Gist-Brocades (1975), para III(1).

players' agents (2005), the Commission argued that an arrangement aimed at raising ethical and professional standards had contributed to economic progress by promoting 'a better operation of the market'.[26]

At other times, economic progress was interpreted more broadly. In addition to the correction of market failure, it was understood to imply a contribution to industrial policy and other non-economic benefits. In *Ford/Volkswagen* (1994), for instance, the Commission advocated interpreting the notion of economic progress as encompassing 'social' progress, such as protecting employment.[27] In *Vacuum Interrupters Ltd* (1980), it explained that the R&D agreement promoted economic progress by ensuring 'an increase in the efficiency, safety, and durability of the vacuum interrupter'.[28] In *Beecham-Parke, Davis* (1979), economic progress was expected via the development of new medicine.[29] In *BBC Brown Boveri* (1988), *Assurpol* (1992), and *CECED* (1999), economic progress was reflected in the promotion of R&D and the use of environmentally friendlier products and production means.[30] In *Interconnector* (1995), economic progress was thought to be realised by the integration of the British and Continental gas markets.[31] Yet, over the years neither the Commission nor the EU Courts have clearly defined the meaning of this term.

Given the above, it is clear that the wording and interpretation of the four alternative benefits in the sense of Article 101(3) TFEU fail to elucidate the role of non-competition interests. Accordingly, the next sub-sections take a different approach to scrutinise balancing under Article 101(3) TFEU by focusing on the categories of benefits that have vindicated the granting of an exemption.

3.3.1.2 Economic and Non-Economic Benefits

Figure 3.2 describes the categories of benefits that were argued before (a) and accepted by (b) the Commission as the basis for an Article 101(3) TFEU exemption.[32]

26 The Commission's position in T-193/02 FIFA rules on players' agents (2005), para 62, which was endorsed by the GC.

27 The Commission's position in T-17/93 Ford/Volkswagen (1994), para 96, 107. Van Houtte (1982, 514) advocated a similar broad interpretation, calling to understand the term progress in light of the goals of the Treaty listed in Article 2 TEU (ex. Article 2 EEC).

28 27442 Vacuum Interrupters Ltd (1980), para III(5).

29 28796 Beecham-Parke, Davis (1979), para 35–37.

30 32368 BBC Brown Boveri (1988), para 23; 33100 Assurpol (1992), para 38-39; 36718 CECED (1999), para 57.

31 IP/95/550 Interconnector (1995).

32 The three categories of benefits are defined in Section 2.2.3.1. Direct economic benefits are cost and qualitative improvements enjoyed by consumers in the relevant market. Indirect economic benefits are cost and qualitative improvements that do not occur on the market in which the agreement takes place or has a direct impact. Non-economic benefits are not directly related to the characteristics of the relevant product or service. They are non-pecuniary and are often more subjective than economic benefits.

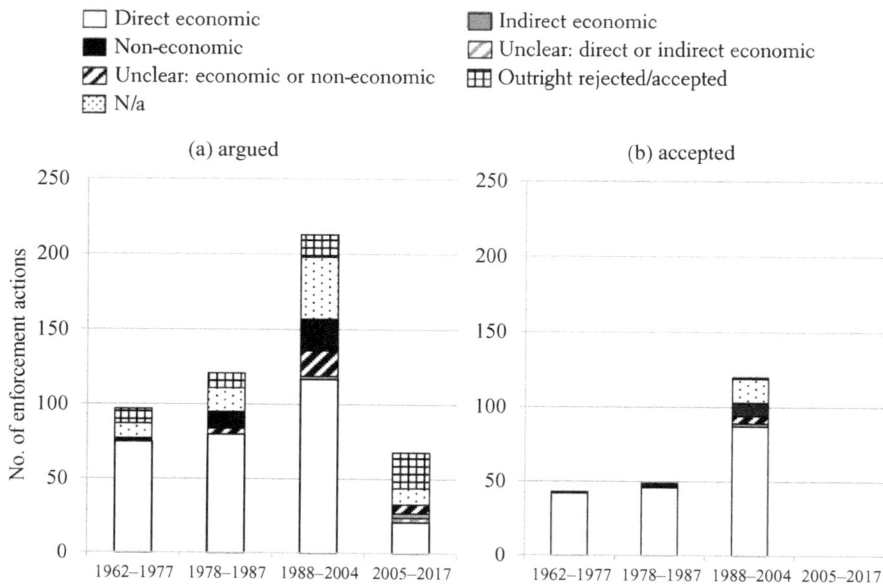

FIGURE 3.2. Article 101(3) TFEU, categories of benefits, Commission[33]
All Article 101 TFEU enforcement actions in which the Commission examined an Article 101(3) TFEU exemption, excluding unpublished comfort letters. In some proceedings, more than one benefit was examined as a justification

Next, Figure 3.3 takes a closer look at the proceedings described in Figure 3.2(b) by outlining the types of non-competition interests that justified exemptions. For the sake of clarity, Figure 3.3(a) includes efficiency and industrial policy-related interests, while Figure 3.3(b) specifies other types of non-competition interests.

Figures 3.2 and 3.3 reveal a remarkable and often overlooked transformation in the types of benefits that were considered relevant under Article 101(3) TFEU. As elaborated in the following sections, during the first enforcement period (i.e. up to 1977), Article 101(3) TFEU was essentially used for balancing competition and industrial policy interests related to the efficiency of production, R&D, or rationalisation. Starting in the second enforcement period, the Commission gradually expanded the scope of the Article to cover broader types of benefits. Yet, following modernisation, the Commission has once again changed its approach, limiting Article 101(3) TFEU to efficiency-related considerations.

3.3.2 *First Enforcement Period: Industrial Policy*

The possibility of relying on indirect and non-economic benefits to justify an Article 101(3) TFEU exemption was rarely discussed during the early days of the EU

[33] Figure 3.2 was originally published in Brook (2019). Reproduced with permission of the Licensor through PLSclear.

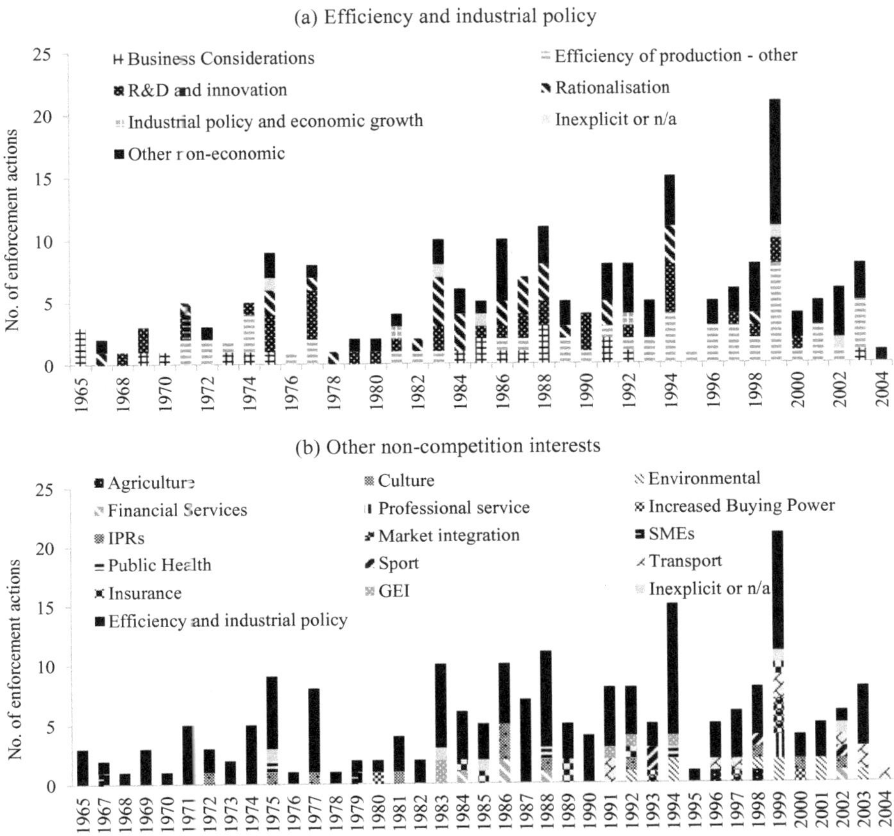

FIGURE 3.3. Types of non-competition interests justifying exemptions, Commission
All Article 101 TFEU enforcement actions exempted by the Commission, excluding unpublished comfort letters. In some cases, more than one interest was accepted as a justification

competition law. During the first enforcement period (1962–1977), the Commission used Article 101(3) TFEU essentially as a tool to balance competition, market integration, and EU industrial policy.[34]

As Figure 3.2 demonstrates, during that period, Article 101(3) TFEU almost exclusively pertained to direct economic benefits (77% of the instances in which the Article was invoked, and 98% of the instances in which it was accepted). The Commission has mostly exempted *horizontal agreements* that furthered the EU's strategic development and growth efforts, such as specialisation agreements, joint research agreements, and joint ventures for the development, manufacture, and marketing of products. It emphasised the economic benefits generated by the agreements, such as lower costs (i.e. setting up long production runs) and better

[34] This is elaborated in Sections 2.5.1 and 3.4.2.

utilisation of production capacities (i.e. specialisation).[35] At the same time, it also noted the positive impact on those horizontal agreements on industrial policy, stressing the importance of promoting R&D, the international competitiveness of EU industry, penetration into new geographical markets, and overcoming the technical difficulties and financial risks linked with the development of technologically advanced products.[36]

Similarly, the Commission exempted a line of agreements setting the rules for participation in *specialised fairs and exhibitions* at which companies present and sell similar products under one roof. Those rules have restricted competition as they limited the freedom of exhibitors to take part in similar activities other than those organised periodically by the organisers of the fair. Nevertheless, the Commission underlined the rationalisation effects of such specialised fairs and exhibitions, affording an opportunity for a periodic comparison to the benefit of both exhibitors and buyers.[37]

This possibility of relying on industrial policy as the basis for an Article 101(3) TFEU exemption was established during the late 1960s. In *Transocean Marine Paint Association (1967)*, the Commission reviewed agreements between manufacturers of marine paint that had agreed to produce and sell paint under a common trademark. The agreements included territorial protection provisions, which prohibited each manufacturer from selling paint in the home territory of another manufacturer without the latter's consent and payment of a fee. The Commission exempted the agreements despite their negative effects on both competition and market integration. It accepted the undertakings' claim that buyers of marine paints would prefer to deal with firms offering paints of identical composition and quality in all large ports. Moreover, it pointed to broader non-economic benefits, noting that the agreements allowed European SME manufacturers to compete with major international companies.[38]

The relevance of industrial policy considerations in the enforcement of Article 101 TFEU was explicitly formulated two years later in the CJEU's preliminary ruling

[35] See Annex A, Section 3.3. See also policy report 1969, 64; policy report 1971, 41; policy report 1972, 43; policy report 1976, 38; policy report 1977, 115. As mentioned in Section 2.5.1, during the first enforcement period, the Commission mainly granted exemptions to horizontal agreements, which were less likely to hinder market integration in comparison to vertical restrictions.

[36] See Annex A, Section 3.4.

[37] 93 European Machine Tool Exhibitions (1969); 181 CEMATEX (1971); 28775 UNIDI (1975); 417 BPICA (1977). See also policy report 1971, 53 and policy report 1977, 97. The Commission exempted similar agreements during the second and third enforcement periods, in 27492 SMM&T Exhibition Agreement (1983); 28959 VIFKA (1986); 31739 Internationale Dentalschau (1987); 31559 Sippa (1991).

[38] 223 Transocean Marine Paint Association (1967), 5–6. This was not a vertical agreement like most of the other agreements assessed during the first enforcement period (see Section 2.5.1). Yet, it raised competition concerns similar to those arising from exclusive distribution agreements.

in *Walt Wilhelm (1969)*. The CJEU declared that the main objective of the EU competition law provisions was to eliminate obstacles to free movement.[39] Thus, the EU institutions were competent to take *negative measures* aimed at increasing market integration by eliminating impediments to trade between Member States. Moreover, the Court added that the EU institutions could also take into account *positive measures* determining the policies for the operation of markets and aimed at promoting EU economic development.[40]

The above illustrates that, during the first enforcement period, the Commission used Article 101(3) TFEU almost exclusively as a tool to promote market integration and EU industrial policy. As Figure 3.2 revealed, during that period the undertakings *did not even attempt* to invoke other types of non-economic benefits as justification for an exemption.

3.3.3 *Second and Third Enforcement Periods: Broadening the Types of Benefits*

3.3.3.1 Metro I and the Workable Competition Standard

The types of relevant benefits under Article 101(3) TFEU were considerably broadened following the CJEU landmark judgement in *Metro I (1977)*.[41] That case examined the operation of Saba, a manufacturer of electronics consumer goods, which had established a selective distribution system in Germany. Saba appointed wholesalers who would purchase its products and resell them to approved specialised dealers. The Commission exempted the selective distribution system under Article 101(3) TFEU.[42] In line with its approach during that time, the exemption was based on an efficiency-inducing argument.[43]

The Commission's decision was challenged by Metro, a wholesaler that had been denied access to Saba's selective distribution system. Remarkably, although the CJEU agreed with the Commission that the agreement had been correctly exempted, it gave a different justification. In particular, while the Commission had based its exemption on economic benefits, the Court resorted to a teleological interpretation of Article 101 TFEU.

39 On the market integration objective of EU competition law and policy, see Section 2.2.1.

40 C-14/68 Walt Wilhelm (1969), para 5. On the differences between negative and positive measures, see also Wesseling (2000, 37).

41 C-26/76 Metro I (1977). For a detailed analysis of the judgement, see also Wesseling (2000, 34–36), Odudu (2006, 160–161), Goyder (2009, 231–232), and Van Rompuy (2012, 150–151).

42 847 Saba (1975), para 38–53. The exemption was granted after certain modifications had been made to the criteria for the appointment of wholesalers. On the Commission's and EU Courts' approaches to selective distribution systems, see Section 5.3.4.

43 The Commission had accepted Saba's submission that the selective distribution system improved the quality of service and facilitated inter-brand competition. See 847 Saba (1975), para 38–42.

The Court held that Article 101 TFEU, read in conjunction with Article 3 EEC,[44] entailed that the appropriate standard for an exemption was not necessarily one of *perfect* competition. Instead, it introduced the notion of *workable* competition, in which the degree of competition protected under Article 101 TFEU is 'necessary to ensure the observance of the basic requirements and the attainment of the objectives of the Treaty, in particular the creation of a single market achieving conditions similar to those of a domestic market'.[45] The nature and intensity of competition, according to the Court, would vary according to what was dictated by the product or service in question and according to the economic structure of the relevant market.

The Court further noted that the requirement of workable competition could be reconciled with the 'safeguarding of objectives of a different nature' if they complied with the latter two conditions of Article 101(3) TFEU.[46] Consequently, the Court concluded that non-economic benefits related to stabilising the provisions of employment justified an exemption.[47]

This statement had opened the door to the consideration of all types of non-competition interests and benefits under Article 101(3) TFEU. Indeed, the empirical findings presented in Figures 3.2 and 3.3 prove that following *Metro I* the Commission posed no restrictions on the types of relevant benefits. In addition to direct and indirect economic benefits, the Commission took non-economic benefits into account including environmental protection, development of sports, and allocation and supply of scarce national resources among states. Furthermore, certain non-economic benefits were also later codified as vindicating granting a block exemption under some of the BERs.[48] Market integration, industrial policy, and efficiencies were no longer the sole justifications for exemption.

The cases in which the Commission maintained that the first benefit condition of Article 101(3) TFEU was not met stated that no real benefit was identified in the specific circumstance of the case.[49] Hence, during the second and third enforcement periods, the Commission had never held that certain types of non-competition interests in general, or non-economic benefits in particular, could not or should not be taken into account to justify an exemption.

The impact of *Metro I* on broadening the types of relevant benefits under Article 101(3) TFEU should be understood in combination with the CJEU's previous statement in *Walt Wilhelm (1969)*. In that case, the Court held that EU institutions could take into account positive measures promoting the development of EU economic

[44] Article 3 EEC laid down a list of the Community 'activities'. A comparable article was not included in the Lisbon Treaties. See Section 2.2.1.

[45] C-26/76 Metro I (1977), para 20. The notion of workable competition was derived from the work of the American scholar Clark (1961) and described in Section 2.5.2.1.

[46] C-26/76 Metro I (1977), para 21–22.

[47] *Ibid*, para 43.

[48] This is elaborated in Chapter 4.

[49] For example, 26186 Central Stikstof Verkoopkantoor (1978), para 88–103; 29133 WANO Schwarzpulver (1978), para III(2); 29869 Italian cast glass (1980), para II(B).

activity when enforcing EU competition law.[50] *Wesseling* has explained that the application of Article 101(3) TFEU after *Metro I* was based on the combination of those two landmark judgements,[51] namely, that when economic circumstances in certain markets (*Metro I* dicta) required the Commission to take certain positive indirect actions to promote the harmonious development of EU economic activity (*Walt Wilhelm* dicta), the Commission would apply Article 101(3) TFEU to take non-competition interests into account under Article 101 TFEU. Similarly, *Evans* has interpreted the first benefit condition as requiring the Commission to determine whether the agreement contributes to the attainment of objectives in the EU interest.[52]

The above illustrates that, up until modernisation, the Commission did not limit the types of benefits that could be examined under Article 101(3) TFEU. The Commission assessed both economic and non-economic benefits that profit either individual consumers or society as a whole. In fact, as the next sub-section shows, the Commission took even broader types of benefits into account than those originally advocated by the CJEU in *Metro I*.

3.3.3.2 The Irrelevance of the Policy-Linking Clauses

The CJEU defined the workable competition standard in *Metro I (1977)* as the degree of competition necessary for the 'attainment of the objectives of the Treaty'.[53] This wording suggests that non-competition interests can justify an Article 101(3) TFEU exemption *only if they constitute an EU objective*.[54]

Indeed, scholars have often linked the consideration of non-economic benefits under Article 101(3) TFEU to the policy-linking clauses.[55] Policy-linking clauses, as discussed in Section 2.5.3.2, require EU institutions to 'take into account', 'aim', or 'pay full regard to' certain public interests when they formulate and implement other policy areas. It was suggested that a teleological interpretation of the policy-linking clauses and the normative structure of the Treaties demands consideration of the protected public interests when applying Article 101(3) TFEU. In this context, the policy-linking clauses could be seen as a formalisation of the need for balancing under the Article. Such an interpretation also entails that public interests listed by

[50] C-14/68 Walt Wilhelm (1969). See Section 3.3.2.

[51] Wesseling (2000, 36). See also Van Rompuy (2012, 151).

[52] Evans (1985, 101).

[53] C-26/76 Metro I (1977), para 20.

[54] According to the Rome Treaty, which was in force when *Metro I* was rendered and throughout the second enforcement period, those objectives included market integration (Articles 3(a)-(c) and (h) EEC); common policy in the sphere of agriculture and transport (Articles 3(d)-(e) EEC); competition (Article 3(f) EEC); balanced payment methods (Article 3(g) EEC); the creation of the European Social Fund and European Investment Bank (Articles 3(i)–(j) EEC) and the association of overseas countries and territories to increase and promote joint economic and social development (Article 3(k) EEC).

[55] Semmelmann (2008, 141), Buttigieg (2009, 53, 129), Lavrijssen (2010, 637), Kingston (2010, 789), Van Rompuy (2012, 219, 223–227), and Nowag (2016, 238).

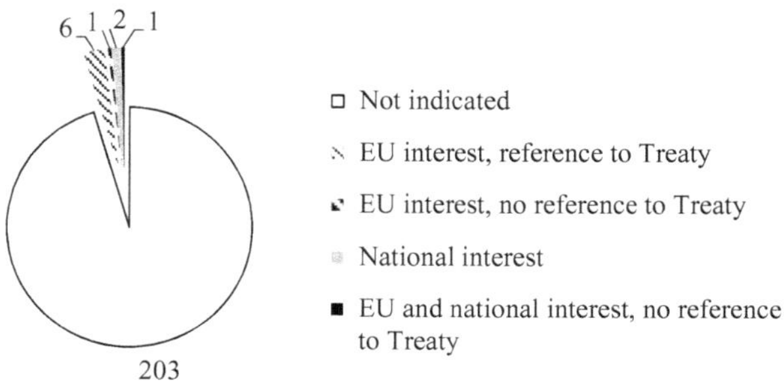

FIGURE 3.4. Legal source of non-competition interests justifying exemptions, Commission (1962–2017)

All Article 101(3) TFEU exemptions granted by the Commission, excluding unpublished comfort letters. In some proceedings, more than one interest was accepted as justification for the exemption. 'National interest' (grey area) includes non-competition interests that are protected by an international treaty signed by a Member State. All of the cases in which the legal source of the non-competition interest was indicated were granted following *Metro I*

the policy-linking clauses enjoy a higher degree of protection compared to non-competition interests that do not enjoy a formal EU status.

However, the empirical findings presented in Figure 3.4 show that, despite the wording of *Metro I* and the emphasis ascribed by various scholars, in practice the Commission did not attach importance to the legal source of the non-competition interests. The figure details the legal sources of the non-competition interests used to justify Article 101(3) TFEU exemptions, as presented by the Commission in each case.

The figure demonstrates, first, that the Commission has almost never specified the legal source of the non-competition interest that justified granting an exemption (white area). In particular, it has usually not invoked a policy-linking clause to justify an exemption.[56]

Second, deviating from the wording of *Metro I*, the Commission had invoked non-competition interests that are not, or were not at that time of the decision, listed as Treaty objectives. For example, it had implicitly accepted employment interests even before the Treaties protected such benefits.[57] In other cases, the

[56] Sections 5.2.5.2 and 7.6.2.2 demonstrate that the policy-linking clauses were used more often as justification for an exemption under Article 101(1) TFEU balancing tools and when accepting commitments.

[57] For instance, in 29525 3000 SSI (1982), para 141, the Commission considered guaranteeing a steady income to tobacco wholesalers and retailers, and in 30299 Grohe's distribution system (1984), para 25–27, and 30261 Ideal-Standard's distribution system (1984), para 26–27, the survival of the traditional plumbing trade. Yet, in those cases, the Commission did not grant exemptions since those restrictions were not limited to what was indispensable to achieve the employment benefits.

Commission referred to *national* non-competition interests to justify an exemption (grey area).[58]

Third, even in the few proceedings in which the Commission identified a policy-linking clause as the legal source for an exemption, it did not always clarify its normative value (thick dashed and black areas). In *Ford/Volkswagen (1992)*, for instance, the Commission mentioned non-economic benefits protected by policy-linking clauses as an additional justification for exempting a joint venture agreement for the development and manufacture of vehicles. The Commission merely stated that in the 'exceptional circumstances' of the case, the joint venture had helped to create jobs and reduce regional disparities, which are basic aims of the Treaties.[59] The Commission, and later the GC on appeal, did not clarify either the role those non-economic benefits had had in granting the exemption or the significance of the policy-linking clause.[60]

The CJEU has implicitly confirmed the Commission's broad reading of *Metro I* in its preliminary rulings. In *Binon (1985)*, the Court reviewed selective distribution systems for press publications, which involved price fixing. The German government submitted that the freedom of the press, as a fundamental right protected by national constitutional law and the CJEU's case law, entailed that competition law could not apply to the press sector without modification.[61] The Court reviewed the freedom of the press under Article 101(3) TFEU, although such an interest was not listed in the Treaty.[62] The CJEU followed a similar approach with regard to employment interests even before they were protected by the policy-linking clauses.[63]

The above demonstrates that both the Commission and the EU Courts have not confined Article 101(3) TFEU to the limited non-competition interests rooted in the Treaties. The workable competition standard has been applied without distinction to all types of benefits, including non-competition interests lacking a formal EU law basis. This is another testament to the fact that prior to modernisation, there was no limitation on the types of non-competition interests or benefits that could be examined under the Article. The next sub-section shows that in a similar vein, the Commission and the EU Courts have also not limited the type of beneficiaries under Article 101(3) TFEU.

58 30525 International Energy Agency (1983), para 28; 34493 37366 37299 37288 37287 37526 37254 37252 37250 37246 37245 37244 37243 37242 37267 DSD (2001), para 143.

59 33814 Ford/Volkswagen (1992), para 28. The practice of invoking non-economic benefits as additional justification is further elaborated in Section 3.3.3.5.

60 T-17/93 Ford/Volkswagen (1994). Later, in T-451/08 CISAC (2013), the GC had once again refrained from clarifying the role of the policy-linking clauses. See Section 3.5.3.1.

61 C-243/83 Binon (1985), para 41–42.

62 *Ibid*, para 43–47. The Commission seemed to agree with this Court's analysis (see in para 43 of the judgement and policy report 1985, 114–115).

63 C-136/86 BINC (1987), para 20–21; C-42/84 Nutricia/de Rooij and Nutricia/Zuid-Hollandse Conservenfabriek (1985), para 39.

3.3.3.3 Relevant Types of Beneficiaries

In addition to broadening the types of relevant non-competition interests under Article 101(3) TFEU, the Commission has also adopted a broad reading of the types of relevant beneficiaries. The CJEU had clearly distinguished between the first and second conditions of Article 101(3) TFEU. According to the Court, while the first condition aims to identify the general public interest generated by an agreement, the second condition aims to ensure that consumers will receive a fair share of such benefits.[64]

Nevertheless, in practice, the Commission had effectively merged the assessment of the two conditions. Although the second condition is worded in a positive way ('any agreement [. . .] allowing consumers a fair share of the resulting benefit'), it did not require proving that consumers will actually benefit from a restrictive agreement. Rather, the Commission applied the condition in a negative way, *assuming* that the remaining competitive pressure in the market will induce the undertakings to pass on part of the benefits to consumers.[65] In *British Airways and Iberia (2003)*, for example, the Commission justified an exemption noting that '[a]lthough there are at this stage only a few concrete indications that the above identified benefits of the co-operation have indeed been passed on to consumers [. . .] there is as such no reason to believe that they would not on those routes where the parties are subject to sufficient competitive constraints from actual and/or potential competitors'.[66]

This, coupled with the broad interpretation granted to the first benefit condition, had expanded the relevant types of beneficiaries under Article 101(3) TFEU. Prior to modernisation, the Article was not limited to individual benefits to direct and indirect consumers, but also exempted collective benefits to society as a whole.[67]

The next sub-section demonstrates the significant impact of such interpretation. It uses the example of environmental benefits to illustrate how the workable competition standard and the Commission's and Courts' interpretations have transformed the scope of Article 101(3) TFEU during the second and third enforcement periods to account for wider types of non-economic benefits.

[64] In C-26/76 Metro I (1977), para 46, for example, the CJEU held that an agreement must 'not only improve the distribution of goods but also allow consumers a fair share of the resulting benefit'. See also Van Houtte (1982, 510), Evans (1985, 102), Buttigieg (2009, 130–137), Townley (2011, 490–491), and Nowag (2016, 234–235).

[65] See Annex A, Section 3.5.

[66] 38479 British Airways and Iberia (2003), para 47.

[67] On the opposite side of the same coin, following modernisation, when the Commission has abandoned the workable competition standard in favour of a consumer welfare standard, the merging of the first two conditions of Article 101(3) TFEU meant that the benefits identified under the first condition are limited to benefits to consumers. See Section 3.3.4.

3.3.3.4 The Case of Environmental Agreements[68]

The need to consider environmental interests within the enforcement of Article 101 TFEU came into vogue only in the 1990s.[69] During the 1970s and 1980s, EU environmental policy was primarily shaped by direct EU regulations.[70] As a result, there was little tension between Article 101 TFEU and EU or national environmental policies This changed in the 1990s when the EU institutions started advocating the use of market-based mechanisms to govern environmental policy.[71] The Council and Member States introduced state subsidies and taxes, tradable permits, and emission schemes and encouraged voluntary environmental initiatives. Those mechanisms were decentralised to the Member State level, leaving the Member States a margin of appreciation for their implementation. The decentralised, market-based mechanisms subjected those new environmental agreements to the application of Article 101 TFEU.[72] Accordingly, the Commission and EU Courts began to balance competition against environmental interests.

In 1992, the Commission first acknowledged in a policy report that environmental protection might justify, in principle, an Article 101(3) TFEU exemption.[73] A year later, it clarified the terms of Article 101(3) TFEU, stating that they were 'sufficiently broad' to allow the inclusion of environmental protection objectives.[74]

However, only as late as 1998 had the Commission first invoked environmental benefits as the main justification for an exemption. In *EACEM (1998)*, the Commission cleared – by means of a comfort letter – a voluntary agreement between the European Association of Consumer Electronics Manufacturers and its members aimed at the reduction of the power consumption of electronic equipment.[75] A year later, in *CECED (1999)*, it exempted a similar agreement between an association of

[68] For a detailed analysis of the development of EU environmental policy, see Kingston (2011, 41–96) and Nowag (2016, 15–21). For an analysis of Article 101(3) TFEU and environmental considerations, see Kingston (2011, 261–293), Nowag (2016, 35–48), Holmes (2020), and van der Zee (2020).

[69] Notably, the Commission exempted agreements promoting 'greener' products and production methods even prior to the 1990s. For instance, agreements creating joint ventures (29428 GEC-Weir Sodium Circulators (1977); 29955 Carbon Gas Technologie (1983); 32368 BBC Brown Bover (1988)) and selective distribution systems (14650 Bayerische Motoren Werke (1974)). However, as described in Section 3.3.3.5, those environmental considerations were expressed as additional justifications for the exemptions.

[70] See Kingston (2011, 42–49).

[71] Article 103r SEA and Articles 2 and 3 EC. The Fifth Environmental Action Programme (1993). See also Kingston (2011, 41–96).

[72] Policy report 1992, 52; policy report 1993, 93.

[73] *Ibid*, 53.

[74] Policy report 1993, 51–52. See also policy report 1998, 56; policy report 2000, 39–43.

[75] 36494 EACEM (1998). The decision is unpublished but is detailed in the Commission's policy report 1998, 56. In previous cases, the environmental considerations were a part of an array of other types of benefits (see 34252 Philips-Osram (1994); 33814 Ford/Volkswagen (1992); 33640 Exxon/Shell (1994)).

manufacturers of domestic appliances and national trade associations and their members. The undertakings agreed not to manufacture or import washing machines that did not meet certain energy efficiency criteria.[76] In *DSD (2001)* and *Austrian system for the disposal of packaging waste (2003)*, the Commission enunciated a similar positive approach to anti-competitive agreements concluded as part of an EU or national environmental initiative.[77]

The exemptions granted in those cases are exceptional to the effect that they entail a particularly broad reading of the four conditions of Article 101(3) TFEU. First, they required a broad interpretation of Article 101(3) TFEU to be able to include non-economic benefits for society as a whole. In addition to the individual economic benefits stemming from the agreements (i.e. cost savings due to lower energy bills), the Commission took into account the collective environmental benefits resulting from a reduction in energy consumption. It stated that the agreement had significantly contributed to the management of energy resources, reduced CO_2 emissions, and, accordingly, to the efforts to counter global warming.[78] The Commission not only took short-term benefits into account but also benefits to 'present and future generations'.[79]

Second, the environmental exemptions required the Commission to balance the harm to competition inflicted on individual consumers with the environmental benefits generated for society as a whole. The Commission explained that environmental benefits 'would adequately allow consumers a fair share of the benefits even if no benefits accrued to individual purchasers'.[80] In other words, the Commission relied on the general *assumption* that consumers would receive a fair share of the environmental benefits without proving or calculating how the agreements actually benefited individual consumers.[81]

Third, in the balance between environmental benefits and the harm to competition, the Commission gave preference to the former. To that end, the Commission exempted the environmental agreements while acknowledging that, in the short term, they were likely to lead to price increases.[82]

Finally, the above cases demonstrate that the Commission had taken into account non-economic benefits even after it planted the first seeds of the more economic

[76] 36718 CECED (1999). Later, in 37893 37894 CECED (2000), the Commission extended the exemption granted to washing machines to other domestic electric appliances.

[77] 34493 37366 37299 37288 37287 37526 37254 37252 37250 37246 37245 37244 37243 37242 37267 DSD (2001). The exemption was granted following voluntary amendments and binding conditions intended to ensure that competition in the relevant markets was not restricted. 35470 35473 Austrian system for the disposal of packaging waste (2003).

[78] 36718 CECED (1999), para 55–56; With respect to EACEM (1998), see policy report 1998, 56.

[79] Policy report 2000, 43. As elaborated in Section 3.3.4, following modernisation, the Commission changed its approach and was strongly opposed to the consideration of such cross-generational benefits.

[80] 36718 CECED (1999), para 56. In para 64, the Commission seems to have ruled out subjective benefits to consumers due to the use of 'greener' washing machines, stating that 'other factors like price, brand image, and technical performance may have more weight in purchase decisions than energy efficiency'.

[81] See Section 3.3.3.3.

[82] 36718 CECED (1999), para 34.

approach in the late 1990s.[83] Taking into account non-economic environmental benefits to society as a whole, therefore, was not considered as standing in conflict with the more economic approach articulated in the Commission's Modernisation White Paper (1999) or the Vertical and Horizontal Guidelines (1999, 2000). Those policy papers were not construed as limiting the relevant types of benefits under the Article, but rather as calling for an effects-based approach and for the use of economic tools when assessing such benefits.

The example of the environmental agreements demonstrates the important role played by non-economic benefits in the enforcement of Article 101(3) TFEU. Up to modernisation, the Commission had not limited the types of relevant benefits under the Article and interpreted the conditions of the Article broadly to reserve a role for benefits for society as a whole.

3.3.3.5 Non-Economic Benefits as an Additional Justification

In addition to the exemptions that were detailed in Figure 3.1 and discussed above, the Commission used non-economic benefits as an additional justification to specify or add weight to Article 101(3) TFEU exemptions that were predominately justified by economic benefits.[84] This section maintains that the use of non-economic benefits as additional justifications has created doubts on their overall role and weight in justifying an exemption.

To this end, Figure 3.5 summarises the use of non-competition interests as additional justification. It details the number of proceedings and categories of benefits that were used as additional justification for an exemption that was primarily based on economic benefits.

The figure shows that the practice of using non-economic benefits as additional justification was particularly prominent during the third enforcement period. The empirical findings further indicate that environmental, employment, and industrial policy considerations were the main types of non-competition interests invoked as additional justifications.[85]

The wording of those decisions makes it hard to understand what weight, if any, was given to the non-economic benefits. In *Synthetic fibres (1984)*, for example, the Commission explained that the coordinated closure of plants 'will also make it easier to cushion the social effects of the restructuring by making suitable arrangements for the retraining and redeployment of workers made redundant'.[86]

Similarly, in *Ford/Volkswagen (1992)*, the Commission exempted a joint venture for the development and manufacture of vehicles. The exemption was primarily

[83] The First seeds of the Commission's more economic approach during the late 1990s were presented in Section 2.5.3.3.

[84] Monti (2007, 115) and Van Rompuy (2012, 263, 279). I have previously identified the role of non-economic benefits as an additional justification in Brook (2019, 134–135).

[85] See Annex A, Section 3.6.

[86] 30810 Synthetic fibres (1984), para 37.

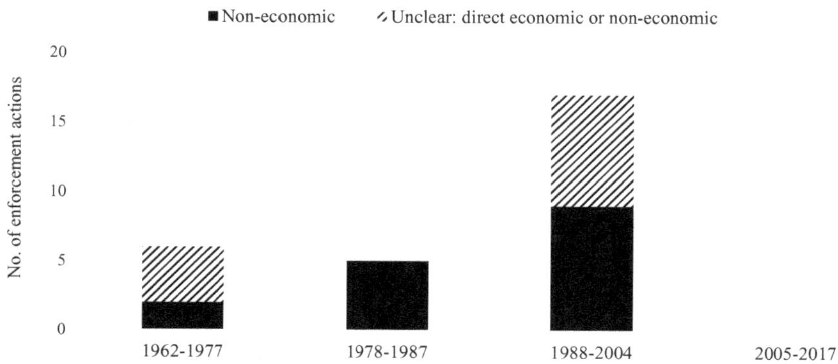

FIGURE 3.5. Non-economic benefits as an additional justification, Commission
All of the Commission's Article 101 TFEU enforcement actions, excluding unpublished comfort letters. In some cases, more than one non-economic benefit was mentioned as an additional justification

based on direct economic benefits.[87] Yet, the Commission also referred to investment, employment, and harmonised development of the EU as interests that were not sufficient for the justification of an exemption but should nevertheless be taken into account.[88] The Commission ambiguously stated that 'this would *not be enough* to make an exemption possible unless the conditions of [Article 101(3) TFEU] were fulfilled, *but it is an element* which the Commission has taken into account'.[89] On appeal, the GC, too, avoided taking a clear stand. It explained that the non-economic benefits 'were taken into account only supererogatorily'.[90]

Scholars disagree as to the role such non-economic benefits have played in the Commission's decisions.[91] *Gyselen*, the former head of DG COMP, has argued that the references to non-economic benefits as additional justification were used as *obiter dicta*, suggesting that they had no independent value.[92] However, *Monti* maintains that the non-economic benefits were decisive in such cases, tipping the balance in favour of granting an exemption.[93] He suggested that the Commission had deliberately chosen to refer to non-economic benefits, knowing that it provided guidance. Thus, Monti has noted 'if ex post we are told that the Commission does not mean what it writes, this casts *grave doubt about the entirety of the decisions*'.[94]

[87] I.e. rationalisation of the product development and manufacturing. See 33814 Ford/Volkswagen (1992), para 25.
[88] *Ibid*, para 36.
[89] Emphasis added. *Ibid*, para 36.
[90] T-17/93 Ford/Volkswagen (1994), para 139, 163.
[91] In general, see Townley (2009, 73–75) and Van Rompuy (2012, 263).
[92] Gyselen (2002, 185).
[93] Monti (2007, 115).
[94] Emphasis added. Monti (2007, 117). See also Van Rompuy (2012, 263).

The reference to non-economic benefits as additional justification has generated further doubts on the role of such benefits under Article 101(3) TFEU.[95] It is unclear if non-economic benefits were invoked in those cases as *obiter dicta*, for the purpose of providing political support to legitimise an exemption, as a 'tie-breaker' in cases where the harm to competition was equal to the economic benefits offered by an agreement, or as interests having an equal footing to the main economic benefits that have vindicated an exemption. In fact, the next section shows that much of the uncertainty surrounding the role of non-economic benefits following modernisation is tied to those decisions in which non-economic benefits were accepted as an additional justification.

3.3.4 *Fourth Enforcement Period: Limiting the Types of Benefits and Beneficiaries*

3.3.4.1 The Commission's Policy Papers

The modernisation of EU competition law at the beginning of the fourth enforcement period has turned the tables on the role of non-economic benefits under Article 101(3) TFEU. While the changes to the balancing method will be discussed in Section 3.4.4, this section will first focus on the types of relevant benefits and beneficiaries under the Article.

As part of its more economic approach, the Commission's policy papers following modernisation have considerably limited the relevant types of benefits under Article 101(3) TFEU to include only 'objective economic efficiencies'.[96] In particular, as discussed in Chapter 2, the Commission Article 101(3) Guidelines (2004) asserted that non-economic benefits should only be taken into account if they are 'goals pursued by other Treaty provisions' and only to the extent that they can be 'subsumed' under the four conditions of Article 101(3) TFEU.[97]

Along the same lines, the Commission Guidelines have also called to limit the relevant types of beneficiaries. As mentioned in Section 3.3.3.3, prior to modernisation, the Commission has merged the first two conditions of the Article. Under the old workable competition standard, this entailed that the Commission had

[95] The possibility of using non-economic benefits as additional justification was also considered in the context of US antitrust law. Pitofsky (1979, 1067), which had later served as the Chairman of the Federal Trade Commission, suggested that political concerns can legitimately serve as a 'tie-breaker' in individual cases. Such non-economic benefits may tilt, for example, the decision whether or not to accept an agreement that produces both anti- and pro-competitive effects. Nevertheless, Pitofsky warned that this *ad hoc* approach to non-economic benefit may be unfair to undertakings, because the results of such balancing are unpredictable. Using non-economic benefits as tie-breakers in certain circumstances was later also discussed by Schwartz (1979, 1080), Kauper (1987, 900), Steuer (2017, 198), and Foer and Durst (2018, 507).

[96] Commission Article 101(3) Guidelines (2004), para 59.

[97] *Ibid*, para 42. See Section 2.5.4.3.

interpreted the second condition broadly, taking into account individual benefits to consumers as well as collective benefits to society as a whole. Following modernisation, the Commission has continued to merge the first two conditions of the Article. Yet, under the consumer welfare standard, merging the two conditions meant that only economic efficiencies occurring to direct and indirect consumers of the product or service ('customers of the parties to the agreement and subsequent purchasers'[98]) should be taken into account.[99]

While the Commission Guidelines have indirectly declared that benefits that were used to justify exemptions during the second and third enforcement periods could no longer be taken into account, they refrained from admitting to a change in the Commission's approach. Instead, the Commission Guidelines argue that this new approach was 'implicitly' indicated in certain paragraphs of *Metro I (1977)* and *Ford/Volkswagen (1994)*.[100] Those two judgements, remarkably, do not seem to support a limiting reading of the types of benefits and beneficiaries relevant under Article 101(3) TFEU.

First, the paragraphs referred to in those two judgements merely confirm that non-economic benefits are relevant for applying the first condition of Article 101 (3) TFEU.[101] As extensively discussed in Sections 3.3.3.1 and 3.3.3.5, in *Metro I*, the CJEU introduced the workable competition standard for Article 101(3) TFEU, thereby confirming an exemption granted to a selective distribution system that stabilised employment. In *Ford/Volkswagen*, the GC affirmed the exemption granted to a joint venture for the development and manufacture of vehicles. The GC explained that while the exemption was predominately based on direct economic benefits, the Commission had also taken into account 'supererogatorily' non-economic benefits of creating jobs and reducing regional disparities.

The two judgements neither limit the types of benefits that can be taken into account nor demand that non-competition interest must be 'subsumed' under Article 101(3) TFEU. Rather, the CJEU and GC have assumed that non-economic benefits are relevant subject to fulfilment of the other three conditions of the Article.

Second, the Commission's new approach does not correspond with the essence of the two judgements.[102] As shown in the previous sections, the EU Courts have not limited the benefits under Article 101(3) TFEU to interests pursued by other provisions of the Treaties. At the time *Metro I* was rendered, employment

[98] *Ibid*, para 84.
[99] See also Townley (2011, 490–491) and Nowag (2016, 234–235).
[100] Commission Article 101(3) Guidelines (2004), footnote 54.
[101] C-26/76 Metro I (1977), para 43; T-17/93 Ford/Volkswagen (1994), para 139.
[102] See also Petit (2009, 6–7) and Van Rompuy (2012, 256–257).

considerations were not yet included in any policy-linking clause. Similarly, in *Ford/Volkswagen*, the GC did not refer to the policy-linking clause as a legal basis for an exemption.[103]

Finally, the Commission Article 101(3) Guidelines have essentially added two new conditions for the consideration of non-economic benefits. They require that the benefits are (i) pursued by other Treaty provisions and are (ii) 'subsumed' under the four conditions of the Article. Adding those new conditions is incompatible with the notion that the four conditions of Article 101(3) TFEU are cumulative and exhaustive. According to the CJEU and the Commission Article 101(3) Guidelines themselves, the granting of an exception cannot be made dependent on any other condition once the four conditions have been met.[104]

Notably, the early draft of Article 101(3) Guidelines was more explicit about a change in the Commission's approach. After declaring that the goals pursued by other Treaty provisions could only be taken into account if they are subsumed by the conditions of Article 101(3) TFEU, the draft Guidelines added that it is not 'the role of Article [101 TFEU] and the authorities enforcing this Treaty provision to allow undertakings to restrict competition in pursuit of general interest aims'.[105] This statement was deleted from the final version of the Guidelines, perhaps aiming to limit the conflict with the earlier case law of the CJEU.

The Commission's new interpretation of Article 101(3) TFEU, as mentioned in Section 2.5.4, has quickly encountered opposition. Commentators have pointed out that such interpretation cannot be squared with the Commission's and the CJEU's previous case law, which reserved a significant room for non-competition interests under that provision by considering broad types of benefits and beneficiaries. The Commission's approach is also not fully consistent with the provisions of some BERs, which exempt categories of agreements on the basis of non-economic benefit, while noting that it is presumed that the four conditions of Article 101(3) TFEU are fulfilled.[106] Clearly, from a constitutional perspective, the Commission does not have the legal competence to ignore the EU Courts' interpretation of the Article. It cannot invoke soft law mechanisms to set aside binding principles established by the EU Courts' case law.

[103] See Section 3.3.3.2. Remarkably, the Commission referred to paragraph 96 of the Court's decision in T-17/93 Ford/Volkswagen (1994), which summarised the Commission's position. The Court did not confirm this statement in its findings.

[104] Commission Article 101(3) Guidelines (2004), para 42 and the case law referred to there. See also Van Rompuy (2012, 255–256).

[105] Draft Article 101(3) Guidelines (2003), para 38.

[106] See Chapter 4.

3.3.4.2 The Commission's Practice

It is difficult to evaluate the degree to which the Commission has implemented in practice the new approach that was advocated in its policy papers. As Figures 3.1 and 3.2 demonstrate, the Commission had not accepted an Article 101(3) TFEU defence following the entry into force of Regulation 1/2003, on the basis of neither economic nor non-economic benefits. This was dubbed as the 'death of Article 101(3)'.[107] The fact that an Article 101(3) TFEU defence was not accepted following the entry into force of Regulation 1/2003 could initially be seen as an implementation of the Commission's approach in its policy papers attempting to narrow down the room for non-competition interests under the Article.

A closer look at the empirical findings presented in Figure 3.2(a), however, shows that the Commission decisions have rarely even considered what types of benefits could justify an Article 101(3) TFEU exception. The limited number of cases in which a possible exception was discussed did not involve non-economic benefits. Rather, they focused on economic benefits, which were typically rejected outright, maintaining that no relevant benefit had been identified or sufficiently substantiated.[108] Those cases will be further elaborated in Section 3.4.4.

Remarkably, the empirical findings show that the Commission's decisions have *never* declared that an Article 101(3) TFEU defence cannot be accepted because it had relied on non-economic benefits. Consequently, while the Commission's policy papers have advocated a change, its decisional practice had not clarified whether the Commission believes that non-economic benefits could still justify an exception in certain circumstances. The Commission did not explain what the (new?) conditions for an Article 101(3) TFEU exception are and if and how such conditions conform to the Commission's and EU Courts' previous case law on balancing.[109]

Chapter 7 argues that the steep decrease in the invocation and acceptance rate of Article 101(3) TFEU defence following modernisation does *not* entail that non-competition interests do no longer play a role in the enforcement. Rather, it suggests that this decline is the result of the procedural pillar of modernisation that has enhanced the Commission's enforcement discretion. Following modernisation, the

[107] De Pablo (2011) and Bailey (2016).

[108] See Annex A, Section 3.7. The Commission has also applied the second fair share condition rigidly. In 39595 Continental/United/Lufthansa/Air Canada (2013), para 62–79, for example, it examined the Star Alliance agreement introducing a revenue-sharing joint venture on transatlantic routes. The Commission provisionally accepted that the agreement fulfilled the first, third, and fourth conditions of the Article. However, the efficiencies were insufficient compensation for the negative effects the agreement had on premium passengers traveling the Frankfurt-New York route. While the agreement could not be exempted under Article 101(3) TFEU, the Commission did accept commitments.

[109] Section 3.5.3.1 suggests that the Courts have not fully endorsed the Commission's attempt to limit the types of relevant benefits under Article 101(3) TFEU.

Commission will use its priority setting powers to 'simply not bring a case or close a case that had already been opened' when it believes that an agreement can be saved by Article 101(3) TFEU.[110]

The continued relevance of non-economic benefits under the Article can also be inferred from the BERs. As elaborated in Chapter 4, each BER is based on the presumption that the protected categories of agreements satisfy all four conditions of Article 101(3) TFEU. Since some BERs continue to protect agreements that promote non-economic benefits also following modernisation, such benefits are also deemed to be relevant for individual exceptions.

To conclude, the Commission's policy papers, combined with the lack of decisions clarifying the application of Article 101(3) TFEU in the decentralised era, create great uncertainties as to the relevant types of benefits under the Article. Indeed, as Section 3.6 discloses, not all of the national competition enforcers have converged to the Commission's new approach.

3.3.5 *Interim Conclusion*

This section has demonstrated that, prior to modernisation, no limitation was placed on the types of non-competition interests or benefits that could be examined under Article 101(3) TFEU or on the types of beneficiaries. Influenced by the workable competition standard of the CJEU, the Commission took a broad range of benefits into account. In addition to direct and indirect economic benefits to individual consumers, it included non-economic benefits to society as a whole and to future generations. During that period, therefore, Article 101(3) TFEU has not only been seen as a tool to balance the harm and benefits to specific undertakings and their customers but had also taken regulatory and social objectives into account such as environmental, employment, and development policies. Moreover, the Commission and CJEU did not attach importance to the legal source of the non-competition interests. The first benefit condition of Article 101(3) TFEU was applied without distinction to benefits that are protected by the policy-linking clauses and to those lacking an EU law basis.

As part of the substantive modernisation, the Commission has advocated a change to its previous practice. Its Article 101(3) Guidelines and policy papers have essentially restricted the types of relevant benefits under Article 101(3) TFEU to include only direct economic benefits that influence short-term narrow consumer welfare. Subsequently, many non-competition interests that had previously been taken into account under Article 101 TFEU were no longer applicable in the Commission's view, at least to the extent they could not be expressed in efficiency or monetary terms.

[110] The Commission's answers to the questionnaire in OECD Role of Efficiency Claims in Antitrust Proceedings (2012), 90.

At the same time, it is unclear if, and how, the Commission actually implemented this new approach. Following modernisation, Article 101(3) TFEU was rarely discussed in proceeding taking place in front of the Commission and did not involve non-economic benefits. Even in the limited number of cases in which a possible exception was discussed, the Commission has mostly rejected outright the fulfilment of the first benefit condition, holding that no relevant benefit has been identified or sufficiently substantiated. This created many uncertainties as to the relevant types of benefits under the Article.

3.4 THE BALANCING METHOD

3.4.1 *Overview*

The previous section discussed the changes in the types of benefits that could be assessed under Article 101(3) TFEU over the span of the four enforcement periods. This section reveals a corresponding transformation in the method that guided balancing. More specifically, it demonstrates how the process of balancing, the intensity of control, and the relative weight given to the four conditions of the Article have developed over the years.

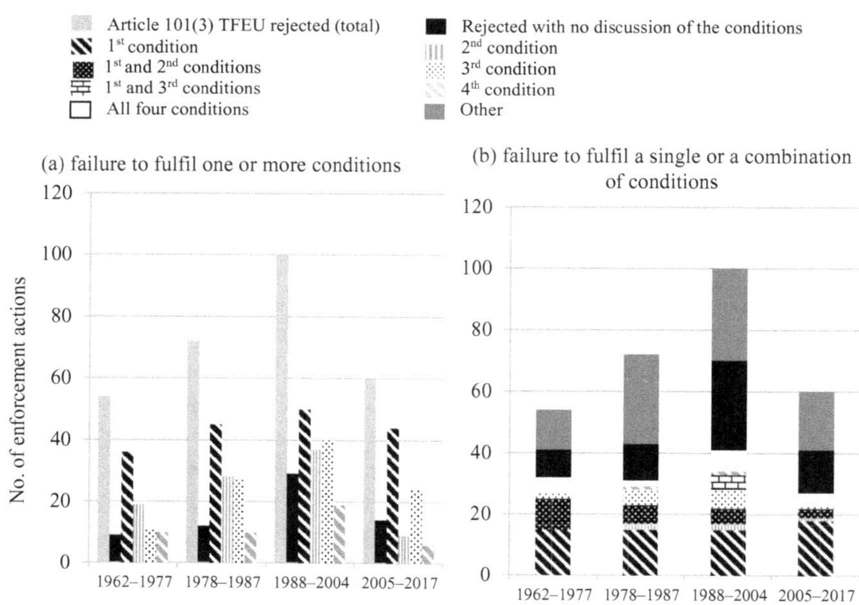

FIGURE 3.6. Denying the application of Article 101(3) TFEU, Commission
All Article 101 TFEU enforcement actions in which Article 101(3) TFEU was argued and rejected, excluding unpublished comfort letters. In some proceedings, Article 101(3) TFEU was argued more than one time

Before discussing those changes in detail, Figure 3.6 provides an overview of the reasons leading the Commission to *reject* applications for Article 101(3) TFEU exemptions. Figure 3.6(a) indicates the number of enforcement actions in which each of the four conditions of the Article was explicitly rejected or in which Article 101(3) TFEU was rejected without discussion of the conditions (black bars). Figure 3.6(b) takes a different perspective to the same question by outlining the number of enforcement actions in which an exemption was refused due to a failure to meet a single condition or a combination of conditions.

The figure illustrates that failing to fulfil the first condition was the reason for rejecting most applications for exemption, excluding the cases in which the Article was rejected without discussion of the conditions. It also reveals that the third condition requiring that the restriction be indispensable has gained growing importance since the second and third enforcement periods. Finally, the figure confirms that the fourth condition for the elimination of competition was rarely the sole reason for denying an exemption. The above trends, as the next sections show, point to fundamental changes in the balancing method.

Before moving to present the changing balancing methods, however, it must be noted that it is possible that the Commission only disclosed parts of its reasons for rejecting an Article 101(3) TFEU claim. Given the time and resources involved, the Commission might have decided to focus its reasoning on the failure to meet some of the four conditions of the Article while considering that also other conditions were not fulfilled. Although it is important to keep this in mind when interpreting Figure 3.6, it does not render the figure insignificant. The following sections show that the conditions that were put forward by the Commission as a reason to refuse an exemption were the very same conditions that were highlighted in decisions granting an exemption. This suggests that the Commission did not attribute equal weights to the four conditions of the Article; some conditions have played a more decisive role than others in guiding balancing, and their relative weights have changed over time to correspond to changes in the overall balancing framework.

3.4.2 *First Enforcement Period: Market Integration and the First Benefit Condition*

During the first enforcement period (i.e. up until 1977), Article 101(3) TFEU, like EU competition policy in general, chiefly served as a mechanism for completing the internal market and developing the EU industrial policy.[111] Along those lines, the empirical findings indicate that the application of Article 101(3) TFEU during that period did not involve a genuine balancing of competition and non-competition

[111] See Section 2.5.1.

interests but rather centred around assessing the agreement's impact on market integration. Accordingly, the Commission had refused to exempt agreements having a negative impact on the internal market, even when they promoted competition interests or had direct economic benefits.[112]

This policy can be traced back to the famous case of *Grundig/Consten (1964, 1966)*.[113] In its first decision refusing to grant an Article 101(3) TFEU exemption, the Commission had examined an exclusive distribution agreement between a German producer of radios and televisions and a French firm appointed as an exclusive distributor in France. As part of the agreement, the producer permitted the distributor to register the products' trademark in France. Emphasising the importance of the single market, the Commission explained that trademarks must not be used to reinforce export prohibitions that result in the isolation of national markets.[114]

The CJEU confirmed this approach. It rejected the undertakings' argument that an increase in trade and inter-brand competition could offset the intra-brand restriction resulting from the exclusive distribution agreement. When assessing the relationship between competition and market integration in Article 101(3) TFEU, the latter prevailed. The Court prioritised the potential risk to the internal market over the effects on competition.[115]

On the opposite side of the coin, during the first enforcement period, the Commission was open to exempting agreements that did not hinder market integration.[116] The empirical findings show that the analysis of those proceedings focused on the first benefit condition. The other three conditions of Article 101(3) TFEU were marginal to the analysis and interpreted loosely.[117] For instance, when applying the second condition, i.e. the fair share, the Commission exempted agreements that

[112] See Annex A, Section 3.8.

[113] 4 and 3344 Grundig/Consten (1964), 5–6; C-56/64 C-58/64 Grundig/Consten (1966).

[114] A similar approach was adopted in cases involving balancing of IPRs, such as 28812 Theal/Watts (1976), para II(B); 28374 Advocaat Zwarte Kip (1974); 28967 Bronbemaling (1975), para III; 26949 AOIP/Beyrard (1975); policy report 1975, 52. See also Evans (1981, 426), Gerber (1998, 352), and Wesseling (2000, 24). On the Commission's and Courts' approach to IPRs, see also Section 5.3.5.

[115] C-56/64 C-58/64 Grundig/Consten (1966), 347–350.

[116] The fact that the agreements contained no territorial restrictions was a decisive factor in granting the exemptions. See Annex A, Section 3.9. See also policy report 1971, 54–65; policy report 1975, 24, 54; policy report 1977, 107.

[117] See Figure 3.6; policy report 1971, 42; policy report 1976, 43. While most of the decisions focused on the first benefit condition, the decisions on specialised exhibitions (see Section 3.3.2) centred on the third indispensability condition. The Commission assumed that the limitation on participation in competing exhibitions was beneficial and merely required that the restriction be limited in time.

benefited society as a whole even when they did not directly advance the interests of the consumers of the product.[118] Similarly, the Commission exempted cooperation agreements while explicitly declaring that the restriction of competition might not have been indispensable.[119]

The degree of harm to competition played almost no role in assessing an exemption. The exemptions issued during the first enforcement period had rarely contained information on the undertakings' market share and economic power or even identified the relevant markets. They did not differentiate between theories of harm from horizontal and vertical restraints. Instead of indicating if, and how, an agreement has restricted competition, the decisions have centred on the form of the agreement and its effects on market integration.[120] Hence, an agreement's effect on market integration was the decisive criterion guiding Article 101(3) TFEU analysis during the early years of EU competition law.

3.4.3 *Second and Third Enforcement Periods: Sectoral Approach and the Third Indispensability Condition*

3.4.3.1 The Workable Competition Standard as a Balancing Method

The workable competition standard, introduced by the CJEU in *Walt Wilhelm (1969) and Metro I (1977)*,[121] changed the Article 101(3) TFEU balancing method in three interrelated manners.

First, it broadened the *types of benefits and beneficiaries* that could be examined under the Article. As described above, during the second and third enforcement periods (i.e. 1978–April 2004), the Commission interpreted the first condition of Article 101(3) TFEU to include all types of non-competition interests and benefits.[122]

Widening the scope of the first two conditions had required the Commission to find other ways to balance competition and non-competition interests. The

[118] In 26940 KEWA (1975), para III(2) and 26940 United Reprocesses GmbH (1975), pata III(2) the Commission exempted reprocessing agreements in the nuclear fuel sector aimed at recovering fissile materials that can be reused in nuclear fuel fabrication. It emphasised the particular characteristics of the reprocessing industry: It was a new industry at a critical stage of the nuclear fuel cycle regarded as economically vital by governments and related to the development and ecological problems arising from the storage of radioactive waste. When applying the second fair share condition, the Commission pointed only to future and uncertain benefits to direct consumers, stating that the agreement 'opens the way to an eventual drop in prices charged to users'. See also policy report 1975, 42–43.

[119] In 26625 Clima Chappée-Buderus (1969), 3 and 27073 Bayer/Gist-Brocades (1975), 7 the Commission exempted cooperation agreements while declaring that the undertakings were part of a business group having sufficient financial resources and technical capabilities to develop their products independently.

[120] See also Witt (2016b, 1114–1117).

[121] On the workable competition standard, see Sections 2.5.2.1 and 3.3.3.1.

[122] See Section 3.3.3.

empirical findings indicate that this was done by adding more weight to the last two conditions of Article 101(3) TFEU and to the indispensability condition in particular. The Commission interpreted the indispensability condition as entailing a legal balancing process, by which it loosely assessed whether the harm to competition was reasonable and proportionate in light of the potential benefits.[123]

Second, the workable competition standard was used to apply Article 101(3) TFEU to new areas of the economy. Whilst during the first enforcement period Article 101 TFEU had only been enforced with regard to agreements in the private sector, from the early 1980s onward the Commission applied the Article to agreements in the public realm, in regulated and liberalised sectors in particular. In this context, the workable competition standard was used to introduce a *sectoral approach* as the new method for balancing. Rather than using a one-size-fits-all balancing tool, the Commission administered a case-by-case approach. It tailored the scope and intensity of the four conditions of Article 101(3) TFEU according to the 'degree of competition necessary' in each sector.[124]

Third, the Commission invoked the workable competition standard for the application of Article 101(3) TFEU as a *market-building tool*. During the second and third enforcement periods, the reasoning for granting exemptions gradually shifted from the *establishment* of the common market to the need to *regulate* economic policy and the competitive process.[125] The Commission proclaimed that Article 101(3) TFEU was 'more than just a means of lifting the ban on restrictive practices'. Rather, it could also foster industrial policy and the rationalisation process.[126] Accordingly, Article 101(3) TFEU was employed to regulate economic policy, shelter national industries from foreign competition, ensure an adequate level of services of general economic interest, protect SMEs, and promote social goals.[127]

The function of Article 101(3) TFEU as a market-building tool was also reflected by the Commission's practice of attaching conditions or obligations to exemptions. As demonstrated by Figure 3.1, about half the exemptions granted during the second and third enforcement periods were subject to general or specific conditions. This

[123] On the legal balancing process, see Section 1.2.2.1.

[124] In its 1981 policy report, 11, the Commission held that 'the Community is essentially based on a market economy [. . ..] However, this policy *is not based on a laissez-faire model*, but is designed to maintain and protect the principle of *workable competition* [. . .] decisive importance is attached to the interaction between competition policy and the policies which contribute to the attainment of a single market, where conditions are similar to those on national markets. The interaction between competition policy and the common commercial policy is equally important'. Emphasis added. On the sectoral approach, see also Section 2.5.3.1.

[125] See also Wesseling (2000, 37) and Van Rompuy (2012, 154).

[126] Policy report 1983, 12.

[127] Policy report 1978, 9, 12, 49; policy report 1979, 9–10; policy report 1980, 10; policy report 1981, 33; policy report 1982, 13–14; policy report 1983, 12, 31, 53; policy report 1984, 11–12, 16, 20, 33; policy report 1985, 11; policy report 1986, 14; policy report 1987, 13.

provided the Commission with an opportunity to shape the market structure and business practices.

This function of the Commission's exemption decisions was endorsed by the CJEU. In *VBBB/VBVB (1984)*, for example, the Court explained that obligation to notify agreements to the Commission was not only intended to prepare the way for infringement decision or an exemption, but 'the procedure also presents an opportunity for the undertakings concerned to adapt the practices at issue to the rules of the Treaty'.[128]

The empirical findings show that most of the specific conditions attached related to the third indispensability condition. Because there was no or little limit on the type of relevant benefits under the first condition, the focus of the analysis centred on ensuring that the restriction of competition is proportionate to achieving those benefits. From the third enforcement period, conditions were also attached to safeguard the fulfilment of the fourth elimination of competition condition. This might reflect a more effects-based approach, which considers the actual effects of the agreement on competition.[129]

The empirical findings presented in the next sub-sections illustrate that the combination of the above effects has prompted an incoherent approach to Article 101(3) TFEU. The four conditions of the Article were applied strictly to agreements impairing market integration, and more flexibly to agreements in liberalised or regulated sectors, agreements in sectors affected by an economic crisis, and agreements promoting EU industrial policy.[130]

3.4.3.2 Market Integration

The analysis of Article 101(3) TFEU continued to focus on market integration during the second and third enforcement periods. The Commission persisted in refusing to exempt most naked horizontal restrictions of competition, vertical agreements that involved elements of exclusivity, export or import bans, and arrangements having similar effects.[131] Such decisions have often justified the refusal with reference to the negative impact of the agreements on market integration rather than on competition.[132]

[128] C-43/82 C-63/82 VBBB/VBVB (1984), para 52.

[129] On the first seeds of the more economic approach, see Section 2.5.3.3.

[130] The Commission's sectoral approach was also evident in certain 'special' markets, such as selective distribution systems of luxury cosmetics and beer distribution agreements. See Annex A, Section 3.10. See also policy report 1991, 98–99; policy report 1992, 114–115; policy report 2000, 39; and Sauter (2016, 41–42).

[131] See Annex A, Section 3.11. See also policy report 1982, 66; policy report 1992, 112; policy report 1998, 36–37. By comparison, the Commission exempted similar agreements that did not hinder market integration. For example, franchising agreements in 32358 ServiceMaster (1988) and 31697 Charles Jourdan (1988).

[132] 29595 Pioneer Hi-Fi Equipment (1979), para 87; 1576 Zanussi (1978), para 12; 30188 Moet et Chandon (London) Ltd (1981), para 15; 30070 National Panasonic (1982), para 59; 30064 Cast iron and steel rolls (1983), para 61; 30696 Distribution system of Ford Werke AG (1983), para 43; 28930 Milchförderungsfonds (1984), para 44; 30809 John Deere (1984), para 34; 30658 Polistil/

In particular, the Commission had often used the indispensability condition to preserve the prominence of market integration by holding that restrictions placed on parallel trade cannot be deemed indispensable.[133] In *Pioneer Hi-Fi Equipment (1979)*, for example, it noted that even if the agreements could have generated certain benefits, restrictions on cross-border trade cannot be regarded as indispensable because they conflict with the basic principles of the common market.[134]

By comparison, the Commission had applied the indispensability condition in a flexible manner to agreements that did not have a negative effect on market integration. In *Carbon Gas Technologie (1983)*, it authorised a joint venture for research and development in the field of coal gasification, by which the undertakings agreed to refrain from competition with the joint subsidiary and with each other. The Commission noted that given the industrial importance of the parties and the developed technology, the agreement carried an appreciable restriction of competition. It also expressly acknowledged that the undertakings were likely to achieve the benefits independently without cooperation.[135] Despite the significant restriction of competition and the possibility to develop the technology independently, in the absence of a negative effect on market integration the Commission exempted the cooperation.

3.4.3.3 Liberalised and Regulated Markets

The Commission's incoherence balancing under Article 101(3) TFEU was also apparent when the Article was applied in liberalised and regulated markets. As the European integration process gathered pace following the Single European Act of 1986 and the Treaty on European Union of 1992, the Commission expanded the substantive scope of EU competition law. It began to apply Article 101 TFEU to newly liberalised markets (insurance, financial services, postal services, energy, telecom, and transport) and to regulated sectors (regulated professions, sports, media, and pharmaceutical products).[136]

In those markets, Article 101(3) TFEU often served as a means to ensure the promotion of the single market and a sufficiently high quality of services, rather than

Arbois (1984), para 58; Sperry New Holland (1985), para 5831143 Peugeot (1986), para 38–40; 35733 VW (1998), para 189; Mercedes-Benz (2001), para 216; 35706 36321 Video Games (2002), para 341.

[133] 29595 Pioneer Hi-Fi Equipment (1979), para 87; 30809 John Deere (1984), para 34; 1576 Zanussi (1978), para 12; 26912 Hennessy/Henkell (1980), para 32; 31192 31507 Tipp-Ex (1987), para 70; 32290 Newitt/Dunlop Slazenger International (1992), para 64; 32725 Viho/Parker Pen (1992), para 20; 32948 34590 Tretorn (1994), para 72.

[134] 29595 Pioneer Hi-Fi Equipment (1979), para 87. See also policy report 1979, 66.

[135] 29955 Carbon Gas Technologie (1983), 4.

[136] For liberalised markers see Annex A, Section 3.12, and for regulated markets Annex A, Section 3.13.

the balance of competition and non-competition interests.[137] Along those lines, the Commission issued designated policy papers adapting the enforcement of Article 101 TFEU to those sectors.[138] It tailored the conditions of Article 101(3) TFEU to the relevant sector to facilitate an *ad hoc*, case-specific balance between social and political non-competition interests.[139]

The Commission interpreted the conditions of the Article flexibly to accommodate agreements that furthered liberalisation of the respective markets. In *Scottish Nuclear Energy Agreement (1991)*, for example, it exempted an exclusive import and export rights agreement, which formed part of a Scottish electricity privatisation scheme. It did not examine in detail whether the claimed benefits were likely to be passed on to consumers. The Commission merely assumed that consumers would benefit from a liberalised market while acknowledging that the agreement would lead to higher prices in the short term.[140] In other words, the liberalisation of the industry was regarded, in itself, as the fair share for consumers.

The application of Article 101(3) TFEU to the insurance and financial markets provides a good example of how the workable competition standard facilitated this balancing. Given their economic and social values, in many Member States, those sectors were traditionally heavily regulated or run by states' monopolies. Consequently, they were not fully subject to competition law. The Commission first enforced Article 101 TFEU in those markets only in the mid-1980s.[141] Even then, it followed a flexible approach, adapting the conditions of Article 101(3) TFEU to limit competition in favour of other policy objectives.

In the financial sector, the empirical findings reveal that the Commission exempted all of the notified agreements during the second enforcement period, of which two cases were subject to certain voluntary modifications.[142] This was true even with respect to highly restrictive agreements with an effect similar to price

[137] See Annex A, Section 3.14.

[138] With respect to energy, see the internal energy market, Commission Working Document, Com (88) 238 1988; with respect to telecom see Guidelines on Competition Rules in the Telecommunications Sector (1991). With respect to transport see Section 4.3.1.2.

[139] See Annex A, Section 3.15.

[140] 33473 Scottish Nuclear Energy Agreement (1991), para 33–37. The undertakings had claimed that the agreement would contribute to the long-term planning required in the industry, the need to ensure the profitability of the nuclear power station to offset investment costs, and the reduction of overcapacity. Similarly, see 36748 REIMS II (1999), para 78–85. However, at the Commission's request, the undertakings reduced the term of the agreement – from the remaining 30-year lifespan of the nuclear power station down to 15 years.

[141] The Commission affirmed the applicability of Article 101 TFEU to horizontal agreements in the insurance sector as early as 1972 (policy report 1972, 60–61). Yet, only towards the end of the second enforcement period did it apply this policy in practice in 30307 Fire insurance (1984). In C-172/80 Züchner (1981), para 6–9, the CJEU first refuted the argument that financial services are, or should be, left outside the scope of EU competition law. Following Züchner, the Commission started to scrutinise payment systems. See also Lista (2013, 17, 130–135).

[142] The exemptions were justified due to the agreements' contribution to improving payment facilities (261 Belgische Vereniging der Banken/Association Beige des Banques (1986), para

fixing. In *Visa International's multilateral interchange fee (2002)*, for instance, the Commission exempted an agreement setting default multilateral interchange fees (MIF).[143] The Commission acknowledged that the agreement limited the banks' pricing policies, amounting to the *de facto* setting of a minimum fee. Yet, it exempted the agreement by emphasising its contribution to market integration (i.e. facilitating and encouraging cross-border purchases).[144]

Similarly, in the insurance sector, while the Commission had prohibited agreements resulting in price fixing or recommendations,[145] it had accepted significant restrictions of competition that would probably not have been accepted if they had been concluded in other markets. In *Nuovo Cegam (1984)*, for instance, it held that a standard tariff constitutes, in itself, a benefit in the meaning of the first condition of Article 101(3) TFEU. The Commission merely stated that the third indispensability condition applied, without explaining why such a tariff was necessary, or why a standards tariff could justify an exemption whereas the setting of an obligatory premium could not.[146]

Moreover, the Commission frequently applied Article 101 TFEU via a negotiation process in which it eventually accepted voluntary commitments.[147] In *P&I Clubs (1985)*, it exempted an agreement between protection and indemnity clubs for marine mutual insurance. The agreement significantly restricted competition by limiting the attractiveness of transferring between clubs by setting up a mechanism relating to the premiums quoted for ships that were already insured. After three years of negotiations, the undertakings agreed to modify the mechanism. While the premiums were opened up to negotiation, their level and the timing for transferring to a new club were still restricted. The Commission held that the modified system was 'a fair compromise between the different interests'. It used industrial policy considerations to justify its flexible application of the fourth condition by noting that there was a 'strong likelihood' that prohibiting the agreement would have 'harmful effects on the mutual insurance system' leading members of the clubs to 'decide to leave the clubs and set up new P&I clubs outside the Community'.[148]

47–49), rationalisation and standardisation of the services (31356 ABI (1986), para 53–60), and integration of the services across Member States (30717 Uniform Eurocheques (1984), para 37).

143 MIF is an interbank payment made for each transaction carried out with a payment card. It is paid to the cardholder's bank by the retailer's bank and is normally passed on by the retailer's bank to retailers.

144 29373 Visa International (2002), para 66–68, 89. In 2007, as described in Section 3.4.4.1, the Commission adopted a different approach to similar agreements. Moreover, in CA98/05/05 MasterCard (2005), as described in Section 3.6.2.1, the UK NCA held that this Commission's reliance on market integration deprived the use of the Commission's findings in the UK national proceeding.

145 30307 Fire insurance (1984), para 24, 42.

146 30804 Nuovo Cegam (1984), para 22–23.

147 *Ibid*, para 22; 30373 P&I Clubs (1985), para 56.

148 30373 P&I Clubs (1985), para 56.

The sectoral approach to Article 101(3) TFEU was also evident in the assessment of environmental agreements.[149] The empirical findings show that during the second and third enforcement periods the Commission refused to exempt agreements on the basis of environmental considerations on only a single occasion. In *Ansac (1990)*, involving an export cartel, it was not convinced that there was a causal link between a market sharing agreement and the alleged benefit.[150]

All of the other environmental agreements were exempted. The Commission applied the four conditions of Article 101(3) TFEU flexibly to favour environmental benefits over competition. It took into account broad non-economic benefits, including benefits for future generations, without requiring solid proof for substantiating the alleged benefits. When exempting the agreement in *CECED (1999)*, for instance, the Commission relied on the identification and quantification of the benefits presented by the undertakings.[151] Similarly, when applying the third indispensability condition, it held that less restrictive alternatives compared to a total ban on high-energy consumption washing machines (e.g. industry-wide target, information campaigns, and a greater focus on fulfilling EU eco-label criteria) would either jeopardise the attainment of the environmental benefits or be less effective. This statement seems debatable given the fact that only 10% of the washing machines sold in the EU fell within the banned category.[152]

3.4.3.4 Sectors Affected by Economic Crisis

The sectoral approach was also evident in the assessment of agreements in sectors affected by the economic crisis of the mid-1970s.[153] Per its declared policy, the Commission adopted a special method for applying Article 101(3) TFEU to those sectors. It differentiated between two types of restrictions of competition. On the one hand, it refused to exempt the so-called crisis cartels aimed at setting prices or quotas.[154] On the other hand, it did exempt industrial-restructuring agreements directed at an orderly reduction of excess capacity.[155] In fact, during the second

[149] On the Commission's approach to environmental agreements, see also Section 3.3.3.4.
[150] 33016 Ansac (1990), para 23.
[151] For example, the decision states '[a]ccording to CECED, [...] the energy consumption of washing machines was reduced by [...]' (para 14); 'According to CECED, the agreement is likely to reduce electricity output by [...]' (para 36); 'According to CECED, were models of phased-out machines to be replaced by an equivalent number of machines [...] TWh would be saved' (para 47); 'CECED estimates the pollution avoided [...]' (para 51).
[152] 36718 CECED (1999), para 58–63, 66.
[153] See Section 2.5.2.2.
[154] 29869 Italian cast glass (1980), para II(B)(3); 30350 Zinc producer group (1984), para 87.
[155] In its policy report (1981), 13, the Commission explained '[w]here there is an irreversible disparity between production capacity and demand, agreements between undertakings aimed at achieving an orderly reduction of excess capacity may be exempted from the ban on restrictive practices, in so far as undertakings do not jointly fix production and delivery volumes and selling prices of the relevant products nor aim at barring imports. Nor can the Commission

enforcement period, the Commission exempted all the restructuring agreements it had under review.[156]

This required a flexible application of the conditions of Article 101(3) TFEU. In *Synthetic fibres (1984)*, for instance, the ten largest EU synthetic fibre manufacturers had agreed to close down 18% of their production capacity for the manufacture of synthetic textiles. The Commission exempted the agreement, noting that free-market forces had failed to achieve the capacity reductions necessary to re-establish and maintain a long-term, effective, and competitive structure.[157]

This conclusion is questionable. In the first place, the restructuring agreement did not generate short-term economic benefits from which consumers could receive a fair share. On the contrary, it clearly aimed to increase the undertakings' profits by raising prices and limiting capacity.[158] Nevertheless, the Commission submitted that the agreement produces benefits as it will raise the profitability and restore the competitiveness of the undertakings in the longer term and will make it easier to cushion the social effects of the restructuring by making arrangements for the retaining redeployment of redundant workers.[159] Hence, while the agreement might possibly have benefited the overall economic and social conditions, it is difficult to explain how the *consumers of the product* received a fair share from such benefits.[160] In the second place, the Commission did not oblige the undertakings to prove that restructuring was the least restrictive way to achieve these benefits. The agreement was classified as indispensable merely because it did not coordinate the use of the remaining capacity.[161]

3.4.3.5 Industrial Policy

Much like in the first enforcement period, the Commission seemed favourable towards agreements promoting EU industrial policy. In particular, it exempted joint ventures and horizontal cooperation agreements that failed to fulfil the conditions of the Horizontal BERs, given the undertakings high market shares. Despite the

tolerate measures which use private or public protectionism to shield a national market from external competition'.

[156] 30810 Synthetic fibres (1984); 30863 BPCL/ICI (1984); 31055 ENI/Montedison (1986). See also policy report 1984, 69–73.

[157] 30810 Synthetic fibres (1984), para 31.

[158] *Ibid*, para 26, 28, 41. See also Hornsby (1987, 92).

[159] *Ibid*, para 37, 39–41. See also policy report 1982, 43–44; policy report 1983, 53–54.

[160] In 30525 International Energy Agency (1983), para 30, the Commission took a similarly lenient approach towards an agreement aimed at ensuring a secure supply in times of crisis, due to its benefits for consumers as well as to the 'general economy of the participating countries'. The exemption was granted although the agreement had significantly restricted competition. See also policy report 1984, 56.

[161] Policy report 1982, 43–44. In 31055 ENI/Montedison (1986), para 40–41, the exemption was granted even though the agreement resulted in a substantial reduction of competition in the market. See also policy report 1986, 76–77.

potential restriction of competition, the Commission maintained that such agreements were a necessary component in the economic strategy of the EU, essential for rationalisation, R&D, innovation, and the dissemination of technology.[162]

Typically, the application of Article 101(3) TFEU to those agreements focused on the indispensability condition while assuming that they produced benefits and granted consumers a fair share.[163] Furthermore, the Commission essentially waived the requirements of the fourth condition when the other three conditions were fulfilled.[164]

The Commission also emphasised the need to ensure the international competitiveness of EU firms and the role of competition law in economic recovery, growth, and employment.[165] For instance, it justified exempting a collective management and copyright licensing agreement by emphasising the need to respond to a changing marketplace driven by globalisation, rapid technological progress, and a dynamic nature.[166] By the same token, it exempted restructuring agreements and cooperation agreements in the vehicle sector, pointing to the structural changes in the sector and to the frequent link-ups between manufacturers.[167]

During the second and third enforcement periods, to conclude, the Commission used the workable competition standard as the method to guide Article 101(3) TFEU balancing. Balancing was administrated according to a sectoral approach, by which the Commission tailored the scope and intensity of the four conditions of Article 101 (3) TFEU according to the 'degree of competition necessary' in each sector. By applying a legal proportionality test, the Commission enjoyed a wide discretion to assess, on a case-by-case basis, whether the restriction of competition was proportionate to and reasonable for achieving a non-competition interest. Informed by the workable competition standard, the four conditions were applied strictly to agreements impairing market integration, and in a flexible manner to agreements in liberalised or regulated sectors, agreements in sectors affected by an economic crisis, and agreements promoting EU industrial policy.

[162] See Annex A, Section 3.16. See also policy report 1994, 23–26, 105. In some cases, the undertakings offered voluntary commitments to meet these conditions, see 33640 Exxon/Shell (1994), para 66; 33863 Asahi/Saint-Gobain (1994), para 31; 34410 Olivetti/Digital (1994); 35855 Scandairy (1997); IP/98/353 Photo-graphic manufacturers (1998); 32173 Continental/Michelin (1998).

[163] This trend was discussed in Section 3.3.3.3. See also policy report 1994, 24, 106.

[164] See also Section 3.4.1 and Figure 3.6.

[165] Commission White Paper on Growth, Competitiveness, Employment (1993). See also policy report 1994, 24.

[166] 38014 IFPI 'Simulcasting' (2002), para 84.

[167] Restructuring agreements: 34456 Stichting Baksteen (1994), para 18–28; IP-96-1183 Roundwood trade (1996). Cooperation in vehicles: 31902 Iveco/Ford (1988), para 31–33; 33814 Ford/Volkswagen (1992); 33031 Fiat/Hitachi (1992), para 25–28; 33863 Asahi/Saint-Gobain (1994); 37889 GM/Fiat (2000). See also policy report 2000, 45.

3.4.4 *Fourth Enforcement Period: Consumer Welfare and Economic Evidence*

The modernisation has brought about considerable changes to the method of Article 101(3) TFEU balancing.[168] As elaborated in the following sub-sections, the Commission introduced the short-term narrow consumer welfare as the standard guiding the enforcement of Article 101 TFEU in general, and Article 101(3) TFEU balancing in particular, increased the nature and evidentiary threshold required to justify an exception, shifted the analysis to the first benefit condition, and revised the Commission's approach to the application of Article 101(3) TFEU to by-object restrictions.

3.4.4.1 Short-Term Narrow Consumer Welfare Standard

The Commission's policy papers following modernisation were the first to introduce *short-term narrow consumer welfare* as the standard guiding the enforcement of Article 101 TFEU in general, and Article 101(3) TFEU balancing in particular.[169] Article 101(3) Guidelines (2004) declare that the aim of EU competition rules is to protect competition 'as a *means of enhancing consumer welfare* and of ensuring an efficient allocation of resources'.[170] Hence, according to the Guidelines, Article 101(3) TFEU saves an agreement that restricts competition if it also carries 'pro-competitive effects by way of efficiency gains' that 'outweigh its anti-competitive effects'.[171]

While not declaring so in these terms, the Guidelines essentially reflect a short-term narrow consumer welfare standard. The Commission states that it will take into account efficiency gains that create additional value by lowering the costs of production, improving the quality of a product, or creating a new product.[172] The analysis focuses on measuring static efficiency, namely, the optimal distribution of resources among alternative production targets at a certain point in time and on the benefits to direct or indirect consumers in the relevant markets.[173]

This new standard has marked a significant change to the balancing method. The Commission has replaced the workable competition standard that guided the application of Article 101(3) TFEU prior to modernisation with an economic-based balancing method. It has transposed the legal balancing process based on a

[168] On the effects of modernisation on balancing more generally, see Section 2.5.4.
[169] As described in detail in Sections 2.5.4.2–2.5.4.4.
[170] Emphasis added. Commission Article 101(3) Guidelines (2004), para 33.
[171] *Ibid*, para 13, 33.
[172] *Ibid*, para 33, 60–72.
[173] ICN Competition Enforcement and Consumer Welfare (2011), 31. See also Sections 1.2.1.3 and 2.5.4.4.

proportionality analysis into an economic balancing process based on an economic welfare assessment.[174]

At the same time, it is unclear if and how the Commission has actually applied the consumer welfare standard in practice. Similarly to the questions surrounding the relevant types of benefits under Article 101(3) TFEU examined in Section 3.3.4, the empirical findings reveal that the Commission has rarely referred to consumer welfare in its decisional practice.

Most of the Commission's decisions lacked a reference to consumer welfare altogether. In a few cases, the Commission merely mentioned the notion of consumer welfare without explaining its meaning and scope or how it applies to Article 101(3) TFEU.[175] Hence, in contrast to many NCAs that have established theoretical and practice-based frameworks,[176] the Commission's decisional practice does not explain how the standard should be applied to a specific case.

3.4.4.2 Robust Economic Evidence

In addition to adopting a new balancing standard, the Commission has increased the nature and evidentiary threshold necessary for granting an Article 101(3) TFEU exception. The previous sections have illustrated that, prior to modernisation, the Commission often settled for a low standard of proof, relying on speculative evidence or general policy arguments. Yet, following modernisation, the Commission has demanded strong economic evidence to prove the fulfilment of the four conditions.

In its Article 101(3) Guidelines (2004), the Commission enacted a high evidential threshold for proving the first benefit condition. Undertakings are expected to substantiate the nature of the claimed efficiencies, a causal link between the agreement and the efficiencies, the likelihood and magnitude of the claimed efficiency, and how and when each claimed efficiency would be achieved. In addition, they are required to calculate, as accurately as possible, the value of such efficiencies.[177] Following modernisation, quantitative and empirical analysis has become an important technique in the Commission's application of the Article.[178]

174 On the definitions of legal and economic balancing processes, see Section 1.2.2.1.

175 34579 36518 38580 MasterCard I (2007), para 60 and footnotes 310 and 834; 39188 Bananas (2008), para 341–342; 39092 Bathroom Fittings and Fixtures (2010), para 990; 39230 Rio Tinto Alcan (2012), para 94; 39612 Perindopril (Servier) (2014), para 1206–1209. On the possible meanings of consumer welfare, see Section 1.2.1.3.

176 See Section 3.6.2.

177 Commission Article 101(3) Guidelines (2004), para 51–58. Similar details are required for applying the other three conditions of Article 101(3) TFEU, in para 76, 78, 94, 109–115. This approach was repeated in the new versions of the Vertical Guidelines (2010), para 6, 19, 60, 96, 122–127, Horizontal Guidelines (2011), para 29, 49, 95–100, 141, 183, 217, 246, and in the BERs adopted after 2004, as detailed in Section 4.3.3.1.

178 See also Bishop and Walker (2010, Part III), Lianos and Genakos (2013), and Witt (2016, 240–244).

Similarly, the Commission has restricted the application of the second fair share condition. Article 101(3) Guidelines have inverted the order of the second and third conditions, ordering an examination of the indispensability condition before calculating the fair share passed on to consumers. Accordingly, the Guidelines have excluded from the calculation of fair share benefits that are the result of a restriction that was not indispensable.[179] In *International Skating Union's eligibility rules (2017)*, for example, the Commission found that benefits resulting from the Skating Union's so-called eligibility rules could not be taken into account for the purpose of calculating the benefits and fair share since such rules go beyond what is necessary to protect legitimate sport-related interests.[180] This was not the Commission's practice in the past. Prior to modernisation, the Commission would examine the indispensability of an agreement only after identifying the relevant benefits and the share passed on to consumers. Hence, the fair share also included benefits resulting from restrictions that were not indispensable.

Moreover, the modernisation has shifted the burden of proof. According to Regulation 1/2003, the competition enforcer only bears the burden of proving an Article 101(1) TFEU infringement. The undertakings bear the burden of proving that the four conditions of Article 101(3) TFEU have been fulfilled.[181] In other words, the Regulation builds on the bifurcated structure of Article 101 TFEU to introduce a new allocation of the burden of proof. This has created an asymmetry: The standard for proving a justification under Article 101(3) TFEU has become significantly higher than the standard for proving an infringement of Article 101(1) TFEU. This asymmetry makes it more difficult to successfully invoke Article 101(3) TFEU.[182] Indeed, as mentioned, the empirical findings point out that the Commission has rejected most Article 101(3) TFEU claims outright following modernisation, noting that no relevant benefit had been identified or substantiated.[183]

The higher evidentiary requirements and shift in the burden of proof can be demonstrated by reviewing the Commission's payment card decisions. As was described above, in *Visa II (2002)* the Commission exempted an MIF system despite its price-fixing effects,[184] assuming that the MIF furthered economic and technical progress by contributing to 'the existence of a large-scale international payment system'.[185] Merely five years later, following modernisation, the Commission established a much higher threshold for fulfilling the first condition of Article 101(3)

[179] Commission Article 101(3) Guidelines (2004), para 39.
[180] 40208 International Skating Union's Eligibility rules (2017), para 293–297.
[181] Regulation 1/2003, Preamble 5 and Article 2.
[182] GCLC Annual Conference (2010, 19–23).
[183] See Section 3.3.4.
[184] Subject to placing a cap on the amount of the MIF that related to the audited costs of services that the banks would be rendering to the retailers and customers. See Section 3.4.3.3.
[185] 29373 Visa International (2002), para 91.

TFEU.[186] Departing from its previous approach, it held that 'there is no presumption' that MIFs enhance the efficiency of card schemes.[187] Rather, it required robust theoretical and empirical evidence.[188] Although it held that the payment systems generated efficiencies, it did not identify a causal link between the efficiencies and the specific restrictions.[189]

3.4.4.3 Focus on the First Benefit Condition

The changes to the evidentiary requirements brought about by modernisation have also affected the relative weight given to the four conditions of Article 101(3) TFEU. In the post-modernisation era, the focus of Article 101(3) TFEU has shifted away from the indispensability condition to the quantification and calculation of benefits, and to a lesser extent to the fair share condition.[190]

Unlike the second and third enforcement periods,[191] the Commission was no longer willing to accept assumptions that consumers received a fair share of the resulting benefit due to some remaining competitive pressure. In *MasterCard I (2007)*, for example, the Commission held that 'without further evidence – which MasterCard failed to submit – it cannot safely be assumed that by pursuing its aim of maximising system output MasterCard is creating objective efficiencies that benefit all customers'.[192]

Since undertakings have almost never managed to produce evidence to quantify and calculate the benefits and to prove the fair share to consumers, the other conditions imposed by the Article have become less significant. One could argue that although the provisions of Article 101(3) TFEU contain four conditions, in practice only the first is a substantive condition, whereas the other three are limitations on, or requirements of, the first.[193]

[186] 37860 Morgan Stanley Dean Witter/Visa (2007); 34579 36518 38580 MasterCard I (2007); 38606 Cartes bancaires (2007), as confirmed by the GC in T-491/07 Cartes Bancaires (2012). In C-67/13P Cartes Bancaires (2014), the CJEU annulled the decision due to insufficient examination of whether there was a by-object restriction.

[187] 34579 36518 38580 MasterCard (2007), para 733.

[188] *Ibid*, para 693.

[189] 37860 Morgan Stanley Dean Witter/Visa (2007), para 312–320; 38606 Cartes bancaires (2007), para 380–477; 34579 36518 38580 MasterCard I (2007), para 679–733. The change in the Commission's approach was scrutinised by the GC. In T-111/08 MasterCard (2012), para 224–226 and 235 and T-491/07 Cartes bancaires (2012), para 95–96, the GC rejected the claim that the Commission departed from its previous position without sufficient explanation. The Court justified the decisions with reference to the lack of a causal link.

[190] See Figure 3.6. This trend was also previously observed by Kjolbye (2004, 573) and Faull and Nikpay (2014, 317).

[191] See Section 3.3.3.3.

[192] 34579 36518 38580 MasterCard I (2007), para 743.

[193] See also Kjolbye (2004, 573), Sufrin (2006, 933), and Faull and Nikpay (2014, 317).

Kjolbye,[194] *Faull*, and *Nikpay*,[195] three competition enforcers writing in a private capacity, have linked the above changes to the procedural modernisation. The notification regime of Regulation 17/62 entailed a reactive enforcement culture in which the Commission devoted most of its enforcement efforts to assessing notified agreements. The indispensability condition was, in their opinion, well suited for this purpose. It served as a type of proportionality test. When the first condition was satisfied and there was a sufficiently competitive market, the Commission would often assume that consumers would receive a fair share of the benefits. On the other hand, Regulation 1/2003 is based on self-assessment. This, in combination with the more economic approach, means that fewer cases will be found to fall within the scope of Article 101(1) TFEU in the first place. The rest of the cases will merit a more careful analysis of all four conditions, which requires greater emphasis on the first two conditions.

3.4.4.4 Hard-Core and By-Object Restrictions

In addition to the above changes to the balancing method, modernisation has altered the Commission's approach to the application of Article 101(3) TFEU to by-object restrictions. The Commission's Article 101(3) Guidelines (2004) declare that although Article 101(3) TFEU does not *a priori* exclude certain types of agreements, hard-core restrictions are 'unlikely' to fulfil the conditions of the Article.[196] The Commission's decisions following modernisation use even stronger language, holding that by-object restrictions are 'in principle' ineligible for an exception as they do not create genuine benefits, do not provide a fair share to consumers, and are not indispensable.[197] The Commission's new approach to by-object restrictions places another limitation on the type of restrictive agreement that could benefit from an Article 101(3) TFEU exception following modernisation.[198]

The empirical findings, however, illustrate that the Commission's position does not reflect its practice prior to modernisation. Figure 3.7 describes the types of restrictions in which Article 101(3) TFEU has been accepted. It differentiates between by-object restrictions (black bars), by-effect restrictions (grey bars), and proceedings that did not indicate the type of restriction (white bars).

194 Kjolbye (2004, 573).

195 Faull and Nikpay (2014, 317).

196 Commission Article 101(3) Guidelines (2004), para 46. See also Commission Guidance on Restrictions of Competition 'by object' (2014), 4.

197 36957 36997 37121 37138 37380 Glaxo Wellcome (2001), para 124 (repealed by the GC and CJEU); 39401 E.ON/GDF (2009), para 265; 39510 Ordre National des Pharmaciens (2010), para 705. The BERs adopted during the fourth enforcement period and described in Chapter 4 follow a similar approach and do not apply to agreements containing hard-core infringements.

198 Arguably, this also goes against the principle that the conditions of Article 101(3) TFEU are cumulative and exhaustive. See Sections 3.3.4 and 2.2.3.

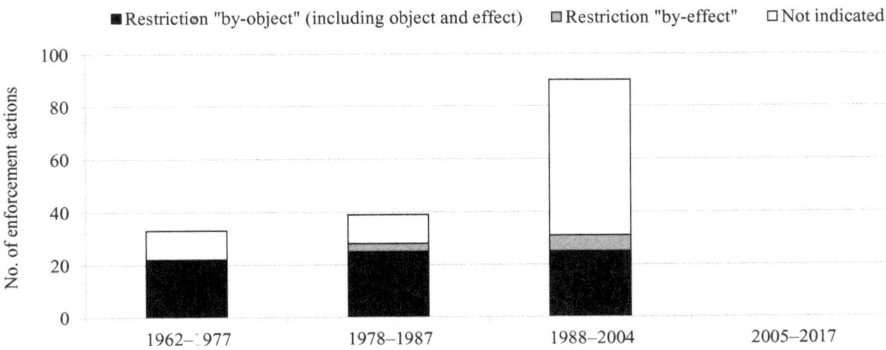

FIGURE 3.7. Exemptions according to restriction type, Commission
All Article 101 TFEU enforcement actions, excluding unpublished comfort letters. The type of restriction is based on the classification of the Commission, as indicated in each case

The figure demonstrates that, prior to modernisation, the Commission exempted a number of restrictions it categorised as by-object.[199] For example, in *REIMS II (1999)*, it approved a price-fixing agreement between European postal operators setting the remuneration for cross-border mail.[200] Similarly, in *Société Air France/ Alitalia Linee (2004)*, rendered only three weeks before the entry into force of Regulation 1/2003, the Commission exempted an air alliance cooperation agreement including provisions on scheduling, marketing, and pricing, which had been classified as a by-object restriction.[201] The number of exemptions granted to by-object restrictions is likely to be even higher than indicated by the figure, as some of the proceedings in which the Commission did not indicate the type of the restriction involved hard-core restrictions (white bars).

The change in the Commission's approach could be linked to a transformation in the classification of a restriction as by-object. The switch to an effects-based approach and the introduction of the ancillary restraints doctrine has narrowed down the scope of Article 101(1) TFEU.[202] Therefore, some of the by-object restrictions that were exempted in the past may no longer fall within the scope of the prohibition of Article 101(1) TFEU. At the same time, this explanation cannot fully account for the Commission's new approach. As shown above, prior to

[199] See, for example, 30810 Synthetic fibres (1984); 30863 BPCL/ICI (1984); 30804 Nuovo Cegam (1984); 31055 ENI/Montedison (1986); 32265 Concordato Incendio (1989); 32408 TEKO (1989); 33100 Assurpol (1992); 36494 EACEM (1998); 36718 CECED (1999); 36748 REIMS II (1999); 8284 Société Air France/Alitalia Linee (2004).

[200] 36748 REIMS II (1999).

[201] 38284 Société Air France/Alitalia Linee (2004).

[202] See Section 5.3.4. See also Jones (2010, 791), Rousseva (2013, 251), and Commission Guidance on Restrictions of Competition 'by object' (2014), 4.

modernisation, the Commission also exempted 'classic' horizontal hard-core restrictions, such as price fixing, which are still classified as hard-core restriction today.

Against this backdrop, the Commission's new approach to by-object restrictions should be viewed as another limitation imposed on the type of restrictive agreement that could benefit from an Article 101(3) TFEU exception. The Commission created a unique balancing framework for by-object restrictions, which is based on neither primary nor secondary EU law, nor on the case law of the EU Courts. In fact, Section 3.5.3 reveals that this new approach to the balancing of by-object restrictions has not been accepted by the EU Courts and has created tension between the Commission's and EU Courts' approaches to Article 101(3) TFEU balancing following modernisation.

3.4.5 *Interim Conclusion*

As EU primary and secondary laws do not offer a clear method to guide Article 101(3) TFEU balancing, the balancing method was chiefly developed by the Commission's practice. Over the years, the Commission has altered its Article 101 (3) TFEU balancing methods. It has changed the balancing process, the evidentiary burden for exemptions, the interpretations and relative weight given to the four conditions of Article 101(3) TFEU, and its approach to by-object restrictions.

Prior to modernisation, balancing was guided by the workable competition standard. This facilitated a legal balancing process based on a proportionality test, which left the Commission a significant margin of discretion to decide whether to exempt an agreement. The Commission did not apply Article 101(3) TFEU in a uniform manner to all types of sectors and agreements. The empirical findings show that the Commission applied the conditions of the Article strictly to agreements impairing market integration, and in a flexible manner to agreements in liberalised or regulated sectors, agreements in sectors affected by an economic crisis, and agreements promoting EU industrial policy.

As part of its substantive modernisation, the Commission has advocated changing the balancing method. Its policy papers have transformed Article 101(3) TFEU into an economic balancing process with the introduction of the short-term narrow consumer welfare standard. According to the Commission's policy papers, balancing is limited to measuring the economic, quantifiable benefits of an agreement against its harm to competition. This balancing method is based on an economic and factual cost–benefit analysis. The core of the analysis has shifted to proving and quantifying the benefit generated for individual consumers, rather than examining whether the restriction of competition is proportionate and justifiable. An Article 101(3) TFEU defence requires a much higher evidentiary threshold, imposes the burden of proof on the undertakings, and effectively excludes excepting by-object restrictions.

Nevertheless, the practical implications of the Commission's new approach remain unclear because the Commission has only rarely applied Article 101(3)

TFEU following modernisation and has mostly rejected outright the possibility of granting an exception. As detailed in this section and elaborated in Chapter 7, the substantive pillar of modernisation has not only transformed the theory of harm for applying Article 101(1) TFEU and the balancing tool of Article 101(3) TFEU but also informed the selection of enforcement targets. Following modernisation, the Commission has chosen to focus its enforcement efforts on hard-core restrictions that are unlikely to be justified by overriding non-competition interests under Article 101(3) TFEU even in line with the Commission's broad interpretation prior to modernisation.

As a result, the Commission's decisional practice did not clarify the particularities of the short-term narrow consumer welfare that was advocated in its policy papers and how it should guide the application of Article 101(3) TFEU. This, taken together with the open questions surrounding the relevant types of benefits under the Article, has created great uncertainty on the role of non-competition interests following modernisation.

This uncertainty has been reinforced because, as the next section reveals, the EU Courts have not fully accepted the changes advocated by the Commission's policy papers. They have not fully accepted either the limitations placed by the Commission on the relevant types of benefit or the balancing method and the new framework for by-object restrictions.

3.5 EU COURTS

3.5.1 *Overview*

Article 101(3) TFEU balancing has been rightly described as *the foremost area of inconsistency* between the Commission's and EU Courts' approaches following modernisation.[203] The empirical findings presented below show that prior to modernisation, the EU Courts had a leading role in shaping Article 101(3) TFEU balancing. They had a decisive influence in determining the types of benefits that could be examined under the Article and the balancing method.

This changed subsequent to modernisation. At the turn of the millennium, the Commission took up the reins on interpreting Article 101(3) TFEU. This section shows that although the EU Courts have not fully endorsed the Commission's new approach to Article 101(3) TFEU, neither did they take a clear stand on how balancing should be applied. Their judgements have often used vague and ambiguous wording and did not directly address questions as to the scope of the Article. This has created much uncertainty as to the current role of non-competition interests under the Article. Moreover, as Section 3.6 illustrates, the lack of guidance from the

[203] Petit (2009, 6) and GCLC Annual Conference (2010, 82–83).

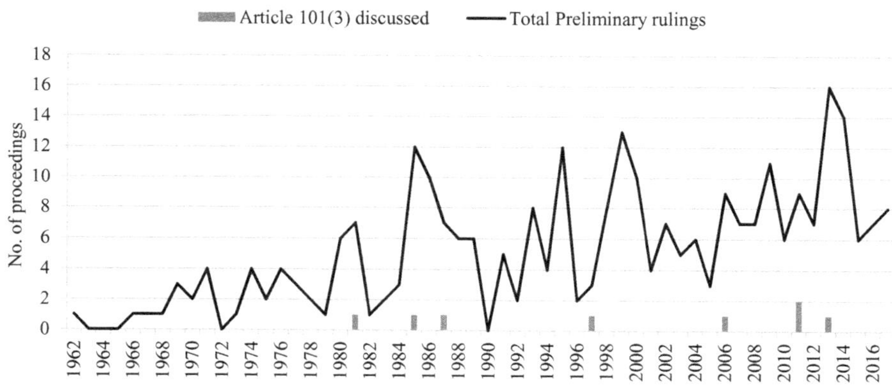

FIGURE 3.8. Article 101(3) TFEU, preliminary rulings

EU Courts has facilitated conflicting national balancing practices, which have hampered the uniformity of balancing throughout the EU.

Before exploring the above in detail, this section shall provide an overview of the proceedings in which the EU Courts have discussed the application of Article 101(3) TFEU. First, Figure 3.8 presents the number of preliminary rulings in which the Article has been discussed (grey bars).

The figure discloses that national courts have referred only a limited number of questions on the interpretation of Article 101(3) TFEU to the CJEU.[204] This can perhaps be explained by the fact that until May 2004, the Commission had the sole power to grant Article 101(3) TFEU exemptions in public enforcement actions. National courts, therefore, only reviewed the application of the Article in a number of private enforcement cases. Moreover, scholars have noted that, since modernisation, national courts have not made any preliminary references concerning matters covered by the Commission's guidelines.[205] Accordingly, although the guidelines are non-binding soft law, they *de facto* have limited the CJEU's opportunities to enunciate its balancing approach.

Interestingly, the empirical findings reveal that the preliminary rulings have focused on the same types of infringements as the ones examined by the Commission during each enforcement period. Up until the third enforcement period (i.e. April 2004), the preliminary rulings have centred on the application of Article 101(3) TFEU to distribution systems. Following modernisation, they have mostly dealt with the application of the Article in regulated sectors.[206]

[204] For a list of preliminary rulings on the interpretation of Article 101(3) TFEU individual exemptions, see Annex A, Section 3.17.

[205] Ibáñez Colomo (2013, 370) and Blockx (2018, 99).

[206] See Annex A, Section 3.17.

Next, Figure 3.9 examines appeals involving the application of Article 101(3) TFEU.[207] It specifies the total number of appeals against the Commission's decisions (black line), appeals in which an individual exemption was discussed (grey line), appeals in which the Courts ratified the exemption granted by the Commission (bars), and appeals in which the Courts overturned a Commission's decision granting or denying an individual exemption (crosses).

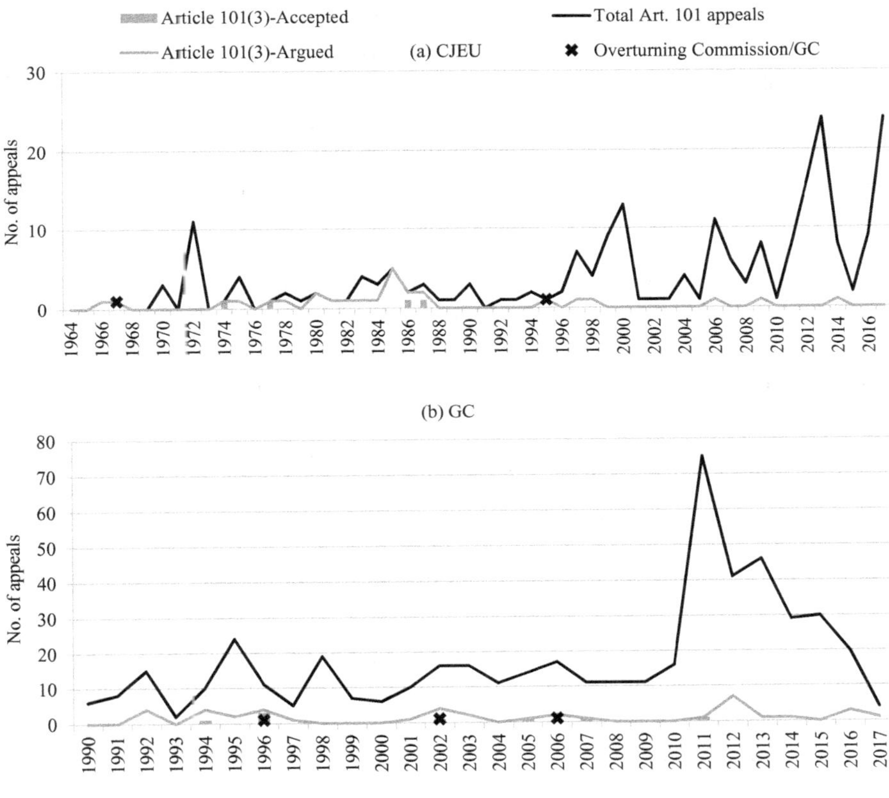

FIGURE 3.9. Article 101(3) TFEU, EU Courts appeals
The seven proceedings heard by the GC in 2012 in which Article 101(3) TFEU was examined appealed only two Commission decisions. Therefore, it does not represent a substantive peak

The figure demonstrates that the EU Courts have had limited opportunities to review the Commission's application of Article 101(3) TFEU[208] and have rarely overturned the Commission's analysis. Despite that, as the next sections reveal, the EU Courts had an important role in shaping Article 101(3) TFEU balancing principles prior to modernisation.

[207] See Annex A, Section 3.18.
[208] See also Bailey (2004, 1327, 1347).

3.5.2 From an Active Role Prior to Modernisation to a Passive Role

From the early days of EU competition law, the CJEU introduced a standard of marginal review to scrutinise the Commission's application of Article 101(3) TFEU. It has consistently emphasised that the Commission has a wide margin of discretion when applying the Article.[209] This principle was particularly true with respect to the consideration of non-competition interests. The EU Courts have acknowledged the Commission's discretion to balance under Article 101(3) TFEU, and the GC explicitly affirmed that the 'Commission is entitled to base itself on considerations connected with the pursuit of the public interest'.[210] Balancing under Article 101(3) TFEU was classified as a matter entailing a complex economic assessment, triggering a less strict standard for control, which is confined to 'verifying whether the facts have been accurately stated, whether there has been any manifest error of appraisal and whether the legal consequences deduced from those facts were accurate'.[211]

Indeed, the empirical findings confirm that the CJEU and GC have mostly confined their appraisal to procedural elements of the Commission's decisions or undertaken a very general appraisal of its analysis. In most cases, they did not question the Commission's substantive assessment of the four conditions of the Article.[212]

This, however, does not mean that the EU Courts have not influenced the balancing principles. As demonstrated in Sections 3.3 and 3.4, the Courts, and the CJEU in particular, have had an immense impact on the development of Article 101(3) TFEU prior modernisation. They have shaped the *types of benefits* that could be examined under the Article by interpreting Article 101(3) TFEU to include broad economic and non-economic benefits. This was summarised by AG *Léger*, noting that '[a]ccording to the case-law, the wording of Article [101(3) TFEU] makes it possible to take account of the particular nature of different branches of the economy, social concerns and, to a certain extent, considerations connected with the pursuit of the public interest'.[213] Moreover, the EU Courts have introduced the workable competition *balancing method*, based on a legal balancing process and with a relatively low evidentiary threshold.

In many of the Article 101(3) TFEU landmark cases prior modernisation, the court did not overturn the outcome of the Commission's decisions. It merely introduced new balancing methods and principles.[214] In parallel, notwithstanding the narrow marginal review standard, the Courts have overturned the Commission's

[209] See Section 2.4.

[210] T-528/93 T-542/93 T-543/93 T-546/93 EBU/Eurovision System (1996), para 118.

[211] T-168/01 GlaxoSmithKline (2006), para 241.

[212] See Annex A, Section 3.19. See also Bailey (2004, 1327, 1347), Cseres (2007b, 160–161), and Kalintiri (2016, 1288–1289). Yet, in some proceedings, the GC also evaluated the Commission's substantive analysis. See, for instance, T-17/93 Ford/Volkswagen (1994); T-29/92 Building and Construction Industry in the Netherlands (1995); T-131/99 Whitbread (2002).

[213] AG Léger opinion in C-309/01 Wouters (2001), para 113.

[214] See, for example, the Courts' judgements in C-56/64 C-58/64 Grundig/Consten (1966), as described in Section 3.4.2; C-26/76 Metro I (1977), as described in Section 3.3.3.1; and T-17/93 Ford/Volkswagen (1994), as described in Section 3.3.3.5.

balancing in some instances. In fact, four out of the five Courts judgements overturning Commission decisions on the application of Article 101(3) TFEU were based on an appraisal of the substantive balancing elements.[215] In those judgements, the Courts actively engaged in complex balancing issues. In particular, the Courts criticised the manner in which the Commission had calculated the benefit condition[216] and applied the indispensability[217] and elimination of competition[218] conditions. Hence, despite the marginal review standard, in the past the EU Courts played a leading role in the development of Article 101(3) TFEU balancing.

This has changed in parallel with modernisation. In the few actions for annulment in which the EU Courts had the opportunity to examine the application of Article 101(3) TFEU following modernisation, they have often concisely affirmed the Commission's analysis[219] or focused on procedural grounds.[220] Similarly, the CJEU's preliminary rulings have mostly briefly addressed the possibility of exception without detailing the application of the conditions of the Article to the specific case[221] or merely referred to the wording of the provision.[222] As such, the EU Courts have not openly clarified the scope of the Article or assessed the Commission's new approach.

Section 8.2.3 suggests that this is in line with the Court's general avoidance of taking a stance on controversial legal, economic, and political questions surrounding the objectives of EU competition law in general, and balancing in particular, following modernisation. The limited involvement of the EU Courts in Article 101 (3) TFEU balancing may also be the result of the change to the balancing process. As elaborated in Section 3.4.4, as part of modernisation, the Commission has called to transform the application of Article 101(3) TFEU from a legal balancing process that is based on an abstract application of the principle of proportionality to an economic balancing process that is linked to a consumer welfare assessment. While the EU Courts often engage with the weighing of interests by examining whether a

[215] In the fifth case, C-8/66 C-9/66 C-10/66 C-11/66 Noordwijks Cement Accoord (1967), 94, the Commission's decision with respect to Article 101(3) TFEU was annulled due to insufficient reasoning.

[216] C-360/92P Net Book Agreements (1995), para 29, annulling the Commission's and GC's decisions in 27393 27394 Net Book Agreements (1988), para 71-86 and T-66/89 Net Book Agreements (1992), para 71–116.

[217] T-528/93 T-542/93 T-543/93 T-546/93 EBU/Eurovision System (1996), para 95–103, annulling the Commission's decision in 32150 EBU/Eurovision System (1993); T-168/01 GlaxoSmithKline (2006) as upheld by C-501/06P C-513/06P C-515/06P C-519/06P GlaxoSmithKline (2009), annulling the Commission's decisions in 36957 Glaxo Wellcome (2001).

[218] T-185/00 T-216/00 T-299/00 T-300/00 Eurovision (2002), para 83–86, annulling the Commission's decision in 32150 Eurovision (2000).

[219] T-193/02 FIFA rules on players' agents (2005), para 100–104.

[220] C-171/05P FIFA rules on players' agents (2006), para 24; T-259/02 T-260/02 T-261/02 T-262/02 T-263/02 T-264/02 T-271/02 Austrian banks – 'Lombard Club' (2006), para 213–214.

[221] C-403/08 C-429/08 Football Association Premier League (2011), para 145; C-439/09 Pierre Fabre (2011), para 50.

[222] C-238/05 Asnef/Equifax (2006), para 65–71; C-1/12 Ordem dos Técnicos Oficiais de Contas, (2013), para 102–103.

measure has gone beyond what is required to attain a legitimate objective (e.g. in free movement cases), they have shown dereference to the Commission's assessment of complex economic matters.

The next section argues that the limited judicial review does not entail that the EU Courts have accepted the Commission's new interpretation to Article 101(3) TFEU balancing. Nevertheless, while the EU Courts did not accept the Commission's new interpretation of Article 101(3) TFEU, they refrained from clarifying the scope of balancing under the Article.

3.5.3 *Not Fully Endorsing the Commission's New Approach*

The first part of this chapter demonstrated that from the outset of the modernisation plans, the Commission has advocated for substantive reform to Article 101(3) TFEU balancing. Under the heading of the more economic approach, it has attempted to alter the EU Courts' previous case law on the types of relevant benefits and balancing method.[223]

In terms of legal hierarchy, however, the Commission does not have the legal competence to change the EU Courts' case law. The Commission is bound by the principles developed in the case law and cannot limit the scope of Article 101(3) TFEU by means of soft law or as a hidden result of Regulation 1/2003.[224] While the Commission is entitled to adopt guidelines indicating its policy on how to exercise its discretion, it may not depart from the rules of the Treaty or previous EU Courts judgements.[225]

Against this background, the uniform enforcement and consistent development of EU competition law would have been well served by clarification from the EU Courts as to the limits of balancing, the scope of Article 101(3) TFEU, and the validity of the Commission's new approach.

The empirical findings presented above showed that the EU Courts did not answer these questions directly. Nevertheless, as the following sub-sections show shows, there are various indications that the EU Courts never fully embraced the Commission's limitation on the types of benefits that could be examined under Article 101(3) TFEU and the reference to the short-term narrow consumer welfare standard as a balancing method.[226]

3.5.3.1 Types of Benefits[227]

There are several indications that the EU Courts have not followed the Commission's new narrow reading of the first condition of Article 101(3) TFEU,

[223] See Sections 3.3.4 and 3.4.4.
[224] See also Schweitzer (2007, 9), Stefan (2008, 763–764), Townley (2009, 70, 178–181), Gerard (2012, 36–38), and Witt (2016, 261–295).
[225] C-439/11P Ziegler (2013), para 59; C-226/11 Expedia (2012), para 29. On the relationship between the Commission's soft law mechanisms and the judgements of the EU Courts, see Stefan (2008), and on national Courts, see Kovacs, Tóth, and Forgacs (2016).
[226] See also Townley (2009, 47), Van Rompuy (2012, 208), Witt (2012, 444), and Gerbrandy (2015, 771).
[227] This section elaborates on similar points I have previously discussed in Brook (2019, 151–152).

limiting it to economic benefits. To this end, Figure 3.10 describes the categories of benefits that were discussed in Article 101(3) TFEU proceedings in front of the EU Courts.

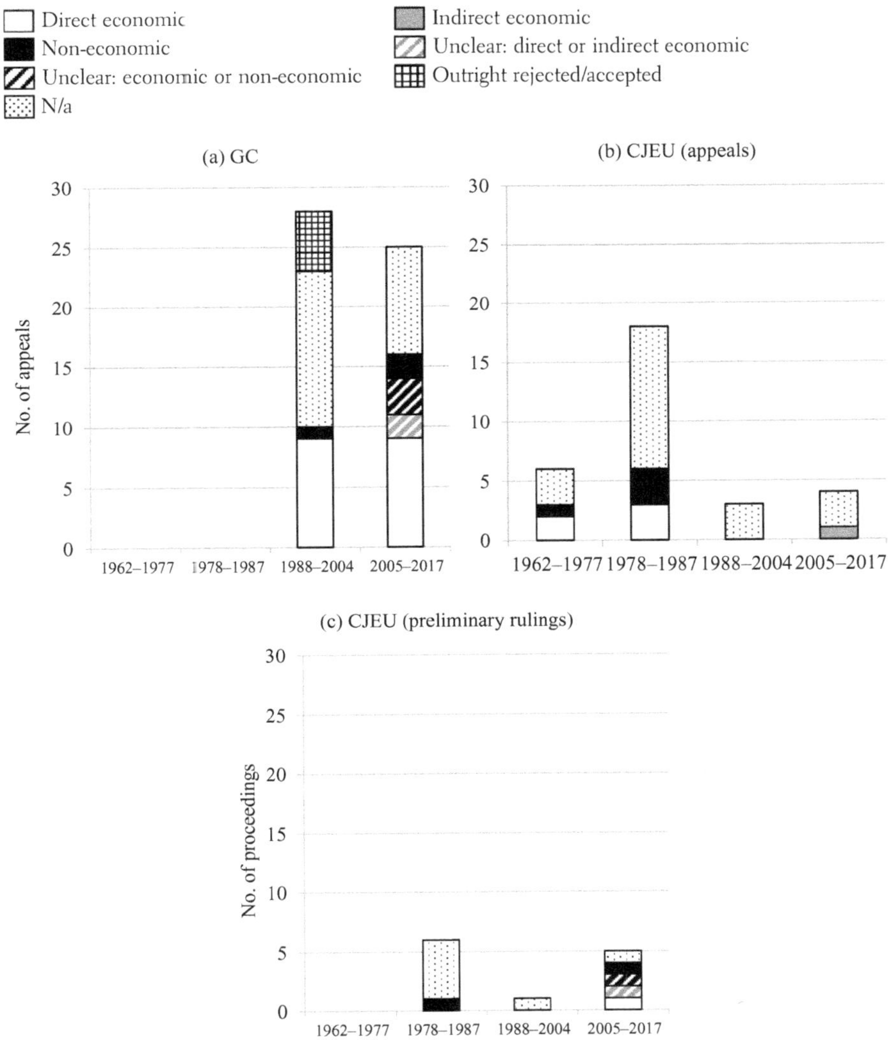

FIGURE 3.10. Article 101(3) TFEU, categories of benefits, EU Courts[228]
All appeals and preliminary rulings on the application of Article 101(3) TFEU. In some proceedings, more than one benefit was accepted as a justification

[228] Figure 3.10 was originally published in Brook (2019). Reproduced with permission of the Licensor through PLSclear.

First, the empirical findings show that the CJEU's preliminary rulings following May 2004 still recognise that the protection of non-economic benefits – such as those relating to financial services, regulated professions, IPRs, and sports – could justify an Article 101(3) TFEU exception (Figure 3.10(c), black and dashed bars).[229] Similarly, the EU Courts upheld a number of Commission decisions that had been adopted prior to May 2004, which exempted agreements on the basis of non-economic benefits. The Courts confirmed that non-economic benefits relating to sports, the environment, and financial services justified Article 101(3) TFEU exceptions and fighting free riding, promoting R&D, and culture were interests that could, in theory, justify an exception.[230] Those Court decisions did not recognise any change in the rules of identifying the relevant benefits under Article 101(3) TFEU following modernisation.

Second, the pertinence of non-economic benefits is also supported by the parallel the CJEU drew between Article 101(3) TFEU and free movement exceptions, in which broad non-economic benefits undoubtedly justify an exemption.[231] In *Football Association Premier League (2011)*, for example, the Court examined an exclusive broadcasting license agreement. The CJEU first affirmed that the agreement restricted the freedom to provide services and could not be justified by IPRs or promotion of sports considerations since it went beyond what is necessary to achieve those aims.[232] The Court also referred to this free movement analysis to explain why the agreement did not fulfil the conditions of Article 101(3) TFEU.[233] The Court assumed, in other words, that non-economic benefits were relevant both under the free movement and the competition law provisions.

Third, the GC has declared that policy-linking clauses create an obligation to consider non-economic benefits under Article 101(3) TFEU. In *CISAC (2013)*, it noted that the policy-linking clause on the protection of culture entails the obligation 'to bear in mind the requirements relating to the respect for and promotion of cultural diversity' when applying the four conditions of the Article.[234] Although the Court did not specify how culture should be taken into account, it emphasised that such non-economic benefit was relevant.

[229] C-238/05 Asnef/Equifax (2006), para 67; C-403/08 C-429/08 Football Association Premier League (2011), para 105–124, 145–146; C-1/12 Ordem dos Técnicos Oficiais de Contas (2013), para 96–103.

[230] See Annex A, Section 3.20.

[231] On the relationship between the conditions for exceptions under EU competition law and free movement rules, see Mortelmans (2001, 635–645), Monti (2002, 1086–1090), O'Loughlin (2003), Forrester (2006), and Enchelmaier (2012).

[232] C-403/08 C-429/08 Football Association Premier League (2011), para 105–124.

[233] *Ibid*, para 145–146.

[234] T-451/08 CISAC (2013), para 103. Yet, the GC upheld the Commission's decision findings that the burden of proof under Article 101(3) TFEU was not reversed merely by the fact that a non-competition interest was protected by the cultural policy-linking clause.

Finally, the EU Courts have also not accepted the Commission's new interpretation of consumers, limiting the *beneficiaries* under Article 101(3) TFEU to direct consumers. In *JCB Services (2006)*, the CJEU held that the restrictions of competition should be 'offset by benefits, *inter alia*, for consumers'. This suggests that not all of the relevant benefits under Article 101(3) TFEU must necessarily be enjoyed by consumers.[235] In *GlaxoSmithKline (2009)*, the Courts affirmed that the promotion of innovation in the pharmaceutical industry should be taken into account.[236] In other words, future benefits to society as a whole could justify a restriction of competition. In *MasterCard (2014)*, the CJEU seemed to take a more restrictive approach, requiring that benefits to direct consumers as well as benefits to indirect consumers in 'separate but connected' markets be taken into account.[237] In any event, the Courts clearly did not accept the Commission's reading that limited the Article to direct economic benefits profiting direct consumers alone.

3.5.3.2 Balancing Method

There are also indications that the EU Courts did not embrace the consumer welfare standard for applying Article 101(1) and (3) TFEU in general, and the narrow short-term consumer welfare in particular. Whereas the EU Courts agreed with the Commission that consumer welfare is a *relevant factor* for the application of Article 101 TFEU, they rejected the Commission's approach *limiting* balancing to an economic balancing based on the consumer welfare standard.[238]

At first, the GC actually appeared to support the Commission's new approach. In *GlaxoSmithKline (2006)*, the GC asserted that Article 101(1) TFEU aims 'to prevent undertakings, by restricting competition between themselves or with third parties, from *reducing the welfare of the final consumer*'.[239] Because this statement referred to Article 101(1) TFEU, it could have been interpreted as suggesting that Article 101(3) TFEU or Article 101 TFEU as a whole might pursue other objectives.[240] Yet, in *Austrian banks – 'Lombard Club' (2006)* rendered only three months later, the GC clarified that Article 101 TFEU as a whole pursued a consumer welfare aim by stating that Articles 101 and 102 TFEU were 'designed to ensure that competition is

[235] Emphasis added. C-167/04P JCB Service (2006), para 162.

[236] Case T-168/01 GlaxoSmithKline (2009), para 248. The CJEU accepted the GC analysis; however, it did not go into details on this point. See C-501/06P C-513/06P C-515/06P C-519/06P GlaxoSmithKline (2009), para 95.

[237] Case C-382/12P MasterCard (2014), para 243. The CJEU pronounced a similar position in C-238/05 Asnef/Equifax (2006), para 73.

[238] In comparison, the US Supreme Court has explicitly accepted the reliance on the consumer welfare standard In Continental Television v. GTE Sylvania (1977), 1003, it held that the 'legislative intent underlying the Sherman Act had as its goal the promotion of consumer welfare'. On the US Courts' approach, see also Ginsburg and Haar (2014, 943–944).

[239] Emphasis added. T-168/01 GlaxoSmithKline (2006), para 118.

[240] Townley (2009, 178–181).

not distorted in the internal market are ultimately intended to enhance the *well-being of consumers*'.[241]

However, the GC's positive approach towards consumer welfare was short-lived. In *T-Mobile (2009)* and *GlaxoSmithKline (2009)*, the CJEU rejected, at least in part, the consumer welfare standard as the sole aim of Article 101 TFEU. It declared that Article 101 TFEU 'is designed to protect *not only* the immediate interests of individual competitors or consumers but also *to protect the structure of the market and thus competition as such*'.[242]

Notably, the CJEU opted for a vague formulation compared to the one suggested by the Advocate General. AG *Kokott* submitted that Article 101 TFEU was not designed 'only or primarily' to protect competitors or consumers, but mainly to 'protect the structure of the market and thus competition as such (as an institution)'.[243] The advancement of consumer welfare, according to her, is only a secondary and indirect effect of competition policy. The CJEU, however, did not repeat this clear statement. Instead, it abstained from taking a clear stand on the goals and method for applying the Article.

The rejection of the sole reliance on the consumer welfare standard was later repeated in *TeliaSonera (2011)*, where the CJEU had referred to its long-established principle declaring that the function of the EU competition rules is to 'prevent competition from being distorted to the detriment of the *public interest, individual undertakings and consumers* thereby ensuring the *well-being of the European Union*'.[244] According to the Court, therefore, modernisation has not limited the EU competition rules to the assessment of the harm to consumer welfare.

In a similar vein, the EU Courts did not clearly embrace the Commission's rhetoric in its policy papers, portraying Article 101(3) TFEU as an economic balancing process. While following modernisation the Commission rebranded the benefits under Article 101(3) TFEU as 'efficiencies' that must be 'calculated' 'as accurately as reasonably possible',[245] the Courts continued to use the wording associated with a legal balancing process that had characterised their older case law. As a consequence, the Courts explain that when applying Article 101(3) TFEU,

[241] Emphasis added. T-259/02 T-260/02 T-261/02 T-262/02 T-263/02 T-264/02 T-271/02 Austrian banks – 'Lombard Club' (2006), para 99.

[242] Emphasis added. C-8/08 T-Mobile (2009), para 38. See also C-501/06P C-513/06P C-515/06P C-519/06P GlaxoSmithKline (2009), para 62; C-68/12 Slovak Banks (2012), para 18. This definition was repeated by the GC in T-461/07 Visa (2011), para 126 and T-357/06 Bitumen (2012), para 11.

[243] AG Kokott opinion in C-8/08 T-Mobile (2009), para 58.

[244] Emphasis added. C-52/09 TeliaSonera (2011), para 22, quoting C-46/87 C-227/88 Hoechst (1989), para 25. This was repeated by the GC, for example, in T-458/09 and T-171/1 Slovak Telekom (2012), para 38; T-357/06 Bitumen (Netherlands) (2012), para 230; T-325/16 Falcon (2018), para 173; T-705/14 Perindopril (2018), para 306; T-701/14 Perindopril (2018), para 236; T-691/14 Perindopril (2018), para 238; T-682/14 Perindopril (2018), para 167; T-680/14 Perindopril (2018), para 88; T-679/14 Perindopril (2018), para 200.

[245] Commission Article 101(3) Guidelines, point 56. On the Commission's approach, see Section 3.4.4.1.

the 'objective advantages' (rather than efficiencies or economic effects) must be 'examined' (rather than calculated) on the basis of 'factual arguments and the evidence provided' (rather than solely on economic data).[246]

Finally, the empirical findings reveal that the EU Courts did not adopt the Commission's new approach to the balancing of by-object restrictions. Following modernisation, as discussed in Section 3.4.4.4, the Commission declared that by-object restrictions are 'in principle' ineligible for an Article 101(3) TFEU exception. Despite such statements, the EU Courts continued to order a full analysis of Article 101(3) TFEU conditions, also with respect to by-object restrictions. They have neither required a different analysis nor indicated a lower likelihood of success in such cases.[247]

3.5.4 *Interim Conclusion*

The empirical findings affirm that prior to modernisation, the EU Courts were active in shaping Article 101(3) TFEU balancing. They had an important role in developing the principles guiding the types of benefits examined under the Article and the balancing method.

This changed following modernisation. On the one hand, the EU Courts did not embrace the Commission's new interpretation of Article 101(3) TFEU, at least in part. They continued to follow the balancing principles established in their case law prior to May 2004, leaving significant room for the consideration of non-competition interests. On the other hand, regrettably, the EU Courts have done so in an indeterminate manner. They were not clear on what types of benefits could be taken into account, the role of the consumer welfare standard, and the balancing method.

The EU Courts' practice generated great uncertainty on the limits of Article 101 (3) TFEU balancing. Because the Commission and the Courts have not articulated clear and coherent balancing principles, it is difficult to predict the applicable balancing framework. As the next section demonstrates, it also opened the door for the national enforcers to adopt diverging approaches to balancing in the era of decentralised enforcement.

3.6 NCAS AND NATIONAL COURTS

3.6.1 *Overview*

The previous sections have exhibited how the substantive and procedural pillars of modernisation have altered Article 101(3) TFEU balancing. This section discusses

[246] C-501/06P C-513/06P C-515/06P C-519/06P GlaxoSmithKline (2009), para 93–95, 102–103, 128–129; C-382/12P MasterCard (2014), para 228, 232, 234–235, 240–241.

[247] C-501/06P C-513/06P C-515/06P C-519/06P GlaxoSmithKline (2009), para 68–167; T-168/01 GlaxoSmithKline (2006), para 214–315. This was also the Court's approach in the past in T-17/93 Ford/Volkswagen (1994) and C-243/83 Binon (1985). See also GCLC Annual Conference (2010, 89).

an additional, less explored effect of Regulation 1/2003 relating to the institutional pillar of modernisation.

The decentralisation of enforcement has empowered the NCAs, for the first time, to apply Article 101(3) TFEU, and as such to engage in the balancing of competition and non-competition interests. Prior to modernisation, NCAs and national courts could have only applied Article 101(1) and (2) TFEU, while the assessment of Article 101(3) TFEU was reserved to the Commission.

The decentralised enforcement is based on the assumption that the obligation to apply the provision of Article 101 TFEU will result in a uniform administration of the law across the EU. Indeed, during the discussions preceding the adoption of Regulation 1/2003, the Council stressed that '[t]he abolition of the Commission exemption monopoly is not meant to pave the way for application of multiple national standards which may be different in content or enforcement from the standard of [EU] competition law [. . ..] Such a situation could seriously hamper the proper functioning of the internal market'.[248] The importance of a uniform application of Article 101(3) TFEU balancing was also shared by the Commission and the European Parliament.[249]

Nevertheless, although Regulation 1/2003 has entrusted NCAs to apply Article 101 (3) TFEU, it has not provided a clear and binding framework to guide the NCAs' new balancing powers. As a consequence, when EU primary and secondary law or the case law of the EU Courts do not prescribe otherwise, the NCAs may shape their national approaches based on their legal, economic, and social traditions. Although the Commission's guidelines and policy papers have stimulated a process of voluntary convergence to the Commission's practices,[250] they are not binding on the Member States.

As mentioned in Section 2.3.3.3, NCAs have a more limited power to apply Article 101(3) TFEU than the Commission. NCAs cannot adopt positive decisions granting an exception but can only adopt non-binding 'no grounds for action' findings, declaring that on the basis of the information in their possession the conditions for establishing an Article 101 TFEU infringement are not met.[251]

This section demonstrates that 'no grounds for action' findings are highly significant because they reveal, shape, and clarify the NCAs' approaches to Article 101(3) TFEU balancing. The empirical findings reveal that there was no single form for such 'no grounds for action' findings. Some were adopted as part of a formal decision in which the findings of inapplicability are not binding in themselves,

[248] Council's Progress Report on Proposal for Modernisation (2001), para 10.

[249] Staff Working Paper on Proposal for Modernisation (2001), para 11; Committee on Economic and Monterey Affairs Report on Proposal for Modernisation (2000), 22. See also Section 2.3.3.2.

[250] Lianos and Geradin (2013, 578–583) and Cseres and Mendes (2014, 486).

[251] Regulation 1/2003, Article 5 and C-375/09 Tele2Polska (2011).

while others were included in informal measures or press releases.[252] Some were short and concise, while others provided a full, detailed analysis.[253]

Since the NCAs' no grounds for action findings are not binding, they are not notified to the ECN or examined by the Commission. While the Commission had exercised some informal controls, the national interpretations of Article 101(3) TFEU balancing are not bound to the safeguards put in place by Regulation 1/2003 to ensure a consistent application of EU competition law.[254]

Indeed, this section illustrates that the NCAs have developed unique balancing approaches. The first group of NCAs (i.e. UK and Hungary) has generally conformed to the Commission's approach following modernisation. The second group (i.e. Netherlands and Germany) has openly deviated from such an approach. The third group (i.e. France) has also done so, but with more subtlety. Before exploring those national differences in detail, Figure 3.11 first presents an empirical overview of the application of Article 101(3) TFEU by the Five NCAs.

The figure records three types of cases. First, it presents the aggregated number of Article 101 TFEU enforcement actions in EU, mixed, and purely national cases (black lines). Second, it indicates the number of EU and mixed-cases in which Article 101(3) TFEU was invoked (dark grey lines). From those cases, it specifies the number of enforcement actions in which the NCAs adopted 'no grounds for action' findings noting that they believe that the conditions of Article 101(3) TFEU were fulfilled in either a formal (triangulars) or informal (triangulars with black border) measure. Third, the figure shows the number of purely national cases in which only the national exception equivalent to Article 101(3) TFEU was examined (dotted light grey lines). From those cases, it details the number of enforcement actions in which the national provision was accepted by a formal (squares) or informal (squares with black border) measure.

[252] See Figure 3.11.

[253] In France, one of the three findings of inapplicability decisions were taken as part of an informal opinion (05-A-23 Electricity purchases by intensive industrial users (2005)), while the other two were part of a formal decision (07-D-05 UFOP (2007) and 10-D-28 Exchanges Check-Image Fee (2010)). In Germany, the three findings of inapplicability were part of decisions to terminate the proceedings (B7–43/09 Fiber telecommunications networks (2010); B4–152/07 Coordination of tenders for sales packaging waste collection services by compliance schemes (2011); Construction of corvettes (2017)). The two former cases included detailed reasoning. In Hungary, all of the ten findings of inapplicability formed part of a formal decision (Vj-169/2003/68 Fertilizers (2004); Vj-132/2004/26 Card issuance (2004); Vj-200/2004/13 Funeral service in Szolnok (2005); Vj-178/2004/5 Pont Audio (2005); Vj-128/2004/23 Tomb construction activities in Túrkeve (2005); Vj-23/2005 Rába Group and Integris (2005); Vj-207/2004/51 Rába IT agreement (2005); Vj-94/2005 British American Tobacco group (BAT) (2006); Vj-191/2006/10 Euronics (2007); Vj-7/2008/178 Motor oils and lubricants (2009)). In the Netherlands, the four findings of inapplicability were part of highly detailed informal opinions (4713 Health insurers preferred suppliers policy (2005); 7011/23.827, MSC Shrimp Fishery (2011); 7512 Geldservice Nederland B.V. (2013); 14.1134.15 ATMs in rural areas (2014)). The impact of findings of inapplicability on balancing will also be examined in Section 7.6.3.

[254] See Section 2.3.3.3.

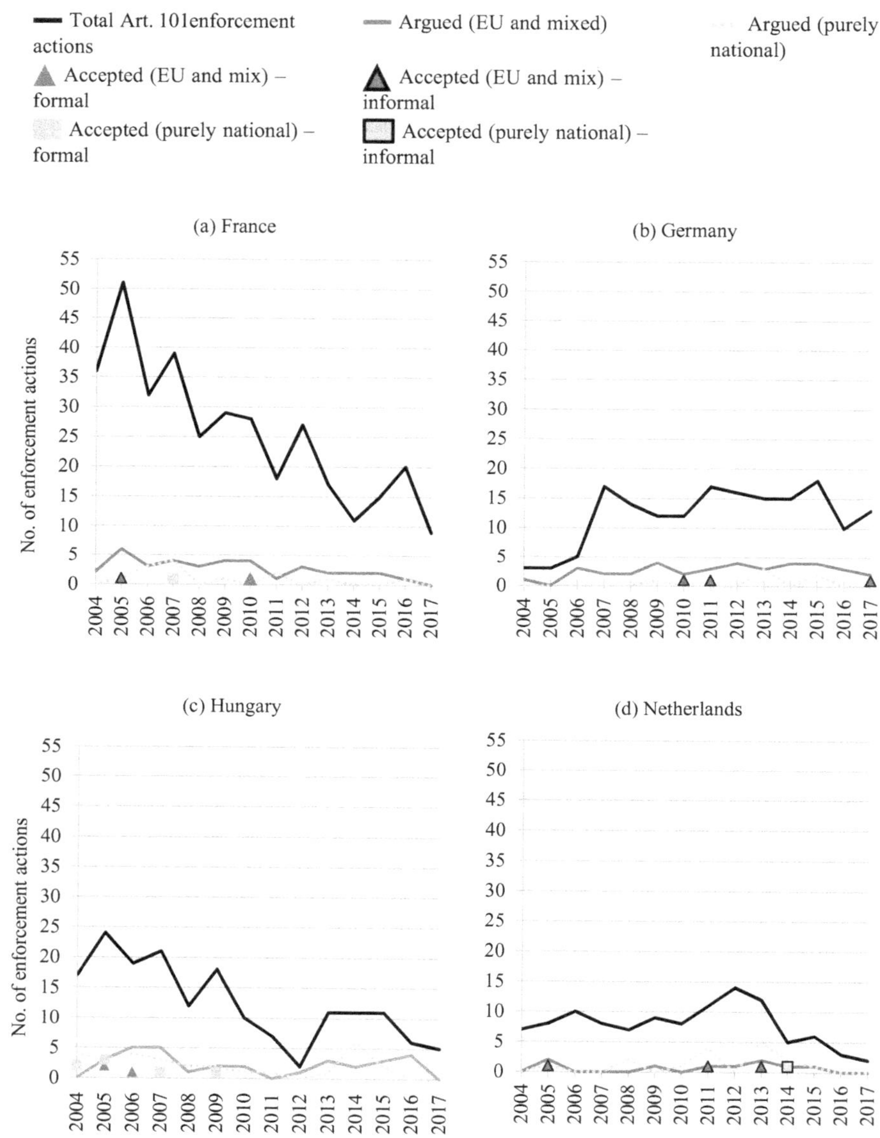

FIGURE 3.11 Article 101(3) TFEU, NCAs
Article 101(3) TFEU refers only to individual exemptions and does not include the application of the BERs. The cases in which Article 101(3) TFEU was accepted refer to 'no grounds for action' findings

The figure reveals that, similarly to the Commission's practice, the NCAs, too, have made little use of Article 101(3) TFEU following modernisation (see also Table 3.1). Moreover, the empirical findings illustrate that like the Commission, they have mostly rejected Article 101(3) TFEU outright without providing detailed reasoning for the application of the four conditions of the Article.[255]

A closer look at the empirical findings, nevertheless, points to the divergence in the national practices. This section, therefore, is dedicated to a discussion of the national balancing approaches. It shows that the NCAs have adopted different positions on the types of relevant benefits, balancing method, and intensity of control for applying the Article's four conditions. Balancing was also affected by the national equivalent provisions, which in some cases differed from the wording of Article 101(3) TFEU. In fact, this section reveals that the differences in the national equivalent provisions have not only affected the balance of purely national cases. They also had spillover effects on the interpretation of Article 101(3) TFEU in cases in which the EU provision applied.

3.6.2 *Types of Benefits and Balancing Method*[256]

The first part of this chapter has demonstrated that neither EU primary and secondary law nor the case law of the EU Courts has restricted the types of benefits that can justify an Article 101(3) TFEU exception. Although the Commission advocated limiting such benefits to economic efficiencies, Member States and competition enforcers may develop their national approaches. Figure 3.12 illustrates

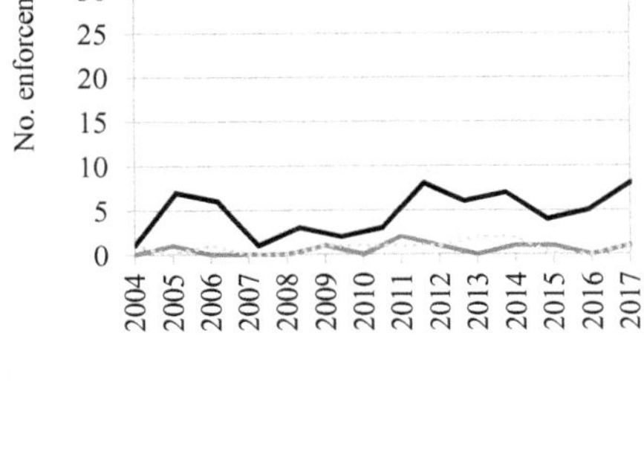

FIGURE 3.11 (cont.)

[255] See Section 3.6.3.

[256] Some of the findings presented in this section with respect to the relevant types of benefits were also examined in Brook (2019, 141–148).

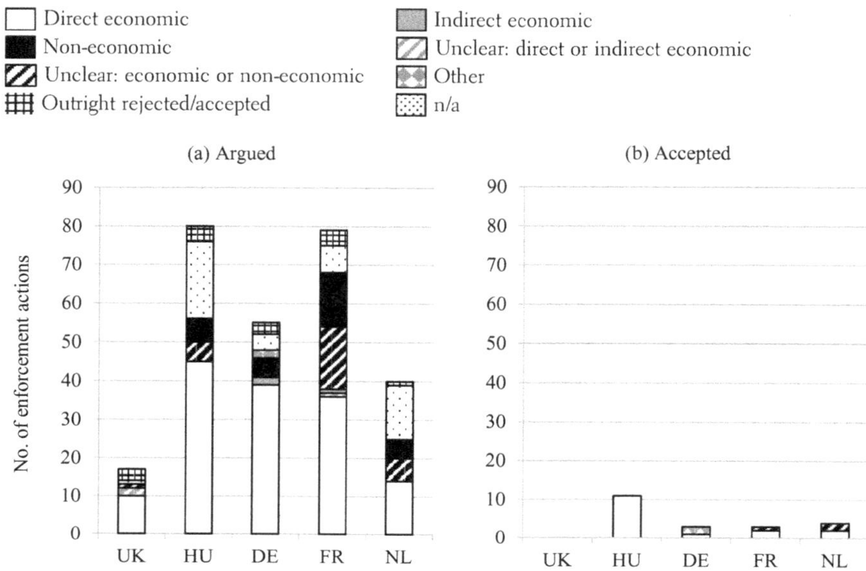

FIGURE 3.12 Article 101(3) TFEU, categories of benefits, NCAs[257]
All Article 101 TFEU enforcement actions in which the NCAs examined an Article 101(3) TFEU exemption. In some proceedings, more than one benefit was examined as a justification

that the NCAs have indeed followed different approaches in this regard. To this end, it summarises the categories of benefits invoked by the undertakings and accepted by the NCAs as justification for an Article 101(3) TFEU exception.

The figure shows that the NCAs' approaches to the relevant types of benefits can be roughly divided into three groups: NCAs that have restricted Article 101(3) TFEU to economic benefits (UK and Hungary); those that have also taken non-economic benefits into account (the Netherlands and France); and those that have not based their decision on the classification of benefits and gave deference to the legal source of the restriction of competition (Germany).

The following sub-sections demonstrate that the NCA's approaches to the relevant types of benefits also match their view on the applicable balancing method.[258] The NCAs that followed a short-term narrow consumer welfare standard to guide balancing have restricted Article 101(3) TFEU to economic benefits. Those which

[257] Figure 3.12 was originally published in Brook (2019). Reproduced with permission of the Licensor through PLSclear.

[258] The various consumer welfare standards and the national approaches were presented in Sections 1.2.1.3 and 2.6.

followed a long-term broad consumer welfare standard have also accepted non-economic benefits, and those which did not base their analysis on the classification of benefits have rejected a consumer welfare standard altogether.

3.6.2.1 Economic Benefits and Short-Term Narrow Consumer Welfare (UK and Hungary)

The first group of NCAs followed a short-term narrow consumer welfare standard and limited the scope of Article 101(3) TFEU to economic benefits, similar to the position advocated by the Commission's subsequent modernisation.

The UK NCA provides a prominent example. The UK NCA declared that it does not consider non-competition interests beyond narrow consumer welfare when applying Article 101(3) TFEU. It only takes quality efficiencies and those detailed in the Commission Article 101(3) Guidelines (2004) into account.[259] The standard set in the Commission's Guidelines was also explicitly used in purely national cases, where only the national equivalent provision was applied.[260]

Even when the UK NCA examined an agreement that might have an impact on non-economic benefits, it has focused on narrow efficiencies. In its informal opinion on *Rural broadband wayleave rates (2012)*, for example, it assessed the rate recommendations proposed to their members by the National Farmers' Union and the Country Land and Business Association for the grant of wayleaves for broadband in rural areas. The analysis centred exclusively on quality and cost-saving efficiencies and did not examine the potential social benefits emanating from improving the service in rural areas.[261] Similarly, in *Modelling Sector (2016)*, the UK NCA examined collusion between model agencies and their trade association involving modelling service pricing.[262] The NCA rejected outright the claim that price fixing was justified due to its effect on improving the working conditions of models. While it acknowledged that trade associations could increase the efficiency of markets, e.g.

[259] CE/2596-03 Tobacco (2010), para 7.58. The decision was quashed by the CAT in 1160/1/1/10 1161/1/1/10 1162/1/1/10 1163/1/1/10 1164/1/1/10 1165/1/1/10 Tobacco (2011); Rural broadband wayleave rates (2012), para 8.12. The role of narrow consumer welfare in the enforcement of Article 101 TFEU and the national equivalent exception was confirmed by UK NCA officials (in their private capacities) as well as by academics. See Townley (2010, 311) and the references there. Remarkably, in CA98/05/05 MasterCard (2005), the NCA cryptically stated in footnote 464 that 'maximizing "social welfare" (according to some economic yardstick) is not necessarily the same as satisfying the exception conditions in Article [101(3)] or section 9 of the CA98'. This remark did not seem to have an impact on future proceedings.

[260] OFT Understanding Competition Law Guidelines (2004), para 5.5; CE/9856-14 Refrigeration (2016), para A.90; CE/9857-14 Bathroom fittings (2016), para A.88; Online sale of posters and frames (2016), para 5.82; 50235 Residential estate agency services (2017), para 5.68; 50283 Cleanroom laundry services (2017), para 5.176; 50343 Light fittings (2017), para 4.180.

[261] Rural broadband wayleave rates (2012), para 8.12, 8.16–8.17. In comparison, the Dutch NCA examined social benefits in a similar case 14.1134.15 ATMs in rural areas (2014).

[262] CE/9859-14 Modelling (2016), para 4.173.

by clearly expressing standard terms and conditions that are transparent to customers, such benefits could only be taken into account if they affected consumers, such as by reducing the consumer price.

Remarkably, the types of benefits that the UK NCA considered under Article 101 (3) TFEU were even narrower than those recognised by the Commission. In *MasterCard (2005)*, the UK NCA reviewed a MIF case, which resembled the Commission's *Visa (2002)* decision.[263] The UK NCA had rejected an Article 101 (3) TFEU exception, contrary to the Commission's decision. It explained that the Commission had exempted the agreement *inter-alia* on the basis of market integration considerations, which are not considered by the NCA when applying Article 101(3) TFEU and the national equivalent provision.[264]

The Hungarian NCA has stated in its policy papers that it follows a long-term broad consumer welfare standard.[265] However, its decisional practice reveals that the Hungarian NCA has actually interpreted the Article in line with the Commission's short-term narrow consumer welfare standard. The Hungarian NCA and courts have held that Article 101(3) TFEU does not cover non-economic benefits – such as employment, price stability, diversity of literature, promotion of research and education, the fight against unlicensed software, and freedom of the press.[266]

3.6.2.2 Non-Economic Benefits and Long-Term Broad Consumer Welfare (the Netherlands and France)

The second group of NCAs opted for a long-term broad consumer welfare standard for applying Article 101(3) TFEU balancing and took into account also non-economic benefits. Long-term broad consumer welfare is based on dynamic efficiency, namely, the increase of welfare over time in light of the incentive to innovate and renew processes and products. Unlike short-term narrow consumer welfare, it also takes non-economic benefits into account. It includes both benefits to the

[263] The Visa (2002) decision was described in Section 3.4.3.3.

[264] CA98/05/05 MasterCard (2005), para 104–106. The appeals tribunal set the decision aside in 1054/1/1/05 1055/1/1/05 1056/1/1/05 MasterCard (2006) after it became apparent that the NCA's defence in appeal was substantially different from the analysis in its decision.

[265] GVH, Fundamental Principles of Competition Policy (2007), 7–8, 18; GVH's Website: The Responsibilities of the Authority (available here: www.gvh.hu/en/gvh/responsibilities_of_the_gvh/2349_en_the_responsibilities_of_the_authority). Although the NCA refers to the notion of long-term consumer welfare, it has overtly decided not to adopt an exact definition of its standard. Instead, it has affirmed that that notion provides general, underlying, conceptual guidance rather than a technical test for enforcement in practice, see ICN Competition Enforcement and Consumer Welfare (2011), 19.

[266] Vj-47/2004 Hungarian Association of Book Publishers and Book Retailers (2004), para 103, 109, 111, as upheld by the Court in 2.Kf.27.280/2008/7 Hungarian Association of Book Publishers and Book Retailers (2009), 10–12; Vj-96/2009-178 Book market (2013), para 321–332; Vj-26/2006 Navigation tools (2007), para 295; 2.Kf.27.672/2008/7 Newspaper distribution I (2009), 18–19.

specific consumer and society as a whole and benefits to current and future generations.[267]

The Dutch NCA has declared that it follows such a standard.[268] Its approach to sustainability agreements demonstrates the implications of this policy choice.

The possibility of taking into account sustainability concerns under Article 101(3) TFEU was confirmed by the Dutch NCA in its informal opinion in *MSC Shrimp Fishery (2011)*. This case involved a control system put in place by national producers and the fishing association to limit the overfishing of Brown-shrimp. The NCA stated that the system may be justified under Article 101(3) TFEU insofar as it is indispensable for meeting sustainability concerns identified by scientific studies. Nevertheless, the NCA held that at the time of the assessment, studies have revealed that the Brown-shrimp population was not in danger. Hence, it concluded that the proposed system would go beyond what was necessary and could not be justified.[269]

These findings have instigated a heated political discussion. Later that year, the Minister of Agriculture submitted a letter to the Dutch House of Representatives demanding the consideration of animal welfare and environmental interests in NCA proceedings related to agreements in the agricultural and nutrition sectors.[270] In early 2013, the House of Representatives requested the Minister of Economic Affairs to instruct the NCA, by means of a policy rule, on how to assess such agreements.[271] Following those requests, in May 2014 the NCA adopted its Vision Document on Competition and Sustainability.[272] Interpreting both Dutch and EU competition law, this policy paper maintains that sustainability considerations can play an important role in the enforcement of Article 101 TFEU. In July 2020, the NCA published Draft Guidelines on Sustainability Agreements, which are expected to replace the Vision Document.[273]

[267] ICN Competition Enforcement and Consumer Welfare (2011), 31–33; Vision Document on Competition and Sustainability (2014), para 2.6; and Claassen and Gerbrandy (2016, 3).

[268] *Ibid*; Guidelines on Price Arrangements between Self-employed Workers (2019), para 53–55. See also Claassen and Gerbrandy (2016, 3). As demonstrated by Figure 3.11, the Dutch NCA expressed a positive view on granting exceptions only in informal proceedings.

[269] 7011/23.827 MSC Shrimp Fishery (2011).

[270] Letter from Henk Bleker (Minister of Agriculture) to the House of Representatives re sustainability initiatives and competition law (22.11.2011).

[271] Dijkgraaf/Geurts motion of 24 January 2013, Parliamentary Documents II, 2012/2013, 33 400 XIII, nr. 99. According to Article 5 of the Dutch Competition Act, the Minister of Economic Affairs can lay down policy rules, in particular, to instruct the NCA on how to take other than economic interests into account in its assessment of competition restrictive agreements.

[272] Vision Document on Competition and Sustainability (2014). The Vision Document also served as the basis for a shorter policy rule issued by the Minister of Economic Affairs and published the same day; see Dutch Government Gazette, Decision of the Minister of Economic Affairs of May 6, 2014, No. WJZ/14052830, Containing the Policy Rule Regarding the Application by the Netherlands Authority for Consumers and Markets of Section 6, Paragraph 3 of the Dutch Competition Act in Anticompetitive Arrangements that have been made for the Purpose of Sustainability (8 May 2014).

[273] Draft Guidelines on Sustainability Agreements (2020).

The Dutch Vision Document and Draft Guidelines pursue a long-term broad consumer welfare approach by interpreting the four conditions of Article 101(3) TFEU broadly. The benefit condition of Article 101(3) TFEU, in the NCA's interpretation, entails that an agreement must have a positive welfare effect through the realisation of efficiencies. Despite the use of the term 'efficiencies', which was employed by the Commission following modernisation to limit exceptions to economic benefits,[274] the Dutch NCA assesses the subjective value consumers attach to certain product features (e.g. as a result of environmentally friendly or animal-friendly production means) as well as benefits resulting from the efficient use of scarce natural resources for the benefit of future consumers.[275] Hence, it is willing to take into account indirect economic and non-economic benefits.

The Draft Guidelines pave the way for an even greater role for non-economic benefits, by abolishing the need to quantify the benefits in certain circumstances: First, when the benefits cannot be easily quantified, for example, in the case of non-economic benefits, undertakings will merely need to identify the nature of the benefits and the likelihood of realising them.[276] Second, if the undertakings involved have a combined market share of no more than 30%, they will only need to demonstrate that the initiative is specifically aimed at certain sustainability objectives and real benefits can be reasonably expected. According to the Draft Guidelines, in those circumstances it can be assumed that the initiative will create benefits for buyers or suppliers and that consumers will receive a fair share.[277] Third, there is no need to quantify the benefits when 'at first glance' it is sufficiently clear that the sustainability benefits offset the competitive harm.[278]

The Draft Guidelines also take into account benefits to society as a whole by including the difference between operational and social costs. The NCA declared that it would examine the actual costs of externalities, for example, by paying living wages and compensating for greenhouse gas emissions.[279]

Along similar lines, according to the Dutch NCA, the fair share condition of Article 101(3) TFEU is fulfilled if the consumers that have suffered anti-competitive harm would be no worse off as a result of the agreement. There is no obligation to demonstrate that consumers actually benefit from an agreement. This interpretation opens the door to accept an agreement that benefits society as a whole rather than produces benefits for specific consumers. In addition, the Dutch NCA has declared

[274] See Section 3.3.4.
[275] Vision Document on Competition and Sustainability (2014), 11, 13.
[276] Draft Guidelines on Sustainability Agreements (2020), para 32–33.
[277] *Ibid*, para 47. The Commission followed a similar approach prior to modernisation, as elaborated in Section 3.3.3.3.
[278] *Ibid*, para 48.
[279] *Ibid*, para 35.

its willingness to offset disadvantages to current consumers with long-term benefits to future consumers.[280]

The Draft Guidelines advocate broadening the second condition even further, by calling to consider benefits for society as a whole when an agreement aims to prevent or limit 'obvious environmental damage' and helps to comply with an international or national environmental standard to which the Dutch government is bound.[281]

The Dutch NCA has also adhered to a broad reading of the last two conditions of Article 101(3) TFEU, noting that they were not applied strictly in practice. The Vision Document explains that the indispensability condition does not mean that there is no less harmful measure available to achieve the sustainability aim. Rather, a 'reasonably necessary' test applies, which considers only realistic and feasible, less far-reaching alternatives that could potentially bring about *significantly* greater efficiencies.[282] Similarly, since the fourth condition is assessed in connection with the three other subtests, significant sustainability benefits are able to compensate for the substantial anti-competitive restrictions of an agreement.

Although the Vision Document and Draft Guidelines are lengthy and detailed, they do not propose a clear balancing method. They maintain that sustainability considerations are relevant but do not explain *how* they should be weighed against competition interests. Indeed, the empirical findings show that the Dutch NCA has used significantly different balancing methods when applying Article 101(3) TFEU to sustainability agreements in specific cases.

First, *Coal power plants (2013)* involved an agreement between energy producers, distributors, the government, and advisory bodies aimed at achieving more sustainable energy production in the Netherlands. As part of the agreement, the parties had planned to accelerate the closing down of five coal-fired power plants. Referring to (the then draft version of) the Vision Document, the Dutch NCA noted that non-economic benefits such as a reduction in emissions and more sustainable energy production could be taken into account under Article 101(3) TFEU.[283] While the Dutch NCA agreed that closing down the plants would lead to emission reductions, it determined that the agreement did not produce environmental benefits. It explained that the EU emissions trading system would have allowed other parties to use the CO_2 emissions that had been saved by shutting down the plants. The CO_2 emission reduction would thus be cancelled out by an increase in emissions elsewhere.[284] Next, the Dutch NCA used *shadow prices* to assess benefits resulting

280 Vision Document on Competition and Sustainability (2014), 14–16; Draft Guidelines on Sustainability Agreements (2020), para 29–30, 36.

281 Draft Guidelines on Sustainability Agreements (2020), para 38, 40–41.

282 Vision Document on Competition and Sustainability (2014), 17. See also Draft Guidelines on Sustainability Agreements (2020), para 56.

283 Coal power plants (2013), 3–4.

284 *Ibid*, 4.

from reducing other types of emissions. It examined the benefits created for the Dutch society as a whole by calculating the estimated reduction in costs as a result of the agreement. Since the estimated increase in price was higher than the expected avoided costs, the Dutch NCA declared that the first two conditions of Article 101(3) TFEU had not been met.[285]

Second, in *De Stroomversnelling (2013)*, the Dutch NCA examined a proposed joint venture between construction companies and public-housing corporations to renovate and turn houses into energy-neutral buildings. The undertakings had planned to use the energy costs paid by lessees to finance the required renovations. In the first phase, the construction companies would experiment with 1,000 homes using different technologies and construction methods. In the next two phases, 110,000 homes would be made energy-neutral. Unlike *Coal power plants*, the Dutch NCA did not calculate the possible environmental or monetary benefits of the project. Instead, it assumed that the exchange of knowledge and experience would make the construction industry more sustainable. However, the Dutch NCA had doubts as to whether the restriction of competition was limited to what was necessary. It noted that certainly after the first phase, other construction companies should be able to compete for contracts from these public-housing corporations as well.[286]

Third, in the much-debated *Chicken of tomorrow (2015)*, the Dutch NCA used a third method to balance sustainability benefits under Article 101(3) TFEU. In this informal opinion, it reviewed an agreement between provincial governments, farmers, animal-fodder producers, veterinarians, and supermarkets aimed at replacing regularly produced broiler chickens with a more sustainable product. The agreement had established a minimum standard for improving the living conditions of chickens and required the use of fewer antibiotics. The Dutch NCA used the *willingness-to-pay* test to apply Article 101(3) TFEU. It explained that animal welfare, environmental, and public health benefits could only be taken into account if consumers attached actual value to them. Based on a consumer survey, it held that consumers were willing to pay only a small amount for achieving those benefits, which could not compensate for the expected increase in price.[287]

The willingness-to-pay test differs from other methods used by the Commission and other NCAs to account for non-competition interests under Article 101(3) TFEU. It quantifies non-economic benefits that cannot be measured using

[285] *Ibid*, 4–6.

[286] ACM/DM/2013/205913 De Stroomversnelling (2013), 2.

[287] ACM/DM/2014/206028 Chicken for tomorrow (2015), 5–6. The consumers were willing to pay an additional 68 eurocents per kilo of chicken filet for the promotion of animal welfare, 15 eurocents for the environmental benefits, and 0 eurocents for the public health considerations. The total benefit of the agreements was 82 eurocents per kilo, while the increase in price was estimated to be EUR 1.46 euro per kilo. Thus, the NCA concluded that the agreement generated no net benefits for consumers. The application of the willingness-to-pay test in this case was further evaluated in the Dutch NCA's Memo on Welfare of Today's Chicken and that of the Chicken of Tomorrow (2020).

traditional economic tools. Rather than focus on the objective benefits arising from an agreement (e.g. the reduction in emissions in *Coal power plants*), it measures the subjective value consumers attach to such benefits. Moreover, while in *Coal power plants* the Dutch NCA had examined the environmental benefits to the entire population, in *Chicken of tomorrow* it only included benefits for chicken consumers (and not, for example, for vegetarians).[288]

Although the Dutch NCA found that on balance the sustainability benefits could not justify the harm to competition in the above proceedings, such benefits played an important role in the analysis. Moreover, there are various indications suggesting that since the rendering of those decisions, sustainability benefits have played a bigger role in the application of Article 101 TFEU in the Netherlands.

In particular, the Dutch executive was unsatisfied with the outcomes of the above proceedings. In July 2015, the Minister of Economic Affairs sent a letter to the House of Representatives declaring his intention to amend the policy rule to demand broader consideration of sustainability issues.[289] A draft policy rule from December 2015 suggested that the NCA was required to take benefits to society as a whole outside the relevant market into account and to assess a package of agreements in its totality (e.g. in the *Coal power plants* scenario).[290] Yet, the Minister withdrew his original proposal a year later after encountering opposition from the Commission[291] and the Dutch NCA,[292] which both raised questions on the compatibility of the proposed regime with EU competition law.[293]

Instead, the Minister adopted three alternative measures. First, in September 2016, he published an amended policy rule.[294] The new rule provided that the

[288] For a critique of the willingness-to-pay test as discriminating against the poor, see Hovenkamp (1982,10–11).

[289] Letter from Mr Kamp, the Dutch Minister of Economic Affairs, Agricultural Affairs and Innovation to the House of Representatives re sustainability initiatives and competition law (July 15, 2015).

[290] Consultatieverslag beleidsregel Mededinging en Duurzaamheid. Available at: www.internetconsultatie.nl/mededingingenduurzaamheid/document/2534.

[291] Letter from DG COMP to the Dutch Minister of Economic Affairs (26.02.2016). Available at: www.rijksoverheid.nl/documenten/brieven/2016/02/26/brief-eu-over-mededinging-enduurz aamheid. DG COMP noted with respect to this proposal that 'EU Competition law, however, allows us to take into account sustainability concerns when and to the extent that these also are perceived as benefits in the eyes of the actual consumer in the relevant market (as compared to society as a whole)'. It also explained that 'while in certain circumstances it may be necessary to assess the package agreement in its entirety, it can certainly not be the rule'.

[292] Letter from the ACM to the Dutch Minister of Economic Affairs (18.02.2016). Available at: www.rijksoverheid.nl/binaries/rijksoverheid/documenten/brieven/2016/02/18/briefacm/briefacm.pdf.

[293] Letter from Mr Kamp, the Dutch Minister of Economic Affairs, Agricultural Affairs and Innovation to the House of Representatives re sustainability initiatives and competition law (June 23, 2016).

[294] Dutch Government Gazette, Decision of the Minister of Economic Affairs of September 30, 2016, No. WJZ/16145098, Containing the Policy Rule Regarding the Application by the Netherlands Authority for Consumers and Markets of Section 6, Paragraph 3 of the Dutch

Dutch NCA had to take benefits occurring in the long-term as well as benefits to society as a whole into account. Second, the Minister declared that he would submit a new legislative proposal to facilitate sustainability initiatives that would exclude the applicability of competition rules. Third, the Minister would engage in talks with the Commission, advocating for more room for sustainability initiatives.

In December 2016, the Dutch NCA published 'basic principles for oversight of sustainability agreements', which could potentially mark a change in approach. The document states that the NCA 'will not take action against sustainability arrangements that enjoy broad social support if all parties involved such as the government, citizen representatives, and businesses are positive about the arrangements'.[295] Consequently, agreements such as those in *Coal power plants* and *Chicken of tomorrow*, which enjoyed the social support and involvement of interest groups, would no longer be enforced even when they failed to fulfil the four conditions of Article 101(3) TFEU.

In practice, this policy rule has a similar impact to 'no grounds for action' findings. In both cases, the NCA will not enforce Article 101 TFEU, given the environmental impact of an agreement. This shift from explicit-substantive to implicit-procedural balancing could endanger the effectiveness of EU competition law and will be discussed in Chapter 7.

The debate over the role of sustainability benefits under Article 101(3) TFEU is still ongoing in the Netherlands. It was revived by a ruling of the Supreme Court of the Netherlands in late 2019, declaring that the State is obliged to ensure that greenhouse gas emissions will have been reduced by 25% by late-2020 compared with 1990.[296] This was one of the motives leading the NCA to publish its Draft Guidelines on Sustainability Agreements, which reserve a greater room for non-economic sustainability benefits and are excepted to replace the Vision Document.[297]

The willingness to take into account non-economic benefits in the Netherlands is not limited to sustainability concerns. The Vision Document deliberately left the term undefined, noting that 'sustainability' could include a wide range of policies, including environmental protection, public health, fair trade production, and animal welfare. Moreover, it emphasises that sustainability considerations do *not*

Competition Act in Anticompetitive Arrangements that have been made for the Purpose of Sustainability (3 September 2016).

[295] ACM, Basic Principles for Oversight of Sustainability Agreements (2016).

[296] 19/00135 State of the Netherlands v. Urgenda Foundation (2019). The Chairman of the Dutch NCA, Martijn Snoep, had declared that the NCA has interpreted the decision as applicable for the purpose of competition law enforcement. See Snoep (2020b).

[297] Draft Guidelines on Sustainability Agreements (2020). See also the Dutch NCA's Memo on Welfare of Today's Chicken and that of the Chicken of Tomorrow (2020).

form a special category. Namely, other non-competition interests ought to be evaluated using the same analytical framework and balancing tools.[298]

In fact, a similarly broad approach to the consideration of non-economic benefits is reflected in the Dutch NCA's Guidelines on Price Arrangements between Self-employed Workers (2019). By reference to the CJEU's ruling in *Metro I (1977)*, those Guidelines declare that '[s]afeguarding the *social protection* of employees and self-employed workers [...] can be *considered a benefit*'.[299] The Guidelines aim to permit self-employed workers to negotiate collectively with their clients and agree on minimum rates and to allow trade organisations to issue recommended rates for self-employed workers. The Guidelines apply exclusively to Dutch competition law. Yet, since they are based on EU law and the EU Courts' case law, they seem to also inform the Dutch NCA's approach in mixed cases.

The Guidelines declare that in order to comply with the national equivalent to Article 101(3) TFEU, such arrangements must (i) safeguard an 'objectively justified level of social protection'. This can be embodied by avoiding a race to the bottom as a result of working below the minimum income level, social dumping, and straining the national social security system;[300] (ii) be reasonably necessary for achieving the objective;[301] (iii) provide current and future direct and indirect buyers a fair sure of such benefits. The fair share can be realised in the form of quality improvements, by preventing self-employed workers from getting dragged into a race to the bottom in terms of price, with the risk that, in the long run, the quality of the services performed will decline. It can also be realised if the buyers subjectively perceive the value of social protection as a quality improvement (the willingness-to-pay test);[302] and (iv) leave a sufficient room for competition between the self-employed workers, for example, on non-price parameters or from self-employed workers that are not part of the price arrangement.[303]

As in the Netherlands, the French NCA also asserted in its policy papers that it adheres to a long-term broad consumer welfare standard.[304] The empirical findings affirm that the long-term broad consumer welfare standard was evident in French practice at least until around 2010. In *UFOP (2007)*, for example, it found that the conditions for an exception were met with respect to a pricing method set by a trade association. The NCA highlighted the benefits arising from the pricing system not only for patients but also for the national social security system as a whole.[305] Similarly, in its informal opinion in *Cinema code (2009)*, it declared that the

[298] Vision Document on Competition and Sustainability (2014), 6.

[299] Emphasis added. Guidelines on Price Arrangements between Self-employed Workers (2019), para 55. These Guidelines are further discussed in Sections 5.2.5.2, 5.4.1.2, 6.3.1, and 7.6.1.1.

[300] Guidelines on Price Arrangements between Self-employed Workers (2019), para 56, 58–59.

[301] *Ibid*, para 62–65.

[302] *Ibid*, para 68–69.

[303] *Ibid*, para 70.

[304] ICN Competition Enforcement and Consumer Welfare (2011), 10, 28, 32.

[305] 07-D-05 UFOP (2007), para 64–65.

assurance of a wider diffusion of cinematographic works in the general interest could be considered as economic progress in the meaning of Article 101(3) TFEU.[306] Section 3.6.4 further shows that the consideration of non-economic benefits in France was also informed by the wording of the French exception equivalent to Article 101(3) TFEU, which applies to agreements aimed at creating or maintaining jobs and agreements governing agriculture products.

This approach guided the three cases in which the French NCA found that the four conditions of Article 101(3) TFEU applied.[307] One of them, *Exchanges Check-Image Fee (2010)*, is particularly noteworthy. While it had a similar factual basis as the Commission's and UK's MIF, it resulted in a different outcome.[308] The French NCA prohibited collusion between French banks for setting check exchange fees. At the same time, it held that fixing six other related services fees was justified. Using a long-term broad consumer welfare standard, the French NCA explained that such fees reflected a proper return for the new services that compensated the relevant costs. Moreover, unlike the Commission and UK decisions, the French NCA did not rely on economic evidence for granting an exception.[309] This is a prominent example of how the different consumer welfare standard affects the outcome of balancing.

The limits of the French approach to Article 101(3) TFEU balancing were examined in *Fair Trade (2006)*, where the French Minister of the Economy asked the NCA to examine the operating conditions of a fair trade trademark system. The system set higher prices for fair trade products, aimed to improve the living conditions of producers and the means of production in developing countries. The NCA held that such price setting might be justified given its positive effects on both the environment and on social conditions in developing countries.

The assessment of both types of benefits has reflected the NCA's willingness to take into account broad non-economic benefits for consumers and for society as a whole. The NCA found little difficulty in concluding that environmental benefits, which are protected by EU and national policy papers, can be taken into account.[310] The assessment of the social benefits has posed greater difficulties. The NCA admitted that improving social conditions in developing countries was a benefit that fell outside the regular scope of Article 101(3) TFEU. It could not be considered

[306] 09-A-50 Cinema code (2009), para 94.

[307] 05-A-23 Electricity purchases by intensive industrial users (2005); 07-D-05 UFOP (2007); 10-D-28 Exchanges Check-Image Fee (2010).

[308] See Sections 3.4.4.1 and 3.6.2.1.

[309] 10-D-28 Exchanges Check-Image Fee (2010), para 390–395, 532–599. The NCA decision was repealed by the Paris Court of Appeal in 2010/20555 Exchanges Check-Image Fee (2012) and cancelled by the Court de Cassation in 12/15971 Exchanges Check-Image Fee (2015) due to procedural issues. In its answer to the questionnaire of the ICN Competition Enforcement and Consumer Welfare (2011), 32, The NCA referred to the case as an example of its unique approach to Article 101(3) TFEU based on long-term consumer welfare.

[310] 06-A-07 Fair trade (2006), para 105.

to constitute economic progress in the meaning of the first condition of the Article. Rather, other instruments such as taxation, social legislation, and public services were better suited to help achieve such aims.[311] The NCA also acknowledged that it was unclear whether benefits to farmers from non-EU countries ('extraterritorial benefits') could be taken into account.[312] Yet, it decided to leave this question open, noting that such benefits could, in any case, be included insofar as they produced effects in EU markets. By interpreting the first benefit condition of Article 101(3) TFEU broadly, the NCA had invoked indirect economic and non-economic benefits such as the establishment of a reference price system, the creation of employment opportunities, and a boost to the competitiveness of EU markets.[313]

The application of the second fair share condition also demanded a flexible interpretation of Article 101(3) TFEU. The French NCA noted that the fair trade system was likely to increase the price of fair trade products.[314] However, the fair share could be realised by means of the improved quality of the product.[315] Alternatively, the fair trade products could be perceived as introducing a new 'service' of solidarity. This assures consumers that the premium paid for the fair trade product is used for the benefit of the third-country workers and population (e.g. improved wages, education, health, or technology) and is not pocketed by EU producers.[316] At first sight, this argument resembles the CJEU's Article 101(1) TFEU case law declaring that agreements operating on solidarity principles are not prohibited by the Article.[317] However, unlike the Article 101(1) TFEU case law, *Fair trade* examined an agreement between economic operators having a commercial purpose. The French NCA's argument thus shifts the classification of solidarity – from a social interest to a commodity.

Gradually, the French NCA's policy papers moved closer to the narrow short-term standard advocated by the Commission. This substantive change had taken place in parallel to the procedural and institutional reform of French competition law.[318] The first seed of this development is evident in a 2009 paper by *Lasserre*, the president of the French NCA at that time. Lasserre called for convergence in the enforcement of competition law throughout the EU and expressed a commitment to following an effects-based approach based on robust economics and strict rules.[319]

In the same vein, the NCA declared that it limited the categories of benefits that could justify an Article 101(3) TFEU exception. In the past, it had maintained that indirect economic and non-economic benefits – such as protection of jobs, living

[311] *Ibid*, para 97.
[312] *Ibid*, para 98–99.
[313] *Ibid*, para 100–104.
[314] *Ibid*, para 113.
[315] *Ibid*, para 111–112.
[316] *Ibid*, para 63, 113.
[317] See Section 5.2.4.
[318] See Section 2.6.1.1.
[319] Lasserre (2009, 16–17).

standards, fair trade rules, stabilisation of prices, increased bargaining power, culture, and protection of SMEs – were relevant under Article 101(3) TFEU.[320] Since 2009, however, the NCA has seemed to restrict the categories of benefits that could justify an exception.

In the *Digital books (2009)* informal opinion, which was rendered only two months after to *Cinema code* described above, the French NCA was hesitant to determine that a single price system for digital books could be justified by cultural interests. Departing from its previous approach, it held that culture was a general interest rather than a true economic justification.[321] Along similar lines, in 2011 the NCA asserted that in the enforcement of competition rules, the notion of consumer welfare should be confined to an economic criterion. It explained that its mandate was limited to making markets work in the best interest of consumers. Promoting other public policies and, if need be, reconciling those with consumer welfare were a task best left to Government and Parliament.[322]

Nevertheless, the empirical findings reveal that the French NCA has continued to examine non-economic benefits such as public health, environmental considerations, and the development of rural areas under Article 101(3) TFEU.[323] While it refused to accept an Article 101(3) TFEU defence by demanding a high threshold of economic evidence or applying the indispensability condition strictly, it did not hold that non-economic benefits – as such – could not justify an exception.[324]

The Dutch and French interpretations of Article 101(3) TFEU are incompatible with the approach of the first group of competition enforcers. In a departure from the Commission's new approach, they were willing to incorporate broad non-economic benefits under the Article, taking into account short- and long-term benefits to the specific consumer and society as a whole. While, admittedly, those NCAs have accepted Article 101(3) TFEU defences in a handful of cases (see Figure 3.11), their interpretations have clearly deviated from the first group of competition enforcers.

3.6.2.3 Rejecting the Consumer Welfare Standard (Germany)

The third group of NCAs has altogether rejected the use of a consumer welfare standard to guide Article 101(3) TFEU balancing. The German NCA, for instance, has done so openly. In 2008, a year before the CJEU questioned such a standard in *GlaxoSmithKline (2009)*,[325] the president of the German NCA opted for a similar

[320] See Annex A, Section 3.21.
[321] 09-A-56 Digital books (2009), para 128.
[322] ICN Competition Enforcement and Consumer Welfare (2011), 25. See also de Silva (2019, 3–4).
[323] See Annex A, Section 3.21.
[324] See Section 3.6.3.2.
[325] See Section 3.5.3.2.

approach. He explained that German competition law focuses primarily on the protection of the competitive process and not on consumer interests. In his opinion, the consumer welfare standard is not only contrary to the German approach but also conflicts with the 'well-established approach of European jurisprudence'.[326] He maintained that a consumer welfare standard did not provide a theoretical toolkit for the purpose of applying competition law but was rather 'an endeavor fraught with numerous uncertainties'.[327]

Later, the German NCA explained that, although consumer welfare plays an important role in its work, it is not the primary goal of enforcement.[328] This policy choice influences the German interpretation of Article 101(3) TFEU balancing. The Article is seen as a mechanism for accepting restrictive agreements that have a positive impact on *competition interests*, namely, on the competitive structure and process. This was repeated in the NCA's mission statement declaring that it 'bases its decisions solely on competitive criteria [. . .] it is *undisputed that there are other important economic and socio-political goals than ensuring competition*. However, it is *not* the Bundeskartellamt's responsibility to realise these'.[329]

Accordingly, the German NCA has limited the *nature* of benefits that can be examined under the first condition of Article 101(3) TFEU. Similarly to the first group of competition enforcers, it has taken only cost and quality efficiencies into account.[330] It maintained that other benefits, such as facilitating highly risky investments, reducing costs that could indirectly improve R&D efforts, and reducing the deficit in health care providers, could not be taken into account.[331]

This was confirmed by the Düsseldorf Higher Regional Court in *Round timber in Baden-Württemberg* (2017). The Court excluded the possibility of examining sustainability benefits, holding that concerns related to the management of forests, climate, water balance, or clean air could not be taken into account under Article 101(3) TFEU.[332] This approach clearly clashes with the Dutch and French interpretations, which were described above.

326 Heitzer (2008, 3). See Section 3.4.4.1.
327 *Ibid*, 4.
328 ICN Competition Enforcement and Consumer Welfare (2011), 19.
329 Emphasis added. Available at www.bundeskartellamt.de/EN/AboutUs/Bundeskartellamt/bundeskartellamtnode.html.
330 See Annex A, Section 3.22.
331 B1–62/13 Rental of retail space in factory outlet centres (2015), para 323; B4–1006/06 Container glass (2007), para 181–186; B3–11/13 Ophthalmologists-AOK (2013), para 41–42; B3–11/13 Ophthalmologists-ÄÄGB (2013), para 61–61. The nature of the benefits relevant under Article 101(3) TFEU was discussed in Section 2.2.3.1.
332 VI-Kart 10/15 (V) Round timber in Baden-Württemberg (2017), para 327–328. Prior to this judgement, While the German NCA has largely limited the possibility of taking non-economic benefits into account under Article 101(3) TFEU, it has not utterly excluded the consideration of environmental benefits. In B4–1006/06 Container glass (2007), for instance, the NCA reviewed the establishment by German container glass manufacturers of a glass recycling company to jointly purchase all the waste glass recovered from household rubbish collection.

At the same time, similarly to the second group of enforcers, the German NCA did not restrict the relevant type of *beneficiaries*. Departing from the Commission's approach following modernisation, it assessed industrial policy considerations that were not directly related to the consumers in the markets in which the infringement had taken place. The German NCA interpreted the provision so as to cover industry-wide benefits related to security of supply, bargaining power, the functioning of online platforms, and elimination of 'white spots' of Internet access.[333]

Furthermore, the German NCA has used Article 101(3) TFEU to examine agreements that formed an *inherent part of the implementation of a national law*. In those cases, the NCA gave deference to the legal source of the restriction of competition. For example, in *Coordination of tenders for sales packaging waste collection services by compliance schemes (2011)*, the NCA found, with reference to the German Packaging Ordinance, that the conditions of Article 101(3) TFEU had been fulfilled. An amendment to the Ordinance had obliged compliance schemes for sales packaging waste to coordinate their tenders via a newly established joint body.[334] Yet, the amendment did not make any stipulations as to the form of the coordination. The NCA affirmed that, while the form of coordination chosen by the undertakings fell within Article 101(1) TFEU, it was justified by Article 101(3) TFEU as a necessary element of the scheme.[335] Notably, the NCA chose to label environmental benefits as cost savings stemming from the collaboration rather than as non-economic benefits. In comparison, when the Commission examined a similar system in *DSD (2001)*, it tied the exemption to environmental protection.[336]

In *Construction of corvettes (2017)*, the German NCA examined a complaint launched by German Naval Yards Kiel (GNYK) for their non-inclusion in a

With reference to the policy-linking clause and an environmental study, the undertakings claimed that the agreement saved natural resources, reduced energy use, and lowered emissions. The NCA admitted that the possibility of taking such benefits into account under Article 101(3) TFEU depends on the broader question of whether the Article is limited to benefits to individual consumers or can also take benefits to society as a whole into account. Yet, the NCA decided to leave this question open, noting that, in any case, less restrictive measures could have achieved the same environmental aims (see para 146, 151, 11, 187–188, 193). See also B1–72/12 Round timber in Baden-Württemberg (2015), para 450–458, 482–485; OECD Horizontal Agreements in the Environmental Context, Note by Germany (2010), para 18–19.

333 See Annex A, Section 3.23. In B4–71/10 Online banking conditions (2016), para 420–421, the German NCA left open the question of whether benefits for the security of online banking qualify as a benefit in the sense of Article 101(3) TFEU, noting that in the case at hand such restrictions were not indispensable.

334 The German Packaging Ordinance (*VerpackV*), Article 6(7).

335 B4–152/07 Coordination of tenders for sales packaging waste collection services by compliance schemes (2011), 6.

336 34493 37366 37299 37288 37287 37526 37254 37252 37250 37246 37245 37244 37243 37242 37267 DSD (2001), para 142–146. In its 2010 comments to the OECD roundtable on horizontal agreements in an environmental context, the German delegation explained that the decision proved that environmental objectives could be achieved just as well in a competitive environment. See OECD Horizontal Agreements in the Environmental Context, Note by Germany (2010), para 13.

consortium for the construction and supply of corvette class ships for the German armed forces. In May 2017, the Public Procurement Tribunal at the Bundeskartellamt accepted the claim, noting that the planned award of the tender to the consortium did not comply with public procurement provisions, as the consortium was the only undertaking that had been invited to participate in the bidding procedure.[337] The appeal on this decision, launched before Düsseldorf Higher Regional Court, was withdrawn after the parties have reached a settlement according to which GNYK will join the consortium. This settlement was reached following significant political pressure imposed by the Federal Government, urging the consortium to complete the transaction prior to the national elections of September 2017.[338]

In July 2017, the German NCA announced that it would not initiate proceedings to examine whether the inclusion of GNYK in the consortium could, in itself, violate the EU and German prohibitions of cartels. In a short press release, it stated that the arrangement 'could meet the legal requirements for an exemption from the prohibition', pointing to a 'number of special features' of the case.[339] The reasoning vindicating the fulfilment of the four conditions of Article 101(3) TFEU was not revealed on account of the confidentiality requirements in the affected defence sector.

The above examples show that, although the German NCA had not declared that Article 101 TFEU was inapplicable to situations of state involvement, it has accepted broader types of non-economic benefits, which would otherwise probably not justify an Article 101(3) TFEU exception. This approach was later enunciated by the German legislator and is elaborated in Chapter 6.[340] Notably, the Commission and most other NCAs have accepted similar agreements by applying Article 101(1) TFEU balancing tools rather than Article 101(3) TFEU.[341]

To conclude, the Five NCAs have adopted very different approaches to the types of benefits that can be examined under Article 101(3) TFEU and the balancing method guiding its application. Some have interpreted the Article broadly, similarly to the Commission's and EU Courts' approach prior to modernisation. Others have narrowed the scope of the Article to economic benefits and short-term consumer welfare, following the Commissions' new approach.

337 See press release from 18.5.2017, available at: www.bundeskartellamt.de/SharedDocs/Publikation/EN/Fressemitteilungen/18_05_2017_VK%20Korvetten.pdf?blob=publicationFile&v=2. See also German annual report (2017), 40–41.

338 German Commercial Law Firms (2017).

339 Construction of corvettes (2017).

340 Section 6.3.4 presents a German law stating that it can be presumed that Article 101(3) TFEU applies to agreements pooling activities relating to state, municipal, and private forests.

341 See Chapter 5.

3.6.3 *Intensity of Control*

In addition to variations in the methods guiding balancing and the types of relevant benefits, the NCAs have applied different levels of intensity of control when assessing the four conditions of Article 101(3) TFEU. The UK, German, and Hungarian NCAs have generally applied the conditions strictly. The Dutch NCA and, to a lesser degree, the French NCA have taken a sectoral approach in which the intensity of control has varied according to the type of agreement or sector concerned.

3.6.3.1 Strict Control (UK, Germany, and Hungary)

The empirical findings reveal a strict application of the four conditions of the Article by the UK, German, and Hungarian NCAs.

Similarly to the Commission's practice following modernisation, the UK NCA has mostly rejected outright the possibility of an exception. In most of the cases, it noted that the undertakings had not invoked Article 101(3) TFEU or had done so in an undetailed manner.[342] In the remaining proceedings, however, the NCA provided an exhaustive analysis of Article 101(3) TFEU. It rejected all claims for exceptions, highlighting that they should be based on robust evidence proving appreciable and objective economic benefits.[343] Like the Commission's approach following modernisation, the UK NCA has inverted the examination of the second and third conditions and taken only benefits resulting from indispensable restrictions into account.[344]

The Hungarian NCA has adopted a similar approach. This, however, was not always the case. Until 2005, the NCA accepted almost all claims invoking an Article 101(3) TFEU defence as long as the agreements had not set prices directly. Those exceptions were mostly justified with reference to the agreements' contribution to rationalising national markets. They merited a flexible interpretation of the conditions of Article 101(3) TFEU, which was not based on quantification of the alleged benefits.[345]

Yet, since 2006, the Hungarian NCA has adopted a stricter approach, leading it to deny exceptions in most cases.[346] This strict approach was especially prominent because the NCA chose to enforce agreements in sectors that were prone to

[342] See Annex A, Section 3.24.

[343] CE/2596-03 Tobacco (2010), para 7.73; CE/9784-13 Ophthalmology sector (2015), para 4.139; CE/9320-10 Hotel online booking (2014), para 6.55; CE/9578-12 Mobility scooters (2014), para 3.237; CE/9531-11 Paroxetine (2016), para 13.65; CE/9859-14 Modelling (2016), para 4.172.

[344] 50283 Cleanroom laundry services (2017), para 5.177. The Commission's approach is detailed in Section 3.4.4.1.

[345] Most of those agreements were notified to the NCA under the old national notification regime. See Annex A, Section 3.25.

[346] See Annex A, Section 3.26.

balancing, such as regulated professions, liberalised markets,[347] and, especially, financial services.[348] Moreover, the NCA has refused claims for an Article 101(3) TFEU defence even when national law protected the relevant non-competition interest. In *Online distribution of contact lenses (2015)*, for instance, the NCA declared that a rebate system for contact lenses that discriminated against online distributors could not be justified for public health reasons. It held that a national regulation requiring all distributors to have a physical shop did not change this analysis since it was not the duty of manufacturers to ensure distributor compliance with relevant sector-specific regulations.[349]

At the same time, the Hungarian NCA adopted a more lenient standard to review agreements that could 'almost' benefit from a provision of a BER or the Commission's guidelines. In *British American Tobacco group (2006)*, for instance, the NCA examined an exclusive distribution agreement between undertakings having a higher market share than the one prescribed by the Vertical BER. The NCA nevertheless granted an exception for the agreement without engaging in a full analysis of Article 101(3) TFEU. It explained that since the BER was denied due only to the high market share, it was sufficient to examine the fulfilment of the fourth elimination of competition condition.[350] The only other two exceptions granted by the NCA following 2006 involved similar circumstances.[351] The NCA relied on the

347 In most of those proceedings, the NCA accepted commitments to rectify the infringement (see Section 7.6.2.3); in those involving price fixing, fines were also imposed. See Annex A, Section 3.27.

348 Vj-74/2011 Mortgage loans (2013), as upheld by the court of first instance in 5.K.33.278/2014/99 Mortgage loans (2015) and court of the second instance in 2.Kf.653.032/2015/28 Mortgage loans (2016); Vj-78/2013 MasterCard and OTP (2015); Vj-18/2008 Uniform interchange fee levels (2009), 201–219. However, the NCA accepted an Article 101(3) TFEU defence in an early case. It exempted the restrictive license agreement in Vj-132/2004/26 Card issuance (2004), para 6, 13–15, due to the benefits of introducing new service with high quality. See also Horváth and Tóth (2016).

349 Vj-55/2013 Online distribution of contact lenses (2015), para 211–214. This conclusion was perhaps reinforced by the CJEU's decision in C-108/09 Online distribution of contact lenses (2010), holding that the national regulation was incompatible with EU free movement rules.

350 Vj-94/2005 British American Tobacco group (BAT) (2006), para 32–36.

351 Vj-191/2006/10 Euronics (2007) and Vj-7/2008/178 Motor oils and lubricants (2009). In *Motor oils and lubricants*, para 26, 29, 61–66, the NCA accepted an Article 101(3) TFEU defence with respect to clauses in distribution agreements including non-compete clauses and RPM. The NCA held that the conditions of the provisions were not met with respect to the RPM and non-compete clauses exceeding five years in length, holding that the alleged benefits – relating to the elimination of free riding, high quality of service that could reduce pollution and promote the safety of cars – were not proven. Yet, the NCA accepted non-compete clauses of up to five years. It did not analyse the conditions of Article 101(3) TFEU but briefly noted that such clauses could automatically benefit from the BER. In *Euronics*, para 20–2, 42–461, the NCA accepted an Article 101(3) TFEU defence with respect to the creation of a joint venture by three commercial and service providers for joining the international supermarket chain Euronics and building up Euronic's Hungarian network. This case came close to being excluded from the application of Article 101 TFEU as a fully functional joint venture. However, it was found to fall within Article 101(1) TFEU since the joint venture developed business relations exclusively,

presumptions set in the BERs and the Commission's guidelines and only assessed the parts of the agreements that failed the BER or guidelines. The Commission and German NCA, by comparison, adopted a different approach to such matters, which will be detailed in Section 4.5.1.

The German NCA took an even stricter approach. It mostly refused to grant exceptions due to failing to fulfil the benefit and indispensability conditions of Article 101(3) TFEU[352] and in a few proceedings due to failure to fulfil the fair share condition.[353] Moreover, even when a non-competition interest was regarded as relevant, the balancing of competition and non-competition interests often tilted in favour of the former. In fact, the empirical findings show that in several instances the NCA was unwilling to accept similar practices that were approved by other competition enforcers. This demonstrates how a strict intensity of control affects the balancing under Article 101(3) TFEU.

First, in *Long-term gas supply (2006, 2007, 2009)*, the German NCA and courts refused to accept an Article 101(3) TFEU defence with respect to long-term gas supply contracts because of their long duration and high purchasing obligations.[354] The non-compete obligations in those contracts were shorter than those prescribed by the Commission's Vertical BERs and restrictions that had been accepted by the Commission.[355]

Second, in *Pecuniary loss liability risks for auditors and chartered accountants (2008)*, the NCA prohibited insurance companies from jointly insuring the pecuniary loss liability risks run by auditors and chartered accountants in an insurance pool. The undertakings referred to the Commission's decision in *P&I Club (1985)* and the insurance BER, arguing that an exception was warranted due to coinsurance benefits.[356] They claimed that although the BER was inapplicable due to the undertakings' high market share, the BER should be understood as the EU legislator's acknowledgment that the three first conditions of Article 101(3) TFEU

on a long-term basis, with its founders. The exception was based on the agreement's contribution to cost- saving effects through the joint purchase and coordination involved in the distribution of goods to the outlets.

352 See Annex A, Section 3.28.

353 Joint selling of media rights (2008); B2–90/01-4 Timber (2008), para III(4); B8–175/11 Titisee-Neustadt (2015), para 151.

354 B8–113/03 Long-term gas supply (2006), 23–26; VI2-Kart 1/06 (V) Long-term gas supply (2007), para 125–134; KVR 67/07 Long-term gas supply (2009). The NCA was willing to accept a maximum duration of four years for resellers who accounted for more than 50% of the overall demand, but only two years above 80%.

355 Regulation 2790/1999 on Vertical Agreements, Article 5(a). In 38348 Repsol (2006), the Commission accepted a five-year duration for contracts with established resellers when the market shares of the dominant firm did not exceed 30% to 50%. In IP/00/297 Gas Natural/Endesa (2006), which involved an Article 102 TFEU infringement, the Commission accepted a duration of twelve years. See also Hauteclocque (2009, 101–102).

356 30373 P&I Clubs (1985), as described in Section 3.4.3.3.

applied.[357] The NCA rejected the argument, noting the agreement did not create benefits and was not indispensable.[358]

Third, the German NCA developed a unique approach to the so-called price parity or most favoured nation (MFN) clauses used in online platforms. While this specific finding was later rejected by the German Court of Appeals, this example sheds light on the German NCA's understanding of Article 101(3) TFEU balancing.

Pursuant to MFN clauses, a supplier agrees to grant a platform the best terms and conditions it makes available to any third party. There are two types of MFN clauses: Those that ensure that the price and terms quoted through the platform are not higher than those available on the upstream supplier's website ('narrow MFN') and also those that apply to other platforms and channels ('wide MFN').[359]

Although many NCAs objected to a wide MFN, the German NCA also opposed narrow MFN clauses. The NCA first prohibited a wide MFN clause in *Amazon (2013)* and *HRS-Hotel Reservation Service (2013)*.[360] In *Booking.com (2015)*, it extended the prohibition to narrow MFN clauses. It rejected the claim that a narrow MFN was justified by general benefits related to online hotel platforms, such as generating traffic, bundling demand, better utilisation rates for hotels, improved access to foreign customers, economies of scale, reduction of search costs for end-consumers, and transparent pricing. It concluded that such benefits were irrelevant under Article 101(3) TFEU and that only direct benefits stemming from a narrow MFN clause could be examined.[361]

The German prohibition of narrow MFNs clearly deviated from the approaches of other NCAs that had accepted the very same clause.[362] In fact, in July 2015, following investigations by several NCAs and with the help of the Commission,

[357] B4–31/05 Pecuniary loss liability risks for auditors and chartered accountants (2007), para 146–150.

[358] *Ibid*, para 159.The Düsseldorf Court of Appeals annulled the decision in VI-Kart 11/07(V) Pecuniary loss liability risks for auditors and chartered accountants (2008). It held that the NCA had defined the market too narrowly. Under the appropriate market definition, the pool could benefit from the BER. The NCA's appeal against the decision was rendered inadmissible in KVR 34/08 Pecuniary loss liability risks for auditors and chartered accountants (2009).

[359] See also Israel and Jakobs (2015), Ezrachi (2015), Heinz (2016), Hunold (2016), Colangelo (2016), and Mackenrodt (2019).

[360] In both proceedings, the German NCA rejected claims that wide MFN clauses generated benefits in the form of elimination of free riding, improvement of the quality of the services, enhancement of competition on quality, or the 'searchability' of products. It held that, even if such benefits persisted, a wide MFN would result in increased prices. Hence, the clause failed to provide consumers with a fair share and went beyond what was necessary to achieve the aim. See B6–46/12 Amazon (2013), 2–3. The case was informally closed after Amazon removed the clauses from their contracts with its dealers; B9–66/10 HRS-Hotel Reservation Service (2013), para 223–234. The Düsseldorf Court of Appeals upheld the HRS Article 101(3) TFEU analysis on the merits in VI-Kart 1/14 (V) HRS (2015), para 127–138.

[361] B9–121/13 Booking.com (2015).

[362] For an interesting discussion, see also Mackenrodt (2019).

Booking.com implemented a narrow MFN clause throughout the EU.[363] A total of 25 NCAs publicly accepted or tacitly endorsed Booking's conduct, some by means of commitments.[364]

The German NCA defended its position by noting that '[w]hile we are of course working with our European neighbours to ensure uniformity, here we are talking about different national markets with different market conditions. In addition, different tools were used by the authorities. There is no inconsistency'.[365] *Mundt*, the president of the German NCA, similarly explained that the divergent German approach was conceivable since the decision concerned the German market.[366] This explanation, however, is unconvincing. The German NCA applied Article 101 TFEU in a case that affected trade between Member States. Therefore, it was bound to the limits of Article 101(3) TFEU.

The conflict between the German NCA and the other NCAs' interpretations of Article 101(3) TFEU was subject to judicial review by the Düsseldorf Higher Regional Court. The undertakings claimed that by adopting a view divergent from the majority of NCAs, the German NCA had breached its obligation to apply Article 101 TFEU in a uniform manner as required under Regulation 1/2003 and derived from the duty of sincere cooperation in the sense of Article 4(3) TEU. The Court, nevertheless, rejected those claims. It maintained that the fact that various NCAs had adhered to interpretations of issues that were not settled by law did not hinder an NCA from issuing a decision. According to the Court, the correct application of the law was the sole decisive factor in the duty of an NCA to enforce EU competition law effectively. Therefore, simply counting the number of NCAs advocating for one or another interpretation of the law was not required.[367]

While the Düsseldorf Higher Regional Court's judgement may comply with the black letter of the Treaties, it does not observe the spirit of Regulation 1/2003. Accommodating conflicting balancing decisions of NCAs with respect to a single

[363] In contrast to wide MFNs, narrow MFNs constitute a less intrusive restriction on pricing or terms and do not involve many of the competition concerns of wide MFN. See Ezrachi (2015, 506–507).

[364] Commitments were adopted in Italy, Sweden, France, Denmark, Ireland, and Austria. See European Commission Daily News 21/04/2015, Ezrachi (2015, 512), and Heinz (2016, 531). Since other NCAs have accepted narrow MFN by way of commitments, they have not discussed in depth how, and if, they complied with the four conditions of Article 101(3) TFEU. One exception is the Swedish NCA decision, which submitted that a narrow MFN reduced the risk of free riding on investments made by Booking.com. See Swedish Competition Authority, Bookingdotcom Sverige AB and Booking.com (15 April 2015) Ref: 596/2013, para 33. A similar positive position to narrow MFN clauses was adopted by the UK NCA in CMA – Private Motor Insurance Market Investigation: Final Report of September 2014, para 8.56.

[365] Vane (2015).

[366] See in Ezrachi (2015, 513).

[367] Kart 1/16 (V) Booking.com (2016), para 107–115.

agreement has detrimental effects on the uniformity and legal certainty of balancing, which lies at the heart of the decentralised enforcement regime.[368]

To make matters even more complicated, in June 2019 the German Court of Appeals has annulled the Düsseldorf Higher Regional Court's Booking.com judgement. The Court of Appeals held that Article 101 TFEU does not prohibit narrow MFN clauses because they ensure a fair and balanced contractual exchange of services between platforms and hotels. The Court of Appeals followed a unique line of reasoning. Whereas the German NCA and Düsseldorf Higher Regional Court – like most other NCAs – have based their analysis on Article 101(3) TFEU, the Court of Appeals referred to the ancillary restraints balancing tool of Article 101(1) TFEU.[369] Finding that narrow MFN clauses are not prohibited under Article 101 (1) TFEU, the Court did not address the applicability of Article 101(3) TFEU. As such, it did not explain if the German NCA's approach to Article 101(3) TFEU balancing differs from those of the other competition enforcers and, if so, how it can be squared with the spirit of Regulation 1/2003.

3.6.3.2 Varying Control (the Netherlands and France)

The French NCA was more flexible in applying the four conditions of Article 101(3) TFEU than the UK, Hungarian, and German NCAs. This is demonstrated in *Fair Trade (2006)*, which was presented in Section 3.6.2.2. As mentioned, the French NCA examined a fair trade trademark system setting higher prices for fair trade products, aimed to improve the living conditions of producers and the means of production in developing countries. The French NCA applied a flexible legal proportionality analysis to evaluate environmental benefits. It held that the agreement could be justified due to its 'general' contribution to the protection of the environment.[370] Referring to the Commission's Horizontal Guidelines (2001) and *Carbon Gas Technologie (1983)* decision,[371] the NCA maintained that when an agreement produces a positive rate of return for consumers in reasonable payback periods, there is no need to calculate the environmental benefits.[372] The NCA overlooked the Commission Article 101(3) Guidelines (2004), which instigated a much stricter standard for the calculation of benefits.[373]

The flexible application of Article 101(3) TFEU was also reflected in other cases heard by the French NCA. For instance, the NCA used the protection of

[368] The objective of uniformity under Regulation 1/2003 is further elaborated in Section 8.3.2. The German NCA and courts have also adopted diverging interpretations of the balancing principles embedded in BERs, as elaborated in Section 4.5.1.

[369] Kart 2/16 (V) Booking.com (2019), para II(2). On ancillary restraints as a balancing tool, see Section 5.3.4.

[370] 06-A-07 Fair trade (2006), para 105.

[371] 29955 Carbon Gas Technologie (1983), as described in footnote 69 (page 111).

[372] 06-A-07 Fair trade (2006), para 105–108.

[373] See Section 3.4.4.1.

non-economic benefits enshrined in national legislation as a benchmark for assessing whether there was a benefit under Article 101(3) TFEU instead of requiring economic evidence. In *Cycle and cycle products (2006)*, it found that safety concerns regulated by national legislation could in theory justify an exception as long as the restriction was limited to what was necessary.[374] On the opposite side of the same coin, in *Heating, ceramic sanitary and plumbing equipment* (2006), manufacturers and sellers concluded a series of agreements limiting the resale of heating products to professional fitters. The French NCA rejected the claim that the restriction was warranted due to safety requirements related to the insulation of heating equipment using fuel and gas. It noted that even if the insulation of such products was unsafe, the applicable national regulations did not restrict their sale to professional installers.[375]

Gradually, however, the French NCA tightened the standard for an Article 101(3) TFEU defence. In addition to the shift from a long-term broad to a short-term narrow consumer welfare standard,[376] the NCA demanded economic evidence to substantiate the alleged benefit and fair share and carefully applied the indispensability condition.[377] Indeed, the empirical findings reveal that, since 2010, Article 101 (3) TFEU has not been successfully invoked in France.[378]

The Dutch NCA had also exhibited a degree of flexibility in applying the conditions of Article 101(3) TFEU. In general, Article 101(3) TFEU was only discussed in a very small number of proceedings in the Netherlands. In most instances, the possibility of granting an exception was promptly rejected without an in-depth analysis.[379] However, the empirical findings reveal that the Dutch NCA had interpreted the conditions of the Article in a flexible manner when they were applied to sustainability agreements.

As already discussed in Section 3.6.2.2, the Dutch NCA's Vision Document on Competition and Sustainability (2014), Draft Guidelines on Sustainability Agreements (2020), and opinions in cases such as *De Stroomversnelling (2013)* and *Chicken of tomorrow (2015)* made use of estimates and proxies rather than exact economic calculations for proving the first benefit condition.[380] In particular, the Dutch NCA took into account also the subjective value consumers attach to greener

[374] 06-D-37 Cycle and cycle products (2006), para 460–461, 473.

[375] 06-D-03 Heating, ceramic sanitary and plumbing equipment (2006), para 1269–1274. The Court confirmed this analysis in 2006/07820 Heating, ceramic sanitary and plumbing equipment (2008), 29–33.

[376] See Section 3.6.3.2.

[377] See Annex A, Section 3.30.

[378] See Figure 3.11(a). Section 7.3.2 maintains that this could also be attributed to a change in the discretional enforcement powers granted to the French NCA, following the 2009 reform to the French enforcement regime.

[379] See Annex A, Section 3.29.

[380] For example, see ACM/DM/2013/205913 De Stroomversnelling (2013), 2; ACM/DM/2014/206028 Chicken for tomorrow (2015), 5–6.

product features.[381] The proof of such benefits, according to the Dutch NCA, mainly requires substantiating *which* sustainability benefits are claimed, *when* they would be realised, and to *whom*.[382] Differing from the Commission's Article 101(3) Guidelines, the NCA does not ask for an accurate calculation of the 'economic importance of such efficiencies'.[383]

The Dutch NCA also adhered to a relaxed reading of the indispensability condition. Arguing that the 'necessity criterion is generally not applied too strictly in practice', it explains that the key factor is whether the restriction 'can be reasonably considered necessary to achieve the intended benefits'.[384] Unlike the Commission, which requires that there will be '*no other* economically practicable and less restrictive means of achieving the efficiencies', the Dutch NCA only requires proof that alternative measures would be 'significantly less efficient'.[385]

This section demonstrated that the NCAs have exhibited different levels of intensity of control when assessing the four conditions of Article 101(3) TFEU. The weight ascribed to non-competition interests, therefore, did not only differ according to their approaches to the relevant types of benefits or to the balancing method. It was also dependent on the nature, degree, and evidence each enforcer required for accepting an Article 101(3) TFEU defence.

3.6.4 *National Equivalent Provisions*

The national approaches to balancing have also been affected by the wording of national provisions equivalent to Article 101(3) TFEU. This section shows that this has not only affected the balance of purely national cases but has also sometimes had spillover effects on the interpretation of Article 101(3) TFEU in mixed-case scenarios in which the EU provision applied.

Regulation 1/2003 obliges the Member States to apply Article 101 TFEU in parallel to national competition law when an agreement affects trade between the Member States.[386] Hence, EU law does not affect the scope of the national provisions equivalent to Article 101(3) TFEU. Consequently, whereas the laws of some Member States closely mirror the wording of Article 101(3) TFEU, others have opted for different formulations. Of the five Member States examined in this book, the wording of the German, Dutch, and UK national equivalent provisions is identical

381 Vision Document on Competition and Sustainability (2014), 11, 13.
382 *Ibid*, 16.
383 Commission Article 101(3) Guidelines (2004), para 50.
384 Vision Document on Competition and Sustainability (2014), 17.
385 Emphasis added. Commission Article 101(3) Guidelines (2004), para 75; Vision Document on Competition and Sustainability (2014), 17.
386 Regulation 1/2003, Article 3. See Sections 2.3.3.2 and 6.1.

to the wording of Article 101(3) TFEU.[387] The wording of the French and Hungarian exceptions, as elaborated below, differs from the EU counterpart.

In Hungary, this difference has had only a limited impact in practice. The Hungarian exception is worded similarly to Article 101(3) TFEU but adds that the first benefit condition is fulfilled when an agreement contributes to 'the protection of the environment'.[388] Since the role of environmental benefits under Article 101(3) TFEU is uncertain, it is unclear to what extent this provision deviates from the EU exception.[389] The empirical findings, in any event, affirm that, in practice, the NCA has not accepted agreements on this basis.[390]

Yet, in France, the different wording of the exception has had an impact in practice, even in mixed cases.[391] As such, it provides an illuminating example of how a national law can affect balancing in a decentralised regime. The French exception differs from Article 101(3) TFEU in two ways.[392] First, it applies to agreements aimed at *creating or maintaining jobs*. This is a non-economic benefit for society as a whole. Second, the French provision grants exceptions for 'practices which may consist of *organising, for agricultural products or products of agricultural origin*, under the same brand or trade name, the production volumes and quality and the commercial policy, including by agreeing to a common transfer price'.

The French NCA had long insisted that the national and EU exceptions were substantively identical.[393] However, this statement was not always supported by its enforcement practices, especially prior to 2008. The NCA held that certain agreements could escape the prohibition of Article 101(1) TFEU due to their positive impact on the job and agriculture markets. In mixed cases, such as *Fair Trade (2006)*, the NCA used the wording of the national exception to apply Article 101(3) TFEU to an agreement having an effect on trade between Member States.[394]

In later proceedings, however, the French NCA limited the impact of the national exception. It interpreted the national provision in light of Article 101(3)

387 German Competition Act, Section 2(1); Dutch competition act, Article 6(3); UK competition act, Section 9.

388 Hungarian Competition Act, Article 17.

389 See, for instance, Sections 3.3.3.4, 3.3.3.5, 3.5.3.1, 3.6.2.2, and 3.6.2.3.

390 Environmental considerations were invoked and rejected in Vj-7/2008/178 Motor oils and lubricants (2009), para 29–30, 61 and Vj-66/2012 Geophysical measuring operations (2014), para 119, 246.

391 Mixed cases are defined as cases in which an NCA enforces both Article 101 TFEU and the national equivalent provision. See Section 1.3.2.1.

392 Emphasis added. French Commercial Code, Article L. 420-4(II). See also OECD Regulatory Reform in France (2003), 8, 11. The exception for agriculture products was introduced through Law 96-588 of 1 July 1996 concerning loyalty and balance in commercial relationships, aiming to allow SMEs to group and participate in the agriculture markets.

393 09-A-50 Cinema code (2009), para 92–93; 09-A-56 Digital books (2009), para 104–105, 126; 12-D-08 Endive (2012), para 564; 15-D-19 Delivery (2015), para 715. See also OECD Regulatory Reform in France (2003), 11.

394 06-A-07 Fair trade (2006), para 102.

TFEU and did not apply it in cases affecting trade between Member States.[395] In *Endive (2012)*, for example, the NCA analysed the national exception with reference to the Commission Article 101(3) Guidelines. It held that when assessing agriculture agreements, the concept of economic progress hinged mainly on two complementary objectives: consumer welfare via the improvement of product quality and the production conditions.[396]

3.6.5 *National Courts*

The national approaches to Article 101(3) TFEU balancing were also shaped by national courts. While Regulation 1/2003 envisioned an essential role for national courts in ensuring consistent and effective enforcement,[397] the influence of the national courts on the enforcement of Article 101 TFEU in general and 101(3) TFEU in particular has been greatly underappreciated by legal scholarship. This might be a result of the limited visibility of national judgements in comparison with the practices of the Commission and NCAs, which operate within the ECN network of EU competition authorities. Unlike the NCAs, national courts are required to transmit judgements concerning the application of Article 101 TFEU to the Commission only *after* they have been notified to the parties. Although the Commission can submit its observations to the national courts, it cannot take over a case the way it can with respect to NCA investigations.[398]

The practice of national courts, however, is a noteworthy subject of study. As clearly illustrated by the German Courts' judgements in *Booking.com* described above,[399] national courts carry a significant influence in devising the national balancing principles. Against this backdrop, Figure 3.13 summarises the number of appeals appearing before national courts that have scrutinised the application of Article 101(3) TFEU by NCAs. It specifies the number of enforcement actions in which the application of Article 101(3) TFEU has been appealed (grey bars) and the number of cases in which the courts have overturned NCA decisions in this regard (black bars).

The figure yields two interesting observations. First, it shows that most national courts have examined the application of Article 101(3) TFEU in only a relatively

395 This was part of a general trend in interpreting Article 101(3) TFEU in light of the Commission's approach, as elaborated in Section 3.6.2.2. See 08-A-07 Organisation of fruit and vegetable processing industry (2008), para 62–74; 09-A-48 Dairy (2009), para 72, 83–89; 12-D-08 Endive (2012), para 561–564. The Appeal Court of Paris in 2012/06498 Endive (2014) quashed the decision, finding that the conduct did not infringe Article 101(1) TFEU. In a second appeal, the Cour de cassation in 14/19589 Endive (2015) referred the question for preliminary ruling. The CJEU rendered its decision in C-671/15 Endive (2017).

396 12-D-08 Endive (2012), para 572.

397 Regulation 1/2003, Preamble 7–8, 21 and Articles 15–16.

398 Regulation 1/2003, Article 15.

399 See Section 3.6.3.1.

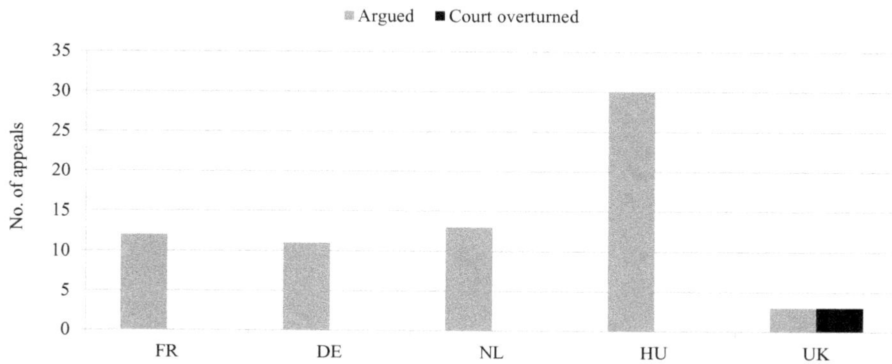

FIGURE 3.13 Article 101(3) TFEU, national courts (May 2004–2017)
Each appeal instance at which a case was examined is counted as an independent appeal

small number of cases. This could be explained by the small invocation rate of Article 101(3) TFEU before NCAs and the use of informal measures to examine Article 101(3) TFEU issues, which are unlikely to be appealed (see Figure 3.11). As a result, national courts have had only a few opportunities to scrutinise Article 101(3) TFEU balancing. Hungary represents a clear exception to this rule. The Budapest Metropolitan has reviewed various appeals on the application of Article 101(3) TFEU, which were often re-examined by the Budapest Appeal Court as a second instance for appeal and by the Curia in the third instance.

Second, the figure reveals that national courts have been exceptionally careful in interfering with NCA decisions on the application of Article 101(3) TFEU balancing. They have mostly affirmed the NCAs' analyses and shown deference to their discretion. This finding is in line with the limited judicial review the EU Courts exercised on the Commission's application of Article 101(3) TFEU. It may also be the result of the deference of national courts to the NCAs' discretion when performing a complex economic assessment.

The UK courts, however, present a special case. In fact, the empirical findings show that the CAT has accepted all of the appeals in which the undertakings raised concerns over the NCA's application of Article 101(3) TFEU.[400] Yet, those judgements were based on flaws in the assessment procedure, rather than on substantive scrutiny of the application of the Article's conditions. As a result, the CAT has not explained how Article 101(3) TFEU balancing ought to be applied in those cases.

[400] 1160/1/1/10 1161/1/1/10 1162/1/1/10 1163/1/1/10 1164/1/1/10 1165/1/1/10 Tobacco (2011), para 55, 61, 95–96; 1226/2/12/14 Hotel online booking (2014), para 116, 125–126, 146, 158, 174. In 1054/1/1/05 1055/1/1/05 1056/1/1/05 MasterCard (2006), para 28–38, the CAT has set aside the NCA's decision upon its request.

The above shows that although national courts may engage in Article 101(3) TFEU balancing, they have done so infrequently. The limited involvement of national courts in Article 101(3) TFEU balancing could also explain the empirical findings that were presented by Figure 3.8, pointing to the low number of preliminary questions referred to the CJEU on the application of the Article. This raises doubts as to the degree that national judiciaries have actually ensured the effectiveness, uniformity, and legal certainty of balancing in practice, as intended by the decentralised enforcement regime of Regulation 1/2003.[401]

3.6.6 *Interim Conclusion*

Regulation 1/2003 has empowered the NCAs, for the first time, to apply Article 101(3) TFEU, and as such to engage in the balancing of competition and non-competition interests. The decentralisation, however, was not complemented by the establishment of a single, binding EU balancing framework. Consequently, national enforcers enjoy a wide margin of discretion to shape their national approaches when EU primary and secondary law or the case law of the EU Courts does not prescribe otherwise.

Indeed, this section showed that the NCAs have adopted different positions on the types of relevant benefits, balancing method, and intensity of control for applying the Article's four conditions. The empirical findings suggest that the NCAs' approaches to Article 101(3) TFEU balancing can be roughly divided into three groups: The first group of NCAs (i.e. UK and Hungary) has generally conformed to the Commission's approach, following a short-term narrow consumer welfare standard, restricting Article 101(3) TFEU to economic benefits, and demanding strong economic evidence. The second group (i.e. Netherlands and France) has deviated from such an approach, using a long-term broad consumer welfare standard and also accepting non-economic benefits and more abstract evidence. The third group (i.e. Germany) did not base their analysis on the classification of benefits and rejected a consumer welfare standard altogether.

The fragmentation of Article 101(3) TFEU balancing, this section concluded, has created serious uniformity concerns. The NCAs have reached conflicting decisions with respect to the same or similar agreements and adopted different balancing principles. This impedes the level playing field and legal certainty of economic actors across the EU, exposing undertakings to multiple balancing standards.

This divergence was not mitigated by the national courts. The empirical findings have shown that although national courts may engage in Article 101(3) TFEU balancing, they have done so infrequently. Most national courts have examined the application of Article 101(3) TFEU in only a relatively small number of cases and have been exceptionally careful in interfering with NCA findings. As such, it is

[401] This is elaborated in Section 8.3.

doubtful whether they fulfil the role envisioned to them by Regulation 1/2003 in ensuring the consistent and effective application.

3.7 CLOSING REMARKS: TRANSITIONS IN ARTICLE 101(3) TFEU BALANCING

This chapter has pointed to remarkable transitions in Article 101(3) TFEU balancing across the enforcement periods and between the competition enforcers.

Prior to modernisation, the Commission used the powers bestowed on it by the centralised notification regime to account for a wide variety of non-competition interests. During the first three enforcement periods (i.e. 1962–April 2004), Article 101(3) TFEU balancing was neither based on coherent economic principles nor on an analysis of the effects of an agreement. Guided by the case law of the CJEU, Article 101(3) TFEU was informed by the workable competition standard. Accordingly, non-competition interests were taken into account via a loose legal proportionality test on an *ad hoc*, case-by-case basis and were frequently found to overpower the competitive harm. The balancing method and outcome were heavily dependent on the relevant sector. Reflecting a sectoral approach, the Commission and EU Courts have applied the conditions of Article 101(3) TFEU strictly to agreements impairing market integration while setting a low threshold for agreements in liberalised or regulated sectors, sectors affected by an economic crisis, or agreements promoting the EU industrial policy.

During that period, the Commission and EU Courts placed no limitation on the types of relevant non-competition interests or benefits. In addition to direct and indirect economic benefits to individual consumers, they examined non-economic benefits to society as a whole and to future generations. Moreover, they did not attach importance to the legal source of the non-competition interests. They examined without distinction benefits that were protected by the policy-linking clauses and those lacking a formal EU law basis.

The Commission took advantage of the notification system to negotiate with the undertakings the terms for exemptions. This allowed the Commission to alter the terms of an agreement prior to its implementation to reflect what the Commission considered to be an appropriate balance between competition and non-competition interests.[402] Article 101(3) TFEU, consequently, was not only an outlet to balance the harm and benefits generated to consumers by a specific agreement. It also reflected a host of legal, economic, and social objectives serving as a regulatory tool to govern and shape the European markets.

The *ad hoc*, case-by-case approach to Article 101(3) TFEU balancing had prevented the emergence of coherent balancing principles prior to modernisation. Nevertheless, one key merit of the old centralised-notification regime was that it

[402] See Figure 3.1 and Section 3.4.3.1.

provided a highly certain and uniform application of Article 101(3) TFEU across the internal market. Undertakings learned of the compatibility of their agreements prior to their implementations (albeit more often than not by means of informal comfort letters).[403] Hence, while Article 101(3) TFEU balancing was not based on a set of clear principles, it was applied in a fairly uniform and predictable manner.

The modernisation of EU competition law aimed to increase the effectiveness of the enforcement. The Commission generally considers the modernisation to be a major success, noting in particular that the reform in the application of Article 101(3) TFEU 'has worked very well in practice without any major difficulties with [its] direct application'.[404] The empirical findings presented in this chapter, however, questioned this conclusion. They demonstrated that the combined effect of the three pillars of modernisation has jeopardised the effectiveness, uniformity, and legal certainty of Article 101(3) TFEU balancing.

First, the chapter argued that the *substantive pillar of modernisation* has failed to produce a set of clear balancing principles. Although the Commission's new policy papers dubbed Article 101(3) TFEU balancing as an objective exercise of measuring economic efficiencies, they have not offered principles that can guide the application of the Article. The assessment of Article 101(3) TFEU still requires the competition enforcers to employ considerable value judgement and to make fundamental policy choices when interpreting its conditions.[405]

Second, this chapter has shown that the lack of clear balancing principles has become particularly problematic in combination with the *procedural pillar of modernisation*. Admittedly, the shift from a prior notification to an *ex-post* self-assessment regime inherently carries legal certainty risks. Because agreements are no longer notified and reviewed *ex-ante* prior to their implementation, certain grey areas in which self-assessment might be difficult to execute are bound to emerge.

Such risks, however, were aggravated due to the Commission's new interpretation of Article 101(3) TFEU balancing. While the Commission proposed the shift to a self-assessment regime in the Modernisation White Paper of 1999, its new interpretation of Article 101(3) TFEU was only presented in its 2004 Guidelines. As a result, when Regulation 1/2003 had entered into force, the old case law that adhered to the workable competition standard of balancing was no longer in line with the Commission's more economic approach to Article 101(3) TFEU.[406] The procedural modernisation was based on the no longer valid assumption that the old notification

[403] The legal certainty was sometimes hindered by the Commission's choice for informal measures. See Sections 2.3.2 and 7.5.3.

[404] Policy report 2009, para 80. See also Report on the Functioning of Regulation 1/2003 (2009), para 7; Report on the Functioning of Regulation 1/2003 (2014), para 6.

[405] See also Piergiovanni and D'Elia (2008, 5–9), Petit (2009, 2–4), and GCLC Annual Conference (2010, 19–20, 58–76).

[406] As empirically demonstrated in Sections 3.3.4 and 3.4.4, and previously observed by Jones (2010, 793), Gerard (2012, 36), Bellamy and Child (2013, 179–180), and Witt (2016, 296–297).

regime had 'enabled the Commission to build up a coherent body of precedent cases'.[407]

The Commission did not fill this gap in its decisional practice. Despite the need for a body of case law to guide balancing, the Commission has only rarely discussed the application of Article 101(3) TFEU following modernisation. Deviating from the pledge it undertook in the Modernisation White Paper, the Commission refrained from issuing positive decisions or informal guidance explaining how the conditions of the Article could be successfully invoked in the context of a specific case.[408] Even in the limited number of enforcement actions in which a possible exception was discussed, the Commission has mostly rejected outright an Article 101(3) TFEU defence. It did not clarify how the conditions of the Article ought to be applied following modernisation and if and how such conditions conform to the Commission's and EU Courts' previous case law on balancing.[409]

The limited number of cases in which the Commission applied Article 101(3) TFEU following modernisation has also prevented the EU Courts from evaluating balancing questions. Because the Commission did not adopt decisions on the application of the Article, the Courts did not have the opportunity to scrutinise the Commission's balancing approach on appeals. What is more, this chapter has suggested that even in the rare cases in which the Courts actually had such opportunity, they did not grasp it to define the scope of the more economic approach and the consumer welfare standard.

Accordingly, while the EU Courts did not embrace the Commission's new interpretation of Article 101(3) TFEU, at least in part, they were not clear on what types of benefits could be taken into account, the role of the consumer welfare standard, and the balancing method. The Courts also did not scrutinise the Commission's guidelines or reveal how they could be squared with the case law rendered prior to modernisation.

Third, the effectiveness, uniformity, and legal certainty of Article 101(3) TFEU balancing were also jeopardised by the *institutional pillar of modernisation*. The decentralisation of the enforcement has empowered the NCAs, for the first time, to apply Article 101(3) TFEU, and as such to engage in the balancing of competition and non-competition interests. At the same time, the decentralisation was not complemented by the establishment of uniform, binding EU balancing principles. Since the Commission's notices and guidelines are binding on the Commission alone, national enforcers may adopt diverging interpretations where EU primary and secondary laws or the EU Courts' case law do not prescribe otherwise. They enjoy a

[407] Modernisation White Paper (1999), para 76.

[408] Ibid, para 14, 88–89, with the exception of the informal guidance issued as part of the Coronavirus Temporary Framework. This is further elaborated in Section 7.6.3.

[409] See the empirical findings presented in Figure 3.2 and Section 3.3.4.

wide margin of discretion to shape their national approaches based on their legal, economic, and social traditions.

Indeed, the empirical findings have pointed to a considerable divergence in national approaches. NCAs have followed different standards for Article 101(3) TFEU balancing (short-term narrow or long-term broad consumer welfare, or rejecting such standards) and took account of different types of benefits (direct and indirect economic and non-economic benefits) to different types of beneficiaries (direct/indirect consumers and society as a whole) while applying various levels of intensity of control. The national balancing approaches were also affected by the national equivalent provisions, which in some cases differed from the wording of Article 101(3) TFEU. Such differences, the empirical findings have shown, have not only affected the balance of purely national cases but also had spillover effects on the interpretation of Article 101(3) TFEU in cases in which the EU provision applied. This chapter submits, therefore, that the safeguards of Regulation 1/2003 were insufficient to ensure the uniformity and legal certainty of Article 101(3) TFEU balancing.[410]

Finally, this chapter has shown that in contrast to the prominence of Article 101(3) TFEU in the EU competition law scholarship and policy papers on balancing, following modernisation the Article was applied only in a limited number of instances. As the next chapters will reveal, following modernisation, much of the consideration given to non-competition interests has shifted away from Article 101(3) TFEU to other national and implicit-procedural balancing tools.

[410] This will be elaborated in Chapter 8.

4

Block Exemption Regulations

4.1 INTRODUCTION

Block exemption regulations (BERs) are traditionally perceived as having the administrative function of reducing the Commission's workload. This chapter, however, submits that BERs have an additional role. BERs, like Article 101(3) TFEU individual exemptions, are also a tool that can be used to balance competition and non-competition interests.[1]

The BER is a legal tool that automatically discharges certain categories of agreements from the prohibition imposed by Article 101 TFEU, without the need to undertake a detailed competition analysis.[2] When an agreement is covered by the terms of a BER, undertakings are protected by a safe haven and are relieved from the burden to prove that the agreement fulfils the conditions of Article 101(3) TFEU. As such, each BER is based on the presumption that the protected categories of agreements satisfy 'with sufficient certainty' all four conditions of the Article.[3] It offers a rule of thumb by establishing a presumption of legality for relatively unproblematic cases, offering undertakings legal certainty as to the validity of an agreement.[4]

BERs were initially introduced to EU competition law to accommodate the enormous number of notifications that resulted from the enforcement set-up of

[1] This was previously identified by Monti (2007, 113–123) and Van Rompuy (2012, 278–279).

[2] The legal source for issuing BERs is found in Articles 101(3) and 103 TFEU.

[3] See, for example, Regulation 330/2010 on Vertical Agreements, Preamble 5; Regulation 2790/99 on Vertical Agreements, Preamble 5; Regulation 1217/2010 on Research and Development, Preamble 7; Regulation 1218/2010 on Specialisation Agreements, Preamble 5; Regulation 772/2004 on Technology Transfer, Preamble 9; Regulation 267/2010 on Insurance, Preamble 8; Regulation 461/2010 on Motor Vehicles, Preamble 14. See also Commission Article 101(3) Guidelines (2004), para 35.

[4] T-51/89 Tetra Pak (1990), para 37, as repeated in the Commission's Policy Brief on EU Competition Rules and the Marketplace (2018), 4.

Regulation 17/62. When the Commission adopted the first BER on Distribution Agreements in 1967, it was already faced with a backlog of 37,450 notifications. The BER successfully reduced the Commission's workload: Of the 40,000 notifications received by the Commission during the first years of application of Articles 101 and 102 TFEU, 29,500 were covered by the BER.[5]

However, this workload-reducing function perished following the entry into force of Regulation 1/2003. Under the self-assessment regime, undertakings, rather than the Commission, are required to examine whether an agreement could benefit from the terms of a BER. Although the workload motivation had lost its value, the Commission decided to keep the special BER instrument.[6] It did not, for example, abolish all BERs, issuing corresponding substitute guidelines for the application of Article 101(3) TFEU instead.

Scholars have already noted that the BER instrument does not fit in with the new enforcement regime. *Marcos and Sánchez Graells*, for example, have described BERs as a 'fossilised' administrative device that enacts a specific competition analysis for certain sectors or types of agreements without any economic justification.[7] As such, BERs cannot be squared with the more economic and effects-based approach of EU competition law. Thus, they have maintained, following modernisation there is no longer any (proper) function for BERs, which distort consistent enforcement across all markets and sectors.

This chapter, nonetheless, advocates a different approach. It concludes that BERs play, and have played in the past, an important role in addition to their administrative function. BERs, like Article 101(3) TFEU individual exemptions, are also a tool for taking into account economic and non-economic benefits within the enforcement of Article 101 TFEU. They offer a pre-determined, explicit balancing tool, promoting the uniformity and legal certainty of balancing within the decentralised, self-assessment regime.

Balancing under the BERs takes place on two levels: First, the adoption of each BER is the result of a lengthy political process involving the Member States and the EU institutions. It entails *ex-ante* balancing between the protection of competition interests on the one hand and the promotion of other economic, industrial, and political interests on the other hand. This process does not only allow the Member States and the EU institutions to shape the role of non-competition interests in a specific BER. Because each BER is based on the presumption that the protected categories of agreements satisfy 'with sufficient certainty' the conditions of Article 101 (3) TFEU, the terms of each BER also inform the balancing principles applicable to

[5] Regulation 67/67 on Distribution Agreements. See policy report 1979, 15–16; policy report 1971, 57; policy report 1987, 33. See also Section 2.3.2.

[6] Modernisation did not affect the validity or legal nature of the BERs. See Commission Article 101(3) Guidelines (2004), para 2.

[7] Marcos and Sanchez-Graells (2010, 190). See also Ehlermann (2000, 566), Riley (2003a, 605), and Goyder (2009, 638–639).

the Article's individual exemptions. These powers are noteworthy, especially since the Member States and the EU institutions carry little influence over the relevant types of benefits, balancing method, and intensity of control applicable to Article 101 (3) TFEU individual exemptions.

Second, the application of a BER to an individual agreement also involves balancing. To this end, this chapter distinguishes between *general BERs* that apply to certain categories of business practices and *sectoral BERs* that apply to specific sectors and industries. It shows that general BERs are mostly restricted to the consideration of economic benefits. They are based on a balancing process by way of exclusion and confine the discretion of the competition enforces to objective factual criteria. Sectoral BERs, by comparison, are often more political in nature and pursue a regulatory balancing that protects a broad range of non-economic benefits. They mostly enact only general balancing standards based on a legal balancing process. Sectoral BERs require the competition enforcer to engage in a full analysis weighing the harm and benefits produced by an agreement, akin to the assessment of an individual Article 101(3) TFEU exemption.[8]

Moreover, this chapter demonstrates that the balancing method has undergone a transformation over the enforcement periods. Up until the end of the third enforcement period (i.e. the late 1990s), BERs were based on a *formalistic* analysis. Yet, most of the BERs adopted since reflect an *effects-based approach*. In fact, this shift represented the first wave of substantive and procedural modernisation in other fields of EU competition law. The development of the various BERs and their categorisation (form or effects based; general or sectoral) are also summarised in Annex B.

The modernisation of BERs, combined with the abolishment of most sectoral BERs during the same period, has represented a trade-off between a more economic approach of the balancing method on the one hand and reduced uniformity and legal certainty on the other hand. The old formalistic and sectoral BERs were highly transparent but less effective at protecting competition since they excluded the application of Article 101 TFEU to certain practices or sectors regardless of the competitive harm. The new effects-based BERs require a higher level of discretion in applying the economic balancing process, a typical downside of the more economic approach that jeopardises the legal certainty and consistent application of balancing across the EU.[9]

Before discussing the balancing embedded in BERs in detail, it should be noted that theoretical and empirical scholarship on BERs is scarce. Perhaps because BERs are often seen as an administrative tool, there are only a few studies on the rationale and function of BERs as a substantive legal instrument. Moreover, because the

8 On the differences between high and low discretion balancing tools and between legal balancing and exclusion processes, see Sections 1.2.2.1 and 4.3.2.2.

9 Bishop (2001, 57, 60). See also Sections 2.5.3.3 and 3.7.

application of the BERs is mostly straightforward, there is a limited number of Article 101 TFEU enforcement actions that have detailed the application of BERs. Even under the old notification regime, agreements falling within the scope of certain BERs were not notified to the Commission.[10] Other agreements that required notification were mostly assessed by means of informal settlements or comfort letters when they were protected by a BER.[11]

The comprehensive quantitative and qualitative coding presented in this book can help fill this gap. Aiming to map the balancing function of BERs, this chapter is constructed as follows: Section 4.2 presents an overview of the empirical findings on the application of BERs by the Commission and EU Courts. Section 4.3 details the balancing function of BERs. It points to the different types of relevant benefits and balancing methods guiding the general and sectoral BERs and analyses their modernisation towards the end of the third enforcement period. Section 4.4 discusses the application of BERs by national enforcers, emphasising a number of legal certainty and uniformity challenges. Section 4.5 explores the relationship between Article 101(3) TFEU individual exemptions and BERs balancing. Finally, Section 4.6 concludes by discussing the transformation in BERs balancing following modernisation.

4.2 LEGAL AND EMPIRICAL BACKGROUND

BERs create a presumption that certain categories of agreements fulfil the four conditions of Article 101(3) TFEU without the need to undertake a full case-by-case analysis. The procedure and rules applicable for benefiting from this presumption have changed over the years.

Up until the late 1990s, BERs contained provisions for three types of clauses: 'White clauses' were provisions in an agreement that were not considered to restrict competition or that could automatically qualify for an exemption; 'grey clauses' were restrictions that could be exempted in certain circumstances and merited a closer examination; and 'black clauses' were restrictions that would not benefit from a safe harbour. Some BERs included an opposition procedure, by which a grey clause had to be notified to the Commission and was deemed to be exempted unless the Commission had actively opposed to the agreement within a designated time slot of typically 6 months.[12] The opposition procedure was gradually abandoned in the

[10] See Section 4.3.3.1.

[11] For statistics on the application of BERs in comfort letters, see Figure 7.5.

[12] Regulation 4087/88 on Franchising Agreements, Article 6; Regulation 2349/84 on Patent Licensing, Article 4; Regulation 556/89 on Know-how Licensing, Article 4; Regulation 240/96 on Technology Transfer Agreements, Article 4; Regulation 418/85 on R&D, Article 7; Regulation 417/85 on Specialisation, Article 4; Regulation 870/1995 on Consortia, Article 7; Regulation 823/00 on Consortia, Article 7. On the opposition procedure, see also Venit (1985) and Greaves (1994, 23–24).

BERs adopted towards the end of the 1990s. Following the entry into force of Regulation 1/2003, all BERs are now fully applied on a self-assessment basis.[13]

The procedure governing the application of BERs has produced only limited empirical data on their application in comparison to the other explicit-substantive balancing tools. Prior to modernisation, the safe haven provided by the BERs had mostly obviated the Commission's need to undertake an individual assessment, and many of the opposition procedures were settled by means of informal and unpublished comfort letters.[14] The empirical data on the application of the BERs is even more limited with respect to the period after the Commission abolished the need to notify such agreements and following the entry into force of Regulation 1/2003.

Keeping this caveat in mind, the empirical findings presented in this chapter nonetheless reveal a number of important insights into the balancing embedded in BERs. To this end, Figure 4.1 provides an overview of the application of BERs, by indicating the number of Article 101 TFEU enforcement actions in which the Commission has examined their application. It details the total number of Article 101 enforcement actions (black line), cases in which the benefits of a BER were investigated (grey line), and cases in which a BER was found to apply (bars). In addition, it specifies the number of enforcement actions in which the withdrawal of a BER was investigated (crosses); this will be discussed in Section 4.5.2.

The figure signals the limited availability of empirical data on the application of BERs. First, it illustrates that BERs have been invoked only in a relatively limited number of proceedings (grey line). This was especially true during the fourth enforcement period, post-modernisation. After May 2004, there was a significant

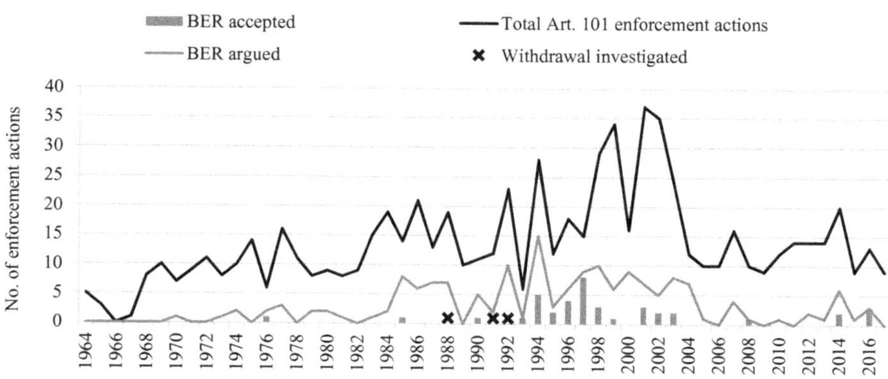

FIGURE 4.1. BERs, Commission
All Article 101 TFEU enforcement actions rendered by the Commission, excluding comfort letters. In some proceedings, more than one BER was invoked, or only certain restrictions exempted

[13] See Section 4.3.3.
[14] See Section 7.5.3 and Figure 7.5. See also Greaves (1994, 23).

drop in the number of proceedings in which the benefit of a BER was examined. As mentioned, this could be explained by the modernisation of BERs in the late 1990s, which released undertakings from the duty to give notification of agreements that benefited from a BER.[15] Since notification of those agreements was no longer given, they are not reflected in the figure. The figure only reflects borderline cases in which the undertakings and the Commission disagreed on whether or not the agreement could benefit from a BER. The decline in the invocation rate of BERs could also be linked to the Commission's enforcement priorities. As elaborated in Sections 7.3 and 7.4, following modernisation the Commission has focused its enforcement efforts on hard-core infringements of competition, in which BERs clearly do not apply.

Second, the figure shows that the Commission found that an agreement benefited from a BER in only a limited number of Article 101 TFEU enforcement actions (bars). As Figure 7.5 demonstrates,[16] the benefits of BERs were mostly acknowledged by means of comfort letters. On the one hand, this could indicate the success of the BER as an instrument; if BERs are clear and predictable legal tools, agreements that fall within the scope of a BER do not require the Commission's analysis and can be exempted informally.[17] This conclusion is reinforced by the observation that most cases in which the benefit of a BER was accepted were related to sectoral BERs. As detailed in Section 4.3, those BERs require a more comprehensive competition analysis involving a wide margin of discretion for the competition enforcer. On the other hand, since most exemptions were settled informally or by means of an unpublished comfort letter, the lack of detailed exemption decisions might lead to uncertainty about the scope of the BERs.[18]

Next, Figure 4.2 summarises the number of Article 101 TFEU enforcement actions in which the EU Courts have reviewed the application of BERs. This includes cases in which the Courts have appraised (CJEU – black line, GC – grey line) and overturned (crosses) the Commission's decisions. In addition, the figure details the number of proceedings in which BERs-related questions were referred for CJEU preliminary ruling (dotted line).

The figure reveals that the CJEU has regularly discussed questions relating to BERs in its preliminary rulings (dotted line). In fact, the Court has answered significantly more preliminary questions on BERs than questions related to Article 101(3) TFEU individual exemptions.[19] Section 4.3.2.1 affirms that those rulings were essential in shaping the substantive scope of the BER and hence of balancing.

In contrast, the Courts have had only limited involvement in reviewing challenges to the Commission's application of BERs. Until the beginning of the 1990s, the Courts

[15] See Section 4.3.3.
[16] See also Section 7.5.3.
[17] Greaves (1994, 9).
[18] This touches upon the greater trend of the limited number of findings of inapplicability, as observed in Section 3.2 and elaborated in Section 7.6.3.
[19] See Figure 3.8.

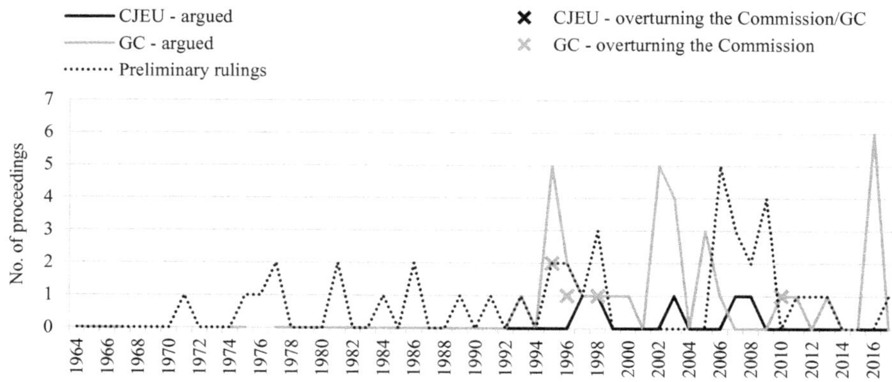

FIGURE 4.2. BERs, EU Courts
In some proceedings, more than one BER was invoked. The six proceedings before the GC in 2016 all related to appeals lodged against a single Commission decision. Thus, they do not represent a significant increase in the number of appeals involving the application of BERs

had not examined any appeals on the application of BERs by the Commission, issuing the first ruling on this matter as late as 1993. Even when the CJEU (black line) and GC (grey line) did appraise the application of a BER, they rarely intervened in the Commission's decision. The few judgments in which the GC did overturn the Commission's assessment were based on procedural errors[20] or insufficient evidence[21] (grey crosses). These findings are a testament to the Commission's margin of discretion to balance under the BER regime, as further elaborated below.

4.3 BERS AS A BALANCING TOOL

Examining the nature of balancing under a BER merits drawing a distinction between two types of BERs: general and sectoral.[22] Annex B provides a comprehensive overview of the BERs in each category. This section shows that the two types of

[20] In T-14/93 Distribution of railway tickets by travel agents (1995), para 64 (as confirmed by C-264/95P Distribution of railway tickets by travel agents (1997)), the GC annulled the Commission's decision that reviewed the agreement under Regulation 17/62 and not the special mechanism established by Regulation 1017/68 on Inland Transport. In T-7/93 Langnese-Iglo (1995), para 207-208 (as confirmed by C-279/95P Langnese-Iglo (1998)), the GC held that the Commission could not withdraw the benefit of a BER with respect to future agreements.

[21] In T-79/95 80/95 Eurotunnel (1996), para 60–65, the GC held that the Commission had misinterpreted the agreements as a matter of fact; in T-374/94 Night Services (1998), para 189, that the Commission did not take a sufficient account of the legal and economic context surrounding the agreement; and in T-427/08 Watch Repair (2010), para 130–142, that the Commission had granted an exemption without sufficiently establishing the market share.

[22] The classification of the two types of BER has previously been studied by Marcos and Sanchez-Graells (2010, 183) and Sauter (2016, 40).

BER vary in the types of benefits that they take into account, their balancing process, and the margin of discretion required in their application. Moreover, it discusses the transformation of BERs balancing following modernisation.

4.3.1 *Type of Benefit: General and Sectoral*

4.3.1.1 General BERs

General BERs exempt agreements that contain specific categories of *business practices* (e.g. vertical agreements, specialisation, or R&D). They are applicable without distinction to all sectors and industries.

General BERs remove two types of agreement from the scope of Article 101 TFEU. First, they exempt agreements that do not bear anti-competitive effects.[23] This does not involve balancing. Second, they exempt agreements that have an anti-competitive effect, but that generate economic benefits that potentially outweigh the harm caused to competition interests. As such, they balance competition- and efficiency-related interests.

The BERs for horizontal and vertical agreements are examples of general BERs. The BERs for horizontal agreements balance competition interests with certain economic benefits such as risk sharing, cost saving, increased investments, pooling of know-how, and enhancement of product quality and variety.[24] They also take R&D and innovation interests into account.[25] BERs for vertical agreements balance competition interests with economic efficiency within a chain of production or distribution by facilitating better coordination. They exempt agreements that are likely to reduce transaction and distribution costs or optimise sales and investment levels.[26] They are also intended to protect SMEs.[27]

In the past, the BERs for horizontal and vertical agreements were also directed at promoting market integration.[28] They did not exempt agreements capable of dividing the internal market even when they did not have a clear anti-competitive effect (i.e. if the parties held low market shares). Consequently, on balance, market integration prevailed over competition interests.[29]

[23] In C-32/65 Italy v the Commission and Council (1969), 405–406, the CJEU held that the authorisation granted under Article 101(3) TFEU to exempt categories of agreements does not imply that because a particular agreement comes within a scope of a BER it necessarily restricts competition in the meaning of Article 101(1) TFEU.

[24] Regulation 1218/2010 on Specialisation Agreements, Preamble 6; Commission's Horizontal Guidelines (2011), para 2.

[25] Regulation 1217/2010 on Research and Development, Preamble 5.

[26] Regulation 330/2010 on Vertical Agreements, Preamble 6.

[27] Green Paper on Vertical Agreements (1997), para 183. See also Maziarz (2014, 346).

[28] Green Paper on Vertical Agreements (1997), iv, para 181. See also Wesseling (2000, 78–79), Monti (2007, 357), and Van Rompuy (2012, 159).

[29] This corresponds with a similar trend in the assessment of Article 101(3) TFEU individual exemptions. See Section 3.4.2.

Classifying the general BERs as entailing balancing is linked to the narrow definition of competition interests adopted by this study.[30] They mostly balance restrictions imposed on the undertakings' commercial freedom with economic efficiencies. Yet, economists have already noted that the general BER acknowledges that certain non-negligible restrictions of competition should be accepted since they promote socially desirable results. Hence, the general BERs cannot rely on a strict welfare analysis and often require a compromise between conflicting and incommensurable values.[31] The same was admitted by the Commission itself, noting that 'strict economic theory is just one of the sources of [the Vertical BERs] policy'.[32]

4.3.1.2 Sectoral BERs

Unlike the General BERs that pertain to specific categories of business practices, sectoral BERs exempt a variety of business practices in *one* specific sector (e.g. maritime transport, motor vehicles). Sectoral BERs are a form of regulatory balancing.[33] They exempt significant restrictions of competition in favour of promoting EU industrial policy and the functioning of the sector, even if there are no directly related efficiencies.[34] Sectoral BERs overtly require the consideration of non-economic benefits, going beyond the regular scope of Article 101(3) TFEU balancing.

The transport BERs provide a good illustration of this point. During the negotiation of the Rome Treaty, the economic, political, and legal conditions of the transport sector differed substantially across the Member States and were subject to both national and international legislation.[35] Because the Member States considered transport to be a national public interest, they decided not to regulate it in the same manner as other economic activities. Transport received a separate chapter in the Rome Treaty and was exempted from the general application of competition rules. The competition rules could apply only to certain means of transport, subject to the adoption of special regulations.[36]

The adoption of such regulations was highly contentious. It took the Commission, Council, and Member States a full three years to agree on the rules governing inland transport, and the rules for maritime and air transport were adopted almost twenty-five years later in 1986 and 1987, respectively.[37] Even then,

[30] See Section 1.2.1.

[31] Jacquemin (1999, 211–215). See also Van Rompuy (2012, 168).

[32] Green Paper on Vertical Agreements (1997), para 86.

[33] Greaves (1994, 6, 115) and Wesseling (2000, 40). On the definitions of corrective and regulatory balancing, see Section 1.2.2.2.

[34] Monti (2002, 1080–1083).

[35] Policy report 1968, 51; policy report 1980, 19–20; Greaves (1991, 17, 105–106).

[36] Regulation 141/62 Exempting Transport from Regulation 17/62, Articles 1–3.

[37] Regulation 4056/86 on Maritime Transport repealed by Regulation 1419/2006 on Maritime Transport; Regulation 246/2009 on Liner Shipping; Regulation 3975/87 on Air Transport, replaced by Regulation 487/2009 on Air Transport.

the Member States refused to give up control, deciding that the Council (which comprises representatives of the Member States) would directly adopt some of the transport BERs, rather than delegating this power to the Commission as was done with most other BERs.[38] This provided the Member States with the power to strike a balance between transport and competition interests.

The Member States also insisted on reserving some degree of control in the application of the transport BERs to a specific agreement. The Inland Transport BER, for instance, obliged the Commission to consult the Council whenever an agreement raised questions of principle concerning the common transport policy and required the approval of crisis cartels by the Council.[39] Similarly, the Regulation ordered that a designated Advisory Committee be consulted before adopting any individual decision.[40]

The transport BERs justified exemptions by reference to a wide array of non-competition interests. For instance, the Inland Transport BER was the result of a political compromise between the Member States. It not only included an exemption for technical agreements promoting efficiencies[41] but also permitted serious restrictions of competition promoting non-economic benefits such as the grouping of SMEs into purchasing cartels and crisis cartels.[42] Comparable provisions requiring the consideration of non-competition interest were also included in future transport BERs.[43] For instance, the Maritime Transport BER exempted agreements concluded by the members of a liner conference that had been designed to fix the rates and conditions of carriage, as well as other market-sharing agreements. While these are clearly anti-competitive agreements, the BER justified the exemption by noting 'the distinctive characteristics of maritime transport'.[44] This rather vague justification was often explained by the historically cartelised structure of the liner trade and the welcome stability it brought to the industry.[45]

Sectoral BERs, involving similar characteristics and broad room for consideration of non-economic benefits, are not limited to the transport sector. Since the mid-1980s, the Commission has gradually adopted additional sectoral BERs. In 1983 it adopted rules for beer supply and petroleum service-station agreements,[46] in 1985 for

[38] Regulation 1017/68 on Inland Transport; Regulation 4056/86 on Maritime Transport. See also Greaves (1994, 131), Goyder (2009, 141–142), and Bailey and Whish (2015, 178). The process of adopting a BER is detailed in Section 4.3.2.1.

[39] Regulation 1017/68 on Inland Transport, Article 17.

[40] *Ibid*, Article 16.

[41] *Ibid*, Articles 3 and 5.

[42] *Ibid*, Articles 4 and 6. On crisis cartels, see also Section 3.4.3.4.

[43] For a detailed discussion, see Greaves (1991, 129–142, 173–183).

[44] Regulation 4056/86 on Maritime Transport, Preamble.

[45] Monti (2002, 1079).

[46] Those sectors were governed by Regulation 1984/83 on Exclusive Purchasing, Articles 6–13. The Regulation was for the most part a general BER.

the motor vehicle sector,[47] and in 1991 for insurance.[48] Notably, the Commission's sectoral approach to BERs has mirrored the workable competition standard that guided Article 101(3) TFEU individual exemptions in that it prescribes that balancing methods be determined according to the relevant sector.[49]

4.3.2 *The Balancing Method*

This section illustrates that balancing under BERs takes place on two levels: first, by the Member States and the EU institutions when adopting a BER; and second, by the competition enforcers when applying a BER to an individual agreement. The balancing method in each of those levels will be explored below.

4.3.2.1 Adopting BERs

The adoption of a BER is the result of a lengthy political process involving the Member States, Council, Commission, EU Courts, Parliament, and members of interest groups. The legislative process is normally carried out at two stages.[50]

First, the *Council* adopts an Enabling Regulation, which empowers the Commission to adopt a BER dealing with a specific category of agreements. This process ensures the involvement of the *Member States* in balancing. In fact, the Commission originally proposed a one-time delegation of powers, allowing it to issue all types of BERs. Such a general delegation would have allowed the Commission to independently shape the balancing embedded in BERs. Yet, the Council, consisting of representatives of the Member States, was unwilling to relinquish complete control. The Council restricted the delegation of powers of each Enabling Regulation to a specific category of agreements.[51] To date, the Council has adopted only three Enabling Regulations: with respect to vertical agreements and the bilateral licencing of IPRs; standardisation, R&D, and specialisation; and insurance.[52]

At the second stage, the *Commission* defines the terms and provisions of the BER.[53] Since the commercial behaviour of undertakings is often shaped by the Commission's views on balancing, this allows the Commission to regulate and not only enforce EU competition policy. To this extent, by adopting BERs, the

[47] Regulation 123/85 on Motor Vehicles, replaced by Regulations 1475/95 1400/2002 and 461/2010 on Motor Vehicles.

[48] Regulation 358/2003 on Insurance, replaced by Regulation 267/2010 on Insurance.

[49] See Section 3.3.3.1. See also Wesseling (2000, 40) and Lista (2013, 30).

[50] BERs in the transport sector followed a different adoption process, as detailed in Section 4.3.1.2.

[51] Greaves (1994, 6, 20).

[52] Enabling Council Regulation 19/65 on Vertical Agreements (as amended by Regulation 1215/99); Enabling Council Regulation 2821/71/EEC on Standardisation, R&D and Specialisation agreements; Enabling Council Regulation 1534/1991 on Insurance.

[53] Goyder (2009, 142). See also policy report 1971, 98–99.

Commission encourages undertakings to conclude agreements that benefit from the terms of a BER and to avoid others.[54]

This stage also involves the *EU Courts*. The terms of each BER must conform to the Courts' case law. Hence, BERs have often been based on or modified to comply with the Courts' approaches to balancing.[55] Especially since the process of adopting a BER is commonly quite lengthy, the Courts have had a number of opportunities to influence the substance of a draft BER. In those cases, the Courts rather than the Commission have settled controversial balancing issues during the process of adopting that BER.

For example, the CJEU was highly influential in shaping the balancing principles embedded in the first BER on distribution agreements. Following the approval of the Enabling Regulation in 1965, the Commission began investigating what types of distribution agreements should be exempted by the prospective BER. Yet, the CJEU was the institution that finally resolved this issue. In *STM (1966)* and *Consten/Grundig (1966)*, which were rendered *before* the Commission had finalised its position, the CJEU held that not all distribution agreements are prohibited by Article 101(1) TFEU.[56] The CJEU also shaped the amendment of the same BER in 1976. The amendment aligned the text of the BER with the CJEU interpretation, which ran counter to the Commission's previous interpretation.[57] Similarly, the Court's judgment in *Maize seed (1982)* clarified the content of the Patent Licensing BER, and its judgment in *Pronuptia (1986)* shaped the Franchising BER.[58]

The *Member States* and *interest groups* both play a role in the legislative process. Each BER is finalised following a consultation with all Member States through the Advisory Committee and with commercial and industrial interest groups. The consultation process takes interests represented by regional, national, and sectoral pressure groups into account.

In various instances, those consultations led to substantial changes to earlier drafts of BERs.[59] Lobbying efforts, for example, have resulted in introducing modifications to the sectoral BERs on insurance and motor vehicles, which exempt agreements that do not fulfil the regular conditions of an Article 101(3) TFEU exemption but promote other industrial or political interests.[60]

54 Wesseling (2000, 40) Marcos and Sanchez-Graells (2010, 190), and Bailey (2016, 119).

55 Greaves (1994, 5–7).

56 C-56/65 STM (1966), 250; C-56/64 C-58/64 Grundig/Consten (1966), 339–340, 344–346.

57 C-63/75 Fonderies (1967), para 11–19; C-47/76 De Norre (1977), para 10–11. See also policy report 1976, 20–21; and Greaves (1994, 50–51).

58 C-258/78 Maize seed (1982) shaped Regulation 2349/84 on Patent Licensing. See policy report 1979, 20; policy report 1982, 30. C-161/84 Pronuptia (1986) shaped Regulation 4089/88 on Franchising Agreements. See policy report 1985, 40. See also Greaves (1994, 63–64) and Goyder (2009, 255).

59 Forrester and Norall (1984, 15) and Goyder (2009, 142).

60 Groves (1995), Faure and Bergh (1995, 83), Marcos and Sanchez-Graells (2010, 199), Colino (2010, 210, 212–213), Wijckmans and Tuytschaever (2011, 299), Vogel (2016, 638), Porrini (2016, 167–168), and Akpinar (2017, 61).

Finally, the *European Parliament* also takes part in shaping balancing. The Commission is required to report to the Parliament on the application of BERs, to which the Parliament can recommend revisions.[61]

Each BER is adopted for a limited time. As demonstrated by Annex B, BERs typically expire after a period of ten or fifteen years. As such, both the Member States and the EU institutions are regularly involved in reviewing, consulting, and modifying the balancing principles applicable under each BER. Their positions are not only based on pure competition interests but also take broader policy considerations into account.

The Member States' and the EU institutions' involvement in adopting the BERs does not only allow them to fashion the role of non-competition interests in that specific BER but also shapes the role of non-competition interests under Article 101 (3) TFEU individual exemptions. Since each BER is based on the presumption that the protected categories of agreements satisfy 'with sufficient certainty' the four conditions of the Article, the terms of each BER also influence the relevant types of benefits, balancing method, and intensity of control applicable to individual exemptions.

4.3.2.2 Applying BERs

In addition to the *ex-ante* balancing embodied in the adoption of a BER, the application of a BER to a specific agreement also entails balancing. The balancing method differs between general and sectoral BERs. Figure 4.3, therefore, summarises the number of Article 101 TFEU enforcement actions in which the Commission has discussed the application of general and sectoral BERs. It presents the number of BERs examined (general – black bars, sectoral – grey bars) and exempted (triangles and crosses).

The figure reveals that, since the third enforcement period (i.e. after 1988), 59% of the BERs invoked and 87% of the BERs accepted were sectoral (grey bars and crosses). This can be explained by the Commission's focus during that period on enforcement in regulated and liberalised markets.[62] Since the Commission directed its enforcement efforts to agreements in areas governed by sectoral BERs, those BERs were more likely to be discussed in Commission decisions.

The high rate of invocation and acceptance of sectoral BERs can also be linked to the balancing process and discretion warranted in their application. Sectoral BERs typically require the competition enforcer to engage in a detailed *legal balancing process* when applying them to a specific case, leaving the enforcer ample discretion.

Some sectoral BERs warrant a full competition analysis comparable to the balancing method of Article 101(3) TFEU individual exemptions. For instance,

[61] Greaves (1994, 131) and Whish (2000, 892).
[62] See Section 2.5.3.1.

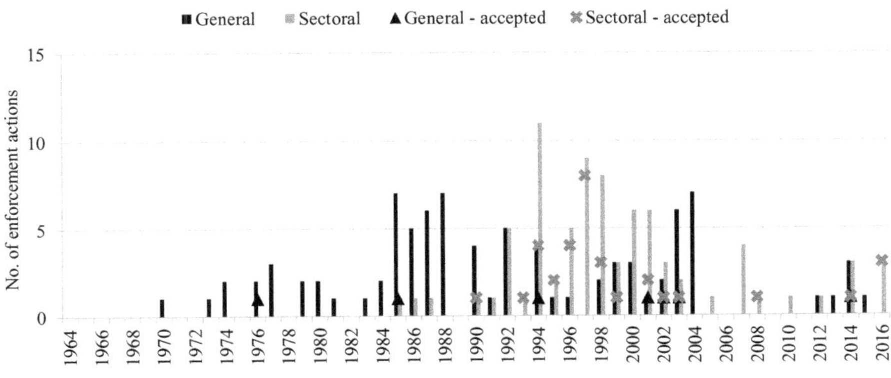

FIGURE 4.3. General and sectoral BERs, Commission
All Article 101 TFEU enforcement actions rendered by the Commission, excluding comfort letters. In some cases, more than one BER was invoked

the Inland Transport BER repeats the wording of Article 101(3) TFEU with only small modifications to adapt it to the sector.[63] When applying that BER, the competition enforcers balance the case-specific harm to competition (often as a result of a cartel) with the case-specific benefits. They must ensure that consumers received a fair share of the benefits, that the restrictions are indispensable, and do not eliminate competition.[64]

This is illustrated by three decisions exempting the creation of transport services between the UK and continental Europe as part of the opening of the *Channel Tunnel (1994)*.[65] Each of the cooperation arrangements involved an agreement between the public rail companies owning the railway infrastructure in their

[63] Regulation 1017/68 on Inland Transport, Article 5 provides that the prohibition of anti-competitive agreements may be declared inapplicable to 'any agreement or category of agreement between undertakings, any decision or category of decision of an association of undertakings, or any concerted practice or category of concerted practice which contributes towards improving the quality of transport services; or promoting greater continuity and stability in the satisfaction of transport needs on markets where supply and demand are subject to considerable temporal fluctuation; or increasing the productivity of undertakings; or furthering technical or economic progress; and at the same time takes fair account of the interests of transport users and neither: (a) imposes on the transport undertakings concerned any restriction not essential to the attainment of the above objectives; nor (b) makes it possible for such undertakings to eliminate competition in respect of a substantial part of the transport market concerned'.

[64] See, for example, 31029 French inland waterway charter traffic-EATE levy (1985), para 52–56; 34494 Tariff structures in the combined transport of goods (1993), para 49–61; 33941 HOV SVZ/MCN (1994), para 99–103; 34518 ACI (1994), para 48–59; IP-94-850 Rapid delivery services (1994); 34600 Night Services (1994), para 59–70; 34446 Trans-Atlantic Agreement (1994), para 462–491; 32490 Eurotunnel (1994), para 86–103; 33218 Far Eastern Freight Conference (1994), para 92–142; 35134 Trans-Atlantic Conference Agreement (1998), para 409–441; 34018 Far East Trade Tariff and Surcharges Agreement (FETTSCA) (2000), para 175.

[65] 32490 Eurotunnel (1994); 34518 ACI (1994); 34600 Night Services (1994). See also policy report 1994, 112–113.

respective countries. The Commission admitted that a joint entry into the emerging international transport market could reinforce the undertakings' already dominant position, making access impossible or extremely difficult for competing providers. Yet, it observed that entry into that market required considerable investment in transport equipment and fixed installations and that the economic viability of such new activities was highly uncertain. Therefore, the Commission concluded that the rapid promotion of these new services for the benefit of the European industry justified the cooperation between the incumbent national rail companies.

Other sectoral BERs prescribe a different balancing method guided by a legal proportionality test. For example, the Motor Vehicles BER states that the exemption does not apply 'where the supplier of motor vehicles refuses to give independent operators access to any technical information, diagnostic and other equipment [...] required for the repair and maintenance of these motor vehicles or for the implementation of environmental protection measures'.[66] According to the Commission, the technical information must be 'proportionate to independent repairers' needs'.[67] The competition enforcer, therefore, must ascertain the legitimate level of access to technical information, diagnostic, and other equipment that is necessary to meet the independent repairers' needs or for the implementation of environmental protection measures.

Arguably, the need to apply a full competition analysis similarly to Article 101(3) TFEU individual exemptions created a degree of uncertainty that had motivated the Commission to examine the application of the sectoral BERs in reasoned and published decisions rather than by means of comfort letters or informal settlements.[68] This could explain the findings in Figure 4.3, showing that sectoral BERs were more visible in Article 101 TFEU enforcement actions.

In comparison, most of the general BERs are based on a balancing process by way of *exclusion*. They leave the competition enforcer only limited discretion to balance when applying the BER in a specific case. A competition enforcer is essentially required to identify the type of agreement (e.g. vertical, horizontal) and to calculate the market share of the undertakings involved. In addition, an enforcer has to verify that the agreement does not include any prohibited clauses ('hard-core restrictions'). Consequently, while the adoption of BERs involves a degree of discretion to balance competition and non-competition interests, the application of a general BER mostly involved a limited degree of discretion. Indeed, the EU Courts repeatedly confirmed that, as a legal exception to competition rules, BERs should be interpreted strictly.[69]

66 Regulation 1400/2002 on Motor Vehicles, Article 4(2). For a detailed discussion of that BER, see also Colino (2010) and Wijckmans and Tuytschaever (2011, Chapter 10).

67 39140 DaimlerChrysler (2007), para 16.

68 This is also supported by the empirical findings presented in Figure 7.2.

69 C-234/89 Delimits (1991), para 46; T-9/92 Eco System (1993), para 37; C-70/93 BMW (1995), para 28; C-306/96 Javico International (1998), para 32; C-230/96 Cabour (1998), para 30, 143; T-395/94 Trans-Atlantic Agreement (2002), para 146; C-439/09 Pierre Fabre (2011), para 57–58.

The empirical findings suggest that the application of general BERs to specific cases was, in general, straightforward. Yet, the competition enforcers were not entirely consistent in this approach. They occasionally deployed a higher margin of discretion, going beyond the strict wording, and applied the benefits of a general BER to situations that are merely compatible with its 'spirit'.

In *Fonderies (1976)*, for example, the CJEU examined the wording of the BER on Exclusive Distribution, stating that the exemption shall not apply to agreements in which 'undertakings from one Member State only are party and which concern the resale of goods within that Member State'.[70] Despite this wording, and contrary to the Commission's submission,[71] the Court interpreted the BER broadly. It held that 'there is no reason based on the objectives of Regulation No 67/67 for failing to allow agreements of *an identical nature* concluded between two undertakings belonging to the same Member State to benefit from this general exemption'.[72] In *BP Kemi (1979)*, the Commission held that, when interpreting a provision of a BER, 'we cannot confine ourselves solely to the letter of the text; *its spirit and purpose* and its function within the general objectives of the Regulation have also to be considered'.[73] As a result, the Commission found that the purchasing agreement concluded by undertakings did not enjoy the exemption provided by the BER on Exclusive Distribution.

Hence, even the application of the relatively inflexible legal tool of the general BER leaves room for discretion when applied in a specific case. Section 4.4.1.1 further shows that certain national enforcers have interpreted the general BERs as setting only a general balancing standard that leaves an even broader margin of discretion. These interpretations have rendered balancing less certain than what at first sight might be expected from general BERs, sometimes resulting in their inconsistent application.

4.3.3 *Modernising BERs*

4.3.3.1 From Form-Based to Effects-Based Balancing

Balancing of competition and non-competition interests under BERs has changed over the enforcement periods. This section shows that until the end of the third enforcement period, BERs were based on a formalistic analysis. Yet, most of the BERs adopted since then reflect an effects-based approach. In fact, this shift planted the first seeds for the advent of an effects-based approach in all other areas of EU competition law.[74]

70 Regulation 67/67 on Distribution Agreements, Article 1(2).
71 See also policy report 1976, 20–21.
72 Emphasis added. C-63/75 Fonderies (1976), para 13.
73 Emphasis added. 29021 BP Kemi/DDSF (1979), para 95.
74 Whish (2000, 887) Sufrin (2006, 932–933), Monti (2007, 357), Goyder (2009, 209–210), Jones (2010, 787–788), and Gerard (2012, 25–29).

The application of the early general and sectoral BERs warranted a formalistic and relatively straightforward examination. The first BER on Distribution Agreements essentially centred on the form of an agreement. The exemption was dependent on whether an agreement contained certain provisions and omitted others.[75] This approach also guided the BERs replacing and supplementing the first BER.[76] Each BER included a detailed list of what could be included in an agreement without infringing Article 101(1) TFEU ('white provisions'), restrictions that could be exempted by the BER ('grey restrictions'), and restrictions that would cause the BER to lose its effect ('black restrictions').[77]

This formalistic 'pigeonholing' approach was well-suited to achieve the administrative motivation of the BERs. It allowed the Commission to quickly review a large number of agreements without overtaking an in-depth competition analysis. It also provided undertakings with legal certainty. Yet, this approach was also condemned as arbitrary. In a seminal 1995 article, *Hawk* argued that this approach forced undertakings to alter their agreements to comply with the forms permitted by the BERs in a manner that benefitted neither themselves nor their consumers.[78] Pointing to what would later be described as the 'straitjacket effect', he argued that the BERs limited the structures of distribution in the EU while ignoring the changing commercial and technological realities. Hawk's line of criticism was widely accepted by practitioners, scholars, and members of the industry alike.[79] By the late 1990s, it was also accepted by the Commission itself. In its 1998 policy report, the Commission acknowledged the need to modernise the BERs.[80]

A year later, the Commission introduced Regulation 2790/99 on Vertical Agreements, replacing a number of earlier BERs. Abolishing the list of white clauses, the new BER covered all types of vertical agreements and followed an effects-based approach. Accordingly, an exemption became dependent on the market power held by the undertakings rather than on the form or types of restrictions contained in the agreement. In the Commission's words, 'the general idea is that there should be a single and very broad block exemption regulation covering all vertical restrictions of competition in respect of all intermediate and finished goods and all services. A limited number of restrictions would be excluded, such as price-fixing agreements for example. These would form a "black list" of clauses that were not exempted by the regulation. The regulation would not seek to list the clauses that were exempted, as is done in the block exemption regulations currently in force,

75 Regulation 67/67 on Distribution Agreements.
76 Regulation 1983/83 on Exclusive Distribution; Regulation 1984/84 on Exclusive Purchasing; Regulation 4087/88 on Franchising Agreements.
77 See Section 4.2.
78 Hawk (1995).
79 Policy report 1996, 31; policy report 1999, 8; Whish (2000, 887); Sufrin (2006, 932–933); Monti (2007, 357); Goyder (2009, 209–210), and Gerard (2012, 25–29).
80 Policy report 1998, 21–22.

and this would immediately remove the straitjacket effect associated with the present white lists, which incite firms to force their agreements into a mould provided by the relevant block exemption regulation'.[81]

The Commission's new effects-based approach was an essential pillar in the overall modernisation of EU competition law. At the substantive level, it marked a shift from a form-based to an effects-based approach. It protected competition by allowing competition enforcers to concentrate their efforts on cases involving market power and eliminate the straitjacket effect. At the procedural level, it was the first step towards diminishing the notification regime. The Vertical BER was the first to dispense with the obligation of prior notification in all vertical agreements covered by the BER by abolishing the opposition procedure.[82] This model was followed by all subsequent general BERs. It was also extended to some, but not all, of the new sectoral BERs.[83]

The modernisation of the BERs is summarised in Figure 4.4. The figure indicates the number of form-based and effects-based BERs invoked (black and grey lines, respectively) and accepted (triangles and crosses, respectively).

The figure highlights that formalistic BERs were invoked much more frequently compared to effects-based BERs and were also accepted more often. Since the adoption of the first effects-based BER in 1999, formalistic BERs accounted for 73% of the BERs examined in the Commission's enforcement actions, and 79% of those accepted. While, as mentioned, the empirical findings on the application of BERs must be interpreted with caution,[84] this could indicate that the effects-based

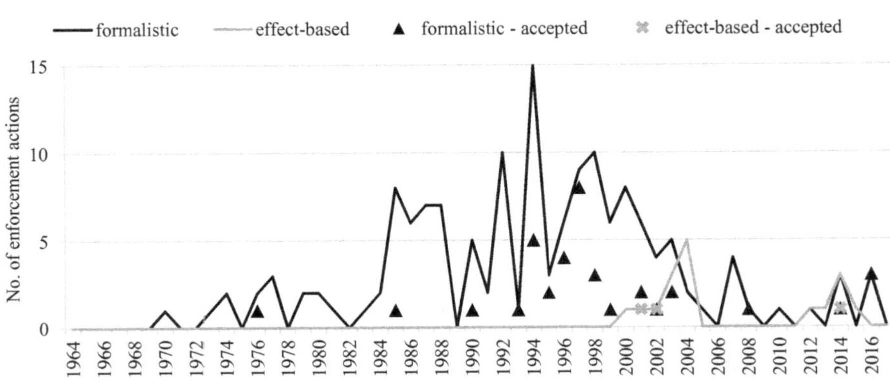

FIGURE 4.4. Form- and effects-based BERs, Commission
All Article 101 TFEU enforcement actions rendered by the Commission, excluding comfort letters. In some cases, more than one BER was invoked

[81] *Ibid*. See also policy report 1999, 7.
[82] See policy report 1999, 8, 29.
[83] See Annex B.
[84] See Section 4.2.

approach did not significantly impede the legal certainty of those BERs. In other words, it seems that undertakings were generally capable of self-assessing their conduct and complying with the requirements of the effects-based BERs.

At the same time, it cannot be denied that BERs still run counter to an effects-based approach. BERs inherently rely on formalistic categories of agreements and sectors rather than on detailed economic case-by-case analyses of their effects, such as in the case of Article 101(3) TFEU individual exceptions.

4.3.3.2 Questioning the Theoretical Justification of Sectoral BERs

The modernisation of the BER has also marked a change in attitude towards sectoral BERs. Sectoral BERs have been increasingly criticised as a form of protectionism sheltering inefficient industries and firms and impeding market efficiency. They were condemned as instruments that were regulatory in nature rather than aimed at competition enforcement.[85]

By the end of the 1990s, the Commission (partly) accepted this criticism. As part of its more economic approach, and similar to its approach to BERs on state aid,[86] it voiced concerns about the economic justification for sectoral BERs. Aiming to prevent 'unjustified differentiation' between sectors, in 1999 the Commission combined various BERs that dealt with specific forms of vertical restraint into a single wide-ranging BER.[87] The Commission further noted that the sector-specific rules for beer and petrol should be withdrawn, as the continuation of a special regime for those sectors 'is not justified on economic or legal grounds'.[88] The Commission was also critical of the transport BERs and has, since the beginning of the 2000s, progressively limited their scope.[89] In 2013, it finally held that there was no longer any need to keep the sector-specific regulations for this sector and subjected it to the regular competition rules.[90] Similarly, in 2016, the Commission decided not to extend the Insurance BER when it expired in March 2017.[91]

85 Wesseling (2000, 40), Marcos and Sanchez-Graells (2010, 199–200), and the references there.

86 Regulation 800/2008 on State Aid General Block Exemption Regulation replaced by Regulation 651/2014. See also Deiberova and Nyssens (2009, 27).

87 Policy report 1998, 30–31.

88 *Ibid*, 31.

89 Regulation 1/2003 repealed the special procedural rules for transport agreements and broadened the Commission's enforcement powers in that sector. In the area of maritime transport, Regulation 1419/2006 repealed Regulation 4056/86 in its entirety; in the area of inland transport, Regulation 169/2009, which repealed Regulation 1017/68, retained some sector specific exemptions. Similarly, while the Council's Enabling Regulation 487/2009, which repealed Regulation 3976/87, allowed for the issuance of BERs for air transport, no such Regulation was adopted. See policy report 2004, 26.

90 Commission Press Release IP/13/122, 19 February 2013.

91 Regulation 267/2010 on Insurance replacing Regulation 358/2003 on Insurance. This decision was based on the Commission's Impact Assessment on the Insurance BERs (2016).

However, there are a number of exceptions to this trend. The motor vehicle sector, for example, still benefits from a sector-specific exemption.[92] Regulation 1400/2002, which was adopted following the modernisation of most BERs, manifested a quasi-regulation of this sector. After an exceptionally long and complex assessment process, it was replaced by Regulation 461/2010, which extended the provisions of the previous BER on new motor vehicles for a transition period of three years, after which they have become subject to the general Vertical BER. Even after the transition period ended, the distribution of spare parts and repair and maintenance services still remains subject to a sectoral exemption.[93] This reflected a political compromise following significant lobbying from dealers.[94]

A sectoral exemption also governs the cooperation of shipping companies for the joint operation of liner shipping service (consortia). This BER was extended in April 2020 for additional four years, despite continuing claims arguing that it is not in line with economic theory and is an instrument for accepting undue restrictions of competition in the maritime transport sector.[95] Interestingly, the exemption granted by the BER is justified not only by reference to economic benefits but also by non-economic benefits as environmental protection via a reduction in fuel consumption and industrial policy by promoting the global competitiveness of the EU's shipping sector.[96] This raises the question of how the Commission's call to limit the Article 101(3) TFEU individual exemptions to economic benefits[97] can be squared with the broad non-economic benefits that justify an exemption under the sectoral BERs.

4.3.4 *Interim Conclusion*

This section has examined the balancing that has taken place in the process of adopting and applying BERs, highlighting that BERs involve considerable room for non-competition interests. This is especially true with respect to sectoral BERs. While general BERs mainly take economic, efficiency-related considerations into account, sectoral BERs examined broad non-economic interests and often reserve greater political power to the Council and Member States. Moreover, sectoral BERs prescribe only general balancing standards. They leave competition enforcers

[92] Regulation 461/2010 on Motor Vehicles replacing Regulations 123/85, 1475/95 and 1400/2002 on Motor Vehicles. See also policy report 1998, 30–31.

[93] Regulation 461/2010 on Motor Vehicles, Articles 2–3.

[94] Colino (2010, 210, 212–213, 216–217) and Wijckmans and Tuytschaever (2011, 293–299). On the role of lobbying in the previous versions of the Motor Vehicles BERs, see Groves (1995).

[95] Regulation 2020/436 extending the period of application of Regulation 906/2009 on Consortia. On the Consortia BER, see also Greaves (1994, 111–112), Townley (2004), and Levitt and Ziegler (2014).

[96] Staff Working Document on the Evaluation of the Consortia BER (2019), 32–33, 47. The industrial policy objective is also apparent in Recital 6 of Regulation 246/2009 on Liner Shipping, declaring that the BER 'can make a positive contribution to improving the competitiveness of shipping in the Community'.

[97] See Section 3.3.4.

greater discretion to balance by way of applying a legal balancing process. General BERs, by comparison, often limit the discretion of competition enforcers. Once a set of criteria apply, they exclude the prohibition of Article 101(1) TFEU without a need to undertake a detailed analysis. Consequently, sectoral BERs facilitate balancing that is less uniform and certain compared with the balancing embodied in general BERs.

The modernisation of the BERs was designed to focus the analysis on the agreement's effects on competition and economic welfare. In particular, it has led the Commission to abolish most sectoral BERs. This combination of the shift to an effects-based BER and the abolishment of the sectoral BERs has marked a move away from using BERs as a regulatory tool towards using them as a measure to ensure the uniform enforcement of competition rules across all sectors and types of agreements.

4.4 NCAS AND NATIONAL COURTS

4.4.1 *NCAs*

As in the case of Article 101(3) TFEU individual exceptions, Regulation 1/2003 has empowered NCAs to apply the conditions of the BERs.[98] As such, the NCAs have been entrusted with new balancing powers. Nevertheless, thus far, only very limited attention was awarded by academics and policymakers to the application of BERs by NCAs and national courts.

One can distinguish between three types of enforcement actions in which NCAs apply BERs: (i) mixed cases[99] in which they apply the EU BERs; (ii) purely national cases[100] in which they apply the EU BERs; and (iii) national and mixed cases in which they apply national BERs. Those three types of proceedings are summarised in Figure 4.5 and elaborated below.

4.4.1.1 EU and Mixed Cases

First, NCAs apply the EU BERs in mixed cases, i.e. when an agreement affects trade between Member States (black lines). The figure shows that the NCAs, like the Commission, have accepted BERs in only a relatively small number of proceedings (black triangles). This confirms the conclusion that the application of the BERs is generally clear and that undertakings manage to self-assess their conduct.[101]

According to Regulation 1/2003, the application of the EU BERs in mixed cases is subject to the same substantive rules that apply to the Commission.[102]

[98] Prior to May 2004, BERs could only be applied by national courts.

[99] Mixed cases are proceedings involving the enforcement of Article 101 TFEU and the national equivalent provision. See Section 1.3.2.1.

[100] Purely national cases are proceedings involving only the enforcement of the national provision equivalent to Article 101 TFEU. See Section 1.3.2.1.

[101] See Section 4.2.

[102] Regulation 1/2003, Preamble 10.

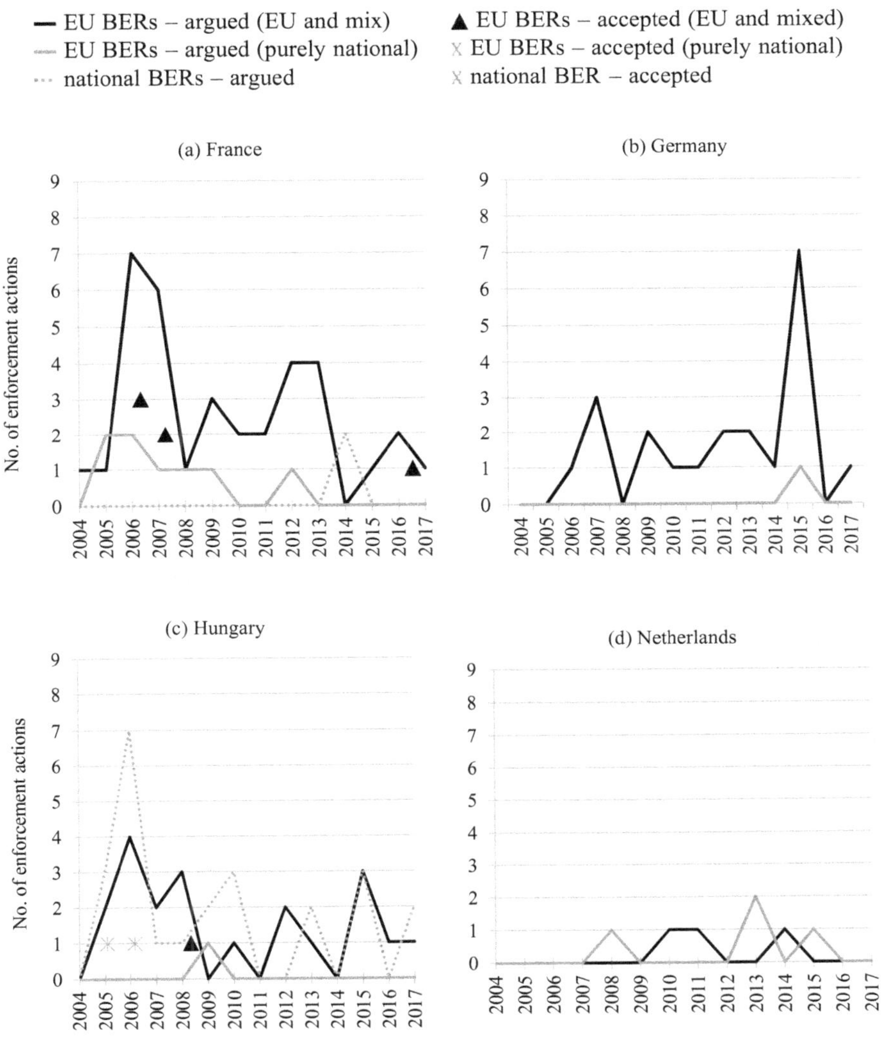

FIGURE 4.5. BERs, NCAs
In some proceedings, more than one BER was invoked

The empirical findings, however, illustrate that the NCAs did not always follow the Commission's and EU Courts' interpretations of the BERs. This was even evident in the application of general BERs, which, as mentioned, leave the competition enforcers a relatively small margin of discretion to determine the scope of balancing.

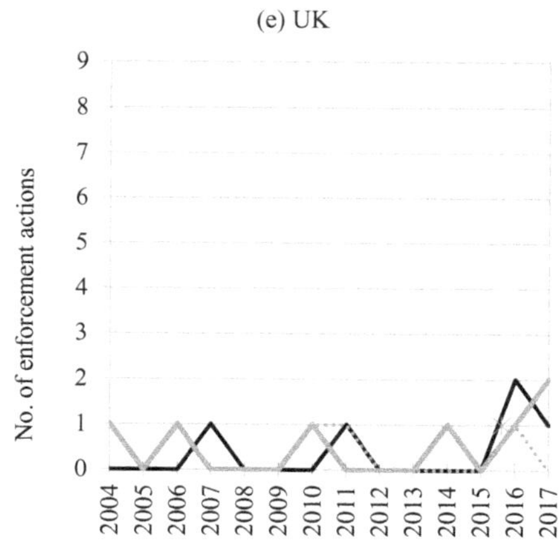

FIGURE 4.5. *(cont.)*

The tension between the EU and German approaches in interpreting the EU Vertical BERs provides an illustrative example. In *ASICS (2015, 2017)*, the German NCA had to determine whether the prohibition – imposed on distributors in a selective distribution system – forbidding participation in online price comparison tools had excluded the benefits of the Vertical BER.[103] At that time, similar questions were already examined by the CJEU in *Pierre Fabre (2011)* and *Coty (2017)*. The CJEU concluded that a *de facto* ban on any online sale amounted to a restriction of authorised distributors' passive sales to end users that excludes the agreement from the BER (*Pierre Fabre*), whereas certain restrictions on specific kinds of online sale may benefit from the safe harbour (*Coty*).[104]

Nevertheless, the German NCA had interpreted the Vertical BERs as prescribing only a general standard. Accordingly, it maintained that the decision of whether an agreement contained a hard-core restriction for the purpose of applying a BER must follow the same principles as classifying a by-object restriction. This entails a full competition analysis of the legal and economic background, including an assessment of whether the agreement was objectively necessary for the functioning of the distribution system. Its analysis followed similar principles as the ancillary restraint exception, which will be elaborated in Section 5.3.4. Based on such an analysis, the German NCA found that the prohibition against participating in online price comparison tools was excluded from the benefit of the BER.

[103] Regulation 330/2010 on Vertical Restrains. See B2–98/11 ASICS (2015), para 380–386.
[104] C-439/09 Pierre Fabre (2011), para 51–59; C-230/16 Coty (2017), para 59–69.

The German NCA's analysis was confirmed by the German courts.[105] The decision of the German High Court in the matter was particularly remarkable because it was rendered one week *after* the CJEU's judgment in *Coty (2017)*. Admittedly, the precise scope of *Coty* is unclear from the judgment itself, for instance, whether its reasoning can be extended to non-luxury goods and other forms of online platforms. Yet, the Commission and various scholars had already pointed out that the reasoning in *Coty* did not appear to be limited to specific product categories or particular market conditions. They noted that because one of the main purposes of a BER is to secure legal certainty about the validity of Article 101 TFEU, the assessment of hard-core restrictions should not depend on the product concerned or an analysis of the market conditions.[106] Nevertheless, the German High Court did not accept this position and prescribed a full case-by-case analysis.[107]

The above shows that diverging interpretations by the competition enforcers might hamper the function of BERs in ensuring the uniform and certain application of Article 101(3) TFEU balancing. This is another testament to the power of national enforcers to facilitate conflicting interpretations of balancing across the EU, as was already discussed in the previous chapter.[108] By dint of interpreting BERs as entailing a wide margin of discretion, NCAs and national courts may impair a consistent application of the BERs across the EU and the undertakings' ability to predict in advance the compatibility of their agreements with Article 101 TFEU.

4.4.1.2 Purely National Cases

Second, NCAs apply EU BERs to purely national cases (grey lines). The normative value of EU BERs in purely national cases is not a matter of EU law. Some Member States, such as Germany, the Netherlands, and the UK, have formally transported EU BERs into national law, so they apply *mutatis mutandis* to purely national cases.[109] In France, EU BERs do not have any formal value. Yet, the French NCA and courts have used them as an 'analytical guide' for competition analysis. Consequently, in practice, EU BERs direct the analysis of purely national cases in France.[110]

105 The German first instance court confirmed this decision in VI-Kart 13/15(V) ASICS (2017), para 91–107. It denied granting leave for a second appeal, noting that this question was indisputable. A few months later, the German High Court rejected an appeal against this refusal in KVZ 41/17 ASICS (2017), para 12–35, holding that it was beyond doubt that the prohibition amounted to a hard-core restriction in the meaning of the BER.

106 Commission Policy Brief on EU Competition Rules and the Marketplace (2018), 4; Waelbroeck and Davies (2018, 9); and Wijckmans (2018, 375).

107 KVZ 41/17 ASICS (2017), para 12–35.

108 See Section 3.6.5.

109 German Competition Act, Section 2(2); Dutch Competition Act, Articles 12 and 13; UK Competition Act, Section 10(2).

110 05-D-48 Taximeters (2005), para 55; 05-D-32 Dry dog food (2005), para 184; 06-D-37 Cycle and cycle products (2006) para 313; 07-D-04 Jeff de Bruges chocolates (2007), para 85. This was approved by the Appeals Court in 2007/00370 Cycle and cycle products (2008).

4.4.1.3 National BERs

Finally, some Member States adopted national BERs in addition to the EU BERs. In some cases, the national BERs exempt the same type of conduct governed by the EU BERs (e.g. in Hungary[111] and the UK[112]). In other cases, national BERs extend beyond the substantive scope of the EU BERs. The latter BERs are a clear example of national balancing.

In France, for instance, national BERs have exempted anti-competitive agreements related to signs of quality and crisis situations in the agriculture sector.[113] In the Netherlands, a national BER exempts retail cooperation, retail exclusivity agreements in shopping centres, and joint bidding in the field of procurement.[114] In the UK, national BERs exempt practices in relation to public transport ticketing schemes,[115] the defence industry, supply of oil and petroleum products, and the coronavirus pandemic.[116]

According to the principle of primacy of EU law, national BERs cannot exempt otherwise prohibited agreements when such agreements affect trade between

[111] For example, Hungary adopted Decree 53/2002 on Specialisation Agreements, Decree 54/2002 on R&D, Decree 55/2002 on Vertical Agreements, Decree 246/1997 on Franchising, Decree 205/2011 on Vertical Agreements, Decree No. 86/1999 on Technology Transfer Agreements, Decree 202/2011 on Specialisation Agreements, Decree 204/2011 on Motor Vehicles, Decree 203/2011 on Insurance Sector, Decree 206/2011 on Research and Development.

[112] The Competition Act 1998 (Land and Vertical Agreement Exclusion) Order 2002 excluded vertical agreements until 2005.

[113] Decree 96-499 on Signs of Quality in the Agricultural Sector, Decree 96-500 on Adaptation Measures for Crisis Situations, Decree 2007-1884 on Motor Vehicles Subsidiaries. See also Vogel (2012, 171–172) and Boudou et al. (2014, 109).

[114] Decree Exempting Cooperation Agreements in Retail Trade (2014); Decree Exempting New Shopping Centres (1997). Policy rules of the Minster of Economic Affairs on Combination Agreements (2013). See also Felsö, Baarsma, and Mulder (2007), Holmes and Davey (2007, 617), and Pree and Molin (2013, 203).

[115] Public Transport Ticketing Schemes Block Exemption (Order 2001), extended by the Public Transport Ticketing Schemes Block Exemption (Amendment) Order 2016.

[116] Competition Act 1998 (Public Policy Exclusion) Order 2006 (maintenance and repair of warships); Competition Act 1998 (Public Policy Exclusion) Order 2007 (strategic and tactical weapons and their supporting technology) (repealed by the Competition Act 1998 (Public Policy Exclusion) (Revocation) Order 2011 (Team Complex Weapons); Competition Act 1998 (Public Policy Exclusion) Order 2008 (design, construction, maintenance and disposal of nuclear submarines); The Competition Act 1998 (Public Policy Exclusion) Order 2012 (supply of oil fuels in an emergency); Competition Act 1998 (Groceries) (Coronavirus) (Public Policy Exclusion) Order 2020; Competition Act 1998 (Health Services for Patients in England) (Coronavirus) (Public Policy Exclusion) Order 2020; Competition Act 1998 (Solent Maritime Crossings) (Coronavirus) (Public Policy Exclusion) Order 2020; Competition Act 1998 (Health Services for Patients in Wales) (Coronavirus) (Public Policy Exclusion) Order 2020; Competition Act 1998 (Dairy Produce) (Coronavirus) (Public Policy Exclusion) Order 2020. The British exceptions are further discussed in Section 6.3.3.

Member States.[117] However, the empirical findings illustrate that the NCAs did not always respect this principle.

In a small number of proceedings, the Hungarian NCA applied national BERs to mixed cases.[118] In *Distribution of tobacco products (2005)*, for example, the Hungarian NCA exempted an agreement under a national BER, while admitting that the agreement might affect trade between Member States. It maintained that it did not have to decide on the issue or assess the compatibility of the agreement with the comparable EU BER, as the exemption was requested by the undertakings that invoked the national BER.[119]

Perhaps even more importantly, the empirical findings confirm that the Member States have generally refrained from taking action against agreements in mixed cases that could otherwise have been protected by a national BER. To this extent, the empirical findings prove that the NCAs rarely pursued agreements in mixed cases when they could also have been covered by a national BER were it not for the circumstance that the agreement affected trade between Member States. In *Paroxetine-IVAX/GSK agreement (2016)*, the UK NCA seemed to admit such practice. After finding that the agreement could have benefited from the national vertical BER, the NCA closed the proceedings, also with respect to Article 101 TFEU infringement, noting that the agreement was unlikely to restrict competition.[120]

Similarly, the UK NCA declared that although its Public Transport Ticketing Schemes BER cannot exempt agreements from the application of Article 101 TFEU in mixed-cases, 'the same principles apply' to determine whether an agreement has countervailing benefits under EU and national competition laws. Accordingly, where a ticketing scheme agreement meets the requirements of the BER, 'it is likely to also be treated as exempt from the prohibition in Article 101 TFEU'.[121]

The above examples support the conclusion that, while national BERs do not formally affect balancing in mixed cases, they may indeed have such a spillover effect. This is yet another example of balancing by enforcement discretion, which is further detailed in Chapter 7.

4.4.2 *National Courts*

Figure 4.6 summarises the judicial review of the application of BERs by NCAs. This includes cases in which the application of BERs was examined (grey bars) and overturned (black bars) by national courts.

[117] Regulation 1/2003, Article 3. See Section 2.3.3.2.

[118] For example, Vj-195/2007/129 Newspaper distribution II (2010), para 85–87, 150; Vj-68/2011 Alt Cash Kft (2013), 18, 22.

[119] Vj-154/2004/16 Distribution of tobacco products (2005), para 21–28.

[120] CE/9531/11 Paroxetine-IVAX/GSK agreement (2016) (case closure summary), para 2.

[121] Public transport ticketing schemes block exemption Guidance (2016), para 2.6

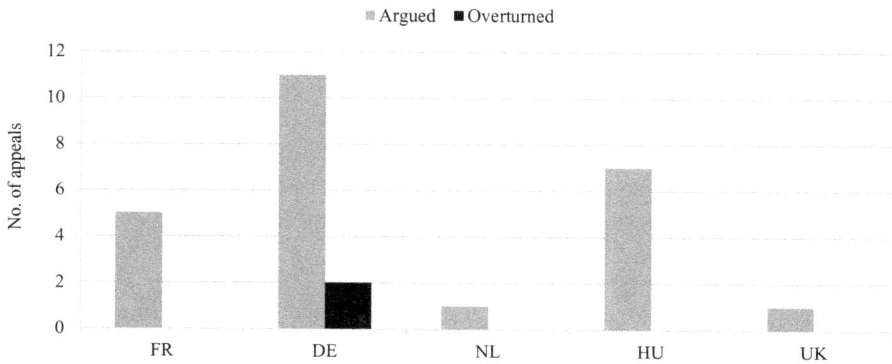

FIGURE 4.6. BERs, national courts (May 2004–2017)
Each appeal instance at which a case was examined is counted as an independent appeal. The figure includes appeals on both EU and national BERs

Like the EU Courts,[122] the national courts examined only a few challenges to the NCAs' application of BERs, and almost never overturned an NCA's decision. The small number of successful national challenges is an additional indication that the application of BERs is relatively certain and has not generally posed legal difficulties.

Yet, the application of the BERs has raised a few legal challenges. The German courts annulled two NCA's decisions refusing to exempt agreements under BERs. [123] Notably, those two judgments related to the manner in which the German NCA defined the relevant market and, accordingly, calculated the market shares in effects-based BERs. This illustrates that effects-based BERs, which are guided by economic balancing process, can give rise to some legal uncertainty concerns.

4.4.3 *Interim Conclusion*

The empirical findings reveal some divergence in the national application of BERs. In particular, they show that NCAs and national courts have sometimes interpreted the BERs as offering a higher degree of discretion compared to the approach of the Commission and EU Courts. In addition, national BERs have sometimes directly or indirectly influenced the application of Article 101 TFEU in mixed cases. As such, they may jeopardise the uniformity and legal certainty of balancing in the decentralised enforcement regime.

[122] See Section 4.2.

[123] VIKart 11/07 (V) Pecuniary loss liability risks for auditors and chartered accountants (2008), para 23–57, as confirmed by the second instance in KVR 34/08 Pecuniary loss liability risks for auditors and chartered accountants (2009); VIKart 5/09 (V) Merck and VWR distribution agreement (2013), para 95–148.

4.5 RELATIONSHIP BETWEEN BERS AND INDIVIDUAL EXEMPTION BALANCING

The function of BERs as a balancing tool must be understood in the wider context of Article 101 TFEU enforcement, and particularly, in connection with Article 101(3) TFEU individual exemptions. This section, therefore, discusses situations in which an individual exemption was granted after the benefit of a BER has been refused, revealing that the competition enforcers had divergent approaches to the application of Article 101(3) TFEU's conditions in those situations. This section also presents the rare number of cases where a competition enforcer withdrew or considered withdrawing the benefits of a BER from a specific agreement.

4.5.1 *Individual Exemption Granted after BER Refused*

Each BER, as mentioned, is based on the assumption that all protected agreements satisfy the four conditions of Article 101(3) TFEU. Yet, the fact that the benefit of a BER has been refused does not mean that an individual exemption is not possible. Indeed, in a number of proceedings, the competition enforcers granted an individual exemption after the benefit of a BER had been considered yet refused (e.g. since the agreement was classified as a hard-core restriction or exceeded the market share threshold prescribed by the BER).

These scenarios were common in the Commission's practice prior to modernisation. Figure 4.7 summarises the number of the Commission's Article 101 TFEU enforcement actions in which an individual exemption was granted after a benefit of a BER had been explicitly refused. It shows that, prior to May 2004, individual exemptions were mostly granted to agreements failing the terms of the vertical BERs (black and white bars), BERs related to technology (grey shaded bars), or sectoral BERs (white and grey bars). The brackets below each enforcement period provide additional context by indicating the number of Article 101(3) TFEU individual exemptions granted in each of the enforcement periods.

The empirical findings also demonstrate that the practice of granting an individual exception after a BER was denied had become rare following the entry into force of Regulation 1/2003. This is hardly surprising in light of the limited number of Article 101(3) TFEU individual exceptions following modernisation. At the EU level, as Figure 4.7 reveals, this situation was irrelevant since the Commission never accepted an Article 101(3) TFEU defence.[124] At the Member States level too, the Five NCAs scarcely ever found that the conditions of Article 101(3) TFEU individual exceptions had been fulfilled.[125] Only the French[126] and

[124] See Section 3.2.

[125] See Section 3.6.1.

[126] In its informal opinion in 13-A-08 Network sharing and roaming (2013), para 69, the French NCA declared that the agreement will need to be examined on a case-specific basis under

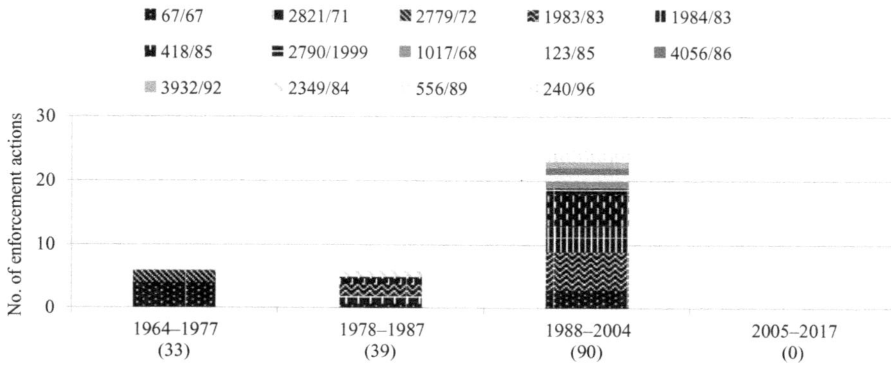

FIGURE 4.7. Individual exemption granted after BER refused, Commission
(in brackets, the total number of Article 101(3) exemptions granted in each enforcement period)
All Article 101 TFEU enforcement actions, excluding unpublished comfort letters. In some proceedings, more than one BER was invoked

Hungarian[127] NCAs have taken a positive view towards granting an Article 101(3) TFEU individual exception after denying the benefit of a BER.

The limited number of cases in which individual exceptions were granted after the benefit of a BER had been refused could be an indication of the relatively high legal certainty of balancing under BERs. As pointed out by *Faull and Nikpay*, if a significant number of agreements that fail to meet the conditions of a BER fulfil the four conditions of Article 101(3) TFEU, the BER in question probably needs to be reformulated.[128]

At the same time, the empirical findings indicate that the legal certainty and uniformity of balancing have been compromised by the Commission's and NCAs' different approaches to applying the four conditions of Article 101(3) TFEU in cases where an agreement could not benefit from a BER. They show that the competition enforcers essentially diverged in their interpretations regarding the following two questions:

First, in situations where an agreement fulfils almost all of the terms of a BER but fails to meet a term that is linked to *one condition of Article 101(3) TFEU*, is it sufficient to examine only the condition that denied the benefit of the BER, or is it necessary to assess all four conditions of Article 101(3) TFEU separately? For

Article 101(3) TFEU, after failing to meet the conditions of Regulation 1218/2010 on Specialisation Agreements.

[127] In Vj-23/2005 Rába Group and Integris (2005) and Vj-94/2005 British American Tobacco group (2006), para 66–71, after failing to meet the conditions of Regulation 2790/1999 on Vertical Agreements; and in Vj-207/2004/51 Rába IT agreement (2005), para 67–76 and Vj-7/2008/178 Motor oils and lubricants (2009), para 60–66, after failing to meet the conditions of the national vertical BER.

[128] Faull and Nikpay (2014, 310).

example, when assessing a vertical agreement that does not contain a hard-core restriction but is concluded between undertakings with a high market share, is it sufficient to examine only whether the agreement eliminates competition (the fourth condition of Article 101(3) TFEU)?

Second, in situations where an agreement fails to meet the conditions of a BER because of a *single provision in the agreement*, is it sufficient to examine whether that single provision can fulfil the conditions of Article 101(3) TFEU while assuming that the rest of the agreement is eligible for an individual exemption? This question relates to the severability of the BER. For example, when assessing a vertical agreement that cannot benefit from the Vertical BER due only to a non-compete obligation exceeding five years in length (a hard-core restriction), is it sufficient to assess the eligibility of the non-compete obligation with Article 101(3) TFEU conditions or should the entire agreement be examined?

Some competition enforcers have answered both questions in the negative. For example, the Commission Vertical Guidelines demand a full Article 101(3) TFEU analysis of an agreement that does not satisfy all of the BER conditions (the first question),[129] or if certain provisions of the agreement do not meet the conditions of the BER (the second question).[130] Similarly, the German NCAs' decision in *Pecuniary loss liability risks for auditors and chartered accountants (2008)* stated that an agreement that could not benefit from the insurance BER because of the undertakings' high market share would necessitate a full analysis of all four conditions of Article 101(3) TFEU. According to the German NCA, it could not be assumed that the first three conditions of the Article were fulfilled with reference to the BER.[131] This approach limits the effects of BERs to the agreements that are fully exempted by them.

Other competition enforcers chose a different path. In *Motor oils and lubricants (2009)*, the Hungarian NCA examined a distribution agreement that included non-compete and RPM clauses. The RPM clause, which was a hard-core restriction under the vertical BER, prevented the agreement from benefiting from the BER's safe harbour. Yet, the NCA maintained that non-compete clauses that did not exceed five years in length were compatible with Article 101(3) TFEU. The Hungarian NCA did not fully examine all four conditions of Article 101(3) TFEU. Rather, it briefly noted that such clauses could automatically benefit from the BER in the absence of an RPM (the first question).[132] Similarly, in *British American*

[129] Commission Vertical Guidelines (2010), para 96.

[130] *Ibid*, para 70–71.

[131] B4-31/05 Pecuniary loss liability risks for auditors and chartered accountants (2008), para 146. The decision was annulled on various grounds by the Düsseldorf Court of Appeals. See Section 4.4.2.

[132] Vj-7/2008/178 Motor oils and lubricants (2009), para 60–66. This case was purely national. However, since the Hungarian vertical BER is based on its EU counterpart, the interpretation of the Hungarian BER could also affect the interpretation of the Hungarian NCA of the EU BER. See also Boronkay and Molnár (2009, 874).

Tobacco group (2006), the Hungarian NCA explained that, since BERs are based on the assumption that they apply to cases that satisfy all four conditions of Article 101(3) TFEU, it is generally enough to examine only the parts of the agreement that fail to fulfil the conditions of the BER. If those 'excess' restrictions are not restrictive in and of themselves, the agreement could be accepted without further analysis (the second question).[133] The Hungarian approach broadens the substantive effect of BERs. The BER balancing tool is also applied indirectly to agreements that are not directly covered by it.[134]

The differences between the Commission and the German NCA approach on the one hand and the Hungarian NCA approach on the other hand to the relationship between BERs and individual exceptions demonstrate how national interpretations can lead to different balancing practices. This could compromise the uniformity and legal certainty of balancing under Article 101(3) TFEU individual exemptions and BERs.

4.5.2 *Withdrawal of BERs*

Questions of the relationship between Article 101(3) TFEU individual exceptions and BERs can also arise when the Commission or NCAs decide to withdraw the benefits of a BER from a specific agreement.[135] Such a withdrawal is appropriate when an agreement that fulfils the terms of a BER does not produce objective advantages that compensate for its negative effects on competition (i.e. an agreement between undertakings having a low market share but holding cumulative effect in parallel networks of similar agreements by competing suppliers or cases of buying power).[136]

The empirical findings presented in Figure 4.1 show that the Commission considered the withdrawal of BERs in only three proceedings. In *Langnese-Iglo (1992)*, it withdrew the benefit conferred by the Exclusive Purchasing Agreement BER from agreements requiring the German retailers Langnese and Scholler to purchase single-item ice cream for resale exclusively from the latter. The withdrawal was justified given the cumulative effects of the agreements.[137] In the other

[133] Vj-94/2005 British American Tobacco group (2006), para 23–33.

[134] Boronkay and Molnár (2009, 873).

[135] Regulation 1/2003, Article 29. See also Commission Article 101(3) Guidelines (2004), para 2 and 36. Prior to modernisation, the possibility to withdraw the application of BERs was set in the Council's Enabling Regulations. Regulation 1/2003 and the BERs adopted after Regulation 2790/99 on Vertical Restrains entrusted also the NCAs to withdraw the benefit of a BER in its Member State's territory if they believe that an exemption is no longer appropriate. See Regulation 1/2003, Article 29(2); Modernisation White Paper (1999), para 95.

[136] *Ibid*. See also policy report 1999, 25.

[137] 31533 and 34072 Langnese/Iglo (1992), para 108–113. The withdrawal was upheld by the GC in T-7/93 Langnese-Iglo (1995), para 133–196 and the CJEU in C-279/95P Langnese-Iglo (1998), para 43–49. Yet, the GC noted that the Commission had no legal basis to withdraw the benefit of the BER from future agreements (para 205–210).

two cases, the threat of withdrawal was sufficient to bring the infringement to an end.[138]

Moreover, the empirical findings indicate that the Five NCAs examined in this study did not use their powers to withdraw the benefits of BERs.[139] This also reflects the practices of other NCAs.[140] The German NCA considered withdrawing the benefits of the Vertical BER from the MFN clause in *HRS (2013)* but found this to be unnecessary because the market share of the undertakings was more than 30% and could not have benefited from the BER.[141] This statement could be seen as a warning to other undertakings that such types of clauses will not be automatically protected by the safe haven of the BER, at least not in Germany.[142]

The very limited use of the competition enforcers' power to withdraw the benefits of the BERs fosters the legal certainty of balancing by BERs and, indirectly, also the uniformity between enforcers. Accordingly, undertakings can be assured that they are protected by the safe haven of a BER if their agreements fulfil its conditions. Yet, the legal certainty and uniformity of the BERs should not be overestimated. As mentioned, in some cases, the competition enforcers used their discretion to interpret and apply BERs to alter the balancing under the BERs.

4.6 CLOSING REMARKS: TRANSITIONS IN BERS BALANCING

This chapter has shed light on the balancing function of BERs. It has shown that while BERs are traditionally perceived as having the administrative function of reducing the Commission's workload, they also serve as a tool to balance competition and non-competition interests.

In the past, BERs were heavily criticised as policy-driven, regulatory balancing tools that did not effectively protect competition interests. This line of criticism was prominent prior to the modernisation of BERs in the late 1990s. Older BERs, and especially sectoral ones, were considered highly political. Both their adoption process and their application left significant room for the consideration of broad non-economic benefits on the basis of a formalistic analysis that did not focus on the

[138] In 33157 Eco System/Peugeot (1991), para 25, the Commission threatened to withdraw the benefit of the motor-vehicle BER from Peugeot's Belgian and Luxembourg dealer networks; In 31043 Tetra Pak I (1988), para 53, the Commission considered withdrawing the benefits of the patent licensing BER from the exclusive license agreement between Tetra Pak and the BTG. The decision was upheld by the GC in T-51/89 Tetra Pak I (1990).

[139] Regulation 1/2003, Article 29(2). In 06-D-11 Turbo Europe (2006), para 26–30, the French NCA refused to withdraw a BER.

[140] According to the national reports presented at the XXIII FIDE Congress in 2008, none of the NCAs withdrew the benefit of a BER, either on the basis of Regulation 1/2003 or the equivalent domestic provisions. See in Marcos and Sanchez-Graells (2010, 197). See also Bailey and Whish (2015, 711).

[141] B9–66/10 HRS best price clauses (2013), para 15, 59, 189, 268–270.

[142] On MFN clauses, see also Section 3.6.3.1.

impact of an agreement on competition interests. As such, BERs were rightly seen as a form of protectionism serving as an instrument with a regulatory character.[143]

The switch to an effects-based approach and the abolishment of most of the sectoral BERs as part of the substantive modernisation were aimed at increasing the effectiveness of BERs. BERs were refocused to protect agreements having little or no effect on competition or which generate economic benefits.[144] Nevertheless, a small number of sectoral BERs are still in force. Leaving room for the consideration of broad non-economic benefits on the basis of a formalistic analysis, they endanger the consistent enforcement of EU competition law across all sectors of the economy.[145]

This chapter has shown that while the modernisation of BERs has increased their effectiveness, it also raised two sets of challenges with respect to the uniformity and legal certainty of balancing.

The first set of challenges relates to the *application of BERs*. BERs may promote legal certainty and uniformity because they outline transparent and predictable balancing rules, which require relatively limited discretion. Yet, this merit of BERs was hindered by their modernisation. The transformation from form-based to effects-based BERs has granted the competition enforcers greater discretion to balance. This has been especially true when the competition enforcers have interpreted BERs as prescribing only a general standard, which require a detailed, economic balancing process. For example, the interpretation of BERs by the CJEU in *Pierre Fabre (2011)* and *Coty (2017)*[146] and the German NCA and courts[147] draws the balancing process under BERs closer to the analysis of Article 101(3) TFEU individual exemptions. While this may increase the effectiveness of balancing, it gives rise to legal certainty concerns and opens the door to inconsistent national interpretations of BER balancing.

Uniformity and legal certainty concerns over the application of BERs were also associated with national BERs, which have sometimes directly or indirectly influenced the application of Article 101 TFEU also in mixed cases.

Despite the above, the empirical findings have suggested that the legal challenges relating to the application of the BERs should not be exaggerated. In practice, BERs have been discussed in a relatively small number of enforcement actions and challenges before EU and national courts, suggesting that overall undertakings have managed to self-assess their behaviour correctly.[148]

The second set of challenges relates to the *relationship between BERs and individual exemptions*. Namely, the extent to which withdrawing the application

143 See Sections 4.3.2, 4.3.1.2, and 4.3.3.
144 See Section 4.3.3.1.
145 See Section 3.7.
146 See Section 4.3.1.1.
147 See Sections 4.4.1.1 and 4.4.2, respectively.
148 See Sections 4.2 and 4.4.1.1.

of a BER or granting an individual exemption to an agreement that has failed to meet the conditions of a BER hampers legal certainty or uniformity. The empirical findings imply that these set of challenges had have only little effect in practice. Section 4.5 above has shown that the benefits of BERs have almost never been withdrawn. Similarly, only in a limited number of cases have individual exceptions been granted after the benefit of a BER was refused. Thus, the reliance on BERs has mostly served as a good indicator of the compatibility of an agreement with Article 101 TFEU.

Studying the balancing function of the BERs is also interesting for exploring the limits of balancing under Article 101(3) TFEU individual exceptions. Since each BER is based on the presumption that the protected categories of agreements satisfy 'with sufficient certainty' the four conditions of the Article, the terms of each BER also influence the relevant types of benefits, balancing method, and intensity of control applicable to individual exceptions. The possibility to take into account broad non-economic benefits via a sectoral approach in BERs challenges the Commission's narrow interpretation of Article 101(3) TFEU individual exceptions following modernisation.

5

Article 101(1) TFEU

5.1 INTRODUCTION

The balancing tools of Article 101(3) TFEU individual exemptions and BERs are based on EU primary or secondary law and were largely developed in the Commission's case law and policy papers. In contrast, the balancing tools of Article 101(1) TFEU are predominantly derived from CJEU case law. This chapter shows that the CJEU introduced those tools to counterbalance the Commission's broad interpretation of what constitutes a restriction of competition that falls within the scope of Article 101(1) TFEU. As elaborated below, the CJEU was of the opinion that agreements restricting the commercial freedom of parties can escape the prohibition of Article 101(1) TFEU if they are necessary for the attainment of social or efficiency-related goals.

The empirical findings demonstrate that despite the CJEU's efforts, the Commission made only little use of those balancing tools in practice and interpreted them narrowly. Furthermore, the CJEU did not establish one overarching concept to guide Article 101(1) TFEU balancing. Instead, it created numerous sector-specific or restriction-specific exceptions, which are applied on a case-by-case basis. The CJEU's *ad hoc* approach, combined with the Commission's limited use of Article 101(1) TFEU tools, creates significant uncertainty as to the scope of and method for Article 101(1) TFEU balancing. Faced with these uncertainties, the Commission, NCAs, and EU and national courts have adopted inconsistent and conflicting balancing approaches.

This chapter offers a comprehensive empirical mapping of Article 101(1) TFEU balancing tools as applied in practice. It is structured as follows: Section 5.1 introduces the balancing function of Article 101(1) TFEU. It demonstrates that the Article contains two categories of balancing tools: those directed at balancing state and public interests (non-economic benefits) and those directed at the attainment of commercial interests (economic benefits). Sections 5.2 and 5.3 elaborate on each of those two categories, respectively. Each section presents the surrounding legal background and the empirical findings on the EU Courts' and the Commission's application of the relevant balancing tools. Next, it discusses the balancing methods of the various balancing tools and critically analyses their implications. Section 5.4 details the practices of the various national enforcers. It points to the significant variation in the manner in which the NCAs and national courts have applied and interpreted those exceptions. Section 5.5 concludes.

5.1.1 *Between a Jurisdictional Provision and a Balancing Tool*

The possibility to balance under Article 101(1) TFEU has been a subject of debate from the outset of EU competition law and continues to do so to this day. The wording of the Article does not explicitly refer to a balancing function. It stipulates that 'the following shall be prohibited as incompatible with the internal market: all agreements between undertakings, decisions by associations of undertakings and concerted practices which may affect trade between Member States and which have as their object or effect the prevention, restriction or distortion of competition within the internal market'.

The Commission has originally understood the Article as a jurisdictional provision. According to this view, Article 101(1) TFEU is designed to determine whether EU or national competition law applies, i.e. if the agreement could affect trade between Member States.[1] Consequently, the Commission had held that the prohibition dictated by Article 101(1) TFEU applies to almost any restriction imposed on the undertakings' freedom of commercial action and that balancing should be confined to Article 101(3) TFEU. As early as *Grundig/Consten (1966)*, it explained that 'the *decisive criterion* for the coming into force of the prohibition [. . .] consists of the finding that the agreement *interferes with the freedom of action* of the parties or with the position of third parties on the market'. In particular, the Commission concluded that Article 101(1) TFEU 'applies *virtually automatically* to [. . .] agreements which establish absolute territorial protection for exclusive distributors. This point is *central to Commission policy*'.[2]

This approach had a significant impact prior to modernisation. Under the enforcement regime of Regulation 17/62, the fact that an agreement fell under the scope of Article 101(1) TFEU not only meant that EU law applied; it also implied that only the Commission, which had a monopoly on granting Article 101(3) TFEU exemptions, could carry out balancing. By classifying Article 101(1) TFEU as a

[1] Odudu (2006, 101), Geyder (2009, 110–114), and Townley (2009, 113). Arguably, classifying an agreement as purely national might also be a form of balancing since some Member States have unique balancing tools under national law. This is discussed in Chapter 6 and Section 7.5.4.

[2] Emphasis added. The Commission's position was presented in the Report for the Hearing in C-56/64 C-58/64 Grundig/Consten (1966), 326.

jurisdictional provision, the Commission in effect barred the NCAs and national courts from engaging in balancing. Hence, interpreting Article 101(1) TFEU as 'catching' as many agreements as possible was linked to the need to ensure effective and uniform balancing throughout the EU.[3]

The Commission's approach was instantly met with fierce criticism.[4] Using Article 101(1) TFEU as a jurisdictional provision conveyed the notion that all agreements had to be notified to the Commission, even when they had an insignificant effect on competition. The Commission was flooded with applications for Article 101(3) TFEU exemptions, creating a serious administrative backlog.[5]

This chapter shows that over the years the CJEU gradually attributed a substantive balancing function to Article 101(1) TFEU. While the Court endorsed the Commission's broad interpretation of the provision for the most part, it did introduce certain exceptions. In particular, the Court submitted that some forms of restriction of the rivalry between undertakings did not fall within the scope of Article 101(1) TFEU if they were necessary for attaining non-competition commercial or public interests. As elaborated in this chapter, some of those balancing tools have served as a substitute to Article 101(3) TFEU individual exemptions.

Before presenting these types of exceptions, it should be emphasised that the differences between Article 101(1) and (3) TFEU balancing tools are still relevant today, post modernisation. It is true that, following modernisation, Article 101(1) TFEU no longer determines the actor applying EU competition law. The Commission, NCAs, and EU and national courts apply both Article 101(1) and (3) TFEU. However, two important differences remain.

First, from a substantive point of view, an agreement that benefits from an Article 101(1) TFEU exception does not necessarily fulfil the four conditions of Article 101(3) TFEU.[6] This is particularly true when an exception is based on non-economic benefits. For example, cultural benefits that do not directly increase consumer welfare may fail to meet the first condition of Article 101(3) TFEU (at least according to the Commission's more economic approach following modernisation[7]) but might

3 Venit (2003, 577) and Komninos (2005, 2–3). In addition, restrictions on the commercial freedom of undertakings were also seen as harmful to market integration. A broad interpretation of Article 101(1) TFEU allowed the Commission to control agreements that hindered the single market, irrespective of the actual impact on competition interests. See Odudu (2006, 89–99).

4 Wolf (1962, 550–559; 1963, 634), Joliet (1967, 189), Korah (1981b), Steindorff (1984), Gyselen (1984), Forrester and Norall (1984, 23–24, 38–40), Whish and Sufrin (1987, 1), Waelbroecht (1988, 695), Green (1988), Hawk (1988, 64–65, 69–70; 1995, 997–978, 982–983), Black (1997, 145–161), Wesseling (1999, 88–93, 422–424), Manzini (2002), Nicolaides (2005, 131–134), Nazzini (2006, 516–518), Odudu (2006, 101), Goyder (2009, 52), and Sauter (2016, 98–99). See also Commission Green Paper on Vertical Restraints (1997), executive summary, para 37.

5 See Section 2.3.2.

6 Wesseling (2000, 105–107), Townley (2009, 246–247), GCLC Annual Conference (2010, 42), and Van Rompuy (2012, para 248).

7 See Section 3.3.4.

justify an Article 101(1) TFEU exception. Similarly, an agreement that promotes environmental benefits but eliminates competition in the market fails the fourth condition of Article 101(3) TFEU but could be accepted under Article 101(1) TFEU.[8]

Second, from a procedural point of view, the two balancing tools entail different burdens of proof.[9] The burden of proving an infringement of Article 101(1) TFEU rests with the competition enforcer alleging the infringement. The burden of proving the conditions of Article 101(3) TFEU, on the other hand, rests with the undertakings concerned and often requires robust economic evidence.[10] Therefore, proving Article 101(1) TFEU exceptions may be preferable from the point of view of the undertakings. Those two differences, as detailed below, affect the types of benefits that can be taken into account under Article 101(1) and (3) TFEU, the applicable balancing method, and the intensity of control.

5.1.2 *Between the Theory of Harm and a Balancing Tool*

Non-competition interests may have a double role under Article 101(1) TFEU. First, non-competition interests may act as a balancing tool, justifying granting an exception to an otherwise anti-competitive agreement. This function is the focus of this chapter.

Second, non-competition interests, in the narrow definition adopted in this study,[11] may also form part of the theory of harm. Especially since the prohibition of Article 101(1) TFEU is open-textured and drafted in a broad manner, not every harm to the competitive process and structure is perceived to justify taking enforcement action. Rather, the enforcement of the prohibition of Article 101(1) TFEU is often vindicated by reference to the harm an infringement causes to one or more of the objectives of EU competition policy (i.e. economic freedom, market integration, and especially following modernisation – economic welfare). The instrumentalisation of EU competition law to protect market integration, for example, was evident in early case law, in which the enforcement focused on eliminating vertical restraints having a similar determinantal effect on cross-border trade as public measures prohibited by free movement laws.[12]

Moreover, at times, the theory of harm went beyond the objectives of EU competition policy, aiming to safeguard 'the proper functioning of normal

8 The GC confirmed that Article 101(1) TFEU exceptions are not subject to proving the elimination of competition condition of Article 101(3) TFEU. See T-712/14 Watch Repair (2017), para 46 and 54.

9 Regulation 1/2003, Article 2 and Preamble 5. See also GCLC Annual Conference (2010, 15–21, 36).

10 On the burden of proof for an Article 101(3) TFEU exception, see Section 3.4.4.1.

11 As elaborated in Section 1.2.1, competition interests are defined as the protection of the competitive process and structure as such.

12 Goyder (2009, 52–69) and Ibáñez Colomo (2016). See also Section 2.5.1.2 and Section 3.4.2.

competition'.[13] The assessment of what constitutes 'normal competition' may take into account non-competition interests and may use normative benchmarks embedded in EU and national norms external to competition law.[14] In *Allianz (2013)*, for example, the CJEU examined whether an agreement between insurance companies and dealers was restrictive by object. The Court invoked Hungarian consumer protection law as the benchmark for determining the degree of independence dealers should maintain from insurance companies to support the 'proper functioning of the car insurance market'.[15] A similar approach has been taken by the German NCA in *Facebook (2019)*, finding that Facebook has abused its dominant position by imposing terms that do not comply with European data privacy rules.[16]

Non-competition interests, therefore, have stimulated the development of innovative, often contentious, theories of harm.[17] Some of the aspects related to the role of non-competition interests in devising the theory of harm will be explored in Chapter 7, examining the selection of enforcement priorities and the imposition of remedies by the competition enforcers. This chapter, however, will focus on cases in which non-competition interests served as an *exception* to an otherwise anti-competitive agreement prohibited by Article 101(1) TFEU.

5.1.3 *Two Categories of Article 101(1) TFEU Balancing Tools*

This chapter submits that the CJEU has not developed a single, overreaching principle to guide Article 101(1) TFEU balancing. Instead, it has created *ad hoc*, sector-specific or restriction-specific balancing tools. Established on an incremental case-by-case basis, those balancing tools overlap and at times even contradict each other.

In fact, the differences between the various Article 101(1) TFEU balancing tools were not always very clear. The competition enforcers were not always explicit on which balancing tool was used, and consequently, various scholars have often disagreed on the classification of the types of balancing tools used in certain cases. Therefore, the empirical findings presented in this chapter should be understood as representing the author's interpretation, which aims to highlight the inconsistencies and theoretical flaws embodied in those balancing tools rather than to provide a precise depiction of their application in practice.

Despite the above, Article 101(1) TFEU balancing tools can be roughly divided into two categories according to their balancing function. The first category includes

[13] See, for example, in C-209/07 Beef Industry (2008), para 17; C-8/08 T-Mobile (2009), para 29; C-67/13P Cartes bancaires (2014), para, 50. See also Section 5.3.4.

[14] Costa-Cabral and Lynskey (2017, 16–17).

[15] C-32/11 Allianz (2013), para 47.

[16] B6–22/16 Facebook (2019).

[17] See, for example, Townley (2009, 205–241), Lianos (2013, 19–20), Ibáñez Colomo (2016), Ibáñez Colomo and De Pablo (2017), Costa-Cabral and Lynskey (2017), Dunne (2020, 8–10, 13–25), and Costa-Cabral (2020, 18–19).

tools aimed at balancing competition interests with *state or public interests*. These balancing tools are used for agreements that are designed to realise a social or national goal or are the expression of state sovereignty. The second category includes tools for balancing competition and *commercial interests*. These balancing tools weigh competition against efficiencies. The balancing tools under each of these two categories are summarised in Table 5.1.

TABLE 5.1. *Article 101(1) TFEU balancing tools*

Balancing tool	Typical non-competition interests	Type of protected benefits	Leading cases	Balancing includes a proportionality test?
Balancing between competition and state and public interests				
State action	Regulated and liberalised markets	Economic and non-economic benefits	INNO (1998); Van Eycke (1988); Suiker-Unie (1975); Leclerc (1985)	No
Notion of undertakings	Social security schemes; regulated entities		Höfner (1991)	No
106(2) TFEU	Liberalised markets		Flugreisen (1989); Eurovision systems (1993, 1996)	Yes, limited to what is necessary for providing a SGEI
Nature and purpose	Collective bargaining between employers and employees		Albany (1999); Pavel Pavlov (2000)	No
Inherent restriction	Regulated professional associations		Wouters (2002); Meca-medina (2002, 2004, 2006)	Yes, limited to what is necessary for the proper practice of a profession
Balancing between competition and commercial interests				
Rule of reason	Pro- and anti-competitive effects	Mostly economic benefits	Polypropylene (1992); Night Services (1998); Métropole (2001)	Yes, balance of pro- and anti-competitive effects

(continued)

TABLE 5.1. (*continued*)

Balancing tool	Typical non-competition interests	Type of protected benefits	Leading cases	Balancing includes a proportionality test?
Objectively necessary agreement	Purchasing association; entry into a new market		Société Technique Minière (1966); Gøttrup-Klim (1994)	Yes, necessary for the existence of an agreement of that type or that nature
Ancillary restraints	Non-compete clauses; selective distribution; franchising; horizontal cooperation		Métropole (2001); MasterCard (2014)	Yes, necessary and proportionate to secure the benefits of a pro-competitive agreement
IPRs	Licensing agreement; sale of business involving IPRs		Grundig/ Consten (1966)	Yes, doctrine of exhaustion
De minimis	SMEs; market integration; pension funds; financial institutions; sports		Volk (1969); Expedia (2012)	Yes, in some cases

5.2 BALANCING COMPETITION AND STATE OR PUBLIC INTERESTS

5.2.1 *Legal and Empirical Background*

The first category of Article 101(1) TFEU balancing tools relates to the issue of whether, and how, the prohibition of Article 101 TFEU applies to agreements linked to state and public interests. The conduct of a state, like the conduct of a private undertaking, can potentially distort competition on the market. For instance, a national law might sacrifice competition in favour of protecting employment conditions or the environment. A state might choose to delegate certain powers to undertakings, which might in turn act in a manner that limits competition. This poses the question of whether Article 101 TFEU applies to an agreement that is the direct result of a state measure (e.g. law, regulation, or the administrative use of public power), is influenced by a state, or substitutes a task that was previously performed by the state.

The structure of the EU Treaties seems to give a definitive answer to this question. The competition law chapter in the TFEU is divided into two sections: first, 'rules applying to undertakings' (Articles 101-106 TFEU) and second, rules governing 'aid granted by states' (Articles 107-109 TFEU). This structure suggests that the use of state power is subject to state aid rules, while Article 101 TFEU only controls the conduct of private undertakings.

The practices of the Commission and CJEU up until the late 1980s reflected this divide. As elaborated below, they applied Article 101 TFEU exclusively to the conduct of private undertakings engaged in economic activity. In parallel, it was *assumed* that Member States pursue the advancement of public interests and should therefore not be subject to the Article. The Member States, consequently, were permitted to advance public policies at the expense of competition.[18]

The launch of the SEA, however, blurred this divide.[19] The EU and Member States delegated former public tasks to private undertakings, assuming that competition forces would advance the general welfare. In particular, the regulation of new sectors (e.g. banking), in combination with delegation, self-regulation, and privatisation (e.g. in the transport, telecommunications, and energy markets), introduced market principles to what was previously perceived as public sectors of the economy. Safeguarding the public interest was no longer seen as a monopoly of the state.[20]

Chapter 3 illustrated that the Commission responded to these changes by expanding the scope of Article 101(3) TFEU to facilitate the consideration of non-economic benefits. Until the end of the third enforcement period (i.e. May 2004), the Commission used Article 101(3) TFEU to exempt certain anti-competitive agreements that promoted state or public interests.

This section reveals that the CJEU has taken a different path to tackle the clashes between competition and public and social interests by introducing various new balancing tools to account for such considerations already within the scope of Article 101(1) TFEU. Such tools did not always directly engage in balancing of competition and non-competition interests. The balancing was often hidden under the disguise of technical questions, examining, for example, whether an alleged anti-competitive behaviour could be attributed to the meeting of the minds of undertakings, rather than to a state measure. Nevertheless, in many cases, the answers to those questions merit a normative, rather than a merely factual, value judgement. Such choices shape the scope of Article 101 TFEU and the equilibrium between the protection of competition to the advancement of state or public interests.

Figure 5.1 outlines the development of those balancing tools in the CJEU preliminary rulings. It indicates the number of enforcement actions in which such balancing tools were discussed (bars), with reference to the total number of preliminary rulings concerning Article 101 TFEU (black line).

18 Ibrahim (2015, 226) and Sauter (2016, 78).

19 Gerber (1994b, 137–138).

20 Wilks (1993, 276), Wesseling (2000, 42–44), Baquero Cruz (2007, 552), and Ibrahim (2015, 226).

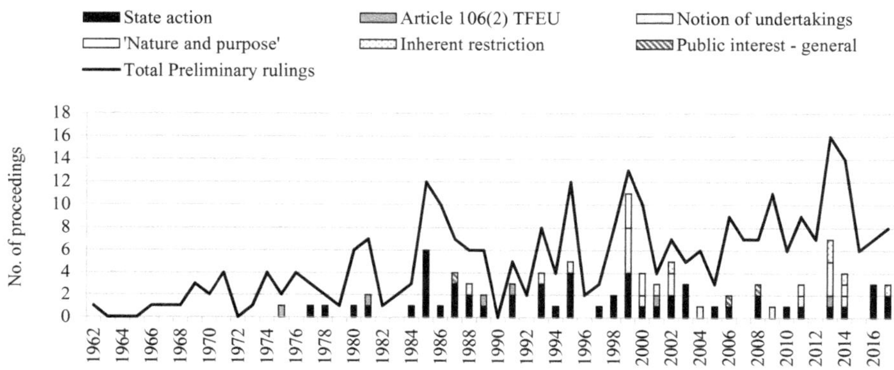

FIGURE 5.1. Article 101(1) TFEU, state or public interests, preliminary rulings
In some proceedings, more than one type of Article 101(1) TFEU state or public exception was discussed

This figure illustrates that the balancing of competition with state and public interests was frequently discussed in the preliminary rulings handed down since the late 1970s. As detailed below, the early balancing tools developed by the CJEU focused on examining whether an agreement was a genuine state measure and not a cartel in disguise (Article 106(2) TFEU, dark grey bars; state action, black bars; and since the mid-1980s the notion of undertakings, light grey bars). Those tools centred on assessing whether the agreement could be attributed to a state. They did not focus on evaluating whether the restriction of competition was actually justified and proportionate. Towards the end of the third enforcement period, however, the CJEU introduced new balancing tools and interpreted the old tools in a way that gave more weight to weighing competition and non-competition interests. This is reflected by the 'nature and purpose' and inherent restriction exceptions introduced in the late 1990s and early 2000s, respectively (white and white and black dotted bars).

Figure 5.2 depicts the application of those exceptions by the Commission and EU Courts in appeals. The figure highlights the number of enforcement actions in which one or more of those exceptions were discussed (grey line) and accepted (bars). With respect to the Courts, it also indicates the number of proceedings in which the previous instance's decision accepting or rejecting an exception was overturned (crosses, corresponding to the colour of the relevant exception).

The figure confirms that the Commission made limited use of the state or public interest balancing tools (a). Consequently, the EU Courts had only a few opportunities to review such tools in appeals (b and c). One clear exception is the state action defence. As the next section shows, while the Commission interpreted this defence narrowly, accepting it only in a few cases (black bars), the EU Courts accorded greater weight to the state's influence (black crosses).

The following sections examine in detail the development of the balancing principles guiding each of the state or public interest exceptions. Each section first

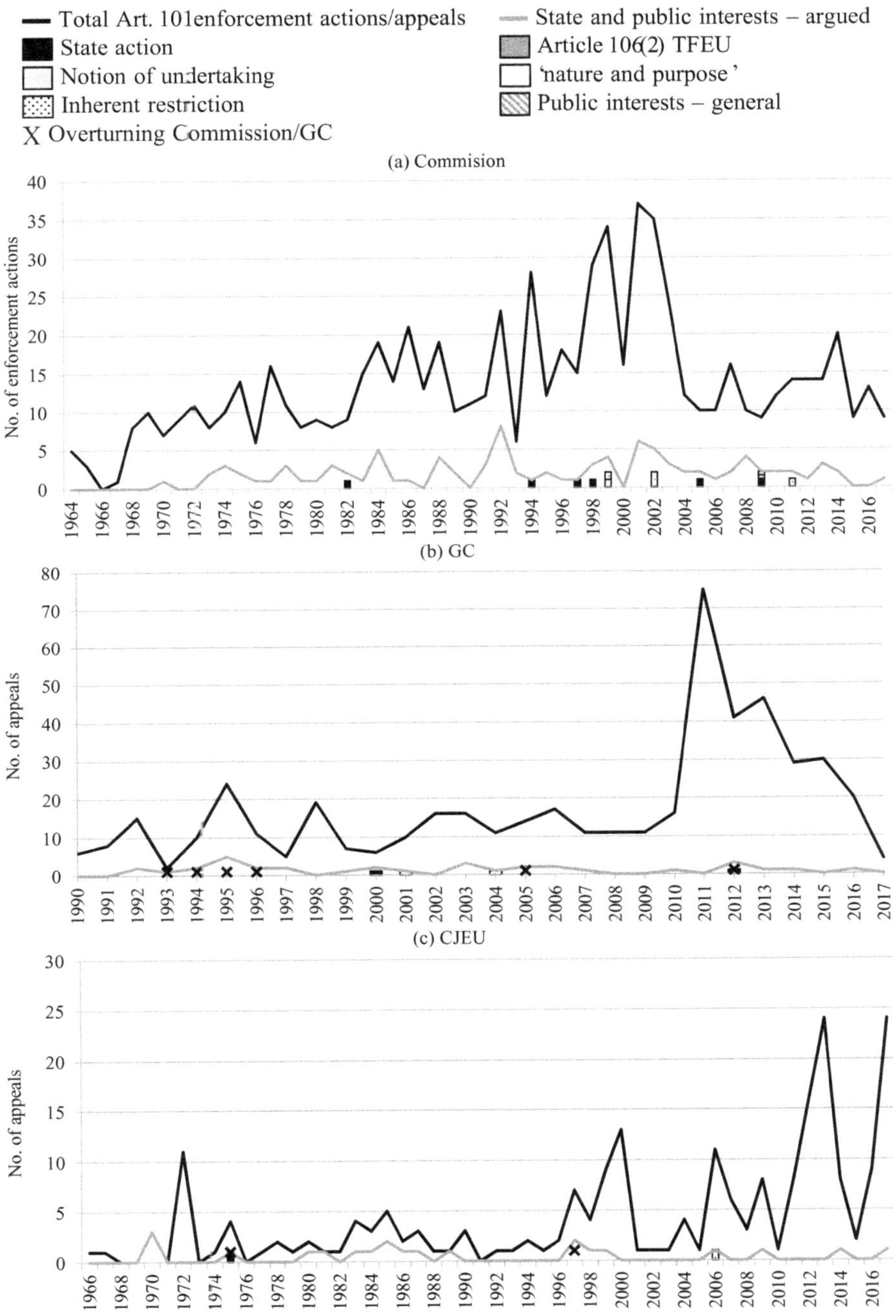

FIGURE 5.2 Article 101(1) TFEU, state or public interests, Commission and EU Courts appeals

In some proceedings, more than one type of Article 101(1) TFEU state or public exception was discussed

explores the extent to which such an exception serves as a balancing tool and the relevant types of benefits before discussing the balancing method.

5.2.2 *State Action Defence*[21]

5.2.2.1 Balancing Tool

The first state and public interest balancing tool is the EU's state action defence. This legal doctrine originated in the United States. The US Supreme Court held that states are shielded from federal antitrust laws when they engage in a *bona fide* exercise of their sovereign regulatory powers and that private entities are immune from antitrust liability when they act in furtherance of an articulated state policy and under active supervision.[22]

Unlike the United States, there is no clear state action defence under EU law.[23] On the contrary, as detailed in this section, the principle of primacy of EU law requires Member States not to introduce or maintain in force legislative or regulatory measures that could render Article 101 TFEU ineffective. Nevertheless, in certain cases, the CJEU has accepted national measures that limited the full application of the Article. This case law reflects a search for balancing.[24] On the one hand, the CJEU has recognised that a state must be allowed to exercise its sovereign power to adopt measures that it deems justified for economic or social reasons, even when they conflict with competition interests. On the other hand, the Court has also acknowledged that the full effectiveness of Article 101 TFEU would be seriously undermined if Member States will use their powers to facilitate anti-competitive agreements. Member States must not allow undertakings to evade the prohibition of the Article by offering them a legislative shield.[25] A restraint would only be tolerated if it is a genuine state measure and not a weakly regulated private agreement.

21 The notion of 'state action defence' is a US term. The comparable EU exception is often linked to the concept of *effet utile* or the duty of sincere cooperation. Nevertheless, this book uses the term state action defence since it encompasses a broad range of situations of state involvement. The term was also used to describe those exceptions in AG's opinions, for example, in C-180/98 C-181/98 C-182/98 C-184/98 C-185/98 Pavel Pavlov (2000), para 87, 91; C-198/01 Consorzio Industrie Fiammiferi (CIF) (2003), para 1–2; C-264/01 C-306/01 C-354/01 C-355/01 AOK Bundesverband (2003), para 73–77. Moreover, some of the Member States' rules are similar to the US version. As elaborated in Section 5.4.1.2, those national rules are not based on the legal sources that have guided the CJEU's reasoning.

22 Muris (2003, 546) and Gerard (2010, 203).

23 The EU's contribution to the OECD Regulated Conduct Defence Report (2011), 195.

24 Bailey and Whish (2015, 228).

25 In the words of AG Tesauro, in his opinion in C-2/91 Meng (1993), para 6.

The case law on the EU state action defence is complex and unclear, giving rise to much controversy on the limits of this balancing tool.[26] The first seeds of the defence were planted in the late 1970s. *INNO (1977)* concerned a Belgian law that required tobacco manufacturers and importers to fix their selling price. In answer to a request for a preliminary ruling, the CJEU held that Article 4(3) TEU, which prescribes that Member States shall 'abstain from any measure which could jeopardise the attainment of the objectives of the Treaty', applies to the Treaties' provisions on competition. It explained that while it is true that the competition rules (in that case, Article 102 TFEU) are directed at undertakings, 'the Treaty imposes a duty on Member States not to adopt or maintain in force any measure which could deprive that provision of its effectiveness'.[27]

As Figures 5.1 and 5.2 demonstrate, the EU state action defence gained importance from the late-1970s to the mid-1980s. In those years, the defence was mostly developed through a line of preliminary references dealing with the prosecution of undertakings by public authorities or their competitors for breach of various national laws that have included a component of price fixing. The undertakings have invoked the defence to argue that Article 4(3) TEU, read in conjunction with Article 101 TFEU, rendered such national laws to be incompatible with EU law and thus unenforceable.[28]

A strict application of the *INNO* principle in those cases would have prohibited the Member States from adopting many of those price-fixing measures, which clearly affected the functioning of free competition on the market. Yet, as detailed below, the Court had shown deference to national sovereignty. Retreating from its initial strict interpretation of Article 4(3) TEU in *INNO*, it sought a more nuanced balance between competition and state and public interests.

Remarkably, the state action defence was not only invoked by undertakings in private cases as a *sword* to contest the compatibility of certain national laws with the provision of Article 101 TFEU. It was also used in public enforcement as a *shield*,

[26] On the EU defence, see Joliet (1988), Verstrynge (1989), Temple Lang (1989), Gyselen (1989), Chung (1995), Bacon (1997), Castillo de la Torre (2005), Baquero Cruz (2007), Blomme (2007), Gerard (2010, 203), Bailey and Whish (2015, 227–233), Wendt (2012, 216–220), and Sauter (2015).

[27] C-13/77 INNO (1977), para 30–31.

[28] C-177/82 C-178/82 Van De Haar (1984), para 24; C-229/83 Leclerc (1985), para 14–20; C-231/83 Cullet (1985), para 12–18; C-299/83 Leclerc (1985), para 9; C-215/84 Ferey (1985), para 5–6; C-209/84 C-210/84 C-211/84 C-212/84 C-213/84 Asjes (1986), para 70–77; C-188/86 Lefèvre (1987), para 7; C-311/85 Vlaamse Reisbureaus (1987), para 9–24; C-136/86 BINC (1987), para 22–25; C-254/87 Syndicat des libraires de Normandie (1988), para 8–13.

suggesting that undertakings should not be culpable to conduct influenced by a state's involvement. In the latter cases, the state action defence was not directly tied to the concept of the Member States' duty of sincere cooperation pursuant to Article 4(3) TEU. It was applied without distinction also when undertakings were influenced by measures adopted by third countries that are not part of the EU.[29]

Following those early developments, the defence was restated at the beginning of the third enforcement period in *Van Eycke (1988)*. The CJEU has provided a more detailed definition, stipulating that the *effet utile* of Article 101 TFEU could be compromised if a Member State either (i) required or favoured the adoption of an anti-competitive agreement (ii) reinforced the effects thereof, or (iii) deprived its own regulation of its official character by delegating to private undertakings responsibility for taking decisions affecting the economic sphere.[30] Those situations developed into three strands of balancing tools, each subject to distinctive balancing methods and intensity of control. The CJEU did not establish an overriding principle to guide the assessment. Conversely, the three strands were split into even smaller issue-specific balancing tools, overlapping and at times inconsistent with one another.

Before moving to discuss *Van Eycke's* three strands of case law in detail, it should be noted that the empirical findings reveal that the EU Courts and the Commission often avoided applying the state action defence by dint of interpretation. They regularly solved tensions between Article 101 TFEU and state measures by holding that the specific anti-competitive conduct of the undertaking went beyond what the state measure demanded. This approach was taken especially to settle politically sensitive issues such as restrictions of competition originating from national constitutions; international agreements; clashes between Article 101 TFEU and other provisions of the EU Treaties, the Charter of Fundamental Rights, or secondary law; and restrictions imposed by statutes governing the conduct of professional associations.[31]

5.2.2.2 Balancing Method (1): State Requiring or Favouring Anti-competitive Agreements

The first strand of cases in which the state action defence was examined dealt with similar situations as *INNO*, where an anti-competitive agreement was required or

[29] See, for example, 27095 Franco-Japanese ballbearings agreement (1974), 5, and implicitly 29395 Windsurfing International (1983), 10–11; 6870 Aluminium imports from eastern Europe (1984), para 10; 32450 French-West African ship-owners' committees (1992), para 35–36; 39258 Airfreight (2010), para 966–1016; 39462 Freight Forwarding (2012), para 404–405.

[30] C-267/86 Van Eycke (1988), para 16. This list was interpreted as unexhaustive. See AG Fennelly opinion in C-140/94 C-141/94 C-142/94 DIP SpA (1995), para 43.

[31] See Annex A, Section 5.1.

favoured by a national measure. In such cases, the restriction of competition was not attributed to the undertakings and, in some cases, was found to constitute an infringement of a state's obligation under Article 4(3) TEU. The empirical findings illustrate that the EU Courts and Commission distinguished between three sub-types of such measures.[32]

First, situations in which a binding state measure *required* undertakings to engage in anti-competitive conduct (state compulsion cases). The Commission and EU Courts interpreted this exception to the undertakings' liability narrowly. They demanded a strong causal link between the state measure and the anti-competitive agreement, showing that the state measure left the undertakings no other choice but to engage in anti-competitive conduct. An exception could be granted only if the agreement was required, rather than merely permitted, approved, or encouraged, by national legislation.[33] Unsurprisingly, the empirical findings show that in light of this strict intensity of control, such a causal link could almost never be established.[34]

Second, the Commission and EU Courts were more open to accepting agreements in situations in which a state measure left *no room for competitive autonomous conduct* on the part of undertakings (lack of autonomy cases).[35] In those situations, the undertakings' freedom of action was so restricted that the anti-competitive conduct could not be perceived as a meeting of the minds of the contracting undertakings.[36]

[32] This was summarised in T-216/13 Telefónica-Portugal Telecom (2016), para 111–120, confirming the Commission's decision in 39839 Telefónica and Portugal Telecom (2013), para 286–287.

[33] 26918 Suiker-Unie (1973), 15; 27010 Deutsche Philips GmbH (1973), 2–3; 28852 29127 29149 Fedetab (1978), para 83; 29702 Johnson & Johnson (1980), para 34; 29525 30000 SSI (1982), para 100; 29395 Windsurfing International (1983), 10–11; 30350 Zinc producer group (1984), para 74; 30307 Fire insurance (1984), para 28; 26870 Aluminium imports from eastern Europe (1984), para 10; 32026 Bayo-n-ox (1989), para 40–41; 33151 33997 Jahrhundertvertrag VIK-GVSt (1992), para 19, 24; 36147 EPI code of conduct (1999), para 26; 36571 Austrian banks – 'Lombard Club' (2002), para 373–375; 38549 Barême d'honoraires de l'Ordre des Architectes belges (2004), para 12, 40–54; 38281 Italian raw tobacco (2005), para 322; 39181 Candle waxes (2008), para 192–194; 39462 Freight Forwarding (2012), para 404–405; 39839 Telefónica and Portugal Telecom (2013), para 286–287; T-37/92 SMMT-JAMA arrangements (1994), para 64–70, in which the GC overturned a Commission's decision that have rejected a compliant since the agreement was permitted by the UK authorities; T-66/99 Greek Ferries (2003), para 190, 196; T-65/99 Greek Ferries (2003), para 136; T-59/99 Greek Ferries (2003), para 102; T-217/03 T-245/03 French beef (2006), para 92; C-198/01 Consorzio Industrie Fiammiferi (CIF) (2003), para 66–80.

[34] Such link was implicitly established in T-325/01 Mercedes-Benz (2005), para 156, overturning the Commission's decision in 36264 Mercedes-Benz (2001).

[35] See Annex A, Section 5.2. See also Commission Report on Competition in Professional Services (2004, 20) and Castillo de la Torre (2005, 408). A similar approach was applied where an EU legislation has limited the residual competition on the market. See, for example, T-142/89 Welded steel mesh (1995), para 91; T-143/89 Welded steel mesh (1995), para 29; C-219/95P Welded steel mesh (1997), para 24–25.

[36] Gyselen (1993, 3) and Goyder (2009, 116–118, 558).

The lack of autonomy principle was first formulated by the CJEU in *Suiker-Unie (1973, 1975)*. The Commission declared that sugar producers had agreed to share markets and rejected the claim that a tendering system introduced by the Italian authorities and the EU quotas system required such conduct.[37] The CJEU, however, annulled the Commission's decision. Rather than analysing the case on the basis of the state compulsion principle (i.e. examining whether the anti-competitive conduct was *required* by the state), it noted that the agreement escaped the prohibition of Article 101(1) TFEU since the regulatory framework left the undertakings almost no room to compete.[38]

In later cases, the Commission and EU Courts have applied the lack of autonomy principle narrowly. Undertakings were found to infringe Article 101 TFEU when the state measure had considerably restricted their autonomy, but not fully limited it.[39] Even when a national regulatory system had fully eliminated the potential for price competition, the Commission and Courts held that the undertakings could have competed on other parameters of competition.[40]

Third, in *Van Eycke (1988)*, the CJEU stated that the *effet utile* of Article 101 TFEU could also be compromised when a state had merely *favoured* an anti-competitive agreement (non-legislative measure cases).[41] The application of the state action defence to such conduct was first examined in *Asia Motor (1994, 1996, 1998)*, in which the Commission rejected a complaint alleging that importers of Japanese cars had fixed import quotas.[42] On the basis of the lack of autonomy justification, it explained that the aforesaid conduct was an integral part of the French authorities' policy, which set the total quantity of vehicles allowed into France each year and determined the rules for the allocation of that quantity. The importers thus had no commercial freedom of action. Yet, on appeal, the GC accepted the French authorities' submission that the anti-competitive conduct was not imposed by a national *legislative* measure. It affirmed that in the absence of binding legislation,

[37] 26918 Suiker-Unie (1973), 15.

[38] C-40 to 48, 50, 54 to 56, 111, 113–114/73 Suiker-Unie (1975), para 65–73.

[39] T-513/93 CNSD (2000), para 60–75; 37614 Interbrew and Alken-Maes (2001), para 171–172, 247–249; T-66/99 Greek Ferries (2003), para 176–198; T-65/99 Greek Ferries (2003), para 119–141; C-198/01 Consorzio Industrie Fiammiferi (CIF) (2003), para 66–80; T-168/01 GlaxoSmithKline (2006), para 106–108.

[40] C-198/01 Consorzio Industrie Fiammiferi (CIF) (2003), para 68–69; T-513/93 CNSD (2000), para 57–73; T-168/01 GlaxoSmithKline (2006), para 67–70, 99–108.

[41] C-267/86 Van Eycke (1988), para 15–16.

[42] Asia Motor France III (1994) (unpublished). The decision is quoted in T-387/94 Asia Motor France III (1996), para 24. Prior to this decision, the Commission rejected a complaint arguing that the system was a state measure in Asia Motor France II (1991), unpublished. The decision is quoted in T-7/92 Asia Motor II (1993), para 64, in which the GC had overturned the Commission's decision that was based on lack of autonomy claims. In other cases, the Commission examined non-legislative measures under the lack of autonomy strand. See, for example, 29021 BP Kemi/DDSF (1979), para 71; 32450 French-West African ship-owners' committees (1992), para 35–36.

the Commission was entitled to reject the complaint 'only if it appears on the basis of objective, relevant and consistent evidence that that conduct was unilaterally imposed upon them by the national authorities through the exercise of *irresistible pressures*'.[43]

It is unclear whether the CJEU has accepted the GC's reasoning. Although the CJEU upheld the GC's judgement, it was not required to address the question of non-legislative measures.[44] A year later, in *Polypropylene (1999)*, the CJEU rejected on factual grounds a claim alleging irresistible pressure, noting that the decision was reached '*without ascertaining whether irresistible pressure* exerted by the authorities of a Member State can exclude an undertaking's liability'.[45] Since the CJEU did not directly address the matter, it is doubtful whether undertakings can escape liability where a state has favoured an anti-competitive agreement by means of a non-legislative measure.

In any event, subsequent Commission and GC decisions have clarified that undertakings will not face liability for actions influenced by non-legislative measures only in exceptional circumstances.[46] The Court noted that the fact that anti-competitive conduct was known or even fostered by a national authority had no bearing on the applicability of Article 101 TFEU. Such pressure did not always even justified mitigating or waiving a fine.[47] In *French beef (2003)*, for example, the Commission noted that while the French Minister for Agriculture had 'strongly encouraged' the conclusion of an anti-competitive agreement, he did so only after he was 'provoked by weeks of farmers' demonstrations, sometimes violent'. According to the Commission, this proves that the farmers enjoyed a margin of autonomous conduct and thereby are liable for an Article 101 TFEU infringement.[48] This strict control makes it extremely difficult for undertakings to benefit from such an exception.[49]

Notably, the undertakings' liability for complying with a state measure that required or favoured an anti-competitive agreement is independent of the state's liability. This is not an obvious conclusion. One could have argued that since Article 101 TFEU has a direct effect, undertakings are obliged not to comply with a national

43 Emphasis added. T-387/94 Asia Motor France III (1996), para 65.
44 C-401/96P Asia Motor France III (1998), para 56–60.
45 Emphasis added. C-235/92P Polypropylene (1999), para 128.
46 See Annex A, Section 5.3.
47 See, for example, the GC's approach in T-259/02 T-260/02 T-261/02 T-262/02 T-263/02 T-264/02 T-271/02 Austrian banks – 'Lombard Club' (2006), para 258–260, 505. See also Section 7.6.1.2.
48 38279 French beef (2003), para 150–156, as confirmed by T-217/03 T-245/03 French beef (2006), para 92.
49 Similarly, in T-216/13 Telefónica-Portugal Telecom (2016), para 118, the GC held that undertakings will not be held liable for infringement only if the irresistible pressures were applied in a way as to deprive them of any autonomy in implementing the decisions of the public authority. In T-387/94 Asia Motor France III (1996), para 64–65, in comparison, the irresistible pressures, in itself, was seen as depriving the autonomy of the undertakings.

measure that requires or favours an anti-competitive agreement.[50] Such a position would have shifted the burden to balance competition with state and public interests to the undertakings.

Nevertheless, in *Ladbroke (1993, 1995, 1997)*, the CJEU had overturned the GC's decision and rejected the AG's opinion by maintaining that the compatibility of national legislation with the competition rules cannot be regarded as decisive when examining the applicability of Article 101 TFEU to the conduct of undertakings.[51] A national measure that required or favoured an anti-competitive agreement will release undertakings from liability, even if the state had breached its obligations under Article 4(3) TEU.

The state's liability, on the other hand, is dependent on the culpability of the undertakings. Accordingly, the Court held that a state did not breach its Treaty obligation by adopting measures that have made the affiliation to sectoral pension fund compulsory upon a request by employers and workers associations when such arrangements were justified on solidarity grounds.[52]

5.2.2.3 Balancing Method (2): State Reinforcing an Anti-competitive Agreement

The second strand of the state action defence involved situations in which a state had merely reinforced the effects of a pre-existing agreement. According to the CJEU, this applies when a state measure 'incorporates either wholly or in part the terms of agreements concluded between undertakings and requires or encourages compliance on the part of those undertakings'.[53] The anti-competitive effect of the state involvement is weaker in comparison with the cases discussed in the previous section. A state does not *require* an anti-competitive agreement but merely reinforces the effects of an existing agreement.

Despite the lesser anti-competitive effect of the state's involvement, the CJEU was strict towards national measures that reinforced an existing agreement. To this end, it found that Member States have breached their obligations even where there was a weaker causal link between the state measure and the anti-competitive agreement as

[50] In a number of cases, the Commission held that undertakings cannot escape the prohibition of Article 101 TFEU by relying on a state measure that is incompatible with the free movement rules. See, for example, 28374 Advocaat Zwarte Kip (1974), 2–3.

[51] C-359/95P C-379/95P Ladbroke (1997), para 31–33, overturning the GC's decision in T-548/93 Ladbroke (1995), para 47–49, which overturned the Commission's decision in 33374 Ladbroke (1993). See also AG Cosmas opinion in C-359/95P C-379/95P Ladbroke (1997), para 65; C-198/01 Consorzio Industrie Fiammiferi (CIF) (2003), para 51.

[52] C-219/97 Maatschappij Drijvende Bokken BV (1999), para 56–58; C-115/97 C-116/97 C-117/97 Brentjens' Handelsonderneming BV (1999), para 66–68; C-67/96 Albany International BV (1999), para 66–68; C-180/98 C-181/98 C-182/98 C-184/98 C-185/98 Pavel Pavlov (2000), para 98; C-437/09 AG2R Prévoyance (2011), para 37–39.

[53] C-267/86 Van Eycke (1988), para 18.

compared to the causal link it required in state compulsion cases. In *Vlaamse Reisbureaus (1987)*, for example, an ethics code of the national association of travel agents precluded agents from giving discounts by renouncing their commissions. The Belgium government transformed the code into a Royal Decree. The CJEU held that the decree could be deemed as reinforcing a pre-existing agreement concluded in the sector, although it had not been established that the private agreement was still in force at the time the dispute arose. In other words, it was sufficient that the state measure in question was based on an anti-competitive agreement, even if it was no longer operative.[54]

In *Meng (1993)*, however, the CJEU had seemed to allow more room for state's measures that have originated from anti-competitive agreements. The Court held, in contrast to the Commission's view, that national rules applicable to a particular branch of insurance cannot be regarded as reinforcing the effects of a pre-existing agreement in another branch of insurance.[55] As summarised by AG *Tesauro*, in the absence of an even indirect link with an anti-competitive conduct attributable to undertakings, state measures will not be declared incompatible with Article 101 TFEU merely because they produced an effect equivalent to an anti-competitive agreement.[56]

A state measure that reinforces an anti-competitive agreement does not remove the conduct from the scope of Article 101 TFEU. Rather, both the state and the undertakings may be liable for infringement of the competition rules.[57] Yet, the empirical findings show that the reinforcement strand was mostly discussed in the context of preliminary rulings examining the validity of state measures,[58] while questions surrounding the undertakings' liability in similar situations were mostly examined under the third strand of the state action defence. As elaborated in the next sub-section, this has left the undertakings some room to escape liability.

5.2.2.4 Balancing Method (3): Delegation of State Powers

The third strand of state action defence expanded the *effet utile* doctrine to situations in which anti-competitive behaviour resulted from a delegation of public powers to

[54] C-311/85 Vlaamse Reisbureaus (1987), para 9–24. As observed by AG Tesauro in his opinion in C-2/91 Meng (1993), para 14. See also Bacon (1997, 284).

[55] C-2/91 Meng (1993), para 17–19.

[56] AG Tesauro opinion in C-2/91 Meng (1993), para 23–24.

[57] C-123/83 BINC (1985), para 23.

[58] C-209/84 C-210/84 C-211/84 C-212/84 C-213/84 Asjes (1986), para 70–77; C-311/85 Vlaamse Reisbureaus (1987), para 9–24; C-136/86 BNIC (1987), para 24–25; C-267/86 Van Eycke (1988), para 18; C-66/86 Flugreisen (1989), para 47–49; C-2/91 Meng (1993), para 14–22; C-245/91 Ohra Schadeverzekeringen (1993), para 9–15; C-219/97 Maatschappij Drijvende Bokken BV (1999), para 53–60; C-115/97 C-116/97 C-117/97 Brentjens' Handelsonderneming BV (1999), para 63–68; C-67/96 Albany International BV (1999), para 54–70; C-180/98 C-181/98 C-182/98 C-183/98 C-184/98 C-185/98 Pavel Pavlov (2000), para 98; C-437/09 AG2R Prévoyance (2011), para 37–39.

private undertakings. This describes a scenario in which a state allows undertakings, such as regulated professional associations, to assume the state's responsibility to govern markets.

The delegation strand of cases distinguishes between two types of state rules. On the one hand, it permits national measures which, even if adopted after consultation with undertakings, do not have the effect of endorsing, favouring, or reinforcing agreements between undertakings. In particular, conveying an opinion on a draft decision was not found to constitute a delegation of powers.[59] In fact, coordinated advocacy and lobbying efforts by professional associations of undertakings were seen as part of the democratic process, necessary when complex technical or knowledge is involved.[60] Such measures are deemed compatible with Article 101 TFEU and Article 4(3) TEU and will not subject the undertakings or the state to liability.

On the other hand, states are prohibited from divesting their own rules of the character of legislation by delegating the responsibility for taking decisions affecting the economic sphere. To this end, they are prohibited from simply rubber-stamping anti-competitive agreements. In such cases, the attribution of liability to private undertakings is not completely clear. In some cases, the Commission stated that undertakings will remain liable for the breach of Article 101 TFEU in addition to the state, yet had not imposed fines.[61]

The delegation strand of case law had emerged from the CJEU's preliminary ruling in *Leclerc (1985)*. A distributor had challenged a French law that obliged national publishers and importers to fix retail prices for books. Applying the first two strands of the state action defence would have probably resulted in a finding that France had infringed Article 4(3) TEU by either requiring or reinforcing a price-fixing arrangement. Such findings would have had the dramatic consequence of limiting the Member States' law-making powers in this regard.

Indeed, the Commission argued that Article 4(3) TEU could *not* be interpreted 'as to deprive Member States of all power in the economic sphere by prohibiting them from interfering with free competition'. Rather, Article 101 TFEU should apply to Member States only in the exceptional circumstances of compulsion and reinforcement cases or when a state has 'pursued the specific aim of enabling undertakings to circumvent the Community competition rules'.[62] Thus, the Commission maintained that the French law should be considered solely in the light of the free movement rules that prohibit quantitative restrictions on imports.

The CJEU used different reasoning to achieve essentially the same outcome. It noted that the French law did not require concluding an agreement, but rather imposed a statutory obligation on the undertakings to fix prices unilaterally.

59 See Annex A, Section 5.4.

60 AG Léger opinion in C-35/99 Manuele Arduino (2001), para 74, 79.

61 33407 CNSD (1993), para 44; 33686 Coapi (1995), para 48; 36147 EPI code of conduct (1999), para 26.

62 C-229/83 Leclerc (1985), para 12.

Accordingly, 'the question arises as to whether national legislation which renders corporate behaviour of the type prohibited by Article [101(1) TFEU] *superfluous*, by making the book publisher or importer responsible for freely fixing binding retail prices, detracts from the effectiveness of Article [101 TFEU]'.[63]

The Court did not answer this question in *Leclerc*. Instead, it noted that the purely national systems and practices of the French law had not yet been made subject to EU competition policy. The Member State obligation under Article 4(3) TEU would thus not be 'specific enough to preclude them from enacting legislation of the type at issue on competition in the retail prices of books'.[64]

The Court continued to circumvent answering similar questions in a series of cases during the 1980s. Instead of examining whether the delegation of state powers had *actually* hindered the effectiveness of the competition rules by making a private agreement unnecessary, the Court focused on the *form and identity* of the body that has formally adopted the anti-competitive measure. When a measure was formally adopted by an association of undertakings, even upon a state order, Article 101 TFEU was found to apply.[65] When public authorities adopted a measure directly, such a measure was not deemed to be incompatible even if it was adopted following consultation with private undertakings.[66]

Nevertheless, from the 1990s onwards, the CJEU had to revisit the question it posed in *Leclerc*, as it was confronted with more complicated cases in which the state ordered the setting of tariffs by so-called mixed bodies. Such bodies were either comprised of both representatives of the state and private undertakings or of private undertakings that were nominated by state authorities as experts.

The CJEU's approach to mixed-bodies was developed in *Reiff* (1993). The Court examined the fixing of road haulage tariffs by the members of a German board, which was then approved and published in a form of a binding governmental order. The members of the board were experts in the relevant branches of the haulage industry, chosen by the Federal Minister of Transport from among the persons suggested to him by undertakings and associations in the sector. Despite the composition of the tariff board, the CJEU held that the German government did not deprive its legislation of its official character. It observed that the German law did not allow the board members to fix the tariffs solely by reference to their private interests as undertakings engaged in transport. Rather, the law ordered the board to take into account public interests of the agricultural sector and of medium-sized undertakings and regions that are economically weak or have inadequate transport facilities and to consult an advisory committee made up of representatives of the

63 Emphasis added. *Ibid*, para 15.
64 *Ibid*, para 20. See also C-254/87 Syndicat des libraires de Normandie (1988), para 8–13.
65 C-123/83 BINC (1985), para 3, 19–26. See also the Commission in 28980 Pabst & Richarz-BNIA (1976), para II(1); 29883 AROW/BNIC (1982), para 54–58.
66 C-231/83 Cullet (1985), para 17; C-215/84 Ferey (1985), para 5–6; C-188/86 Lefèvre (1987), para 7; C-267/86 Van Eycke (1988), para 19.

users of the services. In addition, the law provided that if the tariffs fixed by the board will not serve the public interest, the Minister may fix them independently instead.[67]

Based on this line of reasoning, the Court held that when a state grants regulatory powers to undertakings or professional associations, it is careful to define public interest criteria for the exercise of those powers, sets essential principles with which the rules must comply, and retains the power to adopt decisions in the last resort; such rules will be classified as legitimate state measures that will not be subject to Article 101 TFEU.[68]

The Court, in other words, assumed that mixed bodies that satisfy the above conditions will operate in the general public interest. This presupposes that when a private undertaking is nominated to a mixed body, it will operate as an arm of the state, while ignoring its private commercial interests.[69] Hence, the Court found that the above conditions were satisfied even when a state had almost automatically approved or largely endorsed the recommendations of a mixed body[70] and when a mixed body was composed of a majority of private undertakings.[71]

In *Corsica Ferries France SA (1998)*, for example, the CJEU had taken a favourable view towards the participation of mooring groups in the administrative procedure for drawing up tariffs. The Court reached this conclusion although the national law did not determine the criteria to be observed when laying down the tariffs, and although the tariffs were sometimes set in accordance with agreements concluded between undertakings and later brought into force by a public measure.[72] Similarly, in *Manuele Arduino (2002)*, *Federico Cipolla (2006)*, and *Hospital Consulting (2008)*, the Italian state was found to retain its powers with respect to a law ordering fixing a minimum fee for lawyers on the basis of a draft produced by the national lawyers' association, a body established under the auspices of the Minister of Justice and composed of lawyers elected by their fellow members. While noting that the law contained neither a procedural arrangement nor substantive public interest criteria ensuring that the association will act as an arm of the state, the Court noted that the tariffs were subject to a Minister's approval and that national courts could depart from the tariffs in exceptional circumstances and by duly reasoned decision.[73]

[67] C-185/91 Bundesanstalt für den Güterfernverkehr (Reiff) (1993), para 14–24. See also C-153/93 Delta (1994), para 13–23.

[68] C-309/99 Wouters (2002), para 68.

[69] C-185/91 Bundesanstalt für den Güterfernverkehr (Reiff) (1993), para 22; C-153/93 Delta (1994), para 18; C-140/94 C-141/94 C-142/94 DIP SpA (1995), para 18; C-250/03 Giorgio Emanuele Mauri (2005), para 31–34.

[70] AG Fennelly opinion in C-266/96 Corsica Ferries France SA (1998), para 56.

[71] C-38/97 Autotrasporti Librandi Snc di Librandi F&C (1998), para 34. A minority representation of undertakings in the mixed-bodies, nevertheless, was viewed as an indication of state control. See, for example, C-96/94 Centro Servizi Spediporto Srl (1995), para 23; C-140/94 C-141/94 C-142/94 DIP SpA (1995), para 14–24.

[72] As described in AG Fennelly opinion in C-266/96 Corsica Ferries France SA (1998), para 9.

[73] C-35/99 Manuele Arduino (2002), para 34–44; C-94/04 C-202/04 Federico Cipolla (2006), para 44–54; C-386/07 Hospital Consulting (2008), para 15–27.

The Court, namely, had assessed neither the essence of the anti-competitive effects of the measures nor whether the act of delegation could actually help realise a public interest. Rather, it took a more formalistic approach. The empirical findings confirm that once it had been held that a state maintained some degree of formal control, the conduct was almost automatically classified as compatible with Article 101 TFEU.[74]

5.2.2.5 Modernising the State Action Defence

Commentators have criticised the three strands of the state action defence, as developed by the CJEU case law, as being overly form-based.[75] On the one hand, the case law indicates that genuine state measures are not prohibited by Article 101 TFEU. This is true even when the state has adopted such a restrictive measure it left almost no room for competition (lack of autonomy cases) or has accorded an agreement the full force of law (delegation strand). On the other hand, an agreement is inevitably unlawful, regardless of its merits and possible benefits for the public interest, when undertakings have not acted exclusively on the basis of a state measure. In such a case, the conduct can only be saved if it meets the conditions of an Article 101(1) or (3) TFEU exception.[76]

The EU state action defence, therefore, is based on the assumption that state involvement in private arrangements safeguards an appropriate balance between competition and non-competition interests. This assumption reflects *public interest theories* of regulation. State authorities are perceived as the benevolent maximisers of social welfare and the public interest.[77] According to this approach, the form of the agreement is decisive; it is one thing for economic operators to come together and agree on opening hours (thus removing competition from that sphere), but quite a different matter for Member States to regulate such hours in the public interest.[78] Public interest theories suggest that since state authorities are the maximisers of the public interest, they should be entrusted with the task of balancing. Competition enforcers should avoid frustrating this balance by imposing their own conception of legitimate public interest in areas of domestic social and economic policy.[79]

[74] See Annex A, Section 5.5.

[75] AG Jacobs opinion in C-180/98 C-181/98 C-182/98 C-184/98 C-185/98 Pavel Pavlov (2000), para 164; Verstrynge (1989, 21–25); Chung (1995); Baquero Cruz (2007, 587); Gerard (2010, 204–205); and Sauter (2016, 78).

[76] See also AG Darmon opinion in C-185/91 Bundesanstalt für den Güterfernverkehr (Reiff) (1993), para 34–42, 61–69.

[77] Laffont and Tirole (1991, 1) and Morgan and Yeung (2007, 17–18).

[78] This example was presented by AG Darmon opinion in C-185/91 Bundesanstalt für den Güterfernverkehr (Reiff) (1993), para 38, and later cited by AG Fennelly, in his opinion in C-140/94 C-141/94 C-142/94 DIP SpA (1995), para 39.

[79] AG Darmon opinion in C-185/91 Bundesanstalt für den Güterfernverkehr (Reiff) (1993), para 73. See also AG Fennelly opinion in C-140/94 C-141/94 C-142/94 DIP SpA (1995), para 40.

This assumption, nevertheless, overlooks the very merits that are attributed to self-regulation by public interest theories. Public interest theories command setting and enforcing rules by undertakings and associations of undertakings as promoting the functioning of the profession for the public good.[80] Private actors are perceived as having a greater degree of expertise and technical knowledge, allowing them to govern markets more effectively and with lower compliance costs compared to public authorities. The form of governance, according to public interest theories, should not justify a different treatment in assessing the compatibility of otherwise anti-competitive agreements with Article 101 TFEU.

The assumption that state involvement safeguards an appropriate balance, moreover, ignores the critic voiced by *private interest theories* of regulation. Private interest theories suggest that it would be naïve to assume that public interest justifications fully explain the process of regulation. They are sceptical about the notion that regulation is likely to create welfare for the benefit of all. Studies of *capture* and *interest group theories* argue that as a rule, state measures are designed and operate primarily for the benefit of the undertakings they sought to regulate. Undertakings hold considerable influence over shaping economic governance to serve their private interests, via practices such as lobbying, revolving doors, private relationships with regulators, and influencing the composition of the regulator's management.[81] Such private influence is reinforced when undertakings are invited to self-regulate or take part in regulation via mixed bodies. In such situations, undertakings are prone to over-represent their commercial, ideological, and political interest on account of the general public. Hence, private interest theories too question the assumption that the form of the governance will ensure balancing for the general public interest.

Based on the above, some commentators have advocated reforming the EU state action defence by introducing an effects-based test.[82] They call to focus the analysis on examining whether a state measure has actually contributed to attaining a public policy objective and is proportionate.

An effects-based approach to the EU State action defence was promoted by a number of Advocates General. In *Pavel Pavlov (2000)*, for example, AG *Jacobs* suggested that instead of focusing on the form (i.e. the link between a private agreement and a state measure), the Court should examine whether the practice can be justifiable on public interest grounds. He argued that Member States should be deemed to comply with the Treaties' obligation 'where, although they reinforce the restrictive effects of a concertation between undertakings, they are taken in pursuit of a legitimate and clearly defined public interest objective and where

80 Streeck and Schmitter (1985, 1–28) and Ogus (1995). For an interesting study of the EU competition law's approach to private interest government, see Sauter (2015).

81 Stigler (1971) and Laffont and Tirole (1991).

82 Gerard (2010, 204–205) and Sauter (2016, 78).

Member States actively supervise that concertation'.[83] This, in his opinion, will strike an adequate balance between the prevention of anti-competitive practices and the public interest embedded in preserving the regulatory autonomy in the professions.[84]

Concurring with this approach, in his opinions in *Wouters (2001)* and *Manuele Arduino (2001)*, AG *Léger* added that a state measure that reinforces an anti-competitive practice should be justified if the state measure (i) has exercise effective control over the content of the agreement, (ii) pursues a legitimate aim in the public interest, and (iii) is proportionate to the aim pursued.[85]

While the CJEU had not followed this approach,[86] the Commission embraced a similar effects-based analysis following modernisation, at least in the delegation strand of cases. In its Report on Competition in Professional Services (2004), the Commission held that rules adopted by professional associations by an act of delegation are ultimately bound to a proportionality test. The rules must be objectively necessary to attain a clearly articulated and legitimate public interest objective and the least restrictive measure able to achieve such an objective.[87]

The GC has also appeared to embrace an effects-based approach. In *Ordre national des pharmaciens (ONP) (2010, 2014)*, the Commission and GC have examined the conduct of the French professional association for pharmacists, to which a French code has delegated functions to ensure compliance with professional duties, defend the honour and independence of the profession, supervise the competence of pharmacists, and contribute to promoting public health and the quality of health care.[88] The Commission condemned the association for limiting price reductions through rebates for clinical testing and restricting the development of larger groups of laboratories as to protect the economic interests of the majority of its members. Applying the delegation test, it noted that the vast majority of the governing body members were nominated by private undertakings and were not bound to public interest criteria. The GC concurred, yet on different grounds. Instead of examining the act of delegation, it referred to the inherent restriction exception, examining whether the association's behaviour was necessary for the pursuit of a legitimate objective intended by the law.[89]

83 AG Jacobs opinion in C-180/98 C-181/98 C-182/98 C-184/98 C-185/98 Pavel Pavlov (2000), para 163.

84 *Ibid*, para 162. See also para 86–91.

85 AG Léger opinions in C-309/99 Wouters (2001), para 207 and C-35/99 Manuele Arduino (2001), para 87–92.

86 Yet, as elaborated in Sections 5.2.2.3 and 5.2.4, the Court held that the state did not infringe its obligation since the practice did not amount to an agreement between undertakings in the meaning of Article 101(1) TFEU.

87 Commission Report on Competition in Professional Services (2004), 3–4.

88 39510 Ordre national des pharmaciens (ONP) (2010), para 607–609; T-90/11 Ordre national des pharmaciens (ONP) (2014), para 2.

89 *Ibid*, para 44. On the application of the inherent restriction exception in this case, see Section 5.2.6.2.

Similarly, the GC has shifted the consideration in lack of autonomy cases from the ambit of the state action defence to the theory of harm. In *GDF Suez SA (2012)* and *E.ON/GDF (2012)*, it held that undertakings did not share markets in breach of Article 101(1) TFEU where national legislation had created national monopolies. Instead of focusing on the state's influence in limiting the room for competition, the Court held that the surrounding economic and legal contexts had not left real concrete possibilities for the undertakings concerned to compete.[90]

A more recent decision suggests that the CJEU may have come around to such an approach. In *API (2014)*, the Court examined an Italian decree entrusting a number of road transport activities to a mixed advisory body. The body was composed of the representatives of state authorities, associations of road transport operators and consumer associations, undertakings, and bodies in which the state held a majority stake. A committee comprised of ten members of the advisory body could fix minimum charges payable by consumers in order to ensure road safety.[91] The CJEU declared that the price-fixing arrangement was incompatible with Article 101 TFEU. Based on a formalistic delegation test, it observed that the committee was largely composed of representatives of private undertakings and that the state did not supervise the charge fixing. However, the Court also went on to examine whether the objective of the legislation, namely road safety, was likely to be achieved by the delegation of powers. It observed that the national legislation did not contain any procedural or substantive requirements to ensure that the committee would act as an arm of the state pursuing the public interest.[92] In other words, the Court not only examined the form of delegation but also scrutinised the substance of the rules adopted.[93]

Adding a proportionality test to the state action defence brings this exception closer to the inherent restriction exception, which will be discussed in Section 5.2.6. It shifts the focus away from measuring the degree of state influence over the adoption of an agreement to assessing its actual effect on competition and non-competition interests. This shifts the balancing process away from a formalistic, exclusion-based balancing to a legal balancing process.[94] It requires the competition enforcers to assess whether an anti-competitive agreement went beyond what was required to attain a non-competition interest and whether the claimed benefits exceeded the harm to competition.

While this development might have brought the consideration of state action defence with the effects-based approach to competition law, the Court seemed to retreat to a formalistic approach in the following preliminary rulings in which it examined the defence. In *Salumificio (2016)*, the Court held that an Italian law

[90] T-370/09 GDF Suez SA (2012), para 81–113; T-360/09 E.ON/GDF (2012), para 83–125.
[91] C-184/13 C-185/13 C-186/13 C-187/13 C-194/13 C-195/13 C-208/13 API (2014), para 28–46.
[92] *Ibid*, para 34–41.
[93] See also Lanza (2015, 195) and Sauter (2015, 4).
[94] On the types of balancing processes, see Section 1.2.2.1.

setting minimum prices for road haulage services on the basis of operating costs fixed by the national administration after hearing the position of relevant trade associations had not infringed Article 101 TFEU. The decision focused on the form of the decision. The Court emphasised that the national administration had only *heard* the professional associations rather than delegated its public powers.[95]

Similarly, in *CHEZ (2017)*, the CJEU examined a Bulgarian law setting minimum prices for legal services and prohibiting courts from ordering the reimbursement of fees at an amount lower than the minimum fee. The fees had been fixed by a professional body of lawyers. The Court held that the act of setting a minimum fee should not be regarded as a state action since the law did not contain a specific criterion ensuring that the minimum fee was fair and justified in accordance with the public interest. Adhering to a form-based approach, the Court did not examine the actual criteria that had guided the price-setting by the professional body.[96]

To conclude, this section has shown that while an anti-competitive agreement may be caught by Article 101 TFEU notwithstanding state involvement, the Commission and EU Courts were hesitant to interfere with the sovereignty of Member States and were careful to prohibit national measures even when they restricted the free operation of competition. The state action defence was developed on an *ad hoc*, case-by-case basis and resulted in a complicated and often inconsistent balancing method. As such, it is an unpredictable balancing tool, leaving the competition enforcers ample discretion to strike a balance between competition interests and the level of state involvement in the economy.

To make matters even more complicated, when the Commission published its Coronavirus Temporary Framework in April 2020, it has appeared to depart from the principles developed in the case law on the state action defence. In a surprising statement, the Commission declared that the fact that a cooperation between undertakings in response to situations of emergency stemming from the coronavirus outbreak was 'encouraged and/or coordinated by a public authority (or carried out within a framework set up by the latter) is also *a relevant factor to be taken into account* to conclude that such cooperation would not be problematic under EU competition law or would not be an enforcement priority for the Commission'.[97] The Commission further added that '[i]n the context of an imperative request from public authorities to undertakings to temporarily cooperate in response to urgency situations related to the current COVID-19 outbreak (e.g. to organise production and delivery to meet an urgent need to keep up the functioning of health care for COVID-19 patients), such cooperation is allowed'.[98]

95 C-121/16 Salumificio (2016), para 22–27.
96 C-427/16 C-428/16 CHEZ (2017), para 46–49.
97 Emphasis added. Commissions Coronavirus Temporary Framework (2020), para 15.
98 *Ibid*, para 16.

Section 7.4.3.5 submits that this statement probably ought to be understood as a signal that the Commission is willing to engage in balancing by setting the enforcement priorities, rather than a change to the EU state action defence. Nevertheless, the implications of the Commission's statement in its Coronavirus Temporary Framework are likely to come under scrutiny in the future.

5.2.3 *Article 106(2) TFEU*

5.2.3.1 Types of Benefits

Like the state action defence, Article 106(2) TFEU addresses the relationship between competition rules and a state measure. It provides that undertakings entrusted with the operation of services of general economic interest (SGEI) are subject to Article 101 TFEU only 'insofar as the application of such rules does not obstruct the performance, in law or in fact, of the particular tasks assigned to them. The development of trade must not be affected to such an extent as would be contrary to the interests of the Union'.

Article 106(2) TFEU was drafted as a political compromise between Member States advocating a more trade-oriented economy and those calling for various forms of state involvement.[99] By allowing certain derogations from the competition rules, the Article seeks to reconcile the Member States' interest in using undertakings as an instrument of economic or fiscal policy with the EU's interest in ensuring compliance with competition rules and preservation of the unity of the common market.[100] The political controversy surrounding SGEI also became evident during the discussions in the run-up to the Amsterdam Treaty. A proposal to amend Article 106(2) TFEU was rejected in favour of introducing a new policy-linking clause that expressly preserved Article 106 TFEU in light of the 'place occupied by services of general economic interest in the shared values of the Union as well as their role in promoting social and territorial cohesion'.[101]

Despite its political importance, in practice Article 106(2) TFEU had only a limited function in conjunction with Article 101 TFEU cases.[102] Figure 5.1 shows

[99] Schweitzer (2011, 16–20), Bailey and Whish (2015, 247–253), and Sauter (2016, 218–219).

[100] C-219/97 Maatschappij Drijvende Bokken BV (1999), para 93; C-115/97 C-116/97 C-117/97 Brentjens' Handelsonderneming BV (1999), para 103; C-67/96 Albany (1999), para 103.

[101] Article 14 TFEU provides that 'given the place occupied by services of general economic interest in the shared values of the Union as well as their role in promoting social and territorial cohesion, the Union and the Member States, each within their respective powers and within the scope of application of the Treaties, shall take care that such services operate on the basis of principles and conditions, particularly economic and financial conditions, which enable them to fulfil their missions'. See also policy report 1997, 10; Commission Services of General Interest in Europe (2001), para 2; Ross (2000, 22–38); and Bailey and Whish (2015, 249).

[102] Article 106(2) TFEU was accepted as a defence in a number of Article 102 TFEU cases. See Bailey and Whish (2015, 252–253).

that Article 106(2) TFEU was seldom used before the mid-1980s[103] and was discussed in only a small number of CJEU preliminary rulings. Figure 5.2 further illustrates that the Commission and EU Courts on appeal never used this provision to justify an Article 101(1) TFEU exception.

Nevertheless, several commentators have suggested using Article 106(2) TFEU as a balancing tool to accommodate rules adopted by professional associations and solidarity funds, aimed at the preservation of the public interest.[104] In particular, this approach was advocated by AG *Léger* in his opinion in *Wouters (2001)*, calling to use Article 106(2) TFEU to accept the Dutch Bar association rule prohibiting a partnership between members of the Bar and other professions. AG Léger emphasised the benefit of a Treaty-based exception. He warned against introducing a public policy exception that is not based on the wording of the Treaties. In his opinion, such a balancing tool will negate the effectiveness of Article 101(3) and 106(2) TFEU balancing tools. The CJEU, however, disagreed and has accepted the practice under the newly developed inherent restrictions doctrine instead.[105]

Similarly, in *AOK Bundesverband (2003)*, AG *Jacobs* invoked Article 106(2) TFEU to justify the conduct of sickness funds that are required by national law to join a buying cartel.[106] The CJEU has once again disagreed, holding that the funds were not subject to Article 101 TFEU since they are not undertakings. As elaborated below, the proposed Article 106(2) TFEU route could have stricken a more nuanced balancing between competition and domestic social policies, since the restriction of competition would have to be limited to what is necessary for the performance of the social task.

5.2.3.2 Balancing Method

In its early case law, the CJEU maintained that Article 106(2) TFEU was a specific application of the general principle of Article 4(3) TEU.[107] This led commentators to argue that Article 106(2) TFEU was merely an expression of the principle of proportionality. Measures entrusting undertakings with the operation of an SGEI were simply stated in lieu of granting a separate exception.[108] Notwithstanding this early interpretation, the empirical findings illustrate that the EU Courts later

[103] The Commission and EU Courts mentioned the Article during the 1970s and at the beginning of the 1980s without a full analysis. See C-94/74 IGAV (1975), para 33–37; 28980 Pabst & Richarz/BNIA (1976), 5; C-172/80 Züchner (1981), para 7–8.

[104] Korah (2004, 14, 74, 192), Szyszczak (2004, 195–196), Jones and Sufrin (2008, 266, footnote 227), and Nowag (2015, footnote 10).

[105] AG Léger opinion in C-309/01 Wouters (2001), para 107, 114, 155–201. The inherent restrictions doctrine is detailed in Section 5.2.6.

[106] AG Jacobs opinion in C-264/01 C-306/01 C-354/01 C-355/01 AOK Bundesverband (2003), para 86–102.

[107] C-13/77 INNO (1977), para 42.

[108] Verstrynge (1989, 17), Temple Lang (1989, 124–125, 130), and Chung (1995, 91).

classified Article 106(2) TFEU and the state action defence as two different ways to escape the application of Article 101 TFEU. In fact, the EU Courts sometimes applied both exceptions, albeit separately. In *Flugreisen (1989)*, for instance, the CJEU stated that a tariff agreement approved by the aeronautical authorities has infringed Article 101 TFEU and was incompatible with Article 4(3) TEU but might have been justified under Article 106(2) TFEU.[109]

Accordingly, over the years the Commission and EU Courts have developed a separate set of Article 106(2) TFEU balancing tests based on the four cumulative conditions listed in the Article.

First, the Article provides that an undertaking must be *entrusted* with the operation of an SGEI.[110] The CJEU has clarified that the entrustment must take place by an act of a public authority.[111] The CJEU interpreted this condition in a relatively broad manner. It held that the act of entrustment does not necessarily require a legislative measure. Rather, a concession governed by public law or in order to give effect to the obligations imposed on the undertakings that have been entrusted with the operation of an SGEI was sufficient.[112] In *Albany (1999)*, the Court took a step forward, suggesting by implication that requesting public authorities to make affiliation to sectoral pension funds compulsory was sufficient to constitute an act of entrustment.[113]

The Commission, nevertheless, has interpreted this condition particularly narrowly. The mere approval of an anti-competitive agreement by a Member State,[114] a legal act favouring such an agreement,[115] or a general regulation that does not refer to the specific task[116] were not found to qualify as an act of entrustment. This narrow interpretation precludes using Article 106(2) TFEU as a balancing tool more frequently, for example, in the context of the professional association cases described above.

Second, Article 106(2) TFEU is limited to the *operation of an SGEI*. The notion of 'services of general economic interest' is not defined by the EU Treaties. Member States enjoy a wide margin of discretion to decide what they regard as an SGEI on

[109] C-66/86 Flugreisen (1989), para 49, 54.
[110] The notion of an undertaking under both Articles 101 and 106(2) TFEU is identical. See C-475/99 Ambulanz Glöckner (2001), para 18–19; C-327/12 Ministero dello Sviluppo economico (2013), para 35.
[111] C-66/86 Flugreisen (1989), para 55.
[112] C-159/94 Commission v France (1997), para 66. See also AG Léger opinion in C-309/01 Wouters (2001), para 160.
[113] C-67/96 Albany (1999), para 98–111. For this view, see also AG Léger opinion in C-309/01 Wouters (2001), para 160; and Gyselen (2000, 436–438).
[114] 30717 Uniform Eurocheques (1984), para 29–30. See also Commission Services of General Interest in Europe (2001), para 22.
[115] 30717 Uniform Eurocheques (1984), para 29–30; 30979 31394 Decca Navigator System (1988), para 128–129. See also Commission Services of General Interest in Europe (2001), para 22.
[116] 30979 31394 Decca Navigator System (1988), para 128–129.

the basis of their political and national preferences.[117] That notion can cover any service of an economic nature that is essential to the general public in a manner that justifies a degree of intervention by the public authorities to control the conditions under which it is provided.[118]

Third, Article 106(2) TFEU exception applies *only insofar as* the application of competition rules does not obstruct the performance, in law or in fact, of the particular tasks assigned to the undertakings. This entails a proportionality test. According to the CJEU, Article 106(2) TFEU applies only if the restriction is necessary to enable the undertaking to perform its task of general interest under economically acceptable conditions.[119] The empirical findings show that failing this proportionality test has been the cause for rejecting many Article 106(2) TFEU claims. The EU Courts, and especially the Commission, were sceptical of claims that an anti-competitive agreement was necessary to enable an undertaking to carry out the task assigned to it.[120]

Fourth, Article 106(2) TFEU provides that '[t]he *development of trade* must not be affected to such an extent as would be contrary to the interests of the Union'. This condition is rather unclear in conjunction with Article 101 TFEU. Irrespective of Article 106(2) TFEU, Article 101 TFEU does not apply to an agreement that does not affect trade between Member States. Thus, this condition could be understood as demanding a more significant impact on inter-state trade compared to the level required for the enforcement of Article 101 TFEU.[121] Alternatively, it could be regarded as a clarification of how the third proportionality condition should apply. In *VIK-GVSt (1992)*, for instance, the Commission maintained that the proportionality of an anti-competitive agreement must be measured against the further development of the internal market, balancing the national and EU interests.[122]

Moreover, it remains unclear which institution can apply the fourth condition. Although the CJEU has confirmed the direct effect of the first sentence of Article 106(2) TFEU,[123] some scholars have argued that the application of the fourth condition of Article 106(2) TFEU lays within the exclusive competence of the Commission.[124] This brings Article 106(2) TFEU exception closer to the institutional enforcement setting of Article 101(3) TFEU under the old enforcement regime. Given the political sensitivity of the fourth condition, it is unsurprising that it has received so little attention in decisional practice. In fact, the empirical findings

[117] T-106/95 FFSA (1997), para 99–100; T-17/02 Fred Olsen (2005), para 215–228; Commission Services of General Interest in Europe (2001), para 22. See also Faull and Nikpay (2014, 849).
[118] Faull and Nikpay (2014, 847).
[119] C-475/99 Ambulanz Glöckner (2001), para 57.
[120] See Annex A, Section 5.6.
[121] Bailey and Whish (2015, 253).
[122] 33151 33997 Jahrhundertvertrag VIK-GVSt (1992), para 29–30. See also Faull and Nikpay (2014, 864).
[123] C-127/73 SABAM (1974), para 22.
[124] Faull and Nikpay (2014, 864) and Bailey and Whish (2015, 253).

reveal that the competition enforcers have never rejected the application of Article 106(2) TFEU on that ground alone.[125] Thus, the question of which institution can apply this fourth condition remains open.

In sum, Article 106(2) TFEU represents a Treaty-based exception on the basis of a legal proportionality test for balancing the harm to competition interests with state involvement in economic life. While this provision has been subject to heated political debate, it has hardly ever been used in practice to guide the balancing in Article 101 TFEU cases.

5.2.4 *Notion of Undertakings*

5.2.4.1 Types of Benefits

The interpretation of the notion of undertakings, in its meaning under Article 101(1) TFEU, is another tool to balance state and public interests against the protection of competition. The CJEU has held that Article 101(1) TFEU only governs agreements and concerted practices between *undertakings* or *association of undertakings engaged in economic activity*. It does not apply to the conduct of public bodies exercising their public body prerogative.[126] This divide is based on the abovementioned assumption of public interest theories of regulation, according to which private economic actors normally pursue their own self-interest, while states aim to advance the public interest.[127] Consequently, Article 101 TFEU does not apply to activities connected with the exercise of public powers.[128]

As elaborated below, since the beginning of the 1990s, the CJEU has used the notion of undertakings as a balancing tool not only to exclude state measures from the scope of Article 101(1) TFEU but also to exclude the conduct of *private entities acting in the public interest*.[129] In particular, it has been used to permit anti-competitive agreements between undertakings in regulated and liberalised markets carrying out activities that were previously performed by a state or that had a solidarity aspect or a redistribution function.[130]

[125] Yet, in 32732 Ijsselcentrale (1991), para 47, the Commission noted that even if the other conditions of Article 106(2) TFEU were fulfilled in the case, an obstruction of imports and exports would not be acceptable in light of the EU's efforts to achieve a single energy market.

[126] C-30/87 Bodson (1988), para 18; C-364/92 SAT Fluggesellschaft (1994), para 30; C-343/95 Calì (1997), para 23; C-138/11 Compass-Datenbank (2012), para 36–38. See also Bailey and Whish (2015, 145–146).

[127] AG Jacobs opinion in C-67/96, C-115/97, 116/97 and C-117/97 and C-219/97 Albany (1999), para 184. See also Ibrahim (2015, 267). On public interest theories of regulation, see Section 5.2.2.5.

[128] C-30/87 Bodson (1988), para 18; C-343/95 Cali (1997), 23.

[129] See also AG Jacobs opinion in C-67/96 C-115/97 C-116/97 C-117/97 C-219/97 Albany (1999), para 184–185.

[130] Boeger (2007, 326–328), Ibrahim (2015, 267), Bradshaw (2016, 334), and Kloosterhuis (2017).

Unlike the state action defence and Article 106(2) TFEU exceptions, the notion of undertakings is not exclusively dependent on an act of entrustment or derogation of state powers. Rather, the assessment centres on the function the entity performs. Accordingly, this exception has opened the door to accepting voluntary anti-competitive agreements between private entities aimed at pursuing non-competition interests.

In contrast to the CJEU's approach, Figure 5.2(a) demonstrates that the Commission has almost never used the notion of undertakings for the purpose of balancing. A closer look at the Commission's decisions from the 1970s up until the end of the 1990s shows that the Commission has categorically rejected the use of the balancing method relying on the notion of undertakings. On the contrary, it has emphasised that commercial activities of trade and professional associations are activities of an association of undertakings regardless of their status under national law.[131]

Nevertheless, the Commission has been more open to the use of the notion of undertakings as a balancing tool for sport-related agreements. In fact, the empirical findings show that *Mouscron (1999)* and *AMA (2009)*, both sports-related, were the only two cases in which the Commission has used this exception.[132] In other sports-related cases, the Commission referred to CJEU decisions in the field of free movement to explain that 'purely sporting interest' (e.g. rules of matches and proper conduct, disciplinary actions, and anti-doping) are not economic in nature, while related economic activities (e.g. the sale of tickets for events and competitions, advertising and broadcasting contracts, the commercial exploitation of trademarks and merchandise) do involve the conduct of undertakings.[133] The Commission has held that if a sports association engages in some economic activity, even if secondary to its primary objectives, it could be considered an undertaking within the meaning of Article 101(1) TFEU.[134]

5.2.4.2 Balancing Method

The notion of undertakings is not defined by the EU Treaties.[135] In *Höfner (1991)*, the CJEU established the well-known formula according to which 'the concept of an undertaking encompasses every entity engaged in an economic activity,

[131] See Annex A, Section 5.7.

[132] 36851 Mouscron (1999); 39471 Certain joueur de tennis professionnel/Agence mondiale anti-dopage (2009), para 19–27. In other cases, the Commission accepted sports-related agreements by finding that they did not restrict competition. See Section 5.2.6.2.

[133] See Annex A, Section 5.8.

[134] 40208 International Skating Union's Eligibility rules (2017), para 147.

[135] The notion of undertaking is defined in Article 1 of Protocol 22 EEA as 'any entity carrying out activities of a commercial or economic nature'.

regardless of the legal status of the entity and the way in which it is financed'.[136] The CJEU used three criteria to differentiate economic from non-economic activities. As elaborated below, in some cases the criteria were used cumulatively, and in others as alternatives for an exception.[137]

The first criterion for defining an undertaking is the *comparative markets criterion*. In *Höfner*, the CJEU submitted that employment procurement is economic in nature since it '*has not always been, and is not necessarily*, carried out by public entities'.[138] In later case law involving the activities of professional associations, the CJEU replaced this with a more flexible standard. In *Wouters (2002)*, for example, the Dutch bar association was classified as an undertaking since it did not exercise powers that are '*typically* those of a public authority'.[139]

The comparative markets criterion does not offer clear guidance in the event there is no fully competitive market in which a number of undertakings compete. In *AOK (2004)*, groups of sickness funds had fixed the prices of medicinal products on the basis of German legislation aimed at fighting cost increases in the national statutory health insurance scheme. Because of the German legislation, the CJEU could not examine if the price fixing was an activity that was 'necessarily' or 'typically' performed by a public authority. Instead, the CJEU seemed to accept AG *Jacobs*' position,[140] submitting that in such circumstances the question is whether the activity *could, at least in principle*, be carried by private undertakings in order to make profits.[141]

However, since almost any activity with economic importance could be carried out by private entities, the criterion could potentially cause a broad range of purely public measures to be classified as the operation of undertakings. This interpretation would essentially nullify the general principle that Article 101 TFEU does not apply to state measures.[142]

In light of the over-exclusiveness of the comparative markets criterion, at times the CJEU has used a second *participation criterion* to decide whether a conduct was an economic activity. According to this standard, 'any activity consisting in offering goods and services on a given market is an economic activity',[143] while bodies having

[136] C-41/90 Höfner (1991), para 21. The definition was originally given with respect to Article 102 TFEU but was also repeated in the Article 101 TFEU context; see Annex A, Section 5.9.

[137] AG Poiares Maduro opinion in C-205/03P FENIN (2005), para 10–14. See also Wendt (2012, 91–92).

[138] Emphasis added. C-41/90 Höfner (1991), para 22. See also C-475/99 Ambulanz Glöckner (2001), para 20.

[139] Emphasis added. C-309/99 Wouters (2002), para 58. See also C-1/12 Ordem dos Técnicos Oficiais de Contas (2013), para 46; C-136/12 Consiglio nazionale dei geologi (2013), para 44.

[140] AG Jacobs opinion in C-264/01 C-306/01 C-354/01 C-355/01 AOK Bundesverband (2003), para 27.

[141] C-264/01 C-306/01 C-354/01 C-355/01 AOK Bundesverband (2004), para 54–57.

[142] See also Wendt (2012, 91).

[143] See Annex A, Section 5.10.

'an exclusively social function' are not engaged in an economic activity.[144] The CJEU explained that since EU competition law does not detract from the powers of the Member States to organise their social security systems, Article 101(1) TFEU does not apply when the social objective pursued by the scheme embodies the principle of solidarity.[145] Solidarity, according to the Court, entails the redistribution of income between those who are better off and those who, in view of their resources and state of health, would be deprived of the necessary social cover.[146] This participation criterion has guided the CJEU's assessment of social security schemes, pension funds, old-age insurance, workers' health and accident insurance, and, since the 2010s, also the conduct of professional associations.[147] Thus, whereas by the comparative markets criterion the economic nature of the activity is only implicitly linked to participation in the market, the participation criterion focuses on the fact that the activity is carried out under market conditions.

In more recent years, the CJEU has introduced a third *state influence criterion*, taking into account the exercise of state control for the classification as undertakings. In *Kattner Stahlbau (2009)* and *AGR2 (2011)*, state control over the management of social security schemes was an indicator that the entity should not be classified as an undertaking.[148] In the first decision, the CJEU found that the state influence was sufficiently great to take the conduct outside of the scope of Article 101(1) TFEU, while in the second case the state's limited control indicated that the entity should be classified as an undertaking.

The state influence criterion was also extended to examine regulations adopted by a professional association regulated by national law. In *Ordem dos Técnicos Oficiais de Contas (2013)* and *Consiglio nazionale dei geologi (2013)*, the Court emphasised that because the regulatory power vested in the associations was not subject to any conditions or criteria, the associations had acted as undertakings when adopting the regulation.[149] These cases bring the notion of undertakings exception closer to the formalistic approach to the delegation strand of the EU state action defence, discussed above.[150]

144 C-159/91 C-160/91 Poucet (1993), para 18; C-264/01 C-306/01 C-354/01 C-355/01 AOK Bundesverband (2004), para 51, 58–59; C-350/07 Kattner Stahlbau (2009), para 66.

145 C-159/91 C-160/91 Poucet (1993), para 6; C-218/00 Cisal di Battistello Venanzio & C. Sas (2002), para 31; C-264/01 C-306/01 C-354/01 C-355/01 AOK Bundesverband (2004), para 64; C-350/07 Kattner Stahlbau (2009), para 37, 53.

146 Similarly, in C-70/95 Sodemare SA (1997), para 29, AG Fennelly defined social solidarity as the 'inherently uncommercial act of involuntary subsidization of one social group by another'. See Annex A, Section 5.11, for a list of cases in which the Court classified schemes as based on the solidarity or capitalisation principles.

147 See Annex A, Section 5.12.

148 C-350/07 Kattner Stahlbau (2009), para 60–66; C-437/09 AG2R Prévoyance (2011), para 53–65.

149 C-1/12 Ordem dos Técnicos Oficiais de Contas (2013), para 48–56; C-136/12 Consiglio nazionale dei geologi (2013), para 42–44.

150 See, for example, the following cases that were discussed in Section 5.2.2.5: C-184/13 C-185/13 C-186/13 C-187/13, C-194/13 C-195/13 C-208/13 API (2014), para 41; C-427/16 C-428/16 CHEZ (2017), para 49; C-121/15 Salumificio (2016), para 25–26.

Like the aforementioned strands of the state action defence,[151] the conditions for the notion of undertakings exception are often inconsistent and are not based on a consistent rationale. For instance, the theoretical basis of the state influence criterion runs counter to the rationale underlying the first two criteria. The comparative markets and participation criteria are distinctively functional in nature. The classification as undertakings depends on the nature of the particular *activity* rather than the nature or status of the *actor*.[152] Such a classification is unrelated to the level of influence exerted by the state.[153] The CJEU vindicated this approach by pointing out the need to avoid having the various Member States treat the same situation differently simply because an activity was formally classified as a public service in one Member State and as private in another.[154] In contrast, the state influence criterion focuses on the nature of the actor. It recognises the right of Member States to delegate certain decision-making competencies without falling afoul of the *effet utile* rule of Article 4(3) TEU.[155] Situations that would not be accepted under the state action defence might fall outside the scope of Article 101(1) TFEU by dint of the state influence criterion. This leaves the competition enforcers a wide margin of discretion and could result in conflicting balancing outcomes.[156]

This section has presented the inconsistencies between the various tests of the notion of undertakings and between this balancing tool and other Article 101(1) TFEU exceptions. It has shown that the lack of a consistent rationale guiding the notion of undertakings has created much uncertainty as to the applicable law, making it difficult to predict the outcome of balancing in a specific case.

5.2.5 *'Nature and Purpose': Collective Bargaining Agreements*

The previous sections have discussed exceptions that were mostly based on the *form* of the agreement, namely on the premise that the conduct is related to the exercise or delegation of public powers. Those balancing tools are characterised by an *exclusion* balancing process. Once an agreement has been classified as a public measure, Article 101(1) TFEU is inapplicable. The next two sections deal with forms of *legal balancing processes*, which were introduced by the CJEU towards the end of the third enforcement period (the late 1990s).[157] In those cases, the *promotion of a non-competition interest*, in itself, justified granting an agreement an exception from the

151 See Section 5.2.2.
152 Odudu (2005, 212–213; 2006, 25), Wendt (2012, 90), and Sauter (2016, 76).
153 C-180/98 C-181/98 C-182/98 C-183/98 C-184/98 C-185/98 Pavel Pavlov (2000), para 85–89, 102–119; C-309/99 Wouters (2002), para 65–66; C-1/12 Ordem dos Técnicos Oficiais de Contas (2013), para 48.
154 For example, see C-309/99 Wouters (2002), para 54–55, 67–69. See also Odudu (2006, 24), Sauter (2016, 76), and Kloosterhuis (2017, 121–122).
155 Sauter (2016, 81).
156 See also Boeger (2007, 320), Ibrahim (2015, 267–268), and Kloosterhuis (2017, 117–118)
157 On the differences between exclusion and legal balancing processes, see Section 1.2.2.1.

prohibition imposed by Article 101(1) TFEU. This section is dedicated to the 'nature and purpose' exception, which is uniquely applicable to collective bargaining agreements, while Section 5.2.6 examines the broader inherent restriction exception.

5.2.5.1 Types of Benefits

Social security systems, negotiated through collective bargaining between employers and employee associations, serve an important social objective. They aim to improve working and employment conditions for the public interest and are protected by the Treaties and EU Charter of Fundamental Rights.[158] At the same time, those agreements cannot benefit from the notion of undertakings exception described in the previous section. The CJEU found that despite embodying elements of solidarity, those schemes were based on the principle of capitalisation.[159]

Against this background, the CJEU developed an issue-specific exception governing such agreements. This 'nature and purpose' exception dates back to the *Drijvende Bokken, Brentjens' and Albany (1999)* trilogy. The Court explained that certain restrictions of competition are inherent to agreements between organisations representing employers and workers. According to the Court, the social objectives pursued by such agreements would be 'seriously undermined' if they were subject to Article 101(1) TFEU. Therefore, it concluded that such agreements ought to be regarded 'by virtue of their nature and purpose' as falling outside the scope of the Article.[160]

As elaborated below, the legal basis for this exception and the special protection it affords to workers unions over other types of social policy objectives is not clear. *Korah* has even suggested that this exception was developed by the Court for political reasons to prevent antagonising the unions.[161]

5.2.5.2 Balancing Method

The CJEU set two cumulative conditions for granting the 'nature and purpose' exception.[162] First, the agreement must be the result of collective bargaining

[158] Article 151 and 152 TFEU and EU Charter on Fundamental Rights, Article 28. See also C-219/97 Maatschappij Drijvende Bokken BV (1999), para 56–57; C-115/97 C-116/97 C-117/97 Brentjens' Handelsonderneming BV (1999), para 56–57; C-67/96 Albany (1999), para 59–60; and Bradshaw (2016, 333).

[159] On the notion of undertakings, see Section 5.2.4. For a critique of the Court's analysis, see Bradshaw (2016).

[160] C-219/97 Maatschappij Drijvende Bokken BV (1999), para 56–57; C-115/97 C-116/97 C-117/97 Brentjens' Handelsonderneming BV (1999), para 56–57; C-67/96 Albany (1999), para 59–60.

[161] Korah (2004, 43).

[162] C-219/97 Maatschappij Drijvende Bokken BV (1999), para 56–60; C-115/97 C-116/97 C-117/97 Brentjens' Handelsonderneming BV (1999), para 56–60; C-67/96 Albany (1999), para 59–63. See also C-222/98 Hendrik van der Woude (2000), para 20–27; C-180/98 C-181/98 C-182/98 C-183/98 C-184/98 C-185/98 Pavel Pavlov (2000), para 68–69; C-437/09 AG2R Prévoyance (2011), para 28–36.

between employers and employee organisations. Those types of agreements are protected by Article 153 TFEU, which states that the Commission must promote close cooperation between Member States in the social field, particularly in matters relating to the right of association and collective bargaining between employers and workers (the 'nature'). Second, the agreement must contribute to improving the working conditions of the employees (the 'purpose').

The scope and limits of this exception were assessed in *FNV (2014)*, in which the CJEU examined a collective labour agreement of musicians who substituted for the members of an orchestra. The agreement was concluded pursuant to a Dutch law that allowed employer and employee associations to conclude collective labour agreements on behalf of employees as well as on behalf of independent service providers. The Court noted that although the substitute workers performed the same services as employees, they should nonetheless be classified as undertakings. This led the Court to determine that the employer and employee organisations had acted as associations of undertakings when negotiating the agreements for the substitute workers. Hence, the agreement failed the first 'nature' condition.[163] Notably, despite what could have been seen as a highly formalistic approach, the CJEU added that the exception would apply if the substitute workers were 'false self-employed', i.e. functionally comparable to employees.[164]

To justify its position, the Court invoked the legal protections granted by the Treaties to collective bargaining between employers and employees. It emphasised that, on the contrary, the Treaties did not encourage self-employed service providers to open a dialogue with the employers to whom they provide their services.[165] Hence, the Court limited this exception to agreements promoting non-competition interests that are protected by the Treaty.[166] While there is no case law with respect to agreements pursuing non-competition interests outside the labour context, it might be possible to extend the 'nature and purpose' exception to other non-competition interests covered by the policy-linking clauses.

FNV reveals a theoretical inconsistency between the 'nature and purpose' and notion of undertakings exceptions. The judgement implies that the 'nature and purpose' exception applies to collective bargaining between associations of employers and employees since they *do not* act as associations of undertakings for such

[163] C-413/13 FNV Kunsten Informatie en Media (2014), para 24–30.

[164] *Ibid*, para 31–42. The Court explained that the status of 'worker' within the meaning of EU law is irrespective of classifying a person as self-employed under national law, for tax, administrative or organisational purposes. The concept of 'worker' under EU law entails that the person acts under the direction of his employer as regards, in particular, his freedom to choose the time, place, and content of his work, does not share in the employer's commercial risks and forms an integral part of that employer's undertaking, so forming an economic unit with that undertaking.

[165] *Ibid*, para 29.

[166] See also Witt (2016b, 285).

purposes. However, if such an agreement were not concluded between undertakings, it would be granted an exception from Article 101(1) TFEU by virtue of the notion of undertakings exception. This renders the 'nature and purpose' exception meaningless.[167]

The outcome of *FNV* was criticised, especially with the rise of the gig economy. Scholars have pointed out that the rights of self-employed workers, which are not employees in the traditional sense of the word, would not be protected through collective labour agreements.[168] Such concerns were addressed by the Dutch NCA's Guidelines on Price Arrangements between Self-employed Workers (2019), which will be elaborated in Section 5.4.1.2. A year later, as part of the public consultation on the Digital Services Act Package in 2020, the Commission announced that it would be launching a process to 'ensure that the EU competition rules do not stand in the way of collective bargaining for those who need it'.[169] The Commission's consultation, however, did not explain what legal instrument will be adopted in this context.

5.2.6 *Inherent Restriction*

5.2.6.1 Types of Benefits

Like the 'nature and purpose' exception, the inherent restriction exception is also based on a legal balancing process that weighs an agreement's contribution to achieving a specific public interest against its harm to competition. It provides that Article 101(1) TFEU does not prohibit an anti-competitive agreement that is inherent and proportionate to the pursuit of a legitimate aim.

The case law on the inherent restriction exception is puzzling. The EU Courts and Commission have insisted that the pursuit of a legitimate non-competition interest *could not* justify, as such, an otherwise anti-competitive agreement. In the absence of specific legislation or a derogation of public authority powers, a private undertaking cannot sacrifice competition in favour of attaining a public aim. The inadequacy of a public measure to address the problems of a particular sector does not empower an undertaking to assume a public task.[170] In such situations, an exception is confined to the four conditions of Article 101(3) TFEU. Such statements have been made, in particular, with reference to measures aimed at the alleviation of financial or structural crisis and financial security, consumer protection, health and safety, fight against illegal practices, anti-dumping, functioning of sports associations, social aims, and even measures alleging the promotion of

[167] Bradshaw (2016, 320–321).
[168] Schiek and Gideon (2018, 281–282) and Gerbrandy, Janssen, and Thomsin (2019, 40–42).
[169] Public consultation on the Digital Services Act Package (2020).
[170] See Annex A, Section 5.13. See also Figure 5.1, black and white dashed bars.

competition or correction of market failures.[171] However, as the next sub-section reveals, the inherent restriction exception seems to do just that.

Like the other state and public interest exceptions, the inherent restriction doctrine allows Member States to adopt a diverging degree of national protection of non-economic benefits. In *Wouters*, for example, the Court emphasised that the fact that different rules may be applicable in other Member States does not mean that such rules are incompatible with EU law. Rather, '[e]ven if multi-disciplinary partnerships of lawyers and accountants are allowed in some Member States, the Bar of the Netherlands is entitled to consider that the objectives pursued by the 1993 Regulation cannot, having regard in particular to the legal regimes by which members of the Bar and accountants are respectively governed in the Netherlands, be attained by less restrictive means'.[172]

5.2.6.2 Balancing Method

The origin of the inherent restriction exception is typically ascribed to the CJEU in *Wouters (2002)*, yet the exception was actually introduced three years earlier by the Commission. *EPI code of conduct (1999, 2001)* concerned the code of the association of representatives of the European Patent Office (EPO). The Commission held that some of the code's provisions fell outside the scope of Article 101(1) TFEU as they were necessary to avert misleading advertising, protect professional secrecy, and avoid conflicts of interest. It explained that even if the code could constitute a restriction of competition under other circumstances, it was 'necessary in the economic and legal context specific to the profession in question' to guarantee the representatives' impartiality and to ensure the proper functioning of the EPO.[173]

The GC partly accepted and partially annulled the Commission's decision, implicitly approving the exception. It highlighted the importance of the necessity test, pointing out that the applicant had not demonstrated that the provision of the code was 'objectively necessary' to preserve the dignity and rules of conduct of the profession concerned.[174]

The inherent restriction exception was first formalised by the CJEU preliminary ruling in *Wouters (2002)*, a case similar to *EPI code of conduct*. The CJEU reviewed a rule of the Dutch Bar association prohibiting a partnership between members of the Bar and other professions. The rule was adopted pursuant to a Dutch law that entrusted the Bar with the responsibility for adopting professional rules designed to ensure the proper practice of the legal profession.[175] The CJEU began by declaring

[171] See Annex A, Section 5.14.
[172] C-309/99 Wouters (2002), para 108.
[173] 36147 EPI code of conduct (1999), para 35.
[174] T-144/99 EPI code of conduct (2001), para 78.
[175] Dutch Law on the Bar of 23 June 1952, adopted pursuant to Article 134 of the Constitution of the Kingdom of the Netherlands.

that the Bar was an association of undertakings and that the rule could not be classified as a state measure. This statement was particularly important since the rule had not been notified to the Commission for the purpose of receiving an Article 101(3) TFEU exemption. According to the old enforcement regime of Regulation 17/62 in force at the time, this meant that the rule could not be exempted under Article 101(3) TFEU and should have automatically been deemed void pursuant to Article 101(2) TFEU if it had been found to be in breach of Article 101(1) TFEU.

In *Wouters*, the Court famously added that not every agreement that restricts the freedom of action of undertakings necessarily falls within the prohibition of Article 101(1) TFEU. Instead, the overall context must be examined. In particular, 'account must be taken of its objectives, which are here connected with the need to make rules relating to organisation, qualifications, professional ethics, supervision and liability, in order to ensure that the ultimate consumers of legal services and the sound administration of justice are provided with the necessary guarantees in relation to integrity and experience'.[176] The CJEU explained that this exception is based on a three-step examination: first, whether the potentially anti-competitive measure *pursued a legitimate aim*; second, whether the restriction of competition was *inherent* to the pursuit of this aim; and third, whether the restriction was *proportionate*. In contrast to Article 101(3) TFEU exemptions, there is no need to prove the existence of benefits or the fair share granted to individual consumers.

The CJEU concluded that the rule aimed to ensure compliance with the Bar's professional conduct rules in light of the prevailing perception of the profession in the Netherlands. The Bar was entitled to consider that its members would not have been able to advise and represent their clients independently and in observance of strict professional secrecy if they had concluded partnerships with other professions.[177] Based on the above, the Court held that the Bar could reasonably make that consideration despite its restrictive effects and that the rule was necessary for the proper practice of the legal profession in the Netherlands.[178]

Shortly after the CJEU defined the inherent restriction in *Wouters*, the Commission applied the exception in *Meca-Medina* (2002, 2004, 2006). The Commission examined a complaint filed by two swimmers against anti-doping rules adopted by the International Olympic Committee and implemented by the International Swimming Federation. The swimmers alleged that the definition of doping and the threshold set for doping infringed Article 101 TFEU. The Commission, nevertheless, rejected the complaint. It agreed with the swimmers that such measures could impact the athletes' freedom of action. Yet, by reference to

[176] C-309/99 Wouters (2002), para 97.
[177] *Ibid*, para 105.
[178] *Ibid*, para 110.

Wouters, it observed that the anti-doping rules were necessary to ensure the integrity of sporting events and thus fell outside the scope of Article 101(1) TFEU.[179]

On appeal, the GC applied the notion of undertakings rather than the inherent restriction exception to justify the rules. It noted that the anti-doping rules were purely sporting rules, which did not pursue any economic objective.[180] The CJEU, however, endorsed the Commission's analysis. It began by noting that purely sporting rules could fall within the scope of Article 101 TFEU if adopted by undertakings.[181] Moreover, it agreed with the Commission that the anti-doping rules were inherent to the organisation and proper functioning of competitive sports and necessary by their very purpose ensuring healthy rivalry between athletes.[182]

Remarkably, the Commission and CJEU accepted the sporting rules in *Meca-Medina* by reference to *Wouters*. Both cases were based on the same balancing method and reasoning. Yet, the empirical findings reveal that in subsequent cases the Commission and EU Courts were more open to accepting sporting rules than rules for professional associations. While they accepted almost all of the sporting rules in cases in which the exception was invoked, they refused to accept all of the professional association's rules examined.[183] This was linked to the balancing method and intensity of control applied:

First, the Commission and EU Courts applied a strict proportionality test to the professional association cases, asserting that the professional rules were disproportionate to achieving the alleged public interests.[184] The GC was particularly strict, requiring that the measure be the *sole* possible method for attaining the non-competition interest.[185]

Second, the Commission often used alternative balancing tools to examine comparable situations. For example, the Commission's decision in *Meca-Medina* was clearly based on the inherent restriction exception.[186] Yet, on appeal, the Commission argued that the reference to *Wouters* was used only 'in the alternative' 'for the sake of completeness', whereas the decision was based on the notion of undertakings exception.[187] Such an approach has also been evident in the Commission's policy papers since modernisation. The exception is absent from the Commission Article 101(3) Guidelines (2004), Vertical Guidelines (2010), and

179 38158 Meca-Medina and Majcen/IOC (2002), para 43–55.
180 T-313/02 Meca-Medina and Majcen/IOC (2004), para 50–69. On the notion of undertakings and sporting rules, see Section 5.2.4.
181 C-519/04P Meca-Medina and Majcen/IOC (2006), para 30–31.
182 *Ibid*, para 43–45.
183 See Annex A, Section 5.15. A favourable approach to sporting rules was also evident in applying the notion of undertakings exception; see Section 5.2.4.
184 38549 Barême d'honoraires de l'Ordre des Architectes belges (2004), para 97–99; T-451/08 CISAC (2013), para 92; C-1/12 Ordem dos Técnicos Oficiais de Contas (2013), para 93–100.
185 T-451/08 CISAC (2013), para 92.
186 As also clarified by the Commission in its policy report 2002, 200.
187 T-313/02 Meca-Medina and Majcen/IOC (2004), para 62.

Horizontal Guidelines (2011) and received only a little attention in other relevant policy papers.[188]

Third, the Commission and EU Courts added an additional condition for applying the exception to professional associations cases. In addition to the three conditions mentioned above, they held that the agreement must be *required by national legislation*. In *ONP (2010, 2014)*, for example, the Commission refused to accept foreclosure and price-fixing practices implemented by the French pharmacist association. The refusal was tied, *inter alia*, to the fact that the anti-competitive behaviour was not part of any national legislation.[189]

This condition was affirmed by the CJEU in *API (2014)*, where a body mostly composed of representatives of the economic operators had fixed the prices of haulage services for hire and reward. The prices were fixed on the basis of an Italian law stating that such prices should not be lower than the minimum operating costs. The Court held that although it could not be ruled out that the protection of road safety may constitute a legitimate objective, fixing the minimum operating costs by such a body was not an appropriate means of attaining that objective. The CJEU highlighted that the legislation merely referred, in a general manner, to the protection of road safety, without establishing any link between the minimum operating costs and the improvement of road safety. Such legislation would only have been appropriate if it genuinely reflected a concern to attain it in a consistent and systematic manner.[190]

To conclude, while *Wouters* did not refer to the regulatory function of the Bar as a decisive factor in granting an exception, subsequent case law has limited the exception to private acts based on regulatory powers. This has introduced a new causal link requirement for the inherent restriction exception, bringing it closer to the conditions of the state action defence.[191] In comparison, such a causal link was not needed to justify an exception for sporting rules.[192]

5.2.7 *Interim Conclusion*

This section has examined the balancing tools developed by the CJEU to balance competition and non-competition interests related to state and public interests. Each of those balancing tools protects an array of economic and non-economic benefits,

[188] See, for example, Commission Report on Competition in Professional Services (2004).

[189] 39510 Ordre national des pharmaciens (ONP) (2010), para 684–691. The GC confirmed the Commission's position in this regard in T-90/11 Labco/ONP (2014), para 44, 162.

[190] C-184/13 C-185/13 C-186/13 C-187/13 C-194/13 C-195/13 C-208/13 API (2014), para 46–56.

[191] See Section 5.2.2.

[192] The sports associations were not regulatory bodies. While it can be argued that the International Olympic Committee in Meca-Medina was a semi-regulatory body governed by public international law, it is clear that the Court did not focus on the idea that the measure was a regulated activity of a Member State. See also Townley (2009, 133–134).

safeguarding non-competition interests that have been traditionally protected by the Member States.

Those Article 101(1) TFEU balancing tools are not clearly based on the wording of the Treaty provisions (with the exception of Article 106(2) TFEU that was rarely used in practice). The derogations from the general Treaty principles reflect a pragmatic approach, introduced by the CJEU on a case-by-case basis in response to the expansion of Article 101(1) TFEU's reach to include agreements subject to state influence and in markets that were previously subject to such influence. The CJEU developed those balancing tools to accommodate national welfare provisions with the stricter EU competition law provisions, thereby avoiding destabilising conflicts with Member States.

This practice has resulted in a complicated array of inconsistent and contradictory exceptions, lacking an underlying common rationale.[193] This section showed that similar restrictions of competition were evaluated according to different types of exceptions and tests, sometimes leading to different outcomes in similar cases. In light of the above, it is not surprising that many of the preliminary rulings referred to the CJEU by national courts were dedicated to clarifying the scope of the state and public interest balancing tools (as reflected by Figure 5.1).

The uncertainty surrounding the state and public interest balancing tools has been reinforced by the fact that the EU Courts' case law and Commission's policy papers have provided only general guidance on how to apply them. The Commission has rarely applied those exceptions in practice, and its policy papers have advocated a narrow interpretation that limits their scope. Lacking a definitive method for their application, they leave the competition enforcers an exceptionally large margin of discretion to take into account non-competition interests.

In the past, the state and public interest balancing tools were mostly based on an *exclusion* balancing process.[194] Reflecting public interest theories of regulation, the analysis was focused on evaluating the influence of the state on the agreement and the actual or potential role of the state in the markets concerned (i.e. the state action defence and the notion of undertakings exceptions). The analysis often did not affirm whether the restriction of competition had actually pursued a legitimate aim and whether it was proportionate to protecting non-competition interests.

From the late 1990s, the CJEU introduced new balancing tools (i.e. the 'nature and purpose' and inherent restriction exceptions) and reinterpreted the old tools in a way that gave more weight to balance the effects of the agreement on competition. Yet, while the competition enforcers have opened up the room for a more substantive weighing of competition and non-competition interests, the state and public interest exceptions still involve at most legal balancing processes. The competition

[193] Gyselen (1989, 54–60), Chung (1995, 1–5), Bacon (1997, 284), Gyselen (2002, 2–3), Schepel (2002, 38), Korah (2004, 14), and Baquero Cruz (2007, 587).

[194] On the different balancing processes, see Section 1.2.2.1.

enforcers must examine whether an anti-competitive agreement has gone beyond what is required to attain a legitimate non-competition interest and whether the claimed benefits exceed the harm to competition interests. Unlike Article 101(3) TFEU individual exceptions and BERs, the state and public interest exceptions went mostly untouched by the more economic approach and are not tied to a notion of economic efficiency.

This was not necessarily needed to be the case. Several commentators have called to reinterpret the state and public interest balancing tools through the economic lens of market failure. They suggested that instead of grounding an exception on non-economic benefits and the role of the state, the exceptions could be equally understood on efficiency grounds as market correcting tools aimed at enhancing consumer welfare.[195]

Introducing an economic balancing process may rationalise Article 101(1) TFEU balancing, bringing its conditions closer in line with the effects-based approach to EU competition law following modernisation. A more economic approach, moreover, could also avoid similar situations being regulated differently according to the form of the arrangements adopted by the various Member States. Nevertheless, adopting a more economic approach to Article 101(1) TFEU balancing tools may question the need for the state and public interest balancing tools altogether, as it brings the analysis closer to the consumer welfare-based approach to Article 101 (3) TFEU.

5.3 BALANCING COMPETITION AND COMMERCIAL INTERESTS

5.3.1 *Legal and Empirical Background*

The prior sections have examined cases in which competition interests clashed with state powers or public interests. This section moves to examine another category of Article 101(1) TFEU balancing tools. It covers situations in which the realisation of an efficient market outcome – such as facilitating certain types of commercial transactions, economies of scale and scope, or technological advancements – was taken into account to limit the application of the Article.

This category of balancing tools is tied to the notion of 'restriction of competition' within the meaning of Article 101(1) TFEU. As mentioned in the opening of this chapter, it is unclear what kind of restrictions on undertakings' commercial freedom fall within the scope of the Article. The Commission has traditionally taken the view that almost any restraint on commercial freedom infringes Article 101(1) TFEU. Yet, the CJEU and various scholars have argued that the Article should include a substantive balancing element, namely that Article 101(1) TFEU does not prohibit

[195] For example, see Ibáñez Colomo (2012), Janssen and Kloosterhuis (2016), and Kloosterhuis (2017).

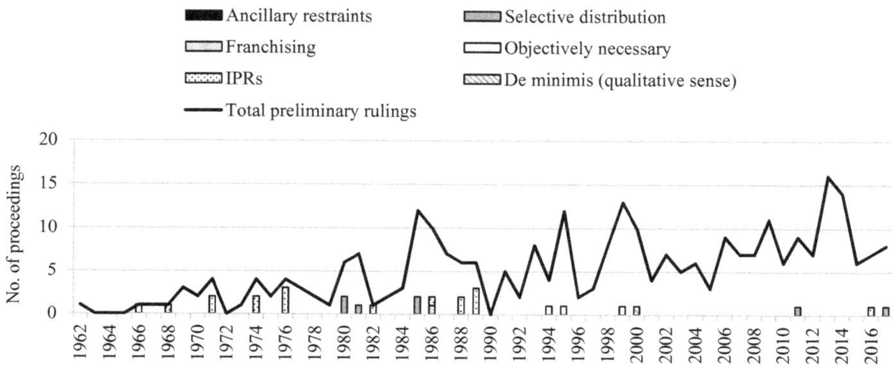

FIGURE 5.3. Attainment of efficient market outcome, preliminary rulings
In some proceedings, more than one type of Article 101(1) TFEU commercial exception was discussed

restrictions that are necessary and proportionate to the attainment of a commercial purpose.[196]

Ascribing this balancing function to Article 101(1) TFEU was heavily influenced by the US 'rule of reason' concept.[197] The US Supreme Court has held that the notion of 'restriction of trade' in the Sherman Act does not prohibit all restraints on trade – only undue or unreasonable ones.[198] The American case law has distinguished between two types of restrictions: *per se* restrictions, which are always prohibited irrespective of their effect on competition and cannot be justified; and other restrictions that are examined under the 'rule of reason'. This merits a full effects analysis, including weighing the agreement's pro- and anti-competitive effects.

This section shows that a fully-fledged rule of reason has not been accepted under Article 101(1) TFEU. At the same time, the CJEU has introduced weaker versions of the rule in the form of objectively necessary agreements, ancillary restraints, IPRs, and the *de minimis* exceptions. Figure 5.3 presents the application of those balancing tools in the CJEU's preliminary rulings. It indicates the number of enforcement actions in which the exceptions have been discussed (bars) and the total number of Article 101 TFEU preliminary rulings (black line).

Figure 5.3 highlights the CJEU's remarkable influence in developing these exceptions. As elaborated below, in a relatively small number of cases, the CJEU has shaped various exceptions that have guided the balancing applied by the Commission, NCAs, and national courts.

Figure 5.4 outlines the use of these exceptions by the Commission and EU Courts in appeals. It presents the number of enforcement actions in which one or more

[196] See Section 5.1.1.
[197] For detailed analysis, see Whish and Sufrin (1987, 5–8), Black (1997, 145–161), Wesseling (1999, 422–424), Manzini (2002, 392–394), and Bailey and Whish (2015, 143–145).
[198] Standard Oil Co. of New Jersey v. United States, 221 U.S. 1 (1911).

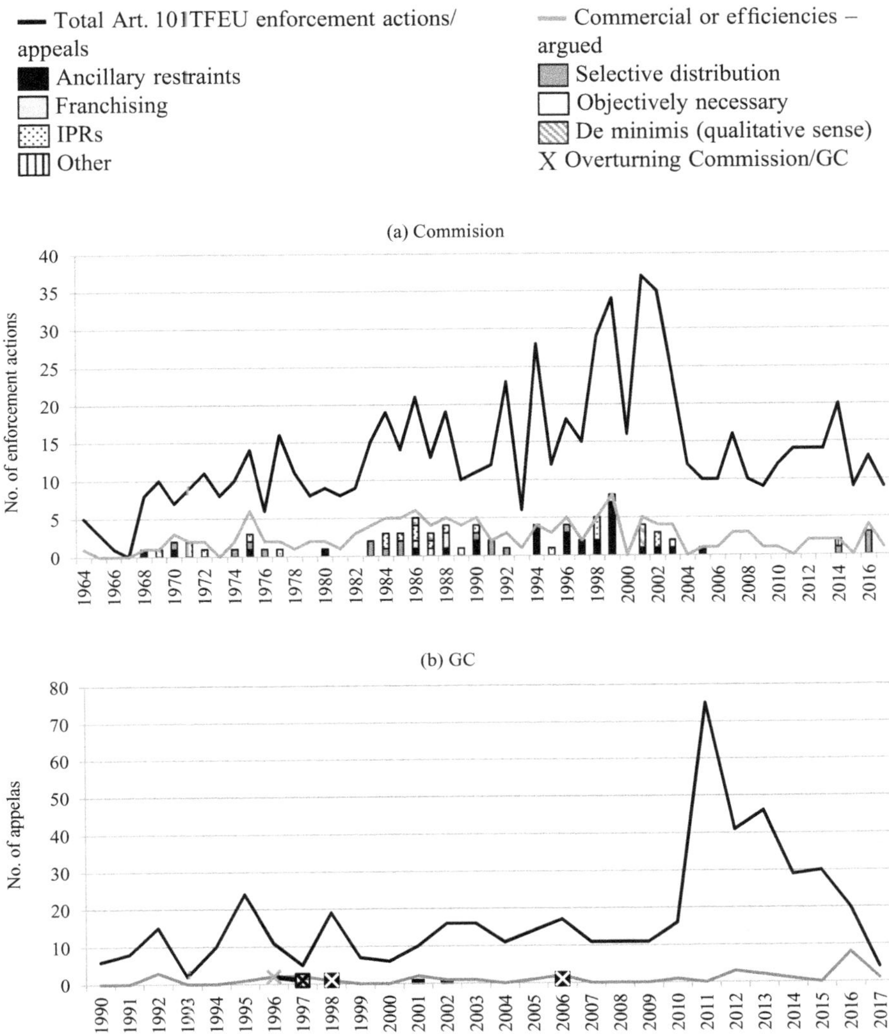

FIGURE 5.4. Attainment of efficient market outcome, Commission and EU Courts appeals

In some proceedings, more than one type of Article 101(1) TFEU commercial exception was discussed

exceptions were discussed (grey lines) and accepted (bars). It also indicates the number of proceedings in which the EU Courts overturned the previous instance's decision accepting or denying such exceptions (crosses, corresponding to the colour of the relevant exception).

The figure demonstrates that the Commission made a limited use of those exceptions in comparison to Article 101(3) TFEU individual exemptions (a). As

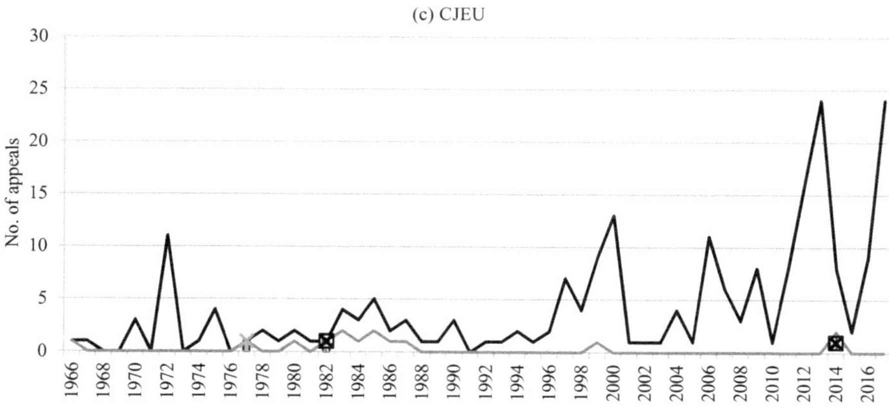

FIGURE 5.4. (*cont.*)

detailed below, despite criticism from the EU Courts, the Commission insisted that efficiency-related considerations would be limited to the scope of Article 101(3) TFEU. In *Bananas (2008)*, for example, it asserted that 'once an anticompetitive object of communications is established, the parties cannot justify them by arguing that they had in mind "efficiency increasing" aims. For an anticompetitive concerted practice to be exempted from the application of Article [101 TFEU], the conditions set out in Article [101(3) TFEU] must be met'.[199]

In addition, Figures 5.3 and 5.4 illustrate that those balancing tools appear to have lost their weight since modernisation. Like Article 101(3) TFEU,[200] they have received limited attention from the EU Courts and the Commission since May 2004 and have almost never been used to justify limiting the scope of the Article 101 (1) TFEU prohibition. Chapter 2 has suggested that this can be partly explained by the more economic approach to the theory of harm, advocated by the Commission following modernisation. Chapter 7 further argues that the limited number of cases examining the commercial interest exceptions could also be explained by the general shift from explicit-substantive to implicit-procedural balancing tools.[201]

The following sections detail the development of those balancing tools, the types of benefits examined, the balancing methods, and the intensity of control. They affirm that the differences in the Commission's and Courts' approaches, together with the sparing use of those exceptions since May 2004, have hindered achieving a clear approach to balancing.

[199] 39188 Bananas (2008), para 303. See also para 278, 282, 300–302.
[200] See Section 3.2.
[201] See Section 2.5.4.4 and Chapter 7.

5.3.2 EU Rule of Reason

The debate over the existence of a rule of reason in EU competition law dates back to *Grundig/Consten (1966)*. The CJEU rejected the undertakings' and the German Government's plea for applying the rule in Article 101(1) TFEU.[202] The Court acknowledged that, like its US counterpart, Article 101(1) TFEU refers to two types of restrictions of competition: by-object and by-effect. Yet, as shown in Section 3.4.4.4, both types of restrictions can be exempted under Article 101(3) TFEU. In other words, there are no *per se* prohibitions under Article 101 TFEU.

Despite its initial rejection, over the years the CJEU has expressed a growing flexibility in applying Article 101(1) TFEU. This implies that it may have accepted a rule of reason. In *Breeders' rights (1982)*, for instance, it overturned the Commission by finding that an open exclusive license was compatible with Article 101(1) given 'the specific nature of the products in question'.[203] A few years later, in *Pronuptia (1986)*, it held that a system of franchises did not fall within the prohibition of Article 101(1) TFEU since it was necessary for the operation of that commercial format.[204] In *Gøttrup-Klim (1994)*, a restrictive membership condition in a purchasing cooperative was granted an exception since it was necessary for the functioning of the cooperative.[205]

During the 1990s, the EU Courts began to explicitly invoke the rule of reason concept. This was especially evident in the GC's decisions that have attempted to import the US notion of *per se* restrictions into Article 101 TFEU. In *Polypropylene (1992)*, the GC explained that the fact that a restriction is listed under Article 101(1)(a) to (e) TFEU 'precludes the application of a rule of reason, assuming such a rule to be applicable in Community competition law, since in that case it must be regarded as an infringement *per se* of the competition rules'.[206] Later, in *Night Services (1998)*, it clarified that when applying Article 101 TFEU, account should be taken of the actual conditions under which an agreement functions 'unless it is an agreement containing obvious restrictions of competition such as price-fixing, market-sharing or the control of outlets'. Pro-competitive effects could only be taken into account under Article 101(3) TFEU

[202] C-56/64 C-58/64 Grundig/Consten (1966), 342.

[203] C-258/78 Breeders' rights – maize seed (1982), para 58.

[204] C-161/84 Pronuptia (1986), para 15–27.

[205] C-250/92 Gøttrup-Klim (1994), para 34–35. Notably, AG Tesauro suggested to grant an exception with reference to the workable competition standard, which was described in Section 2.5.2.1 (see para 18). However, the workable competition standard is not mentioned in the CJEU's judgement, which has focused on the proper functioning of the cooperative.

[206] T-14/89 Polypropylene (1992), para 265. See also T-148/89 Welded steel mesh (1995), para 109.

when examining such obvious restrictions.[207] This was confirmed by the CJEU in *Polypropylene (1999)*.[208]

The modernisation of EU competition law, however, found itself at a turning point when confronted with that approach to an EU-type rule of reason. The Commission's Modernisation White Paper (1999) advocated a narrow reading of the EU Courts' past judgements.[209] First, the Commission maintained that the EU Courts had not established a rule of reason, but rather a more limited concept of ancillary restraints (which will be discussed in Section 5.3.4). According to the Commission, the Courts had accepted a rule of reason 'to a limited extent' in the past. Yet, the structure of Article 101 TFEU prevents any greater use of this approach. If Article 101(1) TFEU was regularly used to balance pro- and anti-competitive effects, Article 101(3) TFEU would be cast aside. This outcome would be paradoxical, as the Commission believed that Article 101(3) TFEU already contained all the elements of a rule of reason. This reasoning was also supported by AG *Léger* in its opinion in *Wouters (2001)*.[210]

Second, the Commission submitted that a rule of reason was undesirable in light of the decentralisation of the enforcement. It pointed out that a rule of reason could be used to limit the prohibition of Article 101(1) TFEU on the basis of political considerations.

The EU Courts' approach converged with the Commission's in this regard. In judgements handed down after the publication of the Modernisation White Paper, the GC stressed that a rule of reason did not and had not existed in Article 101(1) TFEU.[211] Moreover, in *MasterCard (2014)*, the CJEU emphasised that Article 101(1) and (3) TFEU had two distinct objectives. The former relates to the question of whether a restriction of competition exists. Article 101(1) TFEU balancing is thus confined to examining whether an agreement that overall does not impede competition is likely to be implemented without a subordinate restriction to competition. Article 101(3) TFEU, on the other hand, deals with cases in which agreements have an appreciable adverse impact on parameters of competition such as price, quantity, and quality of goods or services. Article 101(3) TFEU balancing thus examines whether the harm to competition is indispensable to the attainment of other non-competition interests.[212]

[207] T-374/94 T-375/94 T-384/94 T-388/94 Night Services (1998), para 136.

[208] C-235/92P Polypropylene (1999), para 133.

[209] Modernisation White Paper (1999), para 55–57.

[210] AG Léger opinion in C-309/01 Wouters (2001), para 103–108.

[211] T-112/99 Métropole (2001), para 72; T-65/98 Van den Bergh Foods (2003), para 106. Notably, in T-49/02 T-50/02 T-51/02 Brasserie (2005), para 85, the GC seemed to go back to its earlier approach by holding that a rule of reason could not apply since it was a by-object restriction. Yet, a year later in T-328/03 O2 (2006), para 69, it once again rejected the existence of a rule of reason.

[212] C-382/12P MasterCard (2014), para 89–94.

Nevertheless, the following sub-sections illustrate that the EU Courts and the Commission have *de facto* accepted weaker versions of the rule of reason, introducing balancing to Article 101(1) TFEU. Differing from the state or public interest exceptions, those balancing tools have mostly taken into account economic benefits, balancing the protection of the competitive process and structure with other legitimate commercial interests.

5.3.3 *Objectively Necessary Agreement*

The first tool introduced by the CJEU to balance competition and commercial interests was the so-called objectively necessary agreement exception. It provides that a restriction of the commercial freedom of undertakings does not infringe Article 101(1) TFEU if it creates competition that would not have existed without it (Figures 5.3 and 5.4, white bars).[213]

This exception dates back to *Société Technique Minière (1966)*, in which the CJEU asserted that an exclusive license did not infringe Article 101(1) TFEU, as the 'agreement seems really necessary for the penetration of a new area by an undertaking'.[214] It was first formalised only many years later by the Commission's Article 101 (3) Guidelines (2004). Therefore, it is not entirely clear how often it was used. In particular, some of the decisions described above as an expression of a rule of reason could alternatively be viewed as an application of the objectively necessary exception.[215] In *Gøttrup-Klim (1994)*, for instance, the CJEU examined the statutes of a cooperative purchasing association forbidding its members from participating in other forms of organised cooperation for purposes of joint purchasing. According to the Court, the prohibition against dual membership did not restrict competition within the meaning of Article 101(1) TFEU since dual membership might have jeopardised the proper functioning of the cooperative and its contractual power. The restriction fell outside the scope of Article 101(1) TFEU as far it was limited to what is necessary to ensure such aims.[216]

Similar reasoning also guided the assessment of cooperation agreements. *Night Services (1994, 1998)* concerned a cooperation agreement for the rail carriage of passengers via the Channel Tunnel. The GC criticised the Commission for not taking into account the actual legal and economic context of the agreement. According to the GC, the Commission failed to determine whether the

[213] On the objectively necessary agreement exception, see also Van Rompuy (2012, 236–238), Faull and Nikpay (2014, 261–264), and Bailey and Whish (2015, 136–137).

[214] C-56/65 Société Technique Minière (1966), 250.

[215] See also 33585 Distribution of railway tickets by travel agents (1992), para 73–74.

[216] C-250/92 Gøttrup-Klim Grovvareforening (1994), para 34–45. See also C-399/93 H. G. Oude Luttikhuis (1995), para 11–20.

undertakings had 'real concrete possibilities' to compete.[217] In a similar vein, in *O2 (2003, 2006)*, the GC held that the Commission should have assessed whether an infrastructure-sharing agreement was necessary and indispensable to enable O2 to function as a competitive operator capable of offering coverage and quality services on the 3G mobile telecommunications market. According to the Court, the Commission should have considered 'whether, in the absence of the agreement, O2 would have been present on the 3G market work'.[218] The GC stressed that a detailed economic analysis of the effects of the agreement was necessary not only for the purposes of granting an Article 101(3) TFEU exemption but also as part of the economic analysis to determine the applicability of Article 101(1) TFEU.[219]

The empirical findings show that despite the Courts' case law, the Commission has scarcely accepted a claim for the objectively necessary exception (Figure 5.4 (a)).[220] Moreover, it construed the expression narrowly in its Article 101(3) Guidelines (2004).[221] The Guidelines emphasise that an exception can only be granted on the basis of objective factors external to the undertakings. The test is not whether the undertakings would not have agreed to conclude a less restrictive agreement, but whether a less restrictive agreement could have been concluded in light of the nature of the agreement and the characteristics of the market.

5.3.4 *Ancillary Restraints*

The previous section has shown that certain restrictive *agreements* fall outside the scope of Article 101(1) TFEU if they are necessary for creating competition that would not have existed without them. This section deals with another type of exception, whereby a *specific clause* restricting rivalry between undertakings is considered necessary for the realisation of the overall legitimate commercial purposes of an agreement.[222] According to this ancillary restraints exception, a provision that is directly related, necessary, and proportionate for securing the benefits of an agreement that is not otherwise restrictive of competition does not fall under the prohibition of Article 101(1) TFEU.

The EU Courts held that the ancillary restraints exception does *not* entail an economic balancing process weighing the pro- and anti-competitive effects of the clause. Rather, it consists of a legal balancing process in which the necessity of the

[217] 34600 Night services (1994); T-374/94 T-375/94 T-384/94 T-388/94 Night Services (1998), para 137.
[218] 38369 Network Sharing Rahmenvertrag (2003); T-328/03 O2 (2006), para 77.
[219] T-328/03 O2 (2006), para 79.
[220] The two exceptions in which the Commission seemed to accept agreements on the basis of an objectively necessary exception implicitly were 30373 37143 P&I Clubs (1999), para 65–74, 85–86, and 38370 UK Network Sharing Agreement (2003), para 93, 101.
[221] Commission Article 101(3) Guidelines (2004), para 18(2).
[222] On the ancillary restraints exception, see Faull and Nikpay (2014, 251–266), Bailey and Whish (2015, 137), and Sauter (2016, 99–100).

restriction for the main operation is being assessed in the 'abstract'.[223] To this end, the ancillary restraints exception differs from the balancing process guiding the application of Article 101(3) TFEU exception, at least according to the Commission's more economic approach following modernisation.

Like the objectively necessary exception, there is no clear point in time at which the ancillary restraints exception was introduced into EU competition law. As elaborated below, the GC first formalised the exception only in *Métropole (2001)*.[224] However, the empirical findings show that up until 2001, the Commission and EU Courts applied it implicitly in various contexts (Figures 5.3 and 5.4, black, dark grey, and light grey bars):[225]

First, the exception was used to examine non-compete clauses attached to the sale of a business. In *Reuter/BASF (1976)*, for example, a sales agreement had limited the future activities of Dr Reuter after he sold his company to BASF. It included a non-compete clause for a period of eight years. The Commission held that the non-compete clause should be examined in consideration of its role in preserving the goodwill of the business sold. Accordingly, the non-compete clause infringed Article 101(1) TFEU since it went beyond what was necessary to secure the legitimate commercial purpose of the agreement.[226]

Second, the ancillary restraints exception was applied to analyse horizontal cooperation agreements[227] and agreements aimed at achieving environmental protection.[228] The principles underlying these exceptions were later codified in the relevant horizontal BERs and guidelines.[229] In *ACEA (1998)*, for instance, the Association of European Automobile Manufacturers (ACEA) undertook on behalf of its members to reduce CO_2 emissions from new passenger cars sold within the EU. The Association aimed to achieve an average reduction of 25% within ten years across all of its members, while not imposing an individual target on each manufacture. Thus, individual members were free to apply more or less stringent levels of CO_2 emissions. The Commission cleared the agreement by issuing a comfort letter. According to the Commission, the agreement was likely to encourage the ACEA

[223] C-179/16 Hoffmann-La Roche (2018), para 70–71; T-112/99 Métropole (2001), para 107–109; T-65/98 Van den Bergh Foods Limited (2003), para 107. On the legal and economic balancing processes, see Section 1.2.2.1.

[224] T-112/99 Métropole (2001).

[225] This was also observed by AG Saugmandsgaard Øe, in his opinion in C-179/16 Hoffmann-La Roche (2018), para 105–106. See also Diaz (1996).

[226] 28996 Reuter-BASF (1976), 46–47. A similar approach was taken by the Commission and CJEU in 30389 30408 Nutricia-de Rooij Nutricia-Zuid-Hollandse Conservenfabriek (1983), para 26–38, and C-42/84 Nutricia-de Rooij and Nutricia-Zuid-Hollandse Conservenfabriek (1985), para 20, finding that a non-compete clause should be shortened.

[227] See Annex A, Section 5.16.

[228] 37231 ACEA (1998); 37634 JAMA (1999); 34493 37366 37299 37288 37287 37526 37254 37252 37250 37246 37245 37244 37243 37242 37267 DSD (2001), para 104–114.

[229] See Section 4.3.2.1.

members to independently develop and introduce new CO_2-efficient technologies.[230]

Third, the exception was used to examine selective distribution systems. As demonstrated in Chapter 4, by the mid-1980s the balancing relating to the functioning of most distribution systems was governed by BERs. Yet, the application of balancing to selective distribution was more complex.[231] On the one hand, selective distribution systems inherently restrict the commercial freedom of undertakings. On the other hand, manufacturers often impose those restrictions to guarantee adequate consumer support and pre- and post-sales services. They were particularly deemed essential to providing support for technically complex products (e.g. electronic equipment and cars) or luxury products (e.g. perfumes and watches).[232] As a result, the rules governing selective distribution systems remained more obscure and were developed on a case-by-case basis.

In a series of cases extending from the 1970s through the 1990s, the Commission and EU Courts have taken the view that selective distribution systems are not caught by Article 101(1) TFEU when a supplier has merely set the qualitative objective criteria dealers are obliged to meet (Figures 5.3 and 5.4, dark grey bars).[233] They introduced a proportionality test to examine selective distribution systems, which is essentially identical to the ancillary restraints principle. In 1999, such principles were finally codified within the scope of the Vertical BER.[234]

Despite its codification, the scope of the selective distribution systems exception has remained unclear and has been the subject of heated debate.[235] This debate was stimulated by the CJEU preliminary ruling in *Pierre Fabre (2011)*. In what appeared to be a clear deviation from its prior case law, the CJEU declared that 'the aim of maintaining a prestigious image is not a legitimate aim for restricting competition' and therefore could not justify a total prohibition on the sale of cosmetic and personal care products via the Internet.[236] Accordingly, in *Watch Repair (2017)*, the GC held, on the basis of *Pierre Fabre*, that the aim of maintaining a prestigious image is not a legitimate aim for restricting competition. According to the GC, the

[230] 37231 ACEA (1998). A similar assessment guided the Commission's decision in 37634 JAMA (1999).

[231] On the EU competition law approach to selective distribution systems, see Goyder (2009, 230–232), Monti (2013), and Bailey and Whish (2015, 680–682).

[232] T-19/91 Vichy (1992); C-19/92 Yves Saint Laurent Perfumes (1996); T-88/92 Perfumes Givenchy system of selective distribution (1996), para 141–148; T-427/08 Watch Repair (2010), para 139–142; 39097 Watch Repair (2014), para 153–169; T-712/14 Watch Repair (2017), para 49. See also Forrester and Norall (1984, 27) and Goyder (2009, 230–232).

[233] See Annex A, Section 5.17.

[234] See Section 4.3.2.1. The Commission continued to apply the exception to systems not covered by the BER, such as in 39097 Watch Repair (2014), para 163–169.

[235] For example, see Monti (2013), Witt (2016a), Ezrachi (2017), Waelbroeck and Davies (2018), and Wijckmans (2018).

[236] C-439/09 Pierre Fabre (2011), para 46.

exception is confined to restrictions necessary for preserving the quality of the products and ensuring their proper use.[237]

Shortly after the GC's decision in *Watch Repair*, the CJEU clarified in *Coty (2017)* that *Pierre Fabre* had not altered the rule established in its prior case law. It declared that a selective distribution system that is primarily designed to preserve the luxury image of goods is compatible with Article 101(1) TFEU insofar as it is uniform, not applied in a discriminatory fashion, and proportionate in light of the objective pursued.[238] The CJEU explained that its statement in *Pierre Fabre* related to the specific situation in that case.[239] Accordingly, it found that a specific prohibition on the use of third-party platforms for online sales could be justified for the purpose of preserving the luxury image of the goods, as long as it met the conditions for the exception.[240]

Fourth, in *Pronuptia (1986)*, the CJEU transposed the selective distribution rationale to franchising agreements. It explained that the franchising business model calls for communicating know-how and necessary assistance to franchisees without running the risk that such communication would benefit competitors. The franchisor must also take the necessary measures for maintaining the identity and reputation of the network bearing its business name or symbol. Therefore, provisions necessary for such purposes do not infringe Article 101(1) TFEU.[241] This approach has guided the examination of other franchising agreements (Figures 5.3 and 5.4, light grey bars)[242] and has, since 1988, been included in BERs.[243]

Despite this impressive array of decisions, the ancillary restraints exception was only formalised towards the end of the third enforcement period. In *Métropole (2001)*, the GC first defined the exception as 'any restriction which is directly related and necessary to the implementation of a main operation'.[244] This definition was incorporated into the Commission's Article 101(3) Guidelines (2004) and confirmed by the CJEU in *MasterCard (2014)* and *Hoffmann-La Roche (2018)*.[245]

Remarkably, the formalisation of the ancillary restraints exception has narrowed its scope by setting three strict conditions for its application.[246] First, the definition provides that an agreement must be directly related and subordinate to the implementation of the main operation. This requires a direct link between the restrictive

[237] T-712/14 Watch Repair (2017), para 65–66.
[238] C-230/16 Coty (2017), para 29.
[239] *Ibid*, para 33–35.
[240] *Ibid*, para 38–58.
[241] C-161/84 Pronuptia (1986), para 16. See also the Commission's decision in 31428 31429 31430 31431 31432 Yves Rocher (1986), para 36–55.
[242] 30937 Pronuptia (1986), para 17–27; 32034 Computerland (1987), para 22–25; 32358 ServiceMaster (1988), para 7–22; 31697 Charles Jourdan (1988), para 26–32.
[243] See Section 4.3.2.1.
[244] T-112/99 Métropole (2001), para 104.
[245] Commission Article 101(3) Guidelines (2004), para 29–31; C-382/12P MasterCard (2014), para 89; C-179/16 Hoffmann-La Roche (2018), para 69–75.
[246] T-112/99 Métropole (2001), para 104–106; C-382/12P MasterCard (2014), para 77–79.

clause and the main agreement. Second, the substantive and geographic scope of the restriction should be proportionate to the implementation of the main operation. Third, the restriction needs to be objectively necessary for the implementation of the main operation.

In *Métropole (2001)*, the GC explained that the third condition entails assessing whether, in the absence of the restrictive clause, the main operation would be *difficult*.[247] However, in *MasterCard (2014)* and *Hoffmann-La Roche (2018)*, the CJEU imposed a higher standard of *necessity*. It declared that the fact that the operation was 'simply more difficult to implement or even less profitable without the restriction' was not sufficient. Rather, the operation must be 'impossible to carry out in the absence of the restriction'.[248]

Possibly aiming to counter these strict conditions for granting an exception, some decisions appear to have *implicitly* accepted a variation on the ancillary restraints exception, resembling the reasoning that guided the exception prior to its formalisation. In *Cartes bancaires (2007, 2012, 2014)*, the Commission held that a co-operative joint venture between competing firms for the creation of a card payment system constituted a by-object restriction. The Commission rejected the undertakings' allegation that the restriction was an ancillary restraint aimed at solving free-riding problems. Since the restriction was not necessary for the creation or existence of the card payment system, the Commission and later the GC maintained that free-riding concerns are confined to Article 101(3) TFEU analysis.[249] The CJEU, however, took a different view. It held that the legitimate objective of fighting free-riding prevented the agreement from being classified as a by-object restriction.[250] The CJEU did not explicitly refer to the ancillary restraints exception. Yet, its judgement was based on similar reasoning, namely that a legitimate objective informs the existence of an infringement of Article 101(1) TFEU.[251]

The Commission followed a similar line of analysis in a decision rendered two months prior to the CJEU's judgement in *Cartes bancaires*. In *Refusal to provide payment services (2014)*, the Commission rejected DataCell's complaint claiming that MasterCard and Visa had prevented it from accepting payments by card. It explained that Visa and MasterCard membership rules prohibited the use of their systems for the processing of illegal transactions or transactions that may damage the scheme's reputation or trademark. In light of those objectives, the Commission maintained that it was unlikely to establish a by-object restriction.[252]

[247] T-112/99 Métropole (2001), para 111.

[248] C-382/12P MasterCard (2014), para 91; C-179/16 Hoffmann-La Roche (2018), para 71.

[249] 38606 Cartes bancaires (2007), para 365–368; T-491/07 Cartes bancaires (2012), para 139–140, 156–158.

[250] C-67/13P Cartes bancaires (2014), para 74–75.

[251] For a similar view, see Ibáñez Colomo and De Pablo (2017, 18–19).

[252] 39921 Refusal to provide payment services (2014), para 74. This type of reasoning also guided the reversal of two decisions of the French NCA by a French Court, as elaborated in Section 5.4.2.

In conclusion, the case law and the balancing principles guiding the ancillary restraints exception are highly unclear. There is no clear point in time at which the ancillary restraints exception was formally introduced into EU competition law. While the exception was only formalised at the beginning of the 2000s, the Commission and EU Courts have implicitly held in various contexts that a provision that is directly related, necessary, and proportionate for securing the benefits of an agreement that is not otherwise restrictive of competition does not fall under the prohibition of Article 101(1) TFEU. Following modernisation, the Commission and EU Courts have stricken the conditions for an exception. Yet, the assessment is still based on a relatively abstract legal proportionality balancing, which is not bound to an economic balancing process weighing the pro- and anti-competitive effects of the clause.

5.3.5 *IPRs*

The relationship between intellectual property rights (IPRs) and Article 101(1) TFEU has provoked debate for many years.[253] While competition law and IPRs are two complementary elements of industrial policy, sometimes they may also clash. IP laws grant owners of IPRs an exclusive right to prevent the unlicensed use of their creations. The owners have significant discretion to decide how, and if, to license or use their inventions. From a competition law perspective, however, the grant of such an exclusive right can significantly impede competition.

Since IPRs are generally protected by national laws, the principle of primacy of EU law suggests that IPRs could not limit competition.[254] As demonstrated by the first part of this chapter, in cases of conflict between national law and Article 101 TFEU, the latter normally prevails.[255] Nevertheless, the Commission and EU Courts have used a different tool to balance competition and IPRs. Instead of focusing on the scope of the national law, they have opted for a balancing method similar to the ancillary restraints exception that focuses on the substance of the agreements and the IPRs (Figures 5.3 and 5.4, white and black dotted bars).

This balancing tool is based on the *doctrine of exhaustion*, which was developed by the CJEU in *Grundig/Consten (1966)*.[256] The Court distinguished between the existence and exercise of IPRs. The *existence* of an IPR is governed by Article 345 TFEU, which limits the application of Treaty provisions that undermine national

[253] On the relationship between IPRs and competition law, see policy report 1971, para 58; Korah (2001), Peeperkorn (2003), Anderman and Kallaugher (2006), Drexl (2008), Goyder (2009, 262–294), Turner (2010), Faull and Nikpay (2014, 1446–1509), and Bailey and Whish (2015, 811).

[254] See T-680/14 Perindopril (Servier) (2018), para 84–85; Korah (2001, 803) and Bailey and Whish (2015, 811).

[255] See Section 5.2.2.

[256] C-56/64 C-58/64 Grundig/Consten (1996), 345–346. See also Korah (2001, 806), Faull and Nikpay (2014, 1447–1454), and Bailey and Whish (2015, 811).

ownership systems. The *exercise* of an IPR, however, is subject to Article 101 TFEU. Hence, once the holder of an IPR puts the protected product on the market in one Member State, the IPR has been exhausted and cannot be invoked to prevent the importation of the product to another Member State. Once the IPR has been exhausted, the exercise of an IPR by the proprietor may give rise to an infringement of the competition rules. According to the CJEU, the prohibition of Article 101 TFEU would be rendered ineffective if undertakings could use IPRs to achieve the same purpose as anti-competitive agreements.[257]

This distinction between the existence and exercise of IPRs in the context of competition law was inspired by the Treaties mechanism to balance between IPRs and the free movement of goods. Article 36 TFEU states that the prohibition on quantitative restrictions between Member States does not preclude restrictions that are justified on grounds of public policy, including the protection of industrial and commercial property, in so far as those restrictions do not constitute a means of arbitrary discrimination or a disguised restriction on trade.[258]

In the past, the particulars of the IPRs exception varied according to the type of IPR covered by an agreement. The competition enforcer first needed to identify the specific subject matter of the agreement, namely the IPR predominantly being exercised (e.g. mostly a patent, a trademark, or know-how). Next, the scope of what was considered the exercise of the IPR was determined according to the subject matter of that right. For example, the specific subject matter of a patent was defined as the exclusive right to utilise an invention and to decide on the first placing of a product on the market to recompense the creative efforts of the inventor.[259] The specific subject matter of the copyright entailed a right to decide on the first placing of a work on the market, the right to require compensation for its public performance, and the right to rent out the work.[260]

The selected form of IPR, therefore, informed the balance between competition and IPRs. This formalistic approach was apparent in the CJEU's and Commission's practices until the end of the second enforcement period (i.e. the late 1980s).[261] However, since then, the CJEU has gradually adopted a more effects-based analysis. Rather than focusing on the *form* of the agreement, it assessed the *commercial and economic rationale* behind it.

Maize seed (1982) marked this change. That case involved an exclusive licence for plant breeders' rights conferring absolute territorial protection. The Commission's

[257] C-56/64 C-58/64 Grundig/Consten (1966), 345.

[258] C-15/74 Centrafarm (1974), para 39; C-262/81 Coditel (1982), para 13; T-680/14 Perindopril (Servier) (2018), para 88–91.

[259] C-15/74 Centeafarm (1974), para 9; C-193/83 Windsurfing surfing International (1986), para 45; 39226 Lundbeck (2013), para 598–604; 39612 Perindopril (Servier) (2014), para 1120.

[260] C-403/08 C-429/08 Football Association Premier League (2011), para 107–108; 40023 Cross-border access to pay-TV (2016), para 40.

[261] See Annex A, Section 5.18.

analysis followed a formalistic approach. Based on the selected form of the agreement, it determined that the agreement was prohibited by Article 101(1) TFEU and could not be exempted by Article 101(3) TFEU.[262] The CJEU, on the other hand, engaged in more nuanced balancing in the scope of Article 101(1) TFEU. It distinguished between an 'open exclusive licence', whereby the licensor agrees not to licence anyone else in the territory, to a 'closed exclusive licence' that eliminates all competition from third parties.[263] The CJEU maintained that a closed exclusive licence conferred absolute territorial protection and would always fall within Article 101(1) TFEU.[264] Yet, an open exclusive licence might be necessary to allow licensees to assume the risk of cultivating and marketing new products and therefore could fall outside the scope of Article 101(1) TFEU. A number of factors need to be examined, including the nature of the product, the novelty and importance of the technology, the investment risks assumed by the licensee, and the development of intra-brand competition.[265]

Hence, *Maize seed* expanded the scope for Article 101(1) TFEU balancing in IPRs cases. In later cases, the CJEU held that licensing agreements, including agreements involving territorial exclusivity, did not infringe Article 101(1) TFEU when they were necessary for the purpose of IPRs.[266] This introduced a legal balancing process, similar to the ancillary restraints exception, to the balance between IPRs and competition interests.[267] In other words, the balancing shifted from exclusion on the basis of the form of the IPR to a legal balancing process assessing the necessity of the relevant restriction on competition.

The BERs adopted since the mid-1980s have reflected this new approach. A substantial part of the balancing between IPRs and competition interests has thus moved to the scope of the BERs.[268] IPRs agreements that do not benefit from a BER are still assessed under Article 101(1) TFEU IPRs exception. The empirical findings show that it has guided the Commission's and EU Courts' balance between IPRs and competition interests in cases involving collecting societies,[269] pay-for-delay settlements,[270] and broadcasting agreements.[271]

[262] 28824 Breeders' rights – maize seed (1978), para 1.E.5, II.B.8.
[263] C-258/78 Breeders' rights – maize seed (1982), para 53.
[264] *Ibid*, para 68–79.
[265] *Ibid*, para 53.
[266] See Annex A, Section 5.19.
[267] On ancillary restraints, see Section 5.3.4.
[268] See Section 4.3.1.1.
[269] 38681 Cannes Agreement (2006); 38698 CISAC Agreement (2008), 159–160.
[270] 39226 Lundbeck (2013), para 598–605, 638–646, as confirmed by the GC in T-460/13 Lundbeck (2016), para 140–151; T-467/13 Lundbeck (2016), para 106–112; T-469/13 Lundbeck (2016), para 243–252; T-470/13 Lundbeck (2016), para 224–234; T-471/13 Lundbeck (2016), para 314–326; T-472/13 Lundbeck (2016), para 117–132; 39612 Perindopril (Servier) (2014), para 1102–1124.
[271] 40023 Cross-border access to pay-TV (2016), para 35–36.

5.3.6 *De Minimis*

The *de minimis* rule excludes from the scope of Article 101(1) TFEU agreements between undertakings with low market shares or agreements having a small impact, which are unlikely to have an appreciable effect on competition.[272] The *de minimis* rule was introduced by the CJEU in *Völk (1969)*.[273] It was followed by the Commission's *de minimis* Notice that defined a safe harbour for agreements between undertakings with a market share that did not exceed a certain quantitative threshold.[274]

The *de minimis* rule is often perceived as applicable to agreements having a limited impact on competition. According to this view, the rule essentially proclaims that the Commission will not assert jurisdiction over agreements between undertakings having a low market share. Indeed, *Völk* and the Commission's Notice dealt with cases in which restrictions were not appreciable in quantitative terms (i.e. the undertakings' low market share). This rule does not involve balancing. Yet, there are strong indications that the *de minimis* rule was also applied to other situations in a manner that entailed balancing between competition and non-competition interests.

First, the Commission and EU Courts applied the *de minimis* rule to situations in which the nature of the restriction itself was not deemed to be appreciable (Figures 5.3 and 5.4, grey and white strips bars).[275] Those cases involved a similar analysis to the ancillary restraints exception discussed above. In *Pavel Pavlov (2000)*, for instance, the CJEU held that the decision of medical specialists to create a pension fund entrusted with the management of a supplementary pension scheme did not restrict competition in an appreciable manner since the cost of the scheme had a marginal and indirect influence on the cost of the services offered.[276]

Notably, such qualitative exceptions were granted in sectors prone to tension between public interest and competition law. In addition to the pension funds in *Pavel Pavlov*, it was applied to agreements related to financial institutions, sports, and R&D.[277] A similar qualitative *de minimis* exception is found in the Commission Horizontal Guidelines (2001). The Guidelines state that an environmental agreement is unlikely to have an appreciable effect on competition irrespective of the undertakings' market share if it contributes to the achievement of a sector-wide

[272] On the *de minimis* doctrine, see also Goyder (2009, 104–107), Bailey and Whish (2015, 148–152), and Wagner-von Papp (2015).

[273] C-5/69 Völk (1969).

[274] Commission de minimis Notice (1970). The notice was revised in 1977, 1986, 1997, 2001, and 2014.

[275] See also Van Rompuy (2012, 238–240) and Bailey and Whish (2015, 151–152).

[276] C-180/98 C-181/98 C-182/98 C-183/98 C-184/98 C-185/98 Pavel Pavlov (2000), para 91–97.

[277] See Annex A, Section 5.20.

environmental target. Yet, the agreement is restrictive if it serves to disguise a cartel rather than achieving genuine environmental benefit.[278]

Second, the *de minimis* rule was also tied to the market integration objective. Although the CJEU's judgement in *Völk* concerned a by-object restriction (absolute territorial protection), the Commission's Notice does not apply to price or territorial restrictions.[279] In *Expedia (2012)*, the CJEU confirmed this approach by declaring that the *de minimis* exception did not apply to a by-object restriction.[280] Put differently, the rule does not accept agreements that hinder market integration even when the undertakings' low market share suggests that it has marginal or no impact on competition. This implies that the EU *de minimis* rule is also aimed at safeguarding market integration.[281]

Finally, the *de minimis* rule also reflects the balance between competition and the protection of SMEs. In fact, until 1997 the Commission's Notices applied the exception only to SMEs. In addition to a low market share, the exception had set a limit on the turnover of the undertakings.[282] The Commission justified this with reference to the importance of SMEs in promoting non-economic benefits such as a source of jobs at times of crisis.[283] Yet, in 1997 the Commission deleted the limitation on turnover, noting that it was unjust to reserve the exception for SMEs.[284] Nevertheless, the protection of SMEs still guides many of the Member States' national *de minimis* rules.[285]

5.3.7 *Interim Conclusion*

This section has shown that from the early days of EU competition law to the present, the Commission and EU Courts have accounted for efficiencies and commercial interests already when defining the scope of Article 101(1) TFEU.

[278] Commission Horizontal Guidelines (2001), para 184–191.

[279] That is, horizontal agreements that fix prices, limit production or sales, share markets or sources of supply, and vertical agreements that fix resale prices or confer territorial protection. See Commission de minimis Notice (1997), para 11; Commission de minimis Notice (2001), para 11.

[280] C-226/11 Expedia (2012), para 35–37. This rule was later codified in Commission de minimis Notice (2014), para 2.

[281] For a similar view, see Lianos (2013, 14).

[282] See also policy report 1971, 16; policy report 1977, 10; policy report 1981, 14; Commission Guide for Small and Medium-Sized Enterprises (1983), 21; and Witt (2016b, 95).

[283] Policy report 1981, 14. See also Regulation 1287/2013 establishing a Programme for the Competitiveness of Enterprises and small and medium-sized enterprises, Preambles 6 and 15.

[284] Press release IP/97/42 'the Commission invites comments on the envisaged revision of the Notice on agreements of minor importance ("de minimis")' (22.1.1997). Yet, the notices still refer to SMEs, holding that the exception is based on the assumption that agreements between SMEs are rarely capable of significantly affecting competition within the common market. Consequently, as a general rule, they are not caught by the prohibition of Article 101(1) TFEU. See Commission de minimis Notice (1997), para 19; Commission de minimis Notice (2014), footnote 5.

[285] See Sections 6.3.1 and 6.3.2.

This has stood in contrast with various Commission's statements insisting that efficiency-related considerations should be limited to the scope of Article 101 (3) TFEU.

Like the balancing of state and public interests, the commercial exceptions were chiefly developed by the CJEU on a case-by-case basis. Consequently, there are numerous form-specific or restriction-specific balancing tools, which do not always have a consolidating, overriding rationale. In fact, scholars have suggested different classifications and justifications for those commercial exceptions.[286]

The scope and terms of those balancing tools remain vague. Until modernisation, the EU Courts hinted that a rule of reason might apply, despite the Commission's fierce opposition. This section has shown that even after the rule of reason was finally rejected, the objectively necessary, ancillary restraints, IPRs, and *de minimis* exceptions merited similar balancing. It is not surprising, therefore, that the Commission, GC, and CJEU have often reached conflicting decisions on the application of these exceptions.

The commercial interest exceptions are generally confined to the consideration of economic benefits, although at times they were also extended to protect non-economic benefits such as environmental or employment protection. At the same time, those exceptions do not entail an economic balancing process. Differing from Article 101(3) TFEU conditions as interpreted by the Commission following modernisation, Article 101(1) TFEU commercial exceptions are mostly based on a relatively abstract legal balancing process, leaving the competition enforcers ample discretion to balance. As such, they are difficult to square with the effects-based approach advocated by the Commission following modernisation.

Indeed, this section has shown that as part of the substantive modernisation, the EU Courts and Commission have sometimes attempted to narrow the scope of the exceptions to reflect a more economic balancing process. These efforts have drawn the assessment of Article 101(1) TFEU closer to the conditions for an Article 101(3) TFEU exception, creating further doubts on the scope of balancing under both provisions and the need for Article 101(1) TFEU balancing tools altogether.

The next section shows that the uncertainties surrounding both Article 101(1) TFEU's state and public interest exceptions and commercial exceptions have led to ambiguity and divergence in the practices of the national enforcers.

[286] Bailey and Whish (2015, 136–138), for instance, differentiate between agreements and provisions that are necessary to achieve an objective purpose. Faull and Nikpay (2014, 235–266) and Van Rompuy (2012, 234–240) identify two different categories: specific clauses that fall outside the scope of Article 101(1) TFEU due to the market context surrounding the agreement and agreements in which goods or services would not have been supplied unless a degree of exclusivity had been assured. See also Section 5.1.3.

5.4 NCAS AND NATIONAL COURTS

The previous sections have shown that the CJEU had developed Article 101(1) TFEU balancing tools on a case-by-case basis, without a clear underlying principle. The Commission often opposed these exceptions by advocating a limitation on the scope of balancing under Article 101(1) TFEU, especially after modernisation. The Commission and EU Courts have not always agreed on the relevant balancing tool applicable to a given case or how it should be applied. This has created much uncertainty as to the scope and conditions of Article 101(1) TFEU balancing tools.

The national enforcers have acknowledged these uncertainties. In the UK, for example, the CAT concluded that the assessment of whether a particular arrangement constitutes an infringement of Article 101(1) TFEU 'is a rather more flexible exercise than the CFI [in Métropole] was perhaps willing to appreciate'.[287] Similarly, the Dutch NCA noted with regard to the inherent restriction exception that it 'has been insufficiently explored yet in the jurisprudence in order to be able to make statements on its application'.[288]

The lack of a clear balancing regime has left the national enforcers considerable discretion to apply Article 101(1) TFEU balancing tools, which has resulted in varying interpretations. In general, as elaborated below, the German and UK NCAs took a similar approach to the Commission, limiting Article 101(1) TFEU balancing. The French, Dutch, and, to an extent, the Hungarian NCAs came closer to the CJEU's approach, leaving greater room to account for non-competition interests within Article 101(1) TFEU. The division into these groups of enforcers resembles the divergent approaches to Article 101(3) TFEU balancing, which was reported in Chapter 3.

5.4.1 *NCAs*

5.4.1.1 Overview

Like with Article 101(3) TFEU exceptions, NCAs have limited powers when applying Article 101(1) TFEU balancing tools. The CJEU has extended the *Tele2Polska (2011)* rule to NCAs' findings that Article 101(1) TFEU was not infringed. Accordingly, NCAs can only adopt non-binding 'no grounds for action' findings, declaring that on the basis of the information in their possession the conditions for establishing an Article 101 TFEU infringement are not met.[289] Some have suggested that these limited powers disincentivise NCAs from using Article 101(1) TFEU balancing tools more often.[290]

287 1035/1/1/04 and 1041/2/1/04 Racecourse Association (2005), para 167.

288 Vision Document Competition & Sustainability (2014), para 3.3.2.

289 C-68/11 Schenker (2013), para 42. On the NCAs' 'no grounds for action' findings, see Section 3.6.

290 Gerard (2013, 647) and Monti and Mulder (2017). See also Section 7.4.3.2.

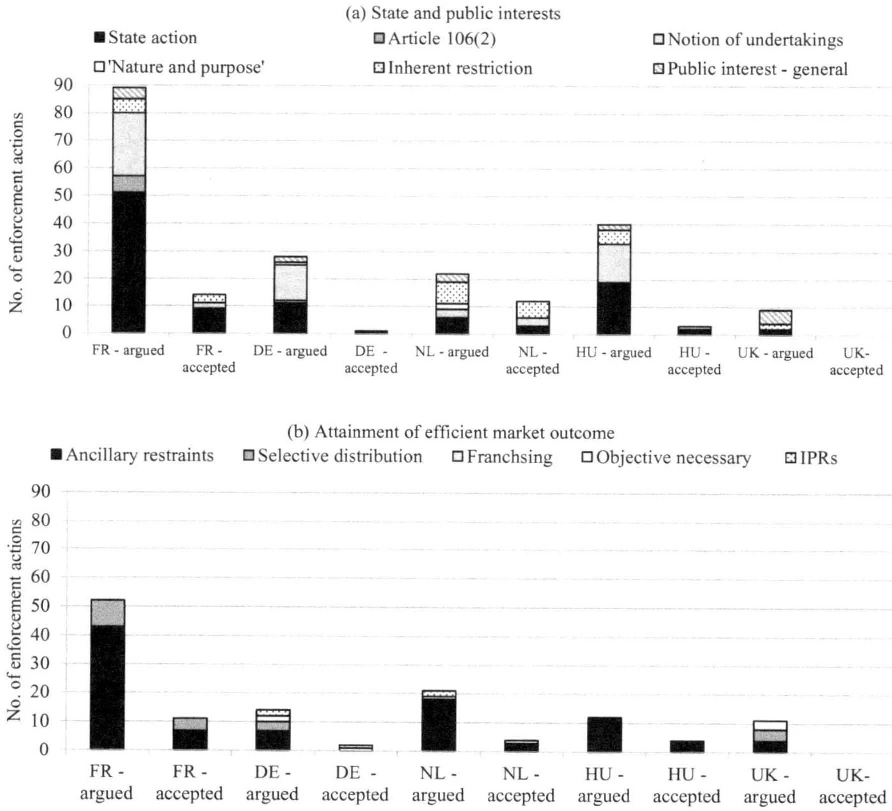

FIGURE 5.5 Article 101(1) TFEU, NCAs

Despite those limited powers, NCAs have made some use of Article 101(1) TFEU balancing tools. Although not binding, those cases are highly significant because they reveal, shape, and clarify the NCAs' approaches to Article 101(1) TFEU balancing. To this end, Figure 5.5 summarises the use of Article 101(1) TFEU balancing tools by the NCAs.

The figure reveals that state and public interest exceptions were invoked by NCAs more often than commercial exceptions. Ultimately, both categories of exceptions were accepted in a similar number of cases. Moreover, it indicates that not all NCAs have used Article 101(1) TFEU balancing tools equally. As in the Commission's practice after May 2004 (see Figures 5.3(a) and 5.4(a)), the German and UK NCAs have almost never accepted Article 101(1) TFEU exceptions. In particular, the German NCA was of the view that some interests related to state influence ought to be examined under Article 101(3) TFEU.[291] The French, Dutch, and, to a lesser

[291] See Section 3.6.2.3.

degree, the Hungarian NCAs have made use of those exceptions, especially those related to state and public interests.

The following sub-sections present various examples demonstrating that the uncertainties surrounding the conditions and scope of Article 101(1) TFEU exceptions have allowed the NCAs to adjust them to reflect their own balancing approaches. In particular, such differences have related to the relevant types of benefits and balancing method, as well as the intensity of control. These differences have seriously jeopardised the uniformity of balancing and given rise to legal certainty concerns.

5.4.1.2 Types of Benefits

Since the scope or rationale for Article 101(1) TFEU exceptions was not clearly identified, the national enforcers varied in the types of benefits they took into account when applying the exceptions. An illustrative example is the application of the ancillary restraints doctrine. Most NCAs examined in this study, like the Commission and EU Courts, have limited the exception to commercial-economic benefits.[292] Yet, the Dutch NCA also examined non-economic benefits such as social interests related to health care and public safety.[293]

National enforcers have also disagreed on whether the commercial interest embedded in the protection of a brand luxury image can justify restricting the commercial freedom of members of selective distribution systems. As mentioned, in *Pierre Fabre (2011)*, the CJEU seemed to alter its previous case law by determining that the protection of a brand luxury image could *not* justify the restriction of competition. Before the Court has taken a more nuanced approach in *Coty (2017)*, the Member States and national enforcers followed diverging interpretations.[294] In fact, such inconstancies were present even within certain Member States:

On the one hand, the German NCA in ASICS *(2015)*,[295] as well as the German and Luxembourg Governments,[296] claimed that qualitative selection criteria for a selective distribution system aimed at preserving the luxury image of goods could *not* be excluded from the scope of the prohibition laid down in Article 101(1) TFEU. This view also guided the GC in *Watch Repair (2017)*.[297] On the other hand, the French, Italian, Dutch, Austrian, and Swedish Governments, as well as the

[292] On the Commission's and EU Courts' strict application following modernisation, see Section 5.3.4.

[293] See Annex A, Section 5.21.

[294] See Section 5.3.4.

[295] B2–98/11 ASICS (2015), 2.

[296] As summarised by AG Wahl in his opinion in C-230/16 Coty (2017), para 61.

[297] See Section 5.3.4.

Commission and AG Wahl, disagreed.[298] Subscribing to this view, certain German courts maintained in a number of civil law decisions that the protection of luxury and prestige goods justified such qualitative selection criteria.[299]

Remarkably, the national enforcers even disagreed on what are luxury products that merited the exception. While the German High Court in *ASICS (2017)* held that sports and running shoes were *not* luxury goods, the District Court of Amsterdam has held two months before that those products did qualify as luxury goods.[300]

5.4.1.3 Balancing Method

In addition to differences in the types of relevant benefits, the NCAs used different balancing tools, methods, and tests to apply Article 101(1) TFEU exceptions. For instance, the NCAs did not adopt a uniform approach towards the existence of an EU rule of reason. The German[301] and UK[302] NCAs rejected a rule of reason under Article 101(1) TFEU, limiting this type of analysis to Article 101(3) TFEU. The French NCA followed a similar approach to the GC cases prior to modernisation, rejecting the rule of reason – at least for by-object restrictions.[303] Yet, the Hungarian NCA seemed to accept a certain form of a rule of reason, noting that a restriction necessary for increasing consumer welfare generally did not fall under Article 101(1) TFEU.[304]

The NCAs also have mixed views on whether the inherent restriction exception must be part of a state measure to justify the restrictive practices of professional associations.[305] While the UK NCA tied the exception to regulatory rules,[306] the French NCA maintained that it might also apply when the professional association was not vested with regulatory powers.[307]

[298] AG Wahl opinion in C-230/16 Coty (2017), para 62.

[299] For instance, the German Higher Regional Court of Frankfurt in 11 U 84/14 Deuter Sport (2015). See also Cicala, Haegeman, and Cuff (2018, 102–103).

[300] The German High Court decision in KVZ 41/17 Online sales of ASICS running shoes (2017), para 12–35. The District Court of Amsterdam decision in C/13/615474/HA ZA 16-959 Nike (2017), para 4.9.3.

[301] B9–121/13 Booking.com (2015), para 180; B4–9/11 B4–94/11 Electronic cash card payment system (2014), para 184.

[302] CP/0090/00/S MasterCard (2005), para 446; CE/9859-14 Modelling (2016), para 4.118.

[303] 06-D-03 Heating, ceramic sanitary and plumbing equipment (2006), para 989.

[304] Vj-18/2008 Uniform interchange fee levels (2009), para 183–186. In that case, the NCA considered that the agreement was not essential to the functioning of the card payment system.

[305] On the debate over the conditions of the inherent restriction exception, see Section 2.6.2.

[306] CP/0090/00/S MasterCard (2005), para 426–430; CE/9859-14 Modelling (2016), para 4.113. and footnote 480.

[307] 08-D-06 Specialist Physicians Overcharging Fees (2008), para 94–96; 10-A-10 Chartered accountants (2010), para 111–117; 15-A-02 Regulated professions (2015), para 6–9.

The differences in the scope and conditions for Article 101(1) TFEU exceptions became particularly obvious when the Member States codified the exceptions in their national laws. While some NCAs have followed the rules developed by the Commission and EU Courts, others have adopted conflicting approaches.

This can be illustrated by comparing the French and Hungarian rules introducing a national state action defence. The Hungarian Competition Act contains a state action defence, by providing that it applies 'unless otherwise provided by law'.[308] Despite this broad wording, which imposes no procedural or substantive conditions for disapplying the national competition act in cases of conflict with other laws, the Hungarian NCA and courts aligned its application with the conditions of the EU state action defence.[309]

In France, by comparison, the Commercial Code states that an agreement that is the result of the implementation of an act or regulation adopted in application thereof is not subject to the national cartel prohibition.[310] The French NCA explained that in addition to being a direct result of the act or regulation, the restriction must also be proportionate to the aim pursued by the national measure.[311] In *Publication of companies' legal information (2013)*, for example, the French NCA examined fixing the fees charged by clerks in commercial courts.[312] The NCA had accepted the national state action defense, noting that the fee was set in a decree as ordered by a provision in the Commercial Code. After establishing that setting the fee was the direct consequence of the national measure, the NCA added that fixing the fees was necessary to ensure equal access to the legal information and that this aim could not have been attained by setting a maximum fee. Hence, unlike the CJEU's mostly formalistic approach, the French NCA maintains that the exception is limited to cases in which the restriction of competition is *substantively* justified.

While the above national state action defences were limited to purely national cases, Section 7.5.4 suggests that they may also carry spillover effects in cases affecting trade between Member States.

Another example of the effects of a national codification of an Article 101(1) TFEU exception is the version of the 'nature and purpose' exception included in the Dutch Competition Act. The Act states that the national cartel prohibition does not apply to collective labour agreements, agreements within an industry or sector between one or more employers' organisations and one or more unions that pertain exclusively to pensions, or agreements or decisions by organisations of professionals

[308] Hungarian Competition Law, Article 1(1).

[309] See Annex A, Section 5.22.

[310] French Commercial Code, Article 420-4-I-1. See also Holmes and Davey (2007, 279); and OECD Regulated Conduct Defence Report (2011), 114. Notably, in 09-A-48 Dairy (2009), para 71–72, the NCA clarified that this exception would apply only to purely national cases.

[311] French NCA Annual Report 2012 (French version), 78.

[312] 13-D-23 Publication of companies' legal information (2013), para 143–160.

that pertain exclusively to participation in an occupational pension scheme subject to the approval of the Minister of Social Affairs and Employment.[313]

Although the wording of the national exception was construed broadly and may apply to agreements that do not satisfy the conditions of the EU 'nature and purpose' exception, the Dutch NCA and courts held that it was a codification of the CJEU's case law.[314] For this reason, the Dutch NCA declared that the national exception also applies to the interpretation of Article 101 TFEU in cases having an effect on trade between Member States.[315] In other words, the national codification may also affect the application of the exception in mixed cases.

For example, the Dutch NCA has *de facto* expanded the scope of the EU 'nature and purpose' exception in situations of price arrangements between self-employed workers. In response to the CJEU's judgement in *FNV (2014)*, it introduced a rule of thumb according to which self-employed workers that work 'side-by-side with one or more employees, and are indistinguishable from those employees in day-to-day operations' will not be deemed to be undertakings for the purpose of contracting price arrangements with their clients.[316] Accordingly, such self-employed workers are allowed to coordinate their rates and other conditions among each other and to collectively negotiate with their clients.

The Dutch NCA justified this interpretation due to the soaring number of self-employed workers in the Netherlands, which is likely to continue to raise upon the emergence of digital platforms. They were adopted following a letter of the Dutch cabinet to the Dutch House of Representatives, in which the cabinet had waived its plans to introduce a statutory minimum rate for self-employed workers, yet declared that self-employed workers should be protected against poverty and prevent clients 'at the lower end' of the labour market from choosing to work with self-employed workers solely because of the lower costs.[317]

The above examples demonstrate that the uncertainties surrounding the scope, conditions, and rationale of Article 101(1) TFEU exceptions have left room for national diverging interpretations on the application of those exceptions.

5.4.1.4 Intensity of Control

The NCAs also used different intensities of control when applying the conditions for exceptions. Given the lack of clear EU balancing principles, the NCAs were free to apply those conditions vigorously or flexibly. This could explain why, as Figure 5.5 illustrates, the French, Dutch, and, to a lesser extent, Hungarian NCAs were

[313] Dutch Competition Act, Article 16.

[314] 5170 VGT (2006), para 27; MEDED 06/4638 STRN VGT (2007), 5–6; Dutch NCA Guidelines on Competition Rules for Independent Contractors (2017), 5.

[315] Guidelines on Price Arrangements between Self-employed Workers (2019), footnote 11.

[316] *Ibid*, para 29. The FNV case and its implications were discussed in Section 5.2.5.2.

[317] Guidelines on Price Arrangements between Self-employed Workers (2019), para 1(3)–(8).

considerably more likely to accept Article 101(1) TFEU exceptions than the Commission and the other NCAs.

The different intensities of control can explain the diverging decisions on the prohibition of the use of third-party platforms in selective distribution systems. While the CJEU took a favourable approach to such restrictions in *Coty (2017)*, the French and German NCAs decided to close their joint investigation into *Adidas (2014, 2015)* only after the sporting goods manufacturer had agreed to abolish the ban on third-party platforms.[318] In *ASICS (2015, 2017)*, the German NCA and courts were highly critical of a similar ban, while not declaring it prohibited.[319] Even following *Coty*, the President of the German NCA hinted that it would continue to take a stricter approach towards such bans. He stated, 'we are still assessing the [Coty] judgment. Prima facie we see however only limited impact on our decision practice'.[320]

A lower intensity of control was also evident when the NCAs stated that an agreement did not fall within the scope of Article 101(1) TFEU without explicitly referring to a specific exception. This is illustrated by the French and Dutch application of the inherent restriction exception. While those NCAs often refused to *formally* accept this exception,[321] they *implicitly* held that Article 101(1) TFEU was not applicable for essentially the same reason. In *Transport to Saint Honorat (2005)*, for instance, the French NCA examined an agreement for transportation to Saint Honorat Island. The Cistercian Congregation of the Immaculate Conception owned most of the island, including its only landing stage. The NCA held that the grant of an exclusive right for use of the landing stage to a single undertaking did not infringe Article 101(1) TFEU. It explained that the agreement was necessary for protecting the site's peculiar geography, the private character of the island, and the need to control the flow of visitors.[322]

Similarly, in *Boar Castration (2008)*, the Dutch NCA issued a positive informal opinion on an agreement concluded under the auspices of the Dutch Minister for Agriculture and the Dutch Animal Protection Agency, which was portrayed as improving animal welfare by putting an end to the castration of boars until 2015. The agreement introduced an interim measure, which effectively required

[318] The German NCA decision in B3–137-12 Adidas (2014), 2, and the French NCA decision in Adidas (2015).

[319] B2–98/11 Online sales of ASICS running shoes (2015), 5; VI-Kart 13-15(V) Online sales of ASICS running shoes (2017), para 57–87; KVZ 41/17 Online sales of ASICS running shoes (2017), para 12–35.

[320] Andreas Mundt, as cited in Cicala, Haegeman, and Cuff (2018, 108).

[321] For example, the French NCA in 08-D-06 Specialist Physicians Overcharging Fees (2008), para 94–96. The Dutch NCA in 6888/435 LHV pace of establishment (2011), para 141–142; 6888/435 LHV pace of establishment (2014), para 282.

[322] 05-D-60 Transport to Saint Honorat (2005), para 62–68. In that case, the NCA used the Article 102 TFEU exception ('objectively necessary') as a basis for also granting an Article 101(1) exception. While not referring to the concept of inherent restriction directly, the NCA essentially followed the same legal test. It applied a similar analysis in 12-D-19 Tooth whitening (2012), para 102–126; 13-D-02 Towing light vehicles (2013), para 59–67.

supermarkets to sell fresh pork only from boars that had not been castrated without the use of anaesthesia. The NCA held that the agreement did not restrict competition despite its purchasing restrictions, *inter-alia*, in light of the animal welfare aim.[323]

5.4.2 *National Courts*

Figure 5.6 summarises the number of proceedings in which Article 101(1) TFEU exceptions were discussed by national courts in appeals on the NCAs' decisions (grey bars), and the number of proceedings in which a national court overturned the NCA decision or the previous instance's decision in this regard (black bars).

The figure indicates that national courts have examined the state and public interest exceptions (a) considerably more often than the commercial exceptions (b). The French and Hungarian Courts have challenged the interpretation given by the NCAs to the state action defence[324] and the commercial interest exceptions.[325] While the Hungarian successful appeals were based on procedural and evidential matters,[326] the French involved substantive balancing questions. The latter may allude to the uncertainty surrounding the application of the state and public interest exceptions.

In *Specialist Physicians Overcharging Fees (2008, 2009, 2010)*, the French NCA found that several medical associations engaged in concerted practices by encouraging physicians in private practices to increase their fees by resorting to 'one-time overcharging'.[327] This fee increase mechanism was codified in national legislation, indicating that it could apply only under exceptional circumstances. The undertakings invoked the state action defence, arguing that the fee increase was necessary after the failure to set new higher rates in negotiations between the medical

[323] 6455 Boars castration (2008). The NCA followed a similar analysis in 5194 Over-the-Counter Payment Services Covenant (2005), para 2.1.1; 12.0256.53 Veterinarian contracts (2013), as confirmed by the Court in ROT 15/1219 Veterinarian contracts (2016), para 9. See also Don (2010, 79) and Lavrijssen (2010, 650).

[324] In France, 2008/08385 Specialist Physicians Overcharging Fees (2009), 7, as confirmed by the Cour de Cassation in 09/13494 09/66021 Specialist Physicians Overcharging Fees (2010), 5–6; in Hungary, 11.K.34.958/2006/23 Waste management (2007), overturned by the Budapest Court of Appeal in ACB 2.Kf.27.027200814 Waste management (2008).

[325] In France, 2010/20555 Exchanges Check-Image Fee (2012), 56–64. In appeal, in 12-15971 Exchanges Check-Image Fee (2015), the Cour de Cassation returned the case to the Court of Appeal due to procedural faults; 2012/06826 Flour mill (2014), 54–66.

[326] 11.K.34.958/2006/23 Waste management (2007); ACB 2.Kf.27.027200814 Waste management (2008).

[327] The NCA in 08-D-06 Specialist Physicians Overcharging Fees (2008), para 94–96, as overturned by the Paris Court of Appeal in 2008/08385 Specialist Physicians Overcharging Fees (2009), 7, and confirmed by the Cour de Cassation in 09/13494 09/66021 Specialist Physicians Overcharging Fees (2010), 5–6.

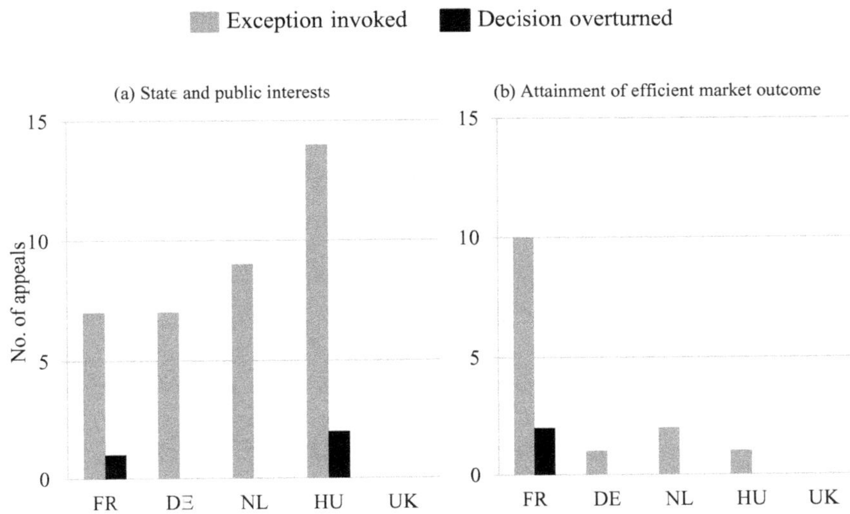

FIGURE 5.6 Article 101(1) TFEU, national courts

associations and the National Union of Health Funds. The NCA rejected the claim, noting that the increase of the fee was not the direct result of the law. Yet, the Paris Court of Appeal accepted the defence. It noted that the regulatory background meant there was no price competition among physicians as the prices are set by central negotiation between the medical associations and the National Union of Health Funds.

The two cases in which the Paris Court of Appeals overturned the NCA's decisions regarding the commercial interest exceptions did not clearly fall into a specific category of an exception. They were both based on similar grounds. In *Exchanges Check-Image Fee (2010, 2012, 2015)*, the NCA held that banks have colluded by agreeing to create new inter-bank fees as part of their discussions, supervised by the French Central Bank, to collectively determine the terms of a new digital system for processing and clearing interbank checks.[328] The banks argued that the uniform fee was intended to compensate the issuing banks for the loss of cash generated by the acceleration of the interbank payment of checks that the new system brought about. Yet, the Paris Court of Appeal disagreed. It held that the agreement setting up the new digital system was a public interest project, creating benefits for all actors concerned. Hence, according to the Court, the

[328] 10-D-28 Exchanges Check-Image Fee (2010); 2010/20555 Exchanges Check-Image Fee (2012), 56–64. In 12-15971 Exchanges Check-Image Fee (2015), the Cour de Cassation returned the case to the Court of Appeal due to procedural faults. After the Paris Court of Appeal issued a second judgement in 2017 that had confirmed the NCA's decision, in 2020 the Cour de Cassation annulled the judgement.

NCA could not have assumed that the agreement had restricted competition by object.

In *Flour mill (2012, 2014)*, based on a leniency application, the NCA held that flour producers have fixed prices and shared markers within a joint venture.[329] The Paris Court of Appeal had once again disagreed, concluding that at the time the joint ventures were created, the milling market was subject to price regulation and production restrictions. In addition, the rapid development of large retail outlet distribution, holding considerable bargaining power, incentivised flour producers to cooperate to safeguard their commercial interests. This objective, according to the Court, meant that the practice could not have been regarded as a restriction of competition by object.

In both cases, despite what would normally be classified as by-object restrictions (i.e. price fixing and market sharing), and similarly to the reasoning of the CJEU in *Cartes bancaires (2014)*, the French Court held that the NCA should not have classified the agreements as by-object restrictions given their positive impact on commercial interests.[330]

Finally, national courts have also influenced Article 101(1) TFEU balancing by critiquing the NCAs' choices of balancing tools. The German Court of Appeals' judgement in *Booking.com (2019)*, which was discussed in Section 3.6.3.1, is a prominent example of how national courts' choices of balancing tools can influence the balancing outcome. As mentioned, while the German NCA and Düsseldorf Higher Regional Court analysed narrow MFN clauses under Article 101(3) TFEU, the Court of Appeals held that such clauses are not prohibited under Article 101(1) TFEU since they are a form of ancillary restraints.[331]

5.5 CLOSING REMARKS: TRANSITIONS IN ARTICLE 101(1) TFEU BALANCING

Article 101(1) TFEU balancing tools were developed by the CJEU on a largely case-by-case basis. While the wording of Article 101(1) TFEU does not explicitly refer to a balancing function, the Court was of the opinion that agreements restricting the commercial freedom of parties can escape the prohibition of Article 101(1) TFEU if they are necessary for the attainment of social or efficiency-related goals. This chapter has distinguished between two categories of Article 101(1) TFEU balancing tools, which differ in the types of benefits they may take into account and the balancing process.

The first category is the state and public interest balancing tools. The CJEU has developed those tools as a response to the expansion of Article 101(1) TFEU's reach

[329] 12-D-09 Flour mill (2012); 2012/06826 Flour mill (2014), 54–66.

[330] See Section 5.3.4. See also Berthol-Balladur and Anselin (2014, 1–2).

[331] Kart 2/16 (V) booking.com (2019), para II(2). This decision was rendered after the cut-off date of the empirical database (see Section 1.3.2), and therefore it is not reflected in Figure 5.6.

to include agreements subject to state influence and in markets that were previously subject to such influence. They leave EU competition law room to accommodate broad non-economic benefits related to national welfare provisions, thereby avoiding destabilising conflicts with Member States.

Prior to modernisation, those balancing tools were mostly form-based. Reflecting public interest theories of regulation, they focused on examining whether an agreement could be attributed to a genuine state measure rather than protecting a cartel in disguise (state action; Article 106(2) TFEU; notion of undertakings).[332] As the state was perceived as the benevolent maximisers of social welfare and the public interest, the CJEU did not require to evaluate whether the restriction of competition was actually justified for and proportionate to achieving the non-competition interests.

During the late 1990s and early 2000s, the CJEU introduced new balancing tools (the 'nature and purpose'; inherent restriction exceptions) and interpreted the old tools in a way that gave more weight to weighing competition and non-competition interests.[333] While this facilitated the weighing up of competition and non-competition interests, the state and public interest exceptions still involve at most a legal balancing process. The competition enforcers must examine whether an anti-competitive agreement has gone beyond what is required to attain a legitimate non-competition interest and whether the claimed benefits exceed the harm to competition interests. Unlike Article 101(3) TFEU individual exceptions and BERs, the state and public interest exceptions went mostly untouched by the more economic approach and are not tied to a notion of economic efficiency.

The second category of Article 101(1) TFEU balancing tools is the commercial interest exceptions. Those exceptions are generally confined to the consideration of economic benefits, although at times they were also extended to non-economic benefits such as environmental or employment protection. Similarly to the state and public interest balancing tools, those exceptions too do not merit an economic balancing process and are based on an abstract legal balancing process.

The scope and terms of the commercial interest exceptions are vague. Until modernisation, the EU Courts hinted that a rule of reason might apply, despite the Commission's fierce opposition arguing that efficiency-related considerations would be limited to the scope of Article 101(3) TFEU. Even after an EU rule of reason was finally rejected, the objectively necessary, ancillary restraints, IPRs, and *de minimis* exceptions merited similar balancing.

Upon modernisation, the EU Courts and Commission have formalised and narrowed down many of those exceptions to reflect a more economic premise.[334] This has drawn the assessment of those exceptions closer in line with the effects-

[332] See Sections 5.2.2, 5.2.3, and 5.2.4.
[333] See Sections 5.2.5, 5.2.6, and 5.2.2.5.
[334] See Sections 5.3.3, 5.3.4, and 5.3.6.

based approach and the Commission's interpretations of Article 101(3) TFEU conditions. At the same time, this development had questioned the aim and necessity of those exceptions in Regulation 1/2003's enforcement regime. While some differences between the Article 101(1) and (3) TFEU balancing tools persist in terms of their conditions and burden of proof,[335] a coherent and simple administration of EU competition law might order integrating the commercial interest exceptions within Article 101(3) TFEU analysis.

Indeed, the commercial interest exceptions have appeared to have lost their weight in parallel to their modernisation. Like Article 101(3) TFEU individual exemptions, they have received limited attention from the EU Courts and the Commission since May 2004 and have almost never been used to justify limiting the scope of the Article 101(1) TFEU prohibition. Chapter 7 argues that this is yet another example of the shift from the implicit-procedural to explicit-substantive balancing tools following modernisation.

This chapter showed that because both categories of Article 101(1) TFEU balancing tools were developed by the CJEU on an *ad-hoc* basis, they have resulted in numerous sector-specific or restriction-specific exceptions. Lacking an underlying conceptual basis, those balancing tools are often inconsistent, overlapping, or contradicting each other. Because balancing is not guided by clear and predictable criteria, the outcome of applying them to a specific case is highly uncertain and leaves ample discretion to each competition enforcer.

The empirical findings have pointed to a similar divergence as the national approaches to Article 101(3) TFEU balancing. On the one hand, following modernisation the Commission and the German and UK NCAs have made only little use of Article 101(1) TFEU balancing tools and interpreted them narrowly. On the other hand, the French, Dutch, and, to an extent, the Hungarian NCAs followed the CJEU's approach, used the balancing tools more frequently, and interpreted them as leaving more room for the consideration of non-competition interests.

The diverging interpretation and use of Article 101(1) TFEU balancing tools were apparent at the EU level (between the Commission, GC, and CJEU),[336] national level between the various Member States,[337] and even within one Member State.[338] At times, Article 101(1) TFEU exceptions seemed to serve as a substitute to Article 101 (3) TFEU individual exemptions. In others, similar restrictions of competition were evaluated according to different types of Article 101(1) TFEU exceptions and tests.

[335] See Section 5.1.1.

[336] For divergence in the state action doctrine, see Sections 5.2.2.2, 5.2.2.4, and 5.2.2.5; notion of undertakings, Section 5.2.4.2; inherent restrictions, Section 5.2.6.2; existence of a rule of reason, Section 5.3.2; and selective distribution systems, Section 5.3.4.

[337] See Section 5.4.1.

[338] For example, the German approach to selective distribution systems, as described in Section 5.4.1.

6

National Balancing Tools

6.1 INTRODUCTION

The previous chapters discussed balancing tools that had their origins in EU primary or secondary law or were developed in the decisional practice of the Commission and EU Courts. They illustrated that national enforcers carried an important role in shaping the role of non-competition interests under those EU explicit-substantive balancing tools. In particular, the NCAs and national courts have adopted divergent interpretations as to the relevant types of benefits, the balancing method, and the intensity of control.

This chapter moves to examine another source of national influence. It explores balancing tools that were adopted by the legislative, executive, or judicial branches of a Member State, limiting the full effect of Article 101 TFEU in favour of promoting non-competition interests. As elaborated below, those unique national tools offer an alternative route to the EU balancing rules set forth in Article 101(1) and (3) TFEU. Many of the national tools are characterised by an *exclusion* balancing process. They do not involve the weighing of competition and non-competition interests by reference to a consumer welfare standard or a legal proportionality test. Instead, they exclude the full application of Article 101 TFEU in favour of protecting other national interests.[1]

The unique national balancing tools not only shaped balancing in purely national cases but were also applicable to agreements that were found to have an effect on trade between Member States.[2] Although this chapter is limited in length, it is essential to highlight the doubts about the compatibility of those national tools with EU competition law, a topic that has been largely overlooked in legal scholarship.

[1] On the different types of balancing processes, see Section 1.2.2.1.

[2] On the difference between purely national, EU, and mixed cases, see Section 1.3.2.1.

National balancing tools bear a significant impact on the consideration of non-competition interests in the decentralised enforcement era. Since the entry into force of Regulation 1/2003, about 90% of Article 101 TFEU enforcement actions have taken place before NCAs.[3] The Commission emphasised in its Modernisation White Paper that 'decentralisation *must not be allowed* to result in inconsistent application of Community competition law. Competition policy will thus *continue to be determined at Community level*'.[4]

To this end, Articles 3(1) and (2) of Regulation 1/2003 express the principles of parallel application and the primacy of and convergence with EU competition law in cases that have an effect on trade between Member States. They stipulate that where national enforcers apply national competition law to agreements that may affect trade between Member States, they should also apply Article 101 TFEU. The application of national competition law may not prejudice the full and uniform application of EU competition law.[5] Articles 3(1) and (2), therefore, are intended to ensure that agreements that are prohibited by EU law will not escape the prohibition of Article 101 TFEU by means of applying national competition rules.

Nevertheless, Article 3(3) of Regulation 1/2003 limits these principles in the event a national law 'predominantly pursues' a different objective from the one of Article 101 and 102 TFEU. Preamble 9 of Regulation 1/2003 clarifies that Member States are not precluded from implementing national rules that protect other legitimate interests than the protection of competition on the market, provided that such rules are compatible with general principles and other provisions of EU law. In particular, they may apply national legislation against unfair trading practices 'irrespective of the actual or presumed effects of such acts on competition on the market'.

Despite the example listed in Preamble 9, Article 3(3) is not limited to unfair trading practices. The broad wording of Article 3(3) entrusts the Member States with wide discretion to favour non-competition national interests over competition. It does not state whether the national rules can be substantive or procedural in nature, or whether or not they can be included within the national competition law as an exception to the rules. Moreover, the Article prescribes neither a limit nor a method to balance competition and non-competition interests. Any type of national interest that 'predominantly pursues' non-competition interests may override Article 101 TFEU irrespective of its actual or presumed harm to competition interests.[6]

This chapter illustrates that in light of the above, the compatibility of some of those national balancing tools with EU competition law is debatable and raises uniformity and legal certainty challenges when an agreement has an effect on trade between

[3] See Section 2.5.4.1.

[4] Emphasis added. Modernisation White Paper (1999), para 83.

[5] Regulation 1/2003, Article 3 and Preamble 8; Commission Staff Working Paper accompanying the Report on Functioning of Regulation 1/2003 (2009), para 139–142. See also Section 2.3.3.2.

[6] See also GCLC Annual Conference (2010, 149–154) and Guidance on Concurrent Application (2014), para 4.2–4.12.

Member States. On the one hand, Article 3(3) may be understood as providing Member States a safe harbour to adopt national balancing tools to pursue non-competition interests. It seems to endorse national rules that protect SMEs or even those that confer special regimes for specific sectors, such as media or agriculture. On the other hand, as detailed in Section 5.2.2, the CJEU has consistently held that the duty of sincere cooperation in its meaning under Article 4(3) TEU prohibits Member States from adopting national legislation that conflicts with EU competition law.

The above questions the Commission's statement that 'Article 3 can be characterised as one of the major successes of Regulation 1/2003'.[7] This statement seemed to refer to the first two paragraphs of the Article while ignoring the difficulties emanating from Article 3(3).[8]

Moreover, national balancing tools may also raise concerns when they are applied or restricted to purely national cases. First, as demonstrated by Section 7.5.4, the effect on trade criterion is an indefinite standard that is open to interpretation. It leaves the NCAs leeway to apply national balancing tools by classifying borderline cases as purely national. Second, this chapter shows that while some of the tools do not formally apply to agreements having an effect on trade between Member States, in practice the competition enforcers have used their enforcement discretion to decide not to open an investigation or bring a proceeding to an end when an agreement that affected trade between Member States could have benefited from a national exception.

This chapter is structured as follows. Section 6.2 provides a legal and empirical background on national balancing tools. It classifies them into four categories, according to the type of norm guiding each balancing tool and type of protected benefits. Section 6.3 explores the types of benefits, balancing method, and intensity of control of each category of national balancing tools. Finally, Section 6.4 discusses the implications of using the national balancing tools as an alternative to the EU explicit-substantive balancing tools in the era of decentralised enforcement.

6.2 LEGAL AND EMPIRICAL BACKGROUND

The national balancing tools presented in this chapter were identified using a bottom-up approach. In other words, they were traced in the process of applying the systematic content analysis to Article 101 TFEU national enforcement actions.[9] The empirical findings highlight the diversity of national balancing tools. To illustrate their different features, the national tools are classified according to two parameters: the level of discretion left to the competition enforcer applying the tool and the relevant types of benefits.[10]

7 Commission Staff Working Paper accompanying the Report on Functioning of Regulation 1/2003 (2009), para 142.

8 For a similar view, see GCLC Annual Conference (2010, 150–151).

9 See Section 1.3.

10 Those parameters were defined in Section 1.2.2.

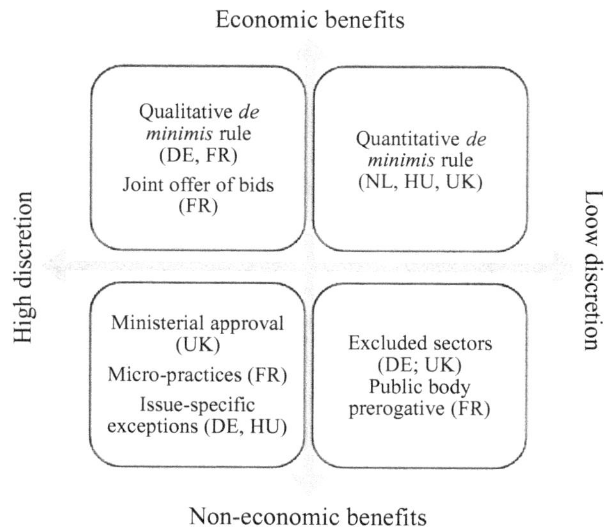

FIGURE 6.1. Classification of national balancing tools

The first parameter is the *level of discretion* left to the competition enforcer when applying each balancing tool. As mentioned, balancing tools that are characterised by a *low level of discretion* apply equally and consistently to all agreements. Once it has been determined that a certain agreement falls within a relevant category, a predetermined categorical rule applies. A balancing tool that is characterised by a *high level of discretion* depends on the specific circumstances of each case and leaves the competition enforcer broader possible courses of action.

The second parameter is the relevant *types of benefits*. A balancing tool that takes only *economic benefits* into account balances cost and qualitative efficiencies against the harm caused to competition. A tool that incorporates broader social and regulatory policies also takes *non-economic benefits* into account. The classification of the national tools detailed in this chapter is exemplified by Figure 6.1.

As the following sections show, each category of national balancing tools entails a different type of balancing, with different effects on the effectiveness, uniformity, and legal certainty of balancing.

6.3 BALANCING TOOLS

6.3.1 *Low Discretion, Economic Benefits*

The first category of national balancing tools is characterised by a low level of discretion, meaning that the tools apply equally and consistently to all agreements and are vindicated by the consideration of economic benefits. Several national *de minimis* rules provide an example of such tools.

Section 5.3.6 examined the EU *de minimis* rule developed by the EU Courts and the Commission. It highlighted that the rule exempts restrictions that do not carry an appreciable effect on competition in quantitative terms (i.e. due to the undertakings' low market share), and as such does not involve the consideration of non-competition interests. Yet, it also showed that the Commission and EU Courts applied the *de minimis* exception to situations in which the nature of the restriction itself was not deemed to be appreciable, adhering to a similar analysis as the ancillary restraints exception. Moreover, up until the third enforcement period (i.e. end of the 1990s), the EU *de minimis* rule had also afforded special protection to SMEs.

In parallel, cases taking place before NCAs and national courts are subject to national *de minimis* rules. This means that national procedural law determines the NCA's jurisdiction to apply Article 101 TFEU and the national equivalent provision. Consequently, an NCA might not have jurisdiction to examine agreements that are caught by the EU *de minimis* rule or *vice versa*.[11]

Table 6.1 summarises the various national *de minimis* rules, illustrating that they differ both from the EU rule and from each other. The table demonstrates that most of the national rules are based on quantitative criteria similar to the EU rule following modernisation (left column) and as such do not involve balancing. Yet, the table also shows that as opposed to the current Commission's rule, the national *de minimis* rules of France, Germany, Hungary, and the Netherlands still afford special protection to SMEs (right column). Some of those national rules are an example of low discretion balancing tools that are restricted to economic benefits and will be elaborated in this section. Others take into account non-economic benefits or merit a higher level of discretion and will be elaborated in the following sections.

Table 6.1 also indicates that the national rules have deviated from the Commission's and EU Courts' position that the *de minimis* rule does not apply to all by-object restrictions (middle column). In all five Member States, the national *de minimis* rule does not apply to a closed list of practices, rather than to all forms of by-object restrictions.[12]

The *de minimis* rules in the Netherland, Hungary, and the UK are characterised by a low level of discretion and are vindicated with reference to economic benefits. In the Netherlands, for example, the national *de minimis* rule (also known as the *bagatelle* exception) applies to agreements between no more than eight undertakings having low turnover or market share.[13] The rule is also applicable to by-object restrictions. For

[11] C-226/11 Expedia (2012), para 28–32.

[12] French Commercial Code, Article L464-6-2; German de minimis Notice (2007), para 14–15; Hungarian Competition Act, Article 13; UK OFT Understanding Competition Law Guidelines (2004), para 2.15–2.21.

[13] That is if the undertakings are not potential or actual competitors, the turnover of the undertakings is not more than EUR 5.5 million when the core activity is the supply of goods, or EUR 1.1 million in all other cases. If the undertakings are potential or actual competitors, their combined market share shall not exceed 5%, and their combined turnover is not higher than EUR 40 million.

TABLE 6.1. *National de minimis rules*

	Criteria	Applicable to by-object restriction?	Special protection of SMEs?
FR[a]	Quantitative: 10% horizontal, 15% vertical Qualitative: improves the management of SMEs[b]	A list of precluded practices	Excluding 'micro-practices'[c]
GR[d]	Qualitative: rationalises economic activities of SMEs Quantitative presumption: 10% horizontal, 15% vertical	A list of precluded practices	The qualitative rule is limited to SMEs[e]
HU[f]	Quantitative: 10% horizontal, 15% vertical (until 2018, 10% for both)	A list of precluded practices (applies to vertical hard-core restrictions)[g]	No, yet a possibility to issue a warning instead of a fine[h]
NL[i]	Quantitative: conduct of no more than eight undertakings having low turnover or market share	Yes, only if the market share is lower than 5% when the agreement affects trade between Member States, and 10% otherwise	A special rule for undertakings with low turnover
UK[j]	Quantitative: 10% horizontal, 15% vertical	A list of precluded practices	No, yet an immunity from fines for 'small agreements'[k]

[a] French Commercial Code, Articles L 464-6-1 and L 464-6-2. See also Vogel (2012, 171).
[b] The French qualitative rule is an example of a high discretion balancing tool that is restricted to economic benefits. Hence, it is discussed in Section 6.3.2.
[c] 'Micro practices' in France are an example of a high discretion balancing tool that takes non-economic benefits into account. Thus, it is discussed in Section 6.3.4.
[d] German Competition Act, Section 3 and German de minimis Notice (2007).
[e] The German qualitative rule is an example of a high discretion balancing tool that is restricted to economic benefits. Hence, it is discussed in Section 6.3.2.
[f] Hungarian Competition Act, Article 13.
[g] *Ibid*. See also Nagy (2017, 60).
[h] As elaborated below, Article 78(8) of the Hungarian Competition Act allows a warning to be issued instead of a fine for first time infringements by SMEs.
[i] Dutch Competition Act, Article 7.
[j] A *de minimis* rule is not expressly mentioned in the UK Competition Act. It applies pursuant to Section 60, which brings the EU case law on this issue into play. The UK *de minimis* doctrine is also explained in OFT Understanding Competition Law Guidelines (2004), para 2.15–2.21.
[k] UK Competition Act, Sections 39–40.

example, the Dutch NCA invoked the rule to allow self-employed workers holding a low market share to collectively fix their rates and commercial terms.[14]

In 2010, the Dutch parliament revised the national *de minimis* rule by raising the market share threshold from 5% to 10%, aiming to provide SMEs more leeway to join forces against buyer power.[15] The Commission, however, objected to this change, noting that it could remove hard-core restrictions from the ambit of Article 101 TFEU.[16] Following this objection, the revision was amended to limit the higher threshold to purely national cases.[17]

Hungary also offers special protection for SMEs. Unlike the EU rule, vertical hard-core restrictions can benefit from the Hungarian *de minimis* rule. In *Plant protection products (2005)*, the Hungarian NCA found that an RPM agreement between undertakings having a low market share had benefited from the national rule. The NCA noted that although the Commission considers RPM to be a hard-core restriction (and therefore cannot benefit from the Commission's *de minimis* rule), this did not preclude the application of the national *de minimis* rule.[18]

Moreover, a 2015 amendment to the Hungarian Competition Act entrusted the NCA with replacing the fines imposed on SMEs for first-time infringements of the national cartel prohibition with a warning.[19] The amendment aimed to bring Hungarian competition law in line with the national Act on Small and Medium-Sized Enterprises and Aid for Their Development (2004), which stipulates that '[w]hen bodies carrying out official inspections of small and medium-sized enterprises [. . .] are required to impose a penalty in respect of the first offence committed, instead of imposing a fine, they shall issue a warning to the enterprises concerned'.[20] Interestingly, the amendment was advocated by the Hungarian NCA itself, after finding that SMEs accounted for more than 70% of the undertakings subject to its enforcement proceedings.[21]

A similar immunity from fines in purely national cases is also provided by the UK Competition Act. Parties to 'small agreements', i.e. non-price-fixing agreements between undertakings with a low turnover or market share, will not face penalties for infringements of UK competition law. This immunity can be withdrawn by the UK NCA in certain circumstances.[22]

[14] Guidelines on Price Arrangements between Self-employed Workers (2019), para 48–52.

[15] Second Chamber, 2007–2008 session, 31 531.

[16] Second Chamber, 2010–2011 session, 32 664.

[17] De Brauw (2011) and Pree and Molin (2013, 203).

[18] Vj-141/2004 Plant protection products (2005), para 43–45.

[19] Hungarian Competition Act, Article 78(8).

[20] Act No. XXXIV on Small and Medium-sized Enterprises and Aid for their Development (2004), Article 12/A.

[21] Sárai (2016, 27).

[22] UK Competition Act, Sections 39–40; The Competition Act 1998 (Small Agreements and Conduct of Minor Significance) Regulations 2000. Immunity was granted (and later withdrawn) in CE/9578-12 Mobility scooters (2014), 4.5–4.6. See also UK Fining Guidelines (2018), para 11.3; Bailey (2014, 237–238); and UK NCA's annual report (2018), 39.

Affording special protection to SMEs, which is sometimes applicable also to by-object restrictions, reflects a unique balance between competition and non-competition interests, departing from the Commission's rule. The compatibility of those national *de minimis* rules with EU competition law and Article 3 of Regulation 1/2003 was reviewed by the CJEU in *Expedia (2012)*. The Court held that when an NCA determines whether or not a restriction of competition is appreciable, it may take into account the quantitative thresholds established in the Commission's *de minimis* notice, but it is not required to do so. Such thresholds, according to the Court, 'are no more than factors among others that may enable that authority to determine whether or not a restriction is appreciable by reference to the actual circumstances of the agreement'.[23]

Notably, the Court has left considerably more room for diverging national *de minimis* rules in comparison to what was suggested by AG *Kokott*. Kokott was of the opinion that although the Commission's *de minimis* notice is a soft law instrument lacking a binding effect, it is of decisive importance for the functioning of the decentralised system. Ensuring the effectiveness and uniformity of Article 101 TFEU, in her opinion, requires obliging national enforces to take 'due account' of the notice and to 'give reasons which can be judicially reviewed for any divergences'.[24] Adopting this approach would have limited the possibility of developing unique balancing approaches within the *de minimis* rules.

To conclude, national de *minimis* rules sometimes provided broader protection to SMEs in comparison with the EU rule and were applied to both mixed and purely national cases. As a result, certain infringements of Article 101 TFEU that could have been reviewed by the Commission could not be scrutinised by NCAs. At the same time, as balancing rules entailing a low level of discretion and vindicated by economic benefits, national *de minimis* rules that are based on quantitative criteria do not raise serious concerns as to the effectiveness, uniformity, and legal certainty of balancing. Despite a certain divergence in their application, they only apply to agreements with limited to no impact on competition. Moreover, each national rule applies in a uniform manner to all agreements on the basis of consistent and unequivocal criteria.

6.3.2 *High Discretion, Economic Benefits*

The second category of national balancing tools is characterised by a high level of discretion and is restricted to economic benefits. Those tools order national enforcers to weigh competition and economic benefits on a case-by-case basis.

For instance, the Paris Court of Appeal introduced a special rule for assessing the joint offering of bids in tenders. The Court submitted that a joint bid did not infringe Article 101(1) TFEU if it could be justified due to technical requirements

[23] C-226/11 Expedia (2012), para 31.
[24] AG Kokott opinion in C-226/11 Expedia (2012), para 39–40.

or cost savings due to economies of scale.[25] This rule guided the examination of a long line of cases before the French NCA,[26] including mixed cases that affected trade between Member States.[27] By contrast, the Commission and other jurisdictions normally assess such efficiencies within the scope of Article 101(3) TFEU.

Another example of a high discretion balancing tool that is restricted to economic benefits is the *de minimis* rule in Germany. While most *de minimis* rules are based on objective quantitative criteria (see Table 6.1), the German rule applicable to SMEs necessitates a case-by-case assessment. It is founded on qualitative criteria, examining whether the agreement rationalises economic activities and serves to improve the competitiveness of SMEs.[28] This rule seeks to allow SMEs to cooperate with competing SMEs and larger companies, helping them to achieve economies of scale and scope and thus offsetting structural disadvantages they suffer compared to larger undertakings.[29]

The EU Courts and Commission, in contrast, normally engage in this type of balancing by using Article 101(1) or (3) TFEU balancing tools. Contrary to Article 101 (3) TFEU (at least according to the Commission's interpretation following modernisation), the German rule does not focus on consumer welfare. Rather, it is dependent on whether the cooperation could lead to the rationalisation of the SMEs' activities. Moreover, unlike the EU *de minimis* rule, it also applies to certain hardcore restrictions that are part of the cooperation agreement.

The French Commercial Code includes a similar provision. In addition to the national equivalent provision to Article 101(3) TFEU, it provides that certain agreements, in particular those that are 'intended to improve the management of small or medium-sized undertakings', may be excluded from the scope of the national prohibition by a decree adopted following a favourable opinion from the NCA.[30] In practice, however, this provision has been used to exclude only very few agreements.[31]

[25] 2000/11303 Somme (2000); BOCCRF 2004–06 FNTV (2004).

[26] See Annex A, Section 6.1.

[27] This exception was accepted in mixed cases, such as 09-D-18 Marseille transportation (2009), para 94–102, and rejected in 09-D-25 Work on railway tracks (2009), para 149–176.

[28] Section 3(1) of the German Competition Act provides: '[a]greements between competing undertakings and decisions by associations of undertakings, whose subject matter is the rationalisation of economic activities through cooperation among enterprises, fulfill the conditions of §2 (1) if: 1. competition on the market is not significantly affected thereby, and 2. the agreement or the decision serves to improve the competitiveness of small or medium-sized enterprises'. See also Klees (2006, 403), Dreher and Korner (2014, 131–133), and Franck (2017). This provision was applied in B1–25/04 Verta/Danzer (2004); B3–06/05 OTC medicines – Land pharmacist associations (2007); B2–90/01-4 Timber (2008); B2–90/01-2 Timber (2009); B2–90/01-3 Timber (2009); B2–90/01-1 Timber (2009); and Yomo (2016).

[29] Bundeskartellamt Information Leaflet of Cooperation of SMEs (2007), para 11.

[30] French Commercial Code, Article 420-4-II.

[31] For a discussion and a list of excluded agreements, see Boudou et al. (2014, 109).

High discretion balancing tools that are restricted to economic benefits raise uniformity and legal certainty challenges and may stand in conflict with the EU balancing tools. As the above examples illustrate, at times they may act as an alternative balancing route to an Article 101(3) TFEU analysis, which is not bound to the four conditions of the Article. Because they entrust NCAs with a wide margin of discretion, those national balancing tools are less predictable and coherent in comparison to the first category of national balancing tools.

6.3.3 *Low Discretion, Economic and Non-Economic Benefits*

The third category of national balancing tools resembles the EU sectoral BERs as they are based on social and political considerations and apply to an entire sector or to all types of practices.[32] Yet, differing from the sectoral BERs, those national tools leave competition enforcers limited discretion when applying the balancing to a specific case.

An illustrative example of such tools is found in the UK Competition Act, which excludes the transfer of newspapers or newspaper assets from the national cartel prohibition. The UK Competition Act also excludes agreements that are subject to scrutiny by other acts, such as those related to financial services, company law, broadcasting, and the environment.[33] Similarly, the German Competition Act excludes from its national cartel prohibition agreements related to agriculture, energy, newspapers, and magazines.[34]

A balancing rule that is characterised by low discretion and takes non-economic benefits into account can also stem from a jurisdictional requirement. One example is the French jurisdictional rule applicable to agreements involving the use of public body prerogative. The French legal order is organised around two separate bodies of law: civil (private) law and administrative (public) law. Each body of laws is subject to the jurisdiction of a separate branch of courts. Accordingly, the assessment of the legality of an administrative decision, including those that concern the conclusion of public contracts, can only be carried out by the administrative courts.[35]

This rule affects the enforcement of both EU and national competition laws. According to the division of competences under French law, only the administrative courts can examine the legality of agreements involving the expression of state powers. The French NCA and the civil courts have no jurisdiction in those cases. For this purpose, the French NCA and the courts distinguish between (i) conduct that involves the use of public body prerogatives, which can only be assessed under

[32] On the sectoral BERs, see Section 4.3.1.2.

[33] UK Competition Act, Section 3(1) and Schedules 1–3.

[34] German Competition Act, Sections 28–30.

[35] Petit and Rabeux (2009, 106–109).

the administrative jurisdiction; and (ii) the conduct of public bodies acting in the economic sphere, independent of any public body prerogative, which can be examined by the NCA and the civil courts.[36]

Cases taking place before the French NCA or the administrative courts are subject to different procedural and substantive rules.[37] As such, agreements involving the use of the French State's prerogative enjoy a favourable standard of review. In practice, the NCA has mostly rejected claims of lack of jurisdiction, at least in part, while in a small number of cases it has found that it was not competent to examine the matter.[38] The Courts have confirmed all challenges to this ground.

Low discretion balancing tools that take non-economic benefits into account may hinder the full effect of Article 101 TFEU in favour of broad types of non-competition interests. At the same time, they are transparent, relatively predictable, and merit only limited discretion when applied to a specific agreement. As such, they provide a relatively high degree of legal certainty and are generally applied quite consistently to agreements in the relevant Member State.

6.3.4 *High Discretion, Economic and Non-Economic Benefits*

The final category of national balancing tools relates to situations in which the national legislative or executive uses its powers to exclude the application of Article 101 TFEU from a specific agreement. Unlike the low discretion balancing rules that take non-economic benefits into account, in which an entire sector or type of practice is excluded, this section examines *issue-specific* balancing tools benefiting certain agreements for essentially political reasons.

There are various examples of such issue-specific balancing tools. The UK Competition Act, for example, provides for a ministerial public policy defence, allowing the Secretary of State to declare the Article 101 TFEU and the national cartel prohibition are inapplicable for 'exceptional and compelling reasons of public policy'. [39] This exception resembles the German ministerial exemption that was deleted shortly after the entry into force of Regulation 1/2003.[40]

[36] 03174 Aéroport de Paris (1999). See also 09-D-18 Marseille transportation (2009), para 21–29; 10-D-13 Le Havre Port (2010), para 148–150; and Perroud (2013, 33–38).

[37] Petit and Rabeux (2009, 106–109) and Perroud (2013, 33–38).

[38] See Annex A, Section 6.2.

[39] Article 7(1) of Schedule 3 of the UK Competition Act provides: '[i]f the Secretary of State is satisfied that there are exceptional and compelling reasons of public policy why the Chapter I prohibition ought not to apply to (a) a particular agreement, or (b) any agreement of a particular description, he may by order exclude the agreement, or agreements of that description, from the Chapter I prohibition'. See also Bailey and Whish (2015, 376).

[40] See Section 2.6.2.2.

In practice, the UK Secretary of State has made careful use of this power. Only a few orders have been issued,[41] three in relation to the defence industry[42] (one of which was repealed[43]), one with respect to arrangements for the supply of oil and petroleum products in the event of significant disruption to the normal supply,[44] and five with respect to the coronavirus pandemic.[45]

When examining the defence industry and the supply of oil and petroleum products, the Secretary of State has interpreted the powers narrowly, i.e. limited to national security concerns. It noted that the orders were not incompatible with Article 101 TFEU because Article 346(1)(b) TFEU provides that provisions of the Treaty shall not preclude a Member State from taking 'measures as it considers necessary for the protection of the essential interests of its security which are connected with the production of or trade in arms, munitions and war material'.[46] Accordingly, prior to Brexit, other public policy concerns unrelated to national security might not have been able to justify an exception by the Secretary of State, at least when there was an effect on trade between Member States. Similar questions were raised, and left unanswered, with respect to the coronavirus pandemic exclusion orders.[47]

Another example of a high discretion balancing tool that takes non-economic benefits into account is the French *de minimis* rule, which sets a separate appreciability threshold for less serious cases ('micro-practices').[48] Those practices cannot be

[41] Since the Secretary of State's orders do not fall within the coding selection criteria, they are not included in the database of this study.

[42] Competition Act 1998 (Public Policy Exclusion) Order 2006 (maintenance and repair of warships); Competition Act 1998 (Public Policy Exclusion) Order 2007 (strategic and tactical weapons and their supporting technology); Competition Act 1998 (Public Policy Exclusion) Order 2008 (design, construction, maintenance and disposal of nuclear submarines).

[43] The Competition Act 1998 (Public Policy Exclusion) (Revocation) Order 2011 (Team Complex Weapons).

[44] The Competition Act 1998 (Public Policy Exclusion) Order 2012 (supply of oil fuels in an emergency).

[45] Competition Act 1998 (Groceries) (Coronavirus) (Public Policy Exclusion) Order 2020; Competition Act 1998 (Health Services for Patients in England) (Coronavirus) (Public Policy Exclusion) Order 2020; Competition Act 1998 (Solent Maritime Crossings) (Coronavirus) (Public Policy Exclusion) Order 2020; Competition Act 1998 (Health Services for Patients in Wales) (Coronavirus) (Public Policy Exclusion) Order 2020; Competition Act 1998 (Dairy Produce) (Coronavirus) (Public Policy Exclusion) Order 2020.

[46] Competition Act 1998 (Public Policy Exclusion) Order 2008 (design, construction, maintenance and disposal of nuclear submarines), Explanatory Memorandom, para 4.2.

[47] Odudu (2020, 76–77).

[48] French Commercial Code, Article L 464-9 provides that upon fulfilment of the following conditions, the Minister of the Economy can order the undertakings in question to cease the infringing behaviour and impose on them a fine of an amount not exceeding EUR 75,000 or 5% of the last known turnover in France, whichever is smaller: The agreement must only affect regional markets and is not likely to affect trade between Member States; the individual turnover of the undertakings does not exceed EUR 50 million; and the cumulative turnover of the undertakings is less than EUR 100 million. See also Vogel (2012, 171) and Boudou et al. (2014, 109).

examined by the French NCA, but only by the Minister of the Economy, who can issue specific injunctions.

While the above examples were limited in scope, Hungary made more significant use of issue-specific balancing tools. This line of cases begins with the NCA's investigation in *Watermelon (2013)*.[49] The case involved a price-fixing agreement concluded between supermarkets and national watermelon producers, which also included measures that hindered the distribution of imported watermelons. The agreement was supported by the Hungarian Minister for Rural Development, aiming to secure a fair income standard for farmers.

After the initiation of an NCA investigation, the Hungarian Parliament amended the Act on Inter-branch Organisations (the 'amendment').[50] The amendment allowed the Minister for Rural Development to exclude from the national provision equivalent to Article 101 TFEU agreements in the agricultural sector that provide a fair income for producers, as far as they do not preclude all market actors from joining the agreement.[51] In such cases, the amendment further stated, the Hungarian NCA could not impose fines for the infringement of EU law. Finally, the amendment provided for a special procedure for agriculture products that were not excluded.[52] It obliges the Hungarian NCA to issue a warning to undertakings prior to establishing that an infringement of EU or national law has occurred, asking them to bring their conduct into conformity with the law within a set deadline. Only if the undertaking has failed to cease the infringement by the deadline can a fine be imposed.

This exception is ultimately based on the Minister's judgement, leaving a political actor the discretion to limit the scope of EU and national competition rules. The amendment had an immediate effect. The Hungarian NCA terminated its proceedings in *Watermelon* after the Minister declared that the conditions for the exception had been met.[53] For the same reason, it terminated the proceedings in *Sugar cartel (2012)*, in which it suspected that the sugar producers had regularly coordinated their prices, divided industrial and retail purchasers, and shared information on the quantities sold.[54]

[49] Vj-62/2012 Watermelon (2013).

[50] Hungarian Act No. CLXXVI of 2012 on inter-branch organisations and on certain issues of the regulation of agricultural markets.

[51] Article 18/A(1) states: '[t]he infringement of §11 of the Competition Act cannot be established in case of agricultural products if the distortion, restriction or prevention of competition resulting from an agreement according to §11 of the Competition Act does not exceed what is necessary for an economically justified, fair income, provided that the actors of the market affected by the agreement are not debarred from benefiting from such income and that Article 101 TFEU was not applied'. English translation from Tóth (2013, 364).

[52] Hungarian Act No. CLXXVI of 2012 on inter-branch organisations and on certain issues of the regulation of agricultural markets, Article 18/A(4).

[53] Vj-62/2012 Watermelon (2013), para 13–15; 42–46; 56–57.

[54] Vj-50/2009 Sugar cartel (2012), para 132.

The amendment was also applied retroactively to *Wheat mill products I (2010, 2012, 2014)*.[55] Prior to the adoption of the amendment, the NCA imposed a fine on a market-sharing and price-fixing agreement concerning wheat mill products. Yet, the Hungarian courts that examined the case following the adoption of the amendment held that the NCA should reconsider its decision in light of the new amendment.[56]

The Hungarian issue-specific, political exception for the agriculture sector was heavily criticised by commentators,[57] as well as by the NCA itself. The latter had warned that the amendment could 'lead [...] to a situation in which *the public interest* that the legislator wishes to protect *is no longer clear*'[58] and give rise to serious concerns over the evaluation of cartel activities concerning agricultural products.[59]

The Commission, too, voiced its concerns. Yet, it did not question the underlying premise of the balancing or the exception itself. It merely focused on the provisions that did not allow the Hungarian NCA to impose fines for an Article 101 TFEU infringement, noting it may conflict with the provision of Article 5 of Regulation 1/2003.[60] Under threat of the possible initiation of an infringement procedure against Hungary, the exception was amended. Accordingly, the agriculture exception included in the Hungarian Competition Act itself clarifies that the NCA could impose sanctions, including fines, when an agreement affects trade between Member States.[61]

Following this amendment, the Commission had closed the procedure without further action. The empirical findings, however, suggest that this clarification has had no impact in practice. They show that, prior to the amendment, Article 101 TFEU was actively enforced in the agriculture sector.[62] However, following the amendment, the NCA did open investigations into this sector (or, at least, an investigation that ended with a published notice). This will be further elaborated in Section 7.4.1 as an example of balancing by priority setting.

Despite the criticism, the Hungarian legislator adopted other issue-specific exceptions. In *Waste materials (2015)*, the Hungarian NCA examined the conduct of a group of Hungarian undertakings that had won the bid for operating the national

[55] Vj-69/2008 Wheat mill products I (2010), para 194–197.
[56] 2.K.31.793/2011/90 Wheat mill products I (2012); 2.Kf.649.964/2013/20 Wheat mill products I (2014).
[57] Szilagyi (2012, 3–4; 2013, 6–8), Tóth (2013, 364–366), Pina (2014, 16), Csépai (2015, 404–405), and Cseres (2020, 4–6, 20–21).
[58] Emphasis added. Vj-62/2012 Watermelon (2013), para 70–72.
[59] GVH, Enforceable Ethical Rules to the Agriculture Sector (2009).
[60] Csépai (2015, 404).
[61] Article 93/A of the Hungarian Competition Act provides that the special exception for agriculture shall only apply 'if the necessity of the application of Article 101 of the TFEU does not arise. The necessity of the application of Article 101 of the TFEU shall be established by the Hungarian Competition Authority in its competition supervision proceeding pursuant to Article 3(1) of Council Regulation (EC) No 1/2003, before making the final resolution'.
[62] See Annex A, Section 6.3.

waste management scheme.[63] The tender was part of the re-structuring and re-nationalisation of the domestic waste management market. The government had excluded the incumbents, largely foreign-owned undertakings, from the bidding by restricting the issuance of operating licenses to undertakings that were controlled by the State or local councils.[64] The NCA suspected that the group of undertakings had colluded to fix prices, coordinated the actual bids, and bid-rigged the public procurement procedures.

Faced with those serious allegations, the Hungarian parliament adopted an issue-specific law. It maintained that no infringement of the national prohibition on cartels could be established with respect to actions carried out in the execution of public procurements procedures published in 2012–2013 for the implementation of the National Waste Plan.[65] As a response, the NCA closed the investigation, noting that there was no public interest in continuing the case in light of the new law.[66]

An issue-specific exception for EU and mixed cases was also adopted by the German legislator. In *Round timber in Baden-Württemberg (2015, 2017, 2018)*, the German NCA examined the conduct of the federal state of Baden-Württemberg, which had sold and invoiced wood on behalf of other forest owners and carried out several services related to the marketing of round timber via its company Forst BW. In July 2015, the German NCA held that because the agreements between the federal state and other forest owners fixed prices and restricted sales, they amounted to by-object restrictions of competition.[67] In early 2017, *after* the federal state of Baden-Württemberg had appealed this decision, the German legislator amended the national Federal Forests Act. The amendment excluded these types of agreements from the scope of national competition law, and effectively also from the scope of EU competition law by setting a presumption that they were justified under Article 101(3) TFEU.[68]

The full force of the amendment was not accepted by the Düsseldorf Higher Regional Court. The Court upheld the NCA's decision, noting that the amendment could entail no more than that the federal state's activity no longer violated German competition law. According to the Court, the German legislator did not have the competence to limit the full application of Article 101 TFEU.[69] Nevertheless, in the end, the conduct of the federal state was not prohibited. In 2018, the Federal Court

63 Vj-67/2014/59 Waste materials (2015).
64 Hungarian Act CL XXXV of 2012 Waste Disposal Act, Article 81. See also Varju and Papp (2016, 1661).
65 Hungarian Act XCIX of 2014 on the financial grounding of the central budget.
66 Vj-67/2014/59 Waste materials (2015), 2–3.
67 B1–72/12 Round timber in Baden-Württemberg (2015).
68 German Federal Forest Act, Section 46(2).
69 Kart 10/15 (V) Round timber in Baden-Württemberg (2017), para 349–369.

of Justice overturned the NCA's decision to open the case in the first place without discussing the compatibility of the amendment with EU competition law.[70]

Issue-specific exceptions are the most problematic type of national balancing tool. As high discretion balancing tools that take non-economic benefits into account, they allow NCAs, national courts, the national parliament, or the executive to limit the application of Article 101 TFEU for essentially political reasons. In addition to the harm to competition, this type of balancing tool is also uncertain and not uniform. The high level of discretion and the *ex-ante* nature of many such exceptions do not make for transparent and predictable balancing tools that can be applied consistently.

6.4 CLOSING REMARKS: TRANSITION TO NATIONAL BALANCING TOOLS

Regulation 1/2003 entrusted the NCAs with the power to apply Article 101 TFEU and to engage in balancing. The decentralisation of the enforcement has mostly facilitated a process of soft convergence and voluntary harmonisation of many national competition rules to the practices of the Commission. When it comes to balancing, however, this chapter pointed to an opposite trend, by which NCAs, national courts, governments, and parliaments have introduced unique national rules that explicitly or implicitly limited the enforcement of EU competition law in favour of promoting non-competition interests.

The empirical findings show that many of the national balancing tools have acted as a substitute for the EU explicit-substantives balancing tools of Article 101(1) and (3) TFEU. While their scopes and conditions vary considerably, many of the national balancing tools entrust national enforcers or political actors with broad discretion to exempt agreements on the basis of broad types of economic and non-economic benefits. They may accept agreements that would not be tolerated under the EU balancing tools of Article 101(1) and (3) TFEU.

National balancing tools inherently hamper the uniformity of the enforcement and may hinder legal certainty, especially when they leave the competition enforcers a high level of discretion. Moreover, the compatibility of those national tools with EU competition law in cases having an effect on trade between Member States is highly questionable. As was described in the opening of this chapter, it is unclear whether such rules can benefit from the safe harbour of Article 3(3) of Regulation 1/2003, or whether they should be deemed an infringement of the Member States' duty of sincere cooperation in the meaning of Article 4(3) TEU.

70 KVR 38/17 Round timber in Baden-Württemberg (2018). The decision was based on the finding that the German NCA should not have re-opened its investigation after it had accepted commitments on this matter in 2008. The Court rejected the NCA claim that the reopening of the proceedings was justified by new information obtained after the commitment decision had been adopted.

Moreover, this chapter has shown that even when the national balancing tools were limited to purely national cases, they have often carried *de facto* effects also on cases having an effect on trade between Member States. In many cases, the competition enforcers have used their enforcement discretion to decide not to open an investigation or bring a proceeding to an end when an agreement that affected trade between Member States could have benefited from a national exception in purely national cases. This will be further elaborated in the next chapter.

7

Enforcement Discretion

'Gouverner, c'est choisir! – to govern is to choose!'[1]

7.1 INTRODUCTION

7.1.1 *Balancing by the Exercise of Enforcement Discretion*

The previous chapters examined balancing tools that have overtly limited the enforcement of EU competition law in favour of promoting non-competition interests. Chapters 3–5 discussed balancing tools based on EU law sources, and Chapter 6 reviewed national balancing tools. This chapter moves on to discuss the often-overlooked implicit balancing embedded in the exercise of the competition enforcers' detection, target, instrument, and outcome discretion.

Setting enforcement priorities is an 'inherent feature of administrative activity' for a competition enforcer.[2] Since it is not possible to enforce every potential infringement of Article 101 TFEU, enforcement discretion is a necessary precondition that allows the Commission and NCAs to make effective use of their scarce resources.[3]

This chapter submits that in addition to this task, enforcement discretion also provides competition enforcers with tools to take non-competition interests into account. In practice, enforcement choices are not just about gaining compliance with Article 101 TFEU but also have the effect of determining what the scope and boundaries of the Article are.[4]

[1] Competition Commissioner Kroes in the ICN Seminar on Competition Agency Effectiveness (2009), 6.

[2] T-24/90 BMW AG and BMW Italia SpA (1992), para 77.

[3] ECN+ Directive (2019), Preamble 13. See also ICN Seminar on Competition Agency Effectiveness (2009).

[4] Paraphrasing Black (2001, 3). This is already hinted at by the empirical findings presented in the previous chapters; see, in particular, Sections 3.3.4.2, 4.4.1.3, 5.1.2, 6.1, and 6.3.4.

More specifically, this chapter explores how the modernisation of EU competition law has enhanced the priority setting powers of competition enforcers, thereby creating new implicit-procedural tools to account for non-competition interests. It shows that under the old enforcement regime of Regulation 17/62, the Commission was obliged to assess all notified agreements by issuing either a formal decision or an informal comfort letter. While this obligation consumed much of the Commission's resources and left it only limited room to shape its enforcement strategy,[5] it also compelled the Commission to actively engage in balancing under the explicit-substantive balancing tools of Article 101(1) and (3) TFEU. The old enforcement regime, accordingly, prompted an abundance of decisions explaining how and in which circumstances non-competition interests could justify a restriction of competition.

This has changed following the entry into force of Regulation 1/2003. The abolishment of the notification regime has enhanced the Commission's enforcement discretion and entrusted the NCAs with powers to enforce Article 101 TFEU and set their priorities. This chapter presents theoretical and empirical evidence suggesting that this has led to a change in the *nature* of agreements examined by the competition enforcers. Following modernisation, the competition enforcers were incentivised to direct their enforcement efforts towards hard-core restrictions and clear-cut infringements of Article 101 TFEU. Those types of restrictions, which were often handled by means of leniency applications and settlements, are unlikely to be justified by overriding non-competition interests.

In parallel, the competition enforcers have either avoided opening investigations against other types of anti-competitive agreements or settled such cases with negotiated remedies or alternative regulatory mechanisms, regardless of whether such agreements could have been justified using the explicit-substantive balancing tools. For example, the Commission has declared that when it finds that an anti-competitive agreement can potentially be saved by Article 101(3) TFEU, it will use its enforcement discretion to 'simply not bring a case or close a case that had already been opened'.[6]

Those non-enforcement decisions, this chapter maintains, bear practical effects similar to 'no grounds for action' findings, in which NCAs declare that the conditions of Article 101(1) or (3) TFEU balancing tools have been fulfilled. In both cases, agreements that promote certain non-competition interests are not enforced.[7] However, the exercise of enforcement discretion is not subject to the rigid substantive and procedural framework applicable to the explicit-substantive balancing tools.

5 This obligation was also criticised as ineffective. See Section 2.3.2.

6 The Commission contribution to the OECD Role of Efficiency Claims in Antitrust Proceedings (2012), 90.

7 In both cases, the Commission and another NCA could still decide to bring an action against the case. However, in light of the limited number of enforcement actions, undertakings face only a limited risk of a second enforcement action.

It is limited by almost no procedural or substantive constraints, and the reasons behind the competition enforcer's decision are often not published or detailed.

Notably, balancing by the exercise of enforcement discretion allows competition enforcers to throw off the shackles of a more economic approach. Such balancing is often not bound to any substantive legal or economic test, it is not explicit, and it is subject to very limited judicial or political scrutiny. There are no constraints on the relevant type of benefits and no clear method guiding their assessment or demands on the intensity of evidence. Remarkably, although the Commission has advocated limiting the room for non-competition interests under the explicit-substantive balancing tools, the Commission and NCAs have not followed the same strict principles when setting their enforcement priorities.

As a result, by exercising enforcement discretion, competition enforcers can account for non-competition interest beyond what is permissible under the balancing tools of Article 101(1) and (3) TFEU, even according to the Commission's and EU Courts' broad interpretation prior to modernisation. It is therefore unsurprising that the balancing of many non-competition interests that had previously taken place under the balancing tools of Article 101(1) and (3) TFEU has now shifted to the exercise of the Commission's and NCAs' enforcement discretion.

It should be emphasised from the outset that this chapter criticises neither the competition enforcers' competences nor their focus on hard-core infringements. The exercise of enforcement discretion is clearly a necessary and important tool to ensure the efficient allocation of competition enforcers' limited resources to combat serious restrictions of competition.[8] It is also widely recognised that in certain circumstances, a decision not to enforce Article 101 TFEU due to countervailing non-competition interests may be preferable. The flexible, at times over-inclusive wording of Article 101 TFEU can rule out agreements that do not fit the economic and legal rationale of the prohibition. In such circumstances, a decision not to enforce Article 101 TFEU might actually enhance the effectiveness of EU competition law.[9]

This chapter merely argues that using enforcement discretion to account for non-competition interests becomes problematic when it systematically shields certain types of anti-competitive agreements or sectors from the full force of the prohibition of Article 101 TFEU, in a manner which is not limited to excluding unforeseeable circumstances in which one can confidently assume that the EU legislature would not want them to be covered or when such decisions are not based on clear economic and legal balancing principles.[10] Such practices, the chapter

8 Modernisation White Paper (1999), para 45; Regulation 1/2003, Preamble 3; ECN+ Directive (2019), Preamble 23.

9 Kovacic (2003, 401–402). On non-enforcement decision to combat over-inclusiveness of the law in general, see Landes and Posner (1975, 38–41), Baxter (1982, 664–673), Turner (1990, 297–298), Odudu (2008, 885–886), and Wils (2011, 376–377).

10 See also Wils (2011, 376–377).

concludes, hinder the effectiveness, uniformity, and legal certainty of Article 101 TFEU enforcement.

7.1.2 *Explicit-Substantive* v. *Implicit-Procedural Balancing Tools*

The balancing tools discussed in this chapter, which take non-competition interests into account by means of exercising enforcement discretion, are fundamentally different from the balancing tools examined in the previous chapters.

Article 101(1) and (3) TFEU and most of the unique national balancing tools are *explicit* and bound by *substantive* legal or economic tests. The consideration of non-competition interests is accomplished in accordance with the rules enshrined in EU or national primary and secondary laws and the principles developed by the decisional practice of the competition enforcers. In comparison, this chapter illustrates that balancing by the exercise of enforcement discretion is often effectuated *implicitly*, under the guise of a *procedural* decision. Competition enforcers *do not need to explain* how, or even *if*, non-competition interests have been taken into account.

Their exercise of enforcement discretion is not limited or directed by EU law: At the EU level, the CJEU has repeatedly emphasised the Commission's broad discretion to set priorities, as a reflection of its responsibility under the Treaty to define and implement the orientation of EU competition policy. In order to perform this task effectively, the Commission is free to select which cases to investigate, when to terminate proceedings, and to devise the procedural instruments.[11]

The same is true of enforcement discretion at the national level. The Treaties and Regulation 1/2003 give the NCAs the *power* to co-enforce EU competition rules but do not address the *means and instruments* for applying them. They do not direct or limit their discretion to set enforcement priorities.[12] Since the NCAs' discretionary powers are mostly bound to national laws, which vary considerably,[13] the allocation of resources is generally left to the discretion of each NCA and Member State. [14]

Consequently, competition enforcers enjoy considerable discretion to decide if, and how, to account for non-competition interests when exercising enforcement discretion. As the ECN observed, NCAs are not limited to selecting cases due to competition concerns (i.e., those having the most harmful effects on competition or consumer welfare) but can also consciously choose *not* to enforce Article 101 TFEU for other reasons. They can prioritise cases on account of considerations related to

[11] Article 105 TFEU. See C-119/97P Ufex (1999), para 88–89; C-344/98 Masterfoods (2000), para 46. See also Wils (2011, 357–360).

[12] As aptly summarised in the Impact Assessment accompanying the ECN+ Directive Proposal (2017), 14; European Court of Auditors, Special Report on the Commission's EU Merger Control and Antitrust Proceedings (2020), para 14.

[13] As elaborated in Section 7.4.2, the ECN Recommendation on the Power to Set Priorities (2013) are general and non-binding recommendations in this regard.

[14] Blanco and De Pablo (2012, 60).

'*public interest*, consumer welfare, market efficiencies, *or other substantive, institutional or procedural considerations*'.[15]

In light of the above, this study distinguishes between (i) Article 101(1) and (3) TFEU and the unique national balancing tools, which will be collectively labelled *explicit-substantive balancing tools* and (ii) the various techniques to account for non-competition interests via the exercise of enforcement discretion, which will be collectively labelled *implicit-procedural balancing tools*.

7.1.3 *Structure and Approach: Studying the Dark Matter of Enforcement*

Revealing the existence of implicit-procedural balancing tools is not an easy task. By its very nature, such a study requires an examination of not only the reasons that led a competition enforcer to take up a certain case but also – and perhaps chiefly – the reasons justifying disregarding a case. Most competition enforcers, however, do not fully reveal such motives in their policy papers or decisional practices. The exercise of the competition enforcers' enforcement discretion was aptly classified as a revolutionary and overlooked dimension of modernisation.[16] Despite some examples that will be presented in the following sections, it is difficult to provide a comprehensive empirical account of the influence of non-competition interests on such decisions. It greatly lies in the 'dark matter' of the enforcement.[17]

Nevertheless, the empirical methodology followed by this study provides a solid basis to test several hypotheses on the existence and scope of balancing within this dark matter. This chapter uncovers areas that have remained untouched by competition enforcement following modernisation by mapping all the Article 101 TFEU enforcement actions rendered by the competition enforcers (when they enjoyed strong enforcement discretion) and comparing them to the Commission's practice prior to modernisation (when it had limited enforcement discretion).

Accordingly, this chapter follows a different methodology than was used to study the explicit-substantive balancing tools. It takes a four-step approach to examine the application of the Commission's and NCAs' enforcement discretion. First, Section 7.2 explores the incentives that influence the setting of enforcement priorities. It poses the hypothesis that the three pillars of modernisation have reduced the competition enforcers' incentives to pursue cases involving a clash between competition and non-competition interests.

Second, Sections 7.3–7.6 evaluate this hypothesis. They demonstrate that the substantive, procedural, and institutional set-up of the EU leaves the Commission and NCAs a wide degree of discretion to set their enforcement priorities. As

[15] ECN Recommendation on the Power to Set Priorities (2013), 2.
[16] Gerard (2012, 21).
[17] See Section 1.3.1.

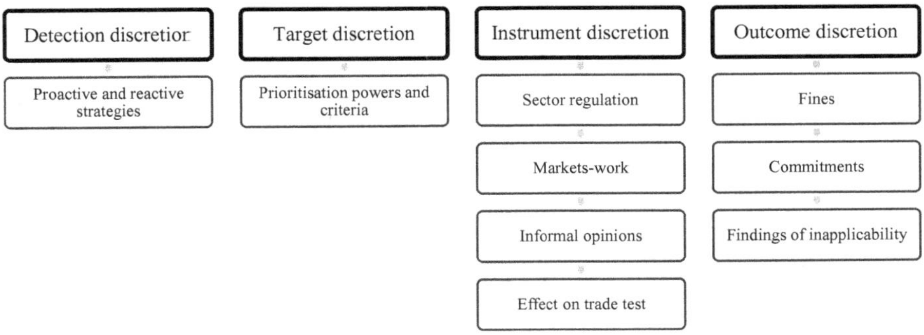

FIGURE 7.1. Four types of enforcement discretion

observed by *Petit*,[18] the competition enforcers have the discretion to devise the detection strategy of anti-competitive agreements ('detection discretion'), decide which investigations to pursue and which to neglect ('target discretion'), apply alternative legal mechanisms to examine a case ('instrument discretion'), and design the remedies ('outcome discretion'). Figure 7.1 shows that each of these four discretionary powers offers an opportunity for balancing. They allow competition enforcers to select cases not only on the basis of competition merits but also to choose *not* to enforce Article 101 TFEU for reasons unrelated to competition interests.

Each of those sections is dedicated to exploring how one particular type of discretion has served as a balancing tool. Each section details the scope of the Commission's and NCAs' discretion and the possibility for judicial review and presents empirical evidence indicating that such discretion has been used to account for non-competition interests in practice. It should be noted that those empirical indications presented in Sections 7.3–7.6 are tentative and suggestive in nature. Rather than offering a decisive proof, they should be understood as indicators, inviting future research into the matter.

Third, Section 7.7 critically assesses the initiative to harmonise the rules governing target discretion as part of the ECN+ Directive. It argues that while the Directive may have contributed to the effective enforcement of EU competition law in general, it is ineffective and counterproductive when it comes to balancing since it fails to address the shortcomings of the current regime.

Finally, Section 7.8 concludes by explaining how modernisation resulted in a shift from the explicit-substantive to the implicit-procedural balancing tools. It maintains that balancing by enforcement discretion is less effective, uniform, and certain compared to the explicit-substantive balancing tools examined in this book.

[18] This classification is heavily based on the one offered by Petit (2010), with some modifications.

7.2 HYPOTHESIS: INCENTIVES GUIDING ENFORCEMENT DISCRETION[19]

The modernisation, as elaborated above, has vested the competition enforcers with enhanced discretional enforcement powers, which can be utilised to account for non-competition interests. This section offers insights from legal, economic, and social-science scholarship in the support of the hypothesis that competition enforcers may *prefer* to use these powers for the purpose of balancing instead of the explicit-substantive balancing tools:

First, competition enforcers have scarce financial, technical, and human resources.[20] The more time they spend on each case, the fewer cases they can deal with.[21] An enforcer must balance the objectives of Article 101 TFEU enforcement, as it understands them, with pragmatic concerns related to the risks and cost associated with the enforcement of a certain agreement, the expected length of the proceeding, and the institutional significance of the case (i.e. how the case relates to the enforcer's portfolio of cases and the potential to establish legal precedent).[22] Those considerations encourage an enforcer to focus on cases that are likely to yield substantial results, namely clear-cut cases having either low risks and costs or high significance. In parallel, an enforcer is discouraged from allocating its efforts to more complicated and costly cases involving balancing issues, which may end without an infringement decision or fine or be overturned by a court. In particular, they may tend to avoid cases that merit a sophisticated analysis.

This trend has been aggravated by the substantive modernisation. As detailed in Section 2.5.4.4, the introduction of the more economic approach has increased the costs for establishing an infringement.[23] Instead of pigeonholing an agreement according to its form and predetermined rules of thumb, the more economic approach demands a case-specific complex economic analysis based on empirical evidence. Balancing under the explicit-substantive balancing tools has thus become a much more costly exercise. In contrast, the exercise of enforcement discretion is not subject to the same rigid legal or economic standards. In many Member States, the competition enforcers are not even required to produce a reasoned decision explaining the exercise of their discretion.[24]

The increased enforcement costs, in turn, have encouraged the competition enforcers to pursue by-object and hard-core restrictions that require only limited

[19] This section expands on similar arguments I have previously presented in Brook (2020, 454–456).
[20] Petit (2010, 45), Blanco and De Pablo (2012, 60), and Jennings (2015, 30).
[21] Vestager (2016).
[22] ICN Seminar on Competition Agency Effectiveness (2009), 17; Posner (2009, 275–276); UNCTAD Prioritization and Resource Allocation (2013), 11; Jennings (2015, 31); CMA Prioritisation Principles (2017).
[23] Gerard (2012, 32–36). See also Witt (2016b, 167–173).
[24] Petit (2010, 44–62); ECN Decision Making Powers Report (2012), 51–53, 70–78.

analysis and which are often supported by leniency applications and settlements. Yet, many of the balancing tools discussed in this book do not apply categorically to hard-core restrictions[25] or are less likely to justify an exception.[26] Thus, by choosing to avert cases that require sophisticated analysis, competition enforcers then rarely have the opportunity to balance competition and non-competition interests in their enforcement practices.

Second, balancing by the exercise of enforcement discretion facilitates a broad variety of non-competition interests, going well beyond what is permissible under the standard of the explicit-substantive balancing tools.[27] This allows the Commission and the NCAs to take into account non-competition interests that could not be accepted under the narrow interpretation of Article 101(1) and (3) TFEU that is advocated by the Commission following modernisation.

Third, favouring the implicit-procedural balancing tools to account for non-competition interests may also be linked to the political and judicial accountability of each competition enforcer to its national government, parliament, the ECN, the Commission, the epistemic community (practitioners and academics),[28] and the general public.[29] Competition enforcers are accountable for the use of their human and financial resources and for the impact of their enforcement choices on achieving effective protection of competition.[30] The accomplishments and prestige of a competition enforcer are often measured by statistics detailing the number of infringement decisions, the level of fines imposed,[31] and the rate of success of judicial review applications.[32] An enforcer might also be disincentivised from engaging in the debate over the role of non-competition interests because the epistemic community questions their relevance under Article 101 TFEU.

25 The EU and some of the national *de minimis* rules (Sections 5.3.6 and 6.3.1) and BERs (Chapter 4).

26 Article 101(3) TFEU (Section 3.4.4.4), ancillary restraints (Section 5.3.4).

27 Compare with Abrams (1971, 2).

28 On the role of the epistemic community in policy design, see in general Haas (1992), and with relation to EU competition law Waarden and Drahos (2002, 928–932) and Townley (2018, 105–106, 154–155).

29 Competition Commissioner Kroes in the ICN Seminar on Competition Agency Effectiveness (2009), 6. More generally, see Cseres and Outhuijse (2017, 97–113).

30 UNCTAD Prioritization and Resource Allocation (2013), 10.

31 This is especially true when an NCA's budget is determined according to the level of fines it imposes. For instance, the Hungarian NCA is allowed to indirectly use 5% of its fines for the funding of conferences and external research projects. See OECD Reforms to Improve the Investment Climate in South East Europe (2006), 119; Sabbatini (2008, 1).

32 The focus on those indicators is made apparent by the annual statistics published in the Commission's and NCAs' policy reports. This was confirmed by the Hungarian NCA in its annual report 2016, 6, noting that 'the total amount of the fines imposed in a competition authority's competition supervision proceedings is an important measure of the effectiveness of its activities'. See also Wils (2004, 217), Sabbatini (2008, 5), Kovacic, Hollman, and Grant (2011, 27), Geradin and Petit (2012, 38), and Kovacic (2015b, 251).

Similar incentives may also guide the behaviour of individual staff members. *Farrell and Katz*, for example, observe that the staff members of the competition enforcers select cases according to their personal preferences and the nature of their compensation. Since the probabilities of success or failure of a case are likely to affect their status and compensation, a rational decision-maker will tend to recommend taking low-risk cases.[33]

In light of the above, enforcers are encouraged to pursue clear-cut infringements, especially those supported by leniency applications, which are unlikely to pose legal difficulties.[34] In comparison, they tend to avoid, settle, or use informal or alternative measures to close more controversial cases.[35] This then runs the risk that the enforcement efforts will excessively centre on cases that draw short-term gains or that are high on the enforcer's regulatory agenda[36] while ignoring cases that involve balancing.

This risk is especially prominent when the Commission's soft law guidelines and notices govern an agreement. As elaborated in Chapters 3 and 5, the role of non-competition interests under Article 101(1) and (3) TFEU remains unclear. The wording of the Article is vague, and the CJEU has refrained from providing clear guidance. At the same time, the Commission has narrowed the scope of the explicit-substantive balancing tools in its soft laws issued following modernisation. It has considerably limited the types of benefits that can be examined, introduced an economic balancing process, and required a high level of economic evidence to justify an exception. Although the soft law mechanisms do not bind NCAs and national courts, diverging cases may encounter legal, academic, or political criticism.

Finally, when accountability mechanisms fail, the enforcement choices of the competition enforcers may also be affected by regulatory capture of personnel, such as revolving doors practices or political and populism-driven motives.[37] A regulated industry may achieve disproportionate influence over the enforcer's decision-making, shifting the enforcement away from the broader public interest and towards its own private interests.[38] In particular, the head of a competition enforcer might be motivated to focus on uncontested headline-grabbing cases, even if such infringements have only a modest impact on competition, and to avoid politically charged issues,[39] such as those involving balancing.

33 Farrell and Katz (2006, 14–15).
34 Harrington (2011, 46).
35 Petit and Rato (2008, 212–213) and Gerse (2010, 335).
36 Forrester (2008, 649) and Wils (2011, 381).
37 Petit (2010, 45), Gerse (2010, 334–336), and Kovacic et al. (2011, 29). More generally, see Posner (2009, 86).
38 Carpenter and Moss (2013, 1).
39 Kovacic et al. (2011, 38).

Against this backdrop, enforcement discretion offers an attractive balancing tool from the standpoint of the competition enforcers. The implicit-procedural balancing tools are not subject to the rigid legal or economic tests that characterise the explicit-substantive balancing tools. Moreover, as detailed below, in many instances the enforcers are not even required to produce a reasoned decision explaining the exercise of their discretion. Balancing by enforcement discretion is also subject to no or limited judicial review. It is not always notified to the Commission and ECN. Hence, discretional enforcement powers leave the enforcers ample room to consider non-competition interests, going well beyond what they could take into account under the explicit-substantive balancing tools. In light of the above, this chapter poses the following hypothesis:

> *Hypothesis: The three pillars of modernisation have incentivised the competition enforcers to direct their enforcement efforts towards clear-cut infringements of Article 101 TFEU that are unlikely to be justified by non-competition interests. Agreements requiring a balance between competition and non-competition interests are likely to be disregarded or resolved by other means, such as negotiated remedies or by closing the probe into the case, even when they do not meet the conditions for an Article 101(1) or (3) TFEU exception.*

The remainder of this chapter is devoted to testing this hypothesis. It presents various case studies in which non-competition interests have explicitly influenced exercising the competition enforcers' enforcement discretion as well as empirical indications of a systematic shift from the explicit-substantive to the implicit-procedural consideration of non-competition interests under Article 101 TFEU. By embedding non-competition interests to their discretionary enforcement powers, the competition enforcers have developed unique prioritisation policies for Article 101 TFEU enforcement, which reflect their own understanding of the role of non-competition interests.

7.3 DETECTION DISCRETION

7.3.1 *Balancing Tool*

A competition enforcer exercises detection discretion when selecting a strategy for identifying anti-competitive behaviour. In this regard, a distinction can be made between two categories of detection strategies[40]: In a *proactive* strategy, a competition enforcer autonomously seeks to reveal anti-competitive agreements by means of *ex-officio* proceedings. Under a *reactive* strategy, on the other hand, the competition enforcer relies on information gathered and submitted by undertakings or third

[40] Petit (2010, 46); ICN Anti-cartel Enforcement Manual (2010), 6–20; Blanco and De Pablo (2012, 60–61); OECD Ex officio Cartel Investigations Report (2013), 12. See also Regulation 1/2003, Article 5.

parties by means of a notification, complaint, whistleblowing,[41] or leniency application. In addition, some national laws compel NCAs to open an investigation upon a referral from other national authorities such as a court, sector regulator, or the executive. The detection strategies are not mutually exclusive. Most enforcers use a combination of detection methods and are not obliged to favour one method over the other.

This section submits that the choice of detection method implicitly comprises balancing. This argument is based on the premise that proactive strategies and certain reactive strategies such as whistleblowing and leniency applications are expected to expose clear-cut infringements of Article 101 TFEU, which are unlikely to be justified by overriding non-competition interests. Other types of reactive strategies are more likely to reveal anti-competitive agreements that raise balancing questions. Therefore, the selection of detection methods implicitly informs the likelihood that an enforcer will face balancing questions. This premise is based on the following grounds:

First, a competition enforcer is unlikely to use *ex-officio* proceedings to detect agreements involving balancing questions. *Ex-officio* proceedings are complex and costly. They track suspicious market behaviour based on expensive economic and statistical data on prices, costs, and market shares.[42] Moreover, this information is just a starting point for the investigation. An infringement can only be established upon proving the existence of an actual agreement or a concerted practice, typically on the basis of correspondence and documents retrieved during an inspection of the undertakings' premises.[43] However, in many Member States, an NCA can only carry out such an inspection if it can prove a high likelihood of establishing *a serious infringement* of the competition rules.[44] Therefore, a competition enforcer will be more inclined to allocate its scarce resources to investigating clear-cut infringements of Article 101 TFEU.[45] Agreements involving balancing questions, in which the legal situation is less clear, are less likely to be assessed by means of a proactive detection strategy.

[41] Whistleblowing programmes grant a monetary award to a private person who provides information that contributes to exposing a cartel. Whistleblowing programmes are not as common as leniency programmes. They were first introduced to proceedings taking place before the Commission in 2017 (see policy report 2017, 4–5). They are also offered by some NCAs, e.g. in the UK since 2008 (UK Whistleblowing Guidelines (2014)), in Hungary since 2010 (Hungarian Competition Act, Article 79/A(3)), and in Germany since 2012 (German NCA annual report 2012, 41). On whistleblowing programmes, see also Polański (2014) and Stucke (2015).

[42] Friederiszick and Maier-Rigaud (2008, 90–93); Petit (2010, 46); OECD Ex officio Cartel Investigations Report (2013), 18.

[43] Friederiszick and Maier-Rigaud (2008, 93–94); OECD Ex officio Cartel Investigations Report (2013), 7, 38, 108.

[44] On the Commission's inspection powers, see Regulation 1/2003, Article 20. See also Friederiszick and Maier-Rigaud (2008, 93–94).

[45] Ibid, 101.; OECD Ex officio Cartel Investigations Report (2013), 41–42.

Second, similarly, leniency and whistleblowing programmes are also unlikely to expose balancing questions. The Commission's leniency programme, as well as those of most Member States, is restricted to revealing *secret cartels* and serious *by-object restrictions*.[46] The same is true for national whistleblowing programmes.[47] Such serious restrictions of competition are unlikely to be justified by overriding non-competition interests. Moreover, it is also unlikely that an agreement that genuinely intends to advance non-competition interests will be kept secret. If undertakings believe that an agreement creates benefits that justify an exception, they typically have no legitimate reason to hide it.[48]

Third, other reactive detection policies are more prone to disclose balancing questions because they limit the competition enforcer's detection discretion. Since the enforcer must act upon information received from an external source, it is less affected by practical considerations related to the enforcement costs, the complexity of the legal questions, or the political sensitivity of the case.[49] Moreover, agreements referred by public authorities are likely to reveal balancing questions because they typically take place in markets that are subject to governmental involvement or regulation.[50]

Finally, the mere availability of a certain detection method may affect the types of agreements detected. An obligation to respond to all complaints and referrals, for instance, consumes the competition enforcer's resources and reduces the prospects of opening *ex-officio* proceedings.[51] Similarly, the availability of leniency applications, which provide quality evidence and low adjudication costs, reduces the enforcer's incentive to pursue risky and expensive investigations of its own accord.[52]

To conclude, the focus on proactive strategies and on reactive strategies such as whistleblowing and leniency applications limits the feasibility of detecting agreements involving balancing questions. The portfolio of cases of a competition enforcer that mostly follows those strategies, as a result, will offer it only a limited opportunity to examine balancing questions within the explicit-substantive balancing tools. Consistently overlooking those agreements means that undertakings will not be deterred from concluding anti-competitive agreements that promote non-competition interests, even if such agreements are incompatible with Article 101

46 The Commission's Leniency Notice (2006), Preamble 1 and 3, states that it aims to reveal 'secret cartels', in which undertakings agree to fix-prices or share markets. National leniency programs are often subject to similar conditions; see the ECN Model Leniency Programme (2012), para 4, 11; Wils (2007, 13–14).

47 Hungarian Competition Act, Article 79/A; UK Whistleblowing Guidelines (2014), 1–2.

48 Similarly, under the old notification regime of Regulation 17/62, an Article 101(3) TFEU exemption was granted only if the agreement was notified to the Commission. A secret agreement could not have benefited from an exemption.

49 On the incentives guiding priority setting, see Section 7.2.

50 See Sections 3.4.3.3, 4.3.1.2, 5.2, and 7.6.2.3.

51 See Section 2.3.2.

52 Petit (2010, 48), Stephan (2013, 229), Idot (2015, 53), Kovacic (2015a, 128–130), and Wils (2016, 350).

TFEU. The next section shows that those very detection policies have guided the practice of many competition enforcers.

7.3.2 *Scope of Detection Discretion*

EU and national rules do not directly dictate the detection strategies of most competition enforcers.[53] At the same time, the applicable substantive, procedural, and institutional frameworks often prompt the use of certain detection methods.[54]

The Commission's practice provides an illustrative example of how *a substantive framework* informs the detection strategy. Prior to modernisation, the Commission's detection strategy was largely reactive. Empirical studies have already confirmed that the obligation to examine all notified agreements has left the Commission only limited capacity to engage in proactive enforcement efforts.[55] This was reinforced by the introduction of the Commission's leniency programme in 1996.[56] Later, the procedural modernisation aimed to initiate, among others, a more proactive detection strategy.[57] Releasing the Commission from the burden of administrative notifications was expected to prompt *ex-officio* investigations.[58]

Nevertheless, in practice, the Commission's strategy remained largely reactive. In fact, the vast majority of the Commission's Article 101 TFEU infringement decisions following modernisation originated from leniency applications. While a small number of infringement decisions were based on complaints, only a few stemmed from *ex-officio* investigations.[59] The sparing use of *ex-officio* investigations is often explained by reference to the substantive modernisation. As mentioned, the more economic approach increased the enforcement costs by demanding a case-specific analysis on the basis of complex economic evidence.[60] Those increased costs incentivise the Commission to make greater use of its less costly leniency programme. The substantive modernisation has, in other words, advanced the use of detection policies that are unlikely to reveal agreements involving balancing questions.

The French enforcement regime is an example of how the *procedural and institutional set-up* of an authority affects its detection policy and, thus, balancing. In the past, the French NCA had only limited investigation powers. While it was

53 However, some Member States have enacted a voluntary or compulsory notification regime for purely national cases. See ECN Questionnaire on Regulation 1/2003 (2013), 2.
54 Petit (2010, 48) and Idot (2015, 53).
55 The source of all the Commission's formal decisions between 1964 and 2004 is presented in Carree, Günster, and Pieter Schinkel (2010, 107–108). See also Wils (2016, 351–352).
56 See Section 2.5.3.3.
57 See Section 7.1.1.
58 Monti (2003).
59 OECD Ex officio Cartel Investigations Report (2013), 104–105; Massadeh (2015, 72–74) and Wils (2016, 351–352). See also Blanco and De Pablo (2012, 60–61).
60 See Section 7.2.

theoretically competent to carry out *ex-officio* investigations, the investigation itself had to be executed by the services of the Ministry of Economy.[61] Consequently, the NCA rarely made use of *ex-officio* investigations. Between 1992 and 2008, only an average of 6% of the investigations per year were initiated of the NCA's own accord.[62] This changed once the 2009 procedural reform granted the French NCA the power to open and conclude investigations.[63] The number of *ex-officio* investigations initiated between 2009 and 2013 increased to an average of 19% of all annual investigations.[64]

The empirical findings presented in Section 3.6.1 suggest that the change of the French detection strategy may have affected balancing. While Article 101(3) TFEU had been successfully invoked by undertakings prior to the procedural reform, the French NCA did not found that the four conditions of the Article were fulfilled in procedures opened following the reform. The French procedural and institutional framework, therefore, shaped the detection methods and thus indirectly affected the likelihood of applying the explicit-substantive balancing tools.

7.3.3 *Empirical Indications*

The empirical findings support the hypothesis that the competition enforcers have focused on leniency applications to detect anti-competitive agreements. Such focus has generated a portfolio of cases that is less likely to raise balancing questions. Figure 7.2 summarises the number of Commission enforcement actions in which the explicit-substantive balancing tools of Article 101(1) and (3) TFEU were discussed, according to the type of procedure (e.g. leniency, commitment decision, settlement). It specifies the number of enforcement actions in which each of the balancing tools was discussed (black bars), compared to the number of proceedings in which it was not mentioned (white bars).

The figure illustrates that following modernisation, the Commission's detection strategy was mainly based on leniency applications, often in combination with a settlement. In fact, 82% of the Commission's infringement decisions under Regulation 1/2003 were conducted by means of a leniency application and/or a settlement.

The figure also shows that the explicit-substantive balancing tools were rarely discussed in proceedings initiated by leniency applications or resolved by a settlement. This is hardly surprising. As mentioned, the Commission's leniency programme is restricted to revealing secret cartels and serious by-object restrictions, which are

[61] French Commercial Code, Article L 462-5.

[62] Based on the statistics presented in Idot (2015, 53). See also Massadeh (2015, 228–237).

[63] French Commercial Code, Article L 462-4.

[64] Based on the statistics presented in Idot (2015, 53). Massadeh (2015, 226) argues that budget constraints have kept the French NCA from initiating an even greater number of *ex-officio* investigations. This reform has also affected the exercise of the French NCA's target discretion, as elaborated in Section 7.4.3.2.

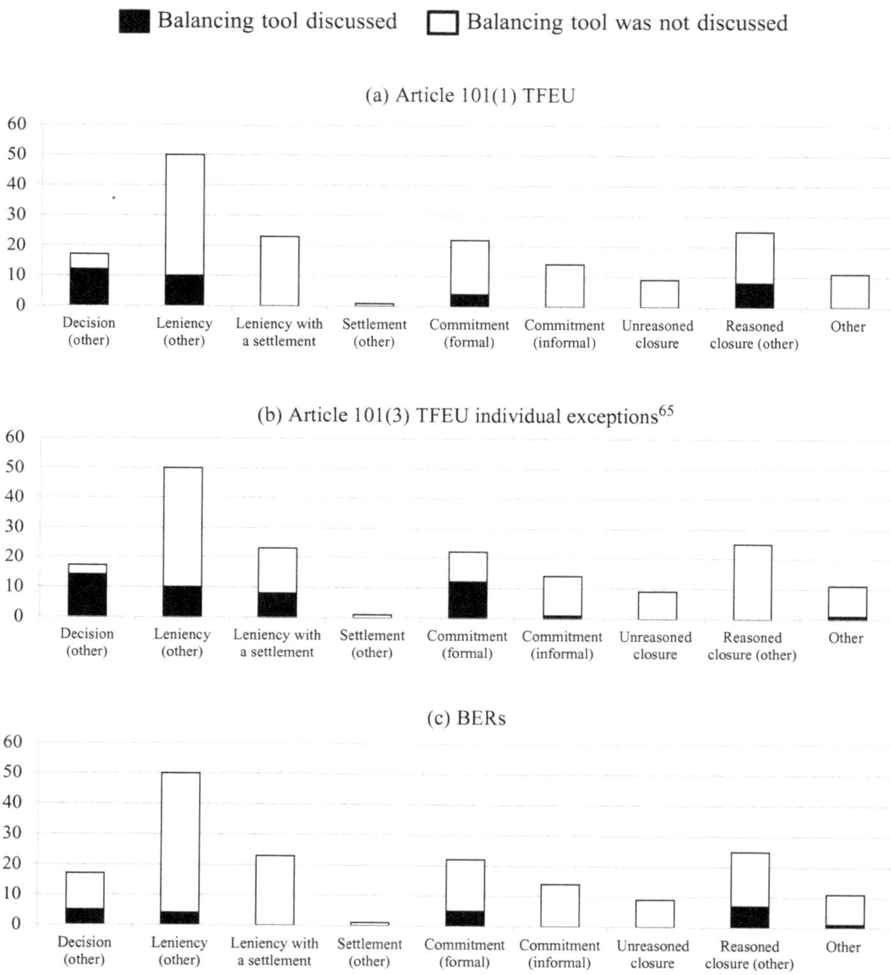

FIGURE 7.2. Balancing tools invoked according to procedure type, Commission (May 2004–2017)[66]

unlikely to be justified by overriding non-competition interests.[67] Arguably, since Article 101(1) and (3) TFEU balancing tools are highly unlikely to apply in such cases, the undertakings have not even attempted to invoke them.

65 Figure 7.2 was originally published in Brook (2020). Reproduced by permission of Oxford University Press.

66 As elaborated in Section 7.6.2, formal commitments are binding commitments accepted pursuant to the procedure specified in Article 9 of Regulation 1/2003. Informal commitments are voluntary behavioural or structural commitments offered by the undertakings, which have led the Commission to close an investigation.

67 See note 46.

In comparison, the Commission has assessed the explicit-substantive balancing tools when examining other types of proceedings. Of the infringement decisions that were not supported by leniency application or concluded by accepting a settlement, 71% have discussed Article 101(1) TFEU balancing tools, 82% have discussed Article 101(3) TFEU individual exemptions, and 30% have discussed BERs. Similarly, Article 101(3) TFEU was frequently discussed when accepting commitments.[68] This confirms the hypothesis that frequent use of leniency applications produces a portfolio of cases that do not require balancing.

Notably, the fact that the explicit-substantive balancing tools were not mentioned more frequently in the Commission's decisions to close the case or accept informal commitments does not mean that non-competition interests did not play a role. As mentioned, the Commission has declared that when it finds that a potential anti-competitive agreement is justified, it would use its priority setting powers to disregard the case or close an investigation.[69] Since the Commission has provided little or no information on the reasons behind those decisions, it is difficult to determine if and how non-competition interests affected the analysis of those cases.

This conclusion that the competition enforcers' detection discretion has produced a portfolio of cases that do not involve balancing questions is also affirmed by comparing the Commission's portfolio of cases to those of the five NCAs examined by this study. Figure 7.3 presents the frequency of use of various procedure types by each competition enforcer.

The figure first demonstrates the divergence in the types of detection strategies used by the competition enforcers. Like the Commission, the German and UK NCAs have devoted much of their effort to leniency and settlements. The same is true, albeit to a less extent for the Dutch NCA. In comparison, the French and Hungarian NCAs have made frequent use of the regular enforcement procedure.

The above, together with the empirical findings presented in previous chapters,[70] reveals a correlation between the types of procedures used and the frequency of examining balancing questions. Enforcers that devoted much of their effort to leniency and settlements (e.g. the Commission and the German and UK NCAs) rarely applied or accepted the explicit-substantive balancing tools of Article 101(1) and (3) TFEU. On the other hand, enforcers that made frequent use of the regular enforcement procedure (e.g. French and Hungarian NCAs) have explicitly engaged in balancing more often.

By the same token, the figure shows that enforcers that dedicated their efforts to issuing informal opinions (e.g. French and Dutch NCAs) and findings of inapplicability (e.g. French, Hungarian, and Dutch NCAs) applied the balancing tools more

[68] The balancing embedded in informal and formal commitments is discussed in Section 7.6.2.

[69] See note 6.

[70] For Article 101(3) TFEU, see Figures 3.1 and 3.11; for BERs, Figures 4.1 and 4.5; for Article 101(1) TFEU, Figures 5.2, 5.4, and 5.5.

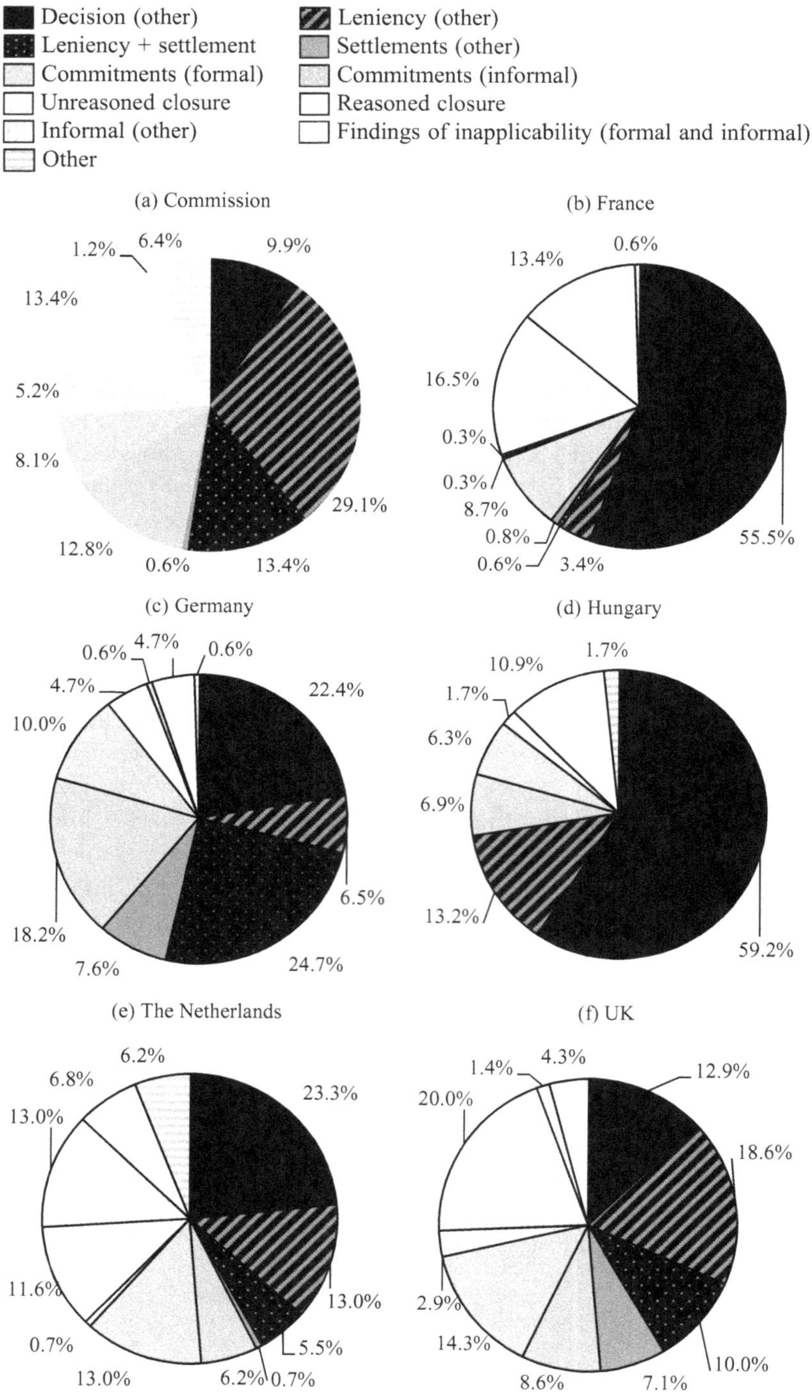

FIGURE 7.3. Detection and outcome discretion, Commission and NCAs (May 2004–2017)

regularly. Those effects of instrument and outcome discretion would be further elaborated in Sections 7.5 and 7.6.

The above findings affirm that procedural choices related to the exercise of detection and outcome discretion influence the composition of the portfolio of cases examined by the competition enforcers and whether or not they are likely to involve balancing questions. Enforcers that devoted much of their effort to leniency and settlements were less likely to be confronted with borderline cases in which they need to balance competition and non-competition interests. As a result, the fact that such enforcers have seldomly applied or accepted the explicit-substantive balancing tools of Article 101(1) and (3) TFEU does not mean that they do not leave room for non-competition interests. Rather, this entails that they have focused on hard-core infringements of competition and did not apply Article 101 TFEU to cases involving balancing questions.

7.3.4 *Interim Conclusion*

This section has proved that following modernisation, the Commission, German, and UK NCAs opted for detection strategies that were less likely to uncover agreements that merited balancing. The French, Hungarian, and Dutch NCAs followed strategies that were more likely to detect agreement raising balancing questions.

The practice of the first group of competition enforcers poses a *threat to the full deterrent effect of Article 101 TFEU*. The reliance on detection strategies that are prone to expose only clear-cut infringements implies that other types of infringements are *de facto* not enforced. As a result, undertakings may assume that anti-competitive agreements that raise balancing questions will not be detected, even when those agreements could not benefit from the explicit-substantive balancing tools of Article 101(1) and (3) TFEU.[71] Therefore, these detection strategies fail to protect competition in agreements that are less likely to be detected by the competition enforcers.

This detection strategy, moreover, threatens the legal certainty of the *explicit-substantive balancing tools*. Competition enforcers that select cases that do not entail balancing have little opportunity to discuss the application of Article 101(1) and (3) TFEU balancing tools in a specific case. This hampers the transparency and predictability of those enforcers' approaches to the explicit-substantive balancing tools.

Finally, the variation in detection strategies may hinder the *uniformity of balancing across the EU*. Undertakings may reasonably expect that certain agreements

[71] This practice also raises concerns as to the effectiveness of leniency policies themselves. Some scholars have pointed out that an effective leniency policy requires a combination of proactive detection strategies. See Kovacic (2015a) and Wils (2016, 350).

raising balancing questions will be detected and enforced by some enforcers and ignored by others. Consequently, non-competition interests are not treated in an equivalent and consistent manner by all competition enforcers.

7.4 TARGET DISCRETION

7.4.1 *Balancing Tool*

Even after a potential anti-competitive agreement has been detected, a competition enforcer may still have the discretion to decide whether to open an investigation and pursue the case. In this context, target discretion refers to the ability of a competition enforcer to concentrate its efforts on a specific infringement, sector, or practice and to avoid enforcing others.[72] Given the scarcity of resources, a degree of target discretion could be seen as an important element for ensuring that competition enforcers prioritise the enforcement of the most serious infringements of competition.[73] At the same time, non-competition interests can influence the exercise of target discretion in three ways:

First, the protection of non-competition interests may *directly* prompt a decision to refrain from pursuing an infringement of Article 101 TFEU. A competition enforcer may choose not to enforce the Article regardless of the agreement's negative effects on competition. Consequently, an anti-competitive agreement will be ignored even if the explicit-substantive balancing tools cannot justify it.[74]

The Dutch NCA's policy on sustainability agreements provides an illustrative example of this effect. In December 2016, the NCA declared that it would no longer exercise its enforcement powers 'against sustainability arrangements that enjoy broad social support if all parties involved such as the government, citizen representatives, and businesses are positive about the arrangements'.[75] This statement has had a significant impact. The NCA will not enforce agreements that are incompatible with Article 101 TFEU on the basis of a political test ('broad social support') that provides the NCA with ample discretion to favour the protection of the environment over competition interests. In fact, the NCA is unlikely to enforce agreements resembling those it had previously prohibited.[76]

Second, target discretion may also serve an *indirect* balancing function. As with the incentives guiding the exercise of detection discretion, a competition enforcer

[72] Lowe (2008, 2); ICN Anti-cartel Enforcement Manual (2010), 32; Petit (2010, 47); ECN Recommendation on the Power to Set Priorities (2013), para 3.

[73] This approach has guided the provisions of the ECN+ Directive, which will be discussed in Section 7.7.

[74] Parret (2009, 34) and Ezrachi (2016, 27).

[75] ACM, Basic Principles for Oversight of Sustainability Agreements (2016). See also Section 3.6.2.2.

[76] As described in Section 3.6.2.2.

may prefer to focus its scarce resources on clear-cut infringements and avoid risky borderline cases.[77] Consequently, a competition enforcer is less likely to pursue cases involving balancing questions that may end in the granting of an exception, the imposition of no or little fine, no observable decision output, or which might be overturned by the reviewing court.

For instance, Chapter 6 discussed the controversial Hungarian law, which has entrusted the Minister for Agriculture and Rural Development to limit competition law enforcement against cartels in the agriculture sector. The Minister may exempt from the national competition law an anti-competitive agreement that guarantees a fair income for farmers. In such a case, the Minister may also order the NCA not to impose a fine for breach of Article 101 TFEU. This law has affected the exercise of the Hungarian NCA's target discretion. The NCA is still competent to investigated anti-competitive agreements in the agriculture sector, to make findings of infringement, and to impose fines where the Minister did not order otherwise. Yet, following the adoption of the law, the NCA has chosen to refrain from enforcement in the agriculture sector altogether. Despite its active enforcement in the past, it has not opened new investigations in this sector and closed all of its active investigations.[78]

Third, the EU *multi-level enforcement regime* provides the Commission and NCAs with additional leeway for balancing. Article 13(2) of Regulation 1/2003 declares that when an NCA or the Commission receives a complaint against an agreement that 'has already been dealt with' by another competition enforcer, it may reject it. The GC has interpreted this provision broadly. In *EasyJet (2015)*, it submitted that the Commission is entitled to reject a complaint that was previously rejected by an NCA on priority setting grounds, even if the NCA had not examined the merits of the case.[79] This principle is applicable even if the NCA rejected the complaint in the course of an investigation conducted under a separate provision of *national law* (e.g. Dutch aviation law, in the case at hand), as long as the review was concluded 'in the light of the rules of EU competition law'.[80] The exercise of target discretion by one enforcer, even as part of applying a sector regulation, may thus preclude the examination of a complaint by another enforcer.

In *Agria Polska (2017)*, the GC further extended the competition enforcers' discretion to reject complaints on priority setting grounds. The Court affirmed the Commission's decision to reject a complaint that had previously been rejected by the Polish NCA for failure to meet the one-year limitation period specified under

77 ICN Anti-cartel Enforcement Manual (2010), 44. See also Sections 7.2 and 7.3.1.

78 See Section 6.3.4.

79 T-355/13 EasyJet (2015), para 27. See also T-201/11 Si.mobil (2015), para 47–50. In T-531/18 LL-Carpenter (2020), para 48, the GC clarified that a complaint would be deemed to be 'dealt with' when a competition enforcer had *examined* the complaint on the basis of EU competition law, even when the competition enforcer has not adopted a decision on the matter. See also T-574/14 EAEPC (2018), para 134–135.

80 T-355/13 EasyJet (2015), para 46.

Polish law.[81] Hence, a national procedural law, detached from any substantive competitive analysis, had justified the rejection of a complaint by the Commission.

The GC's judgments in *EasyJet* and *Agria Polska* mean that a competition enforcer can dispose of legally or politically sensitive agreements without weighing their bearing on competition and non-competition interests. The competition enforcers are motivated to 'play hot potato' – i.e. reject a complaint on priority setting grounds or on the basis of other laws that are not related to competition.[82] Instead of applying the complex analysis of Article 101(1) or (3) TFEU exceptions, an enforcer can simply elect to close the case.

Target discretion, therefore, can serve as a balancing tool. A decision not to pursue an agreement due to non-competition interests carries an impact similar to an NCA's no grounds for action findings.[83] In both cases, competition enforcers elect not to enforce Article 101 TFEU because of certain benefits produced by the agreement. Nevertheless, unlike the explicit-substantive balancing tools, the conditions for balancing by target discretion are not bound by EU law. Moreover, as the next section shows, the scope of such discretion varies between the various competition enforcers.

7.4.2 *Scope of Target Discretion*

EU law neither directs nor restricts the exercise of target discretion.[84] Rather, as mentioned, the ECN has explicitly acknowledged that the selection of cases may centre on non-competition interests.[85] Since the rules governing the exercise of target discretion are subject to national laws, they differ across the EU.[86] This section describes the varying degrees of target discretion. It illustrates that while some enforcers enjoy wide target discretion, others are subject to a specific prioritisation criterion or are required to examine every case brought to their attention. The degree for target discretion informs the scope of balancing.

7.4.2.1 Wide Target Discretion: Commission, German, and UK NCAs

The first group of competition enforcers has a wide margin of discretion to select and prioritise their enforcement targets.[87] The Commission is a good example of an

81 T-480/15 Agria Polska (2017), para 5, 64, 77–78.

82 As aptly described by De Pablo (2015).

83 On no grounds for action decisions, see Sections 7.6.3 and 2.3.3.3.

84 In particular, in T-355/13 EasyJet (2015), para 20, the GC emphasised that the review of the exercise of the NCAs' target discretion is a matter for national courts alone. Nevertheless, pursuant to Article 2 TEU, the enforcement of EU law in general, and priority setting in particular, is subject to the general requirements of the rule of law, which underpin the EU legal system. See Cseres and Mendes (2014, 489).

85 See note 15.

86 Commission Impact Assessment accompanying the ECN+ Directive Proposal (2017), 17. See also Petit (2010, 6) and Blanco and De Pablo (2012, 62–63).

87 ICN Anti-cartel Enforcement Manual (2010), 33, 43.

authority having wide target discretion.[88] The EU Courts have regularly affirmed the Commission's broad discretion to prioritise its enforcement efforts in matters that do not fall within its exclusive competence.[89] In *Masterfoods (2000)*, the CJEU linked this discretion to the Commission's task of defining and implementing the orientation of EU competition policy. Performing this task effectively, according to the Court, requires the Commission to be able to decide whether to pursue a case.[90]

Chapter 2 illustrated that up to the middle of the third enforcement period, the Commission focused its enforcement efforts towards practices hampering market integration. Yet, starting in the mid-1990s, the Commission decided to refocus its target discretion on cartels, noting that they bear the most harm on consumer welfare.[91] From the 2000s onwards, the harm to consumer welfare has become the declared principle guiding the Commission's target discretion.[92]

As with the Commission, the German[93] and UK[94] NCAs enjoy wide target discretion. At times, the German NCA has explicitly used its target discretion to account for non-economic benefits that could not have been accepted under the explicit-substantive balancing tools. In *Associations of ophthalmologists (2012)*, for example, it closed the investigation after finding that a joint bid of several associations of ophthalmologists for a public health insurance fund tender had infringed the national provision equivalent to Article 101(1) TFEU. The NCA linked the termination of the proceedings to a German law providing that the association of

88 EU law only binds the Commission's priority setting powers when dealing with complaints, as elaborated in Section 7.4.2.3. This is reflected by Regulation 773/2004 relating to the Conduct of Proceedings (2004), Articles 2, 5 and 7. See also Blanco (2006, 194–206); ECN Decision Making Powers Report (2012), 51.

89 T-24/90 Automec (1992), para 75; Commission Notice on Handling Complaints (2004), para 41. Under the old enforcement regime of Regulation 17/62, the Commission examined all notifications for negative clearance and exemptions. Under Regulation 1/2003, this principle is only relevant in the context of the withdrawal of BERs in individual cases by virtue of Article 29 of the Regulation.

90 C-344/98 Masterfoods (2000), para 46, as repeated in T-355/13 EasyJet (2015), para 17; T-480/15 Agria Polska (2017), para 34; T-712/14 Watch Repair (2017), para 34. In the same vein, the EU Courts held that an undertaking could not escape a Commission's investigation solely by claiming that the Commission had failed to investigate or prosecute other infringements. Prioritisation decisions would only be considered a misuse of power when it was evident that they had been taken with the exclusive or main purpose of achieving an end other than the enforcement of Articles 101 TFEU. See T-219/99 British Airways (2003), para 66–70; C-186/02P C-188/02P Ramondín (2004), para 44; T-48/00 Corus (2004), para 212; T-271/03 Deutsche Telekom (2008), para 243, 270.

91 Policy report (2000), 35; policy report (2001), 24, 30.

92 Policy report (2002), 32; policy report (2003), 5; policy report (2004), 14; policy report (2005), 199; policy report (2010), 5–7. This also applies with respect to Article 102 TFEU enforcement. See Commission Article 102 Guidance (2009), para 19.

93 ECN Decision Making Powers Report (2012), 53. See also Petit (2010, 49) and Wils (2011, 374–375).

94 1071/2/1/06 Cityhook (2007), para 148. Yet, the UK NCA is required to investigate 'super-complaints' filed by a designated consumer body, as detailed in Section 7.4.2.3.

health insurance physicians could lawfully submit such an offer.[95] It explained that although the result of the case was 'unsatisfactory', as it hampers the goals of competition in terms of quality and price, the German law justified the termination of the proceedings.[96]

Similarly, the German NCA was requested to examine an array of sustainability initiatives by which industry members have agreed on voluntary standards aiming at environmental protection, animal welfare, and social aims. Some of those initiatives were also supported by political parties. The NCA noted the difficulty of assessing the compatibility of those agreements with Article 101 TFEU, given the unclear role of non-competition interests and the need to strike a balance between the competing aims. Hence, while it made reservations with respect to some arrangements, it had explicitly made use of its discretionary powers to decide not to enforce others.[97]

The UK NCA has constrained its target discretion powers by adopting designated prioritisation rules.[98] It has declared that it targets cases that deter and influence anti-competitive behaviour that poses the greatest threat to consumer welfare.[99] Indeed, the UK NCA has closed probes into serious restrictions of competition (i.e. hardcore restrictions) because they had little effect on consumer welfare.[100] The NCA states that the impact on consumer welfare is balanced on a case-by-case basis against the strategic significance of the case (i.e. if the case establishes or tests a new legal or economic approach or clarifies the law in areas of practical commercial importance).[101] Moreover, political forces also influence the prioritisation. The NCA has proclaimed that when setting its priorities, it gives regard to the UK government's non-binding ministerial statement of strategic priorities of the NCA.[102]

Their wide target discretion entrusts the Commission and the German and UK NCAs with an implicit-procedural balancing tool. They may close an investigation due to non-competition interests without publishing or explaining their decisions. Such balancing will remain in the dark matter of the enforcement.

[95] Sozialgesetzbuch Fünftes Buch, Section 73c SGB V.

[96] B3–130/11 Associations of Ophthalmologists (2012), 2–3. See also Kleine and Rübel (2015, 69).

[97] German NCA's activity report (2015/2016), 54.

[98] CMA Prioritisation Principles (2017). This guidance is based on the earlier OFT Prioritisation Principles (2008). On target discretion in the UK, see also Lester (2009).

[99] CMA Prioritisation Principles (2017), para 1.3, 2.1.

[100] In CE/2471-03 Oakley (2008), the UK NCA closed an investigation into a price-fixing agreement after the parties agreed to terminate the agreement, noting that a further investigation would yield only 'extremely limited' consumer benefit. In Visa sponsorship arrangements for Olympics 2012 (2011), the UK NCA closed an investigation into Visa's sponsorship arrangements with the London Organising Committee of the Olympic Games and Paralympic Games, which conferred payment card exclusivity on Visa for the purchase of official Olympic merchandise and for the use of ATM machines at official Olympic Games venues. The NCA explained that the agreements were 'unlikely to give rise to material consumer harm'.

[101] CMA Prioritisation Principles (2017), para 4.

[102] *Ibid*, para 2.1.

7.4.2.2 Public Interest Criterion: Dutch and Hungarian NCAs

The second group of competition enforcers is required to consider a 'public interest' criterion when deciding whether or not to take up a case.[103] Accordingly, such enforcers are obliged to pursue all potential infringements of Article 101 TFEU that come to their attention unless public interests justify otherwise. As detailed below, the substance of this obligation is reliant on national interpretation.

In the Netherlands, for example, the NCA has declared that it exercises its target discretion on the basis of the following two-fold criteria:[104] First, as with the Commission and UK NCA, the Dutch NCA assesses the impact of an agreement on consumer welfare. Yet, the Dutch assessment is distinctive from the other enforcers. In line with the Dutch NCA's broad definition of consumer welfare,[105] the prioritisation focuses not only on short-term economic benefits.[106] The Dutch NCA pursues cases leading to '*sustainable* welfare growth in the *broadest sense of the word*'.[107] It takes into account '*any potential harm* and *social harm* that can be avoided or limited by an enforcement action'. It balances the short- and long-term harm to consumers, as well as indirect effects on innovation, quality, and other markets.[108]

Second, the Dutch NCA examines the *social relevance* of its actions, namely the magnitude of the public interest for an enforcement action. In particular, well-functioning markets, the optimal regulation of legal and natural monopolies, and consumer protection must be given priority.[109]

The combination of a broad consumer welfare standard with the public interest test openly requires the Dutch NCA to take non-competition interests into account when exercising its target discretion. This leaves room for the consideration of economic and non-economic benefits, affecting both current and future consumers.[110]

[103] ECN Decision Making Powers Report (2012), 51.

[104] ACM Prioritisation of Enforcement Investigations (2016). In addition, the Dutch NCA takes into consideration how well it will be able to enforce the case effectively and efficiently.

[105] See Sections 2.6.3.2 and 3.6.2.2.

[106] Conforming to its general practice, the UK NCA adheres to a narrow definition of consumer welfare in this regard, focusing essentially on static and dynamic efficiencies. See CMA Prioritisation Principles (2017), para 4.

[107] Emphasis added ACM Strategy and Enforcement Priorities with regard to Vertical Agreements (2015), 11.

[108] Emphasis added. ACM Prioritisation of Enforcement Investigations (2016), 2. See also ACM Strategy and Enforcement Priorities with regard to Vertical Agreements (2015), 11. In 6824 Health insurers (2010), 2, for example, the NCA rejected a complaint from health care insurers, noting that there was little evidence that the alleged infringement would increase prices and thus harm consumers. See also 7213 NPO (2012), 6–7; 7377 SGR c.s. (2013), 2.

[109] ACM Prioritisation of Enforcement Investigations (2016), 2.

[110] A similar rationale is reflected by the Dutch NCA policy on sustainability agreements, as detailed at the beginning of this section.

The Dutch NCA's decision in *VGT (2005, 2006)* illustrates how target discretion can strike a balance between competition and labour interests.[111] In that case, textile retailer trade unions had negotiated a new collective labour agreement with the Association for Wholesale Retailers in the Textile Business (VGT). After negotiation failed, VGT advised its members to unilaterally modify the employment conditions applicable to new personnel. Subsequently, the trade unions submitted a complaint to the NCA, arguing that the proposed employment conditions contained anti-competitive price arrangements. The NCA initially rejected the complaint on the basis of an Article 101(1) TFEU balancing tool. It asserted that VGT had not acted as an undertaking when negotiating the collective labour agreements.

Upon reassessment of the case, however, VGT's recommendation was found to infringe Article 101(1) TFEU.[112] Nevertheless, the Dutch NCA decided to reject the complaint with reference to its priority setting powers. It declared that the dispute merited striking a balance between competition and social interests. Although the NCA was formally competent to balance the competing interests, it believed that this task ought to be performed by the legislator, or at least by a civil court.[113] Consequently, an infringement of Article 101 TFEU that would not have been accepted under Article 101(1) or (3) TFEU explicit-substantive balancing tools ended up not being enforced.

The Hungarian NCA, like its Dutch counterpart, is also obliged to consider public interest criteria when deciding whether to pursue an infringement.[114] The NCA's policy papers have interpreted this obligation along the lines of the UK NCA's prioritisation approach, focusing on the degree of competitive harm, the number of affected consumers, and the significance of the case for the evolution of competition policy.[115]

The decisional practice of the Hungarian NCA, nevertheless, had actually taken account of a broader range of non-competition interests. In *Network of Pharmacists (2008)*, for example, the Hungarian Chamber of Pharmacists and other associations allegedly exchanged information on drug prices and attempted to hinder the distribution of drugs outside a network of pharmacies. The undertakings claimed that the practice was justified as a state action since a national law called for the price recommendations to be issued. Yet, the NCA rejected the claim, explaining that a national law could not trump Article 101 TFEU. At the same time, the NCA closed the investigation on the grounds of a lack of public interest. It noted,

111 5170 VGT (2005) and 5170 VGT (2006), as confirmed by the Court in MEDED 06/4638 STRN VGT (2007), 5–6. The 2005 decision, although unpublished, is summarised in the 2006 decision.

112 On the reassessment procedure, see Section 2.6.3.3.

113 5170 VGT (2006), para 31. See also Dutch NCA annual report (2006), 63.

114 Hungarian Competition Act, Article 67(2). See also Hegymegi-Barakonyi (2009, 10); ECN Decision Making Powers Report (2012), 72–73.

115 GVH Fundamental Principles of Competition Policy (2007), 11–12; GVH Strategy for Competition Procedure Initiation (2013), Section 3.

inter-alia, that imposing a fine for an infringement would be inappropriate in light of the national law.[116] Consequently, while the national law could not justify an exception based on Article 101 TFEU, it did, however, vindicate a decision not to enforce it.

Competition enforcers that are bound by a public interest criterion are overtly required to examine non-competition interests when exercising their target discretion. As such, non-competition interests directly and openly play a role in exercising target discretion.

7.4.2.3 Legality Principle: French NCA and Complaints

The third group of competition enforcers enjoys no target discretion. They are bound by the so-called legality principle, entailing that they must commence an investigation into any potential infringement that comes to their attention.[117] Such an obligation limits the possibility of using target discretion as a balancing tool.

The French NCA, for example, is obliged to open a formal investigation unless a case is deemed inadmissible (e.g. falls outside the NCA's competence) or manifestly lacks supporting evidence. Closing an investigation requires a formal and reasoned decision.[118] Since 2009, however, this rule has not applied to *ex officio* investigations.[119]

Similarly, certain competition enforcers that for the most part enjoy wide target discretion are bound by a more limited legality principle when assessing complaints.[120] While those enforcers are not required to investigate each complaint, they do have a duty to examine all matters of fact and law brought to their attention and to provide reasoning for their decisions.[121] Such a rule applies to the Commission,[122] the Dutch NCA,[123] and the UK NCA with respect to 'super-complaints' lodged by designated consumer organisations.[124]

7.4.3 *Empirical Indications*

The exercise of target discretion, as mentioned, is often not fully published or reasoned. As it mostly lies in the dark matter of the enforcement, it is difficult to provide comprehensive empirical evidence on balancing by target discretion. Yet,

[116] Vj-33/2007 Network of Pharmacists (2008), para 5, 39, 51.

[117] ICN Anti-cartel Enforcement Manual (2010), 32; ECN Decision Making Powers Report (2012), 51; ECN Recommendation on the Power to Set Priorities (2013), para 3.

[118] Idot (2015, 53–54) and Lachnit (2016, 46).

[119] French Commercial Code, L 462-8.

[120] ECN Decision Making Powers Report (2012), 71–72.

[121] With respect to the Commission's duty, see C-450/98P IECC (2001), para 57; T-355/13 EasyJet (2015), para 18; T-480/15 Agria Polska (2017), para 36. See also Wils (2017, 38).

[122] Regulation 773/2004 relating to the Conduct of Proceedings (2004), Article 7; Commission Notice on the Handling of Complaints (2004), para 41–44; C-210/81 REVOX (1983), para 19; C-119/97P Ufex (1999), para 86; T-24/90 Automec (1992), para 77, 85; T-219/99 British Airways (2003), para 68. See also Cseres and Mendes (2014, 491–494).

[123] ECN Decision Making Powers Report (2012), 73.

[124] UK Enterprise Act, Section 11(1); ECN Decision Making Powers Report (2012), 73.

this section offers a number of empirical indications supporting the hypothesis that target discretion may have been used as a substitute to Article 101(1) and (3) TFEU balancing tools following modernisation. Those indications relate to the large number of discontinued investigations, the steep decrease in Article 101(3) TFEU claims following modernisation, the influence of national approaches to the relevant types of benefits under the explicit-substantive balancing tools, and the manner in which the competition enforcers addressed the challenges arising from the coronavirus crisis.

7.4.3.1 Discontinued Investigations

The empirical findings demonstrate that the Commission and NCAs closed a large number of investigations without adopting a formal decision. This suggests that there was room for balancing by target discretion that may be hidden within the dark matter of the enforcement. Figure 7.4 summarises the number of Article 101 and 102 TFEU investigations notified to the ECN network between May 2004 and December 2017. It shows that while the competition enforcers opened 2361 investigations, only 1233 draft decisions were notified to the ECN pursuant to Article 11(4) of Regulation 1/2003. In other words, almost half the investigations were closed without a decision and thus were not notified.

As *Svetlicinii et al.* have noted, this ratio demonstrates that a significant number of investigations are not subject to the scrutiny of the Commission

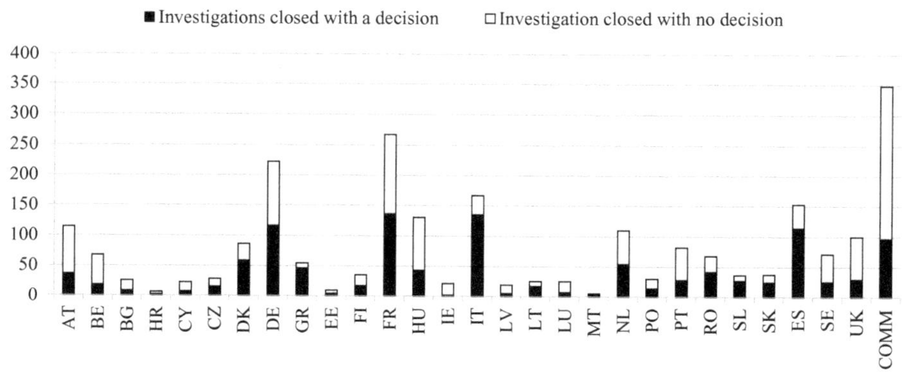

FIGURE 7.4. Discontinued investigations, Commission and NCAs (May 2004–2017)
Data processed from the ECN website. See http://ec.europa.eu/competition/ecn/statistics.html. The number of investigations opened refers to formal investigation measures commenced by the NCAs and notified to the ECN pursuant to Article 11(3) of Regulation 1/2003. The number of investigations closed without a decision refers to open investigations for which the Member States adopted neither a decision requiring that an infringement be brought to an end nor a decision accepting commitments or withdrawing the benefits of a BER, or failed to make notification of any such decision

and ECN.[125] Clearly, not all of those cases involve balancing questions. It is fair to assume that many of the investigations were discontinued due to lack of evidence or since the practice was unlikely to infringe Article 101 TFEU. Yet, the existence of such dark matter implies that the NCAs have the opportunity to balance when applying their target discretion. This, together with the competition enforcers' incentives to use target discretion as a balancing tool, reinforces the hypothesis that such balancing is taking place to a certain extent.

7.4.3.2 Steep Decrease in Article 101(3) TFEU Defence Claims[126]

The use of target discretion for balancing purposes is supported by the empirical findings pointing to a shift in the *nature* of the agreements reviewed by the competition enforcers following modernisation. Chapters 3–5 have indicated that prior to modernisation, when the Commission had a limited target discretion, it had examined a relatively large number of agreements involving balancing questions. Since the Commission could not fully choose its cases, it had to resolve those balancing questions by applying the explicit-substantive balancing tools.

This has changed when the modernisation has enhanced the Commission's target discretion. Since May 2004, per the Commission's declared policy,[127] it has applied Article 101 TFEU almost exclusively to clear-cut and hard-core restrictions of competition.[128] Accordingly, while the Commission's total number of Article 101 TFEU enforcement actions was reduced following modernisation,[129] the number of prohibition decisions against hard-core cartels significantly increased. During the 1990s, the Commission issued an average of 2 prohibition decisions per year against cartels. From the beginning of the 2000s, however, it issued an average of around 6.5 prohibition decisions per year against cartels.[130] As the number of proceedings against cartels tripled, the fines increased by more than tenfold, indicating that the Commission dealt with particularly serious violations.[131]

Even when the Commission examined an Article 101(3) TFEU defence following modernisation, an exception was often promptly rejected. The empirical findings indicate that since May 2004, the Commission has applied Article 101(3) TFEU mainly to cases involving clear-cut infringements such as price fixing, market

[125] Svetlicinii et al. (2018, 2). On the dark matter of the enforcement, see also Section 1.3.1.
[126] I have made a similar argument in Brook (2020, 463–465, 467–470).
[127] Policy report (2004), 36; policy report (2005), 4, 62; policy report (2006), 11.
[128] This was also established by the empirical findings presented in Section 7.3.3.
[129] See Figure 3.1.
[130] Commission's cartels statistics (updated as of March 2018), see http://ec.europa.eu/competition/cartels/statistics/statistics.pdf, Tables 1.9 and 1.10.
[131] *Ibid*, Table 1.2.

sharing, and restrictions having equivalent effects.[132] In such cases, the Commission typically rejected the possibility of granting an exception outright.[133] In other words, the focus on clear-cut infringements following modernisation entails that the Commission will rarely be required to balance competition and non-competition interests in a specific case.

The change in the nature of the cases enforced also explains the decrease in the number of cases in which the undertakings *invoked* Article 101(3) TFEU as a defence (which was dubbed as the 'death' of Article 101(3) TFEU).[134] As mentioned, prior to the entry into force of Regulation 1/2003, the Article was examined in 57% of the Commission's Article 101 TFEU enforcement actions. Yet, *immediately* after Regulation 1/2003 came into force, there was a steep decline in the number of proceedings in which Article 101(3) TFEU was invoked as a defence. Not only has the Commission never accepted an Article 101(3) TFEU defence following May 2004, but the defence was only examined in 25% of the enforcement actions.

The limited use of Article 101(3) TFEU was also evident in cases taken place in front of the NCAs. The empirical findings presented in Section 3.6.1 revealed that like the Commission, most of the NCAs have discussed the conditions of Article 101 (3) TFEU only in a small percentage of their proceedings. While some of them have accepted an Article 101(3) TFEU defence, they have done so only in a handful of cases.

Some commentators have tied this limited consideration of Article 101(3) TFEU in national proceedings to the NCAs' limited competences to apply this Article. They maintained that the provision of Article 5 of Regulation 1/2003, as interpreted by *Tele2Polska*, disincentivises NCAs from dedicating their scarce resources to issuing 'no grounds for action' findings that are concluded without an observable decision output.[135] Arguably, NCAs are likely to prefer using their target discretion to settle cases that raise balancing questions instead of engaging in a complex and resource-intensive Article 101(3) TFEU analysis.

The hypothesis that competition enforcers will tend to use their target discretion to balance instead of applying the explicit-substantive balancing tools is further supported by studying the effects of national procedural reforms on the enforcement patterns. From the five NCAs examined in this study, such reforms have occurred in France and Hungary.

In the past, the French NCA had only limited target discretion. Until 2009, it was obliged to undertake a formal investigation and issue a reasoned decision with respect to any possible infringement that had come to its attention.[136] This changed

[132] See Annex A, Section 7.1.
[133] See Annex A, Section 3.7.
[134] This decrease was presented and discussed in Section 3.2 and Figure 3.1.
[135] Petit (2011) and Svetlicinii et al. (2018, 428). The implications of *Tele2Polska* were discussed in Section 2.3.3.3.
[136] Idot (2015, 53–54) and Lachnit (2016, 46).

when a reform has bestowed the NCA with the powers to open and conclude investigations on its own motion.[137] When concluding such investigations, the NCA is no longer obliged to reason its decision for taking on or disregarding a case.[138] The empirical findings show that the NCA's enhanced powers have changed its enforcement patterns. In particular, Section 3.6.1 disclosed that shortly after the reform, the French NCA ceased to issue 'no grounds for action' findings.

A similar trend is observed in Hungary. The old national regime had afforded the NCA limited enforcement discretion. Like the old EU regime, the national enforcement was based on a notification system, in which the NCA had to explain whether or not the notified agreement has infringed competition or could be justified by overriding non-competition interests. The empirical findings indicate that most of the agreements in which an Article 101(3) TFEU defence was accepted in Hungary were actually notified to the NCA.[139] After a national reform switched to a self-assessment regime in July 2005, the Hungarian NCA has rarely adopted 'no grounds for action' findings.

In light of the above, the fact that Article 101(3) TFEU was hardly discussed and accepted by the competition enforcers following modernisation is not necessarily tied to limiting the role of non-competition interests under the Article in the post-modernisation era. Rather, the empirical findings insinuate that the competition enforcers might have preferred to use their target discretion to take into account non-competition interests instead of applying the conditions of Article 101(3) TFEU. By focusing their enforcement efforts on clear-cut infringements that are unlikely to be justified under Article 101(3) TFEU, the Commission and NCAs have avoided the need to assess the role of non-competition interests under this provision altogether. Moreover, this gave them the freedom to account for non-competition interests without being constrained by or needing to deviate from the principles developed in their policy papers and decisional practice on the application of Article 101(3) TFEU.

7.4.3.3 Influence of National Approaches to the Relevant Types of Benefits under the Explicit-Substantive Balancing Tools

The empirical findings presented in Chapters 3–5 have shown that the competition enforcers that have interpreted Article 101(1) and (3) TFEU balancing tools as limited to the consideration of narrow economic benefits have rarely rendered decisions in which they have explicitly rejected the possibility to take non-economic benefits into account.[140]

[137] French Commercial Code, Article L 462-4. This reform was already discussed in Section 7.3.2.

[138] French Commercial Code, L 462-8.

[139] Vj-169/2003/68 Fertilizers (2004); Vj-132/2004/26 Card issuance (2004); Vj-200/2004/13 Funeral service in Szolnok (2005); Vj-178/2004/5 Pont Audio (2005); Vj-23/2005 Rába Group and Integris (2005); Vj-207/2004/51 Rába IT agreement (2005).

[140] See Figures 3.2 and 3.12 and Sections 4.4.1.3 and 5.4.1.2.

For instance, while the Commission and UK NCA pronounced a strict-narrow approach to the Article in their policy papers, they almost never declared that a specific agreement cannot be justified by overriding non-economic benefits. In contrast, NCAs that were willing to consider non-economic benefits under Article 101(3) TFEU, such as the Netherlands and France, have taken up cases involving the consideration of such benefits.

This does not necessarily entail that the first group of competition enforcers has not taken into account non-economic benefits. Arguably, competition enforcers that have excluded the consideration of non-economic benefits from the scope of Article 101(1) and (3) TFEU were bound to use their target discretion in some cases to avoid deviating from their declared balancing approaches. To this extent, they used their target discretion to account for non-competition interests they were not willing to take into account under the explicit-substantive balancing tools. By refraining from investigating such agreements in the first place, they averted the need to engage in contentious balancing issues, which are likely to encounter legal or political opposition.

7.4.3.4 Influence of Unique National Balancing Tools

The use of target discretion instead of applying the explicit-substantive balancing tools is also supported by examining the effects of national balancing tools on cases having an effect on trade between Member States.

The empirical findings presented throughout this book revealed that when a Member State limited the application of the national equivalent prohibition, the NCAs have also mostly refrained from enforcing Article 101 TFEU against the same agreement. For instance, NCAs did not apply Article 101 TFEU to mixed cases that would have qualified for an exception under a national BER.[141] Comparably, following the codification of the 'nature and purpose' exception for purely national cases under Dutch law, the NCA did not bring actions against collective bargaining agreements affecting trade between Member States.[142]

The competition enforcers were also influenced by issue-specific laws. Chapter 6 has shown that after a Hungarian law protected certain national agriculture agreements from the national cartel prohibition, the Hungarian NCA stopped investigating agriculture agreements altogether. After a German law granted an exception from the national cartel prohibition to forest-related services, the German court opposed opening a case on this matter on procedural grounds.[143]

Put differently, there are several indications that NCAs have used their target discretion to extend the protection afforded by national balancing tools to cases

[141] See Section 4.4.1.3.
[142] See Section 5.4.1.
[143] See Section 6.3.4.

having an effect on trade between Member States. Although such agreements could not have been formally exempted, the NCAs have decided not to pursue such cases.

7.4.3.5 Addressing Coronavirus Challenges

The use of target discretion to account for non-competition interests was particularly evident in the competition enforcers' responses to the outbreak of the coronavirus pandemic. Competition enforcers around the globe had quickly come to a consensus that the unprecedented health, social, and economic challenges have justified a temporary relaxation of the competition rules. A degree of cooperation between competitors was deemed necessary to safeguard an array of non-competition interests related to the protection of public health and safety and ensuring a stable supply of essential products.[144]

In particular, shortly after the outbreak of the pandemic in Europe in early 2020, the ECN published a joint statement on behalf of the NCAs. The statement declares that the ECN understands the need for cooperation among companies in order to ensure the supply and fair distribution of scarce products to all consumers. Therefore, it concludes that '[i]n the current circumstances, the ECN *will not actively intervene* against *necessary and temporary* measures put in place in order to avoid a shortage of supply'.[145]

Two weeks later, the Commission published its Coronavirus Temporary Framework (2020), setting out the main criteria it would follow when assessing cooperation projects aimed at addressing a shortage of supply. The Framework had mostly justified the consideration of non-competition interests with reference to Article 101(3) TFEU, as interpreted by the Commission's Article 101(3), Horizontal, and Vertical Guidelines.[146] The Commission added that undertakings might need specific guidance on their cooperation initiatives in order to facilitate their self-assessment. Accordingly, it noted that it would be willing to provide undertakings with *ad hoc* feedback or comfort letters discussing the legality of specific cooperation initiatives related to the coronavirus outbreak.[147]

The Commission observed that cooperation in the health sector might even need to go further than what is permissible under the regular competition rules. For example, cooperation may be required to overcome critical supply shortages by increasing and optimising production, where such re-organisation would allow

[144] See, for instance, ICN Statement on Competition During and After the COVID-19 Pandemic (2020); ECN Statement on Application of Competition Law During the Corona Crisis (2020); Commissions Coronavirus Temporary Framework (2020), para 3–4, 19; DoJ and FTC Joint Antitrust Statement Regarding COVID-19 (2020).

[145] Emphasis added. ECN Statement on Application of Competition Law During the Corona Crisis (2020).

[146] Commissions Coronavirus Temporary Framework (2020), para 6–13.

[147] *Ibid*, para 7, 17–18. The use of comfort letters is a form of instrument discretion, which will be discussed in Section 7.5.3.

producers to satisfy the demand for urgently needed medicine across the EU. The Commission held that while such information exchange and coordination between undertakings are problematic, 'in the current exceptional circumstances, such measures would not be problematic under EU competition law or – in view of the emergency situation and temporary nature – *they would not give rise to an enforcement priority* for the Commission, to the extent that such measures would be: (i) *designed and objectively necessary* to actually increase output in the most efficient way to address or avoid a shortage of supply of essential products or services, such as those that are used to treat COVID-19 patients; (ii) *temporary in nature* (i.e. to be applied only as long there is a risk of shortage or in any event during the COVID-19 outbreak); and (iii) *not exceeding what is strictly necessary* to achieve the objective of addressing or avoiding the shortage of supply'.[148]

The legal basis for tolerating cooperation agreements in the health sector is unclear. It seems that the Commission has created a new balancing tool, tailored to the coronavirus pandemic. This new balancing tool is not anchored in any of the traditional explicit-substantive balancing tools. Instead, the Commission used its target discretion – the power not to initiate an infringement proceeding – to introduce a new tool based on a proportionality legal balancing test.

Moreover, as presented in Section 5.2.2.5, the Temporary Framework has also deviated from the normal application of the EU state action defence. Contrary to the CJEU case law, the Commission has stated that the fact that cooperation is encouraged or coordinated by a public authority would be a 'relevant factor' supporting a conclusion that such cooperation 'would not be problematic under EU competition law or *would not be an enforcement priority* for the Commission'.[149] By arguing that in such cases cooperation may not be incompatible with the EU competition rules, the Temporary Framework seems to attempt to alter the explicit-substantive balancing tool embedded in the EU state action defence.

In other words, instead of interpreting Article 101(1) and (3) TFEU balancing tools in light of the exceptional circumstances arising from the coronavirus outbreak, the Commission has referred to its target discretion, noting that certain anti-competitive agreements that contribute to stable supply and to public health will not be enforced. This created an alternative route to the explicit-substantive balancing tools. As a form of enforcement discretion, balancing under this new tool goes mostly unpublished, is not fully reasoned, and is not subject to judicial review. Moreover, it is not binding on other competition enforcers.

The downside of this new balancing tool was illustrated by the comfort letter in *Medicines for Europe (2020)*, issued by the Commission on the same day the Temporary Framework was published. The letter was addressed to an association of pharmaceutical manufacturers, the members of which supply around 70% of the

[148] Emphasis added. *Ibid*, para 15–16.
[149] *Ibid*.

medicine in Europe, examining its voluntary cooperation project to address the risk of shortages of critical hospital medicines for the treatment of coronavirus patients. The initiative was supported and monitored by the Commissioner for Health and Food Safety and the Directorate-General for Health and Food Safety (DG SANTE). On the basis of the criteria set forth in the Temporary Framework and additional informal commitments provided by the association, the Commission concluded that 'in the present exceptional circumstances the cooperation practices as set out above *do not raise concerns* under Article 101 [TFEU]'.[150]

The Commission did not explain if the project was permitted due to the EU's or its Member States' involvement, if it can be justified under Article 101(3) TFEU or as an inherent restriction, or whether it was tolerated under the Commission's target discretion. While the comfort letter may have addressed the concerns of the association of pharmaceutical manufacturers and its members, it cannot be used by other undertakings to self-assess the compatibility of their agreements with Article 101 TFEU. It also does not enable the public or EU Courts to critique the balance struck between competition and non-competition interests in that case. Finally, as a non-binding comfort letter, "the Commission's analysis also does not preclude another competition enforcer or a private applicant from bringing an action against this project".

Many of the NCAs have also declared that they will tolerate or refrain from enforcing anti-competitive agreements necessary for safeguarding public policy during the exceptional circumstances of the coronavirus. Similarly to the Commission's Temporary Framework, the NCAs have also not identified a clear legal basis for balancing. They created alternative balancing tools based on legal proportionality tests, sometimes with slightly different conditions than those identified by the Commission, to guide the exercise of their target discretion.

For example, the president of the German NCA declared that 'the Bundeskartellamt *will not actively intervene* against co-ordinations put in place in order to cope with the COVID-19 crisis under the following conditions: (i) they do not *go beyond what is necessary* to generate efficiencies, (ii) the undertakings concerned *keep the Bundeskartellamt informed* about the further development of the co-ordination, and (iii) the co-ordination has to *end without due delay* after the end of the COVID-19 crisis'.[151] Unlike the test created by the Commission's Temporary Framework, informing the German NCA about the cooperation is a necessary precondition for the relaxation of the competition rules.

In *Crisis Management Measures in the Automotive Industry (2020)*, the German NCA reviewed a proposal of the German Association of the Automotive Industry (VDA), setting up stakeholder groups and exchanges of information between owners, employees, customers, creditors, and public authorities on the solvency, credits, aid measures or operational problems of a company and for quickly

[150] Emphasis added. COMP/OG-D(2020/044003) Medicines for Europe (2020), 2.
[151] Emphasis added. Mundt (2020, 254).

developing effective restructuring measures. VDA argued that such temporary measures were necessary to overcome challenges caused by the pandemic. Instead of explaining if, and how, such a system can be justified under Article 101(1) and (3) TFEU balancing tools, the German NCA simply declared that it 'decided, within its scope of discretion, to refrain from examination under competition law in more detail'.[152]

The UK NCA created a similar balancing tool, albeit with some different emphasis. It declared that it 'will not take enforcement action' where temporary measures to coordinate action taken by businesses '(a) are *appropriate and necessary* in order to avoid a shortage, or ensure security, of supply; (b) are *clearly in the public interest*; (c) contribute to the benefit or *wellbeing of consumers*; (d) deal with critical issues that arise as a *result of the COVID-19 pandemic*; and (e) last *no longer than is necessary* to deal with these critical issues'.[153] Unlike the Commission's and the German tests, the British conditions hint towards the consideration of a consumer welfare standard for the exercise of target discretion.

The French and Dutch NCAs have also designed balancing tools to tackle the coronavirus pandemic challenges, yet have not defined a specific criterion for their application. The Dutch NCA explained that '[s]everal companies and trade organizations have already contacted us with questions about what opportunities exist for collaboration. We always *try to find the right balance between the interests* of all parties involved. *ACM will not take any action* if that balance is found and the collaboration is therefore in the general interest of people and businesses'.[154] This approach was repeated in a press release in which the Dutch NCA had endorsed a collaboration between hospitals, pharmacies, and pharmaceutical wholesalers to prevent or reduce a shortage of essential drugs. It noted that it will 'not take any action if collaborations involve transparent, temporary and necessary measures that do not go beyond than what is needed'.[155]

The French NCA has invoked the ECN Statement. While not referring to target discretion directly, it noted that '[t]he current situation is also leading to temporary cooperation movements between companies, notably to guarantee the production and fair distribution of essential products to all consumers. The Autorité de la concurrence supports this type of initiative and is ready to assist them'.[156] Unlike the other NCAs, its informal guidance letters have actually provided a legal basis to explain why it believes that certain initiatives have not infringed competition law.[157]

[152] Crisis Management Measures in the Automotive Industry (2020).

[153] CMA Approach to Business Cooperation in Response to COVID-19 (2020), para 2.3. See also para 1.4–1.5.

[154] Emphasis added. ACM's Oversight During the Coronavirus Crisis (2020). See also Snoep (2020a, 267).

[155] Distribution of Essential Drugs for COVID-19 Patients (2020).

[156] Autorité de la concurrence Action During the COVID-19 Coronavirus Epidemic (2020).

[157] In its opinion on Professional Association Members' Rent (2020), for instance, the French NCA examined an initiative of the professional association representing opticians to send a letter to a number of lessors requesting an adjustment of its members' commercial rents. It confirmed

To conclude, there are various case studies and empirical indications suggesting that the Commission and NCAs have made use of their target discretion to refrain from enforcing Article 101 TFEU when an agreement merited a complex balance between competition and non-competition interests. While the competition enforcers would have been unable to accept some of those anti-competitive agreements by means of the explicit-substantive balancing tools of Article 101(1) or (3) TFEU – at least according to their interpretation – they could, however, invoke the procedural-implicit balancing tools to refrain from enforcing Article 101 TFEU altogether.

7.4.4 *Interim Conclusion*

Wide target discretion is often seen as enabling effective competition law enforcement. Prioritisation allows competition enforcers to make more effective use of their limited resources, focusing on deterring behaviour that poses the greatest threat to competition and consumers.[158] Therefore, both the Commission and the ECN have maintained that increased target discretion helps to enhance the effectiveness of EU competition law enforcement.[159]

At the same time, this section submits that target discretion is problematic when it is used systematically as an implicit-procedural balancing tool. The Commission's and NCAs' choice to refrain from pursuing anti-competitive agreements that could not be justified by the explicit-substantive balancing tools imposes serious risks on the effectiveness, uniformity, and legal certainty of balancing.

First, balancing by target discretion negatively affects those cases that the competition enforcers have *refrained from pursuing*. This balancing tool is not effective, given that the enforcers facilitate broad types of economic and non-economic benefits based on neither a legal nor an economic test. As a result, balancing by target discretion does not necessarily weigh the harm to competition against possible overriding benefits. Target discretion can also lead to fragmentation because the Commission (in addition to certain NCAs) does not observe uniform prioritisation criteria. Moreover, the fact that competition enforcers are not required to publish or reason the exercise of their target discretion jeopardises legal certainty. Thus, neither the observation that balancing is taking place nor the balancing method itself is transparent or fully liable to judicial review. This poses the risk of the arbitrary discrimination of undertakings on the basis of enforcement discretion.[160]

Second, balancing by target discretion also affects the development of EU *competition policy* in general. Targeting only clear-cut infringements renders a

that the terms of the proposed initiative do not appear to infringe the prohibition of Article 101 (1) TFEU.

[158] ECN Recommendation on the Power to Set Priorities (2013), para 1.

[159] *Ibid*, para 4; ECN+ Directive Proposal (2017), Article 4(2)(e) and Preamble 17, as elaborated in Section 7.7.

[160] Petit (2010, 50).

paradoxical outcome: While the more economic approach calls for balancing the positive and negative impacts of an agreement on consumer welfare, enforcement has, in practice, come to revolve around clear-cut infringements of competition that do not require such an exercise.[161] The selection of cases thus renders the enforcement form-based. This generates uncertainty about the role of non-competition interests in the grey zone and the applicable balancing principles.

7.5 INSTRUMENT DISCRETION

Instrument discretion refers to the possibility of using alternative regulatory mechanisms to assess an anti-competitive agreement. For instance, certain competition enforcers may apply rules of sector regulation, undertake markets-work (i.e. sector inquiries or market studies), or issue informal opinions instead of pursuing an Article 101 TFEU infringement proceeding. In addition, the NCAs have a wide margin of discretion to decide whether to classify an agreement as mixed or purely national (i.e. whether it has an effect on trade between Member States). Classifying an agreement as purely national may subject it to a different balancing regime.

Instrument discretion is an important part of the competition enforcers' enforcement discretion. Enforcers not only have the power to refrain from enforcing Article 101 TFEU but can also address anti-competitive agreements by employing alternative enforcement instruments. This section demonstrates how those mechanisms each strike a different balance between competition and non-competition interests.

7.5.1 *Sector Regulation*

Certain anti-competitive agreements may fall under the scope of both Article 101 TFEU and specific rules of sector regulation. In such an event, the competition enforcer and/or the relevant sector regulator must decide whether to enforce Article 101 TFEU, the rules of sector regulation, or both.

The prospect of enforcing rules of sector regulation instead of Article 101 TFEU is embedded in Article 3 of Regulation 1/2003. Article 3(1) orders NCAs and national courts to apply Article 101 TFEU when they apply national competition law. Yet, the Article does not prohibit decisions *not to apply* EU or national competition law. On the contrary, as detailed in Section 6.1, Article 3(3) provides that EU competition law does not preclude the application of a national law that predominantly pursues a different objective. Therefore, an NCA or a sector regulator may apply the rules of a sector-specific regulation instead of enforcing Article 101 TFEU.

Applying sector regulation instead of Article 101 TFEU has a significant impact on balancing. First, sector regulation often does not have the same aim as competition law. Sector regulation does not necessarily focus on either making markets more

[161] Gerard (2012, 38–40), Witt (2016, 212), and Witt (2018, 426).

competitive or on enhancing short-term narrow consumer welfare. It is often directed at securing a broad range of social objectives in situations of market failure, such as ensuring the security of supply, providing an essential but uneconomic service, protecting vulnerable consumers, and reaching environmental or redistributive goals. Consequently, sector regulation strikes a different balance between competition and non-competition interests.[162]

Second, the application of sector regulation is grounded on different substantive, procedural, and institutional enforcement settings, which in turn confers a different balancing method. Most noticeably, contrary to the enforcement of Article 101 TFEU following modernisation, sector regulation is typically applied *ex-ante*, aiming to dictate the behaviour of undertakings. In this sense, such a balancing method resembles balancing by accepting commitments, as will be discussed in Section 7.6.2.

Finally, rules of sector regulation are more prone to political influence in comparison with Article 101 TFEU. Sector regulation is based on national laws that are controlled by the national parliaments and governments.[163] Furthermore, their application is not subject to scrutiny on behalf of the Commission and ECN to assess their compatibility with EU competition law.[164]

The choice between Article 101 TFEU and rules of sector regulation is especially critical for NCAs that are mandated to enforce sector regulation in addition to competition law (e.g. the Dutch, French, UK, and more recently also the German NCAs).[165] The UK enforcement regime provides an illustrative example. According to British law, the CMA and certain sector regulators are vested with concurrent powers to apply EU and national competition laws.[166] Each case is allocated to the authority that is 'better or best placed to do so'.[167] When a case is allocated to a sector regulator, the regulator must decide whether to use its competition law or dedicated sectoral powers At the same time, not all sector regulators primarily aim to ensure competition goals. The UK House of Lords Select Committee on Regulators, for instance, has noted that the promotion of competition is just one of the sector regulators' objectives and that the manner of balancing between the objectives is not

[162] Freeman (2008, 3), Monti (2008, 136), Almunia (2010, 3), Cseres (2013, 27–36), Dunne (2014a, 230), and Bailey and Whish (2015, 1031–1032). In the context of Article 102 TFEU, the Commission has noted that the setting of enforcement priorities would be based on the specific regulatory environment. See Commission Article 102 Guidance (2009), para 8.

[163] Monti (2008, 128–129) and Sauter (2010, 6).

[164] See Section 2.3.3.3.

[165] On the synergies and drawbacks of NCAs having an integrated or separate mandate to enforce competition and sector regulation, see Cseres (2013), Hyman and Kovacic (2013), and Jenny (2016, 9–21).

[166] See Section 2.6.4.3. Similar concurrent models are in effect in Ireland, Greece, and Cyprus. See Stern (2015, 896).

[167] UK Guidance on Concurrent Application (2014), para 3.22–3.25.

obvious.[168] In particular, the UK health regulator does not have an active duty to *promote* competition. It is merely required to protect choices and *prevent* anti-competitive agreements.[169]

The UK's sector regulators have regularly refrained from enforcing Article 101 TFEU when sector-specific rules are available. Possibly due to this reason, Article 101 TFEU was applied considerably less often in the UK than in other, even much smaller, jurisdictions.[170] The sector regulators seldom used Article 101 TFEU and preferred to rely on their sector regulation powers.[171] In *Energy Trade Association (2013)*, for instance, the British Gas and Electricity Markets Authority (Ofgem) explained that it 'considers that its resources would likely be better devoted to further work on the regulatory environment' rather than conducting an Article 101 TFEU proceeding.[172] Moreover, the vast majority of the few Article 101 TFEU enforcement actions examined by the sector regulators in the UK have resulted either in commitments or in non-infringement decisions.[173] In fact, as a result of the sparing use of Article 101 TFEU, the Enterprise and Regulatory Reform Act of 2013 required each sector regulator, for the first time, to determine on a case-by-case basis whether the use of its competition law powers was 'more appropriate' than using its special sectoral powers.[174] Nevertheless, the empirical findings do not indicate an increase in the enforcement of Article 101 TFEU by sector regulators since the reform.

Moreover, balancing by opting for sector regulation was also evident in the Netherlands and Germany, where the NCAs abstained from pursuing anti-competitive agreements that were protected by sector regulation. In the Netherlands, the Healthcare Market Regulation Act of 2006 introduced a system

168 House of Lords Select Committee on Regulators (2007), para 1.31, 3.16–3.34, 7.12. See also National Audit Office (2010) and National Audit Office (2016, 25).

169 UK Health and Social Care Act of 2012, Section 62(3). See also CMA, 'Baseline' Annual Report on Concurrency (2014), para 299–300; Sanchez-Graells (2014).

170 See Figure 3.11. This is also reflected in the ECN statistics, available at: http://ec.europa.eu/competition/ecn/statistics.html.

171 The empirical findings show that between May 2004 and 2017, sector regulators have enforced Article 101 TFEU in seven cases. Five of those cases were closed without a finding of an infringement (Electric trackside lubricators (2005); 213479.02 Supply of grease for use in electric trackside lubricators (2005); CW/00842/06/05 BBC broadcast's provision (2007)) or closed on priority setting grounds (Energy trade association (2013); Price comparison websites (2016)). The other two cases were closed by accepting commitments (Provision of Deep Sea Container rail transport services between ports and key inland destinations in Great Britain (2016)) and a settlement (East Midlands International Airport (2017)). In all of those cases, no fine was imposed for the infringement of Article 101 TFEU.

172 Energy Trade Association (2013), 1.

173 See note 171. See also UK National Audit, Report on the UK Competition Regime (2016), 31–32.

174 Enterprise and Regulatory Reform Act, Section 51 and Schedule 14; UK Guidance on Concurrent Application (2014), para 4.1. This obligation does not apply to the health regulator.

of sector-specific competition that enjoys primacy over general competition rules.[175] The healthcare authority is entrusted with the application of *ex-ante* controls, including the power to impose general obligations on all market parties by intervening in contract terms.[176] In *NZA (2012)*, the Dutch NCA held that in light of such a regulation, it would not give priority to complaints alleging anti-competitive behaviour in the health insurance market.[177] Similarly, in Germany, if an agreement falls under a sector-specific regulation beyond the NCA's competence, it will generally refrain from investigating it, leaving the matter to the relevant sector regulator instead.[178]

7.5.2 *Markets-Work (Sector Inquiries and Market Studies)*

As with reliance on rules of sector regulation rather than Article 101 TFEU, a competition enforcer may circumvent the application of this provision by ordering a markets-work. Markets-work is defined as the powers vested with an enforcer to conduct an investigation into the functioning of a specific sector, market, or type of an agreement outside the scope of an infringement procedure.[179] The name, scope, and methodology for carrying out such investigations vary considerably between competition enforcers.[180] Yet, all of the investigations are characterised by the fact that they aim to *understand* competition concerns rather than *correct* a specific infringement. As with sector regulation, the enforcers have the discretion to decide whether to address the matter by using Article 101 TFEU, markets-work, or both.[181] This choice dictates the role reserved to non-competition interests.

Former Competition Commissioner *Kroes* has asserted that the Commission's power to conclude sector inquiries provides it with a means to strike the right balance between competition policy and regulatory intervention.[182] Indeed, the

[175] Dutch Healthcare Market Regulation Act of 2010, Article 18.

[176] See also Sauter (2010, 11, 13–14).

[177] 7489 NZA (2012), 2.

[178] Dreher (2009, para 4.2).

[179] Lachnit (2016, 159–160). See also Kovacic (2020).

[180] For a survey of the NCAs' powers to issue markets-work, see ECN Questionnaire on Regulation 1/2003 (2013), 6. The French and UK NCAs are good examples at two ends of the spectrum. The French NCA has the power to perform market scans as part of its powers to issue informal advice. Those scans are applied on an irregular basis and yield only informal recommendations. On the other hand, as elaborated below, the UK sector investigations, which are known as market studies, are highly formalised and subject to a strict procedure. See also Dunne (2014a, 235–248) and Lachnit (2016, 162).

[181] See the Commission's website: http://ec.europa.eu/competition/antitrust/sector_inquiries.html. Although the investigation is not targeted at any specific infringement, it may later serve as a basis for an Article 101 or 102 TFEU investigation. There are no strict rules guiding which tool to choose. The UK NCA, for example, is competent to use sector inquiry instead of Article 101 TFEU if the former is deemed 'more appropriate'. See OFT Market Investigation Guidance (2006), 5.

[182] Kroes (2007, 5).

Commission has mainly used sector inquiries to assess regulated markets that raise balancing questions, such as telecommunications, healthcare, energy, and financial services.[183]

The use of markets-work instead of Article 101 TFEU allows the Commission to recommend introducing *ex-ante* sector-specific measures to regulate markets and to take non-competition interests into account beyond what it would be willing to consider under Article 101(3) TFEU.[184] Moreover, it has been suggested that political interests have influenced the Commission's sector inquiries. Scholars have voiced concerns about the politicisation of the Commission's sector inquiries, whereby the investigation is deployed to achieve political aims rather than merely as an information-gathering exercise.[185]

The Commission is attempting to enhance its markets-work powers. In June 2020, it published a public consultation suggesting introducing a 'new competition tool' to deal with structural competition problems across digital markets. Using the module of the UK's market studies tool that will be described below, this new tool could enhance the Commission's competence to undertake markets-work, empowering it to impose remedies even if no competition law violations exist.[186]

The UK practice provides another example of how non-competition interests may be assimilated into markets-work. The UK investigations, known as market studies,[187] demand consideration of the effect of the proposed remedy on consumer detriment and the conditions of regulated sectors.[188] This has been interpreted to include a variety of non-competition interests, including innovation, promoting well-informed consumers, and needs of regulated sectors.[189] Moreover, the

[183] The Commission's sector inquiry powers are subject to Article 17 of Regulation 1/2003, replacing Article 12 of Regulation 17/62. A list of the Commission's sector inquires can be found at http://ec.europa.eu/competition/antitrust/sector_inquiries.html. This record illustrates that the Commission has made regular use of its sector inquires powers only since the late 1990s. On balancing in liberalised and regulated markets, see Sections 3.4.3.3 and 7.6.2.3.

[184] See also Kroes (2007, 5) and Almunia (2010, 3).

[185] Olsen and Roy (2006, 83–84) and Dunne (2014a, 246).

[186] Commission's Public Consultation for a New Competition Tool (2020).

[187] The UK market studies are distinct from comparable tools in other jurisdictions since they are highly formalised and subject to strict procedure and may result in imposing remedies to correct adverse effects on competition. See Enterprise Act, Sections 131–153, as amended by the Enterprise and Regulatory Reform Act, Sections 33–38. Those sections provide that the UK CMA, relevant sector regulators, and the Secretary of State in some circumstances have the power to make a reference for a market investigation. Following such a reference, the CMA (prior to 2014, the Competition Commission) investigates and issues an extensive report. See also OFT Market Investigation Guidance (2006) and Lachnit (2016, 170–182).

[188] The consideration of consumer detriment is required by the Enterprise Act, Section 134(4). The consideration of regulated sector is derived from sector regulation. See Bailey and Whish (2015, 490–491) for a list of the UK market studies. See also Freeman (2008, 5–6).

[189] Ibid.

balancing embodied in market studies is also supported by the power of the UK Secretary of State to intervene in cases that raise defined public interest issues.[190]

Freeman, the former chairman of the UK Competition Commission, has explained that market investigations often involve the consideration of even broader non-economic benefits, noting that the NCA balanced harm to competition against interests related to industrial policy, intellectual property, public health, social policy, environmental protection, and defence.[191] He also noted that 'the resolution and synthesis – choosing which policy should prevail over others' was central to the process of the NCA's administration.[192] Markets-work, therefore, may take a broader range of non-competition interests into account in comparison to the enforcement of Article 101 TFEU.

Competition enforcers may also prefer to use markets-work to take into account non-competition interests since the balancing does not need to fit within their competition law precedent or policy. This gives enforcers the freedom to carry out their analysis without being constrained by or needing to deviate from their explicit-substantive balancing principles developed in their decisional practice and policy papers.[193] Hence, competition enforcers can strike a balance between competition and non-competition interests that does not necessarily correspond to the approaches developed in their Article 101(1) and (3) TFEU balancing tools.

7.5.3 *Informal Opinions*

Informal opinions are another instrument that may facilitate balancing. Such an instrument was at the core of Article 101 TFEU enforcement prior to modernisation. From the early 1970s, the Commission used informal comfort letters to terminate proceedings without issuing a formal decision. As elaborated in Section 2.3.2, the Commission declared that it used comfort letters to deal with notified agreements 'which at first sight' did not raise competition concerns.[194] While Regulation 1/2003 instigated the *ex-post* enforcement regime, the Commission and some of the NCAs are still competent to issue informal opinions analysing the compatibility of specific agreements with the Article.[195] Those informal opinions may provide a general analysis of the competition concerns, declare that an agreement is compatible or incompatible with Article 101 TFEU, or offer recommendations to address the competition concerns.

190 Enterprise and Regulatory Reform Act, Section 35. See also UK Supplemental Guidance on Market Studies and Market Investigations (2014), para 2.18–2.19, 3.8–3.9.

191 Freeman (2008, 6–10).

192 *Ibid*, 9.

193 Compare with Fletcher (2020, 5).

194 Policy report 1981, para 15.

195 On informal guidance generally, see Petit and Rato (2008, 205–206) and Lachnit (2016, 199–230).

Like many other aspects of enforcement discretion, EU law dictates neither the scenarios in which issuing an informal opinion would be appropriate nor their form. As a result, some opinions were detailed and reasoned to a similar extent to infringement decisions. Others were concise, merely summarising the basic facts of the case and concluding whether or not the competition enforcer believes that Article 101 TFEU was infringed.

Informal opinions may examine a host of legal questions and, in particular, provide competition enforcers with an attractive balancing instrument for a number of reasons. First, informal opinions that are *published and reasoned* can offer enforcers an opportunity to clarify the law on the compatibility of an agreement with Article 101 TFEU without undertaking the lengthy and costly competition law analysis necessary for issuing a formal decision. For instance, a number of the Commission's landmark balancing cases, such as *EACEM (1998)*,[196] were adopted in the form of comfort letters. Although the Commission's comfort letters are not binding on national courts, NCAs, or third parties, they have clarified the Commission's position on balancing principles. Such letters also constitute a matter of fact that national courts could take into account in national proceedings.[197] The same is true with respect to national opinions. As detailed below, many of the NCAs' landmark cases that shaped their approach to balancing under Article 101(1) and (3) TFEU were issued in the form of informal opinions.

Second, since informal measures are not binding, they are not liable to judicial review[198] or to notification and scrutiny by the ECN.[199] Accordingly, competition enforcers may examine sensitive balancing issues with a lower risk of facing legal or political challenges.[200]

Third, informal opinions allow competition enforcers to negotiate the terms of agreements with undertakings, entrusting them with market regulation tools similar to markets-works, commitments, or the Commission's Article 101(3) TFEU exemptions prior to modernisation.[201]

Fourth, informal opinions may bring infringements to an end without declaring so openly or imposing a fine. This may be of a particular benefit when a competition enforcer wishes to condemn an agreement in a politicly sensitive sector, which produces some non-competition interests that are insufficient to justify an exception. For example, in *Royal Dutch Society for Physical Therapy (2011)*, the Dutch NCA held that advice given by the society to its members to coordinate their agreements

[196] 36494 EACEM (1998), as detailed in Section 3.3.3.4.

[197] C-253/78 C-3/79 Procureur de la République (1980), para 13; C-31/80 L'Oréal (1980), para 11–12.

[198] With respect to the Commission's comfort letters, see Commission Notification Procedure Notice (1983). See also Van Bael (1986, 78). With respect to the judicial review of informal opinions in France, UK, and the Netherlands, see Lachnit (2016, 206, 211, 216, respectively).

[199] Regulation 1/2003, Article 11(4). See also Section 2.3.3.3.

[200] See Section 7.2.

[201] Forrester (1994, 470–471) and Doren and Wilks (1996, 25). On the use of commitments as a market regulation tool, see Section 7.6.2.

with health insurers might be incompatible with competition law. Yet, it issued an 'informal warning' instead of a prohibition decision.[202] Similarly, the UK NCA issued warning and advisory letters to address possible infringements in areas that had not been prioritised by the authority.[203]

Finally, similarly to sector regulation and markets-works, informal opinions that are *not published or fully reasoned* offer competition enforcers an opportunity to deviate from the balancing principles of Article 101(1) and (3) TFEU balancing tools without admitting so openly or being bound to this change in future cases. This will be further discussed in Section 7.6.3, exploring the balancing function of published and reasoned findings of inapplicability.

The above characteristics of informal opinions may explain why many of the competition enforcers have chosen this instrument to address balancing concerns related to the coronavirus pandemic. As was elaborated in Section 7.4.3.5, the Commission and NCAs (individually and as part of the ECN) have declared that they would be willing to provide undertakings with informal guidance as to the compatibility of their cooperation initiatives with Article 101 TFEU given the exceptional circumstances of the pandemic.[204]

Although informal opinions may be an attractive balancing tool from the point of view of the enforcers, they raise legal certainty and uniformity concerns. Since informal opinions are mostly unpublished, have no binding effect, and could not be challenged in a court, they cannot contribute to fully clarifying the balancing approach advocated by the Commission or NCAs. They also do not afford the EU and national courts an opportunity to challenge the Commission's and NCAs' analysis, thereby hindering the creation of a body of case law detailing the courts' interpretation and stimulating a uniform application by national courts.

This was demonstrated in the case of *Shrimp Fishery (2011, 2013, 2016)*. In 2011, the Dutch NCA examined an agreement between the members of shrimp-fishing trade associations aimed at sustainability-related interests. The NCA was generally supportive of the initiative. It held that mandatory sustainable fishing techniques could contribute to more sustainable fisheries and that such a benefit could be justified under Article 101(3) TFEU.[205] Yet, when the Commission re-examined some of the same restrictions of competition two years later, it rejected the undertakings' claim that the Dutch NCA's informal opinion should be taken into account. The Commission maintained that the NCA's assessment was informal, applied *ex-ante*

[202] Royal Dutch Society for Physical Therapy (KNGF) (2011). See also Dutch NCA annual report (2014), 30.

[203] CMA Essential Information for Businesses: Warning and Advisory Letters (2016). A register of such letters is available on the CMA's website.

[204] Commissions Coronavirus Temporary Framework (2020), para 7, 17–18; ECN Statement on Application of Competition Law During the Corona Crisis (2020).

[205] 7011/23.827 MSC Shrimp Fishery (2011), 5–7. On the other hand, the NCA was hesitant with respect to the association's plan to set catch limits. It held that such a measure would not be deemed indispensable if the shrimp population was not in danger.

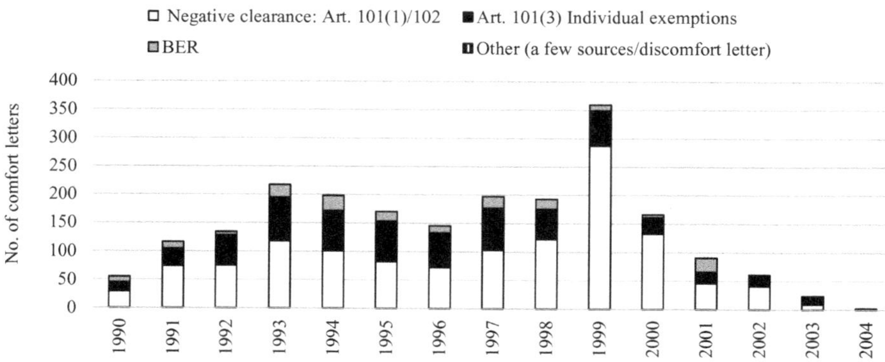

FIGURE 7.5. Comfort letters, Commission 1990–2004

to the relevant agreements, and without full knowledge of the facts.[206] In fact, the NCA's opinion did not even qualify as a mitigating factor for calculating the fines.[207] This demonstrates that although informal opinions are an important source for understanding the NCAs' approaches to balancing, the Commission or the EU Courts might not ascribe significant weight to them.

The empirical findings indicate that informal opinions have played a significant balancing role. At the EU level, as mentioned, they were mainly used prior to modernisation. The publicly available information specifying the Commission's reasons for closing a case by means of a comfort letter (only available for the period between 1990 and 2004[208]), which is summarised in Figure 7.5, illustrates that comfort letters have regularly been used to conclude investigations into agreements that benefited from Article 101(3) TFEU individual exemptions and BERs.

The empirical findings also show that following modernisation, the Commission has chosen not to issue informal guidance, although it is competent to do so. This perhaps corresponds to the warning voiced by several commentators that frequent use of informal opinions would reintroduce the notification regime through the back door.[209] The only exception was the Commission's comfort letter in *Medicines for Europe (2020)*, examining cooperation in the healthcare sector admits the coronavirus outbreak.[210]

206 39633 Shrimp (2013), para 362–364.

207 *Ibid*, para 439. On the role of public policy aims in calculating the fines, see Section 7.6.1.2.

208 See Sections 1.3.2.3 and 2.3.2.

209 Ehlermann (2000, 566), Blanco (2006, 207), and Lachnit (2016, 202). Similar concerns were voiced by some Member States in response to the Modernisation White Paper (1999). See Summary of the observations on the White paper on modernisation (2000), para 4.4, 4.6.

210 COMP/OG-D(2020/044003) Medicines for Europe (2020). This case was discussed in detail in Section 7.4.3.5.

TABLE 7.1. *Explicit-substantive balancing tools in informal opinions*

	Article 101(1) TFEU	Article 101(3) TFEU	BERs
FR	78% (43%)[a]	34% (10%)	34% (10%)
NL	38% (32%)	34% (14%)	7% (8%)
UK[b]	100% (19%)	50% (28%)	0% (35%)

[a] In addition to Article 101(1) TFEU balancing tools that were discussed in Chapter 5, this figure includes the French rules for the joint offering of bids in tenders and the public body prerogative, discussed in Sections 6.3.2 and 6.3.3, respectively.
[b] In the UK, the data in this table only refers to short-form opinions and not to advisory and warning letters that are not fully published. By the end of 2017, the UK NCA had issued only two short-form opinions examining Article 101 TFEU.

At the Member States level, nevertheless, informal opinions were used to examine the application of many of the explicit-substantive balancing tools. Various examples demonstrating the significance of such opinions were presented in Section 3.6 and Figure 3.11. In addition, the empirical findings point to the great divergence in the forms and frequency[211] of issuing informal opinions. The process was formalised for some competition enforcers (Commission,[212] France,[213] Netherlands,[214] and the UK[215]), but not for others (Germany[216] and Hungary[217]).

Table 7.1 examines the debate over the explicit-substantive balancing tools that has taken place before the competition enforcers that have formalised the process of issuing informal opinions. It indicates the percentage of informal opinions in which the balancing tools of Article 101(1) and (3) TFEU were discussed, in comparison

[211] See Figure 7.3.
[212] An informal guidance letter can be issued at the request of undertakings in cases posing a novel legal question. See Regulation 1/2003, Preamble 38; Commission Notice on Informal Guidance (2004). See also Section 2.5.4.5.
[213] According to Article L. 462-4 of the French Commercial Code, the French NCA may issue advisory opinions on competition law questions and make recommendations for the improvement of the competitive situation. The advisory opinions are produced upon the request of Ministers, governmental bodies, a number of sectoral regulators, and professional and consumer organisations. As mentioned in Section 2.6.1.3, since 2009, the NCA also has the power to issue an advisory opinion of its own accord. The NCA's recommendations do not have the same legal value as formal decisions and cannot be appealed before the courts. Yet, they contain detailed analysis and are published. See also French NCA Report, 25 Years of Enforcement (2012), 24–25; Lachnit (2016, 163–170).
[214] The procedure for adopting informal opinions by the Dutch NCA is less formalised in comparison with its French and UK counterparts. See Lachnit (2016, 212–215).
[215] The UK NCA introduced the possibility of issuing so-called short-form opinions in 2010, and on a trial basis only. The CMA has declared that it would issue such opinions on the basis of its prioritisation principles if the issue raises novel or unresolved questions. See UK Short-form Opinions Guidance (2014); Lachnit (2016, 207–210).
[216] Dreher (2009, 3). Yet, the draft of the 10th amendment of the German Competition Act of January 2020, Section 32c(3), suggests introducing an informal opinion measure.
[217] ECN Questionnaire on Regulation 1/2003 (2013), 6.

with the number of other types of proceedings in which those balancing tools were discussed (in brackets).

The table shows that informal opinions delivered by the French, Dutch, and UK NCAs were more likely to involve a discussion about the explicit-substantive balancing tools in comparison with other types of proceedings. This, taken in combination with the competition enforcers' incentives discussed in the opening of the section, might imply that informal opinions offer a more attractive balancing venue from the standpoint of the NCAs, despite their aforementioned uniformity and legal certainty challenges.

7.5.4 *Effect on Trade Test*

After commencing an investigation, an NCA must decide whether to apply Article 101 TFEU or to examine the case solely under national law. In other words, it must determine whether the agreement affects trade between Member States. This choice may have significant bearing on the applicable procedural and substantive rules.[218] In turn, it may also have an impact on balancing.

First, the classification determines the applicable law. As detailed in the previous chapters, some Member States have adopted unique balancing tools and principles that solely apply to purely national cases.[219] Hence, only an agreement that is classified as purely national could be granted an exception under such national rules.

Second, the classification defines the applicable procedural safeguards. In particular, Regulation 1/2003 demands that NCAs inform the Commission before taking certain enforcement actions with respect to mixed cases.[220] This allows the Commission to intervene if there is a serious risk of incoherence, by taking up a case and relieving an NCA of its competence to apply Article 101 TFEU to such an agreement. Purely national cases are not subject to a similar scrutiny.

The various substantive laws and procedural safeguards may induce an NCA to classify a borderline case as purely national, especially when the case involves complex balancing questions. As *Riley* has maintained, 'no public official will rationally choose a procedure that places additional evidential and procedural burdens upon his or her case, when another procedure, often word for word the same text, relying on the same case law, and with the same legal effect, is available'.[221]

This is especially true since NCAs enjoy a wide margin of discretion to determine whether an agreement affects trade between Member

[218] For an illuminating overview, see Botta et al. (2015).

[219] See Sections 3.6, 4.4.1.3, and 5.4 and Chapter 6.

[220] Regulation 1/2003, Articles 11(3), 11(4), and 11(6). See Section 2.3.3.3.

[221] Riley (2003a, 613); see also Riley (2003b, 664). Gerber (1998, 398) further suggests that NCA officials may favour national proceedings since they are primarily responsible for the development and enforcement of their own national competition laws, and it is the performance of this task for which they are likely to be primarily evaluated. He claims that these laws reflect national values and objectives, which the national officials are committed to professionally and often personally.

States.[222] Despite its great significance, there is no clear and harmonised test for measuring such an effect. It is not defined in EU primary or secondary law, and the EU Courts have not provided a precise definition.[223] The Commission's Effect on Trade Notice (2004) offers only non-binding guidance.[224] Ironically, the effect on trade test, which aims to define 'the boundary between the areas respectively covered by Community law and national law',[225] is defined by national law.

Indeed, empirical studies have already revealed that some NCAs have adopted a narrow interpretation of the test in comparison to the CJEU's and Commission's approaches.[226] Moreover, some national courts have adopted different approaches than their respective NCAs.[227] The German *Verta/Danzer (2004, 2005)* decisions provide an illustrative example. As described in Section 2.6.2.2, German competition law provides for a special exception for purely national agreements aimed at rationalising economic activities and improving the competitiveness of SMEs. In *Verta/Danzer*, the NCA relied on the Commission's Effect on Trade Notice to refuse to apply this exception.[228] However, the appeals court overturned that finding. It held that the agreement was purely national since it did not affect trade by its very nature. The Court criticised the NCA for basing its assessment on the Commission's Notice, which was not binding on the Member States.[229]

For essentially the same reasons, it is difficult to use an empirical method to pinpoint cases that have been classified as purely national for the purpose of benefiting from a national balancing tool. Since there is no single test for this classification, it is difficult to challenge the validity of an NCA's decision in a specific case.

Nevertheless, an aggregated overview of the NCAs' classifications can provide some indication of the existence of a balancing by the effect on trade test. To this end, Figure 7.6 presents the ratio of enforcement actions that were classified by the NCAs as mixed cases (black areas) and purely national (grey areas). In some cases, the NCAs did not indicate whether the case was mixed or purely national (white areas).

The figure hints at the possibility of balancing under the effect on trade test, especially in certain Member States. For instance, it illustrates that Article 101(1) TFEU balancing tools were frequently accepted in purely national cases. The figure also reveals that informal commitments were more frequently accepted in purely national cases (with the exception of Germany). While those examples are far from decisive and require further research, they could suggest that NCAs prefer to use their own national laws to balance instead of relying on Article 101 TFEU.

222 Botta et al. (2015, 1249, 1271).

223 See Burnley (2002), Cleynenbreugel (2014, 1393–1400), and Botta et al. (2015).

224 Effect on Trade Concept Notice (2004), para 3, as confirmed by the CJEU in C-439/11P Ziegler (2016), para 59–61.

225 In the words of the CJEU in C-56/64 C-58/64 Grundig/Consten (1966), 341.

226 Botta et al. (2015, 1271).

227 See a list of examples in Commission Staff Working Paper accompanying the Report on Functioning of Regulation 1/2003 (2009), para 150.

228 B1–25/04 Verta/Danzer (2004), 26.

229 I2 Kart 12/04 (V) Verta/Danzer (2005), para 27–36.

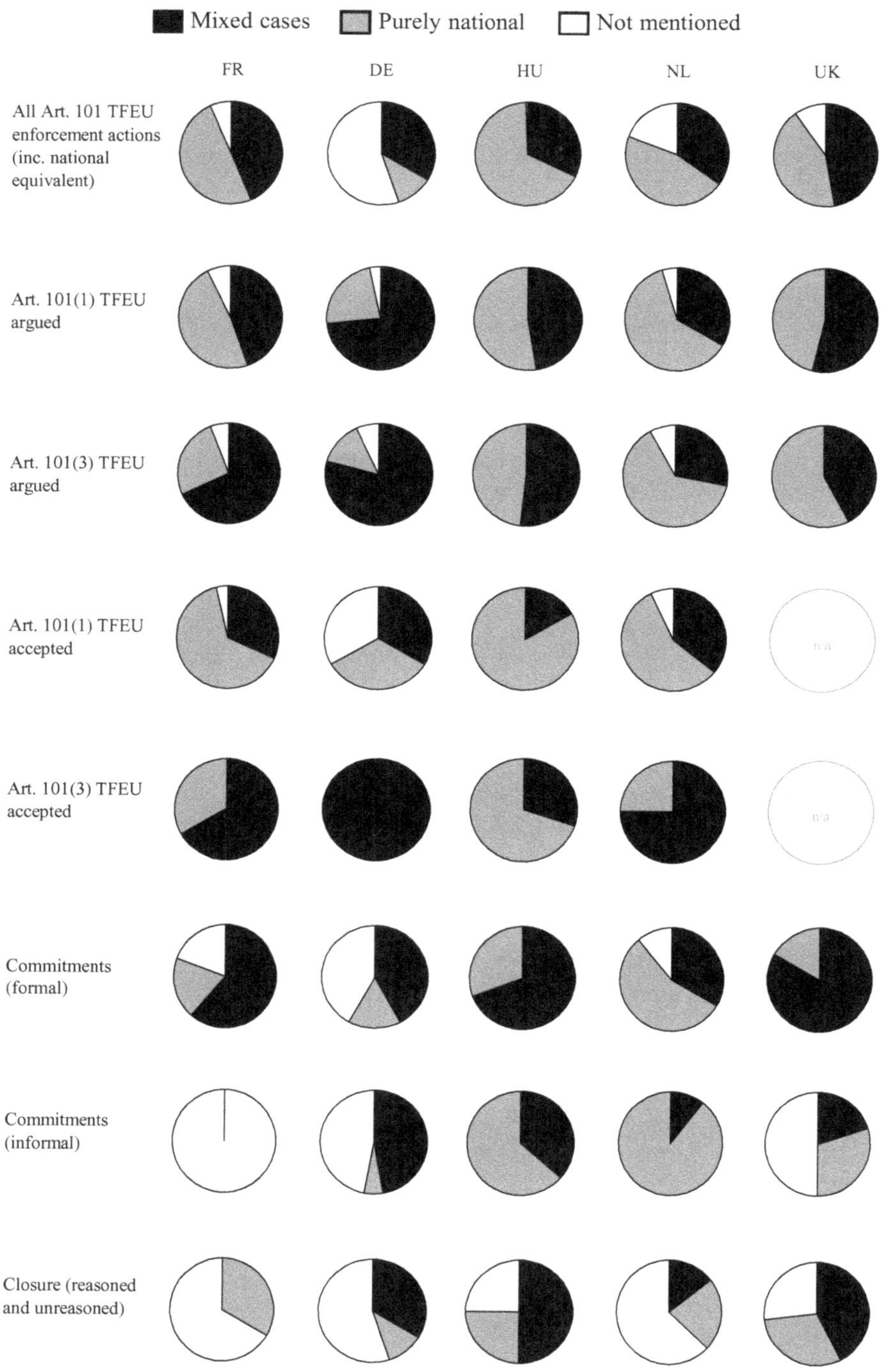

FIGURE 7.6. Balancing tools in mixed and purely national cases, NCAs

7.5.5 *Interim Conclusion*

This section has shown that competition enforcers enjoy significant instrument discretion to apply rules of sector regulation, conduct markets-work, adopt informal opinions, or apply national competition law instead of enforcing Article 101 TFEU. By using these alternative legal mechanisms, they can take account of non-competition interests outside the substantive scope of EU competition law, and often without declaring so explicitly. This opens the door to taking a wide range of non-economic benefits into account and the use of exclusion and legal balancing processes instead of economic analysis. Those balancing tools often pursue regulatory balancing aims to shape markets, thus going beyond a mere correction of the anti-competitive behaviour of the undertakings concerned.[230]

Furthermore, because balancing by instrument discretion is not bound by the rules of EU competition law, such balancing raises uniformity and legal certainty concerns. Similar balancing questions may be addressed by divergent legal mechanisms in the various Member States, leading to fragmentation and hindering the predictability of the legal framework governing balancing.

7.6 OUTCOME DISCRETION

The competition enforcers have outcome discretion, namely the power to select from a wide array of remedies to bring an enforcement proceeding to an end: First, a competition enforcer may adopt an *infringement decision*. In that case, the enforcer must decide whether to impose a fine for the infringement and, if so, to set its level. Second, as an alternative, an enforcer can choose from a toolbox of *negotiated remedies*, such as formal and informal commitments or settlements.[231] Third, if a competition enforcer finds that no infringement of Article 101 TFEU has taken place, it may *bring the proceeding to an end*. This can take the form of a reasoned formal or informal decision, a short summary of the competition analysis, or by terminating the proceedings with no further notice or reasoning.

This section argues that at times, the selection of the measure to bring an enforcement proceeding to an end has taken into account or was affected by non-competition interests. In fact, the empirical findings presented in this section illustrate that following modernisation, the balancing of many non-competition interests that had previously taken place under the explicit-substantive balancing tools of Article 101(1) and (3) TFEU has now shifted to the procedural remedy stage. The following sections will examine in turn the balancing embedded in accepting commitments, setting the fines, and issuing findings of inapplicability.

[230] On the differences between corrective and regulatory balancing, see Section 1.2.2.2.

[231] On commitments as an extension of the competition enforcers' outcome discretion, see also Wathelet (2015, 553) and Sauter (2016, 129).

7.6.1 *Fines*

7.6.1.1 A Balancing Tool

Fines are the main EU law instrument for deterring violations of Article 101 TFEU.[232] This section discusses situations in which achieving such deterrence by imposing high fines (indirectly aimed at safeguarding competition interests) results in adverse effects to the undertakings or to society. It demonstrates that in certain circumstances, the competition enforcers chose to moderate the fines or to refrain from imposing a fine altogether in favour of protecting other non-competition interests.

The rules governing the imposition of fines raise important questions of multi-levelled governance, as such rules have not been harmonised throughout the EU. At the EU level, up until the late 1990s, the Commission did not articulate the method guiding the calculation of fines. Nevertheless, its decisional practice reveals that the fines were based on neither the violator's economic gain nor consumers' economic loss. In contrast to the fines imposed in the United States and certain Member States,[233] the EU fine represents an arbitrary administrative figure, reflecting the gravity of the offence and adjusted by a number of factors. The empirical findings confirm that in the past, the Commission's decisions merely mentioned the relevant elements for assessing the gravity and the duration of the infringement, without detailing their weight.[234] Prompted by several court judgments calling for greater transparency,[235] in 1998 the Commission first adopted its Fining Guidelines, which were subsequently amended in 2006.

At the Member State level, NCAs differ in the nature of the fines they may impose (i.e. in administrative, civil, or criminal proceedings), the methodology for calculating those fines, and the entities that are liable to them.[236] The Five NCAs examined in this study have all adopted policy papers governing the calculation of fines, which, as described below, largely follow the Commission's approach.[237]

[232] See Fining Guidelines (2006), para 4; Report on the functioning of Regulation 1/2003 (2009), para 124; Report on the Functioning of Regulation 1/2003 (2014), para 35; ECN+ Directive Proposal (2017), 16–17 and Preamble 29. The Commission's power to impose fines on the infringement of Article 101 TFEU is established by Regulation 1/2003, Article 23.

[233] Veljanovski (2007, 79).

[234] See also Geradin and Henry (2004, 401, 407) and Lianos et al. (2014, 136).

[235] See, for example, T-148/89 Welded steel mesh (1995), para 142; in T-309/94 Cartonboard (1998), para 77–78, the GC even implied that the Commission was obliged to fully set out its calculation method in its decisions. Yet, this was reversed on appeal by CJEU in C-248/98P Cartonboard (2000), para 44–48. See also Torre (2010, 405).

[236] ECN+ Directive Proposal, 16–17; ECN Questionnaire on Regulation 1/2003 (2013), 5.

[237] French Fining Guidelines (2011); German Fining Guidelines (2006), as amended by the German Fining Guidelines (2013); Dutch Fining Guidelines (2009) as amended by the Dutch Fining Guidelines (2014, 2016); Hungarian Fining Guidelines (2003), as amended by the Hungarian Fining Guidelines (2005, 2012, 2014, 2015, 2017); UK Fining Guidelines (2004), as amended by the UK Fining Guidelines (2012, 2018).

Since the calculation of fines at the EU and national levels is not linked to a precise notion of harm caused to markets or consumers, competition enforcers enjoy a wide margin of discretion when setting them.[238] They may even depart from their fining principles, and not impose a fine at all 'provided there is a legitimate interest in doing so'.[239] This margin of discretion has allowed the Commission and NCAs to take non-competition interests into account when setting fines.

Empirical findings presented below show that over the years some of the explicit-substantive balancing tools of Article 101(1) and (3) TFEU were abandoned in favour of balancing by moderating the fines. For example, rather than balance the promotion of public policy (e.g. sports, industrial policy) or the consequences of economic crisis under Article 101(1) and (3) TFEU,[240] competition enforcers instead take those considerations into account when calculating fines. In addition, some competition enforcers have moderated fines when an agreement is related to the operation of SMEs.

Before moving to discuss those examples, it should be noted that while in those cases the competition enforcers have taken into account similar non-competition interests as the explicit-substantive balancing tools, the moderation of the fine results in a different outcome than an exception under Article 101(1) or (3) TFEU. The imposition of a fine, even if moderated, acknowledges an infringement of Article 101 TFEU and penalises it. Infringement decisions can serve to promote competition even when small, or even no, fines are imposed. Such decisions order undertakings to cease the infringement. They take a clear stand on the law and clarify the boundaries of Article 101 TFEU. They also increase deterrence as they can be used as irrefutable evidence in a follow-up private action,[241] or as an aggravating circumstance increasing the fine for a reoccurring infringement.[242]

Yet, this section suggests that when taken together with the other means to balance via enforcement discretion, undertakings may not be sufficiently discouraged from concluding anti-competitive agreements that promote some non-competition interests but cannot be justified under the explicit-substantive balancing tools. If undertakings grow to expect low fines in certain circumstances, infringement might be considered an economically rational choice. The following sub-sections present examples of policy papers and practices in which the competition enforcers have moderated the fines due to non-competition interests.

[238] C-189/02P Dansk (2005), para 172; Commission Fining Guidelines (1998), para 1; Commission Fining Guidelines (2006), para 2. See also Geradin and Henry (2005, 401, 404), Sauter (2016, 138), and Dunne (2016, 458); European Court of Auditors, Special Report on the Commission's EU Merger Control and Antitrust Proceedings (2020), para 68–72.

[239] Regulation 1/2003, Preamble 11.

[240] See Sections 3.4.3.4 and 5.2.

[241] Damages Directive (2014), Article 9.

[242] Commission Fining Guidelines (2006), para 28.

7.6.1.2 Public Policy Aims

A legitimate public policy aim of an anti-competitive agreement has sometimes played a role in setting the fine. In the past, for instance, the Commission reduced the fines imposed on anti-competitive agreements aimed at solving market fluctuations and remedying past tariff discrimination.[243]

In *Zinc producer group (1984)*, for instance, the Commission declared that zinc producers have infringed Article 101 TFEU by fixing prices, setting export quotas, and sharing the markets of nearly all the zinc smelters and ore producers in the Western world. Despite this serious and prolonged infringement, and despite the fact that the agreement was not duly notified to the Commission, the Commission decided to considerably mediate the fine, noting that the undertakings 'were genuinely attempting to overcome the problems caused by erratic fluctuations in the zinc price quoted on the [London Metal Exchange]'.[244] This finding was particularly noteworthy as the Commission also noted that it was 'doubtful' that the agreement had actually promoted price stability for the benefit of consumers in the meaning of Article 101(3) TFEU or helped control inflation for the benefit of the Member States.[245]

The Commission has also agreed to waive a fine when an infringement occurred in a market undergoing liberalisation. In some cases, it did not explain why no fine was imposed in such circumstances.[246] In others, the waiver was explained by the profound changes in the commercial practices of the undertakings in such sectors, adding that those cases were the first to apply Article 101 TFEU in those sectors.[247] Similarly, the Commission has relinquished the fine in a number of infringements by trade associations, often without clear reasoning.[248] While waiving the fines in those cases could be understood in light of the novelty of the legal questions or the limited culpability of the undertakings due to state involvement, they can also

[243] 30350 Zinc producer group (1984), para 99–101; 33941 HOV SVZ/MCN (1994), para 108–112. In 33384 33378 Distribution of package tours during the 1990 World Cup (1992), para 125, the Commission accepted the claim indirectly, noting that while safety concerns were not a justification for the anti-competitive conduct, they nevertheless complicated the case.

[244] 30350 Zinc producer group (1984), para 99.

[245] *Ibid*, para 87.

[246] 32732 Ijsselcentrale (1991).

[247] 38662 GDF-ENEL (2004), para 163; 38662 GDF-ENI (2004), para 133. A similar justification guided the Commission and CJEU in 26918 Suiker-Unie (1973), para V(2); C-40/73 C-41/73 to 48/73 C-50/73 C-54/73 to 56/73 C-111/73 C-113/73 C-114/73 European sugar industry (1975), para 613–624.

[248] 26349 Besluiten van de Vereniging G.I.S.A. (1972); 27095 Franco-Japanese ballbearings (1974); 28980 Pabst & Richarz/BNIA (1976); 29535 White lead (1978); 29869 Italian cast glass (1980); 29988 Italian flat glass (1981); 28930 Milchförderungsfonds (1984); 33494 Scottish Salmon Board (1992); 33407 CNSD (1993); 33686 Coapi (1995). In 33585 Distribution of railway tickets by travel agents (1992), it imposed a fine, but it was moderated. See policy report (1992, 118).

express the desire to strike a new balance of competition and non-competition interests in liberalised and regulated markets.[249]

From the beginning of the 2000s onwards, the Commission has mostly rejected claims for a fine reduction on the basis of public policy grounds.[250] Nevertheless, in *International Skating Union eligibility rules (2017)*, the Commission decided to waive the fine due to the Union's function in promoting worldwide sports as a public interest recognised in the Treaty. The Commission justified its decision due to the following three cumulative reasons: (i) as this was the first infringement decision adopted by the Commission with respect to rules set by sports governing bodies. The Commission referred to the policy-linking clause, adding that 'the specific nature of sport is recognised in Article 165 of the Treaty'; (ii) that the Eligibility rules have been in place and were publicly known upon their adoption; and (iii) that the Union is an international sports federation that, 'besides being involved in commercial activities, *acts to promote the sport* of speed skating worldwide including by *devolving part of its revenues to the development of the sport*'.[251] Once again, the Commission has agreed to waive the fine *inter alia* on public policy grounds, while at the same time declaring that such aims do not justify an exception under the explicit-substantive balancing tools.[252]

Also some of the national enforcers have accepted public policy aims as a justification for a fine reduction. A number of Dutch policy papers have openly declared that the NCA will not impose a fine on agreements pursuing specific types of public policies. For example, the Dutch NCA issued its Guidelines on Price Arrangements between Self-employed Workers (2019) as a response to a letter sent by the Dutch cabinet to the Dutch House of Representatives. In the letter, the cabinet abandoned its plans to introduce a statutory minimum rate for self-employed workers, yet declared that self-employed workers should be protected against poverty and that clients 'at the lower end' of the labour market should be prevented from choosing to work with self-employed workers solely because of the lower costs. The Guidelines clarify the opportunities that competition law offers to conclude price arrangements between self-employed to achieve such aims. In addition to certain

249 Section 7.6.2 maintains that the need to strike this balance in regulated and liberalised markets had led the competition enforcers to settle many of those cases by accepting commitments.

250 The Commission rejected such claims in 37027 Zinc Phosphate (2001), para 333–334, with respect to an agreement promoting safety; in 37370 Sorbates (2003), para 316–320, with respect to agreement aimed at avoiding anti-dumping; and 39612 Perindopril (Servier) (2014), para 3081, with respect to an agreement aimed at encouraging settlements in litigation with respect to pay-for-delay cases. The CJEU rejected similar claims in C-100/80 C-101/80 C-102/80 C-103/80 Pioneer Hi-fi equipment (1983), para 88–90, with respect to an agreement aimed at solving unfair conditions of competition. In T-456/10 Animal feed phosphates (2015), para 212, the GC clarified that the changes brought about by the Lisbon Treaties in 2009, including the introduction of the objectives of Article 3 TEU and Protocol 27, did not alter the manner in which fines should be calculated in this regard.

251 Emphasis added. 40208 International Skating Union's Eligibility rules (2017), para 348.

252 *Ibid*, para 211–266. See also Section 5.2.6.

exceptions from the national equivalent of Article 101 TFEU, the Guidelines add that the NCA 'will not impose any fines on arrangements between and with self-employed workers that aim to set a minimum rate for self-employed workers that is not higher than necessary for safeguarding the subsistence level'.[253] According to the Guidelines, such a minimum rate shall ensure that self-employed workers are able to support themselves and, additionally, can take out insurance or save some money in case they are unable to work.[254]

A similar approach is proposed by the Dutch NCA's Draft Guidelines on Sustainability Agreements (2020). According to those Guidelines, no fine for infringement of Article 101 TFEU will be imposed if an agreement that pursues a sustainability aim has been published and follows the provisions of the Guidelines 'in good faith as much as possible'.[255]

In addition to the scenarios covered by the above Guidelines, the Dutch NCA had also moderated a fine given the public role of an agriculture association.[256] In other cases, it refused to reduce the fine imposed on agreements purporting to fight tax fraud or protect consumers.[257] It is not completely clear while public policy aims justified fine reductions in some scenarios, but not in others.

Similarly to the Commission's approach prior to modernisation, the process of liberalisation of markets was also sometimes seen as vindicating a fine reduction at the national level. In Hungary, structural transformation in the flour market warranted a reduction,[258] and in the Netherlands, in the health care market.[259]

7.6.1.3 Economic Crisis and Weak Financial Situation

Fine reductions have also been used to account for crisis situations. Section 3.4.3.4 revealed that during the second enforcement period (i.e. 1978–1987), the Commission considered economic crisis as a justification for an Article 101(3) TFEU exemption (the so-called 'crisis cartels'). In the course of the 1980s and the 1990s, the Commission gradually stopped accepting economic crisis as a justification for an exemption. Nevertheless, this sub-section shows that instead of

[253] Guidelines on Price Arrangements between Self-employed Workers (2019), para 7.
[254] *Ibid.*
[255] Draft Guidelines on Sustainability Agreements (2019), para 62.
[256] 7036 1/386 Bell peppers (2012), para 381–386.
[257] 3031 Temporary employment bureau (2004), para 83–84; 7244/597 Magazine packs (2013), para 601.
[258] Vj-74/2003/117 White flour (2004), para 107.
[259] 2688 Tilburg pharmacies (2004), para 119; 2501 Assen pharmacies (2004), para 102; 5851-121 Thuiszorg 't Gooi (2008), para 263–267; 6108/258 Thuiszorg Kennemerland (2008), para 234–236; 6442 WMO Friesland (2012), para 293–296; 6274/569 Midden Ijssel (2010), para 275; 6109/814 Caraat (2011), para 306–311; 6888/435 LHV pace of establishment (2011), para 385–388; AWB 15/431 WMO Friesland (2017), para 7.

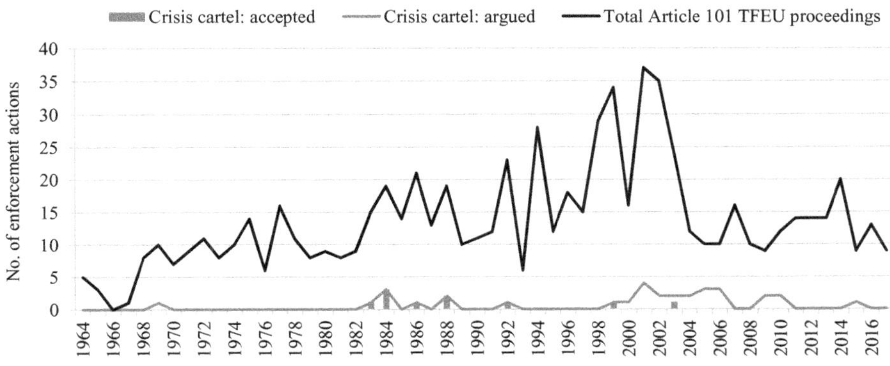

FIGURE 7.7. Crisis cartels, Commission

considering economic crisis under the explicit-substantive balancing tool of Article 101(3) TFEU, the Commission took it into account when setting the fines.

A fine reduction in situations of economic crisis reflects the premise that achieving deterrence by imposing high fines could bring about harmful economic and social side effects. A high fine might bankrupt an undertaking, thereby indirectly increasing market concentration. Imposing a high fine on a strategically important undertaking might also deter economic activity and lead to unemployment in a region or a state.[260] Hence, at times, competition enforcers have balanced the protection of competition interests with other economic and social interests via deterrence.

The possibility to account for crisis situations when calculating fines was first expressed in *Cast iron and steel rolls (1983)*.[261] The Commission maintained that the undertakings' financial situation and the task of aiding the recovery of the sector concerned warranted refraining from the imposition of high fines, despite the existence of a long-term price-fixing agreement. As summarised by Figure 7.7, the Commission accepted similar claims from the 1980s to the late 1990s when a serious crisis led to difficult trading conditions,[262] a hard economic situation,[263] low

[260] Wils (2006a, 197, 204), Reynolds, Macrory, and Chowdhury (2009, 1670), and Torre (2010, 397–398).

[261] 30064 Cast iron and steel rolls (1983), para 72–74. Prior to that, in 26623 Quinine (1969), para 38, the Commission was willing to take into account difficulties confronting members of a cartel with regard to the supply of their raw material. It noted that the two countries that were the leading source of the raw material – Indonesia and the Congo – were in precarious economic and political circumstances that may have prompted a degree of cooperation to assure a steady supply. Yet, it refused to moderate the fines since the restrictions imposed by the cartel went way beyond the coordination of the supply of raw material.

[262] 30988 Flat-glass in the Benelux (1984), para 55.

[263] 30350 Zinc producer group (1984), para 105; 32450 French-West African ship-owners committees (1992), para 74h.

profitability,[264] or losses.[265] The figure specifies the number of cases in which undertakings pleaded for a fine reduction due to crisis cartels (grey line) and in which the Commission accepted them (bars).

Fine reductions for crisis cartels were formalised by the Commission Fining Guidelines (1998). Article 5(b) of the Guidelines states that the Commission will take 'certain objective factors such as a specific economic context' into account. Curiously, Figure 7.7 demonstrates that formalisation actually led to the abandonment of this type of fine reduction.[266] In fact, with the exception of a case in the late 1990s, following the adoption of the 1998 Guidelines, the Commission stopped accepting crisis situations as justification for a fine reduction.[267] Rather, it repeatedly held that loss-making or economic difficulties within a sector did not warrant moderating the fines imposed.[268] The change in the Commission's approach became particularly apparent against the backdrop of the 2008 financial crisis.[269] Departing from the Commission's practice until the 1990s, Competition Commissioner *Kroes* declared that the financial crisis did not justify moderating fines.[270]

French beef (2003, 2006) was the one exceptional case in which the mitigating circumstances of Article 5(b) of the Guidelines prompted the Commission to reduce the fine by 60%, which was further lowered by 70% by the GC.[271] The reasons for this significant fine reduction are not completely clear from the wording of the decision itself. Yet, the GC in appeal and the Commission in later cases attributed it to the exceptional circumstances of the case.[272] Those circumstances included an infringement that was limited to the public behaviour of trade associations whereby the sector had experienced a dramatic decline in consumption and after public measures had proved ineffective. In other words, the circumstances that vindicated the application of Article 5(b) went beyond a mere crisis in the sector.

While economic crisis in a sector in and of itself no longer seems to justify a fine reduction, the Commission still takes notice of situations of economic crisis when calculating fines. The Commissions' new Fining Guidelines (2006) replaced the crisis cartel principle with an 'inability to pay' test. The new Guidelines provide that 'in exceptional cases, the Commission may, upon request, take account of the

[264] 30809 John Deere (1984), para 41.

[265] 31149 Polypropylene (1986), para 108; 31865 PVC (1988), para 52; 31866 LdPE (1988), para 7.

[266] In 2009, the Commission confirmed that although it had in the past accepted the crisis cartel justification, it had not done so after 1998. See 39396 Calcium carbide and magnesium based reagents (2009), para 331; 38589 Heat stabilisers (2009), para 735.

[267] 35860B 39041 Seamless steel tube (1999), para 168–169, as confirmed by T-44/00 Seamless steel tubes (2004), para 271; T-50/00 Seamless steel tubes (2004), para 318–334. See also Faull and Nikpay (2014, 1321, 1327).

[268] See Annex A, Section 7.2.

[269] See also Reynolds et al. (2009) and Torre (2010).

[270] Kroes (2009).

[271] 38279 French beef, para 182–185; T-217/03 T-245/03 French beef (2006), para 356–361.

[272] T-217/03 T-245/03 French beef (2006), para 356–361; 38281 Raw Tobacco Italy (2005), para 384.

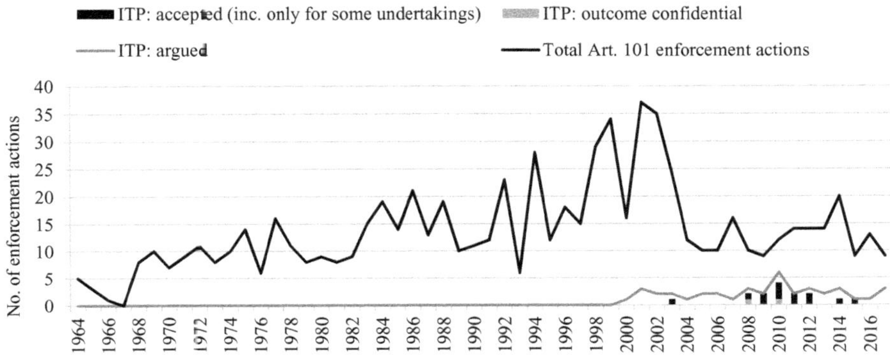

FIGURE 7.8. Inability to pay, Commission

undertaking's inability to pay in a specific social and economic context. It will not base any reduction granted for this reason in the fine on the mere finding of an adverse or loss-making financial situation. A reduction could be granted solely on the basis of objective evidence that imposition of the fine as provided for in these Guidelines would irretrievably jeopardise the economic viability of the undertaking concerned and cause its assets to lose all their value'.[273]

The purpose of this provision, according to the Commission, is to avoid driving financially distressed but competitive undertakings out of the market, thus bearing adverse social and economic consequences.[274] The Commission has repeatedly emphasised that the mere risk of bankruptcy or liquidation was not sufficient. A fine reduction was only justified if the undertakings' assets stood to lose their value because of the fine and only to the extent that it made a takeover by another undertaking or a separate sale of the assets unlikely.[275]

Figure 7.8 summarises the Commission's practice in assessing and accepting the inability to pay claims. The figure presents the total number of cases in which undertakings raised inability to pay claims (grey line) and the number of cases in which the plea for fine reduction was accepted (black bars). In a small number of cases, the result of the claim was unclear due to confidentiality concerns (grey bars).[276]

As becomes apparent from the figure, there was an increase in the inability to pay claims after the outbreak of the economic crisis of 2008 and in the number of cases

[273] Commission Fining Guidelines (2006), para 35. The empirical findings reveal that the Commission also took those considerations into account prior to the 2006 Guidelines, but less regularly. See, for example, 38359 Electrical and mechanical carbon and graphite products (2003), para 36c.

[274] Commission Inability to Pay Information Notice (2010), para 6.

[275] T-71/03 T-74/03 T-87/03 T-91/03 Speciality Graphite (2005), para 332–333; T-406/09 Calcium carbide and magnesium based reagents for the steel and gas industries (2014), para 286.

[276] 39188 Bananas (2008), para 490–491; 39258 Airfreight (2010), para 1381–1399.

in which the Commission has accepted such claims. The empirical findings also show that while almost all inability to pay fine reductions have emphasised the specific *economic context*,[277] some have also invoked the adverse effect in the *social context*, for instance, when the payment of the fine might stimulate unemployment or deteriorate upstream or downstream economic activity.[278]

Once again, the 2006 Guidelines failed to define a clear methodology for assessing an undertaking's inability to pay. In 2010, following the increase in inability to pay claims, the Commission published an information notice to clarify its position.[279] However, even after this clarification had been published, there was no single, unanimously accepted method for such an assessment.[280]

It should be noted that the inability to pay test leaves less room for the consideration of non-competition interests in comparison to the crisis cartel principle. Crisis cartel situations had justified fine reductions for all the undertakings concerned on the basis of the economic crisis in the relevant sector during the time of the infringement (e.g. *French Beef*). Yet, inability to pay claims only justify reducing the fines imposed on a specific undertaking on the basis of its inability to pay at the time the infringement decision is rendered.[281] They take the economic context into account only to the extent that it directly affects an undertaking's ability to pay the fine.[282] Moreover, the inability to pay test is narrower in scope since it is subject to a cumulative requirement. This entails that the inability to pay is linked to both the specific social and economic context.[283]

[277] See Annex A, Section 7.3.

[278] 39396 Calcium carbide and magnesium based reagents (2009), para 372; 38866 Animal Feed Phosphates (2010), para 224–238. The social context was also emphasised by the Courts in C-308/04P Graphite electrodes (2006), para 106; T-352/09 Calcium carbide and magnesium based reagents for the steel (2012); T-406/09 Calcium carbide and magnesium based reagents for the steel and gas industries (2014), para 282–314. Yet, the social context alone did not justify granting a fine reduction. For example, in T-352/09 Calcium carbide and magnesium based reagents for the steel and gas industries (2012), para 180–181 and 201–209, the undertakings, supported by the Slovak Republic, argued that the effects of its bankruptcy would be detrimental in the social and regional contexts. As one of the major employers in Slovakia, having strategic importance for the economic life of the Slovak region of Upper Nitra, its closure would lead to job loss for 2000 employees and the closure or substantial reduction in operation of a number of other undertakings in the same region, including its suppliers. The Court, however, rejected the claim. It explained that while the applicant had proven the special social circumstances, it had failed to prove the economic circumstances. See also T-406/09 Calcium carbide and magnesium based reagents for the steel and gas industries (2014), para 282–314.

[279] Commission Inability to Pay Information Notice (2010).

[280] See also Torre (2010, 402).

[281] Commission Inability to Pay Information Notice (2010) explains that inability to pay may also be taken into account subsequent to the adoption of the decision. This was used in a small number of cases, for instance in 39168 PO/Hard Haberdashery (2011). See also Lianos et al. (2014, 225–228).

[282] Torre (2010, 402).

[283] Commission Fining Guidelines (2006), para 35. The cumulative nature was confirmed in 38069 Copper plumbing tubes (2004), para 822; C-308/04P Graphite electrodes (2006), para 106; T-352/09 Calcium carbide and magnesium based reagents for the steel and gas industries

At the national level, in line with the Commission's practice since the 2000s, the Five NCAs, too, did not regard difficulties in a sector (crisis cartels) as a stand-alone justification for fine reduction.[284] In France, the NCA and courts explicitly rejected this possibility, referring to both EU and national case law.[285]

Yet, some NCAs have taken into account crisis situations when they were combined with other special circumstances, such as those in *French Beef*. In *Bell peppers (2012)*, for example, the Dutch NCA held that the combination of the role of a growing cooperative, together with the financial crisis in the sector, justified a fine reduction.[286] In *Bid rigging in the construction industry in England (2009)*, the UK NCA noted that it would not be appropriate to reduce fines across the board due to the worldwide economic climate but granted all undertakings a more extended period in which to pay.[287] In *Dairy retail price initiatives (2011)*, the UK NCA took into account the farmgate prices for raw milk that were not high enough to cover the dairy farmers' costs, the significant number of dairy farmers leaving the industry, and the resulting pressure to take action to help farmers.[288] It noted that while none of these factors justified the infringements, those exceptional circumstances moderated the seriousness of the infringements and, therefore, the fine.

Like the Commission, all Five NCAs fining guidelines include inability to pay provisions.[289] Contrary to the Commission, in all Five NCAs guidelines, this fine reduction depends solely on the financial circumstance of the undertakings, without reference to the social context. The national provisions, therefore, leave greater

(2012), para 201–209; T-406/09 Calcium carbide and magnesium based reagents for the steel and gas industries (2014), para 282–314; T-393/10 Prestressing steel (2015), para 296; C-523/15P Prestressing steel (2016), para 46.

284 Referring to B12–14/10 Household porcelain in Germany (2013), the President of the German NCA noted 'economic difficulties in a particular sector cannot justify the consumer having to pay more for a product than he would if effective competition were in place. We have borne in mind the difficult economic situation in the porcelain sector in the current proceedings. We have therefore imposed relatively moderate fines, which take account of the financial situation of the individual companies involved'. However, this comment seems to relate to consideration of the inability to pay, rather than directly to the economic crisis.

285 French Fining Guidelines (2011), para 62; the French NCA decisions in 10-D-35 Welding electrodes (2010), para 244–245; 11-D-17 Laundry detergents (2011), para 664–666; 14-D-20 Wallpaper (2014), para 255–257; Paris Court of Appeal in 2008/12495 Plywood manufactures (2009), 15; 2009/03532 Temporary employment sector (2010), 23–24, as confirmed by the Cour de Cassation in 10-12913 10-13686 Temporary employment sector (2011), 7.

286 7036_1/386 Bell peppers (2012), para 381–386.

287 CE/4327-04 Bid rigging in the construction industry in England (2009), para VI.289–290.

288 CE/3094-03 Dairy retail price initiatives (2011), para 7.46–7.47.

289 French Fining Guidelines (2011), para 48, 62–64; German Fining Guidelines (2006), para 24; Dutch Fining Guidelines (2016), para 2.6, read in conjunction with Section 5:46(2) of the Dutch General Administrative Law Act, and Dutch NCA decision in 7244-597 Magazine packs (2015), para 251–254; Hungarian Fining Guidelines (2017), para 79–80; UK Fining Guidelines (2018), para 2.33.

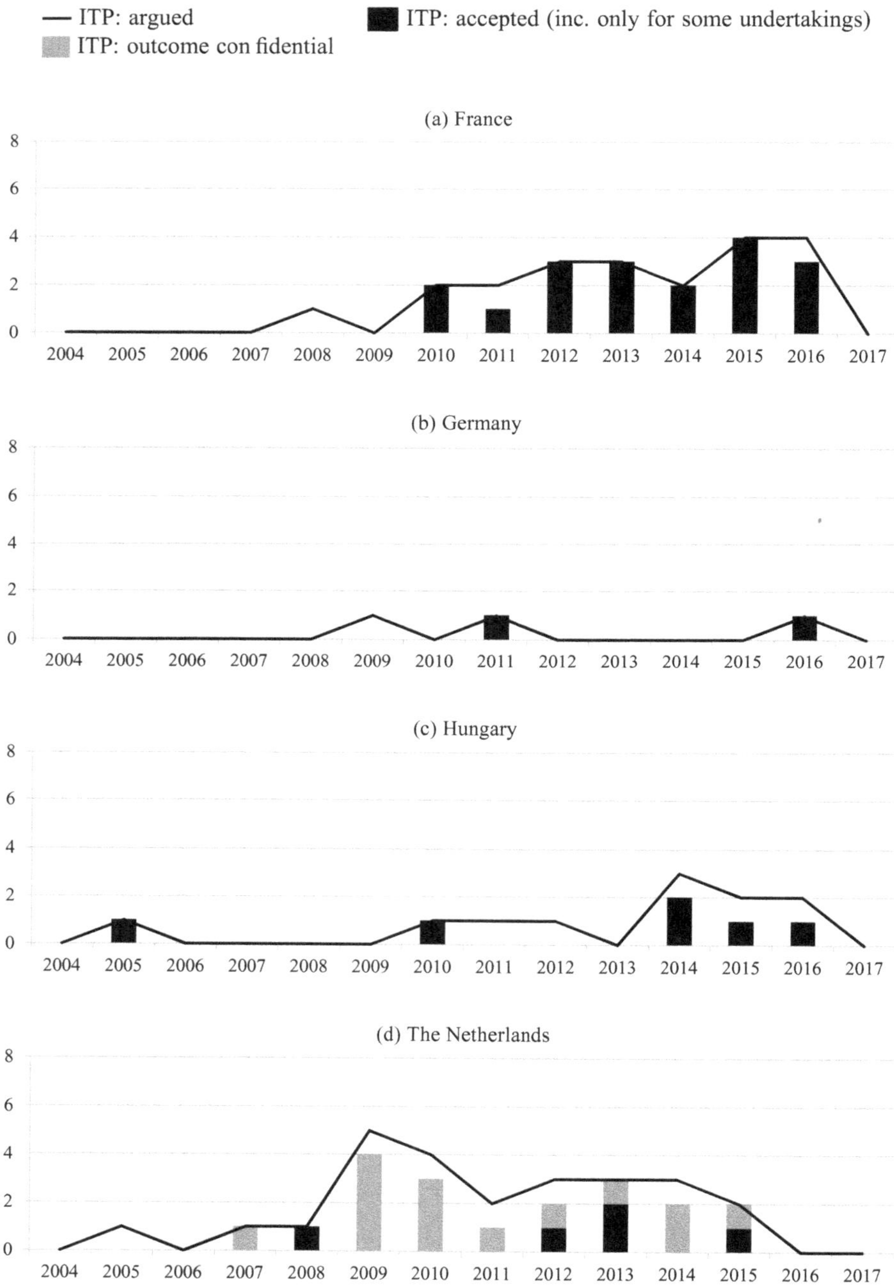

FIGURE 7.9 Inability to pay, NCAs

room for consideration of the financial position of undertakings.[290] Figure 7.9 outlines the inability to pay claims argued (lines) and accepted (bars) before the Five NCAs.

The figure shows that following the financial crisis of 2008, undertakings in almost all the five Member States increased their invocation of inability to pay claims.[291] The figure also reveals that the NCAs were more likely to accept inability to pay claims than the Commission. This might perhaps be the result of their more relaxed approach to such claims.

The exact degree of financial hardship that justifies a fine reduction varies between the Member States For example, the Dutch NCA, unlike the Commission and UK NCA and courts,[292] held that a risk of bankruptcy justifies a fine reduction.[293] Moreover, in a number of cases, the UK NCA, outside the regular financial hardship test, moderated the fines imposed on undertakings noting that they would be disproportionate to the financial position of the undertakings.[294] In some cases, this fine reduction was given after noting that the undertaking did not meet the inability to pay test.[295]

The economic and social crisis in the aftermath of the coronavirus outbreak is likely to revive the debate over the conditions for a fine reduction in crisis situations. In a remarkable ruling in 2020, for example, the Dutch Trade and Industry Appeals

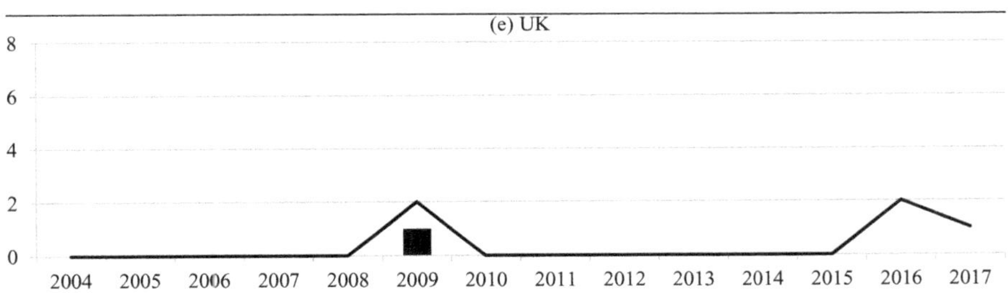

FIGURE 7.9 *(cont.)*
In the Netherlands, most NCA decisions do not indicate whether the plea was accepted on account of confidentiality considerations (grey bars)[296]

[290] See also the CAT in 1067/1/1/06 Price fixing and market sharing in stock check pads (2006), para 43.

[291] See Annex A, Section 7.5.

[292] 1067/1/1/06 Price fixing and market sharing in stock check pads (2006), para 55–56.

[293] Explanatory Memorandum of the Dutch Competition Act, para 57; 7244-597 Magazine packs (2015), para 258–259.

[294] CE/7691-06 Airline passenger fuel surcharges for long-haul flights (2012), para 443; CE/9857-14 Bathroom fittings (2016), para 7.48; CE/9856/14 Refrigeration (2016), para 7.47; CE/9691/12 Galvanised steel tanks – Main (2016), para 5.44; 50343 Light fittings (2017), para 5.49; 50230 Golf equipment (2017), para 5.89.

[295] 50223 Posters and frames (2016), para 6.37, 6.44–6.45; CE/9859-14 Modelling (2016), 5.74–5.92, 5.99.

[296] See Annex A, Section 7.4.

Tribunal has reduced the fine imposed on a cartel member from €1,000,000 to a mere €10,000.[297] This 99% fine reduction was granted although the undertaking had already paid the fine when it was financially liable and although there was no basis to moderate the fine on the basis of the inability to pay test. Yet, the Tribunal held that the undertaking would need to wait too long for a final decision in appeal and would probably go bankrupt due to the circumstances surrounding the coronavirus crisis. It should be noted that since this decision was not fully reasoned, it is unclear how it may affect the calculation of future cases.

7.6.1.4 SMEs

The previous chapters discussed the role of non-competition interest related to the protection of SMEs. They demonstrated that the competition enforcers and Member States have enacted rules that allow SMEs to engage in conduct that would otherwise be classified as an anti-competitive behaviour.[298] In addition, infringements by SMEs have also sometimes warranted a fine reduction or waiver. The Commission has been inconsistent in this regard. In the past, it accepted that claim in some cases[299] but rejected it in others.[300] In *Pre-Insulated Pipe Cartel (2002)*, however, the GC held that the fact that the applicant was a medium-sized family undertaking did not constitute a mitigating circumstance.[301]

Some NCAs continue to take this consideration into account. The UK Competition Act, for example, provides immunity from fines in purely national cases for 'small agreements', i.e. non-price-fixing agreements between undertakings with a low turnover or market share.[302] In Hungary, a 2015 amendment to the Competition Act provides that the Hungarian NCA may issue a warning instead of a fine for a first-time infringement of SMEs in purely national cases.[303] SMEs that cannot benefit from a warning will still enjoy a fine reduction of up to 10%.[304] In fact, SMEs received fine reductions in Hungary even prior to the said amendment.[305] This was also considered a mitigating factor in Germany[306] and sometimes in the Netherlands.[307]

[297] 19/162 Applicant A (2020).

[298] See Sections 5.3.6, 6.3.1, and 6.3.2.

[299] 29290 Vaessen/Moris (1979), para 26–27; 36516 Nathan-Bricolux (2000), para 130.

[300] 37027 Zinc Phosphate (2001), para 342–343.

[301] T-23/99 Pre-Insulated Pipe Cartel (2002), para 338.

[302] Section 6.3.1.

[303] Hungarian Competition Act, Article 78(8). Remarkably, in 1.Kf.650.154/2016/10 Mosquito control (2017), 8, the Hungarian Court applied this amendment retroactively, revoking a fine imposed by the Hungarian NCA prior to the amendment of the Act. See also Section 6.3.1.

[304] Hungarian Fining Guidelines (2017), para 65.

[305] Vj-96/2009-177 Book market (2013).

[306] B3–144/08 Colistin antibiotics (2009); Sanitary sector (2016).

[307] A fine reduction was granted in 6425 Window cleaners (2011), para 328, but rejected in 4814-31 Installation (2005), para 27–28; 6431_1/172 Kazerne II (2009), para 171–173; 6429_1/176 Kazerne

7.6.1.5 Damage to the Economy (France)

This section has thus far described situations in which a fine was *mitigated* to account for non-competition interests. The French NCA, however, has also been prone to *aggravate* fines when an infringement harmed not only competition but also other public policies. The French Commercial Code provides that the fine imposed for an infringement must be proportionate, *inter-alia*, to the resulting 'scale of the damage caused to the economy'.[308] The French NCA has explained that this is not limited to illegal profits that undertakings have reaped due to an infringement (i.e. due to the harm to competition interests), but also to other direct or indirect disturbances to the market.[309] In particular, the fine must reflect the adverse effect on the incentives of other market players and is not limited to precisely measurable loss (i.e. economic and non-economic benefits).

Accordingly, in *Temporary employment sector (2009)*, the French NCA aggravated the fine imposed on France's largest staffing firms. It observed that the firms employing temporary workers, as well as the temporary workers themselves, were harmed by the anti-competitive practice, hindering national employment and economic growth policies.[310] In *Football rights (2009)*, the French NCA aggravated the fine imposed on the French Football Federation and Sportfive for collusion in the awarding of the Federation's marketing rights. It maintained that the anti-competitive practice limited the available resources of the Federation and therefore indirectly hindered the development of amateur football in France.[311] Remarkably, those two decisions were given in mixed cases, in which the French NCA had applied both Article 101 TFEU and the national equivalent provision. Hence, it provides an example of how national fining provisions incorporate national policies in the enforcement of EU law.

7.6.1.6 Scope of Discretion

The previous sections demonstrated how non-competition interests have influenced the setting of fines. They illustrated that EU and national laws have left room for the consideration of non-competition interests when setting the fines. The Commission and NCAs have taken a broad range of benefits into account, especially those related to public policy aims and situations of economic crisis. While, in most cases, EU and national laws left the competition enforcers a considerable margin of discretion

I (2009), para 164–166; 6430_1/131 Meiveld (2009), para 187–188; 6492_1/146 De Tongelreep (2009), para 195–197; 6091_1/204 Distributors of sodium hypochlorite (2009), para 224–225; 6601_1/141 Meerhoven (2009), para 136–137.

[308] French Commercial Code, Article L424-2.

[309] French Fining Guidelines (2011), para 27.

[310] 09-D-05 Temporary employment sector (2009), para 116.

[311] 09-D-31 Football rights (2009), para 364–366.

to account for non-competition interests, some competition enforcers are bound by procedural safeguards.

At the EU level, although the Commission has wide discretion in setting the fine, it must properly justify and explain its calculation. This is particularly true when the Commission decides to deviate from its Fining Guidelines and even when it does so in the favour of the undertakings.[312] Moreover, the Commission's decision is subject to judicial review. Article 261 TFEU and Article 31 of Regulation 1/2003 grant the EU Courts unlimited jurisdiction to review the Commission's decisions on fines. The Courts control not only the lawfulness of the fine but also its merits. They may substitute their own appraisal for the Commission's.[313] The Commission's Fining Guidelines, as a mechanism of soft law, are not binding on EU Courts.[314]

However, the empirical findings reveal that the EU Courts have hardly ever used those powers to appraise the consideration of non-competition interests. While the EU Courts, and especially the GC, have often intervened in the calculation of fines,[315] they have almost always respected the Commission's assessment with respect to balancing.

The EU Courts have consistently held that factors like crisis in the sector and inability to pay are mitigating circumstances which the Commission may, but is not obliged to, take into account.[316] Moreover, they have stated that the mere fact that the Commission may have taken a factor into account in earlier cases does not mean that it must continue to observe such practices in future cases.[317] Specifically, they have confirmed the change in the Commission's approach to crisis situations in which the conditions of a sector can no longer be taken into account but rather only the ability of specific undertakings to pay.[318]

At the Member State level, some of the national courts were relatively active when reviewing inability to pay claims.[319] Interestingly, the next section shows that national courts that intervened in such cases – France, the Netherlands, and the UK – were the same courts active in reviewing the acceptance of commitments. This validates the importance of the national substantive and procedural rules in determining the scope of balancing via outcome discretion.

[312] T-58/14 Shrimps (2018), para 313–317.

[313] See also Forrester (2011, 153–156) and Paz (2014, 218–219).

[314] C-338/00P VW (2003), para 147; T-49/02 T-50/02 T-51/02 Brasserie (2005), para 169; T-101/05 T-111/05 BASF UCB (2007), para 213. See also Torre (2010, 406).

[315] Geradin and Petit (2012, 62) show that 45% of the applications to the GC for reduction of fine for infringement of Article 101 TFEU between 2000 and 2010 were successful. See also Geradin and Henry (2005, 458) and Veljanovski (2007, 76).

[316] See Annex A, Section 7.6.

[317] T-347/94 Cartonboard (1998), para 368; C-23/99 Pre-Insulated Pipe Cartel (2002), para 337. See also Faull and Nikpay (2014, 1289).

[318] See Annex A, Section 7.7.

[319] See Annex A, Section 7.8.

7.6.2 Commitments

7.6.2.1 A Balancing Tool[320]

Regulation 1/2003 granted the Commission and NCAs a novel enforcement instrument in the form of the commitment decision procedure. These powers are often seen as an extension, or a special case of the competition enforcers' priority setting discretion. Originally, this procedure was directed at securing early closure of cases, thereby promoting administrative efficiency.[321] This section reveals that despite this original aim, commitments have also served as an open-ended legal tool to account for non-competition interests. Balancing by accepting commitments is especially significant given the frequent use of this procedure. While it was initially presumed that commitments would be used in 'unusual and rare' circumstances,[322] they quickly became the hallmark of the Commission's enforcement regime[323] as well as of many of the NCAs.

The Commission's power to accept commitments was first formalised by Regulation 1/2003.[324] The Regulation authorises the Commission to close an Article 101 TFEU investigation by accepting behavioural or structural commitments offered by the undertakings ('formal commitments'). This provision codified a long-standing practice in which the Commission resolved investigations by accepting voluntary commitments ('informal commitments').[325] The empirical findings affirm that the Commission continued to accept informal commitments even once Regulation 1/2003 had come into force.[326]

The power to accept formal and informal commitments is not bound to *any substantive test*. Regulation 1/2003 merely prescribes that 'commitment decisions should find that there are *no longer grounds for action* by the Commission without

[320] For a discussion on how commitments can serve as a substitute for an Article 101(3) TFEU balancing, see also Brook (2020, 470–477).

[321] C-441/07P Alrosa (2010), para 35; Report on the Functioning of Regulation 1/2003 (2009), para 13; Commission Staff Working Paper accompanying the Report on Functioning of Regulation 1/2003 (2009), para 94; Report on the Functioning of Regulation 1/2003 (2014), para 21. For empirical data on the duration of the commitment procedure compared to Article 7 decisions, see Gerard (2013, 9).

[322] Temple Lang (2006, 270). See also Schweitzer (2008, 4), GCLC Annual Conference (2010, 62), and Jenny (2015, 702, 709).

[323] As demonstrated by the empirical findings presented in Figure 8.1. See also Schweitzer (2012, 4–5); Report on the Functioning of Regulation 1/2003 (2014), 7.

[324] Regulation 1/2003, Articles 5 and 9 and Preamble 13. See also Commission's Commitment Decision Press Release (2004).

[325] Van Bael (1986, 64), Waelbroeck (1986, 268–280), Wils (2006b, 347), Cengiz (2010a, 2–3, 7–8), Van Rompuy (2012, 270), and Jenny (2015, 703–706). See also policy report (1975, 9); Section 2.3.2.

[326] See Figure 8.1. See also discussion in Wils (2006b, 364).

concluding whether or not there has been or still is an infringement'.[327] It leaves open the questions of whether the agreement actually violated Article 101 TFEU in the first place or whether the modified agreement is compatible with the exceptions of Article 101(1) or (3) TFEU. As a result, the Commission has the extraordinary discretion to accept commitments, which is not bound by the regular competition analysis of Article 101 TFEU.[328]

As elaborated below, commentators have already suggested that these features offer competition enforcers an indirect way to account for non-competition interests.[329] The lack of a substantive test for accepting commitments, combined with their *ex-ante* nature, allows competition enforcers to regulate markets and to promote broad non-competition interests that are not directly related to the economic consequences of the anti-competitive behaviour of the undertakings concerned. In particular, after the Commission attempted to narrow down the scope for balancing under the explicit-substantive tools of Article 101(1) and (3) TFEU as part of modernisation, commitments provide the enforcers with a flexible tool to negotiate and tailor the application of Article 101 TFEU to a specific context.

The lack of a substantive test for accepting commitments was confirmed by the CJEU in *Alrosa (2010)*. The Court held that when accepting commitments, the Commission is only subject to general EU principles, the principle of proportionality in particular. This principle, according to the Court, has a different meaning in the context of a regular infringement or a commitment decision.[330] In the latter case, this simply entails that the offered commitments address the competition concerns expressed by the Commission in its preliminary assessment. The Commission is only required to verify that the proposed commitments do not manifestly go beyond what is necessary to address the competition concerns and that the undertakings have not offered less onerous commitments that could equally address those concerns. The Commission is not obliged to compare the commitments offered with measures that it could have used in the context of an infringement decision.

Despite the lack of a substantive test, the formalisation of commitments by Regulation 1/2003 introduced several *procedural safeguards*. It provides that when the Commission intends to accept a formal commitment, it must publish a concise summary of the case and the proposed commitment and invite interested third parties to submit their observations (the so-called 'market test').[331] Yet, because the

[327] Emphasis added. Regulation 1/2003, Preamble 13. See also C-547/16 Gasorba (2017), para 25–26.

[328] See also Forrester (2008, 640–641), Cengiz (2010a, 3), and Van Rompuy (2012, 272).

[329] Schweitzer (2008, 553), Cengiz (2010a, 11), Blanco and De Pablo (2012, 80–82), Van Rompuy (2012, 270, 274), and CMA's Roundtable on the Use of Commitments in Competition Enforcement (2015), para 11.

[330] C-441/07P Alrosa (2010), para 36–50.

[331] Regulation 1/2003, Article 27(4). The empirical findings confirm that the Commission has often taken third parties' observations into account and ordered that the commitments be modified. See Annex A, Section 7.9.

procedure for accepting informal commitments has not been formalised, the procedural safeguards of Regulation 1/2003 do not apply. By the same token, apart from the general principle of protection of legitimate expectations, there is no legal mechanism to force undertakings to comply with the informal commitments offered.[332]

Regulation 1/2003 had also vested the NCAs with powers allowing them to accept commitments.[333] To make use of such powers, nevertheless, the Member States must adopt national laws that prescribe the applicable substantive and procedural rules. The five Member States examined in this study,[334] like most other Member States,[335] have adopted such laws. Because such rules are not harmonised, national commitments are not identical to the Commission's procedure.[336] There is considerable divergence, in particular, with respect to the legal and procedural frameworks, the application of the proportionality test, the requirement of a market test, and the rights of third parties.[337] The rules governing the judicial review of commitment decisions also differ considerably.[338]

The lack of a harmonised substantive test for accepting commitments gives the competition enforcers a blank check to use commitments as a balancing tool. Consequently, the balancing method guiding the acceptance of commitments can take various forms:

First, a commitment may *apply the law* by following the same balancing method as the explicit-substantive balancing tools. A commitment might, for instance, aim to amend an anti-competitive agreement to bring it into compliance with the four conditions of Article 101(3) TFEU.[339] Competition enforcers might have several reasons to prefer accepting a commitment rather than openly applying an explicit-substantive balancing tool. Commitments provide a flexible, relatively fast, and informal measure for balancing. Since there is no substantive test for accepting commitments, a competition enforcer does not need to explain how and why the

332 Van Rompuy (2012, 270) and Lachnit (2016, 281).

333 Regulation 1/2003, Article 5.

334 French Commercial Code, Article L 464-2 and French Notice on Competition Commitments (2009); German Competition Act, Section 32b; Dutch Competition Act, Article 49a; Hungarian Competition Act, Article 75 and Hungarian Commitment Notice (2018); UK Competition Act, Sections 31A–31E.

335 For a detailed analysis, see ECN Decision Making Powers Report (2012), 28–35. See also ECN Recommendation on Commitment Procedures (2013), para 3.

336 ECN Decision Making Powers Report (2012), para 9, recommends further convergence in national laws on commitments.

337 *Ibid*, 28–35; Schweitzer (2012). Notably, the Commission did not criticise this divergence in its ECN+ Directive Proposal (2017). It merely pointed out in Article 11 that NCAs should have the power to adopt commitments to meet the concerns expressed by them.

338 See Section 7.6.2.4.

339 The Commission declares that commitments can be used to settle a case in which Article 101 (3) TFEU is likely to apply. See Commission Staff Working Paper accompanying the Report on Functioning of Regulation 1/2003 (2009), para 26, 34.

conditions for an exception have been fulfilled. Other enforcers, or the Commission itself, could depart from the Commission's narrow interpretation of the role of non-competition interests without declaring so openly.[340] An enforcer can take broader types of benefits into account, give preference to non-competition interests, or accept a low threshold of evidence.

Second, a commitment may *extend or change the law*. A competition enforcer may accept a commitment as a means of balancing that stays outside the framework of Article 101 (1) and (3) TFEU balancing tools altogether.[341] A competition enforcer may accept a commitment even if the original agreement is not prohibited by Article 101 TFEU, i.e. if the agreement does not infringe Article 101(1) TFEU or fulfil the conditions of Article 101(3) TFEU. By the same token, an enforcer may also accept a commitment that does not remedy all competition concerns. To this end, commitments can be used to protect non-competition interests and non-economic benefits that could not have been considered otherwise or to impose conditions that could not have been attached in the context of an infringement decision.[342]

Third, a commitment may *regulate business behaviour*.[343] Whereas following May 2004, the explicit-substantive balancing tools have typically been applied in an *ex-post* manner, competition enforcers can use commitments as a forward-looking tool aimed at shaping market structures and affecting business conduct.[344] Rather than applying Article 101 TFEU *reactively* to *preserve* competition on the market, commitments can be used to *proactively regulate* an industry.

Balancing by commitments is particularly attractive from the standpoint of the competition enforcers following modernisation. In the face of the Commission's attempt to limit the scope for balancing under Article 101(1) and (3) TFEU, commitments offer an indirect way to facilitate balancing. As *Schweitzer* has aptly summarised it, 'there appears to be a real need, perceived both by the Commission and the undertakings concerned, for a flexible procedural framework outside the normal infringement proceeding to negotiate conditions and obligations fine-tuned to the requirements of Art. [101(3) TFEU]. Commitment decisions here serve as a substitute for exemption decisions in application of [Article 101(3) TFEU] with conditions and obligations'. [345]

[340] On the Commission's narrow interpretation of Article 101(3) TFEU following modernisation, see Sections 3.3.4 and 3.4.4.

[341] Wils (2006b, 357), Schweitzer (2008, 1), Van Rompuy (2012, 274), and CMA's Roundtable on the Use of Commitments in Competition Enforcement (2015), para 11.

[342] Schweitzer (2012, 3). See also Forrester (2008, 646), Cengiz (2010a, 10), and Wathelet (2015, 553).

[343] For the definition of a regulatory balancing tool, see Section 1.2.2.2.

[344] Petit (2010, 32); Ibáñez Colomo (2010, 286); Dunne (2014b, 407); CMA's Roundtable on the Use of Commitments in Competition Enforcement (2015), para 11; and OCED Commitments Report (2016), para 38–30.

[345] Schweitzer (2008, 6).

Yet, balancing by way of accepting commitments also carries serious risks. Although commitments do not have any formal precedential value, they could have that effect in practice. The Commission has already acknowledged that notwithstanding the limited legal effects of commitment decisions, they can serve as a model for addressing similar situations.[346] This position was formalised more recently in *Gasorba (2017)*, in which a Spanish Court asked the CJEU whether a commitment decision adopted by the Commission precludes a national court from declaring that the relevant agreement infringes Article 101 TFEU. The CJEU held that although national courts were not bound by a Commission's commitment decision, both the principle of sincere cooperation laid down in Article 4(3) TEU and the objective of applying EU competition law effectively and uniformly require national courts to take into account 'the preliminary assessment carried out by the Commission and regard it as an *indication, if not prima facie evidence*, of the anticompetitive nature of the agreement at issue'.[347]

When applied to the question of balancing, this means that although the Commission's commitments are not binding on national courts, the balancing embedded in them may carry a legal effect. Under those circumstances, the opportunity to balance outside the explicit-substantive balancing tools could have serious implications that extend beyond the case at hand.

7.6.2.2 Unclear Boundaries

The lack of a substantive standard for accepting commitments has created considerable legal uncertainty as to the role of non-competition interests. This section submits that the legal uncertainty surrounding balancing by accepting commitments has been further aggravated by the Commission's contradictory statements and practices.

The Commission has not always been consistent when defining the boundaries of the commitment tool. The Commission's policy on accepting commitments for by-object restrictions provides a good example. Regulation 1/2003 states that commitments are inappropriate when the Commission intends to impose a fine.[348] By the Commission's interpretation, this entails that it should not accept commitments to remedy hard-core restrictions.[349] Nevertheless, the empirical findings presented in Figure 7.10 reveal that the Commission has accepted both formal (solid bars) and

[346] Commission Staff Working Paper accompanying the Report on Functioning of Regulation 1/2003 (2009), para 109.

[347] C-547/16 Gasorba (2017), para 29.

[348] Regulation 1/2003, Preamble 13.

[349] Commission's Commitment Decisions Press Release (2004). See also Cengiz (2010a, 5). Most Member States have declared that they follow a similar approach. Others, such as the Czech Republic and Slovenia, accept commitments to remedy hard-core infringements – see OCED Commitments Report (2016), para 23.

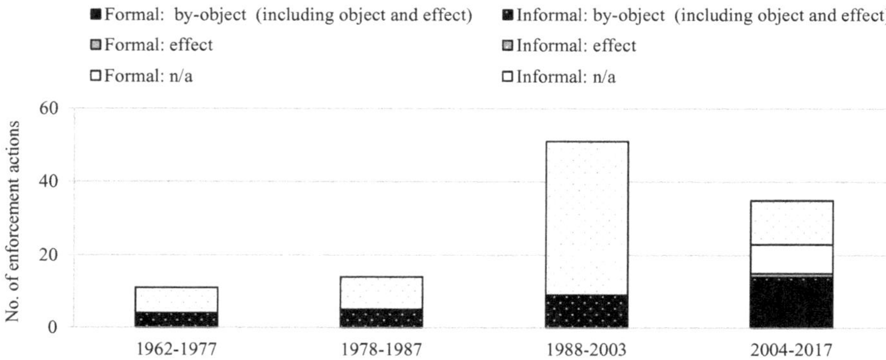

FIGURE 7.10. Commitments for by-object restrictions, Commission

informal (dotted bars) commitments, also when the agreement was classified as a by-object infringement (black bars).[350]

For instance, in *Container Shipping (2016)*, the Commission examined a widespread practice of major global carriers for announcing general rate increases. Those announcements indicated the amount of the intended increase per transported container unit, the affected trade route, and the intended date of implementation. The announcements were made in rounds, by which one party would declare its intended price increase 3–5 weeks before the implementation date, following which other parties would announce their intended price increases in a similar magnitude, for the same route, and with a similar or identical implementation date. Moreover, intended price increases were sometimes postponed or modified to align them with the pricing strategies of the other parties.[351]

Referring to its Horizontal Guidelines (2011), the Commission held that such public exchanges of pricing intentions, even if unilateral, might constitute a by-object restriction. Its preliminary assessment had raised the concern that this practice had the objective of communicating pricing intentions to competitors rather than informing customers about price developments.[352] At the same time, despite this potential serious infringement of competition, the Commission accepted commitments permitting 'timely, transparent and committal price announcements'.[353] It did not adopt an infringement decision or imposed a fine.

In a similar vein, the Commission has expressed inconsistent positions on the regulatory or corrective aim of commitments. In some cases, the Commission has

[350] See Annex A, Section 7.10.
[351] 39850 Container Shipping (2016), para 26–27.
[352] *Ibid*, para 52; Commission Horizontal Guideline (2011), para 72–74. See also Rabinovici (2016, 152).
[353] 39850 Container Shipping (2016), para 84. See also Commission Horizontal Guidelines (2011), para 99.

overtly used commitments as a *regulatory balancing tool*.[354] For example, in *Ship Classification (2009)*, the Commission suspected that the International Association of Classification Societies (IACS) had prevented non-members from joining the association, participating in its technical working groups, and accessing technical background documents. According to the Commission, such behaviour had hindered the entry and development of classification societies, which were not members of IACS, in the ship classification market.[355] IACS proposed a series of commitments, including the adoption of qualitative membership criteria, allowing non-members to participate in IACS' working groups, and full access to its technical resolutions and related background documents. The Commission had accepted the commitments, noting that they were not only necessary to address the competitive concerns but also to promote the efficiency and quality of the classification society's technical work and standards.[356]

Similarly, in *Virtual Print Fee agreements (2011)*, the Commission examined provisions in contracts between major Hollywood film studios and the integrators relating to the financing and installation of digital projection equipment in cinemas. The Commission was concerned that certain provisions that have given the film studio the right to benefit from the most favourable terms, including lower virtual print fee payments, will hinder the access of small film distributors to digital cinemas. The Commission had ended the proceeding after the studios agreed to modify the contracts, to facilitate the release of independent and art house films in new state-of-the-art cinemas. When accepting those informal commitments, the Commission stated not only that the proposed changes will address the preliminary competition concerns but also that the commitments were justified by cultural motives, i.e. providing access to independent films.[357]

Yet, in other cases, the Commission has claimed that commitments should be confined to *corrective balancing* purposes.[358] According to this approach, non-competition interests can only be taken into account to the extent that they are required to safeguard the rights of third parties within the market test. The Commission has maintained that it would not use commitments to *promote* non-competition interests on account of competition, but only to ensure that the steps taken to restore competition did not *harm* the non-competition interests of third parties.

This position was advocated, for instance, in *eBooks (2012)*.[359] The Commission's preliminary assessment had provisionally concluded that four publishers and Apple

[354] On the definition of a regulatory balancing tool, see Section 1.2.2.2.

[355] 39416 Ship Classification (2009), para 13.

[356] *Ibid*, para 31–36.

[357] 39673 Virtual Print Fee agreements (2011), 1. This resembles the use of non-competition interests as additional justification for Article 101(3) TFEU exemptions, as discussed in Section 3.3.3.5.

[358] On the definition of a corrective balancing tool, see Section 1.2.2.2.

[359] 39847 eBooks (2012), para 127.

have adopted a global strategy aiming at raising the retail prices of electronic books. The undertakings have offered to terminate their on-going agency agreements and to exclude certain MFN clauses in their agency agreements for a period of five years. They also offered to give retailers the freedom to discount electronic books, subject to certain conditions, for a period of two years.

When conducting the market test, third parties had claimed that the proposed commitments would negatively impact cultural diversity. By reference to the policy-linking clause on culture, the Commission noted that it is obliged to take cultural considerations into account when accepting commitments. However, the Commission interpreted this obligation narrowly. It stated that the purpose of commitments is to restore the conditions of competition that existed prior to the anti-competitive practice. Since commitments are not intended to promote cultural interests, the Commission is only required to verify that the proposed commitments are not 'adversely affecting cultural diversity'.[360] Hence, the Commission viewed the commitment decision procedure as confined to corrective balancing. The policy-linking clauses could not impose an obligation to actively promote non-competition interests.[361]

7.6.2.3 Empirical Indications

The possibility that commitments could be used for purposes that go beyond their original administrative efficiency aim to account for non-competition interests has already been observed by various commentators.[362] *Ibanez Colomo*, for example, concluded that commitments were used to settle practices that are similar 'in their nature, purpose and impact' to those which have been exempted by Article 101(3) TFEU prior to modernisation.[363] Similarly, *Dunne* pointed to the regulatory nature and function of the Commission's commitment decisions, noting that they have essentially 'replicate[d] the functions performed by the Regulation 17 notification procedure'.[364] They have emphasised that the lack of a substantive test for accepting commitments, in combination with their *ex-ante* nature, allows competition enforcers to regulate markets and to promote non-competition interests that are not directly related to the anti-competitive behaviour of the undertakings concerned.

360 *Ibid*, para 152. A similar approach was repeated in 40023 Cross-border access to pay-TV (2016), para 73–74.

361 A similar rationale guided the Commission's decision in 39398 Visa MIF (2014), para 46. The Commission declared that it could not accept commitments that aimed to promote non-competition interests – in that case, market integration – if there was no anti-competitive harm.

362 Schweitzer (2008, 11), Forrester (2008, 646), GCLC Annual Conference (2010, 65), Van Rompuy (2012, 274), Wagner-von Papp (2012, 961–966), Blanco and De Pablo (2012, 76–78), Wathelet (2015, 554); CMA's Roundtable on the Use of Commitments in Competition Enforcement (2015), para 11; and Sauter (2016, 130, 286–287).

363 Ibáñez Colomo (2018, 288).

364 Dunne (2014b, 406).

While commentators have pointed to the balancing function of commitments, it is difficult to identify the existence and method of balancing in each individual case. In fact, most commitment decisions do not reveal whether non-competition interests have played a role, and if so, how. Instead, competition enforcers have often accepted commitments without explaining whether the original agreement violated Article 101 TFEU and if the proposed commitment could remedy such a violation.

Nevertheless, this section argues that the empirical findings can assist in filling this gap. Although they cannot *prove* the existence of balancing by accepting commitments, they offer *proxies* indicating that balancing might have taken place.

The first proxy relates to the *types of sectors* in which commitments were accepted. The empirical findings summarised in Figure 7.11 reveal that almost all the commitments accepted by the Commission and NCAs following modernisation were related to agreements in the same sectors that had facilitated much of the Article 101(1) and (3) TFEU balancing prior to modernisation. As suggested by *Dunne*,[365] these sectors can be divided into three groups: (i) regulated and liberalise-d markets (grey areas), (ii) technology markets (white areas), and (iii) financial services (black areas). As the previous chapters have shown, those sectors inherently invite balancing questions.[366] Hence, it is highly likely that commitments have functioned, at least in some of those cases, as a balancing tool to take non-competition interests (including non-economic benefits) into account.

The first group, agreements in regulated and liberalised markets, represents the majority of commitments accepted. As described in Section 3.4.3.3, those markets typically require balancing between competition and the need to ensure affordable prices, quality, and equal access. The empirical findings reveal that commitments were accepted in relation to agreements having similar features to those exempted under Article 101(3) TFEU during the third enforcement period (i.e. 1988–April 2004).[367]

In fact, many of the agreements subject to the Commission's first commitment decisions under Regulation 1/2003 had actually initially been notified to the Commission under the old notification regime for the purpose of receiving exemptions.[368] Commitments were seen as an appropriate measure to deal with those transitional cases.[369] They often involved a process of negotiation with the

365 *Ibid*, 406. See also Commission Staff Working Paper accompanying the Report on the Functioning of Regulation 1/2003 (2014), para 21; CMA's Roundtable on the Use of Commitments in Competition Enforcement (2015), para 11, 13; CA98/03/2005 TV Eye (2005), para 51.

366 See Sections 3.4.3.3 and 4.3.1.2, and Chapter 5.

367 During the third enforcement period, Article 101(3) TFEU exemptions were often granted as a result of accepting informal commitments. See Section 3.4.3.1 and Figure 3.1.

368 37214 Joint selling of the media rights to the German Bundesliga (2005), para 7; 38173 The Football Association Premier League Limited (2006), para 11; 38348 Repsol (2006), para 5; 38681 Cannes Agreement (2006), para 13; 39151 39152 SABAM and BUMA (2006).

369 Gippini-Fournier (2008, 43).

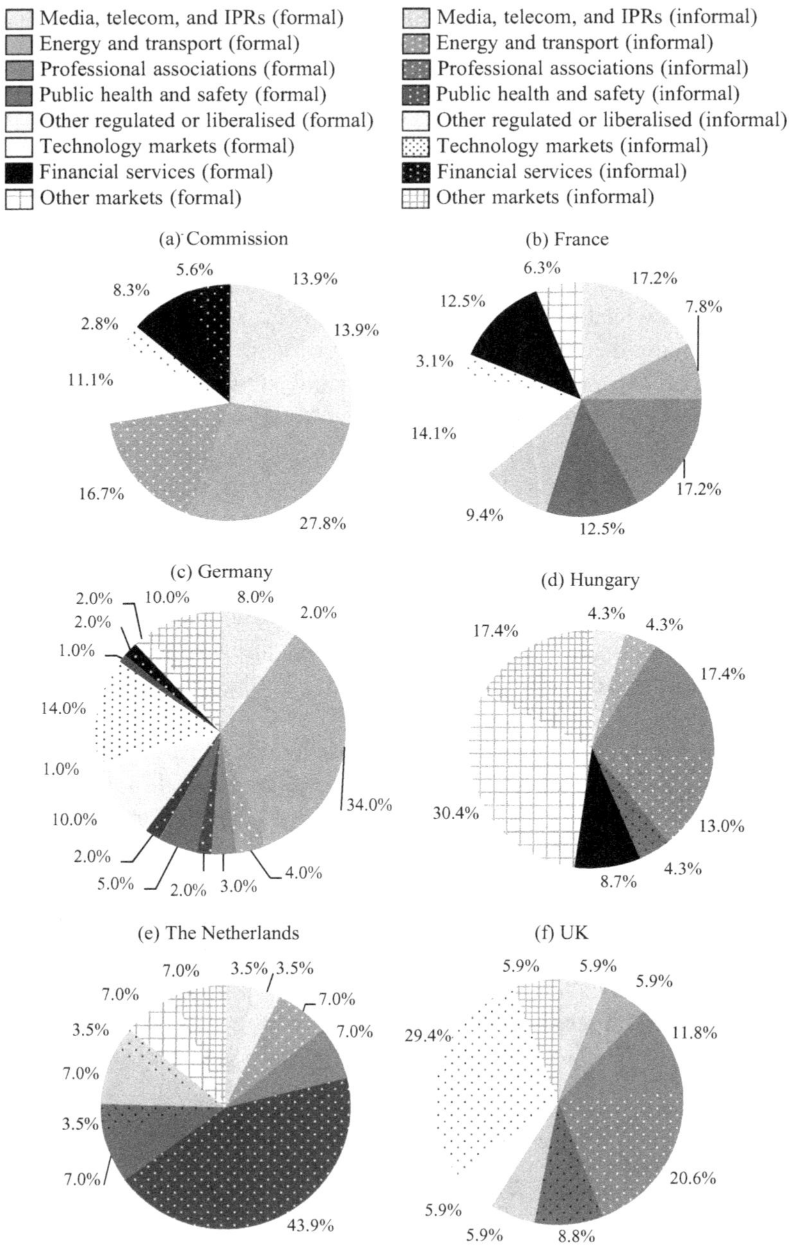

FIGURE 7.11. Commitments by sector, Commission and NCAs (May 2004–2017)[370]
All formal and informal commitments adopted by the competition enforcers. Commitments that do not fit into any of those three groups of sectors are classified as 'other'

[370] Figure 7.11 was originally published in Brook (2020). Reproduced by permission of Oxford University Press. For a list of cases in each category, see Annex A, Section 7.11.

undertakings, modifying the terms of the potentially anti-competitive agreements to strike a case-specific balance between competition and non-competition interests related to the liberalisation of markets and sector-regulation.

In *Joint selling of the media rights to the German Bundesliga (2005)* and *The Football Association Premier League (2006)*, for example, the Commission secured amendments to systems of central marketing of media exploitation rights in new emerging media markets.[371] In *Repsol (2006)*, it accepted commitments in newly liberalised gas and electricity markets, revising the terms of standard supply agreements of oil companies.[372] In *Cannes (2006)*, commitments were given to extend an agreement between collecting societies and music publishers that was previously exempted under Article 101(3) TFEU by means of a comfort letter.[373]

Also, in later cases, which were not notified, commitments emphasised the applicable regulatory frameworks governing the agreements and their sector-specific aims. Such regulatory frameworks have often pursued a host of non-economic benefits, going beyond the narrow competition concerns stemming from the relevant agreement. They were typically directed at securing a broad range of social objectives, such as ensuring the security of supply, providing an essential but uneconomic service, protecting vulnerable consumers, and reaching environmental or redistributive goals.

For example, the Commission accepted commitments in a number of cases related to access to *Technical information for car repairs (2007)*, which altered the provisions of standard agreements between car manufacturers and their after-sales services partners. It explained that those commitments would be binding for a transitional period, after which the EU vehicle emission regulation will govern them.[374] In *Cross-border access to pay-TV (2016)*, the commitments modified the provisions of a licensing agreement involving geo-blocking provisions aimed at the industrial policy aim of the Digital Single Market.[375] The Commission, moreover, had used commitments to address by-object restrictions in regulated markets.[376] The

[371] 37214 Joint selling of the media rights to the German Bundesliga (2005), para 7; 38173 The Football Association Premier League Limited (2006). See also policy report (2005), para 104.

[372] 38348 Repsol (2006). See also policy report (2005), para 58.

[373] 38681 Cannes Agreement (2006).

[374] 39140 DaimlerChrysler (2007); 39141 Fiat (2007); 39141 Toyota Motor Europe (2007); 39143 Opel (2007); policy report (2007), para 67.

[375] 40023 Cross-border access to pay-TV (2016). See also policy report (2016), 7. The GC's judgment rejecting an appeal on the Commission's decision was quashed by the CJEU in C-132/19P Cross-border access to pay-TV (2020).

[376] See Section 7.6.2.2.

choice to use the soft commitments instrument instead of imposing a fine for clear-cut infringements of competition suggests that the Commission may have taken into account broader non-competition interests.

The empirical findings support the conclusion that commitment decisions that balanced competition and regulatory objectives were also adopted by NCAs. Although the NCAs have not always acknowledged this explicitly, many of those commitments essentially involved the negotiations of the terms and conditions of agreements in regulated and liberalised markets, in a similar manner as was done by the Commission when attaching conditions and obligations to Article 101(3) TFEU exemptions prior to modernisation.

NCAs have also used commitments to address balancing challenges associated with agreements governing the function of professional associations. As described in Section 5.2, these agreements often necessitate striking a balance between the economic, social, and regulatory function of the associations. Indeed, the empirical findings show that the NCAs accepted commitments for agreements similar to those that had qualified for an Article 101(1) TFEU exception during the third enforcement period.

The second group of commitments relates to practices in technology markets, and especially to online platforms. This line of cases has typically involved novel legal and economic questions on the applicability of Article 101 TFEU and the balance of competition, innovation, and IPRs. The use of commitments in technology markets was vindicated by the need to adopt timely solutions in fast-changing markets where traditional enforcement mechanisms might not have been fast enough to reflect rapid changes in the industry.[377] When accepting the commitments in *eBooks (2012)*, for example, the Commission noted that traditional enforcement mechanisms might not have been rapid enough to reflect the quick changes in the industry, thus rendering a decision redundant.[378] Similarly, the NCAs have used commitments to solve new and open questions regarding the applicability of Article 101 TFEU to restrictions of online sales by members of selective distribution systems[379] and the use of online platforms.[380] In those cases, commitments served as a tool to overcome the so-called 'regulatory disconnect' problem, i.e. when

[377] Almunia (2013, 3); OCED Commitments Report (2016), para 16; Jenny (2015, 731–735); CMA's Roundtable on the Use of Commitments in Competition Enforcement (2015), para 12.

[378] 39847 eBooks (2012), para 146. Similar justifications were invoked by the UK NCA, for instance in 50408 Live online bidding auction platform (2017), para 4.16.

[379] In France: 06-D-28 Home Cinema (2006); 06-D-24 Bijourama (2006); 07-D-07 Sale of cosmetic products on the internet (2007); 15-D-06 Online hotel booking (2015); Adidas (2015). In Germany: B5–100/10 Sanitary fittings (2011); B7–1/13-35 Sennheiser (2013); B2–98/11 ASICS (2015).

[380] The Commission: 40360 Production and distribution of audiobooks (2017). In Germany: B6–46/12 Amazon (2013). In the UK: Yamaha musical instruments (2006); CE/9692/12 Amazon's price parity policy (2013); CE/9320-10 Hotel online booking (2014); CE/9857-14 Bathroom fittings (2016); BMW car comparison sites (2017); 50408 Live online bidding auction platform (2017).

innovation on the market slows because the legal framework is unable to keep up with technological developments.[381]

The third group of commitments focused on practices in financial services markets. Commitments were used to impose price regulation on financial products. While some of those commitments were directed at eliminating specific competition constraints,[382] others were used to regulate the prices of financial products.[383] In *Visa MIF (2010)*, for instance, the commitments accepted by the Commission have capped the interchange fees that could be charged by an association of banks with relation to certain debit card payments.[384] Similar price regulating commitments were also accepted by NCAs.[385] Those commitments not only aimed to *resolve* the competition concerns but also *regulated* the future development of EU financial markets.

In view of the above, the empirical findings presented in Figure 7.11 indicate that commitments were used to assess the same types of agreements that had been resolved using the balancing tools of Article 101(1) and (3) TFEU prior to modernisation. This suggests the commitments have served as substitutes for the explicit-substantive balancing tools.

This conclusion is further reinforced by examining the debate over the application of the explicit-substantive balancing tools prior to accepting commitments. This debate can serve as another proxy, suggesting that balancing questions were relevant in such cases. Accordingly, Figure 7.12 specifies the number of cases in which the Commission accepted formal and informal commitments (white bars) after discussing the balancing tools of Article 101(1) and (3) TFEU (black and grey bars, respectively).

The figure demonstrates that the Commission regularly accepted formal and informal commitments after the role of non-competition interests had been discussed under the balancing tools of Article 101(1) and (3) TFEU.[386] This was true both prior to modernisation when accepting informal commitments and post-modernisation when accepting formal commitments. This supports the hypothesis

[381] On regulatory disconnect, see Brownsword and Somsen (2009, 26–31), Moses (2013, 1), Brownsword and Goodwin (2012, 369–420), and Butenko and Larouche (2015).

[382] 39177 Tickets for the 2006 World Cup (2005); 39876 EPC Online Payments (2013); 39745 CDS Information Market (2016).

[383] See also Dunne (2014b, 410).

[384] 39398 Visa MIF (2010).

[385] In France: 11-D-11 'CB' payment card (2011); 12-D-17 Non-cash means of payment (2012); 13-D-18 Visa (2013); 13-D-17 MasterCard (2013). In Hungary: Vj-152/2006/86 Budapest Stock Exchange (2008).

[386] The number of commitment decisions discussing Article 101(1) and (3) TFEU balancing tools is probably under-represented in Figure 7.12 because the Commission is not required to explain the application of those provisions when accepting commitments. For a comparison with the consideration of the explicit-substantive balancing tools in other types of procedures following modernisation, see Figure 7.2.

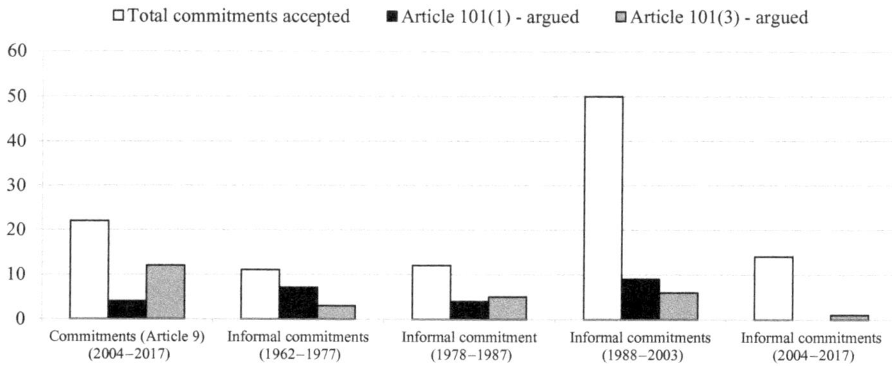

FIGURE 7.12. Article 101(1) and (3) TFEU balancing tools in commitments, Commission

that commitments were accepted to deal with cases that would otherwise have been examined using the explicit-substantive balancing tools.

In sum, there are strong theoretical and empirical indications that commitments are used to account for non-competition interests. Despite such indications, the balancing in a specific case is largely invisible. A competition enforcer is not required to explain whether balancing *has taken place*, which *non-competition interests* were taken into account, and which *balancing method* has been applied. This raises serious concerns as to the uniformity and legal certainty of such balancing tools.

7.6.2.4 Scope of Discretion

The competition enforcers' broad margin of discretion to balance by accepting commitments was also affected by the very restricted judicial review applied by the EU and national courts. As the empirical findings summarised in Figure 7.13 show, this explains the limited number of challenges on decisions accepting commitments in general, and on the merits of balancing in particular. The figure specifies the number of challenges submitted (solid bars) and accepted (dashed bars) on the Commission's and NCA's decisions to accept commitments. It includes appeals on both formal (black bars) and informal (grey bars) commitments.

The limited number of challenges on decisions accepting commitments is not surprising. Commitments are (formally) proposed by undertakings and adopted subject to their consent. Therefore, they are only likely to be challenged by third parties.[387] Previous empirical studies have already pointed out the scarcity of third-party appeals on the grounds of Article 101 TFEU and their low likelihood of

[387] Schweitzer (2008, 10), Wathelet (2015, 554), and Sauter (2016, 128).

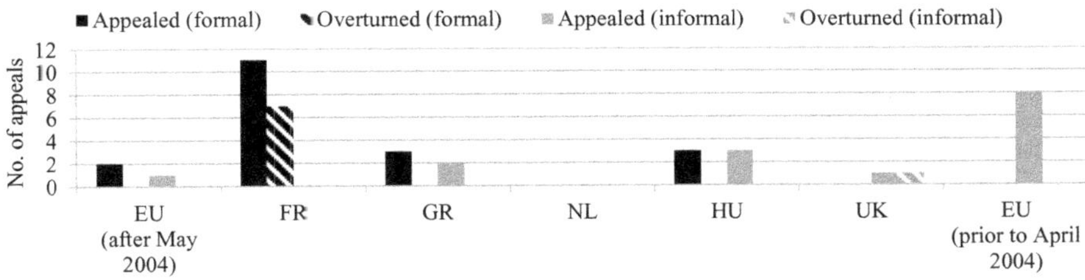

FIGURE 7.13. Commitments, national (May 2004–2017) and EU (1962–2017) courts
The overturned decisions reflect the judgments that overturned the previous instance's ruling with respect to Article 101 TFEU commitments

success.[388] Moreover, since decisions accepting commitments do not always detail the justifications for accepting them, they are difficult to attack on appeal.

In addition to the small number of appeals in general, the empirical findings show that appeals rarely involved an examination of the merits of balancing. At the EU level, the only three appeals launched against Article 101 TFEU formal and informal commitment decisions after modernisation were resolved without a decision on the merits.[389]

Also, at the Member State level, national court judgments overturning NCA decisions accepting commitments did not involve substantive balancing grounds. In France, they were based on procedural grounds,[390] and in the UK, on a lack of consideration of third-party interests.[391] Hence, in practice, the EU and national courts did not engage with the substantive elements of balancing.

The limited appraisal by EU and national courts is often attributed to the judicial review standard adopted by the CJEU in *Alrosa (2010)*.[392] As mentioned, the CJEU had declared that it would give more deference to the Commission's commitment decisions than to its infringement decisions. It would only interfere with commitment decisions involving a *manifest error of appreciation*.[393] Consequently, the

[388] Geradin and Petit (2012, 58).

[389] The appeals in T-300/04 Société Air France/Alitalia Linee Aeree Italiane SpA (2007) and T-447/12 Visa MIF (2010) were withdrawn by the appellant; the appeal in T-274/06 Repsol (2007) was rendered inadmissible since it was lodged out of time.

[390] 2007/13915 Distribution of Medicine (I) (2008), as overturned by 08/70449 Distribution of Medicine (I) (2010); 2008/00508 Distribution of Medicine (II) (2008) as overturned by 08/70449 Distribution of Medicine (II) (2010); 2008/01095 Distribution of Medicine (III) (2009) as overturned by 08/70449 Distribution of Medicine (III) (2010); 07/27275 Access of local radios to national advertisement (2008).

[391] 1226/2/12/14 Hotel online booking (2014).

[392] C-441/07P Alrosa (2010). See Section 7.6.2.1.

[393] C-441/07P Alrosa (2010), para 44. Arguably, in C-132/19P Cross-border access to pay-TV (2020) the CJEU has somewhat limited the Commission's discretion in accepting commitments. The Court distinguished between the assessment of proportionality in the context of the Commission's competition concerns and the impact on the contractual rights of third parties. In the latter case, the principle of proportionality entails that the rights of third parties should 'not be deprived of their substance'.

CJEU vested the Commission with wide discretionary powers to accept commitments, which considerably limited the success of appeal.

Many commentators have strongly criticised this limited standard of judicial review, noting in particular that commitments often go virtually unsupervised by the courts.[394] By expecting the Commission to exercise self-restraint with regard to the remedies it is prepared to accept, the CJEU has excessively restricted the scope of judicial control.[395] This critique was particularly directed at the balance of competition and non-competition interests, for which the law is still unclear.[396] Since commitments allow competition enforcers to take non-competition interests into account in an implicit manner, they may be tempted to use commitments as a substitute for taking a clear stand on the role of those interests under Article 101 TFEU. Subsequently, the competition enforcers' balancing approaches remain unclear and outside the control of the EU and national courts.

Forrester has offered an interesting thought experiment to illustrate this point.[397] He posed the question of how established EU competition law principles might have turned out if the Commission had accepted commitments rather than issuing infringement decisions, meaning that those decisions could not have been discussed before the EU Court. Forrester shows that fundamental EU competition law doctrines would never have been established if such a practice had been followed. Applying this thought experiment to balancing yields similar results. The scope of Article 101(3) TFEU balancing would surely have taken a different turn if the CJEU had not had the opportunity to issue *Metro I (1977)*, in which it spelt out the types of benefits that could be examined under the Article and the workable competition standard.[398] The state action defence of Article 101(1) TFEU would not have been developed equally if the Commission had accepted commitments from the sugar producers instead of issuing its infringement decision in *Suiker-Unie (1975)*.[399]

Indeed, the two Member States in which NCA decisions accepting commitments were overturned – France and the UK – followed a stricter standard of judicial review compared to *Alrosa*. In France, the Paris Court of Appeals granted broad standing to third parties affected by commitment decisions.[400] In the UK, the Enforcement Guidelines and the CAT's case law order a judicial review of

[394] See, for example, Wagner-von Papp (2012, 178), Schweitzer (2013, 40), Gerard (2013, 27), Jenny (2015, 762–765), and OCED Commitments Report (2016), para 49–50.

[395] Jenny (2015, 763).

[396] Schweitzer (2008, 11), Wagner-von Papp (2012, 961–966), and Wathelet (2015, 554). More generally, see GCLC Annual Conference (2010, 65); Van Rompuy (2012, 274); CMA's Roundtable on the Use of Commitments in Competition Enforcement (2015), para 11; and Sauter (2016, 130, 286–287).

[397] Forrester (2008, 646–649).

[398] See Section 3.3.3.1.

[399] See Section 5.2.2.

[400] 2006/18379 Access of local radios to national advertisement (2007), 6; Notice on Competition Commitments (2009), para 47.

commitments at the same standard applicable to the NCA's decisions on mergers and imposition of remedies following a market investigation.[401] The CAT tied this standard to the balancing function embedded in commitments, 'striking a balance' between intervention in a sector and competition.[402]

The limited judicial review of commitments in general and balancing in particular increases the attractiveness of using commitments as a balancing tool from the standpoint of the Commission and NCAs. Commitments are strategically desirable for competition enforcers because they moderate the administrative strain and reduce the risk of overturning the enforcer's decisions on appeal.[403] Arguably, such incentives may lead the competition enforcers to demonstrate a bias in favour of commitments. In particular, they may use such enforcement tools to deal with cases that are ill-suited to such procedures.[404]

7.6.3 *Findings of Inapplicability*

7.6.3.1 A Balancing Tool

If following an investigation a competition enforcer believes that no infringement of Article 101 TFEU has taken place, it may bring the proceeding to an end. This can take the form of a reasoned formal or informal decision, a short summary of the competition analysis, or by terminating the proceedings with no further notice or reasoning.

Prior to modernisation, the Commission had regularly published formal positive decisions and informal comfort letters declaring that an agreement did not fall under Article 101(1) TFEU or that it could be exempted under Article 101(3) TFEU.[405] As part of the switch from a notification to a self-assessment regime, the enforcement of Article 101 TFEU now focuses on infringement decisions. The Commission has declared that when undertakings provide a valid justification for their conduct, for example, if Article 101(3) TFEU is likely to be fulfilled, it will often not pursue a case any further and will not publish the reasons for such findings.[406]

Yet, Regulation 1/2003 still leaves room for publishing findings of inapplicability in the form of formal positive decisions[407] and informal guidance letters.[408] The Commission stated in its Modernisation White Paper that it would use such

[401] UK Commitments Guidelines (2004), para 4.26; 1226/2/12/14 Hotel online booking (2014), para 43.

[402] *Ibid*, para 130–132.

[403] Blanco and De Pablo (2012, 76).

[404] See also Forrester (2008, 646–654), Petit (2010, 56), and Blanco and De Pablo (2012, 75–80).

[405] See Figures 3.1 and 7.5.

[406] Report on the Functioning of Regulation 1/2003 (2009), para 26. See also the Commission in OECD Role of Efficiency Claims in Antitrust Proceedings (2012), 90.

[407] Regulation 1/2003, Article 10. See also Section 2.3.3.

[408] See Section 7.5.3.

measures when 'a transaction raises a question that is new', thereby aiming to 'provide the market with guidance regarding the Commission's approach to certain restrictions'.[409]

At the national level, the NCAs have just a limited power to adopt inapplicability decisions. Article 5 of Regulation 1/2003 provides that an NCA may merely decide that there are 'no grounds for action' on its part.[410] In *Tele2Polska (2011)*, the CJEU clarified that Article 5 entails that an NCA does not have the power to *formally* declare that Article 102 TFEU is inapplicable, even if it is competent to do so under national procedural law.[411] The same logic also applies to Article 101 TFEU. In other words, an NCA's finding of inapplicability is not binding on the Commission or on other NCAs.

Commentators have contended that the CJEU's interpretation of Article 5 discourages NCAs from pursuing complex cases.[412] NCAs would avoid dedicating their scarce enforcement efforts to cases that might be concluded without generating any observable decision output. Accordingly, NCAs would be unlikely to pursue borderline cases (e.g. cases involving balancing) and more inclined to investigate clear-cut infringements regardless of their impact on competition.

Reasoned and published findings of inapplicability are an important enforcement instrument as they clarify the boundaries between lawful and unlawful conduct. Since the wording of Article 101 TFEU is vague, the role of non-competition interests is defined by the decisions of the Commission and NCAs and the judgments of EU and national Courts. Findings of inapplicability, therefore, afford the competition enforcers an opportunity to use their outcome discretion to demonstrate how the explicit-substantive balancing tools can be successfully applied in the context of a specific case. As such, they are crucial for the development of the law, policy, and practice on the balance between competition and non-competition interests.[413] Reasoned and published findings of inapplicability may foster compliance with EU competition law, promote legal certainty, and help prevent fragmentation in the interpretation of Article 101 TFEU.[414]

However, findings of inapplicability may have the opposite effect on balancing if they are not published or fully reasoned. For example, in *Medicines for Europe (2020)*, the Commission has issued a comfort letter with respect to a voluntary cooperation project between pharmaceutical manufacturers aiming to prevent a shortage of medicines for the treatment of coronavirus patients. After presenting the

[409] Modernisation White Paper (1999), para 88.
[410] On 'no grounds for action' findings, see Section 2.3.3.3.
[411] C-375/09 Tele2Polska (2011), para 27–30.
[412] Petit (2011) and Svetlicinii et al. (2018, 8).
[413] GCLC Annual Conference (2010, 64–65) and Bailey (2016, 112, 136–139).
[414] Petit and Rato (2008, 206), Wils (2009, 5–6), GCLC Annual Conference (2010, 64–65), National Audit Office (2010), Blanco and De Pablo (2012, 68–69), Gerard (2012, 33), Bailey (2016, 121–132), Witt (2016, 296–297), National Audit Office (2016, 31), and Mano and Jones (2018, 26–27).

facts of the case, the Commission merely declared that 'in the present exceptional circumstances the cooperation practices as set out above do not raise concerns under Article 101 [TFEU]'.[415] While this conclusion appears to be justified by non-competition interests related to public health, the Commission did not specify its legal basis. It is unclear if the cooperation can be justified under the balancing tools of Article 101(1) TFEU (e.g. as an inherent restriction or a state action), if it satisfies the conditions of Article 101(3) TFEU, or if it falls under the Commission's Coronavirus Temporary Framework as a stand-alone exception.[416] Hence, the Commission's findings could carry only very limited weight in guiding national decisions or helping undertakings to self-assess other initiatives.

Similarly, in *Animal Welfare Initiative (2017)*, the German NCA issued a press release declaring that it had 'no objections' to the Tierwohl project aimed at promoting animal welfare in livestock production.[417] The project involved an agreement between players in the agriculture, meat production, and food retail sectors, introducing labels indicating that the meat was produced subject to animal welfare criteria. It was mainly financed by the four largest food retailers, which paid a fixed amount for any poultry meat sold via the initiative. The German NCA explained that although the project involved the coordination of 'factors relevant to competition', it would be 'tolerated' as far as 'the consumer really benefits from such an initiative'.

The press release does not specify the legal source that led the NCA to 'tolerate' the agreement (e.g. Article 101(3) TFEU or one of the Article 101(1) TFEU balancing tools), the restrictions imposed and the competition concerns, the benefits justifying an exception, the balancing process, or the evidence supporting it. Hence, it is very difficult to evaluate the NCA's decision, to deduce the relevant balancing principles, and to compare it with similar decisions of other NCAs on sustainability agreements (e.g. the Dutch *Chicken of Tomorrow (2015)* and French *Fair Trade (2006)*).[418] Consequently, the German press release has only created further uncertainty as to the German approach to non-competition interests under Article 101 TFEU.

7.6.3.2 Empirical Indications

The empirical findings presented throughout this book have outlined the use of findings of inapplicability by the various competition enforcers. They have illustrated that in the past, the Commission regularly issued formal and informal

[415] COMP/OG -D(2020/044003) Medicines for Europe (2020), 2.

[416] The Temporary Framework was discussed in Section 7.4.3.5.

[417] Animal Welfare Initiative (2017), press release of 28 September 2017. See also German annual report 2017, 20–21 and annual report 2018, 19.

[418] Those cases were discussed in Sections 3.6.2.2 and 3.6.3.2.

inapplicability decisions.[419] This changed, however, following modernisation. Since May 2004, the Commission has never adopted a formal positive decision or an informal individual guidance,[420] with the exception of the informal guidance in *Medicines for Europe (2020)* described above. By exercising its outcome discretion, the Commission consciously chose *not* to engage in the debate on the role of non-competition interests under Article 101 TFEU. Instead, it closed investigations into agreements that may raise balancing questions by virtue of its enforcement discretion. Consequently, the Commission has not grasped the opportunity to clarify many of the open questions about balancing in the realm of Regulation 1/2003 and the more economic approach.[421]

At the same time, the Commission has issued a number of reasoned inapplicability findings rejecting complaints *inter-alia* because an agreement could be justified by an Article 101(1) TFEU exception. Chapter 5 demonstrated that many of those clarifications are essential to understanding the Commission's approach to balancing.

In contrast, some of the NCAs published findings of inapplicability. The form and frequency of such measures are dependent on national law.[422] For example, the German and Hungarian NCAs are competent to adopt positive decisions, including *formal* findings of inapplicability (despite not being binding in and of themselves).[423] The French, Dutch, and UK NCAs may also adopt *informal* findings of inapplicability.[424] Although the frequency and form of national findings of inapplicability varied considerably, they provided an important source of information for understanding the national approaches to balancing. As was elaborated throughout this book, many of those findings provide a rich source of information to understand, analyse, and evaluate the NCAs' approaches to balancing.

At the same time, it should be noted that national inapplicability findings are not notified to the ECN and as such are not subject to the Commission's or the ECN's scrutiny.[425] Consequently, the national interpretations of the balancing tools of Article 101 TFEU may evolve in different directions, resulting in fragmented balancing.

[419] See Sections 3.2, 4.2, 5.2.1, 5.3.1, and 7.5.3.

[420] See Figure 3.1.

[421] Commentators have suggested that the Commission's choice to refrain from adopting inapplicability decisions could be the result of a too high standard for adopting those decisions, or alternatively a fear that such procedures would lead to the backdoor reintroduction of the notification regime. See note 209.

[422] ECN Decision Making Powers Report (2012), 36–39.

[423] *Ibid*, 36–37. See also Petit (2010, 58). For Germany, see also Dreher (2009, para 2.4); for Hungary, see also Hegymegi-Barakonyi (2009, 22–23); for the UK, see also Lester (2009, 14).

[424] In the form of informal opinions, as described in Section 7.5.3.

[425] Regulation 1/2003, Article 11(4). See also Section 2.3.3.3.

7.6.3.3 Scope of Discretion

Not all findings of inapplicability are subject to judicial review. As non-binding measures, *informal* inapplicability findings are not liable to judicial review.[426] On the other hand, the Commission's positive decisions,[427] as well as the *formal* decisions of most NCAs, are in principle subject to judicial review.[428] Yet, in practice, they are unlikely to be appealed. Undertakings usually have no incentive to challenge a declaration that an agreement is not prohibited, and third-party appeals against findings of inapplicability are not available in all jurisdictions (e.g. in Hungary).[429] In light of the above, the balancing reflected in findings of inapplicability is less likely to be reviewed by EU or national courts.

7.6.3.4 Interim Conclusion

This section illustrated that the competition enforcers' outcome discretion was another measure that allowed to take into account non-competition interests. It has shown that the modernisation of EU competition law has shifted much of the balancing away from the explicit-substantive balancing tools of Article 101(1) and (3) TFEU towards procedural decisions to moderate fines, accept commitments, or close the investigation without publishing reasoned findings of inapplicability.

Balancing by outcome discretion provides competition enforcers with an extraordinarily wide margin of discretion to account for non-competition interests. The exercise of outcome discretion is not bound to a clear legal or economic balancing process. Competition enforcers are not required to explain *if* balancing took place, *which* non-competition interests were taken into account, and which balancing tests were applied. Consequently, although there are strong indications that fines, commitments, and decisions to end the enforcement proceedings are used for balancing, the balancing in a specific case is largely invisible.

Accordingly, outcome discretion can be used as an alternative to Article 101(1) and (3) TFEU exceptions, to balance outside the scope of the legal tests of Article 101 TFEU altogether, or to regulate the future conduct of undertakings and markets and to promote non-competition interests that are not directly related to the anti-competitive behaviour of the undertakings concerned.[430] It allows competition enforcers to engage in implicit and flexible balancing and to take broader types of

[426] See Section 7.5.3.

[427] There is neither a clear provision establishing judicial review of the Commission's inapplicability decisions nor any precedent in case law. Yet, this is the prevalent view in the literature. See Blanco (2006, 216–217), Geradin and Petit (2005, 10–11), and Sufrin (2006, 975).

[428] For a survey of the right to judicial review of inapplicability decisions, see ECN Decision Making Powers Report (2012), 39.

[429] *Ibid.*

[430] On corrective and regulatory balancing, see Section 1.2.2.2.

benefits into account than those that can be examined under the explicit-substantive balancing tools. As such, the shift brought by modernisation to an effects-based approach has not been extended to include the practice of setting the remedies.

7.7 ECN+ DIRECTIVE: TOWARDS HARMONISATION OF PRIORITY SETTING?

As elaborated in the previous sections and summarised in Section 7.8, the discretional enforcement powers conferred to the Commission and NCAs by Regulation 1/2003 have a significant bearing on the effectiveness, uniformity, and legal certainty of balancing. Nevertheless, the Modernisation White Paper and Regulation 1/2003 attach few obligations to the application of those powers.

Over the years, the Commission has gradually acknowledged the impact of the discretional enforcement powers under the decentralised enforcement regime.[431] In March 2017, as part of its ECN+ Directive Proposal, it took the first steps to regulate their exercise by the NCAs. The Directive was adopted in early 2019, and the transposition period ended in December 2020.

Notably, the Directive does not regard the effectiveness of priority setting as a stand-alone concern. Priority setting is seen as merely an instrument for guaranteeing the NCAs' independence from external intervention and political pressure from governments and other private or public entities and that NCAs will have the resources and the enforcement and fining powers necessary to apply Articles 101 and 102 TFEU effectively. The Directive seeks to ensure that the NCAs will not lack adequate human and financial resources and operational independence to prevent them from taking any action or limiting their enforcement actions.[432] Therefore, the Directive harmonises three aspects of the NCAs' target discretion.[433]

First, the Directive submits that NCAs should enjoy a degree of target discretion, namely the power to set their priorities for carrying out tasks related to enforcing Article 101 TFEU.[434] This obligation does not significantly alter the previous legal framework, as all NCAs were already competent to open *ex-officio* investigations.[435]

Second, the Directive states that NCAs should have the power to reject complaints on priority grounds.[436] Accordingly, a duty to investigate all complaints, such

[431] For instance, in its Report on the functioning of Regulation 1/2003 (2009), para 33, the Commission referred to the NCAs' priority setting powers as an important aspect of divergence that 'may merit further examination and reflection'. See also Report on the functioning of Regulation 1/2003 (2014), para 34.

[432] ECN+ Directive (2019), Preamble 3, 5, 8, 17.

[433] This section will only examine the Directive's provisions on prioritisation. For a general discussion of the ECN+ Directive, see Wils (2017, 38) and Sinclair (2017).

[434] ECN+ Directive (2019), Preamble 23 and Article 4(5).

[435] Idot (2015, 51) and Wils (2017, 38).

[436] ECN+ Directive (2019), Preamble 23 and Article 4(5).

as the one stemming from the French legality principle,[437] would no longer be compatible with EU law. This obligation may affect the types of cases investigated by the NCAs. As elaborated in Section 7.4.1, a wide target discretion is prone to focus on clear-cut infringements of Article 101 TFEU and avoid borderline balancing cases.

Finally, the Directive declares that NCAs should set their enforcement priorities independently, i.e. without taking instructions from public or private entities.[438] Yet, it adds that this 'is without prejudice to the right of a government of a Member State to issue to national administrative competition authorities general policy rules or priority guidelines' as long as they are not related to a specific Article 101 TFEU enforcement proceeding.[439]

As illustrated throughout this book, this wording is not sufficient to shield NCA staff and management decisions from political influence. For instance, the Dutch NCA's priority setting rule on sustainability agreements, described in Section 7.4.1, provides that the NCA will not enforce an agreement that receives governmental support. This policy is not prohibited by the Directive. While the government's view with regard to a specific agreement is an influential factor in the Dutch NCA's policy choice, in the end, the decision is taken by the NCA alone. Similarly, as presented in Section 6.3.4, several Hungarian and German laws limited the NCAs' competence or incentive to pursue infringements of Article 101 TFEU in politically sensitive areas (e.g. agriculture, waste management tender, and forest services). Those rules were not worded in such a way that they related to 'a specific proceeding' and therefore might not be prohibited by the Directive.

Against this background, the ECN+ Directive regulates merely the tip of the iceberg of enforcement discretion. The Directive does not govern the substantive principles of exercising such discretion. It simply covers procedural elements related to target discretion and aims to enhance the independence of NCAs when allocating their enforcement efforts. The Directive does not deal with many of the core weaknesses of the enforcement regime, which allows competition enforcers to directly or indirectly take non-competition interests into account when exercising enforcement discretion. For instance, it does not limit the types of benefits that can be taken into account, it does not explain how they ought to be balanced against competition interests, and it does not deal with other concerns related to detection, instrument, and outcome discretion.

The ECN+ Directive is not only insufficient but also runs counter to the main findings of this chapter. As discussed above and summarised below, the competition enforcers' almost unrestricted enforcement discretion has been used to account for

[437] See Section 7.4.2.3.

[438] ECN+ Directive (2019), Preamble 23 and Article 4(5); ECN+ Directive Proposal (2017), Explanatory Memorandum, 2.

[439] ECN+ Directive (2019), Preamble 23.

non-competition interests in a manner that impedes the effectiveness, uniformity, and legal certainty of balancing. Yet, this section has revealed that instead of restricting or harmonising the use of such powers, the ECN+ Directive calls for enhancing the NCAs' enforcement discretion. As a result, while the Directive may benefit the enforcement of Article 101 TFEU in general, it may prove to be counter-productive with respect to the future role of non-competition interests in the enforcement.

7.8 CLOSING REMARKS: TRANSITION TO BALANCING BY ENFORCEMENT DISCRETION

The previous chapters have illustrated that upon modernisation, the Commission advocated narrowing the room for non-competition interests under the balancing tools of Article 101(1) and (3) TFEU. It called to limit the types of relevant benefits that could be taken into account, introduced an effects-based approach aimed at enhancing short-term narrow consumer welfare, and increased the quality and strength of evidence required to justify an exception. Subsequently, the Commission, as well as most of the NCAs, rarely invoked or accepted those balancing tools to justify anti-competitive agreements.[440]

This does not mean, however, that non-competition interests no longer play a role in the enforcement. This chapter has argued that modernisation has merely changed the *nature* of agreements that are being examined, which in turn shifted the consideration of non-competition interests from the explicit-substantive to the implicit-procedural balancing tools:

Prior to modernisation, when the Commission had limited discretion to set its enforcement priorities, it was compelled to apply the explicit-substantive balancing tools. The enforcement regime had prompted an abundance of decisions on the application of Article 101(1) and (3) TFEU balancing tools, explaining how and in which circumstances non-competition interests may justify an otherwise anti-competitive agreement.

Yet, this has changed following the entry into force of Regulation 1/2003. The chapter presented case studies, empirical and theoretical evidence supporting the hypothesis that following modernisation the competition enforcers have chosen to dedicate their enforcement efforts to combating clear-cut infringements of competition. Often handled by means of leniency applications and settlements, those agreements are unlikely to be justified under Article 101(1) and (3) TFEU balancing tools altogether. Other types of agreements were mostly not investigated, handled by means of alternative regulatory instruments, or settled by means of negotiated remedies. Accordingly, such agreements were *de facto* tolerated, even when they

[440] See Sections 3.2, 4.2, 5.2.1, and 5.3.1.

have not fully met the conditions for an exemption under the explicit-substantive balancing tools.

This chapter does not criticise the change in the nature of agreements that are being enforced. It recognises that prioritisation choices are necessary to ensure an efficient allocation of the enforcers' scarce resources and that in certain circumstances, non-enforcement decisions that are vindicated by overriding non-competition interests may be desirable.[441] Nevertheless, it warned against a systematic shift in the consideration of non-competition interests, which is *not based on economic or legal balancing principles*. Such shift may hinder the effectiveness, uniformity, and legal certainty of Article 101 TFEU balancing.

First, balancing by enforcement discretion may lead to *ineffective outcomes in specific cases*. The chapter illustrated that the competition enforcers mostly enjoy a wide discretion to set their enforcement priorities. As procedural-administrative decisions, the exercise of detection, target, instrument, and outcome discretion is often not bound to a legal or economic test, in neither the EU nor the national levels. There is almost no limit to the types of benefits they can take into account, balancing process, or the intensity of control. The allocation of enforcement efforts is not necessarily based on a detailed analysis of each agreement's effect on competition or consumer welfare.[442]

Furthermore, in many cases, the exercise of enforcement discretion is not published or reasoned. Laying in the *dark matter of the enforcement*, prioritisation choices allow competition enforcers to account for non-competition interests beyond what is permissible under Article 101(1) and (3) TFEU balancing tools, even according to the Commission's and EU courts' broad interpretations prior to modernisation.

For the above reasons, this chapter submitted that paradoxically, modernisation has hampered the effectiveness of balancing. Although the Commission called to reformulate the explicit-substantive balancing tools to reflect a more economic approach, the assessment of an agreement's effects, including weighing competition and non-competition interests, shifted to the almost unregulated dark matter of enforcement discretion.

Hence, this chapter submits that although modernisation may have enhanced the effectiveness of EU competition law enforcement in general, it is counterproductive when it comes to the role of non-competition interests. Rather than bringing the consideration of non-competition interests in line with the legal and economic principles that guide EU competition law, it has aggravated the already questionable EU competition law's approach to balancing.[443]

441 See Section 7.1.1.

442 This was also observed by the European Court of Auditors, Special Report on the Commission's EU Merger Control and Antitrust Proceedings (2020), para V, 37–38.

443 This is further elaborated in Section 8.3.4.

Second, the shift from explicit-substantive to implicit-procedural balancing tools is also ineffective to the extent it hampers the *overall development of EU competition policy*. The competition enforcers' prioritisation choices are not just about gaining compliance with Article 101 TFEU but are also about determining what the scope and boundaries of the Article are.[444] Competition law and policy are, to a large extent, the result of a dynamic give and take between the Commission, NCAs, EU and national courts, EU institutions, Member States, industry, and other interest groups. Selecting cases in a manner that facilitates non-competition interests on an unsystematic case-specific basis has prevented the emergence of a body of case law in which the relevant institutions could have clarified if and how such policies should be taken into account under the explicit-substantive balancing tools.

As such, modernisation has not only limited the consideration of non-competition interests under the explicit-substantive balancing tools but has also almost eliminated the *debate* over the role of non-competition interests from the competition enforcers' practices. In particular, following modernisation, such decisions and case law might have defined the limits and implications of the more economic approach.[445]

The choice to balance by reference to the implicit-procedural balancing tools is especially noteworthy in cases where agreements were likely to be justified by the explicit-substantive balancing tools. Section 7.6.3.1 showed that reasoned and published findings of inapplicability are an important enforcement instrument for clarifying the boundaries between lawful and unlawful conduct. They provide the competition enforcers opportunities to explain how the explicit-substantive balancing tools can be successfully applied in the context of a specific case and as such are crucial for the development of the law, policy, and practice of balancing.

Third, the shift may lead to fragmentation in the *de facto* scope of Article 101 TFEU. As was elaborated in the previous chapters, due to the open texture of the law and limited guidance from the EU Courts, competition enforcers enjoy a significant degree of discretion in shaping their interpretations of Article 101(1) and (3) TFEU balancing tools. They have some leeway to take account of non-competition interests in a manner that reflects their own understanding of Article 101 TFEU. At the same time, competition enforcers are confined to the substantive limits of the law governing these balancing tools and are susceptible to judicial review.

By comparison, competition enforcers have considerable discretion to balance by setting their enforcement priorities. While they cannot change the content of Article 101 TFEU, their enforcement discretion allows them to overcome the limits of the law and to take non-competition interests into account to a degree beyond what would have been possible otherwise. Indeed, 'choices of priority are, to an important

[444] See note 4.

[445] See also GCLC Annual Conference (2010, 58–76) and Bailey (2016, 131–132). More generally, see UNCTAD Competition Authorities and Judiciaries (2016), 2.

extent, a function of the competition law objectives and the country history, and its legal, political and economic culture'.[446] The *de facto* scope and interpretation of the prohibition of Article 101 TFEU, as a result, differ considerably across Member States, exposing undertakings to multiple balancing standards.

Fourth, the shift impairs the overall *deterrent effect of EU competition law*. Prioritisation choices may lead to *under-deterrence*. To this end, effective deterrence does not require that every infringement be prosecuted, but rather that the expected fine exceeds the expected gains. In many cases – especially those involving balancing questions – the cost of enforcement may exceed the economic gains from correcting specific competitive harm.[447] Yet, even if such enforcement actions are ineffective from a standalone perspective, they may carry an overall deterrent and precedent effects. Such decisions are critical to discourage undertakings from concluding agreements that cannot be justified under the explicit-substantive balancing tools of Article 101(1) and (3) TFEU despite promoting some non-competition interests.[448]

But prioritisation choices may also lead to *over-deterrence*. As mentioned above, the tendency to settle balancing questions by means of enforcement discretion has generated uncertainties as to the role of non-competition interests under the explicit-substantive balancing tools. This unclear scope of balancing can produce a chilling effect, discouraging undertakings from conducting welfare-enhancing agreements that may be justified by Article 101(1) and (3) TFEU balancing tools.[449]

The impact of the shift from the explicit-substantive to the implicit-procedural balancing tools will be further criticised and analysed in the next concluding chapter.

446 UNCTAD Prioritization and Resource Allocation (2013), 17.

447 See Section 7.2.

448 See, for example, the Dutch NCA's decisions and informal opinions in Coal power plants (2013), De Stroomversnelling (2013), and Chicken of tomorrow (2015), discussed in Section 3.6.2.2.

449 Such chilling effects were reported, for example, by members of the British grocery sector. See Fair Trade Foundation (2019). See also Gerbrandy (2017, 545).

8

Conclusion

8.1 INTRODUCTION

This study has examined three questions: How have the rationale, method, and limits for the balancing of competition and non-competition interests in the enforcement of Article 101 TFEU evolved in the first sixty years of its existence? How has this process of evolution affected the attainment of the objectives of Regulation 1/2003, namely effectiveness, uniformity, and legal certainty? And what role should non-competition interests play in order to conform to such objectives?

The empirical findings have disproved the commonly-held view that the modernisation of EU competition law in May 2004 removed non-competition interests from the enforcement of Article 101 TFEU. Based on a quantitative and qualitative analysis of all decisions rendered by the Commission, five representative NCAs, and EU and national courts, it has shown that non-competition interests – including economic and non-economic benefits – have played and continue to play an important role in the enforcement of Article 101 TFEU.

Nevertheless, this study calls attention to a remarkable three-fold shift in the manner in which non-competition interests are being taken into account in the post-modernisation era: First, the study has revealed a shift in the types of *balancing tools* employed in practice, transitioning from explicit-substantive to the dark matter of the enforcement embedded in the implicit-procedural balancing tools; second, it has identified a shift in the *locus of the balancing tools*, from EU-based to Member States-based balancing; and third, it has demonstrated a change in the *institutional dynamics* governing balancing. It has shown that while the EU Courts, and especially the CJEU, have played an active role in shaping the balancing principles in the past, following modernisation the courts have only played a passive-reactive role.

This chapter submits that the three shifts in balancing have hindered the attainment of the very objectives of Regulation 1/2003, namely an effective, uniform, and legally certain enforcement. Consequently, as elaborated below and summarised in

TABLE 8.1. *Transitions in balancing*

Shift	Pre-modernisation	Post-modernisation	Effect on balancing
Types of balancing tools	Explicit-substantive: Article 101(1) and (3) TFEU, BERs	Implicit-procedural: enforcement discretion	Less effective
Locus of balancing tools	EU	Member States	Less uniform
Role of EU Courts	Active	Passive	Less legal certainty

Table 8.1, it argues that while the modernisation of EU competition law may have been successful in general, its effect on the role of non-competition interests under Article 101 TFEU has been counterproductive.

This concluding chapter is structured as follows. Section 8.2 summarises the three transitions in balancing that emerge through modernisation, and Section 8.3 discusses their impact on the effectiveness, uniformity, and legal certainty of the enforcement. Section 8.4 offers policy recommendations on how non-competition interests should be taken into account in the enforcement of Article 101 TFEU, and Section 8.5 concludes.

8.2 TRANSITIONS IN BALANCING

The first research question examined in this book is of an empirical nature. It seeks to identify how the rationale, method, and limits for the balancing of competition and non-competition interests in the enforcement of Article 101 TFEU have evolved in the first sixty years of its existence. This section shows that while both economic and non-economic benefits continue to play a role in the enforcement of Article 101 TFEU following modernisation, the balancing tools, locus of balancing, and the institutional setting surrounding the balancing have shifted.

8.2.1 A *Shift in the Balancing Tools: From Explicit-Substantive to Implicit-Procedural*

The debate over the role of non-competition interests in the enforcement of Article 101 TFEU can be traced back to the establishment of the European Economic Community when the Article was first included in the Rome Treaty. The vague wording of this provision facilitated a decades-long debate over how non-competition interests could and should be examined.

The empirical findings presented throughout this book have shown that, prior to modernisation, the Commission accounted for non-competition interests by reference to the *explicit-substantive balancing tools* of Article 101(3) TFEU, in the form of individual exemptions and BERs. It interpreted Article 101(3) TFEU as leaving ample room for taking non-competition interests into account. When the Commission assessed the application of an individual exemption during the first three enforcement periods (i.e. 1962–April 2004), it did not limit the types of benefits that could justify an exemption. Both economic and non-economic benefits were taken into account, and the Commission had set a low evidential threshold for proving the existence of benefits for consumers.

Moreover, the Commission interpreted Article 101(3) TFEU individual exemptions as entailing a legal balancing process. It followed the vague proportionality test of the workable competition standard to strike a case-specific balance between the competing interests.[1] The same was true for BERs, especially the sectoral ones. Both the adoption process of the BERs, as well as their application, left significant room to integrate broad non-economic benefits.[2] Hence, the individual exemptions and BERs were rightly seen as regulatory instruments, serving as a form of industrial policy and protectionism. Article 101 (3) TFEU did not function merely as an outlet to balance competition with benefits for specific consumers but also reflected political, regulatory, and social objectives.

In addition to the Treaties-based balancing tools of Article 101(3) TFEU individual exemptions and BERs, the CJEU has introduced numerous sector-specific or restriction-specific balancing tools based on the interpretation of various elements of Article 101(1) TFEU. The Court has developed those balancing tools on an *ad hoc* basis to counterbalance the Commission's broad interpretation of what was considered a restriction of competition under Article 101(1) TFEU. According to the Court, agreements restricting the commercial freedom of parties may escape the prohibition of this provision if they are necessary for the attainment of social or efficiency-related goals.[3]

The Commission's and EU Courts' case-specific approaches to balancing have prevented the emergence of a well-defined and systematic framework to guide the explicit-substantive balancing tools of Article 101(1) and (3) TFEU. While their case law could have established a set of coherent balancing principles, the Commission and EU Courts have mostly offered *ad hoc* solutions tailored to the specific legal, economic, and social context of a case.

Indeed, the empirical findings point to the advent of a so-called sectoral approach, with balancing practices that were incoherent and did not comply with a legal or

[1] See Section 3.3.3.1.
[2] See Section 4.3.1.2.
[3] See Section 5.1.3.

economic theory.[4] The balancing tools were applied strictly to agreements impairing market integration and loosely to agreements in liberalised or regulated sectors, sectors affected by an economic crisis, or agreements promoting the EU industrial policy. The balancing principles and tests that guided the case law in one sector, consequently, were often inapplicable to others.

Despite the absence of a well-defined and systematic framework to guide the explicit-substantive balancing tools, prior to modernisation, balancing was applied in a relatively uniform manner across the EU, which provided undertakings with legal certainty. Under the centralised notification regime of Regulation 17/62, all potential anti-competitive agreements needed to be notified to the Commission prior to implementation in order to qualify for an exemption, and the Commission held the sole power to grant Article 101(3) TFEU exemptions. The Commission and undertakings negotiated the terms of exemptions to strike what the Commission considered an appropriate balance between competition and non-competition interests.

The EU's approach to the balancing of competition and non-competition interests has changed since the turn of the millennium, upon the modernisation of EU competition law at the beginning of the fourth enforcement period (i.e. from May 2004 onwards). In the course of modernisation, the Commission has advocated a comprehensive three-pillared reform to the enforcement of Article 101 TFEU, which, in turn, has transformed balancing.

The first substantive pillar of modernisation introduced greater economic thinking to EU competition policy, aiming to increase its effectiveness. Under the heading of a more economic approach, the Commission gradually deployed economic theory and tools to apply Article 101 TFEU. The Commission revised the BERs and its policy papers to focus the competition analysis on the market power held by the undertakings and on the effect of agreements on consumer welfare.

As part of the substantive modernisation, the Commission called to limit the role of non-competition interests under Article 101 TFEU. Its policy papers restricted the types of benefits that could be taken into account under the explicit-substantive balancing tools to direct economic benefits, which ought to be assessed under a narrow short-term consumer welfare standard. Those policy papers advocated reliance on economic and empirical methodologies and substantially increased the evidentiary requirements for exceptions. Subsequently, many non-competition interests that had previously warranted Article 101(1) TFEU exceptions and Article 101(3) TFEU exemptions were no longer applicable in the Commission's view.[5]

Arguably, the Commission's new approach to balancing was influenced not only by the substantive pillar of modernisation but also by the institutional reform. Limiting the scope for balancing under Article 101 TFEU was aimed at safeguarding

[4] On the sectoral approach, see Section 2.5.3.1.
[5] See Sections 3.3.4, 4.3.3, 5.2.7, and 5.3.7.

the effectiveness of EU competition law against undue political national interference in the context of the decentralised enforcement regime. Moreover, narrowing the room for non-competition interests was expected to promote consistent enforcement of the Article and the balancing principles, thereby ensuring the uniformity and legal certainty of their enforcement across the EU.[6]

In line with the Commission's attempts to limit the role of non-competition interests under the explicit-substantive balancing tools, the empirical findings presented throughout this book prove that, after May 2004, those tools were seldom accepted or even invoked. This limited use of the explicit-substantive balancing tools could initially be perceived as confirmation that non-competition interests no longer play a role in the enforcement of Article 101 TFEU. According to this view, the Commission's endeavours to narrow the room for non-competition interests in the substantive and institutional pillars of modernisation have changed the substantive scope of the Article.

Nevertheless, this book has argued that the above view fails to consider the effects emanating from the procedural pillar of modernisation. The switch from a notification to a self-assessment regime has granted the Commission and NCAs new *implicit-procedural balancing tools* to account for non-competition interests in the course of exercising enforcement discretion. This study has offered theoretical and empirical evidence to support the hypothesis that, following the entry into force of Regulation 1/2003, the Commission and NCAs predominantly used those tools to account for non-competition interests. In some instances, the competition enforcers *directly* invoked their enforcement discretion to account for non-competition interests, while in others they did so *implicitly* by devising their detection, target, instrument, and outcome discretion.[7]

The implicit-procedural balancing tools have significant advantages from the perspective of competition enforcers. In particular, instead of engaging in a complex balancing under the explicit-substantive balancing tools, competition enforcers can simply opt to refrain from pursuing a case against an anti-competitive agreement that promotes non-competition interests or to terminate the case by accepting commitments. They are often not required to provide reasoning for their decisions or even to acknowledge that any such balancing took place. Consequently, the exercise of the implicit-procedural balancing tools is largely part of the *dark matter* of EU competition law enforcement.[8]

The shift from explicit-substantive to implicit-procedural balancing tools is summarised in Figure 8.1, which combines the empirical findings presented throughout the book by specifying the number of enforcement actions that were handled or concluded by (i) closing the case due to administrative considerations, e.g. a lack of

[6] See Section 2.5.4.1.
[7] See Section 7.1.3.
[8] On the dark matter, see Sections 1.3.1 and 7.1.3.

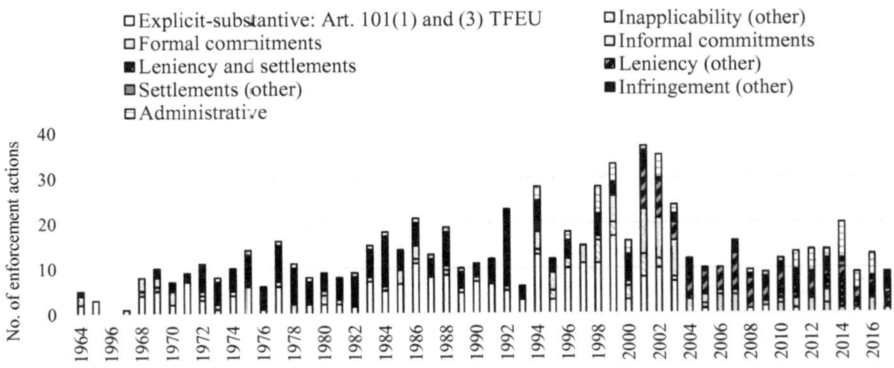

FIGURE 8.1. From explicit-substantive to implicit-procedural balancing tools
All of the Commission's Article 101 TFEU enforcement actions, excluding unpublished comfort letters. In some proceedings, only certain restrictions were exempted. In this figure, Article 101(1) TFEU balancing tools include cases where *a de minimis* claim was accepted

evidence or an expired limitation period (white and grey horizontal striped bars); (ii) accepting formal and informal commitments (light grey and grey dotted bars, respectively); (iii) leniency applications (black and dark grey stripes and black and white dotted bars); (iv) settlements (black and white dotted and dark grey bars); (v) applying the explicit-substantive balancing tools of Article 101(1) and (3) TFEU (white bars); (vi) other infringement decisions (black bars); and (vii) other inapplicability decisions (white and grey diagonal stripes).

The figure proposes that prior to modernisation, when the Commission held limited discretional enforcement powers, it was compelled to balance competition and non-competition interests under the explicit-substantive balancing tools. Consequently, it had the opportunity to issue inapplicability decisions, explaining the circumstances in which non-competition interests warranted Article 101(1) TFEU exceptions or Article 101(3) TFEU exemptions (white bars).

Yet, once the Commission had been vested with enhanced priority setting powers in the post-modernisation era, it dedicated much of its enforcement efforts to cases that were unlikely to raise balancing questions, such as those handled by means of leniency applications and settlements (black and dark grey stripes, black and white dotted, and dark grey bars). In parallel, the Commission mostly disregarded cases that raised balancing questions or resolved them by accepting commitments (light grey and grey dotted bars). As such, the modernisation of EU competition law not only *limited the scope of the explicit-substantive balancing tools* but also *eliminated the debate* over the role of non-competition interests from the Commission's practice.

A similar shift from explicit-substantive to implicit-procedural balancing tools was evident at the national level. The book has demonstrated that this shift was especially prominent in NCAs that followed the Commission's new approach and limited the scope of the explicit-substantive balancing tools (e.g. the German, UK, and Hungarian NCAs). Those NCAs may have been bound to use the implicit-procedural balancing tools available to them to avoid deviating from their declared interpretations of the explicit-substantive balancing tools.[9]

The shift from explicit-substantive to implicit-procedural balancing tools was also prominent in NCAs that had chosen to reserve some room for non-competition interests under the explicit-substantive balancing tools (e.g. the Dutch and French NCAs), but to a more limited degree. While those NCAs made use of their enforcement discretion to account for non-competition interests, they also engaged in balancing under the explicit-substantive tools. As such, they have had the opportunity to discuss and clarify their views on the role of non-competition interests under Article 101(1) and (3) TFEU balancing tools.

8.2.2 *Shifting the Locus of Balancing: From the EU to the Member States*

The institutional pillar of modernisation, as mentioned, entrusted the NCAs with the power to fully apply Article 101 TFEU and to engage in balancing. The decentralisation of enforcement has generally facilitated a process of soft convergence and voluntary harmonisation of many national competition rules with the practice of the Commission. Yet, this study has suggested that when it comes to balancing, the decentralised enforcement regime has brought about an opposite shift, transitioning from EU-based to national-based balancing principles. More specifically, it has revealed two legal sources that have facilitated national-based balancing:

First are the national enforcers' interpretations of Article 101 TFEU *explicit-substantive balancing tools*. This study has confirmed that NCAs and national courts were certainly influenced by the Commission's guidance on Article 101(1) and (3) TFEU balancing tools. The Commission conspicuously kept to its decisive role in shaping EU competition policy in the realm of decentralised enforcement. Nevertheless, because the Commission's guidelines and policy papers are not binding on the Member States, the national enforcers have often shaped their national approaches based on their legal, economic, and social traditions.

In particular, the national enforcers have adopted individual interpretations of the objectives of Article 101 TFEU, the types of relevant economic or non-economic benefits, the balancing process, and the intensity of control. Such choices have sometimes been informed by the wording of the national equivalent provisions of Article 101 TFEU. As such, the national provisions have not only affected the

[9] See Sections 3.6, 4.4, and 5.4.

balance of purely national cases but have also had spillover effects on the interpretation of Article 101 TFEU in cases in which the EU provision applied.[10]

National balancing approaches have also been influenced by the choice between explicit-substantive balancing tools. The empirical findings reveal that the national enforcers have applied the explicit-substantive balancing tools with differing frequency and at times used different balancing tools to address similar situations.[11] Since each tool assigns a different weight and function to non-competition interests, the choice between explicit-substantive balancing tools, in and of itself, is also a form of national balancing approach.

Overall, the book has identified three groups of national enforcers. The first group, which includes the UK and Hungarian NCAs and courts, has generally followed the Commission's interpretation of the explicit-substantive balancing tools. A second group, including the Netherlands and Germany, has sometimes openly deviated from that approach. A third group, including France, has also done so, but with more subtlety.

Second, national balancing practices have also been influenced by *national balancing tools*. This book has illustrated that some Member States shield certain agreements from the prohibition of Article 101 TFEU by adopting national rules that explicitly or implicitly limit the enforcement of EU competition law in favour of promoting non-competition interests. For instance, some Member States have adopted public policy defence clauses or issue-specific rules by which the national government or parliament has limited the enforcement of a specific agreement or type of restriction.[12] Member States have also implemented sector regulation or alternative enforcement mechanisms that subject certain anti-competitive agreements to alternative balancing instruments.[13] Furthermore, balancing has been embedded in national jurisdictional rules (e.g. national *de minimis* rules, and in France, the public body prerogative rule) and in implicit-procedural rules (e.g., enforcement discretion).[14]

In light of the above, the book has called attention to the mutually determinative connection between EU and national balancing principles. It has shown that Member States were not only affected by EU balancing rules when they enforced Article 101 TFEU; they also affected the scope of the prohibition of Article 101 TFEU by interpreting the EU balancing tools and adopting unique national balancing tools. Consequently, decentralisation has afforded the Member States a new opportunity to introduce national balancing principles that interpret and supplement the EU balancing framework.

[10] See Section 3.6.4.
[11] See Sections 3.2 and 5.4.
[12] See Chapter 6.
[13] See Section 7.5.
[14] See Sections 6.3.1 and 6.3.3 and Chapter 7.

8.2.3 A *Shift in the Role of the EU Courts: From Active to Passive*

The third shift in post-modernisation balancing pertains to the role of the EU Courts in guiding balancing. Prior to modernisation, the CJEU had a leading role in the development of balancing. In a series of landmark cases, the Court laid out several fundamental balancing principles. It shaped the *types of benefits* that can be recognised under the Article to include both economic and non-economic benefits.[15] It introduced the workable competition standard as the *balancing process* guiding Article 101(3) TFEU, by which balancing is based on a legal method and requires a relatively low evidentiary threshold.[16] Moreover, it devised *new balancing tools* to account for state involvement and commercial interests under Article 101(1) TFEU.[17] The GC also influenced balancing, especially with respect to Article 101(1) TFEU balancing tools, albeit to a lower degree than the CJEU. While the EU Courts did not produce a detailed balancing framework, their case law had an immense influence on shaping the balancing principles.

This all changed following modernisation. When the Commission embarked on the substantive modernisation in the early 2000s, it likewise took the reins for the development of the balancing principles. The Commission's new balancing approach, which is distinctly incompatible with the CJEU's old case law and opposed by various Member States and EU institutions,[18] had created an urgent need for judgments clarifying the scope of balancing in the post-modernisation era. In particular, the EU Courts could have defined the boundaries and explained the processes for integrating non-competition interests under the Article and the limits of the explicit-substantive and implicit-procedural balancing tools. Moreover, CJEU preliminary rulings could have explored the compatibility of national balancing rules, interpretations, and practices with EU law.[19]

Nevertheless, the EU Courts' judgments have merely created further uncertainty. On the one hand, the EU Courts did not embrace the Commission's new approach to the explicit-substantive balancing tools, at least in part. The empirical findings indicate that the courts have continued to follow the balancing principles established in their old case law, leaving significant room for consideration of non-competition interests. They have not fully endorsed the Commission's new approach to the types of benefits that can be examined under the Article, the reference to the short-term narrow consumer welfare standard, the sole reliance on economic evidence, and the Commission's new approach to by-object restrictions.[20]

[15] See Sections 3.5 and 4.3.2.1.
[16] See Sections 2.5.2.1 and 3.4.3.1.
[17] See Chapter 5.
[18] See Sections 2.5.4 and 8.4.
[19] See Sections 3.5 and 6.4.
[20] See Sections 3.5.3, 5.2.7, and 5.3.7.

On the other hand, the EU Courts have not staked out a clear position on those matters. Departing from their previously active role, the Courts have missed the opportunity to shape the balancing framework following modernisation. In the few cases in which they examined balancing questions, they issued vague and implicit judgments, generating much uncertainty as to the current role of non-competition interests. This trend has been aggravated by the shift from explicit-substantive to implicit-procedural balancing tools, as described above. The Commission's and NCAs' policy choices to focus the enforcement on clear-cut restrictions of competition, which are unlikely to raise balancing questions, have limited the EU Courts' prospects to scrutinise their balancing approaches. Since the Commission and NCAs have rarely enforced agreements that raise balancing questions, the EU Courts have had limited opportunity to clarify the role of non-competition interests in appeals and preliminary rulings.[21]

8.3 HINDERING THE OBJECTIVES OF ARTICLE 101 TFEU ENFORCEMENT

After identifying the three transitions brought by modernisation in the previous section, this section turns to the second research question. It evaluates how the three shifts have affected the attainment of the objectives of Article 101 TFEU enforcement.

The objectives of Article 101 TFEU enforcement are specified in Regulation 1/2003, which states that enforcement must ensure three main objectives: *effectiveness*, *uniformity*, and *legal certainty*.[22] The exact meaning of those three objectives is not clearly defined by the Regulation and can be interpreted in multiple ways. As elaborated below, for the purposes of the second research question, effectiveness is understood as an administrative law concept, uniformity as linked to the harmonisation of laws in the EU decentralised enforcement regime, and legal certainty as transparency and predictability.

The proposed definitions are intended to facilitate the discussion on the empirical findings and link them to normative policy recommendations. It is certainly possible to advance different understandings of each of those objectives, and this section does not intend to discuss all possible interpretations in depth. In any event, the analysis proposed in the following sections may also be of interest to those who put forward alternative understandings of the three objectives and wish to use the empirical findings to propose different arguments.

21 See Chapter 7.

22 Regulation 1/2003, Preamble 1, 3, 22; Modernisation White Paper (1999), para 44–51. Those objectives also guided the old enforcement regime. See Regulation 17/62, Preamble; Modernisation White Paper (1999), para 3–4, 6, 16–18, 24.

8.3.1 *Effectiveness*

Regulation 1/2003 declares that Article 101 TFEU must be applied 'effectively' across the EU.[23] Nevertheless, it does not offer a specific standard by which this effect should be measured. It merely specifies that the enforcement system must ensure that competition in the market is not distorted, guarantee rigorous enforcement, and allow the Commission to refocus its enforcement efforts on combatting the most serious restrictions of competition.[24] Hence, the precise meaning of effectiveness in the context of Regulation 1/2003 remains unclear.

This study ascribes a substantive-administrative element to effectiveness. This definition is not the only possible meaning of effectiveness in the sense of Article 1/2003 and differs from other meanings ascribed to it in EU law.[25] It is inspired by *Galligan*'s writing on the effective use of discretion in the process of administrative decision-making. According to Galligan, the effectiveness of an administrative action refers to the degree by which it contributes to realising the statutory goal of such action.[26] When applied to the act of balancing, this definition entails that its effectiveness is assessed in reference to the objectives of Article 101 TFEU.[27] Balancing is considered effective if it ensures that competition is not distorted, and it is considered ineffective if it fails to achieve that outcome.[28]

As Galligan points out, although the statutory goal is the focal point of the administrative action, the effective achievement of such a goal is not a simple matter of finding a suitable means to achieving a given end. It would be unrealistic to assume that a simplistic, technical relationship exists between a specified goal and the means adopted for its achievement. Rather, the administrative authority's action is always affected by other policy goals, as well as by the need to accommodate

23 Regulation 1/2003, Preamble 1; Modernisation White Paper (1999), para 11, 43–47. On effectiveness in Regulation 1/2003, See also Simonsson (2010, 17–18).

24 Regulation 1/2003, Preamble 3; see also Modernisation White Paper (1999), para 11, 43–47.

25 For example, effectiveness could also be defined in quantitative terms, namely the number of Article 101 TFEU enforcement actions. According to this definition, which guided the Commission's assessment of the application of Regulation 1/2003, more proceedings means greater effectiveness (see, in the Report on the Functioning of Regulation 1/2003 (2009), para 18; Report on the Functioning of Regulation 1/2003 (2014), para 43–44). Some scholars have suggested that effectiveness should be seen as an application of the general EU principle of equivalence and effectiveness. According to this approach, enforcement of Article 101 TFEU must not be made virtually impossible or excessively difficult by national procedural rules (see, for example, Sauter (1997, 16)). Yet, such approaches are not suitable for the purposes of this study, as they do not offer any relevant benchmark for assessing balancing.

26 Galligan (1990, 129).

27 For a similar definition of effectiveness, see Ehlermann (2000, 561–562), Cengiz (2009, 5, 7–9), Kovacic, Hollman, and Grant (2011, 30–31), Cleynenbreugel (2014, 1383), Nazzini (2014, 282–283), and implicitly in German Monopolies Commission (2000, para 73), and Blanco and De Pablo (2012).

28 On the objectives of Article 101 TFEU, see Section 2.2.1.

procedural and financial constraints. Therefore, an administrative action is likely to achieve a more modest level in pursuit of the overall statutory goal.[29]

For the purpose of this study, the definition of effectiveness acknowledges that enforcement of Article 101 TFEU does not purely aim to protect competition interests. A competition enforcer must take other non-competition interests into account, in addition to being bound by procedural and institutional constraints. The effectiveness of balancing should thus be thought of as an ideal. The closer the means adopted arrives at achieving the objectives of Article 101 TFEU, the more effective the balancing is.

Chapters 3–5 illustrate that, prior to modernisation, Article 101(1) and (3) TFEU balancing tools were often criticised as policy-driven, regulatory balancing tools that did not effectively protect competition interests. They were based on a formalistic analysis, excluding the application of Article 101 TFEU to certain practices or sectors regardless of the competitive harm. The modernisation of EU competition law in May 2004 was designed to increase the effectiveness of the enforcement.[30] It aimed to allow the competition enforcers to make more effective use of their limited resources, focusing on deterring behaviour that poses the greatest threat to competition and consumers.

In line with the above, the Commission aspired to modernise the explicit-substantive balancing tools. It rebranded Article 101(1) and (3) TFEU balancing tools as market-driven instruments that take only *direct economic benefits* into account. The balancing process was transformed from *exclusion and legal balancing processes* into an *economic balancing process* applying to agreements that have little or no effect on competition or which generate economic benefits on the basis of a short-term narrow consumer welfare standard. Moreover, the explicit-substantive balancing tools were no longer seen as instruments to further EU industrial policy and regulatory aims. The Commission called for *corrective balancing* that can be applied uniformly across all sectors and types of agreements and is directed at restoring the situation that would have occurred in the absence of the anti-competitive agreement. As a result, the explicit-substantive balancing tools became more effective at protecting competition.

The modernisation of the explicit-substantive balancing tools did not, however, increase the effectiveness of balancing in practice. The empirical findings have revealed that the Commission and NCAs had made only limited use of those explicit-substantive balancing tools following modernisation. Instead, investigations into agreements that raised balancing questions were often settled with negotiated remedies or terminated by closing the probe into the case altogether.

Consequently, undertakings could reasonably assume that restrictions of competition that produced certain non-competition benefits would not be subject to

29 Galligan (1990, 113).
30 See Sections 2.3.3 and 2.5.4.

TABLE 8.2. *Effectiveness of balancing tools (post-modernisation)*

Level of effectiveness	Balancing tool
High	Article 101(3) TFEU, general BERs, Article 101(1) TFEU commercial exceptions
Medium	Sectoral BERs, Article 101(1) TFEU state and public interest exceptions
Low	Enforcement discretion

The effectiveness of the national balancing tools is not indicated, as it differs according to the specific tool

Article 101 TFEU enforcement, even when they do not meet the conditions for an exception under Article 101(1) or (3) TFEU. On the opposite side of the same coin, the study has shown that the uncertainties as to the role of non-competition interests under the explicit-substantive balancing tools may also have had a chilling effect, discouraging undertakings from conducting welfare-enhancing agreements that may be justified by Article 101(1) and (3) TFEU balancing tools.[31]

As a result, the shift from explicit-substantive to implicit-procedural balancing tools has jeopardised the effectiveness of balancing. As elaborated in Chapters 3– 7 and summarised in Table 8.2, the implicit-procedural balancing tools are generally less effective at protecting competition interests, compared to explicit-substantive balancing tools.

The negative impact of the shift to implicit-procedural balancing tools on the effectiveness of balancing is two-fold. First, implicit-procedural balancing tools are less effective, in and of themselves. Competition enforcers have *carte blanche* when balancing by enforcement discretion. There is no limit to the types of benefits they can take into account, the process of balancing, the intensity of control, or the types of remedies pursued by balancing (i.e. corrective or regulatory). Hence, the implicit-procedural balancing tools have allowed the competition enforcers to account for non-competition interests beyond what would be deemed permissible under the explicit-substantive balancing tools of Article 101(1) and (3) TFEU, even in their broad interpretation prior to modernisation.

Second, implicit-procedural balancing tools also hamper the effectiveness of the explicit-substantive balancing tools. The competition enforcers' prioritisation choices should not merely focus on achieving compliance with Article 101 TFEU but should also determine the scope and boundaries of the Article.[32] Selecting cases that do not involve balancing questions has prevented the emergence of a body of case law in which the Commission and NCAs could have clarified if and how non-competition interests should be taken into account under the substantive assessment of Article 101 TFEU. This has created a paradox: While the explicit-substantive

[31] See Section 7.8.
[32] Ibid.

balancing tools have been considerably limited by modernisation, the modernisation itself has introduced new implicit-procedural balancing tools that allow the inclusion of broader non-competition interests than ever before.

In light of the above, the book has questioned the Commission's contention that the modernisation has contributed to effective enforcement by promoting more effective use of the enforcers' limited resources.[33] By calling for a broader yardstick for measuring the effectiveness of enforcement, the book submits that effective enforcement cannot exclusively focus on cartels. The overall success of competition enforcement must also evaluate the exercise of the competition enforcers' priority setting discretion. In particular, a systematic shift to consideration of non-competition interests via the implicit-procedural balancing tools, in a manner that is not based on economic or legal theory, hinders the effectiveness of balancing.

8.3.2 *Uniformity*

The second objective of Article 101 TFEU enforcement relates to the multi-level nature of the enforcement. Following the decentralisation of enforcement, the Commission and NCAs apply Article 101 TFEU in parallel. The pursuit of uniform application is a core objective of Regulation 1/2003. To this end, the Commission has already stressed in its Modernisation White Paper that the multi-governance enforcement regime should not compromise the creation of a single corpus of rules to be developed and applied in the same manner throughout the EU.[34]

The uniform enforcement of Article 101 TFEU in the multi-level governance system of Regulation 1/2003 is generally thought to be a major success.[35] The Commission has emphasised that the EU competition rules 'have to a large extent become the "law of the land" for the whole of the EU'.[36] While the Commission has admitted that a certain level of divergence persists, this has largely been ascribed to differences in the institutional position of NCAs, their national procedures, and sanctions. Some of those differences are further likely to be eliminated following the implementation of the ECN+ Directive.[37]

The uniform enforcement of Article 101 TFEU, and hence of balancing, has two aspects. First, Regulation 1/2003 states that decentralised enforcement must not lead to the adoption of *conflicting decisions* by two or more competition enforcers with

[33] Report on the Functioning of Regulation 1/2003 (2009), para 18; Report on the Functioning of Regulation 1/2003 (2014), para 43–44.

[34] Modernisation White Paper (1999), para 11, 24; On uniformity in Regulation 1/2003, see also Simonsson (2010, 10–15), Blanco and De Pablo (2012, 91–104), and Adinolfi (2015, 68–100).

[35] Report on the functioning of Regulation 1/2003 (2009), para 7; Report on the functioning of Regulation 1/2003 (2014), para 6.

[36] Report on the functioning of Regulation 1/2003 (2009), para 23.

[37] See Section 7.7.

respect to *a single agreement*.[38] For the purposes of this study, this means that two or more competition enforcers should not reach different outcomes when applying balancing to the same agreement. As elaborated in Section 2.3.3.3, Regulation 1/2003 introduced various coordination mechanisms to mediate this risk. While this has not completely prevented contradictory balancing decisions, such decisions are rare. A prominent example is the *Booking.com* saga in which, as detailed in Section 3.6.3.1, the German NCA and courts issued conflicting decisions regarding an agreement that had been examined by twenty-five other NCAs.

The second aspect of uniformity refers to the *consistent enforcement* of Article 101 TFEU by the various competition enforcers. Regulation 1/2003 pursues the creation of a level playing field on which the Article is applied in a similar, if not identical, manner across the EU. Its main thrust is to ensure that NCAs and national courts interpret the law in the same way to avoid forum shopping.[39]

To this end, the decentralisation of EU competition law enforcement has attempted to enhance *vertical institution diversity*.[40] This type of institutional setting is based on a federalist model, whereby the federal level – the Commission – has capacious rulemaking competencies and the Member States have only limited competencies to design their own rules. Reflecting this approach, Regulation 1/2003 endeavours to eliminate the multitude of national competition rules by requiring NCAs and national courts to apply the EU competition rules when an agreement affects trade between Member States, and this is complemented by a host of coordination and soft convergence mechanisms. Those mechanisms attempt to marginalise the scope of national competition rules.

Applying this principle to balancing suggests that in similar situations, a degree of equivalence and consistency should inform the choice of balancing tools, the relevant types of benefits, the balancing processes, and the intensity of control.[41] However, the empirical findings presented throughout the book have illustrated that the provisions of Regulation 1/2003 and its accompanying coordination and soft convergence mechanisms have not sufficiently achieved this aim:

First, the mere obligation to apply Article 101 TFEU to cases affecting trade between Member States has not led to the uniform administration of EU competition policy. As observed by *Basedow*, the former chairman of the German Monopoly Commission, even if one were inclined to accept the assumption that an obligation to apply a single substantive standard relating to a technical private law provision would result in uniform practice, that assumption would not apply to competition

[38] Regulation 1/2003, Article 16 and Preamble 1, 22; Modernisation White Paper (1999), para 44, 47.

[39] Monti (2014b, 117).

[40] On horizontal and vertical institutional diversity of competition law systems, see Budzinski (2003).

[41] For instance, Commissioner Monti stressed that the competition enforcers must follow 'sufficiently similar' approaches when applying Article 101(3) TFEU. See Monti (2000, 14).

law, where national interests and political involvement are more strongly felt.[42] The far-reaching differences in the social, economic, and political traditions of the Member States cast serious doubt as to whether a mere obligation to apply the same provision would secure uniform administration of the law.

Indeed, this study has found that national approaches have introduced a degree of *horizontal institution diversity*, whereby the Member States and the national enforcers design and implement their own balancing rules. This has impeded the consistent application of both the explicit-substantive and the implicit-procedural balancing tools.

The *EU explicit-substantive balancing tools*, as shown in Chapters 3– 5, mostly lay out general balancing principles that leave ample discretion to the competition enforcers. In the absence of a harmonised and binding EU framework on the substantive and procedural aspects of balancing, Member States and national enforcers are allowed to craft national rules, methods, and approaches. The varying national interpretations, coupled with the adoption of unique national balancing tools, have exposed undertakings to multiple procedural and substantive standards when applying the explicit-substantive balancing tools, which undermines the pursuit of identical application sought by Regulation 1/2003.

The horizontal diversity is even more pronounced when it comes to the *implicit-procedural balancing tools* embedded in the exercise of enforcement discretion. Since those implicit-procedural balancing tools have not been harmonised and are not bound by any substantive balancing test, the competition enforcers have failed to apply consistent criteria to account for non-competition interests.

Second, the study indicated that the coordination and cooperation mechanisms enacted by Regulation 1/2003 were insufficient to ensure the uniformity of the explicit-substantive balancing tools.[43] In particular, although Regulation 1/2003 relies on national courts to safeguard the consistent application of Article 101 TFEU,[44] the empirical findings show that the courts did not always promote uniformity. This was the result of a combination of several developments. Because of this shift from explicit-substantive to implicit-procedural balancing tools, national courts had only limited opportunity to discuss Article 101(1) and (3) TFEU balancing tools. Furthermore, in the absence of a detailed and binding EU balancing framework, NCAs and national courts are not barred from adopting diverging interpretations.[45]

Finally, the study also questioned the success of the rule, embedded in Article 5 of Regulation 1/2003 and the CJEU's *Tele2Polska (2011)* judgment, prohibiting NCAs from adopting binding findings of applicability. This rule was vindicated by

[42] Basedow (2007, 430–431).

[43] On the coordination and cooperation mechanisms of Regulation 1/2003, see Section 2.3.3.3.

[44] See Section 3.6.5.

[45] See Section 3.6.

reference to the first aspect of uniformity, namely avoiding conflicting decisions with respect to a single agreement. The CJEU has explained that empowering NCAs to take binding inapplicability decisions would have called into question the uniformity of the decentralised system and would have undermined the power of the Commission because it would have prevented the Commission from subsequently finding that the practice in question infringed the provisions of EU competition law.[46]

Nevertheless, this rule is detrimental to the second aspect of uniformity – consistent application. Chapter 7 suggests that this rule could discourage NCAs from pursuing cases involving complex balancing questions because such cases might be answered without generating any observable decision output. In its place, NCAs are incentivised to close such cases by exercising their discretional enforcement powers irrespective of the impact of the relevant agreement on both competition and non-competition interests.[47]

Allowing NCAs to adopt binding inapplicability decisions might have encouraged them to publish reasoned 'no grounds for action' findings in which they applied the explicit-substantive balancing tools. Such decisions could have revealed, shaped, and clarified the NCAs' approaches to Article 101(1) and (3) TFEU balancing. Moreover, since those decisions would have been subject to judicial review, this would have provided national courts with an opportunity to engage in the balancing debate. Despite the abovementioned leeway to adopt diverging interpretations, national courts could have referred certain balancing questions to the CJEU for preliminary ruling, asked the Commission for information or an opinion, and received the Commission's written observations.[48]

The level of uniformity attributable to the various balancing tools has been discussed in Chapters 3– 7 and is summarised in Table 8.3.

TABLE 8.3. *Uniformity of balancing tools (post-modernisation)*

Level of uniformity	Balancing tool
High	BERs
Medium	Article 101(1) and (3) TFEU
Low	National balancing tools; enforcement discretion

It should be noted that not all agree that the uniform enforcement of EU competition law is desirable. *Svetiev*, for example, suggests using national divergence as a form of experimentalist architecture.[49] *Townley* and *Turk* similarly question the benefits of the status quo and call for a system of co-ordinated

46 C-375/09 Tele2 Polska (2011), para 27–28.
47 See Section 7.6.3.
48 See Sections 2.4 and 3.5.
49 Svetiev (2010). For a critique, see Monti (2014b).

diversity.[50] While the desirability of uniformity in the decentralised enforcement regime is not discussed in this book, the empirical findings invite further discussion on the advantages, disadvantages, and limits of uniformity.

8.3.3 *Legal Certainty*

Regulation 1/2003 and the Modernisation White paper emphasise that enforcement of Article 101 TFEU must take place in compliance with the principle of legal certainty.[51] More specifically, the Modernisation White Paper asserts that the switch to a self-assessment regime was based on the premise that, after 35 years of enforcement, EU competition law had been clarified and thus become more predictable for undertakings. As the scope of Article 101 TFEU became more predictable, *ex-ante* analysis by the Commission was rendered superfluous.[52]

In the context of balancing, achieving a degree of legal certainty requires a transparent balancing regime in which the role of non-competition interests is clearly defined to allow undertakings to self-assess their restrictive practices.[53] The competition enforcers should actively communicate the legal rules and their application in each case to allow undertakings to predict to a sufficient degree of certainty whether an agreement violates Article 101 TFEU and if, and how, balancing will be administered.[54] For this purpose, the competition enforcers must develop consistent and durable balancing methods, worthy of respect over time. The balancing should not be applied on an *ad-hoc* basis and should not fluctuate frequently.[55]

This book has demonstrated that each of the three transformations in balancing following modernisation has impeded the legal certainty of balancing. First, the shift from explicit-substantive to implicit-procedural balancing tools has rendered balancing less *transparent*. As mentioned, prior to modernisation, the Commission regularly published formal positive decisions and informal comfort letters declaring that an agreement did not fall under Article 101(1) TFEU or that it could be exempted under Article 101(3) TFEU. As part of the switch from a notification to a self-assessment regime, the enforcement of Article 101 TFEU now focuses on infringement decisions. The Commission has declared that when undertakings provide a valid justification for their conduct, it will often not pursue a case any further and will not publish the reasons for such findings.[56] The same is mostly true

50 Townley (2018) and Townley and Turk (2019).

51 Regulation 1/2003, Preamble 22, 38; Modernisation White Paper (1999), para 48–51.

52 Modernisation White Paper (1999), para 48.

53 *Ibid*, para 48–51. See also Townley (2009, 42) and Lavrijssen (2010, 655–656).

54 Hawk and Denaeier (2001, 124, 130), Townley (2009, 235), and Peeperkorn (2016, 390).

55 Compare with Kovacic, Hollman, and Grant (2011, 37).

56 Report on the Functioning of Regulation 1/2003 (2009), para 26. See also the Commission in OECD Role of Efficiency Claims in Antitrust Proceedings (2012), 90.

at the national level, especially since NCAs have only limited powers to adopt 'no grounds for action' findings.[57]

Second, the shift from EU to Member States-based balancing has rendered balancing less uniform, and as such also less *predictable*. Even in cases where national enforcers have examined balancing questions by means of the (EU or national) explicit-substantive balancing tools, the role of non-competition interests could not have been predicted – and only determined *ex post* by the enforcer that takes on the case. This is because national enforcers have adopted diverging interpretations of Article 101(1) and (3) TFEU balancing tools and applied their unique national balancing tools.

Finally, the shift in the role of the EU Courts has also increased *legal uncertainty*. EU Courts play an important role in securing predictability. Legal certainty is enhanced when judges and the Commission reach coherent decisions, which can then serve to help undertakings predict the outcome of future cases.[58]

The empirical findings have shown that although the EU Courts have not fully endorsed the Commission's new approach to balancing following modernisation, neither have they taken a clear stand on how balancing should be applied. Due to the shift to implicit-procedural balancing tools, the Courts have had only limited opportunity to review balancing questions in preliminary rulings or appeals against the Commission's decisions. Even in the limited opportunities the Courts have had to address balancing questions, their judgments have often used vague and ambiguous wording and failed to directly address such questions.

The EU Courts' silence on the objectives of Article 101 TFEU, the relevant types of benefits, the balancing process, the intensity of control, and the room for divergence in national interpretations has given the Commission and NCAs additional leeway to shape their respective interpretations regarding the particularities of balancing. Because the EU Courts have not fleshed out the open-textured Treaty provisions on competition, they have entrusted the competition enforcers with additional discretion to determine the role of non-competition interests.

The level of legal certainty associated with the various balancing tools has been discussed in Chapters 3–7 and is summarised in Table 8.4.

8.3.4 *Modernisation as a Double-Edged Sword*[59]

The three shifts in balancing brought about by modernisation, this study has suggested, act as a *double-edged sword*. On one metaphoric edge of the blade, the substantive and institutional pillars of modernisation have increased the *effectiveness*

[57] See Section 8.3.2.
[58] UNCTAD (2016, 2).
[59] This argument was previously presented in Brook (2020), with respect to Article 101(3) TFEU individual exemptions.

TABLE 8.4. *Legal certainty of the balancing tools (post-modernisation)*

Level of legal certainty	Balancing tool
High	BERs
Medium	Article 101(3) TFEU
Low	Article 101(1) TFEU, enforcement discretion

The legal certainty of the national balancing tools is not mentioned, as it differs according to the specific tool

of the explicit-substantive balancing tools. The Commission has used modernisation as a sword to protect the integrity of EU competition law against undue non-competition interests. As a result, the competition enforcers have rarely accepted, let alone discussed, the possibility of justifying an agreement with overriding non-competition interests.

However, reducing the scope of the explicit-substantive balancing tools and the debate over the role of non-competition interests has not eliminated the role of such interests. On the other edge of the sword, the procedural pillar of modernisation has granted competition enforcers new *implicit-procedural* balancing tools in the form of enforcement discretion.

These new implicit-procedural balancing tools are generally less effective at protecting competition and suffer from serious uniformity and legal certainty weaknesses. In other words, although the modernisation of EU competition law may have enhanced the enforcement of EU competition law in general, it has been counter-productive when it comes to balancing. Instead of improving the manner in which non-competition interests are considered under Article 101 TFEU, it has hindered the objectives of the enforcement.

8.4 POLICY RECOMMENDATIONS

In 1979, FTC Commissioner *Pitofsky* submitted that '[i]t is bad history, bad policy, and bad law to exclude certain political values in interpreting the antitrust laws'.[60] This study has shown that the above statement, which was made with respect to US antitrust law in light of the growing influence of the Chicago School, holds equally true for the role of non-competition interests under Article 101 TFEU, post-modernisation.

Bad history: The study has demonstrated that EU competition law and policy were designed to achieve multiple economic, social, and political objectives. Over the years, EU competition law and policy were used to maximise consumer welfare and economic efficiency, integrate the internal market, support the EU's industrial

[60] Pitofsky (1979, 1051).

policy, and ensure personal freedom and Ordoliberal aims. In more recent years, the application of Article 101 TFEU has continued to raise questions on how to strike the right balance between competition, sustainability, data protection, employment rights, the survival of small businesses, innovation, democracy, and the distribution of political power. To this extent, competition law is, and is likely to remain, polycentric.

Bad policy: The Council, Commission, EU Courts, European Parliament, and Member States have repeatedly endorsed consideration of non-competition interests within the enforcement of Article 101 TFEU. They have emphasised that EU competition law is not an end unto itself, but rather an instrument for achieving the EU Treaty's economic and social goals.[61]

Only recently has the European Parliament declared 'the fact that competition rules are treaty based and, as enshrined in Article 7 of the TFEU, should be seen in the light of the wider European values underpinning Union legislation regarding social affairs, the social market economy, environmental standards, climate policy and consumer protection'. According to the Parliament, the application of EU competition law thus 'should address all market distortions, including those created by negative social and environmental externalities'.[62]

Even the Commission continues to insist that Article 101 TFEU leaves room for non-competition interests. Although the Commission's policy papers maintain that only objective economic efficiencies can be taken into account when applying Article 101 TFEU,[63] Commissioner *Vestager* has declared that 'EU competition rules leave *ample room* for taking into account impact on society'.[64]

An approach calling to effectively eliminate the role of non-competition interests in the enforcement of Article 101 TFEU, this study has maintained, amounts to ignoring the basis of EU competition law policy and the political consensus that supports it.[65]

Bad law: Finally, this study has shown that, in practice, non-competition interests – comprising both economic and non-economic benefits – have always played a role in the enforcement of Article 101 TFEU and are likely to continue to play a role in the future. More specifically, it proved that even when the Commission has attempted to limit the role of non-competition interests in the process of modernisation, competition enforcers have always found new ways to account for non-competition interests. Balancing was never eliminated; it merely shifted from the explicit-substantive balancing tools to implicit-procedural and national balancing

[61] See Section 2.2.1.
[62] European Parliament resolution of 31 January 2019 on the Annual Report on Competition Policy (P8_TA(2019)0062), para 7.
[63] Commission Article 101(3) Guidelines (2004), para 59.
[64] Emphasis added. Commission, Parliamentary Questions: Answer Given by Ms. Vestager on Behalf of the Commission (1 June 2017).
[65] Compare with Pitofsky (1979, 1075).

tools, which are generally less effective at protecting competition and suffer from serious uniformity and legal certainty weaknesses.

The above conclusion that Article 101 TFEU should leave room for the consideration of non-competition interests is *not* linked to the desirable normative value of such interests in EU competition law. It is neither at odds with the belief that the main objective of EU competition policy should be the protection of the competitive process and structure nor with the notion that EU competition policy should focus on the enhancement of consumer welfare. This study has deliberately taken an *agnostic view* of normative questions that ask what the objectives of Article 101 TFEU are and how much room the Article leaves for non-competition interests.[66]

This study merely observes that competition interests and economic benefits cannot exclusively explain the application of Article 101 TFEU. The competition enforcers' practices have shown that attempts to limit the consideration of non-competition interests under the explicit-substantive balancing tools were a *double-edged sword*. They have resulted in the reintroduction of those interests, through the back door, in the form of the implicit-procedural balancing tools that are less effective, uniform, and legally certain.

Hence, instead of asking *whether* non-competition interests should play a role in Article 101 TFEU enforcement, this study submits that one should ask *how* non-competition interests should be taken into account in a manner that respects the effectiveness, uniformity, and legal certainty of the enforcement. To this end, the study advocates three policy reforms.

8.4.1 *Re-shifting Balancing to the Explicit-Substantive Tools*

First, the study calls to re-shift the consideration of non-competition interests towards the ambit of the explicit-substantive balancing tools. The empirical findings presented in this book have revealed that despite certain challenges and open questions regarding the application of those tools, they facilitate a more effective, uniform, and legally certain balancing in comparison to the implicit-procedural balancing tools.

An active and transparent application of the explicit-substantive balancing tools, the study argues, will oblige the *Commission and* NCAs to clarify many of the open questions surrounding balancing in the post-modernisation era. They will need to explain what the objectives of EU competition law are and what types of benefits are relevant, define the limits of the consumer welfare standard, demonstrate how to apply the proportionality test, and spell out the appropriate burden of proof. These questions can only be answered if the Commission and NCAs actually apply the explicit-substantive balancing tools.

[66] See Section 1.2.1.1.

Application of the explicit-substantive balancing tools is also essential to provide *EU and national courts* with the opportunity to bridge the gaps in the current EU balancing framework. By examining appeals against the Commission's and NCAs' application of the explicit-substantive balancing tools, the Courts could help to shape the scope, limits, and future of EU competition law and policy and the more economic approach. Active national enforcement of such agreements is especially necessary for examining the compatibility of unique national exceptions and national interpretations of the EU balancing tools with EU competition law.

Active application of the explicit-substantive balancing tools is also vital for safeguarding the democratic and political legitimacy of EU competition law and policy. By taking a clear stand on the open questions surrounding balancing, the competition enforcers could provide the *Member States, EU institutions, other political bodies*, and *the general public* with opportunities to review, comment, and reform the EU approach to non-competition interests.

Above all, the study calls on competition enforcers to use the primary balancing procedure prescribed by the EU Treaties, namely Article 101(3) TFEU. As opposed to balancing by enforcement discretion, the balancing tool of Article 101(3) TFEU ensures that non-competition interests do not overly impede the effectiveness of the enforcement by ordering the weighing of competition and non-competition interests and emphasising that only proportionate and necessary restrictions are allowed. It also puts in place procedural and institutional safeguards to ensure the effectiveness of balancing in the form of the ECN network and judicial review. Hence, the principles and procedures embedded in this tool should guide balancing.

8.4.2 *Enforcing Cases Involving Balancing Questions*

Second, the study recommends that the Commission and NCAs should use their enforcement discretion to build a diverse and balanced portfolio of cases. Competition enforcers should not limit themselves to issuing decisions against clear-cut infringements of competition. They should also choose cases that will help the development of EU competition law by defining the scope and boundaries of Article 101 TFEU.

Accordingly, although competition enforcers should focus most of their detection and target efforts on serious and clear-cut infringements, some of their resources should be allocated for discussing and clarifying the role of non-competition interests under the explicit-substantive balancing tools in formal decisions.[67] Cases involving balancing questions should not only be investigated by means of alternative or informal procedures or negotiated remedies; balancing questions should be

[67] As described in Section 7.6.3, this is of value even if the finding of inapplicability itself is not binding.

subject to transparent prohibition and inapplicability decisions, which are then notified to the ECN network and liable for judicial review.

The study has argued that selecting cases involving balancing questions is also indispensable to facilitating a public debate on political issues related to the objectives of Article 101 TFEU, the types of benefits that can be taken into account, the balancing method, and the limits of the implicit-procedural and national balancing tools. Those balancing questions are not only about law and economics but also have a strong political component. Therefore, a public debate is necessary to ensure the continued legitimacy of and support for EU and national competition laws. While EU and national courts might be able to fill some of the gaps, the focus should be on a more comprehensive balancing framework influenced by EU and national political-democratic processes.

8.4.3 *Codifying and Formalising the Balancing Principles*

Third, further to the previous point, this study suggests that the public debate on balancing could later be leveraged to codify in EU secondary law the scope, principles, and methods of both the explicit-substantive and implicit-procedural balancing tools. To this end, the study observes that neither the cooperation mechanisms of Regulation 1/2003 nor the Commission's soft law policy papers ensure the effective, uniform, and legally certain application of Article 101 TFEU. The role of non-competition interests under Article 101 TFEU is still glaringly unclear, and it differs between Member States according to their respective national traditions.

Thus, this study proposes that, much like the harmonisation of the institutional aspects of decentralised enforcement by the recent ECN+ Directive, it may be the time for a complementary, substantive harmonisation of balancing in EU secondary law. This could take the form of a Regulation that amends or complements Regulation 1/2003's framework. Alternatively, the public debate surrounding the harmonisation of balancing may very well decide to leave some room for divergence in the national interpretations of the EU balancing tools and the adoption of national balancing tools. In that event, a more general balancing framework and corresponding principles could be codified in the form of a directive.

In parallel, the EU Courts should become more active in rendering judgments that bridge the gaps in the balancing framework. When appropriate opportunities arise, the EU Courts should strive to take a clear stand on the objectives of Article 101 TFEU, the precise role of non-competition interests under Article 101 TFEU, and the validity of the Commission's more economic approach.

Further attention should be given to the scope and impact of national rules, interpretations, and practices. The EU Courts should assess the compatibility of the unique national exceptions and the national interpretations of the EU balancing tools with the principle of the primacy of EU competition law, as enshrined in

Article 4(3) TEU and Article 3 of Regulation 1/2003. Doing so would ensure that the objectives of uniformity and effectiveness envisaged by modernisation can be realised while preserving the richness of national experiences.

8.5 FINAL REMARKS

It is not easy to conclude a study on the role of non-competition interests under Article 101 TFEU. New balancing challenges, case law, and policy papers covering such areas as digital markets, the gig economy, sustainability, and means of tackling economic, political, and health crises regularly prompt further debate on the future of non-competition interests. Because the debate on the role of non-competition interests is never-ending, this chapter has aimed to provide an anchor to understand past balancing practices and help shape the future.

This chapter calls for rationalisation of the role of non-competition interests under Article 101 TFEU and the balancing principles. It advocates moving away from *ad hoc* and case-specific solutions to a set of transparent and systematic principles guiding the consideration of non-competition interests.

Such balancing principles are likely to be contentious and might need to be modified over time to meet emerging legal, economic, and social preferences and challenges. Nevertheless – and to some extent regardless of their initial substance – they are likely to be of value to both those who believe that non-competition interests should play a greater role in enforcement and those who advocate limiting that role. This study suggests that only by articulating clear balancing principles that are actively and transparently applied (i.e. via the explicit-substantive balancing tools) will a rational debate emerge – legal, economic, and public – on the role of non-competition interests.

ANNEX A:

References

CHAPTER 2: HISTORY OF ARTICLE 101 TFEU BALANCING

2.1 *First Enforcement Period: Commission Prohibited Horizontal Agreements That Impede Market Integration (Footnote 136)*

26623 Quinine (1969); 597 V.V.V.F. (1969); 128 Julien/Van Katwijk (1970); 324 Vereniging van Cementhandelaren (1971); 581 Cementregeling voor Nederland (1972); 243 244 245 Cimbel (1972); 26918 Suiker-Unie (1973); 791 1373 1374 1498 1499 1500 SCPA (1973); 795 Kali und Salz/Kali Chemie (1973); 400 Agreements between manufacturers of glass containers (1974); 426 Papiers peints de Belgique (1974); 26602 FRUBO (1974); 712 Stoves and Heaters (1975); 256 Bomee-Stichting (1975); 28980 Pabst & Richarz/BNIA (1976); 147 Centraal Bureau voor de Rijwielhandel (1977); 28948 Cauliflowers (1977); 29176 Vegetable parchment (1977); 312 COBELPA/VNP (1977)

CHAPTER 3: ARTICLE 101(3) TFEU INDIVIDUAL EXEMPTIONS

3.1 *Referring to All Four Alternatives of Article 101(3) TFEU Together (Footnote 13)*

26940 KEWA (1975), para III(1); 26940 United Reprocessors GmbH (1975), para III(1); 27093 De Laval/Stork (1977), para 10, extended by 27093 De Laval/Stork (1987), para 6; 29428 GEC-Weir Sodium Circulators (1977), para III(1); 30099 Schlegel/CPIO (1983), para 19; 30804 Nuovo CEGAM (1984), para 19; 30810 Synthetic fibres (1984), para 29–38; 31055 ENI/Montedison (1986), para 29–32; 31302 Boussois/Interpane (1986), para 20; 32075 Bayer/BP Chemicals (1988), para 25–26; 3640 Exxon/Shell (1994), para 67–70; 35280 Sicasov (1998), para 74; 36539 British Interactive Broadcasting (1999), para 159–162; 36748 REIMS II (1999), para 69; 32150 Eurovision (2000), para 84–90; 34493 DSD (2001), para 142–146; 38477 British Airways/SN Brussels Airlines (2003), para 56; 38370 UK Network Sharing Agreement (2003), para 140; 38369 Network Sharing Rahmenvertrag (2003), para 127–128; 37398 Joint selling of the commercial rights of the UEFA Champions League (2003), para 161; 35470 35473 Austrian system for the disposal of packaging waste (2003), para 271, 322; 38479 British Airways and Iberia (2003), para 44; 38284 Société Air France/Alitalia Linee (2004), para 132

3.2 *Technical and Economic Progress (Footnotes 444 and 446)*

Technical and economic progress, taken together, have vindicated exemptions granted in the following cases:

Joint ventures and R&D agreements: 26917 Henkel/Colgate (1971), para III; 27442 Vacuum Interrupters (1977), para 20; 28796 Beecham-Parke, Davis (1979), para 35–37; 29955 Carbon Gas Technologie (1983), para II(B)(1); 30971 BP/Kellogg (1985), para 15(c); 31206 Rich Products/Jus-rol (1987), para 41; 32306 Olivetti/Canon (1987), para 54; 32368 BBC Brown Boveri (1988), para 23; 32006 Alcatel Espace/ANT Nachrichtentechnik (1990), para 18; 34857 PT/MCI (1994), para 53; 34891 Fujitsu AMD Semiconductor (1994), para 41; IP/95/550 Interconnector (1995); 35830 Unisource (1997), para 85–89; 35738 Uniworld (1997), para 68–75; 36592 Cégétel (1999), para 57; 36213 GEAEP&W (1999), para 79

Patent, know-how licensing, and collective management of IPRs agreements: 4204 Velcro/Aplix (1985), para III(1); 36849 MPEG-2 (1998); 31498 Delta ChemieDDD (1988), para 41; 37506 DVD Patent Licensing Programme (2000); 38014 IFPI 'Simulcasting' (2002), para 84–88

Environmental agreements: 36718 CECED (1999), para 57

Rationalisation for avoiding structural overcapacity: 31846 Enichem/ICI (1987), para 34–37; 34456 Stichting Baksteen (1994), para 18–28

Coordination of international payment systems: 29373 Visa International (2002), para 81–91. In 34579 36518 38580 MasterCard I (2007), para 679, while the Commission did not grant an exception, it noted in, that '[i]t is not disputed that payment card schemes such as MasterCard may represent, as such, economic and technical progress'

Cooperation for setting up national-wide mail and communication systems: 35617 Phoenix/GlobalOne (1996), para 58–59; 38170 REIMS II renotification (2003), para 105–117

Insurance: 33100 Assurpol (1992), para 38–39

Economic progress and the promotion of distribution, taken together, have justified exemptions granted in the following cases:
Specialised fairs and exhibitions: 93 European Machine Tool Exhibition (1969), III(1)(c); 181 CEMATEX (1971), para III(1); 28775 UNIDI (1975), para III(2); 417 BPICA (1977), para III(2); 93 European Machine Tool Exhibition (1978), para 14; 417 BPICA (1982), para 12; 27492 SMM&T Exhibition Agreement (1983), para 19; 28959 VIFKA (1986), para 18; 31739 Internationale Dentalschau (1987), para 21; 31593 British Dental Trade Association – BDTA (1988), para 32; 31559 Sippa (1991), para 18
International cooperation in the field of energy to avoid supply disruptions: 30525 International Energy Agency (1983), para 29; 30525 International Energy Agency (1994), para 6(a)
Distribution of pay-TV: 38287 Telenor/Canal+/Canal Digital (2003), para 202

3.3 *First Enforcement Period: Industrial Policy Considerations Justify Exemptions (Footnote 36)*

Specialisation agreements: 26437 Jaz/Peter (1969, 1977); 26625 Clima Chappée-Buderus (1969); 26418 Sopelem/Langen (1971); 26624 F.N.-C.F. (1971); 26612 MAN/SAVIEM (1972); 642 Papier mince (1972); 26825 PRYM-BEKA (1973); 27073 Bayer/Gist-Brocades (1975)
Joint research agreements: 26917 Henkel/Colgate (1971); 26603 Rank/Sopelem (1974)
Joint ventures for the development, manufacture, and marketing of products: 26940 KEWA (1975); 26940 United Reprocessors GmbH (1975); 27442 Vacuum Interrupters (1977); 27093 De Laval/Stork (1977); 29428 GEC-Weir Sodium Circulators (1977); 29236 Sopelem/Vickers (1977)

3.4 *First Enforcement Period: Focus on Industrial Policy Benefits (Footnote 37)*

R&D: 26437 Jaz/Peter (1969); 26625 Clima Chappée-Buderus (1969); 26418 Sopelem/Langen (1971)
International competitiveness or EU industry: 26612 MAN/SAVIEM (1972)
Penetration into new geographic markets and overcoming difficulties in developing advanced technology products: 27442 Vacuum Interrupters (1977); 27093 De Laval/Stork (1977); 29428 GEC-Weir Sodium Circulators (1977); 29236 Sopelem/Vickers (1977)

3.5 *Second and Third Enforcement Periods: Assuming That Consumers Receive a Fair Share (Footnote 66)*

171 856 172 117 28173 Campari (1977), para III(B); 26437 Jaz/Peter (1977), para III(B); 29236 Sopelem/Vickers (1977), para III(3); 28796 Beecham/Parke, Davis (1979), para 38; 27958 National Sulphuric Acid Association (1980), para 47; 30517 Amersham Buchler (1982), para 12; 30437 Rockwell/Iveco (1983), para 9; 29329 VW-MAN (1983), para 34; 30099 Schlegel/CPIO (1983), para 20; 29955 Carbon Gas Technologie (1983), para II(B)(2); 29598 SABA's EEC distribution system (1983), para II(B)(2); 29420 Grundig' s EEC distribution system (1985), para II(B)(2); 31302 Boussois/Interpane (1986), para 20; 31340 Mitchell Cotts/Sofiltra (1986), para 26; 32306 Olivetti/Canon (1987), para 55; 27093 De Laval/Stork (1987), para 7; 31914 ARG/Unipart (1987), para 41; 31902 IVECO/FORD (1988), para 41; 33473 Scottish Nuclear Agreement (1991), para 37; 35679 Novalliance/Systemform (1996), para 71; 36718 CECED (1999), para 56–57; 35470 35473 Austrian system for the disposal of packaging waste (2003), para 272; 38479 British Airways and Iberia (2003), para 47.

This trend was prominent already during the first enforcement period but became more noticeable as the Commission broadened the scope of Article 101(3) TFEU to include non-economic benefits. See, for example, 223 Transocean Marine Paint Association (1967), para III(2); 26045 A.C.E.C/Berliet (1968), para III(2); 26625 Clima Chappée-Buderus (1969), para III(2); 26825 PRYM-BEKA (1973), para III(2); 26603 Rank/Sopelem (1974), para III(2); 5715 Junghans (1976), para 35

3.6 *Non-Economic Benefits as Additional Justification (Footnote 86)*

Environmental considerations: 14650 Bayerische Motoren Werke AG (1974), para 24; 29428 GEC-Weir Sodium Circulators (1977), para III(1)(a); 29955 Carbon Gas Technologie (1983), 3; 32368 BBC Brown Boveri (1988), para 23

Employment considerations: 30810 Synthetic fibres (1984), para 37; 33814 Ford/Volkswagen (1992), para 36; 34456 Stichting Baksteen (1994), para 27

Industrial policy: 26612 MAN/SAVIEM (1972), para 29; 14650 Bayerische Motoren Werke AG (1974), para 124; 26940 United Reprocessors GmbH (1975), para III(3)(a); 29955 Carbon Gas Technologie (1983), 3; 30373 37143 P&I CLUBS (1985), para 56; 30320 Optical fibres (1986), para 59; 32368 BBC Brown Boveri (1988), para 23; 33814 Ford/Volkswagen (1992), para 36; 34857 PT/MCI (1994), para 53–54; 35617 Phoenix-GlobalOne (1996), para 60; 35337 Atlas (1996), para 51; 36718 CECED (1999), para 50; 30373 37143 P&I CLUBS (1999), para 106–108; 38014 IFPI 'Simulcasting' (2002), para 91; 38370 UK Network Sharing Agreement (2003), para 139

3.7 *Fourth Enforcement Period: Commission Rejects Outright the Possibility of Article 101(3) TFEU Exemptions (Footnote 109)*

37980 Souris (2004), para 143–158; 37750 French beer market (2004), para 75; 38549 Barême d'honoraires de l'Ordre des Architectes belges (2004), para 104–110; 38456 Bitumen Nederland (2006), para 162–168; 39181 Candle waxes (2008), para 317; 39188 Bananas (2008), para 340–343; 38698 CISAC (2008), para 231–237; 39510 Ordre National des Pharmaciens en France (ONP) (2010), para 703–706; 39633 Shrimps (2013), para 438; 39226 Lundbeck (2013), para 1221–1231; 39685 Fentanyl (2013), para 406–439; 39612 Perindopril (Servier) (2014), para 2074–2122; 39574 Smart card chips (2014), para 334–335; 39964 Air France/KLM/Alitalia/Delta (2015), para 42; 40055 Parking heaters (2015), para 59–60; 40028 Alternators and Starters (2016), para 68; 39850 Container Shipping (2016), para 57–58; 39824 Trucks (2016), para 87–88; 40023 Cross-border access to pay-TV (2016), para 51–52; 399904 Rechargeable battery (2016), para 54–55; 39960 Thermal Systems (2017), para 80; 40013 Lighting Systems (2017), para 53

3.8 *First Enforcement Period: Refusal to Exempt Agreements That Impede Market Integration (Footnote 113)*

Distribution agreements with elements of export restrictions, RPM, or other limitations on production or sales: 26894 26876 26892 Pittsburgh Corning Europe (1972); 24510 GERO-fabriek (1976); 29018 Miller International (1976); 28282 The Distillers Company Limited (1977); 29146 BMW Belgium NV and Belgian BMW dealers (1977); 29418 Spices (1977)

Uniform discounts and rebates protecting domestic manufacturers: 25963 Gas water-heaters and bath-heaters (1973)

Technical standards: 29151 Video cassette recorders (1977)

3.9 *First Enforcement Period: Exemptions Emphasising the Lack of Harm to Market Integration (Footnote 117)*

Distribution agreements: 3036 D.R.U.-Blondel (1965); 22491 Maison Jalatte (1965); 10498 11546 12992 17394 17395 17971 18772 18888 3213 Omega

(1970); 14650 Bayerische Motoren Werke AG (1974); 847 Saba (1975); 5715 Junghans (1976)

Horizontal technical cooperation and joint R&D agreement: 26045 ACEC/Berliet (1968), 4

Patent licensing: 17545 6964 26858 26890 18673 17448 Davidson Rubber Co. (1972); 21353 Kabelmetal/Luchaire (1975)

3.10 *Second and Third Enforcement Periods: Sectoral Approach in 'Special' Markets (Footnote 131)*

Selective distribution systems in luxury cosmetics markets: 33242 Yves Saint Laurent Parfums (1991); 33542 Parfums Givenchy system of selective distribution (1992)

Beer distribution agreements: 35079 Whitbread (1999), para 150–154. In other cases, the Commission accepted voluntary commitments: IP/19/94/345 Interbrew exclusive right (1994); 35612 Tuborg/Pripps (1998)

Horticultural market: 35280 Sicasov (1998)

3.11 *Second and Third Enforcement Periods: Refusal to Exempt Agreements Impeding Market Integration (Footnote 132)*

Horizontal agreements: 29453 SNPE-LEL (1978); 29535 White lead (1978); 29672 Floral (1979); 197 Industrieverband Solnhofener Natursteinplatten eV (1980); 29525 30000 SSI (1982); 29629 Rolled zinc products and zinc alloys (1982); 30174 Vimpoltu (1983); 30064 Cast iron and steel rolls (1983); 30907 Peroxygen products (1984); 29702 26870 Aluminium imports from eastern Europe (1984); 29725 Wood pulp (1984); 28930 Milchförderungsfonds (1984); 30739 Siemens/Fanuc (1985); 30988 Flat-glass in the Benelux (1984); 31128 Fatty Acids (1986)

Vertical agreements: 29430 Kawasaki (1978); 28852 29127 29149 Fedetab (1978); 29440 Arthur Bell and Sons Ltd – conditions of sale (1978); 28859 Wm. Teacher and Sons Ltd-conditions of sale (1978); 1576 Zanussi (1978); 29595 Pioneer Hi-Fi Equipment (1979); 29011 Rennet (1979); 29021 BP Kemi/DDSF (1979); 29702 Johnson & Johnson (1980); 26912 Hennessy-Henkell (1980); 30188 Moet et Chandon (London) Ltd (1981); 25757 Hasselblad (1981); 30070 National Panasonic (1982); 30077 Cafeteros de Colombia (1982); 28748 AEG-Telefunken (1982); 30696 Distribution system of Ford Werke AG (1983); 30809 John Deer (1984); 30299 Grohe's distribution system (1984); 30261 Ideal-Standard's distribution system (1984); 30658 Polistil/Arbois (1984); 30839 Sperry New Holland (1985); 31143 Peugeot (1986); 31741 Sandoz (1987); 31017 Fisher-Price/Quaker Oats Ltd-Toyco (1987); 31192 31507 Tipp-Ex (1987);

31503 Konica (1987); 27393 27394 Net book agreements (1988); 30979 31394 Decca Navigator System (1988); 32879 Viho/Toshiba (1991); 32290 Newitt/Dunlop Slazenger International (1992); 32725 Viho/Parker Pen (1992); 31550 31898 Zera Montedison/Hinkens Stahler (1993); 32948 34590 Tretorn (1994); 35733 VW (1998); 36264 Mercedes-Benz (2001); 35587 35706 36321 Video Games (2002)

3.12. *Third Enforcement Period: Article 101(3) TFEU in Newly Liberalised Markets (Footnote 137)*

Post services: 36748 REIMS II (1999)

Energy: 33151 33997 Jahrhundertvertrag VIK-GVSt (1992); IP-95-550 Interconnector (1995); 37732 Synergen (2002)

Telecom: 32737 Eirpage (1991); 35617 Phoenix/GlobalOne (1996); 34857 BT/MCI (1994); 35337 Atlas (1996); 35830 Unisource (1997); 35738 Uniworld (1997); 36237 TPS (1999); 36592 Cégétel (1999); 36539 British Interactive Broadcasting (1999); IP/01/1845 Scandinavian digital satellite TV broadcasting (2001); 38370 UK Network Sharing Agreement (2003); 38369 Network Sharing Rahmenvertrag (2003); 38287 Telenor/Canal+/Canal Digital (2003)

Transport: 32792 IATA agency programs (1991); 32659 IATA Passenger Agency Programme (1991); 33585 Distribution of railway tickets by travel agents (1992); 32450 French-West African shipowners' committees (1992); 32448 32450 Cewal, Cowac and Ukwal (1992); IP/96/400 Baltic Liner Conference Agreement (1996); 35545 LH/SAS (1996); 36213 GEAE/P&W (1999); 34250 Europe Asia Trades Agreement (1999); 36253 P&O Stena Line (1999); 37812 Bmi British Midland/Lufthansa/SAS (2001); 37396 Revised Trans-Atlantic Conference Agreement (2002); 37730 AuA/LH (2002); 38477 British Airways/SN Brussels Airlines (2003); 38479 British Airways and Iberia (2003); 38284 Société Air France/Alitalia Linee Aeree Italiane (2004)

3.13 *Third Enforcement Period: Article 101(3) TFEU in Regulated Sectors (Footnote 137)*

Regulated professions: 33407 CNSD (1993); 33686 Coapi (1995); 36147 EPI code of conduct (1999)

Sports: IP/98/355 Danish Tennis Federation (1998); 37124 FIFA rules on players' agents (2002); 37398 Joint selling of the commercial rights of the UEFA Champions League (2003)

Television and film: 32524 Screensport/EBU members (1991); 32745 Astra (1992); 35617 Phoenix/GlobalOne (1996); IP/01/82 Broadcasting in Belgium of French horseraces (2001)

Pharmaceutical products: 34279 ADALAT (1996); 32026 Bayo-n-ox (1989); 36957 Glaxo Wellcome (2001)

3.14 *Third Enforcement Period: Sectoral Approach Focusing on Market Integration (Footnote 138)*

Financial services: 34607 Banque Nationale de Paris-Dresdner Bank (1996); 29373 Visa International (2002)
Post: 36748 REIMS II (1999)
Pharmaceutical products: 34279 ADALAT (1996); 32026 Bayo-n-ox (1989); 36957 Glaxo Wellcome (2001)
Sports: IP/98/355 Danish Tennis Federation (1998); 37124 FIFA rules on players' agents (2002); 37398 Joint selling of the commercial rights of the UEFA Champions League (2003)

3.15 *Third Enforcement Period: Exemptions in Special Sectors to Agreements That Do Not Directly Fix Prices or Quotes (Footnote 140)*

Financial services: 31291 Uniform Eurocheques (1988); 31499 Dutch Banks (1989)
Regulated professions: 36147 EPI code of conduct (1999)
Sports: IP/98/355 Danish Tennis Federation (1998); 37124 FIFA rules on players' agents (2002); 37398 Joint selling of the commercial rights of the UEFA Champions League (2003)
Transport: 32792 IATA agency programs (1991); 32659 IATA Passenger Agency Programme (1991); 35545 LH/SAS (1996); IP/96/400 Baltic Liner Conference Agreement (1996); 36253 P&O Stena Line (1999); 37812 bmi British Midland/Lufthansa/SAS (2001); 37730 AuA/LH (2002); 37396 Revised Trans-Atlantic Conference Agreement (2002); 38477 British Airways/SN Brussels Airlines (2003); 38479 British Airways and Iberia (2003); 38284 Société Air France/Alitalia Linee Aeree Italiane (2004)

3.16 *Third Enforcement Period: Exemptions for Joint Ventures and Cooperation Agreements That Do Not Fall within the BERs (Footnote 163)*

Rationalisation: 31902 lveco/Ford (1988); 32368 BBC Brown Boveri (1988); 34252 Philips-Osram (1994)
R&D and innovation: 32368 BBC Brown Boveri (1988); 32681 Cekacan (1990); 32363 KSB/Goulds/Lowara/ITT (1990); 33814 Ford/Volkswagen (1992); 34410 Olivetti/Digital (1994); 34252 Philips-Osram (1994); 33640 Exxon/Shell (1994); 33863 Asahi/Saint-Gobain (1994); 34891 Fujitsu

AMD Semiconductor (1994); 35855 Scandairy (1997); IP/98/353 Photographic manufacturers (1998); 36213 GEAE/P&W (1999); 37802 Precision Blasting (2000); 37889 GM/Fiat (2000)

3.17 *Preliminary Rulings (Footnote 207)*

Prior to modernisation – focus on distribution systems: C-126/80 SALONIA (1981); C-243/83 Binon (1985); C-41/96 VAG-Händlerbeirat eV (1997). In C-136/86 BNIC (1987), the CJEU also examined fixing of production quotas by a trade association.

Following modernisation – regulated markets: C-238/05 Asnef-Equifax (2006) (financial sector); C-403/08 C-429/08 Football Association Premier League (2011) (broadcasting of sports programs); C-1/12 Ordem dos Técnicos Oficiais de Contas (2013) (chartered accountants). Distribution via the internet in C-439/09 Pierre Fabre (2011)

3.18 *Article 101(3) TFEU Appeals (Footnote 208)*

CJEU: C-56/64 C-58/64 Grundig/Consten (1966), 347; C-8/66 C-9/66 C-10/66 C-11/66 Noordwijks Cement Accoord (1967), 92; C-17/74 Transocean Marine Paint Association (1974); C-71/74 Frubo (1975); C-26/76 Metro I (1977); C-28/77 Theal/Watts (1978); C-30/78 The Distillers Company Ltd (1980); C-209/78 C-210/78 C-211/78 C-212/78 C-213/78 C-214/78 C-215/78 C-218/78 Fedetab (1980); C-61/80 Rennet (1981); C-258/78 Breeders' rights-maize seed (1982); C-96/82 C-97/82 C-98/82 C-99/82 C-100/82 C-101/82 C-102/82 C-103/82 C-104/82 C-105/82 C-108/82 C-110/82 AVEWA-ANSEAU (1983); C-43/82 C-63/82 VBBB/VBVB (1984); C-35/83 Tokecs/Dorcet (1985); C-42/84 Nutricia-de Rooij and Nutricia-Zuid-Hollandse Conservenfabriek (1985); C-25/84 C-26/84 Distribution system of Ford-Werke AG (1985); C-240/82 C-241/82 C-242/82 C-261/82 C-262/82 C-268/82 C-269/82 SSI (1985); C-260/82 SSI (1985); C-193/83 Windsurfing International (1986); C-75/84 SABA (1986); C-45/85 Fire insurance (1987); C-43/85 UINDI (1987); C-360/92P Net Book Agreements (1995); C-137/95P Building and Construction Industry in the Netherlands (1997); C-8/95P UK Agricultural Tractor Registration Exchange (1998); C-171/05P FIFA rules on players' agents (2006); C-501/06P C-513/06P C-515/06P C-519/09P GlaxoSmithKline (2009); C-382/12P MasterCard (2014).

GC: T-19/91 Vichy (1992); T-14/89 Polypropylene (1992); T-61/89 Hudson's Bay-Dansk (1992); T-66/89 Net Book Agreements (1992); T-39/92 T-40/92 Eurocheque (1994); T-34/92 UK Agricultural Tractor Registration Exchange (1994); T-35/92 UK Agricultural Tractor Registration

Exchange (1994); T-17/93 Ford/Volkswagen (1994); T-9/93 Langnese-Iglo (1995); T-29/92 Building and Construction Industry in the Netherlands (1995); T-19/92 Yves Saint Laurent Perfumes (1996); T-88/92 Perfumes Givenchy system of selective distribution (1996); T-528/93 T-542/93 T-543/93 T-546/93 EBU/Eurovision System (1996); T-575/93 Buma (1996); T-213/95 T-18/96 Stichting Certificatie Kraanverhuurbedrijf and the Federatie van Nederlandse Kraanverhuurbedrijven (1997); T-112/99 TPS (2001); T-231/99 Bass (2002); T-131/99 Whitbread (2002); T-185/00 T-216/00 T-299/00 T-300/00 Eurovision (2002); T-395/94 Trans-Atlantic Agreement (2002); T-65/98 Van den Bergh Foods Limited (2003); T-67/01 JCB (2003); T-193/02 FIFA rules on players' agents (2005); T-259/02 T-260/02 T-261/02 T-262/02 T-263/02 T-264/02 T-271/02 Austrian banks – 'Lombard Club' (2006); T-362/02 Bitumen (2006); T-289/01 DSD (2007); T-419/03 Austrian system for the disposal of packaging waste (2011); T-359/06 Bitumen (2012); T-357/06 Bitumen (2012); T-354/06 Bitumen (2012); T-353/06 Bitumen (2012); T-362/06 Bitumen (2012); T-491/07 Cartes Bancaires (2012); T-111/08 MasterCard (2012); T-451/08 CISAC (2013); T-544/08 Candle Waxes (2014); T-469/13 Lundbeck (2016); T-470/13 Lundbeck (2016); T-472/13 Lundbeck (2016); T-699/14 Licensing of intellectual property rights for football collectibles (2017)

3.19 *Basis for EU Courts Scrutiny (Footnote 213)*

Procedural requirements: C-8/66 C-9/66 C-10/66 C-11/66 Noordwijks Cement Accoord (1967), 91–92; T-19/91 Vichy (1992), para 90; T-14/89 Polypropylene (1992), para 271; T-61/89 Hudson's Bay-Dansk (1992), para 148; T-66/89 Net Book Agreements (1992), para 69, 76; T-29/92 Building and Construction Industry in the Netherlands (1995), para 288; T-575/93 Buma (1996), para 40, 56; C-171/05P FIFA rules on players' agents (2006), para 24–25

Very general appraisal of the Commission's discretion: C-28-77 Theal/Watts (1978), para 57; C-30/78 The Distillers Company Ltd (1980), para 23; C-61/80 Rennet (1981), para 18; C-8/08 C-96/82 C-97/82 C-98/82 C-99/82 C-100/82 C-101/82 C-102/82 C-103/82 C-104/82 C-105/82 C-108/82 C-110/82 AVEWA-ANSEAU (1983), para 38; C-35/83 Tokecs-Dorcet (1985), para 40–41; C-240/82 C-241/82 C-242/82 C-261/82 C-262/82 C-268/82 C-269/82 SSI (1985), para 85; C-260/82 SSI (1985), para 62; C-193/83 Windsurfing surfing International (1986), para 101; T-39/92 T-40/92 Eurocheque (1994), para 109–115; T-34/92 UK Agricultural Tractor Registration Exchange (1994), para 99; T-35/92 UK Agricultural Tractor Registration Exchange (1994), para 105; T-29/92 Building and Construction Industry in the Netherlands (1995), para 256, 288; T-9/93 Langnese-Iglo (1995), para 140–149; T-19/92 Yves Saint Laurent Parfums (1996), para 197–205; T-88/92 Parfums Givenchy system of selective distribution (1996), para 197–205; T-213/95 T-18/96 Stichting Certificatie Kraanverhuurbedrijf and the Federatie van Nederlandse Kraanverhuurbedrijven (1997); T-395/94 Trans-Atlantic Agreement (2002), para 251–264; T-231/99 Bass (2002), para 36; T-65/98 Van den Bergh Foods Limited (2003), para 120–144; T-544/08 Candle Waxes (2014), para 263–267; T-469/13 Lundbeck (2016), para 353–354; T-470/13 Lundbeck (2016), para 56–58; T-472/13 Lundbeck (2016), para 712–714

3.20 *Fourth Enforcement Period: Appeals on Commission's Old Exemptions Involving Non-Economic Benefits (Footnote 231)*

Confirming exemptions granted: On the basis of sports: T-193/02 FIFA rules on players' agent (2005); C-171/05P FIFA rules on players' agent (2006). Environmental considerations: T-289/01 DSD (2007), para 38; T-419/03 Austrian system for the disposal of packaging waste (2010), para 23. Financial services: T-259/02 T-260/02 T-261/02 T-262/02 T-263/02 T-264/02 T-271/02 Austrian banks – 'Lombard Club' (2006)

Appeals affirming that in theory non-economic benefits could justify an exemption: On the basis of free riding: T-491/07 Cartes bancaires (2012), para 77, 259. R&D: T-168/01 GlaxoSmithKline (2006), para 268. Culture: T-451/08 CISAC (2013), para 103

3.21 *France: Consideration of Broad Non-Competition Interests (Footnotes 321 and 324)*

Prior to 2009:

Protection of jobs: 05-D-03 Bleach (2005), para 117–121

Living standards of agriculturists: 05-D-10 Fruit and vegetables in Brittany (2005), para 130–132

Stabilisation of prices: 05-D-10 Fruit and vegetables in Brittany (2005), para 130–132; 05-D-55 Essential Oils of Lavandin (2005), para 78–85

Increased bargaining power: 05-A-17 Collective bargaining on deadlines intercompany payment (2005), para 31–37; 05-D-55 Essential Oils of Lavandin (2005), para 78–85

Public health and safety: 06-D-03 Heating, ceramic sanitary and plumbing equipment (2006), para 1254–1261; 07-D-49 Defibrillators (2007), para 323–325

Protection of SMEs: 07-D-49 Defibrillators (2007), para 321–325

Fair trade rules: 06-A-07 Fair trade (2006)

Agriculture: 07-A-04 Quality label (2007)

After 2009:
Increased bargaining power: 13-D-14 Strasbourg vets (2013), para 147–150
Survival of industry: 15-D-19 Standard and express delivery (2015), para 717–725
Broadcasting of sports: 09-D-31 Football rights (2009), para 299–300; 04-A-09 Broadcasting rights for sporting competitions (2009)
Investment: 08-A-16 Mobile virtual network operators (MVNO) (2016), para 123; 11-A-20 Relay masts (2011), para 9–33; 13-A-08 Network sharing and roaming (2013), para 65
Culture: 09-A-50 Cinema code (2009), para 94–95
Public health: 11-A-20 Relay masts (2011), para 9–33
Environmental considerations and development of rural areas: 13-A-08 Network sharing and roaming (2013), para 65

3.22 *Germany: Consideration of Cost and Quality Benefits (Footnote 331)*

B1-25/04 Verta/Danzer (2004), 19; B8-113/03-1 Long-term gas supply (2006), 23–28; B1-116/04 Sand-lime Brick (2006), para 134; B10-148/05 Lottery (2006), para 422–425; B4-1006/06 Container glass (2007); Joint selling of media rights (2008); B2-90/01-4 Timber (2009); B1-232/07 Association of the German construction industry (2009), 2; B3-64/05 Merck and VWR distribution agreement (2009), para 105–110; B10-44/09 B10-45/09 B10-47/09 B10-48/09 B10-10/10 B10-11/10 B10-13/10 B10-14/10 B10-18/10 B10-19/10 B10-20/10 B10-21/10 B10-22/10 B10-23/10 B10-24/10 B10-25/10 Gas and electricity supplier resale bans (2010); B3-134/09 Federal Guild of Hearing Aid Acousticians (2011), para 44–46; B6-114-10 Joint selling of media rights for the German football leagues (2012); B9-96/09 Lufthansa (2012), para 51; B7-11/13 Bosch Siemens (2013), 4; B6-46/12 Amazon (2013), 2–3; B9-66/10 HRS-Hotel Reservation Service (2013), para 199–212; B7-46/13 Telekom and Telefónica (2014), para 90; B3-93/15 Lighters (2015), para 43

3.23 *Germany: Industrial Policy Considerations (Footnote 334)*

B8-113/03-1 Long-term gas supply (2006), 24–26; B7-22/07 Basic Encryption of TV Programs – Commitments (2012), 41; B7-1/13-35 Sennheiser (2013), 1–2; B3-137/12 Adidas (2014), 6–7; B2-98/11 ASICS (2015), para 613–622; B6-81/11 ARD/ZDF online platform 'Germany's Gold' (2014); B7-46/13 Telekom and Telefónica (2014), para 88–89

3.24 *UK: NCA Outright Reject Article 101(3) TFEU Exceptions (Footnote 343)*

CE/2464-03 UOP/prices for desiccant (2004); CE/2890-03 Future fees by certain independent fee-paying schools (2006); CE/4327-04 Bid rigging in the construction industry in England (2009); CE/7510-06 Construction Recruitment Forum (2009); CE/8950/08 Loans to large professional services firms (2011); CE/3094-03 Dairy retail price initiatives (2011); CE/7691-06 Airline passenger fuel surcharges for long-haul flights (2012); CE/9161-09 Distribution of Mercedes-Benz commercial vehicles (vans) (2013); CE/9248-10 Access control and alarm systems to retirement properties (2013); CE/9627/12 Supply of prescription medicines to care homes in England (2014)

3.25 *Hungary: Broad Interpretation of Article 101(3) TFEU until 2005 (Footnote 346)*

Rejecting exceptions in cases of price-fixing: Vj-74/2004/58 Public procurement bidding for building a block of flats with respect to bid-rigging (2004); Vj-138/2004/14 Hungarian Bakers Guild (2004), para 17–19; Vj-60/2004 Budapest Sports Stadium (2005), para 185 as upheld by the Budapest Metropolitan Court in 7.K.34341/2005/15 Budapest Sports Stadium (2006)

Granting exceptions to other types of agreements: Vj-169/2003/68 Fertilizers (2004), para 6.32; Vj-132/2004/26 Card issuance (2004), para 6, 13–15; Vj-200/2004/13 Funeral service in Szolnok (2005), 5–6, 8; Vj-128/2004/23 Tomb construction activities in Túrkeve (2005), para 40; Vj-178/2004/5 Pont Audio (2005), para 35; Vj-23/2005 Rába Group and Integri (2005), para 67, 76; Vj-207/2004/51 Rába IT agreement (2005)

3.26 *Hungary: NCA Refusal to Grant Exceptions for Agreements since 2006 (Footnote 347)*

Vj-161/2004/59 Animal Feed Phosphates II (2006); Vj-162/2004 Universities IT tender (2006); Vj-199/2005 Egg cartel (2006); Vj-71/2005 Sara Lee price restrictions (2007); Vj-158/2005/148 Hyundai Motors Hungary (2007); Vj-140/2006 newspaper distribution I (2007); Vj-26/2006 Navigation tools (2007); Vj-81/2006/74 Medical equipment (2007); Vj-166/2006 Car navigation tools (2009); Vj-195/2007/129 Newspaper distribution II (2010); Vj-69/2008 Wheat mill products I (2010); Vj-134/2008 Wheat mill products II (2010); Vj-151/2009/260 Model contracts for programme (2013); Vj-115/2010 Dental headpieces (2013); Vj-66/2012 Geophysical measuring operations (2014); Vj-96/2010 Contact lenses (2014); Vj-29/2011-522 Ready-mix concrete (2014); Vj-45/2008-641 Colour television tubes (2014); Vj-2/2010 Car refinishing paints (2014); Vj-23/2011 Daily newspapers (2014); Vj-40/2013 Driving schools in Győr (2014); Vj-48/2013 Tenders in Nagylóc and Szécsényfelfalu (2014); Vj-49/2011

Hungarian beer market (2015); Vj-73/2011 Mosquito control (2015); Vj-11/2014 Media Service Support and Asset Management Fund (2016); Vj-156/2004/68 Ice-cream (2006); Vj-2/2015 lead-acid batteries (2016); Vj-37/2014 Meat products temporary sales (promotions) (2016)

3.27 *Hungary: Infringement Findings in Professional Association Cases (Footnote 348)*

Vj-180/2004 Hungarian Bar Association of attorneys (2006); Vj-51/2005 The Hungarian Association of Automobile Dealers (2006), confirmed by the Budapest Metropolitan Court in 7.K.31.11612007144 The Hungarian Association of Automobile Dealers (2009); Vj-201/2005 Hungarian Chamber of Architects (2007), upheld by the Budapest Metropolitan Court in 11.K.31.445/2008/11 Hungarian Chamber of Architects (2010) and the Budapest Appeal Court in 2.Kf.27.463/2009/5 Hungarian Chamber of Architects (2010); Vj-36/2008 Association of journalists (2008), upheld by the Budapest Metropolitan Court in 3.K.30.051/2009/12 Association of journalists (2010) and the Budapest Court of Appeals in 2. Kf.27.217/2010/4 Association of journalists (2010); Vj-3/2008 Rail freight transport services (2012); Vj-51/2008 Professional Guild of Hairdressers (2009), as partially altered (not with respect to Article 101(3) TFEU) by the Budapest Metropolitan Court in 7.K.34.976/2009/9 Professional Guild of Hairdressers (2010), and revised to the GVH's position by the Budapest Court of appeals in 2.Kf.27.333/2010/6 Professional Guild of Hairdressers (2010); Vj-143/16/2008 Chamber Of Plant Protection In Hungary (2010)

3.28 *Germany: NCA Refusal to Grant Exceptions on Basis of the First and Third Conditions (Footnote 353)*

B1-25/04 Verta/Danzer (2004), 19–25; B8-113/03-1 Long-term gas supply (2006), 23–28; B1-116/04 Sand-lime brick (2006), para 134–138; B10-148/05 Lottery (2006), para 422–425; B4-1006/06 Container glass (2007), para 144, 153; B1-232/07 Association of the German construction industry (2009), 2; B3-64/05 Merck and VWR distribution agreement (2009), para 105–110; B10-44/09 B10-45/09 B10-47/09 B10-48/09 B10-10/10 B10-11/10 B10-13/10 B10-14/10 B10-18/10 B10-19/10 B10-20/10 B10-21/10 B10-22/10 B10-23/10 B10-24/10 B10-25/10 Gas and electricity suppliers resale bans (2010); B3-134/09 Federal Guild of Hearing Aid Acousticians (2011), para 44–46; B9-96/09 Lufthansa (2011), para 51; B7-11/13 Bosch Siemens (2013), 4; B1-62/13 Rental of retail space in factory outlet centres (2015), para 323–354; B1-72/12 Round timber in Baden-Württemberg (2015), para 455–458, 482–485; B3-93/15 Lighters (2015), para 43; B7-1/13-35

Sennheiser (2013), 1–2; B3-137/12 Adidas (2014), 6–7; B2-98/11 ASICS (2015), para 613–622; B6-81/11 ARD/ZDF online platform 'Germany's Gold' (2014); Sanitary sector (2016); B6-32/15 Joint selling of media rights to matches of the German Bundesliga (2016); B4-71/10 Online banking conditions (2016), para 421–436

3.29 *Netherlands: NCA Rejects Outright Article 101(3) TFEU Exceptions (Footnote 380)*

4014 Horticultural Services (2005), para 117–120; 5851/121 Thuiszorg 't Gooi (2008), para 224; 108/258 Thuiszorg Kennemerland (2008), para 184–185; 6274/569 Midden Ijssel (2010), para 224–231; 6538 Houses merchants foreclosure auctions (2011), para 219; 6425 Window cleaners (2011), para 246–251; 6888/435 LHV pace of establishment (2011), para 151–154; 7036_1/386 Bell peppers (2012), para 280–281; 7401/106 Demolition firms bid-rigging – Bergambacht & Dilettant (2013), para 128–129; 7244/597 Magazine packs (2013), para 279–284; 13.0612.53 Mobile operators (2014), para 83; 7571/40.O1018 Mandatory flood insurance (2013), para 61–64; ACMDM2015201065_oV Proton therapy (2015), 6

3.30 *France: Strict Intensity of Control (Footnote 378)*

Demanding economic evidence to substantiate the existence of the first two conditions of Article 101(3) TFEU: 09-A-48 Dairy (2009), para 86; 09-A-50 Cinema code (2009), para 166–170; 10-D-13 Le Havre Port (2010), para 321–332, 435–441; 10-D-20 Electronic discount coupons (2010), para 57; 11-D-02 Restoration of historic monuments (2011), para 566–567; 12-D-08 Endives (2012), para 576; 12-D-09 Flour mills (2012), para 663–664, 725–726; 15-D-19 Standard and express delivery (2015), para 720–725, 757–763

Strict application of the indispensability condition: 09-D-31 Football rights (2009), para 299–301; 09-A-48 Dairy (2009), para 85; 10-D-20 Electronic discount coupons (2010), para 58; 11-D-01 Port handling sector on Reunion Island (2011), para 129; 12-D-08 Endives (2012), para 580–584; 12-D-09 Flour mills (2012), para 673–677; 13-D-03 Pork slaughtering (2013), para 252; 13-D-14 Strasbourg vets (2013), para 148–150; 14-A-04 Seed (2014), para 105–107

CHAPTER 5: ARTICLE 101(1) TFEU

5.1 *State Action Defence: Settling Politically Sensitive Issues (Footnote 31)*

Member States' constitutions: 28824 Breeders' rights – maize seed (1978), para 1.E.5, II.B.8; 31734 Film purchases by German television stations (1989), para 39; T-14/89 Polypropylene (1992), para 318–319

Trade and international agreements: 27095 Franco-Japanese ballbearings agreement (1974), 5; C-43/82 C-63/82 VBVB (1984), para 33–40; 33585 Distribution of railway tickets by travel agents (1992), para 85–90; 32450 French-West African shipowners' committees (1992), para 33, 37–38; C-126/97 Eco Swiss China Time Ltd (1999), para 36–41; 39180 Aluminium Fluoride (2008), para 68–72; 38698 CISAC (2008), para, 93–95; T-406/08 Industries chimiques du fluor (ICF) (2013), para 208–214

EU Treaties: C-172/80 Züchner (1981), para 8; C-45/85 Fire insurance (1987), para 12–25; 34073 34395 35436 Van den Bergh Foods Limited (1998), para 211–214

EU Charter of Fundamental Rights: C-43/82 C-63/82 VBVB (1984), para 33–40; 38279 French beef (2003), para 114

EU secondary law: C-90/76 Van Ameyde (1977), para 15; 29525 30000 SSI (1982), para 100; 33151 33997 Jahrhundertvertrag VIK-GVSt (1992), para 19, 24; T-229/94 HOV SVZ-MCN (1997), para 41; 34579 36518 38580 MasterCard I (2007), para 439–444; 38698 CISAC (2008), para 107–110, 161–163; 39401 E.On/GdF (2009), para 252–253

Professional associations: 27000 IFTRA rules for producers of virgin aluminium (1975), 6; 28980 Pabst & Richarz-BNIA (1976), 4; 29883 AROW-BNIC (1982), para 54–58; 33686 Coapi (1995), para 34–35; 36147 EPI code of conduct (1999), para 26–27, 42, as confirmed by the GC in T-144/99 EPI code of conduct (2000), para 49–50; 38549 Barême d'honoraires de l'Ordre des Architectes belges (2004)

National unfair competition and fair trading rules: 400 Agreements between manufacturers of glass containers (1974), para 33–39; 27000 primary aluminum (1975), para III(A)

Other: C-811/79 ARIETE S.P.A. (1980), para 14–17; C-246/88 Roofing felt (1989), para 17–18; 36693 Volkswagen (2001), para 72; 36571 Austrian banks-'Lombard Club' (2002), para 373–375

5.2 *State Action Defence: Lack of Autonomy Strand of Cases (Footnote 35)*

Exception accepted in: Asia Motor France III (1994) (unpublished). The decision quoted in T-387/94 Asia Motor France III (1996), para 24; 33014 Asia Motor France IV (1998) (unpublished). The decision quoted in T-154/98 Asia Motor France IV (2000), para 52.

Exception partially accepted in: 39401 E.ON/GDF (2009), para 288–298

Exception rejected in: 28852 29127 29149 Fedetab (1978), para 88, 105 as confirmed by the CJEU in C-209/78 C-210/78 C-211/78 C-212/78 C-213/78 C-214/78 C-215-78 C-218/78 Fedetab (1980), para 130–131; 1576 Zanussi (1978), para 13; 29133 WANO Schwarzpulver (1978), 6–7; 29021 BP

Kemi/DDSF (1979), para 71; 29525 30000 SSI (1982), para 100–105 as confirmed by the CJEU in -240/82 C-241/82 C-242/82 C-261/82 C-262/82 C-268/82 C-269/82 SSI (1985), para 23–37, 40 and C-260/82 SSI (1985), para 26–30; 31055 ENI/Montedison (1986), para 25; 32450 French-West African shipowners' committees (1992), para 35; 34279 ADALAT (1996), para 202–206; 37614 Interbrew and Alken-Maes (2001), para 171–172, 247–249; 38238 Spanish Raw Tobacco (2004), para 349–355; 39258 Airfreight (2010), para 964–1016; 39510 Ordre national des pharmaciens (ONP) (2010), para 603–604; T-7/92 Asia Motor II (1993), para 68–73; T-513/93 CNSD (2000), para 59–75; 34466 Greek Ferries (1998), para 43–44, 53, 98–108, as confirmed by T-66/99 Greek Ferries (2003), para 176–198; T-65/99 Greek Ferries (2003), para 134–137; T-59/99 Greek Ferries (2003), para 104–105; T-168/01 GlaxoSmithKline (2006), para 67–70, 99–108; T-216/13 Telefónica-Portugal Telecom (2016), para 111–120; C-198/01; Consorzio Industrie Fiammiferi (CIF) (2003), para 66–80

5.3 *State Action Defence: Non-Legislative Measures (Footnote 46)*

GC: T-387/94 Asia Motor France III (1996), para 60–65; T-66/99 Greek Ferries (2003), para 192–195; T-65/99 Greek Ferries (2003), para 138–141; T-216/13 Telefónica-Portugal Telecom (2016), para 117–120

Commission: 32732 Ijsselcentrale (1991), para 21; 31370 31446 UK Agricultural Tractor Registration Exchange (1992), para 49; 38279 French beef (2003), para 150–156; 38238 Spanish Raw Tobacco (2004), para 349–355; 38281 Raw tobacco Italy (2005), para 315–324; 38456 Bitumen Nederland (2006), para 159; 39181 Candle waxes (2008), para 192–194; 39258 Airfreight (2010), para 977–982, 995–1016

5.4 *State Action Defence: An Opinion or Draft Decision on the Basis of Public Interest Criteria Is Not a Delegation of Powers (Footnote 59)*

C-185/91 Bundesanstalt für den Güterfernverkehr (Reiff) (1993), para 14–24; C-96/94 Centro Servizi Spediporto Srl (1995), para 19–34; 35591 35634 Weyl-PW+SSR (1997). The decision was not published, yet is was summarised by the GC in T-197/97 T-198/97 Weyl-PW+SSR (2001), para 67, 79; C-266/96 Corsica Ferries France SA (1998), para 50–54; C-38/97 Autotrasporti Librandi Snc di Librandi F&C (1998), para 26–37; C-35/99 Manuele Arduino (2002), para 40–43; 38401 EMC-Producteurs européens de ciment (2005), para 91, 28–32, as confirmed by the GC in T-432/05 EMC Development AB (2010), para 122; C-94/04 C-202/04 Federico Cipolla (2006), para 44–54; C-386/07 Hospital Consulting (2008), para 15–27; C-121/16 Salumificio (2016), para 22–23; C-532/15 C-538/15 Eurosaneamientos (2016), para 36–40

5.5 *State Action Defence: A Formalistic Approach towards the Delegation of State Powers (Footnote 74)*

The Court held that such conditions were satisfied in: C-153/93 Delta (1994), para 13–23; C-96/94 Centro Servizi Spediporto Srl (1995), para 19–34; C-140/94 C-141/94 C-142/94 DIP SpA (1995), para 14–24; C-38/97 Autotrasporti Librandi Snc di Librandi F&C (1998), para 26–37; C-35/99 Manuele Arduino (2002), para 34–44; C-250/03 Giorgio Emanuele Mauri (2005), para 31–34; C-94/04 C-202/04 Federico Cipolla (2006), para 44–54; C-386/07 Hospital Consulting (2008), para 15–27; C-121/16 Salumificio (2016), para 22–23; C-532/15 C-538/15 Eurosaneamientos (2016), para 36–40

The Commission and EU Courts held that such conditions were not satisfied in: 33407 CNSD (1993), para 42, as upheld by the GC in T-513/93 CNSD (2000), para 55–56; C-309/99 Wouters (2002), para 67–69; 38549 Barême d'honoraires de l'Ordre des Architectes belges (2004), para 42–49; T-193/02 FIFA rules on players' agents (2005), para 74; 39510 Ordre national des pharmaciens (ONP) (2010), para 607–609; C-184/13 C-185/13 C-186/13 C-187/13 C-194/13 C-195/13 C-208/13 API (2014), para 26–41

The question was left to the national court's discretion in: C-198/01 Consorzio Industrie Fiammiferi (CIF) (2003), para 76–80

5.6 *Article 106(2) TFEU: Failing the Proportionality Test (Footnote 120)*

EU Courts: T-289/01 DSD (2007), para 207–210; C-1/12 Ordem dos Técnicos Oficiais de Contas (2013), para 107

Commission: 28980 Pabst & Richarz/BNIA (1976), 5; 29995 ANSEAU-NAVEWA (1981), para 66–67; 30979 31394 Decca Navigator System (1988), para 130; 31734 Film purchases by German television stations (1989), para 40; 32732 Ijsselcentrale (1991), para 43–46; 32524 Screensport/EBU Members (1991), para 68–69; 33151 33997 Jahrhundertvertrag VIK-GVSt (1992), para 28; 32150 EBU/Eurovision System (1993), para 78–79; 36748 REIMS II (1999), para 91–92; 38698 CISAC (2008), para 256–259

5.7 *Notion of Undertakings: Commercial Activities of Associations Irrespective of status under National Law (Footnote 131)*

299 Belgisch Syndikaal Verbond van de Parfumerie (ASPA) (1970), 3; 28980 Pabst & Richarz/BNIA (1976), 4; 26870 Aluminium imports from eastern Europe (1984), para 9.2; 31029 French inland waterway charter

traffic: EATE levy (1985), para 37–39; 31734 Film purchases by German television stations (1989), para 38; 33407 CNSD (1993), para 40–41; 33686 Coapi (1995) para 32–33; 34179 34202 Stichting Certificatie Kraanverhuurbedrijf and the Federatie van Nederlandse Kraanverhuurbedrijven (1995), para 18; 36147 EPI code of conduct (1999), para 23–24; 30373 37143 P&I CLUBS (1999), para 50–51

5.8 *Notion of Undertakings: Sports-Related Economic Activities (Footnote 133)*

Commission: 33384 33378 Distribution of package tours during the 1990 World Cup (1992), para 43–60; 32150 EBU/Eurovision System (1993), para 45–46; 36851 Mouscron (1999); 37576 UEFA Broadcasting Regulations (2001), para 47; 37806 ENIC/UEFA (2002), para 25–26; 38158 Meca Medina (2002), para 33–39; 39471 Certain joueur de tennis professionnel/Agence mondiale antidopage (2009), para 19–27; 40208 International Skating Union's Eligibility rules (2017), para 146–153

GC: T-313/02 MecaMedina and Majcen/IOC (2004), para 35–69; T-193/02 FIFA rules on players' agents (2005), para 68–72

5.9 *Notion of Undertakings: Definition (Footnote 136)*

C-159/91 C-160/91 Poucet (1993), para 17; C-244/94 Federation Française des Sociétés d'Assurance (1995), para 14; C-219/97 Maatschappij Drijvende Bokken BV (1999), para 67; C-115/97 C-116/97 C-117/97 Brentjens' Handelsonderneming BV (1999), para 77; C-67/96 Albany (1999), para 77; C-180/98 C-181/98 C-182/98 C-183/98 C-184/98 C-185/98 Pavel Pavlov (2000), para 74; C-475/99 Ambulanz Glöckner (2001), para 19; C-218/00 Cisal di Battistello Venanzio & C. Sas (2002), para 22; C-309/99 Wouters (2002), para 46; C-264/01 C-306/01 C-354/01 C-355/01 AOK Bundesverband (2004), para 46; C-350/07 Kattner Stahlbau (2009), para 34; C-1/12 Ordem dos Técnicos Oficiais de Contas (2013), para 35; C-327/12 Ministero dello Sviluppo conomic (2013), para 27

5.10 *Notion of Undertakings: Offering Goods and Services in a Market (Footnote 143)*

C-180/98 C-181/98 C-182/98 C-183/98 C-184/98 C-185/98 Pavel Pavlov (2000), para 75; C-475/99 Ambulanz Glöckner (2001), para 19; C-218/00 Cisal di Battistello Venanzio & C. Sas (2002), para 23; C-309/99 Wouters (2002), para 47; C-1/12 Ordem dos Técnicos Oficiais de Contas (2013), para 35–36; C-327/12 Ministero dello Sviluppo economico (2013), para 27

5.11 *Notion of Undertakings: Solidarity (Footnote 146)*

Schemes based on solidarity principles: C-159/91 C-160/91 Poucet (1993), para 8–19; C-218/00 Cisal di Battistello Venanzio & C. Sas (2002), para 31–45; C-264/01 C-306/01 C-354/01 C-355/01 AOK Bundesverband (2004), para 47–65; C-350/07 Kattner Stahlbau (2009), para 44–68 (the Court noted that this finding is subject to verification of relevant factors by the referring court)
Schemes based on capitalisation principles: C-244/94 Federation Française des Sociétés d'Assurance (1995), para 16–22; C-219/97 Maatschappij Drijvende Bokken BV (1999), para 70–77; C-115/97 C-116/97 C-117/97 Brentjens' Handelsonderneming BV (1999), para 81–87; C-67/96 Albany (1999), para 78–87; C-180/98 C-181/98 C-182/98 C-183/98 C-184/98 C-185/98 Pavel Pavlov (2000), para 74–89

5.12 *Notion of Undertakings: The Participation Criterion (Footnote 147)*

Social security schemes: C-159/91 C-160/91 Poucet (1993); C-264/01 C-306/01 C-354/01 C-355/01 AOK Bundesverband (2004)
Pension funds: C-219/97 Maatschappij Drijvende Bokken BV (1999); C-67/96 Albany (1999); C-115/97 C-116/97 C-117/97 Brentjens' Handelsonderneming BV (1999); C-180/98 C-181/98 C-182/98 C-183/98 C-184/98 C-185/98 Pavel Pavlov (2000)
Old-age insurance: C-244/94 Federation Française des Sociétés d'Assurance (1995)
Workers' health and accident insurance: C-218/00 Cisal di Battistello Venanzio & C. Sas (2002); C-350/07 Kattner Stahlbau (2009); C-437/09 AG2R Prévoyance (2011)
Professional associations: C-1/12 Ordem dos Técnicos Oficiais de Contas (2013), para 35–37; C-327/12 Ministero dello Sviluppo conomic (2013), para 29; C-413/13 FNV Kunsten Informatie en Media (2014), para 33

5.13 *Inherent Restrictions: Inadequacy of a Public Measure Does Not Empower an Undertaking to Assume a Public Task (Footnote 170)*

C-136/86 BNIC (1987), para 21; T-29/92 Building and construction industry in the Netherlands (1995), para 96, 104, 178, 186–187; 37124 FIFA rules on players' agents (2002), para 30; T-217/03 T-245/03 French beef (2006), para 87; C-209/07 Beef Industry (2008), para 21; 39510 Ordre national des pharmaciens (ONP) (2010), para 604; 39226 Lundbeck (2013), para 653; 39612 Perindopril (Servier) (2014), para 1205; T-90/11 Ordre national des pharmaciens (ONP) (2014), para 675

5.14 *Inherent Restrictions: Balancing Is Confined to Article 101(3) TFEU (Footnote 171)*

Financial or structural crisis and financial security: C-41/69 Quinine (1970), para 47, 125–127; C-45/69 Quinine (1970) para 33; 27039 Preserved mushrooms (1975), III.2; 28948 Cauliflowers (1977), 7; 30188 Moet et Chandon (London) Ltd (1981), para 7, 15; 30350 Zinc producer group (1984), para 73; 31865 PVC (1988) para 36; 31866 LdPE (1988), para 43; 31572 32571 Building and construction industry in the Netherlands (1992), para 71–75, 117, as confirmed by the GC in T-29/92 Building and construction industry in the Netherlands (1995), para 96, 104, 178, 186–187; T-14/89 Polypropylene (1992), para 298–301; T-305/94 T-306/94 T-307/94 T-313/94 T-314/94 T-315/94 T-316/94 T-318/94 T-325/94 T-328/94 T-329/94 T-335/94 PVC (1999), para 740–741; 36571 Austrian banks – 'Lombard Club' (2002), para 392

Consumer protection: 27000 Primary aluminium (1975), 8; 28980 Pabst & Richarz/BNIA (1976), 2, 4–5

Health and safety: 31624 Vichy (1991) para 18; 38370 UK Network Sharing Agreement (2003), para 83–85

Fight against illegal practices: 38281 Raw Tobacco Italy (2005), para 291

Anti-dumping: 26870 Aluminium imports from eastern Europe (1984), para 12.2; 36604 Citric acid (2001) para 162–166

Sporting rules: 40208 International Skating Union's Eligibility rules (2017), para 171

Social aims: C-61/80 Rennet (1981), para 12; T-61/89 Hudson's Bay-Dansk (1992), para 52

Promote competition or correct market failures: T-14/89 Polypropylene (1992), para 296; 32290 Newitt/Dunlop Slazenger International (1992), para 56 as confirmed by the Court in T-43/92 Newitt/Dunlop Slazenger International and Others (1994), para 131; 36957 Glaxo Wellcome (2001), para 127

5.15 *Inherent Restrictions: Regulated Associations and Sporting Rules (Footnote 183)*

Accepted with respect to sporting rules: 37806 ENIC/UEFA (2002), para 3, 28–42; 39471 Certain joueur de tennis professionnel/Agence mondiale antidopage (2009), para 28–32; 39732 Certain Formula One engine manufacturers (2011), para 34–40

Rejected with respect to sporting rules: 40208 International Skating Union's Eligibility rules (2017), para 225–266

Rejected with respect to professional associations: 38549 Barême d'honoraires de l'Ordre des Architectes belges (2004), para 97–99; T-217/03 T-245/03 French beef (2006), para 89; T-451/08 CISAC (2013), para 86–97; C-1/12 Ordem dos Técnicos Oficiais de Contas (2013), para 93–100; C-136/12 Consiglio nazionale dei geologi (2013), para 53–57; C-184/13 C-185/13 C-186/13 C-187/13 C-194/13 C-195/13 C-208/13 API (2014), para 47–57

5.16 *Ancillary Restraints: Horizontal Cooperation Agreements (Footnote 227)*

Restrictions subordinate to the creation of joint ventures: 34857 BT/MCI (1994), para 46; 34891 Fujitsu AMD Semiconductor (1994), para 36; 34252 Philips-Osram (1994) para 19–20; 35617 Phoenix/GlobalOne (1996), para 53; 35337 Atlas (1996), para 42; 35830 Unisource (1997), para 82; Uniworld (1997), para 65; 39258 Airfreight (2010), para 938–963; 39736 SIEMENS/AREVA (2012), para 32, 42, 43

Cooperation in technology markets: 32688 Konsortium ECR 900 (1990), 33; 34410 Olivetti/Digital (1994), para 20; 35518 Iridium (1996), para 42–49; 35742 EUCAR (1998), 36237 TPS (1999), para 99–109; 36581 Télécom Developpement (1999), para 41–48

Pooling R&D: 26352 Eurogypsum (1968), 2; 28796 Beecham/Parke, Davis (1979), para 33

Specialisation agreements: 29869 Italian cast glass (1980), 6

Standardisation: 197 Industrieverband Solnhofener Natursteinplatten eV (1980), para 35–40; 31458 X/Open Group (1986), para 36–38; 38401 EMC/European Cement Producers (2005), para 9–106

Joint purchasing and selling: 28838 Intergroup (1975)

5.17 *Ancillary Restraints: Selective Distribution Systems Based on Qualitative Objective Criteria (Footnote 233)*

Commission: 10498 11546 12992 17394 17395 17971 18772 18888 3213 Omega (1970), para 5; 24055 Kodak (1970), para 21–24; 14650 Bayerische Motoren Werke AG (1974), para 22; 847 SABA (1975), para 34–41; 5715 Junghans (1976), para 20–26; 25757 Hasselblad (1981), para 63; 28748 AEG-Telefunken (1982), para 53–54; 30668 Murat (1983), para 13–17; 29598 SABA's EEC distribution system (1983), para 2; 30849 IBM personal computer (1984), para 16–17; 30299 Grohe's distribution system (1984) para 15; 30261 Ideal-Standard's distribution system (1984), para 15; 29420 Grundig's EEC distribution system (1985), 5–6; 30665 Villeroy & Boch (1985), para 22; 32026 Bayo-n-ox (1989), para 43; 32595 d'Ieteren motor oils (1990), para 12; 31624 Vichy (1991), para 18; 33242 Yves Saint Laurent Parfums (1991), para 4–7; 33542 Parfums Givenchy system of selective distribution (1992), para 15–18; 29420 Grundig's EC distribution system (1993), para 23–35; 33714 VAG FRANCE (1996), 3–4; 39855 Volkswagen Group Italia (Audi) 5 (2016), para 46–50; 39836 Volkswagen Group Italia (Audi) 3 (2016), para 46–50; 39828 Volkswagen Group Italia (Audi) 2 (2016), para 46–50

EU Courts: C-26/76 Metro I (1977), para 20–21; C-209/78 C-210/78 C-211/78 C-212/78 C-213/78 C-214/78 C-215-78 C-218/78 Fedetab (1980), para 138; C-99/79 Lancôme (1980), para 20–21; C-31/80 L'ORÉAL (1980), para 15–21; C-126/80 SALONIA (1981), para 24–27; C-210/81 REVOX (1983), para 20; C-107/82 AEG-Telefunken (1983), para 42–43, 135-13; C-243/83 Binon (1985), para 31–35; C-31/85 ETA (1985), para 16–18; C-45/85 Fire insurance (1987), para 40–43; T-19/91 Vichy (1992); C-19/92 Yves Saint Laurent Parfums (1996); T-88/92 Parfums Givenchy system of selective distribution (1996), para 141–148; C-439/09 Pierre Fabre (2011), para 46; T-712/14 Watch Repair (2017), 95; C-230/16 Coty (2017), para 24

5.18 *IPRs: Formalistic Approach (Footnote 261)*

Commission: 5405 Burroughs/Geha-Werke (1971), 2; 5400 Burroughs-Delplanque (1971), 2; 17545 6964 26858 26890 18673 17448 Davidson Rubber Co. (1972), para 7–9; 26813 Raymond-Nagoya (1972), 40–42; 28374 Advocaat Zwarte Kip (1974), 14–15; 27879 Sirdar-Phildar (1975), 29; 21353 Kabelmetal/Luchaire (1975), para 8; 28967 Bronbemaling (1975), 28–29; 171 856 172 117 28173 Campari (1977), 73–75; 29246 Penneys (1977), 25–26; 29290 Vaessen-Moris (1979), para 15, 23; 30128 Toltecs/Dorcet (1982), 24–25; 29395 Windsurfing International (1983), 10–17; 30129 Carlsberg (1984), 33–34; 4204 Velcro/Aplix (1985), 27–29; 30017 Breeders' rights-roses (1985), para 23–25; 31302 Boussois-Interpane (1986), para 16–17; 31340 Mitchell Cotts-Sofiltra (1986), para 18–24; 31206 Rich products (1987), para 29–38; 314798 Delta Chemie/DDD (1988), para 30–36; 31734 Film purchases by German television stations (1989), para 40–47; 32026 Bayo-n-ox (1989), para 57–61; 32736 Moosehead/Whitbread (1990), para 15; 31550 31898 Zera/Montedison and Ihinkens/Stähler (1993), para 125; 33375 PMI-DSV (1995), para 10–12; 34279 ADALAT (1996), para 207–211; 36219 Micro Leader/Microsoft (1998), para 29; 35280 Sicasov (1998), para 50–62; Sony licensing agreements for video games (1998); 38014 IFPI 'Simulcasting' (2002), para 61–80; 37920 3G Patent Platform (2002); 37398 Joint selling of the commercial rights of the UEFA Champions League (2003), para 120–124

EU Courts: C-24/67 Parke, Davis and Co (1968), 17–18; C-78/70 Metro-SB-Grossmarkte (1971), para 5–10; C-40/70 SIRENA (1971), para 9–12; C-15/74 Centeafarm (1974), para 38–41; C-8/74 Dassonville (1974), 38–41; C-51/

75 EMI Records I (1976), para 31–34 and C-86/75 EMI Records II (1976), para 28–31; C-96/75 EMI Records III (1976), para 15–18

5.19 *IPRs: Licensing Agreements (Footnote 266)*

C-262/81 Coditel (1982), para 14–19; C-35/83 Tokecs-Dorcet (1985), para 33; C-193/83 Windsurfing surfing International (1986), para 45–49; C-161/84 Pronuptia (1986), para 15–27 C-27/87 Erauw-Jacquery (1988), para 10–11; C-320/87 Ottung (1989), para 17–18; T-504/93 Tierce Ladbroke/PMU-DSV (1997), para 146–162; C-567/14 Genentech (2016), para 35–43; T-460/13 Lundbeck (2016), para 140–141; T-472/13 Lundbeck (2016), para 117–118; T-469/13 Lundbeck (2016), para 243–244; T-470/13 Lundbeck (2016), para 224–225; T-471/13 Lundbeck (2016), para 315–316

5.20 *De Minimis: Qualitative Test (Footnote 277)*

Pension funds: C-180/98 C-181/98 C-182/98 C-183/98 C-184/98 C-185/98 Pavel Pavlov (2000), para 91–97

Financial institutions: 31362 Irish Banks' Standing Committee (1986), para 16; 31764 Baltic International Freight Futures Exchange Limited (1987), 26; 31499 Dutch banks (1989), para 47–49; 37462 Identrus (2001), para 54–55; 29373 Visa International (2001), para 42–44, 54, 58, 64

Sports: 37576 UEFA Broadcasting Regulations (2001), para 51–59

R&D: 242 295 Convention chaufourniers (1969), para II

5.21 *Netherlands: Non-Economic Benefits in the Ancillary Restraints Exception (Footnote 293)*

3022 Breda pharmacies (2004), para 99–101; 5709 Day-care (2008), para 32–35; 5851/211 Thuiszorg 't Gooi (2008), para 195–196 as upheld on this point 5851/262 Thuiszorg 't Gooi (2010), para 77–84; 6091_1/204 Distributors of sodium hypochlorite (2009), para 127–132; 6895 Amsterdam hospitals (2010), para 13, 48; 7138 Home care (2011), para 17. In ACM-DM-2013-202346 Independent pharmacies (2013), the NCA declared that such interests justified collaborations negotiating between independent pharmacies and health insurers, without referring to the ancillary restraints exception explicitly

5.22 *Hungary: Following the EU State Action Defence (Footnote 309)*

Vj-199/2005 Egg cartel (2006), para 372–400, 454–462, as upheld by 7. K.30.838/2007/33 Egg cartel (2008); Vj-180/2004 Hungarian Bar

Association of attorneys (2006), para 20, as upheld by the Court on this point in 2K.30863/2009/8 Hungarian Bar Association of attorneys (2009), 17; Vj-16/2005 Deontological rules of auditors (2006), para 48–50; Vj-51/2005 The Hungarian Association of Automobile Dealers (2006), para 622–645; Vj-60/2006/37 Hungarian Chamber of Pharmacists (2007), para 46–50, 73; Vj-44/2007/19 Taxi in Győr (2007), para 25; Vj-201/2005 Hungarian Chamber of Architects (2007), para 127–133; Vj-1/2008 Hungarian Real Estate Association (2008), para 42–46; Vj-36/2008 Association of journalists (2008), para 5, 15–36 as upheld by the court in 3.K.30.051/2009/12 Association of journalists (2010) and 2 Kf. 27. 217/2010/4 Association of journalists (2010), 7; Vj-143/16/2008 Chamber of Plant Protection In Hungary (2010), para 41; 7.K.34.976/2009/9 Professional Guild of Hairdressers (2010); Vj-3/2008 Rail freight transport services (2012), para 189; 306-314. As upheld by the Court in 3.K.28.763/2013/48 Rail freight transport services (2014), 2.Kf.650.115/2014/5 Rail freight transport services (2015), 18–19 and Kfv.II.37.646/2015/14 Rail freight transport services (2016), 22–23

CHAPTER 6: NATIONAL BALANCING TOOLS

6.1 *France: Joint Offering of Bids in Tenders (Footnote 37)*

The defence was accepted in: 04-D-57 Road surfacing work in the Pyrénées Orientales (2004), para 31–39, 40–47; 05-D-24 Public roads in Somme (2005), para 51–67; 05-D-61 Highway A51 (2005), para 150–160; 05-D-74 Storage of aggregates (2005), para 36–41; 06-D-32 Departmental roads in Aveyron (2006), para 32–41; 06-D-33 Public procurement contracts in the building sector in Auvergne (2006), para 135, 154; 07-D-01 Piping work in the Morbihan (2007), para 99–105; 07-D-11 Road works in Marne (2007), para 99–107; 07-D-34 Saint-Léon Hospital (2007), para 23–42; 08-D-28 Aggregates in Ille-et-Vilaine (2008), para 122–149; 09-D-35 General Hospital Centre Jean (2009), para 16–29; 09-D-18 Marseille transportation (2009), para 94–102

The defence was rejected in: 04-D-43 Grasse school and extracurricular transportation (2004), para 101–115; 04-D-50 Vallée des Lacs (2004), para 28–53; 05-D-26 Public works in the Meuse department (2005), para 152–153; 05-D-47 Weapon destruction (2005), para 193, 200; 06-D-07 Ile-de-France Bid Rigging (2006), para 470, as confirmed by the court in 2006/06913 Ile-de-France Bid rigging (2008), 47; 06-D-25 Work on the Rouen cathedral, para 48; 07-D-47 Aerial navigation (2007), para 173–174, 240–243; 08-D-15 Renovation of boiler rooms in Saône-et-Loire (2008), para 59, 106, 110; 08-D-22 Property surveyors in Haut-Rhin (2008), para 104–121; 08-D-28 Aggregates in Ille-et-Vilaine (2008), para 157–158; 09-D-03 Coach transportation (2009), para 105–108, as upheld by the court in 2009/02679 Coach transportation (2010), 9; 09-D-25 Work on railway tracks (2009), para 149–176; 10-D-10 Landscaping (2010), para 38–45; 11-D-07 Industrial painting (2011), para 134; 16-D-02 School bus transportation in the Lower Rhine (2016), para 125–130

6.2 *France: Public Body Prerogative (Footnote 49)*

Claims for lack of jurisdiction were accepted in: 05-D-04 Gaz de Strasbourg (2005), para 12–16; 05-D-02 Maritime Transport to Hyère (2005), para 12–14; 05-D-20 Casino du Lac de la Magdeleine (2005), para 23–28, as upheld by the court in 2005/11128 Casino du Lac de la Magdeleine (2005), 4; 05-D-23 France Fire installers (2005), para 14–23; 06-D-05 Emergency health transport in the Doubs and Jura (2006), para 24–26; 06-D-14 CPPAP (2006), para 15–17; 10-D-13 Le Havre Port (2010), para 148–150; 11-D-02 Restoration of historical monuments (2011), para 279–281, as upheld by the court in 2011/03298 Restoration of historical monuments (2012); 11-D-16 Telecare for senior (2011), para 20–23; 12-D-13 Control of heavy vehicles (2012), para 76–103; 13-D-10 Press Distribution (2013), para 97–100; 16-D-30 Banking (2016)

Claims for lack of jurisdiction were partially rejected in: 04-D-39 Public slaughterhouse of Laval (2004), para 86–93, as upheld by the court in 2004/14592 Public slaughterhouse of Laval (2006) and the Cour de Cassation in 05-13048 Public slaughterhouse of Laval (2006); 05-D-60 Transport to Saint Honorat, para 15–17, as upheld by the court in 2005-23732 Transport to Saint Honorat, 6; 07-D-10 CIGC (2007), para 64–71; 07-D-27 Professional training (2007), para 64–74, as upheld by the court in 2007/15305 Professional training, 4; 07-D-28 Coal handling in the Havre port (2007), para 43–63, as upheld by the court in 2007-17386 Coal handling in the Havre port, 3; 09-D-17 Pharmacists in Lower Normandy (2009), para 29–37; 12-D-26 Fire extinguishers (2012), para 164–169; 12-A-14 Veterinary medicines (2012), para 76–78

Claims for lack of jurisdiction were fully rejected in: 05-D-41 Vocational Training (2005), para 38–43; 05-D-43 Dental surgeons in Puy-de-Dôme (2005), para 190, as upheld by the court in 2005/15784 Dental surgeons in Puy-de-Dôme (2007), 7 and the Cour de Cassation in 06-13498 Dental surgeons in Puy-de-Dôme (2006), 4–5, 196–197; 05-D-47 Weapon destruction (2005), para 38–42; 07-D-08 Corsican cement (2007), para 64–71; 09-D-18 Marseille transportation (2009), para 21–29; 09-D-07 Supplementary health insurance (2009), para 21–29, as upheld by the court in 2009/06049 (2010) Supplementary health insurance, 8 and the

Cour de Cassation in 10-12038 Supplementary health insurance (2011), 4; 12-D-03 AURAL-Lyon (2012), para 76; 12-D-28 Consortium Stade de France (2012), para 53–55; 12-D-19 Tooth whitening (2012), para 70–79; 13-D-02 Towing light vehicles (2013), para 36–41; 15-D-15 Suburban station of North of Paris (2015), para 38–43

6.3 *Hungary: NCA Decisions in the Agriculture Sector prior to the Amendment (Footnote 73)*

Vj-89-2003/58 Hunting cartel (2004), as upheld by the court in 3.K.33.949/2010/17 Hunting cartel (2011); Vj-132/2003/37 Council for Wild Animals Products and Services (2005) as upheld by the court in 3.K.31.984/2005/30 Council for Wild Animals Products and Services (2008); Vj-199/2005 Egg cartel (2006) as upheld by 7.K.30.838/2007/33 Egg cartel (2008); Vj-69/2008 Wheat mill products I (2010)

CHAPTER 7: ENFORCEMENT DISCRETION

7.1 *Target Discretion: In the Fourth Enforcement Period, Article 101(3) TFEU Was Applied to Price-Fixing, Market-Sharing, and Equivalent Restrictions (Footnote 132)*

37980 Souris (2004), para 141–158; 37750 French beer market (2004), para 75; 38549 Barême d'honoraires de l'Ordre des Architectes belges (2004), para 104–110; 38662 GDF-ENEL (2004), para 143–145; 38662 GDF-ENI (2004), para 120–122; 38456 Bitumen Nederland (2006), para 162–168; 39181 Candle waxes (2008), para 317; 39188 Bananas (2008), para 339–343; 39125 Carglass (2008), para 529–532; 38698 CISAC (2008), para 231–247; 39092 Bathroom fittings & fixtures (2010), para 989–990; 39596 BA/AA/IB (2010), para 77–80; 39258 Airfreight (2010), para 1040–1045; 39510 Ordre National des Pharmaciens en France (ONP) (2010), para 703–706; 39462 Freight Forwarding (2012), para 635–636; 39736 SIEMENS/AREVA (2012), para 82–83; 39839 Telefónica and Portugal Telecom (2013), para 439–446; 39633 Shrimps (2013), para 438–440; 39861 Yen Interest Rate Derivatives (YIRD) (2013), para 84–85; 39914 Euro Interest Rate Derivatives (2013), para 66; 39610 Power cables (2014), para 689; 39574 Smart card chips (2014); 40055 Parking heaters (2015); 40028 Alternators and Starters (2016); 39824 Trucks (2016); 39850 Container Shipping (2016), para 57–58; 399904 Rechargeable battery (2016); 39960 Thermal Systems (2017); 40013 Lighting Systems (2017)

7.2 *Fines: Rejecting Crisis Cartel Situations as Justification for a Reduction of the Fine (Footnote 270)*

34018 Far East Trade Tariff and Surcharges Agreement (FETTSCA) (2000), para 197–198; 36490 Graphite electrodes (2001), para 194–197; 37614 Interbrew and Alken-Maes (2001), para 321; 37027 Zinc Phosphate (2001), para 337–341; 36212 Carbonless paper (2001), para 430–431; 36571 Austrian banks-'Lombard Club' (2002), para 526–530; 37978 Methylglucamine (2002), para 252–253; 38240 Industrial tubes (2003), para 370–372; 38069 Copper plumbing tubes (2004), para 741–746; 37533 Choline chloride (2004), para 215–216; 38337 Thread (2005), para 376–378; 38281 Raw Tobacco Italy (2005), para 384; 38354 Industrial bags (2005), para 810–811; 38620 Hydrogen peroxide (2006), para 488–490; 38645 Methacrylates (2006), para 389–390; 38121 Fittings (2006), para 804–805; 39396 Calcium carbide and magnesium based reagents (2009), para 331; 38589 Heat stabilisers (2009), para 735; 39258 Airfreight (2010), para 1258–1261; 39092 Bathroom fittings & fixtures (2010), para 1397; 39563 Retail food packaging (2015), para 1051

7.3 *Fines: Inability Claims Mostly Based on the 'Economic Situation' (Footnote 279)*

38359 Electrical and mechanical carbon and graphite products (2003), para 358–360; 38543 International Removal Services (2008), para 617, 655–662; 38589 Heat stabilisers (2009), 774–795; 39092 Bathroom fittings & fixtures (2010), para 1326, 1388; 38344 Pre-stressing steel (2010), para 1131–1189; 39168 PO/Hard Haberdashery: Fasteners (2011), para 5–9; 39600 Refrigeration compressors (2011), para 97; 39452 Mountings for windows and window-doors (2012), para 548–550; 39437 TV and computer monitor tubes (2012), para 1164–1182; 39780 Envelopes (2014), para 106; 39563 Retail food packaging (2015), para 1096–1109

7.4 *Fines: Netherlands – Confidential Inability to Pay Decisions (Footnote 293)*

5210 Metal grilles (2007); 5211 Nurseries (2009); 6431_1/172 Kazerne II (2009); 6429_1/176 Kazerne I (2009); 6430_1/131 Meiveld (2009); 6274/569 Midden Ijssel (2010); 6494 6836 Southern Dutch construction companies (2010); 6306 Flour (2010); 6929_1/205 Ship-generated waste collection cartel (2011); 6306 Flour (2012); 7237 7268 Houses merchants foreclosure auctions (2013); 7237 7268 Houses merchants foreclosure auctions (2014); 6538 Houses merchants foreclosure auctions (2014); 7244/597 Magazine packs (2015)

7.5 *Fines: Inability to Pay Claims, NCAs (Footnote 294)*

France

Accepted: 10-D-35 Welding electrodes (2010), para 280–289; 10-D-39 Road sign (2010), 460, 467–468; 11-D-02 Restoration of historical monuments (2011), para 744; 12-D-02 Géfil (2012) para 166–169, 206–208, 233–235, 241–243, 254–256; 12-D-08 Endive (2012), para 663, 680–681, 689–690; 12-D-09 Flour mills (2012), para 954–956; 13-D-03 Pork slaughtering (2013), para 460–472; 13-D-09 Miradors Perpignan (2013), para 202–203; 13-D-12 Distribution of commodity chemicals (2013), para 1132–1336; 14-D-16 Relocation of military personnel in Martinique (2014), para 161–165; 14-D-20 Wallpaper (2014), para 340–348; 15-D-03 Fresh dairy products (2015), para 397–401; 15-D-04 Bakery flour (2015), para 407–409; 15-D-08 Sale of poultry meat (2015), para 383–390; 15-D-19 Standard and express delivery (2015), para 1389–1400; 16-D-02 School bus transportation in the Lower Rhine (2016), para 222–226; 16-D-17 Liquid fuel backup heating units (2016), para 245–247; 16-D-20 Modelling sector (2016), para 520

Rejected: 08-D-32 Steel trading (2008), para 481–488; 10-D-39 Road signs (2010), para 450; 11-D-02 Restoration of historical monuments (2011), para 736, 739, 755; 11-D-13 Electrification and electrical installation (2011), para 417; 12-D-09 Flour mills (2012), para 942–953, 957–959; 13-D-03 Pork slaughtering (2013), para 460–472; 15-D-03 Fresh dairy products (2015), para 402–403; 15-D-04 Bakery flour (2015), para 410–411; 16-D-20 Modelling sector (2016), para 519; 16-D-28 Property management (2016), para 191

Germany

Accepted: B11-13/06 Flour mills (2011); B1-164/13 B1-167/13 B1-87/14 B1-47/15 Furniture (2016)

Rejected: B11-20/05 Sale of liquefied petroleum gas (LPG) (2009)

Hungary

Accepted (including requests to pay the fine in instalments): Vj-120/2004/35 Bio-traditional fruits (2005), para 49; Vj-69/2008 Wheat mill products I (2010), para 324–325, 328-342; Vj-2/2010 Car refinishing paints (2014), para 591–601; Vj-48/2013 Tenders in Nagylóc and Szécsényfelfalu (2014), para 261–262; Vj-65/2012 Public procurement in Komló (2015), para 328–334; Vj-8/2012 Hungarian Banking Association (2016), para 1383–1388

Rejected: Vj-69/2008 Wheat mill products I (2010), para 324–325, 328–342; Vj-134/2008 Wheat mill products II (2011), para 124; Vj-3/2008 Rail freight transport services (2012), para 379; Vj-45/2008-641 Colour television tubes (2014), para 329; Vj-48/2013 Tenders in Nagylóc and Szécsényfelfalu (2014), para 256–262; Vj-73/2011 Mosquito control (2015), para 578–584; Vj-11/2014 Media Service Support and Asset Management Fund (2016), para 504–507

The Netherlands

Accepted: 6108/258 Thuiszorg Kennemerland (2008), para 238–244; 7130/216 Taxi transport Ijssel cities (2012), para 191–193; 6306 Flour (2013), para 8–12; 6538 Houses merchants foreclosure auctions – Pierhagen Vastgoed vof (2013), 360–364; 7244/597 Magazine packs (2015), para 256–266

Rejected: 4014 Horticultural Services (2005), para 195–205; 6108/348 Thuiszorg Kennemerland (2008), 154–160; 6091/204 Distributors of sodium hypochlorite (2009), para 250; 6108/348 Thuiszorg Kennemerland (2010), para 154–158; 6425 Window cleaners (2011), para 340; 6442 WMO Friesland (2012), para 152; 7237 7268 Houses merchants foreclosure auctions (2013), par 373; 6888/435 LHV pace of establishment (2014), para 401–405

UK

Accepted: CE/7510-06 Construction Recruitment Forum (2009), para 5.261–5.270

Rejected: CE/4327-04 Bid rigging in the construction industry in England (2009), para VI.276–288; CE/7510-06 Construction Recruitment Forum (2009), para. 5.261–5.270; CE/9859-14 Modelling (2016), para 5.99; 50223 Posters and frames (2016), para 6.44–6.45; 50235 Residential estate agency services (2017), para 6.60–6.61

7.6 *Fines: EU Courts – Crisis in Sector and Inability to Pay as Mitigating Circumstances (Footnote 318)*

Crisis in sector: T-6/89 Polypropylene (1991), para 285–291, 290; T-7/89 Polypropylene (1991), para 327–336, 335; T-8/89 Polypropylene (1991), para 305–306; T-11/89 Polypropylene (1992), para 350–352; T-13/89 Polypropylene (1992), para 372; T-14/89 Polypropylene (1992), para 379; T-213/00 Far East Trade Tariff Charges and Surcharges Agreement (FETTCSA) (2003), para 351–354; T-85/10 Concrete reinforcing bars, re-adoption (2014), para 111–114; T-70/10 Concrete reinforcing bars, re-adoption (2014), para 399–400; T-69/10 Concrete reinforcing bars, re-adoption (2014), para 241–242; T-489/09 T-490/09 T-56/10 Concrete reinforcing bars (2014), re-adoption, para 193. See also T-141/89 Welded steel mesh (1995), para 146–147; T-142/89 Welded steel mesh (1995), para 117; T-148/89 Welded steel mesh, para 125

Inability to pay: T-23/99 Pre-Insulated Pipe Cartel (2002), para 308; T-213/00 Far East Trade Tariff Charges and Surcharges Agreement (FETTCSA) (2003), para 351–356; T-71/03 T-74/03 T-87/03 T-91/03 Speciality Graphite (2005), para 332–333; C-308/04P Graphite electrodes (2006), para 105; T-452/05 PO/Thread (2010), para 93–97; T-11/06 Raw tobacco-Italy (2011), para 255–256; T-51/06 Industrial bags (2011), para 161–166; T-400/09 Calcium carbide and magnesium based reagents for the steel and gas industries (2012), para 92–120; T-392/09 Calcium carbide and magnesium based reagents for the steel and gas industries (2012), para 111–149; T-352/09 Calcium carbide and magnesium based reagents for the steel and gas industries (2012), para 185–210; C-40/12P Industrial bags (2013), para 107–108; C-58/12P Industrial bags (2013), para 98–101; T-406/09 Calcium carbide and magnesium based reagents for the steel and gas industries (2014), para 285; T-393/10 Prestressing steel (2015), para 288; T-54/14 Shrimp (2016), para 131–142; T-426/10 T-427/10 428/10 T-429/10 T-438/12 439/10 440/10 T-441/12 Prestressing steel (2016), para 489–499

7.7 *Fines: The EU Courts Confirm Change in the Commission Approach to Crisis Situations (Footnote 320)*

T-236/01 T-239/01 T-244/01 T-245/01 T-246/01 T-251/01 T-252/01 Graphite electrodes (2004), para 345, as confirmed by C-328/05P Graphite electrodes (2007), para 100; T-38/02 Interbrew and Alken-Maes (2005), para 413–416; T-64/02 Zinc phosphate (2005), para 139–140; T-259/02 T-260/02 T-261/02 T-262/02 T-263/02 T-264/02 T-271/02 Austrian banks – 'Lombard Club' (2006), para 510; T-109/02 T-118/02 T-122/02 T-125/02 T-126/02 T-128/02 T-129/02 T-132/02 T-136/02 Carbonless paper (2007), para 657–666; T-127/04 Industrial tubes (2009), para 122; T-25/05 Copper plumbing tubes (2010), para 129; T-29/05 Raw tobacco-Spain (2010), para 147; T-12/06 Raw tobacco-Italy (2011), para 289; T-39/06 Raw tobacco-Italy (2011), para 352–354; T-30/05 PO/Needles (2007), para 207–208; T-456/05 T-457/05 PO/Thread (2010), para 195–196

7.8 *Fines: National Courts View Inability to Pay as Mitigating Circumstances (Footnote 321)*

France

The court overturned the NCA's position in 2009/00334 Steel trading (2010), 29–30, 43; 2014/22811 Electrification and electrical installation (2016), 12–13

The Court accepted only some of the undertakings' claims in 2012/06826 Flour mills (2014), 86–89

The Court confirmed the NCA's position in 2005/14062 A84 motorway (2005), 2; 2009/03532 Temporary employment sector (2010), 23–24; 10/12913 10/13686 Temporary employment sector (2011), 30–34; 2011/01228 Road signs (2012), 38–39; 2011/03298 Restoration of historical monuments (2012), 76–77; 2014/09272 Restoration of historical monuments (2015), 8

Germany

The Court confirmed the NCA's position in VI-2 Kart 1/15 (V) Titisee-Neustadt (2015), para 72–74; Kart 1/16 (V) Booking (2016), para 116–117

The Netherlands

The court overturned the NCA's position in ROT 13/892 Houses merchants foreclosure auctions (2014), para 22; ROT 13/1085-13/1096 ROT Houses merchants foreclosure auctions (2014), para 22.1; ROT 14/5426 14/5428 15/540 to 15/552 15/554 15/556 to 15/569 15/585 to 15/591 Houses merchants foreclosure auctions (2016), para 21; ROT 15/592 Houses merchants foreclosure auctions (2016), para 18–19; ROT 15/622 Houses merchants foreclosure auctions (2016), para 16–17; ROT 15/674 Houses merchants foreclosure auctions (2016), para 20; ROT 15/513 Houses merchants foreclosure auctions (2016), para 15; ROT 15/1325 Houses merchants foreclosure auctions (2016), para 15; ROT 15/555 Houses merchants foreclosure auctions (2016), para 20; ROT 15/593 Houses merchants foreclosure auctions (2016), para 17; ROT 15/421 Houses merchants foreclosure auctions (2016), para 15; ROT 15/385 Houses merchants foreclosure auctions (2016), para 20; ROT 14/8992 Houses merchants foreclosure auctions (2016), para 17; ROT 15/6391 Magazine packs (2017), para 17

The outcome of the Court's assessment was confidential in ROT 15/6388 Magazine packs (2017), para 17; ROT 15/6387 Magazine packs (2017), para 26; ROT 15/6209 Magazine packs (2017), para 11

The Court confirmed the NCA's position in AWB 08/1143 MEDED-T1 Housing and Utility Engineering cartel (B&U) (2009), 14; AWB 09/1868 MEDED-T1 Nurseries (2010), 15; 08/2341 MEDED-T1 Housing and Utility Engineering cartel (B&U) (2010), 9; AWB 08/2227 MEDED-T1 Housing and Utility Engineering cartel (B&U) (2010), 9–10; ROT 13/1174 Houses merchants foreclosure auctions (2014), para 18.1–18.3; ROT 12/1784 Flour (2014), 19; ROT 12/1810 Flour (2014), 19–20; ROT 12/1762 Flour (2014), 18; AWB 16/188 Flour (2016), para 7.3.1–7.3.7; AWB 14/583 Flour (2016), para 7.3.1–7.3.7; ROT 15/6389 Magazine packs (2017), para 17; ROT 15/6212 Magazine packs (2017), para 12; ROT 15/6210 Magazine packs (2017), para 12

UK

The court overturned the NCA's position in 1120/1/1/09 Bid rigging in the construction industry in England (2011), para 193

The Court accepted only some of the undertakings' claims in 1117/1/1/09 1123/1/1/09 1134/1/1/09 1135/1/1/09 1138/1/1/09 1139/1/1/09 Bid rigging in the construction industry in England (2011), para 222–237, 261–262; 1125/1/1/09 1128/1/1/09

1130/1/1/09 1131/1/1/09 1136/1/1/09 1137/1/1/09 Bid rigging in the construction industry in England (2011), para 105–116, 135, 177, 193, 206–207

The Court confirmed the NCA's position in 1067/1/1/06 Price fixing and market sharing in stock check pads (2006), para 42–43, 55–56; 1072/1/1/06 Aluminium double glazing spacer bars (2007), para 104–106; 1114/1/1/09 1119/1/1/09 1127/1/1/09 1129/1/1/09 1132/1/1/09 1133/1/1/09 Bid rigging in the construction industry in England (2011), para 309; C3/2011/1965 Bid rigging in the construction industry in England (2012), para 73–82

7.9 *Commitments: Modifications Required Following a Market Test (Footnote 333)*

38173 The Football Association Premier League Limited (2006), para 15–17; 38348 Repsol (2006), para 40; 39596 BA/AA/IB (2010), para 12–13; 39398 Visa MIF (2010), para 8; 39847 eBooks (2012), para 14; 39230 Rio Tinto Alcan (2012), para 12; 39595 Continental/United/Lufthansa/Air Canada (2013), para 15; 39398 Visa MIF (2014), para 11; 39964 Air France/KLM/Alitalia/Delta (2015), para 16; 39745 CDS Information Market (2016), para 7; 40023 Cross-border access to pay-TV (2016), para 16–17

7.10 *Commitments: By-Object Restrictions (Footnote 352)*

Informal commitments

Export/imports bans: 704 25410 SEIFA (1969), para II(4); 597 V.V.V.F. (1969), para II. 29018 Miller International (1976), para 11; 29440 Arthur Bell and Sons Ltd – conditions of sale (1978), para II(1); 30174 Vimpoltu (1983), para 34; 32877 Bayer Dental (1990), para 10–16.

Licensing: 26813 Raymond-Nagoya (1972), para II.

Price-fixing: 197 Industrieverband Solnhofener Natursteinplatten eV (1980), para 27–29; 30804 Nuovo Cegam (1984), para 14; 32797 32798 Lloyd's Underwriters' Association and The Institute of London Underwriters (1992), para 30–38; IP/01/1690 Bank J.Van Breda & Co (2001); IP/01/650 Dutch and Belgian banks (2001); IP/01/635 Ulster Bank (2001); IP/01/634 Bayerische Landesbank Girozentrale (2001); IP/01/554 SNS (2001).

Specialised fairs and exhibitions: 27492 SMM&T Exhibition Agreement (1983), para 14.

Air alliance: IP/01/1433 IATA (2001); 38284 Société Air France/Alitalia Linee (2004), para 38. Distribution: 38287 Telenor/Canal+/Canal Digital (2003), para 156

Formal commitments

Licensing: 38681 Cannes Agreement (2006), para 35; 40023 Cross-border access to pay-TV (2016), para 47–49; 39745 CDS Information Market (2016), para 3.

Long-term exclusive supply agreements: 38348 Repsol (2006), para 2. MIF: 39398 Visa MIF (2010), para 21; 39398 Visa MIF (2014), para 23.
Air alliance: 39596 BA/AA/IB (2010), para 33–34; 39595 Continental/United/Lufthansa/Air Canada (2013), para 36–41; 39964 Air France/KLM/Alitalia/Delta (2015), para 39–43.
MFN clauses: 39847 eBooks (2012), para 64; 39847 eBooks (2013), para 69.
Non-compete clauses: 39736 SIEMENS/AREVA (2012), para 80.
Information exchange: 39850 Container Shipping (2016), para 48–55.

7.11 *Commitments: By Sector (May 2004 to 2017) (Footnote 369)*

	Formal commitments	Informal commitments
	Regulated and liberalised markets	
Media, telecom, and IPRs		
Commission	37214 Joint selling of the media rights to the German Bundesliga (2005); 38173 The Football Association Premier League Limited (2006); 40023 Cross-border access to pay-TV (2016); 38681 Cannes Agreement (2006); 39151 39152 SABAM and BUMA (2006)	38427 Pay Television Film Output Agreements (2004); 39673 Virtual Print Fee agreements (2011); 39943 E5 – Cooperation among large telecom operators (2013); 38767 FIPCOM/Koninklijke Philips Electronics N.V. (2006); 39636 Rights Agency Ltd/SCAPR a.o. (2011)
France	06-D-29 Access of local radios to national advertisement (2006); 06-D-40 Association conducting surveys on magazine press (2006); 07-D-32 Remuneration of press distributors (2007); 05-D-12 EUROPQN (2005); 07-D-17 Films (2007); 07-D-31 Citroën (2007); 10-D-01 iPhone marketing (2010)	
Germany	B6-114/10 Joint selling of media rights (2008); B7-22/07 Basic Encryption of TV Programs – Commitments (2012); B7-17/06 T-Mobile, Vodafone and O2 (2007); B6-32/15 Joint selling of media rights to matches of the German Bundesliga (2016)	Arena and Premiere (2017)
Hungary		Vj-51/2004 Remittance via mobile phone (2004)
The Netherlands	13.0612.53 Mobile operators (2014)	KPN customer call data (2006)
UK	CE/2558-03 TV Eye (2005); CE/2 479/03 London-wide newspaper distribution (2006)	

	Formal commitments	Informal commitments
	Energy and transport	
Commission	38348 Repsol (2006); 39140 DaimlerChrysler (2007); 39141 Fiat (2007); 39142 Toyota Motor Europe (2007); 39143 Opel (2007); 39416 Ship Classification (2009); 39596 BA/AA/IB (2010); 39595 Continental/United/Lufthansa/Air Canada (2013); 39964 Air France/KLM/Alitalia/Delta (2015); 39850 Container Shipping (2016)	36246 Marathon (2004); 38284 Société Air France/Alitalia Linee (2004); 38307 PO/Territorial restrictions Germany (Gazprom) (2005); 37811 Algerian gas export contracts (2007); 39699 Baltic Max Feeder (2010); IP/13/82 European Minibulk and Container Feeder cooperatives (2013)
France	08-D-26 UAT taxis Abbeilles (2008); 09-D-01 Pleasure boats (2009); 13-D-15 Europe-Antilles Sea Freight (2013)	
Germany	B8-113/03-1 to B8-113/03-12 and B8-113/03-15 Long-term gas supply (2006); B10-44/09 B10-45/09 B10-47/09 B10-48/09 B10-10/10 B10-11/10 B10-13/10 B10-14/10 B10-18/10 B10-19/10 B10-20/10 B10-21/10 B10-22/10 B10-23/10 B10-24/10 B10-25/10 Gas and Electricity suppliers resale bans (2010); B10-6/11 Dinkelsbühl (2011); B10-17/11 Markkleeberg (2011); B9-96/09 Lufthansa (2011)	Verivox (2015); Tank & Rast (2017)
Hungary		Vj-7/2008/178 Motor oils and lubricants (2009)
The Netherlands		VSS (2012); APX and Endex (2006)
UK	11/2013 Provision of Deep Sea Container rail transport services between ports and key inland destinations in Great Britain (2015)	
	Professional associations	
Commission		
France	10-D-18 Veterinary analyses (2010); 12-D-29 FFGolf (2012); 06-D-40 Association conducting surveys on magasine press (2006); 08-D-26 UAT taxis Abbeilles (2008); 09-D-01 Pleasure boats (2009); 05-D-12 EUROPQN (2005); 07-D-17 Films (2007)	
Germany	B3-11/13 Ophthalmologists-AOK (2013); B3-11/13 Ophthalmologists-AÄGB (2013); B3-123/11 Pharmacists association in Westphalia-Lippe (2014)	B1-232/07 Association of the German construction industry (2009)

(continued)

(*continued*)

	Formal commitments	Informal commitments
Hungary	Vj-60/2006/37 Hungarian Chamber of Pharmacists (2007); Vj-44/2007/19 Taxi in Gyor (2007); Vj-84/2007 Bar Association of Békés (2009); Vj-97/2013 Driver training ethics code (2015)	Vj-93/2004/14 Hungarian Chamber of Pharmacists (2005); Vj-16/2005 Deontological rules of auditors (2006); Vj-1/2008 Hungarian Real Estate Association (2008)
The Netherlands	6895 Amsterdam hospitals (2010); 7245/151 Federation Textile Management Netherlands (2011); 7191/138 National Association of General Practitioners (2012)	Orthobanda industry association (2004); Royal Dutch Society for the Advancement of Pharmacology (KNMP) (2006); APX and Endex (2006); Architects (2006); The Royal Dutch Notarial Society [Koninklijke Notariële Beroepsorganisatie (KNB)I (2007); Dutch Association for Real estate Agents (NVM) (2007); ROTA (2007); Frisian horses (2008); Breed association (2009); flower-bulb (2008); Royal Dutch Institute of Chartered Accountants (NIVRA) and the Dutch Association of Accounting Consultants (NovAA) (2009); Royal Dutch Notarial Society [Koninklijke Notariële Beroepsorganisatie (KNB) II (2012); Travel Agents and Tour Operators General Agency Conditions (2012); VSS (2012); Foundation for Appraisals and Validations (2013)
UK	CE/2558-03 TV Eye (2005); CE/2479/03 London-wide newspaper distribution (2006); 50243 Showmen's Guild of Great Britain (2017)	OFT946 Scottish legal 'mixed doubles' rule (2008); Bar Council of Northern Ireland (2011); School suppliers (2011); Asbestos awareness training (2013)
	Public health and safety	
Commission		
France	07-D-22 Distribution of Medicine (I) (2007); 07-D-45 Distribution of Medicine (II) (2007); 07-D-46 Distribution of Medicine (III) (2007); 11-D-18 CT and MRI (2011)	
Germany	B3-11/13 Ophthalmologists-AOK (2013); B3-11/13 Ophthalmologists-AÄGB (2013); B3-123/11 Pharmacists association in Westphalia-Lippe (2014); B7-30/07-1 Fire detection systems in Düsseldorf (2013)	B12-11/08 Ophthalmic lenses (2009)

	Formal commitments	Informal commitments
Hungary		Vj-57/2008/23 Gyöngy Strategic Association (2008)
The Netherlands	6895 Amsterdam hospitals (2010); 7138/47-BT930 Home care providers (2011); 7191/138 National Association of General Practitioners (2012)	Orthobanda industry association (2004); Royal Dutch Society for the Advancement of Pharmacology (KNMP) (2006)
UK		NHS trusts (2012); Asbestos awareness training (2013)
	Other regulated and liberalised markets	
Commission		
France	08-D-34 Funeral services in Marseille (2008); 09-D-27 MGSR (2009); 17-D-12 Sugar production (2017)	
Germany	B4-32/08 Quantity transfer contracts (2008); B2-90/01-1 to B2-90/01-4 Timber (2009)	
Hungary		
The Netherlands	5709 Day-care (2008); 5998 Insurance pool (2010)	UvA and VU tuition fees (2012)
UK	CE/9388-10 Motor Insurers (2011)	
	Technology markets	
Commission	39847 eBooks (2012); 39230 Rio Tinto Alcan (2012); 39736 SIEMENS/AREVA (2012)	40360 Production and distribution of audiobooks (2017)
France	06-D-24 Bijourama (2006); 06-D-28 Home Cinema (2006); 07-D-07 Sale of cosmetic products on the internet (2007); 10-D-20 Electronic discount coupons (2010); 15-D-06 Online hotel booking (2015)	Adidas (2015)
Germany	B4-9/11 B4-94/11 Electronic cash card payment system (2014)	B5-100/10 Sanitary fittings (2011); B7-1/13-35 Sennheiser (2013); B6-46/12 Amazon (2013); B3-137/12 Adidas (2014); B2-98/11 ASICS (2015); Audible (2017); Digital cement trading platform (2017)
Hungary		
The Netherlands		
UK	50408 Live online bidding auction platform (2017)	Yamaha musical instruments (2006); CE/9692/12 Amazon's price parity

(*continued*)

(*continued*)

	Formal commitments	Informal commitments
		policy (2013); CE/9320-10 Hotel online booking (2014); CE/9857-14 Bathroom fittings & fixtures (2016); BMW car comparison sites (2017)
	Financial services	
Commission	39398 Visa MIF (2010); 39398 Visa MIF (2014); 39745 CDS Information Market (2016)	39876 EPC online payments (2013); 39177 Which?/DFB + Mastercard + FIFA (2013)
France	11-D-11 'CB' payment card (2011); 12-D-17 Non-cash means of payment (2012); 13-D-17 MasterCard (2013); 13-D-18 Visa (2013)	
Germany	B4-9/11 B4-94/11 Electronic cash card payment system (2014)	B4-13/10 B4-117/15 Fees for ATM withdrawal (2017)
Hungary	Vj-152/2006/86 Budapest Stock Exchange (2008); Vj-78/2013 MasterCard and OTP (2015)	
The Netherlands		
UK		
Other		
Commission		
France	09-D-08 Motorway breakdown services (2009); 11-D-08 Multi-brand gift card (2011)	
Germany	B3-93/15 Lighters (2015)	B5-144/13 GARDENA (2013); B7-11/13 Bosch Siemens (2013); B2-118/10 Procurement of raw milk (2011); B5-35/14 Lego II (2016); B2-31/17 Edeka/Tengelmann (2017)
Hungary	Vj-71/2005 Sara Lee (2007); Vj-63/2006/122 Inform Média (2007); Vj-158/2005/148 Hyundai Motors Hungary (2007); Vj-28/2007 Beer supply agreements (2008); Vj-49/2011 Hungarian beer market (2015); Vj-111/2014 Ferrous and non-ferrous scrap (2015); Vj-104/2016 Nemak-Cevher (2017)	Vj-91/2004/18 Comix (2005); Vj-156/2004/68 Ice-cream (2006); Vj-157-2004/73 Frozen food (2006); Vj-96/2009-113 Book market (2013)
The Netherlands	7533-22 Art auctions (2013); 15.0959.29 Ready-mix concrete (2016)	Concert organisation and ticket sales (2006); Ballast Nedam (2013)
UK		OFT1415 Street furniture advertising (2012)

ANNEX B:

BERs Development

Formalistic BER	Effects based
General BER	Sectoral BER

1960 1970 1980

Vertical (E

67/67 Exclusive Distribution and Purchasing

1983

198

The BER is mainly a general one, yet it es

2349/84

123/8

Horizontal (En

41

417/85

Insurance (

Air transport (Regulatio

141/62 Exempting transport from the application of Regulation 17/62
End of validity: April 2004 (entry into force of Regulation 1/2003)

267
C

267
Passe
Ta
Confe

267
Ground
Ser

Transport by rail, road and inland wat

141/62 Exempting transport

1017/1968 Rail, roa

Liner conferences (BER a

141/62 Exempting transport from the application of Regulation 17/62
End of validity: April 2004 (entry into force of Regulation 1/2003)

Consortia (Enab

141/62 Exempting transport from the application of Regulation 17/62
End of validity: April 2004 (entry into force of Regulation 1/2003)

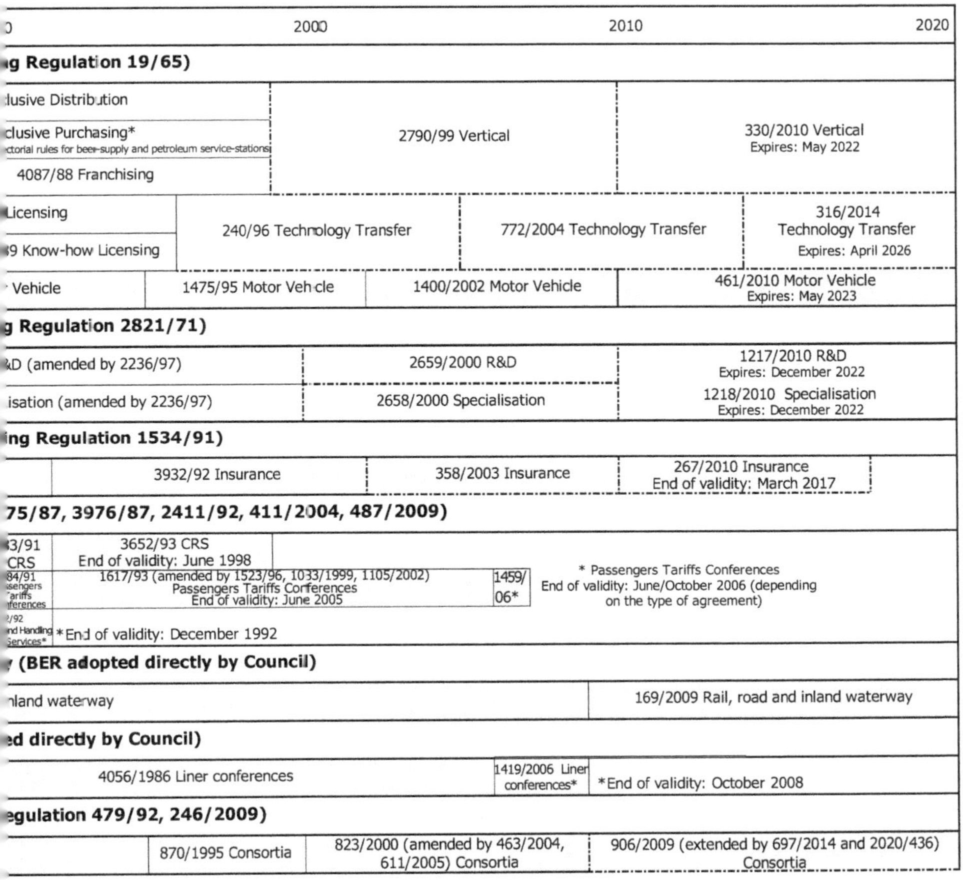

2000
2010
2020
g Regulation 19/65)
lusive Distribution
clusive Purchasing*
ctorial rules for beer-supply and petroleum service-stations
4087/88 Franchising
2790/99 Vertical
330/2010 Vertical
Expires: May 2022
Licensing
9 Know-how Licensing
240/96 Technology Transfer
772/2004 Technology Transfer
316/2014
Technology Transfer
Expires: April 2026
Vehicle
1475/95 Motor Vehicle
1400/2002 Motor Vehicle
461/2010 Motor Vehicle
Expires: May 2023
g Regulation 2821/71)
D (amended by 2236/97)
2659/2000 R&D
1217/2010 R&D
Expires: December 2022
isation (amended by 2236/97)
2658/2000 Specialisation
1218/2010 Specialisation
Expires: December 2022
ing Regulation 1534/91)
3932/92 Insurance
358/2003 Insurance
267/2010 Insurance
End of validity: March 2017
75/87, 3976/87, 2411/92, 411/2004, 487/2009)
3/91
CRS
3652/93 CRS
End of validity: June 1998
84/91
ssengers
ariffs
ferences
1617/93 (amended by 1523/96, 1033/1999, 1105/2002)
Passengers Tariffs Conferences
End of validity: June 2005
1459/
06*
* Passengers Tariffs Conferences
End of validity: June/October 2006 (depending
on the type of agreement)
/92
nd Handling
Services*
*End of validity: December 1992
(BER adopted directly by Council)
nland waterway
169/2009 Rail, road and inland waterway
d directly by Council)
4056/1986 Liner conferences
1419/2006 Liner
conferences*
*End of validity: October 2008
gulation 479/92, 246/2009)
870/1995 Consortia
823/2000 (amended by 463/2004,
611/2005) Consortia
906/2009 (extended by 697/2014 and 2020/436)
Consortia

Laws, Regulations, Reports, and Policy Papers

EUROPEAN UNION

Treaties and International Agreements

Agreement on Social Policy (1992)	Agreement on social policy concluded between the Member States of the European Community with the exception of the United Kingdom of Great Britain and Northern Ireland (OJ 1992 C 191, p. 91), annexed to Protocol (No 14) on social policy, annexed to the Treaty establishing the European Community
Charter of Fundamental Rights	Charter of Fundamental Rights of the European Union (2000/C 364/01)
TFEU and TEU	Consolidated versions of the Treaty on European Union and the Treaty on the Functioning of the European Union (2012/C 326/01)

Regulations

Enabling Council Regulation 1534/1991 on insurance	Council Regulation 1534/91/EEC of 31 May 1991 on the application of Article 85(3) of the Treaty to certain categories of agreements, decisions and concerted practices in the insurance sector, consolidated with amendments introduced by Council Regulation 1/2003/EC of 16 December 2002 (OJ L 143/1, 7.6.1991)
Enabling Council Regulation 19/65 on Vertical Agreements	Council Regulation 19/65/EEC of 2 March 1965 on application of Article 85(3) of the Treaty to certain categories of agreements and concerted practices (OJ P 36, 6.3.1965)
Enabling Council Regulation 2821/71/EEC on Standardisation, R&D and Specialisation Agreements	Council Regulation 2821/71/EEC of 20 December 1971 on application of Article 85(3) of the Treaty to categories of agreements, decisions and concerted practices, (OJ L 285, 29.12.1971)

Regulation 1/2003	Council Regulation (EC) No 1/2003 of 16 December 2002 on the implementation of the rules on competition laid down in Articles 81 and 82 of the Treaty (OJ L 1, 04.01.2003)
Regulation 1017/68 on Inland Transport	Council Regulation (EEC) No 1017/68 of 19 July 1968 applying rules of competition to transport by rail, road and inland waterway (OJ L 175, 23.7.1968)
Regulation 1215/99 amending Enabling Council Regulation 19/65 on Vertical Agreements	Council Regulation (EC) No. 1215/1999 of 10 June 1999 amending Regulation No 19/65/EEC on the application of Article 81(3) of the Treaty to certain categories of agreements and concerted practices (OJ L 148, 10.06.1999)
Regulation 1217/2010 on Research and Development	Commission Regulation 1217/2010/EU of 14 December 2010 on the application of Article 101(3) of the Treaty on the Functioning of the European Union to certain categories of research and development agreements (OJ L 335/36, 18.12.2010)
Regulation 1218/2010 on Specialisation Agreements	Commission Regulation 1218/2010/EU of 14 December 2010 on the application of Article 101(3) of the Treaty on the Functioning of the European Union to certain categories of specialisation agreements (OJ L 335/43, 18.12.2010)
Regulation 123/85 on Motor Vehicles	Commission Regulation (EEC) No 123/85 of 12 December 1984 on the application of Article 85(3) of the Treaty to certain categories of motor vehicle distribution and servicing agreements (OJ L 015, 18.01.1985)
Regulation 1287/2013 establishing a Programme for the Competitiveness of Enterprises and small and medium-sized enterprises	European Parliament and of the Council Regulation (EU) No 1287/2013 of 11 December 2013 establishing a Programme for the Competitiveness of Enterprises and small and medium-sized enterprises (COSME) (2014–2020) (OJ L 347, 20.12.2013)
Regulation 1400/2002 on Motor Vehicles	Commission Regulation (EC) No 1400/2002 of 31 July 2002 on the application of Article 81(3) of the Treaty to categories of vertical agreements and concerted practices in the motor vehicle sector (OJ L 203, 1.8.2002)
Regulation 141/62 on Transport	Council Regulation No. Regulation 141/62 exempting transport from the application of Council Regulation No 17 (OJ L 124, 28.11.1962)
Regulation 1419/2006 on Maritime Transport	Council Regulation (EC) No 1419/2006 of 25 September 2006 repealing Regulation (EEC) No 4056/86 laying down detailed rules for the application of Articles 85 and 86 of the Treaty to maritime transport, and amending Regulation (EC) No 1/2003 as regards the extension of its scope to include cabotage and international tramp services (OJ L 269, 28.9.2006)
Regulation 1475/95 on Motor Vehicles	Commission Regulation (EC) No 1475/95 of 28 June 1 995 on the application of Article 85(3) of the Treaty to certain categories of motor vehicle distribution and servicing agreements (OJ L 145, 29.06.1995)
Regulation 169/2009 on Inland Transport	Council Regulation 169/2009/EC of 26 February 2009 applying rules of competition to transport by rail, road and inland waterway (OJ L 61/1, 5.3.2009)

Regulation 17/62	Council Regulation 17/1962/EEC of 6 February 1962: First Regulation implementing Articles 85 and 86 of the Treaty (OJ L148/5, 21.02.1962)
Regulation 1983/83 on Exclusive Distribution	Commission Regulation (EEC) No 1983/83 of 22 June 1983 on the application of Article 85(3) of the Treaty to categories of exclusive distribution agreements (OJ L 173, 30.6.1983)
Regulation 1984/83 on Exclusive Purchasing	Commission Regulation (EEC) No 1984/83 of 22 June 1983 on the application of Article 85(3) of the Treaty to categories of exclusive purchasing agreements (OJ L 173, 30.6.1983)
Regulation 2020/436 extending the period of application of Regulation 906/2009 on Consortia	Commission Regulation (EU) 2020/436 of 24 March 2020 amending Regulation (EC) No 906/2009 as regards its period of application (OJ L 90, 25.3.2020)
Regulation 2349/84 on Patent Licensing	Commission Regulation (EEC) No 2349/84 of 23 July 1984 on the application of Article 85(3) of the Treaty to certain categories of patent licensing agreements (OJ L 219, 16.8.1984)
Regulation 246/2009 on Liner Shipping	Council Regulation 246/2009/EC of 26 February 2009 on the application of Article 81(3) of the Treaty to certain categories of agreements, decisions and concerted practices between liner shipping companies (consortia) (OJ L 79/1, 25.3.2009)
Regulation 267/2010 on Insurance	Commission Regulation 267/2010/EU of 24 March 2010 on the application of Article 101(3) of the Treaty on the Functioning of the European Union to certain categories of agreements, decisions and concerted practices in the insurance sector (OJ L 83/1, 30.3.2010)
Regulation 2790/99 on Vertical Restrains	Commission Regulation (EC) No 2790/1999 of 22 December 1999 on the application of Article 81(3) of the Treaty to categories of vertical agreements and concerted practices (OJ L 336, 29.12.1999)
Regulation 330/2010 on Vertical Restrains	Commission Regulation 330/2010/EU of 20 April 2010 on the application of Article 101(3) of the Treaty on the Functioning of the European Union to categories of vertical agreements and concerted practices (OJ L 102/1, 23.4.2010)
Regulation 358/2003 on Insurance	Regulation (EC) No 358/2003 of 27 February 2003 on the application of Article 81(3) of the Treaty to certain categories of agreements, decisions and concerted practices in the insurance sector (OJ L 53, 28.2.2003)
Regulation 3975/87 on Air Transport	Council Regulation (EEC) No 3975/87 of 14 December 1987 laying down the procedure for the application of the rules on competition to undertakings in the air transport sector (OJ L 374, 31.12.1987)
Regulation 4056/86 on Maritime Transport	Council Regulation (EEC) No 4056/86 of 22 December 1986 laying down detailed rules for the application of Articles 85 and 86 of the Treaty to maritime transport (OJ L 378, 31.12.1986)
Regulation 4087/88 on Franchising Agreements	Commission Regulation (EEC) No 4087/88 of 30 November 1988 on the application of Article 85(3) of the

	Treaty to categories of franchise agreements (OJ L 359, 28.12.1988)
Regulation 411/2004/EC on Air Transport	Council Regulation 411/2004/EC of 26 February 2004 repealing Regulation (EEC) No 3975/87 and amending Regulations (EEC) No 3976/87 and (EC) No 1/2003, in connection with air transport between the Community and third countries (OJ L 68, 6.3.2004)
Regulation 417/85 on Specialisation	Commission Regulation (EEC) No 417/85 of 19 December 1984 on the application of Article 85 (3) of the Treaty to categories of specialization agreements (OJ L 53/5, 22.2.1985)
Regulation 418/85 on R&D	Commission Regulation (EEC) No 418/85 of 19 December 1984 on the application of Article 85 (3) of the Treaty to categories of research and development agreements (OJ L 53/5, 22.2.1985)
Regulation 461/2010 on Motor Vehicles	Commission Regulation 461/2010/EU of 27 May 2010 on the application of Article 101(3) of the Treaty on the Functioning of the European Union to categories of vertical agreements and concerted practices in the motor vehicle sector (OJ L 129/52, 28.5.2010)
Regulation 487/2009 on Air Transport	Council Regulation 487/2009/EU of 25 May 2009 on the application of Article 81(3) of the Treaty to certain categories of agreements and concerted practices in the air transport sector (OJ L 148/1, 11.6.2009)
Regulation 622/2008 on Settlement Procedure	Commission Regulation (EC) No 622/2008 of 30 June 2008 amending Regulation (EC) No 773/2004, as regards the conduct of settlement procedures in cartel cases (OJ L 171, 1.7.2008)
Regulation 651/2014 State Aid General Block Exemption Regulation	Commission Regulation (EU) No 651/2014 of 17 June 2014 declaring certain categories of aid compatible with the internal market in application of Articles 107 and 108 of the Treaty (OJ L 187, 26.6.2014)
Regulation 67/67 on Distribution Agreements	Regulation No 67/67/EEC of the Commission of 22 March 1967 on the application of Article 85(3) of the Treaty to certain categories of exclusive dealing agreements (OJ 57, 25.3.1967)
Regulation 772/2004 on Technology Transfer	Commission Regulation 772/2004/EU of 27 April 2004 on the application of Article 81(3) of the Treaty to categories of technology transfer agreements (OJ L 123/11, 27.4.2004)
Regulation 773/2004 relating to the Conduct of Proceedings (2004)	Commission Regulation (EC) No 773/2004 of 7 April 2004 relating to the conduct of proceedings by the Commission pursuant to Articles 81 and 82 of the EC Treaty (OJ L 123, 27.04.2004)
Regulation 800/2008 State Aid General Block Exemption Regulation	Commission Regulation (EC) No 800/2008 of the Commission of 6 August 2008 declaring certain categories of aid compatible with the common market in application of Articles 87 and 88 of the Treaty (OJ L 214, 9.8.2008)
Regulation 823/00 on Consortia	Commission Regulation (EC) No 823/2000 of 19 April 2000 on the application of Article 81(3) of the Treaty to

	certain categories of agreements, decisions and concerted practices between liner shipping companies (consortia) (OJ L100, 20.4.2000)
Regulation 870/1995 on Consortia	Commission Regulation (EC) No 870/95 of 20 April 1995 on the application of Article 85 (3) of the Treaty to certain categories of agreements, decisions and concerted practices between liner shipping companies (consortia) pursuant to Council Regulation (EEC) No 479/92 (OJ K 89, 21.4.1995)
Regulation 906/2009 on Liner Shipping	Commission Regulation 906/2009 of 28 September 2009 on the application of Article 81(3) of the Treaty to certain categories of agreements, decisions and concerted practices between liner shipping companies (consortia) (OJ L 256/31, 29.9.2009)

Directives

Damages Directive (2014)	Directive 2014/104/EU of the European Parliament and the Council of 26 November 2014 on certain rules governing actions for damages under national law for infringements of the competition law provisions of the Member States and of the European Union (OJ L 349/1, 5.23.2014)
ECN+ Directive (2019)	Directive 2019/1/EU of the European Parliament and the Council to empower the competition authorities of the Member States to be more effective enforcers and to ensure the proper functioning of the internal market (OJ L 11, 14.1.2019)

Decisions and Opinions

The Economic and Social Committee Opinion on Competition Policy (1982)	The Economic and Social Committee, Opinion on the Commission's tenth report on competition policy (published in conjunction with the fourteenth general report on the activities of the European Communities in 1980) (C 112/23, 3.5.1982)
The Fifth Environmental Action Programme (1993)	The Fifth Environmental Action Programme, approved by the Resolution of the Council and the Representatives of the Governments of the Member States meeting within the Council of 1 February 1993 on a European Community programme of policy and action in relation to the environment and sustainable development (OJ C 138, 17.5.1993)

Policy Papers and Other Documents

Article 101(3) Guidelines (2004)	Commission Notice, Guidelines on the application of Article 81(3) of the Treaty (OJ C 101/97, 27.4.2004)

Article 102 Guidance (2009)	Guidance on the Commission's enforcement priorities in applying Article 82 of the EC Treaty to abusive exclusionary conduct by dominant undertakings (OJ C 45/7, 24.2.2009)
Best Practices Notice (2011)	Commission Notice on the best practices for the conduct of proceedings concerning Articles 101 and 102 TFEU (OJ C 308/6, 20.10.2011)
Clarifications on Transport Infrastructure Projects (1997)	Clarification of the Commission recommendations on the application of the competition rules to new transport infrastructure projects (OJ C 298/5, 30.9.1997)
Commission Policy Brief on EU Competition Rules and the Marketplace (2018)	Competition policy brief: EU competition rules and marketplace bans: Where do we stand after the Coty judgment? (ISBN 978-92-79-81339-9, ISSN: 2315-3113, April 2018)
Commission's Commitment Decisions Press Release (2004)	Commission's Press Release of 17.9.2004, Article 9 of Council Regulation 1/2003 – Providing for a Modernised Framework for Antitrust Scrutiny of Company Behaviour (MEMO/04/217, 17.9.2004)
Commissions Coronavirus Temporary Framework (2020)	Communication from the Commission, Temporary Framework for assessing antitrust issues related to business cooperation in response to situations of urgency stemming from the current COVID-19 outbreak (2020/C 116 I/02, 8.4.2020)
Committee on Economic and Monterey Affairs Report on Proposal for Modernisation (2000)	European Parliament, Committee on Economic an Monterey Affairs Report on the proposal for a Council regulation on the implementation of the rules on competition laid down in Articles 81 and 82 of the Treaty and amending Regulations (EEC) No 1017/68, (EEC) No 2988/74, (EEC) No 4056/86 and (EEC) No 3975/87 (COM(2000) 582. C5-0527/2000 2000/0243(CNS))
Communication on Expiry of the ECSC Treaty (2002)	Communication from the Commission concerning certain aspects of the treatment of competition cases resulting from the expiry of the ECSC Treaty (OJ C 152, 26.6.2002)
Council and the Commission ECN Statement (2004)	Commission Notice on cooperation within the Network of Competition Authorities (OJ C 101/43, 27.4.2004)
Council's Progress Report on Proposal for Modernisation (2001)	Progress report from the Presidency of the Council of the European Union to COREPER (13563/01, 20.11.2001)
De minimis Notice (1970)	Commission Notice of 2 June 1970 concerning agreements of minor importance which do not fall under Article 85(1) of the Treaty establishing the European Economic Community (OJ C 64, 2.6. 1970)
De minimis Notice (1977)	Commission notice of 19 December 1977 concerning agreements of minor importance which do not fall under Article 85(1) of the Treaty establishing the European Economic Community (OJ C 313, 29.12.1977)
De minimis Notice (1986)	Commission Notice on agreements of minor importance which do not fall under Article 85(1) of the Treaty establishing the European Economic Community (OJ C 231, 12.9.1986)

De minimis Notice (1997)	Notice on agreements of minor importance which do not fall within the meaning of Article 85(1) of the Treaty establishing the European Community (97/C 372/04 09.12.1997)
De minimis Notice (2001)	Commission Notice on agreements of minor importance which do not appreciably restrict competition under Article 81(1) of the Treaty establishing the European Community (OJ C 368/13, 22.12.2001)
De minimis Notice (2014)	Notice on agreements of minor importance which do not appreciably restrict competition under Article 101(1) of the Treaty on the Functioning of the European Union (2014/C 291/01 30.08.2014)
Draft Article 101(3) Guidelines (2003)	Draft Notice: Communication from the Commission, Guidelines on the application of Article 81(3) of the Treaty (OJ C 243/62, 10.10.2003)
Draft Treaty Establishing a Constitution for Europe (2004)	Draft Treaty establishing a Constitution for Europe (OJ C 310/1, 16.12.2004)
ECN+ Directive Proposal (2017)	Proposal for a Directive to empower the competition authorities of the Member States to be more effective enforcers and to ensure the proper functioning of the internal market (SWD(2017) 114, 22.3.2017)
Effect on Trade Notice (2004)	Commission Notice, Guidelines on the effect on trade concept contained in Articles 81 and 82 of the Treaty (OJ C 101/81, 27.4.2004)
European Court of Auditors, Special Report on the Commission's EU Merger Control and Antitrust Proceedings (2020)	European Court of Auditors, Special Report 24/2020 on the Commission's EU Merger Control and Antitrust Proceedings: a Need to Scale Up Market Oversight (OJ C 400/07, 24.11.2020)
Fining Guidelines (1998)	Guidelines on the method of setting fines imposed pursuant to Article 15(2) of Regulation No 17 and Article 65(5) of the ECSC Treaty (OJ C 9, 14.1.1998)
Fining Guidelines (2006)	Guidelines on the method of setting fines imposed pursuant to Article 23(2)(a) of Regulation 1/2003/EC (OJ C 210/2, 1.9.2006)
Green Paper on Vertical Restraints (1997)	Green Paper on Vertical Restraints in EC Competition Policy (OJ C 244, 11.8.1997)
Guidance on Restrictions of Competition 'by object' (2014)	Commission Staff Working Document, Guidance on restrictions of competition 'by object' for the purpose of defining which agreements may benefit from the De Minimis Notice Accompanying the document Communication from the Commission Notice on agreements of minor importance which do not appreciably restrict competition under Article 101 (1) of the Treaty on the Functioning of the European Union (SWD (2014) 4136 final)
Guide for Small and Medium-Sized Enterprises (1983)	EEC Competition Rules, Guide for Small and Medium-Sized Enterprises, European Documentation Periodical 1 (983/1984, 21)
Guidelines on competition rules in the telecommunications sector (1991)	Guidelines on the application of the EEC competition rules in the telecommunications sector (OJ C 233/02 6.9.1991)

Horizontal Guidelines (2001)	Commission Notice, Guidelines on the applicability of Article 81 of the EC Treaty to horizontal cooperation agreements (OJ C 3, 6.1.2001)
Horizontal Guidelines (2011)	Guidelines on the applicability of Article 101 of the Treaty on the Functioning of the European Union to horizontal cooperation agreements (OJ C 11/1, 14.1.2011)
Impact Assessment accompanying the ECN+ Directive Proposal (2017)	Commission Staff Working Document 'Impact Assessment' accompanying the document proposal for a Directive of the European Parliament and of the Council to empower the competition authorities of the Member States to be more effective enforcers and to ensure (SWD/2017/0114 final, 22.3.2017)
Impact Assessment On the Insurance BERs (2016)	Commission Staff Working Document 'Impact Assessment' (HT.4012 – IBER, 14.12.2016)
Inability to Pay Information Notice (2010)	Information Notice – Inability to pay under paragraph 35 of the 2006 Fining Guidelines and payment conditions pre- and post-decision finding an infringement and imposing fines (SEC(2010) 737/2, 12.06.2010)
Informal Guidance Notice (2004)	Commission Notice on informal guidance relating to novel questions concerning Articles 81 and 82 of the EC Treaty that arise in individual cases (OJ C 101, 27.04.2004)
Insurance Guidelines (2010)	Communication from the Commission on the application of Article 101(3) of the Treaty on the Functioning of the European Union to certain categories of agreements, decisions and concerted practices in the insurance sector (OJ C 82/02, 30.3.2010)
Leniency Notice (1996)	Commission's 1996 notice on the non-imposition or reduction of fines in cartel cases (OJ C 207, 18.7.1996)
Leniency Notice (2002)	Commission's notice on immunity from fines and reduction of fines in cartel cases (OJ C 45, 19.2.2002)
Leniency Notice (2006)	Commission's notice on immunity from fines and reduction of fines in cartel cases (OJ C 298, 8.12.2006)
Maritime Transport Services Guidelines (2008)	Guidelines on the application of Article 81 of the EC Treaty to maritime transport services (OJ C 245/2, 26.9.2008)
Modernisation White Paper (1999)	White Paper on modernisation of the rules implementing Articles 85 and 86 of the EC Treaty (OJ 1999 C132/1, 28.04.1999)
Notice on the handling of Complaints (2004)	Commission Notice on the handling of complaints by the Commission under Articles 81 and 82 of the EC Treaty (OJ C 101/65, 27.4.2004)
Notification Procedure Notice (1983)	Notice from the Commission on procedures concerning notifications pursuant to Article 4 of Council Regulation No 17/62 (OJ 1983, C 295/7 2.11.1983)
Policy Report(s)	Annual report from the Commission to the European Parliament, the Council, the European Economic and Social Committee and the Committee of the Regions on Competition Policy. Available at: http://ec.europa.eu/competition/publications/annual_report/index.html

Proposal for a Council Modernisation Regulation (2000)	Proposal for a Council Regulation on the implementation of the rules on competition laid down in Articles 81 and 82 of the Treaty and amending Regulations (EEC) No 1017/68, (EEC) No 2988/74, (EEC) No 4056/86 and (EEC) No 3975/87 (Regulation implementing Articles 81 and 82 of the Treaty) (OJ C 365E, 19.12.2000)
Public Consultation for a New Competition Tool (2020)	Antitrust: Commission consults stakeholders on a possible new competition tool (IP/20/977, 2.6.2020)
Public consultation on the Digital Services Act Package (2020)	Competition: The European Commission launches a process to address the issue of collective bargaining for the self-employed (IP/20/1237, 30.6. 2020)
Report on Competition in Professional Services (2004)	Communication from the Commission – Report on Competition in Professional Services (COM(2004) 83 final, 09.02.2004)
Report on the Functioning of Regulation 1/2003 (2009)	Communication from the Commission to the European Parliament and the Council – Report on the functioning of Regulation 1/2003 (SEC(2009)574, 9.7.2014)
Report on the Functioning of Regulation 1/2003 (2014)	Communication from the Commission to the European Parliament and the Council Ten years of antitrust enforcement under regulation 1/2003: Achievements and future perspectives (COM(2014) 453, 9.7.2014)
Report on the Future Competition Law Framework applicable to the Motor Vehicle Sector (2009)	Communication from the Commission, Report on the Future Competition Law Framework applicable to the motor vehicle sector (COM(2009) 388 final, 22.7.2009)
Services of General Interest in Europe (2001)	Communication from the Commission, Services of general interest in Europe (C 17/44, 19.1.2001)
Settlement Notice (2008)	Commission Notice on the conduct of settlement procedures in view of the adoption of Decisions pursuant to Article 7 and Article 23 of Council Regulation (EC) No 1/2003 in cartel cases (OJ C 167/01, 2.7.2008)
Settlement Notice (2008)	Commission Notice on the conduct of settlement procedures in view of the adoption of Decisions pursuant to Article 7 and Article 23 of Council Regulation 1/2003/EC in cartel cases (OJ C 167/1, 2.7.2008)
Staff Working Document on the Evaluation of the Consortia BER (2019)	Commission Staff Working Document, evaluation on of the Commission Regulation (EC) No 906/2009 of 28 September 2009 on the application of Article 81(3) of the Treaty to certain categories of agreements, decisions and concerted practices between liner shipping companies (consortia) (SWD(2019) 412 final, 20.11.2019)
Staff Working Paper accompanying the Report on Functioning of Regulation 1/2003 (2009)	Commission Staff Working Paper accompanying the Communication from the Commission to the European Parliament and council Report on the functioning of regulation 1/2003 (com(2009)206 final, 29.4.2009)
Staff Working Paper accompanying the Report on Functioning of Regulation 1/2003 (2014)	Commission Staff Working Document SWD (2014) 230 – Ten Years of Antitrust Enforcement under Regulation 1/2003 (SWD(2014) 230/2, 9.7.2014)

Staff Working Paper on Article 3 – The Relationship Between EU and National Law (2001)	Commission Staff Working Paper, proposal for a Council regulation on the implementation of the rules on competition laid down in Articles 81 and 82 of the Treaty and amending Regulations (EEC) No 1017/68, (EEC) No 2988/74, (EEC) No 4056/86 and (EEC) No 3975/87 – Commissions Staff Working Paper, Article 3 – the Relationship Between EU and National Law (2000/0243(CNS), 15.06.2001)
Staff Working Paper on Corporate Social Responsibility (2019)	Commission Staff Working Document, Corporate Social Responsibility, Responsible Business Conduct, and Business & Human Rights: Overview of Progress (SWD(2019) 143 final, 20.3.2019)
Staff Working Paper on Proposal for Modernisation (2001)	Commission Staff Working Paper, Commission's Proposal for a new Council Regulation Implementing Articles 81 and 82 (SEC(2001) 871, 31.5.2001)
Supplementary Guidelines on Motor Vehicles (2010)	Supplementary guidelines on vertical restraints in agreements for the sale and repair of motor vehicles and for the distribution of spare parts for motor vehicles (OJ C 138/5, 28.5.2010)
Technology Transfer Guidelines (2004)	Guidelines on the application of Article 81 of the EC Treaty to technology transfer agreements (OJ C 101/2, 27.4.2004)
Technology Transfer Guidelines (2014)	Guidelines on the application of Article 101 of the Treaty on the Functioning of the European Union to technology transfer agreements (OJ C 89/3, 28.3.2014)
Vertical Guidelines (2000)	Commission Notice, Commission Guidelines on Vertical Restraints (OJ C 291/01, 13.10.2000)
Vertical Guidelines (2010)	Commission Guidelines on Vertical Restraints (OJ C 130/1, 19.5.2010)
White Paper on Growth, Competitiveness, Employment (1993)	Growth, Competitiveness, Employment: The Challenges and Ways Forward into the 21st Century – White Paper (COM (93) 700 final/A and B, 5.12.1993).

FRANCE

Codes

Civil Procedure Code	Code de procédure civile français Version consolidée au 1 janvier 2018
Commercial Code	Code de Commerce, Version consolidee au 16 mars 2016, Book IV. English translation of the 2006 version in (WIPO, 2006b)
Penal Code of 1810	Code Penal 1810

Laws

Chapelier Law of 1791	Loi Le Chapelier of 14 June 1791. English translation in (Stewart, 1951), 165-166

Competition Law of 1977	Loi n°77-806 du 19 juillet 1977 relative au contrôle de la concentration économique et à la répression des ententes illicites et des abus de position dominante
Law on Provisional Organisation of Industrial Production of 1940	La loi du 16 août 1940, moyen d'économie dirigée et source d'organisation professionnelle
Law on the Modernisation of the Economy of 2008	Loi de modernisation de l'économie 2008-776 du 4 ao.t 2008
Law on the Organisation of the Nation in Time of War of 1938	Loi du 11 juillet 1938 sur l'organisation générale de la nation pour le temps de guerre

Ordinances and Decrees

Decree 2007-1884 on Motor Vehicles Subsidiaries	Décret n° 2007-1884 du 26 décembre 2007 pris en application de l'article L. 420-4 (II) du code de commerce, concernant un accord relatif aux délais de paiement dans la filière automobile
Decree 96-499 on Signs of Quality in the Agricultural Sector	Décret n°96-499 du 7 juin 1996 pris en application du dernier alinéa de l'article 10 de l'ordonnance n° 86-1243 du 1er décembre 1986 relatif aux accords entre producteurs bénéficiant de signes de qualité dans le domaine agricole
Decree 96-500 on Adaptation Measures for Crisis Situations	Décret n°96-500 du 7 juin 1996 pris en application du dernier alinéa de l'article 10 de l'ordonnance n° 86-1243 du 1er décembre 1986 relatif aux accords entre producteurs agricoles ou entre producteurs agricoles et entreprises concernant des mesures d'adaptation à des situations de crise
Ordinance 2004-1173 adapting French Competition Law to EU Competition Law	Ordonnance n° 2004-1173 du 4 novembre 2004 portant adaptation de certaines dispositions du code de commerce au droit communautaire de la concurrence
Ordinance 2008-1161 on Modernisation of Competition Regulation	Ordonnance n° 2008-1161 du 13 novembre 2008 portant modernisation de la régulation de la concurrence
Ordinance 86-1243 on Competition and Freedom of Prices	Ordonnance n° 86-1243 du 1er décembre 1986 relative à la liberté des prix et de la concurrence. English translation in (Vogelaar, Stuyck and Reeken, 2000), 647
Price Decree 53-704	Decret no. 53-704 du 9 ao.t 1953, relatif au maintien ou au retablissement de la libre concurrence industrielle et commercial. English translation in (Graupner, 2012)
Price Ordinance 45-1483	Ordonnance n°45-1483 du 30 juin 1945 relative aux prix. English translation in (Graupner, 2012)

French NCA Documents

Fining Guidelines (2011)	Communiqué du 16 mai 2011 relatif à la méthode de détermination des sanctions pécuniaires (Autorité de la concurrence's English version)
Notice on Competition Commitments (2009)	Communiqué de procédure du 2 mars 2009 relatif aux engagements en matière de concurrence (Autorité de la concurrence's English version)

Report – 25 Years of enforcement (2012)	Autorité de la concurrence, 25 years of enforcement (2012)
Action During the Covid-19 Coronavirus Epidemic (2020)	Autorité de la concurrence, action during the Covid-19 Coronavirus epidemic, Available here: https://www.autoritedelaconcurrence.fr/en/basic-page/covid-19

GERMANY

Laws and Regulations

Act on Compulsory Cartels of 1933	Gesetz über die Errichtung von Zwangskartellen, 15 Juli 1933
Competition Act	Gesetz gegen Wettbewerbsbeschränkungen. English translations of the original 1957 version in (Graupner, 1965), 164; the Fourth Amendment of 1980 in (Mueller, Heidenhain and Schneider, 1991); the Sixth Amendment of 1998 in (Hengeler Mueller Weitzel Wirtz Law Firm, 2000); the Eight Amendment of 2013 at http://www.gesetze-im-internet.de/englisch_gwb/englisch_gwb.html.
Federal Frosts Act	Gesetz zur Erhaltung des Waldes und zur Förderung der Forstwirtschaft (Bundeswaldgesetz)
Regulation Against Abuse of Economic Power Position of 1923	Verordnung gegen Missbrauch wirtschaftlicher Machtstellungen, 2 November 1923. English translation in (Liefmann, 1932), 351

German NCA Documents

Bundeskartellamt Information leaflet of cooperation of SMEs (2007)	Information leaflet of the Bundeskartellamt on the possibilities of cooperation for small and medium-sized enterprises, March 2013 (Bundeskartellamt's English version)
De minimis Notice (2007)	Bekanntmachung Nr. 18/2007 des Bundeskartellamtes über die Nichtverfolgung von Kooperationsabreden mit geringer wettbewerbsbeschränkender Bedeutung ("Bagatellbekanntmachung") vom 13. März 2007 (Bundeskartellamt's English version)
Fining Guidelines (2006)	Bekanntmachung Nr. 38/2006 über die Festsetzung von Geldbußen nach § 81 Abs. 4 Satz 2 des Gesetzes gegen Wettbewerbsbeschränkungen [GWB] gegen Unternehmen und Unternehmensvereinigungen – Bußgeldleitlinien – vom 15. September 2006 (Bundeskartellamt's English version)
Fining Guidelines (2013)	den Leitlinien für die Bußgeldzumessung in Kartellordnungswidrigkeitenverfahren, 25 Juni 2013 (Bundeskartellamt's English version)

HUNGARY

Constitution and Codes

Civil Code of 1959	1959. IV. Törvény a Magyar Köztársaság Polgári Törvénykönyvéről
Constitution	1949. évi XX. törvény A Magyar Köztársaság Alkotmánya. English translation in (Refworld, 1990)

Laws and Regulations

Act No. CL XXXV of 2012 Waste Disposal Act	2012. évi CLXXXV. törvény a hulladékról
Act No. CLXXVI of 2012 on inter-branch organisations and certain issues of the regulation of agricultural markets	2012. évi CLXXVI. Törvény a szakmaközi szervezetekről és az agrárpiaci szabályozás egyes kérdéseir szervezetekrőll szóló 2012. évi CXXVIII. törvény módosításáról
Act No. IV on the Prohibition of Unfair Economic Activities of 1984	1984. évi IV. törvény a tisztességtelen gazdasági tevékenység tilalmáról
Act No. LVII of 1996 on the Prohibition of Unfair and Restrictive Market Practices	1996. évi LVII. Törvény a tisztességtelen piaci magatartás és a versenykorlátozás tilalmáról
Act No. LXXXVI of 1990 on the Prohibition of Unfair Market Practice	990. évi LXXXVI. Törvény a tisztességtelen piaci magatartás tilalmáról, English translation in (WIPO, 1990)
Act No. V on Unfair Competition 1923	1923. évi V. törvénycikk a tisztességtelen versenyről
Act No. XCIX of 2014 on the financial grounding of the central budget	2014. évi XCIX. Törvény Magyarország 2015. évi központi költségvetésének megalapozásáról
Act No. XX on Agreements Regulating Economic Competition of 1931	1931. évi XX. Törvénycikk a gazdasági versenyt szabályozó megállapodásokról
Act No. XXXIV on Small and Medium-sized Enterprises and Aid for their Development (2004)	2004. évi XXXIV. Törvény A kis- és középvállalkozásokról, fejlődisük támogatásáról szóló
Competition Act	Act LVII on the Prohibition of Unfair and Restrictive Market Practices. English translation following the Amendment of 2000 in (UAIPIT, 2000); Following the Amendment of 2005 in (WIPO, 2006a); Following the Amendment of 2010, from http://www.gvh.hu/en//data/cms998393/Microsoft%20Word%20-%20jogihatter_magyarpiac_versenytorveny_2009_06_01_a.pdf.

Ordinance and Decrees

Decree 205/2011 on vertical agreements	205/2011. (X. 7.) Korm. Rendelet a vertikális megállapodások egyes csoportjainak a versenykorlátozás tilalma alóli mentesítéséről

Decree 246/1997 on Franchising	246/1997. (XII. 20.) Korm. Rendelet a franchise-megállapodások egyes csoportjainak a versenykorlátozás tilalma alól történő mentesítéséről
Decree 53/2002 on specialization agreements	53/2002. (III. 26.) Korm. Rendelet a szakosítási megállapodások egyes csoportjainak a versenykorlátozás tilalma alól történő mentesítéséről. English translation available: http://www.gvh.hu/en//data/cms1024046/55_2002_vertikalis_a .pdf
Decree 54/2002 on R&D	54/2002. (III. 26.) Korm. Rendelet a kutatási és fejlesztési megállapodások egyes csoportjainak a versenykorlátozás tilalma alól történő mentesítéséről. English translation available: http://www. gvh.hu/en//data/cms1022230/ 54_2002_kutatas_a.pdf
Decree 55/2002 on vertical agreements	55/2002. (III. 26.) Korm. Rendelet a vertikális megállapodások egyes csoportjainak a versenykorlátozás tilalma alól történő mentesítéséről. English translation available: http://www.gvh.hu/en//data/cms1022231/55_2002_vertikalis_a .pdf
Decree No. 202/2011 on specialisation agreements	202/2011. (X. 7.) Korm. Rendelet a szakosítási megállapodások egyes csoportjainak a versenykorlátozás tilalma alóli mentesítéséről
Decree No. 203/2011 on insurance sector	18/2004. (II. 13.) Korm. rendelet a biztosítási megállapodások egyes csoportjainak a versenykorlátozás tilalma alól való mentesítéséről
Decree No. 204/2011 on motor vehicles	204/2011. (X. 7.) Korm. Rendelet a gépjármű utópiacra vonatkozó megállapodások egyes csoportjainak a versenykorlátozás tilalma alóli mentesítéséről
Decree No. 206/2011 on research and development	206/2011. Korm. Rendelet a kutatási és fejlesztési megállapodások egyes csoportjainak a versenykorlátozás tilalma alóli mentesítéséről
Decree No. 86/1999 on technology transfer agreements	86/1999. (VI. 11.) Korm. Rendelet a technológia-átadási megállapodások egyes csoportjainak a versenykorlátozás tilalma alól történő mentesítéséről. English translation available: http://www. gvh.hu/en//data/cms1022232/ 86_1999_technologia_a.pdf

Hungarian NCA Documents

GVH Fundamental Principles of Competition Policy (2007)	Fundamental Principles of Competition Policy as Applied by the GVH (GVH's English version)
GVH Strategy for Competition Procedure Initiation (2013)	A gvh versenyfelügyeleti eljárás-indítási stratégiája
Hungarian Commitment Notice (2018)	A Gazdasági Versenyhivatal elnökének és a Gazdasági Versenyhivatal Versenytanácsa elnökének 1/2018. közleménye a Tpvt. 75. §-a szerinti kötelezettségvállalásról
Hungarian Fining Guidelines (2003)	Notice No. 2/3003 of the president of the Hungarian Competition Authority and the Chair of the Competition Council of the Hungarian Competition

	Authority – the method of setting fines in antitrust cases (GVH's English version)
Hungarian Fining Guidelines (2005)	Notice No 2/2005, on the amendment of Notice No 2/2003 on the method of setting fines in antitrust cases, of the President of the Hungarian Competition Authority and the Chair of the Competition Council of the GVH (GVH's English version)
Hungarian Fining Guidelines (2012)	Notice No 1/2012 of the President of the Hungarian Competition Authority and the Chair of the Competition Council of the Hungarian Competition Authority on the method of setting fines in case of market practices infringing Articles 11 and 21 of Act LVII of 1996 on the Prohibition of Unfair Restrictive Practices (Competition Act), and Articles 101 and 102 of the Treaty on the Functioning of the European Union (GVH's English version)
Hungarian Fining Guidelines (2014)	A Gazdasági Versenyhivatal elnökének és a Gazdasági Versenyhivatal Versenytanácsa elnökének 5/2014. számú közleménye egyes korábbi közlemények módosításáról
Hungarian Fining Guidelines (2015)	A Gazdasági Versenyhivatal elnökének 3/2015. (III. 12) GVH utasítása egyes utasítások szervezeti változásokkal, valamint bels ügyintézési szabályok megállapításával összefügg módosításáról
Hungarian Fining Guidelines (2017)	A Gazdasági Versenyhivatal elnökének és a Gazdasági Versenyhivatal Versenytanácsa elnökének 11/2017. közleménye a versenykorlátozó megállapodásokra és összehangolt magatartásokra, a gazdasági erőfölénnyel való visszaélésre, valamint a jelentős piaci erővel való visszaélésre vonatkozó tilalmakba ütköző magatartások esetén a bírság összegének megállapításáról

THE NETHERLANDS

Constitution

Constitution of the Kingdom of the Netherlands	Grondwet voor het Koninkrijk der Nederlanden van 24 augustus 1815

Laws and Regulations

Act Establishing the Authority for Consumers and Markets of 2013	Wet van 28 februari 2013, houdende regels omtrent de instelling van de Autoriteit Consument en Markt (Instellingswet Autoriteit Consument en Markt). English translation available: https://www.acm.nl/en/publications/publication/13190/Rules-of-the-Netherlands-Authority-for Consumers-and-Markets-have-been-harmonized/
Business Regulation Act of 1951	Wet Schorsing Bedrijfsregelingen van 11 April 1951
Competition Act	Mededingingswet, English translation of the original version of 1998 in (Vogelaar, Stuyck and Reeken,

	2000), 753. Following the 2009 Amendment. Available: http://www.dutchcivillaw.com/legislation/competitionact.htm
Dutch Law on the Bar of 1952	Advocatenwet van 23 juni 1952
Healthcare Market Regulation Act of 2006	Wet marktordening gezondheidszorg van 7 Juli 2006
Healthcare Market Regulation Act of 2010	Wet van 7 juli 2006, houdende regels inzake marktordening, doelmatigheid en beheerste kostenontwikkeling op het gebied van de gezondheidszorg (Wet marktordening gezondheidszorg)
Industrial Agreements Act of 1935	Ondernemersovereenkomsten van 15 December 1935
Industrial Organisation Act of 1950	Wet op de bedrijfsorganisatie van 27 Januari 1950. English translation available: https://www.ser.nl/en/publications/publications/2011/2011_ industrialorganisationact.aspx
Law Regulating Economic Competition of 1956	Wet economische mededinging van 28 juni 1956
The Competition (Independent Administrative Authority) Amendment Act of 2015	Wet tot wijziging van de Mededingingswet in verband met het omvormen van het bestuursorgaan van de Nederlandse mededingingsautoriteit tot zelfstandig bestuursorgaan

Ordinances and Decrees

Cartel Ordinance of 1941	Kartelbesluit van 5 November 1941
Dutch Decree Exempting New Shopping Centres (1997)	Besluit van 25 november 1997, houdende vrijstelling van branchebeschermingsovereenkomsten in nieuwe winkelcentra van het verbod van mededingingsafspraken (Besluit vrijstelling branchebeschermingsovereenkomsten)
Dutch Decree Exempting Cooperation Agreements in Retail Trade (2014)	Besluit van 12 december 1997, houdende enige vrijstellingen voor samenwerkingsovereenkomsten in de detailhandel van het verbod van mededingingsafspraken (Besluit vrijstellingen samenwerkingsovereenkomsten detailhandel), As amended in August 2014
Policy rules of the Minster of Economic Affairs on Combination Agreements (2013)	Beleidsregels van de Minister van Economische Zaken van 31 maart 2013, nr. WJZ/12354959, met betrekking tot de toepassing door de Autoriteit Consument en Markt van artikel 6 van de Mededingingswet ten aanzien van combinatieovereenkomsten (Beleidsregels Combinatieovereenkomsten 2013)

Dutch NCA Documents

ACM Prioritisation of enforcement investigations (2016)	Prioritisation of enforcement investigations by the Netherlands Authority for Consumers and Markets, Dutch Government Gazette No 14564 on March 18, 2016, ACM/DJZ/2016/200888 (ACM's English version)
ACM strategy and enforcement priorities with regard to vertical agreements (2015)	ACM's strategy and enforcement priorities with regard to vertical agreements (ACM's English version)

ACM's Oversight During the Coronavirus Crisis (2020)	Press release, ACM's oversight during the Coronavirus crisis of 24 June 2020. Available here: https://www.acm.nl/en/publications/acms-oversight-during-coronavirus-crisis
Draft Guidelines on Sustainability Agreements (2020)	Guidelines Sustainability agreements: opportunities within competition law of July 2020 (ACM's English version)
Fining Guidelines (2009)	Policy Rules No. 14079 of the Minister of Economic Affairs of 11 September 2009, no. WJZ/9150320, containing guidelines on the imposition of administrative fines under legislation the enforcement of which has been entrusted to the Board of the Netherlands Competition Authority (ACM's English version)
Fining Guidelines (2014)	Policy rule of the Minister of Economic Affairs of 4 July 2014, no. WJZ/14112617, on the imposition of administrative fines by the Netherlands Authority for Consumers and Markets (ACM's English version)
Guidelines on Competition Rules for Independent Contractors (2017)	Leidraad Tariefafspraken voor zzp'ers in cao's 24 februari 2017
Guidelines on Price Arrangements between Self-employed Workers (2019)	Guidelines on Price arrangements between self-employed workers of November 2019
Memo on Welfare of Today's Chicken and that of the 'Chicken of Tomorrow (2020)	Memo on Welfare of Today's Chicken and that of the 'Chicken of Tomorrow, of 13 August 2020
Vision Document on Competition and Sustainability (2014)	Vision Document, Competition & Sustainability of May 2014 (ACM's English version)

UNITED KINGDOM

Laws and Regulation

Competition Act of 1980	Competition Act of 1980 c. 21
Competition Act of 1998	Competition Act 1998 c. 41
Enterprise Act of 2002	Enterprise Act 2002 c. 40
Enterprise and Regulatory Reform Act of 2013	Enterprise and Regulatory Reform Act of 2013 c. 24
Fair Trading Act of 1973	Fair Trading Act of 1973 c. 41
Health and Social Care Act of 2012	Health and Social Care Act of 2012 c. 7
Other Enactments (Amendment) Regulations of 2004	The Competition Act 1998 and Other Enactments (Amendment) Regulations 2004 No. 1261
Resale Price Act of 1964	Resale Prices Act 1964 c. 53
Restrictive Trade Practices Act of 1956	Restrictive Trade Practices Act of 1956 c. 68
Restrictive Trade Practices Act of 1968	Restrictive Trade Practices Act of 1968 c. 66
	The Competition Act 1998 (Small Agreements and Conduct of Minor Significance) Regulations of 2000 No. 262

The Competition Act 1998 (Small Agreements and Conduct of Minor Significance) Regulations 2000	
The Monopolies and Mergers Act of 1965	Monopolies and Mergers Act of 1965 c. 50
The Monopolies and Restrictive Practices (Inquiry and Control) Act of 1948	The Monopolies and Restrictive Practices (Inquiry and Control) Act of 1948 c. 66

Orders

Competition Act 1998 (Dairy Produce) (Coronavirus (Public Policy Exclusion) Order 2020	The Competition Act 1998 (Dairy Produce) (Coronavirus) (Public Policy Exclusion) Order 2020, SI 2020/48
Competition Act 1998 (Groceries) (Coronavirus) (Public Policy Exclusion) Order 2020	The Competition Act 1998 (Groceries) (Coronavirus) (Public Policy Exclusion) Order 2020 (SI 2020/369)
Competition Act 1998 (Health Services for Patients in England) (Coronavirus) (Public Policy Exclusion) Order 2020	The Competition Act 1998 (Health Services for Patients in England) (Coronavirus) (Public Policy Exclusion) Order 2020, SI 2020/368
Competition Act 1998 (Health Services for Patients in Wales) (Coronavirus) (Public Policy Exclusion) Order 2020	The Competition Act 1998 (Health Services for Patients in Wales) (Coronavirus) (Public Policy Exclusion) Order 2020, SI 2020/435
Competition Act 1998 (Land and Vertical Agreement Exclusion) Order 2002	The Competition Act 1998 (Land and Vertical Agreements Exclusion) Order 2000
Competition Act 1998 (Public Policy Exclusion) Order 2006 (maintenance and repair of warships)	The Competition Act 1998 (Public Policy Exclusion) Order 2006, SI 2006/605 (maintenance and repair of warships)
Competition Act 1998 (Public Policy Exclusion) Order 2007 (strategic and tactical weapons and their supporting technology)	The Competition Act 1998 (Public Policy Exclusion) Order 2007, SI 2007/1896 (strategic and tactical weapons and their supporting technology
Competition Act 1998 (Public Policy Exclusion) Order 2008 (design, construction, maintenance and disposal of nuclear submarines)	The Competition Act 1998 (Public Policy Exclusion) Order 2008, SI 2008/1820 (design, construction, maintenance and disposal of nuclear submarines)
Competition Act 1998 (Public Policy Exclusion) Order 2012 (supply of oil fuels in an emergency)	The Competition Act 1998 (Public Policy Exclusion) Order 2012, SI 2012/710 (supply of oil fuels in an emergency)
Competition Act 1998 (Solent Maritime Crossings) (Coronavirus) (Public Policy Exclusion) Order 2020	The Competition Act 1998 (Solent Maritime Crossings) (Coronavirus) (Public Policy Exclusion) Order 2020, SI 2020/370
Public Transport Ticketing Schemes Block Exemption	Public Transport Ticketing Schemes Block Exemption (Order 2001) (SI 2001 No 319)

Public Transport Ticketing Schemes Block Exemption (Amendment) Order 2016	The Competition Act 1998 (Public Transport Ticketing Schemes Block Exemption) (Amendment) Order 2016, No. 126
The Competition Act 1998 (Public Policy Exclusion) (Revocation) Order 2011 (Team Complex Weapons)	The Competition Act 1998 (Public Policy Exclusion) (Revocation) Order 2011, SI 2011/2886 (Team Complex Weapons)

UK NCA Documents

CMA Approach to Business Cooperation in Response to COVID-19 (2020)	CMA, Approach to Business Cooperation in Response to COVID-19 of March 2020
CMA Prioritisation principles (2014)	CMA Prioritisation principles of April 2014
CMA Roundtable on the Use of Commitments (2015)	CMA, roundtable on the use of commitments in competition enforcement, Summary note of September 2015
Commitments Guidelines (2004)	Incorporating the Office of Fair Trading's guidance as to the circumstances in which it may be appropriate to accept commitments, Understanding competition law of December 2004
Essential Information For Businesses: Warning and Advisory Letters (2016)	CMA Essential Information For Businesses: Warning and Advisory Letters of 14 January 2016
Fining Guidelines (2004)	OFT, Guidance as to the appropriate amount of a penalty of December 2004
Fining Guidelines (2012)	OFT, Guidance as to the appropriate amount of a penalty of September 2012
Fining Guidelines (2018)	CMA, Guidance as to the appropriate amount of a penalty of April 2018
Guidance on Concurrent Application (2014)	CMA, Regulated Industries: Guidance on concurrent application of competition law to regulated industries of March 2014
OFT Market Investigation Guidance (2006)	OFT, Market Investigation Reference: Guidance about the making of references under Part 4 of the Enterprise Act of 2006
OFT modernisation Guidance (2004)	OFT Guidance Competition law modernisation of December 2004
OFT Prioritisation Principles (2008)	OFT, Prioritisation Principles of October 2008
OFT Roundtable on Narrow versus Broad Definition of Benefits (2010)	OFT, Article 101(3) – A Discussion of Narrow versus Broad Definition of Benefits. Discussion note for OFT breakfast roundtable of 2010
OFT Understanding Competition Law Guidelines (2004)	OFT, Agreements and concerted practices, Understanding competition law of December 2004
Public transport ticketing schemes block exemption Guidance (2016)	CMA, The public transport ticketing schemes block exemption: CMA guidance, of 16 September 2016
Short-form Opinions Guidance (2014)	Guidance on the CMA's approach to Short-form Opinions of April 2014

Supplemental Guidance on Market Studies and Investigations (2014)	Market Studies and Market Investigations: Supplemental Guidance on the CMA's approach of January 2014 (revised July 2017)
Whistleblowing Guidelines (2014)	CMA, Rewards for Information about Cartels of March 2014

INTERNATIONAL ORGANISATIONS

ECN

ECN Decision Making Powers Report (2012)	Decision Making Powers Report, ECN Working Group Cooperation Issues and Due Process of 31 October 2012
ECN Recommendation on Commitment Procedures (2013)	Recommendation on Commitment Procedures of December 2013
ECN Recommendation on the Power to Set Priorities (2013)	Recommendation on the power to set priorities of December 2013
ECN Model Leniency Programme (2012)	ECN Model Leniency Programme, as revised in November 2012
ECN Statement on Application of Competition Law During the Corona Crisis (2020)	Antitrust: Joint statement by the European Competition Network (ECN) on application of competition law during the Corona crisis of March 2020
ECN Questionnaire on Regulation 1/2003 (2013)	ECN Working Group on Cooperation Issues, Results of the questionnaire on the reform of Member States (MS) n of national competition laws after EC Regulation No. 1/2003 of 22 May 2013

ICN

ICN Anti-cartel Enforcement Manual (2010)	Cartel Working Group, Anti-Cartel Enforcement Manual, Chapter 4, Cartel Case Initiation of March 2010
ICN Competition Enforcement and Consumer Welfare (2011)	ICN 10th Annual Conference, Competition Enforcement and Consumer Welfare, Setting the Agenda, 17-20 of May, 2011
ICN Report on Interface Between Competition Policy and Other Public Policies (2010)	Report on Interface Between Competition Policy and Other Public Policies. Prepared by the Turkish Competition Authority, presented at the 9th ICN Annual Conference Istanbul, Turkey
ICN Seminar on Competition Agency Effectiveness (2009)	Competition Policy Implementation, Working Group, Seminar on competition agency effectiveness, Summary Report of January 2009
ICN Statement on Competition During and After the COVID-19 Pandemic (2020)	ICN Steering Group Statement: Competition during and after the COVID-19 Pandemic of April 2020

OECD

OCED Commitments Report (2016)	Commitment decisions in antitrust cases, Background paper by the Secretariat, DAF/COMP of 22 January 2016

OECD Ex officio Cartel Investigations Report (2013)	Ex officio cartel investigations and the use of screens to detect cartels, DAF/COMP(2013)27, of 7 of July 2014
OECD Fighting Hard-Core Cartels (2002)	Report, Fighting Hard-Core Cartels: Harm, Effective Sanctions and Leniency Programs, of 2002
OECD Food Chain Industry Report, Note by France (2013)	Policy Roundtable, Competition Issues in the Food Chain Industry, DAF/COMP(2014)16, of 15 May 2014
OECD Horizontal Agreements in the Environmental Context, Note by Germany (2010)	Policy Roundtables, Horizontal Agreements in the Environmental Context, DAF/COMP(2010)39, of 24 of November 2011
OECD Reforms to Improve the Investment Climate in South East Europe (2006)	Progress in Policy Reforms to Improve the Investment Climate in South East Europe, of 2006
OECD Regulated Conduct Defence Report (2011)	Policy Roundtables, Regulated Conduct Defence Report, DAF/COMP(2011)3, of 1 September 2011
OECD Regulatory Reform in France (2003)	Reviews of Regulatory Reform, Regulatory reform in France, of 2003
OECD Regulatory Reform in Germany (2004)	Reviews of Regulatory Reform, Regulatory reform in Germany, of 2004
OECD Regulatory Reform in Hungary (2000)	Reviews of Regulatory Reform, Regulatory reform in Hungary, of 2000
OECD Regulatory Reform in the Netherlands (1998)	Reviews of Regulatory Reform, Regulatory reform in the Netherlands, of 1998
OECD Role of Efficiency Claims in Antitrust Proceedings (2012)	Policy Roundtables, The Role of Efficiency Claims in Antitrust Proceedings, DAF/COMP(2012)23, of 2 May 2012

UNCTAD

UNCTAD Coherence Between Competition and Government Policies (2011)	The importance of coherence between competition policies and government policies, Note by the UNCTAD secretariat, of 10 May 2011
UNCTAD Competition Authorities and Judiciaries (2016)	Enhancing legal certainty in the relationship between competition authorities and judiciaries, Note by the UNCTAD secretariat. of 17 August 2016
UNCTAD Prioritization and Resource Allocation (2013)	Prioritization and resource allocation as a tool for agency effectiveness, Note by the UNCTAD secretariat, of 26 April 2013
UNCTAD Priority Setting and Discretionary Powers of Competition Authorities (2013)	Priority setting and discretionary powers of competition authorities, Note by the UNCTAD secretariat, of 26 April 2013

Case Law

COMMISSION

Commission decision no. COMP 36264 Mercedes-Benz, of 10 October 2001
Commission decision no. COMP/29373 Visa International, of 24 July 2002
Commission decision no. COMP/29373 Visa International, of 9 August 2001
Commission decision no. COMP/34493 COMP/37366 COMP/37299 COMP/37288 COMP/37287 COMP/37526 COMP/37254 COMP/37252 COMP/37250 COMP/37246 COMP/37245 COMP/37244 COMP/37243 COMP/37242 COMP/37267 DSD, of 17 September 2001
Commission decision no. COMP/34579 COMP/36518 and COMP/38580 MasterCard I, of 19 December 2007
Commission decision no. COMP/35470 COMP/35473 Austrian system for the disposal of packaging waste, of 16 October 2003
Commission decision no. COMP/36516 Nathan-Bricolux, of 5 July 2000
Commission decision no. COMP/36571 Austrian banks-'Lombard Club', of 11 June 2002
Commission decision no. COMP/37027 Zinc Phosphate, of 11 December 2001
Commission decision no. COMP/37214 Joint selling of the media rights to the German Bundesliga, of 19 January 2005
Commission decision no. COMP/37370 Sorbates, of 1 October 2003
Commission decision no. COMP/37614 Interbrew and Alken-Maes, of 5 December 2001
Commission decision no. COMP/37800 Luxembourg Brewers, of 5 December 2001
Commission decision no. COMP/37860 Morgan Stanley Dean Witter/Visa, of 2 October 2007
Commission decision no. COMP/38014 IFPI 'Simulcasting', of 8 October 2002
Commission decision no. COMP/38069 Copper plumbing tubes, of 3 September 2004
Commission decision no. COMP/38158 Meca-Medina and Majcen/IOC, of 1 August 2002
Commission decision no. COMP/38173 The Football Association Premier League Limited, of 22 March 2006
Commission decision no. COMP/38238 Raw Tobacco Spain, of 20 October 2004
Commission decision no. COMP/38279 French beef, of 2 April 2003
Commission decision no. COMP/38281 Raw Tobacco Italy, of 10 October 2005
Commission decision no. COMP/38284 Société Air France/Alitalia Linee, of 7 April 2004
Commission decision no. COMP/38348 Repsol, of 12 April 2006
Commission decision no. COMP/38359 Electrical and mechanical carbon and graphite products, of 3 December 2003
Commission decision no. COMP/38369 Network Sharing Rahmenvertrag, of 16 July 2003

Commission decision no. COMP/38549 Barême d'honoraires de l'Ordre des Architectes belges, of 24 June 2004
Commission decision no. COMP/38589 Heat stabilisers, of 11 November 2009
Commission decision no. COMP/38606 Cartes bancaires, of 17 October 2007
Commission decision no. COMP/38662 GDF-ENEL, of 26 October 2004
Commission decision no. COMP/38662 GDF-ENI, of 26 October 2004
Commission decision no. COMP/38681 Cannes Agreement, of 4 October 2006
Commission decision no. COMP/38698 CISAC Agreement, of 16 July 2008
Commission decision no. COMP/38866 Animal Feed Phosphates, of 20 July 2010
Commission decision no. COMP/39092 Bathroom Fittings and Fixtures, of 23 June 2010
Commission decision no. COMP/39097 Watch Repair, of 29 July 2014
Commission decision no. COMP/39140 DaimlerChrysler, of 14 September 2007
Commission decision no. COMP/39151 39152 SABAM and BUMA, of 4 October 2006
Commission decision no. COMP/39188 Bananas, of 15 October 2008
Commission decision no. COMP/39226 Lundbeck, of 19 June 2013
Commission decision no. COMP/39230 Rio Tinto Alcan, of 21 December 2012
Commission decision no. COMP/39258 Airfreight, of 9 November 2010
Commission decision no. COMP/39396 Calcium carbide and magnesium based reagents, of 22 July 2009
Commission decision no. COMP/39401 E.ON/GDF, of 22 July 2009
Commission decision no. COMP/39416 Ship Classification, of 14 October 2009
Commission decision no. COMP/39471 Certain joueur de tennis professionnel/Agence mondiale antidopage, of 13 October 2009
Commission decision no. COMP/39482 Exotic fruit (Bananas), of 12 October 2011
Commission decision no. COMP/39510 Ordre National des Pharmaciens, of 8 December 2010
Commission decision no. COMP/39595 Continental/United/Lufthansa/Air Canada, of 23 May 2013
Commission decision no. COMP/39612 Perindopril (Servier), of 9 July 2014
Commission decision no. COMP/39633 Shrimps, of 27 November 2013
Commission decision no. COMP/39673 Virtual Print Fee agreements, of 4 March 2011
Commission decision no. COMP/39685 Fentanyl, of 10 December 2013
Commission decision no. COMP/39839 Telefónica and Portugal Telecom, of 23 January 2013
Commission decision no. COMP/39847 Ebooks, of 12 December 2012
Commission decision no. COMP/39921 Refusal to provide payment services, of July 2014
Commission decision no. COMP/40023 Cross-border access to pay-TV, of 26 July 2016
Commission decision no. COMP/40208 International Skating Union's Eligibility rules, of 8 December 2017
Commission decision no. COMP/50343 Light fittings, of 21 June 2017
Commission decision no. IV/ 39563 Retail food packaging, of 24 June 2015
Commission decision no. IV//29329 VW-MAN, of 5 December 1983
Commission decision no. IV/10498 IV/11546 IV/12992 IV/17394 IV/17395 IV/17971 IV/18772 IV/18888 IV/3213 Omega, of 28 October 1970
Commission decision no. IV/128 Julien/Van Katwijk, of 28 October 1970
Commission decision no. IV/14650 Bayerische Motoren Werke, of 12 December 1974
Commission decision no. IV/147 Centraal Bureau voor de Rijwielhandel, of 2 December 1977
Commission decision no. IV/1576 Zanussi, of 23 October 1978
Commission decision no. IV/171 IV/856 IV/172 IV/117 IV/28173 Campari, of 23 December 1977
Commission decision no. IV/17545 IV/6964 IV/26858 IV/26890 IV/18673 IV/17448 Davidson Rubber Co., of 9 June 1972
Commission decision no. IV/181 CEMATEX, of 24 September 1971
Commission decision no. IV/1914 ARG-Unipart, of 22 December 1987
Commission decision no. IV/197 Industrieverband Solnhofener Natursteinplatten eV, of 16 October 1980
Commission decision no. IV/21353 Kabelmetal-Luchaire, of 18 July 1975

Commission decision no IV/223 Transocean Marine Paint Association, of 27 June 1967
Commission decision no IV/22491 Maison Jalatte, of 17 December 1965
Commission decision no IV/243 IV/244 IV/245 Cimbel, of 22 December 1972
Commission decision no IV/24510 GERO-fabriek, of 22 December 1976
Commission decision no. IV/25007 IMA Rules, of 18 September 1980
Commission decision no. IV/256 Bomee-Stichting, of 21 November 1975
Commission decision no. IV/25757 Hasselblad, of 2 December 1981
Commission decision no. IV/25963 Gas water-heaters and bath-heaters, of 3 July 1973
Commission decision no. IV/26045 ACEC/Berliet, of 17 July 1968
Commission decision no. IV/261 Belgische Vereniging der Banken/Association Beige des Banques, of 11 December 1986
Commission decision no. IV/26186 Central Stikstof Verkoopkantoor, of 20 July 1978
Commission decision no. IV/26418 Sopelem/Langen, of 20 December 1971
Commission decision no. IV/26437 Jaz/Peter, of 23 December 1977
Commission decision no. IV/26602 FRUBO, of 25 July 1974
Commission decision no. IV/26603 Rank/Sopelem, of 20 December 1974
Commission decision no. IV/26612 MAN/SAVIEM, of 17 January 1972
Commission decision no. IV/26623 Quinine, of 16 July 1969
Commission decision no. IV/26624 F.N.-C.F., of 28 May 1971
Commission decision no. IV/26625 Clima Chappée-Buderus, of 7 August 1969
Commission decision no. IV/26813 Raymond-Nagoya, of 9 June 1972
Commission decision no. IV/26825 PRYM-BEKA, of 8 October 1973
Commission decision no. IV/26870 Aluminium imports from Eastern Europe, of 18 December 1984
Commission decision no. IV/26894 IV/26876 and IV/26892 Pittsburgh Corning Europe, of 23 November 1972
Commission decision no. IV/26912 Hennessy-Henkell, of 11 December 1980
Commission decision no. IV/26917 Henkel/Colgate, of 23 December 1971
Commission decision no. IV/26918 Suiker-Unie, of 2 January 1973
Commission decision no. IV/26940 KEWA, of 23 December 1975
Commission decision no. IV/26940 United Reprocessors GmbH, of 23 December 1975
Commission decision no. IV/26949 AOIP/Beyrard, of 2 December 1975
Commission decision no. IV/27000 primary aluminum, of 15 July 1975
Commission decision no. IV/27010 Deutsche Philips GmbH, of 5 October 1973
Commission decision no. IV/27073 Bayer/Gist-Brocades, of 15 December 1975
Commission decision no. IV/27093 De Laval/Stork, of 22 December 1987
Commission decision no. IV/27093 De Laval/Stork, of 25 July 1977
Commission decision no. IV/27393 IV/27394 Net book agreements, of 12 December 1988
Commission decision no. IV/27442 Vacuum Interrupters Ltd, of 11 December 1980
Commission decision no. IV/27442 Vacuum Interrupters Ltd, of 20 January 1977
Commission decision no. IV/27492 SMM&T Exhibition Agreement, of 5 December 1983
Commission decision no. IV/27958 National Sulphuric Acid Association, of 9 July 1980
Commission decision no. IV/28282 The Distillers Company Limited, of 20 December 1977
Commission decision no. IV/28374 Advocaat Zwarte Kip, of 24 July 1974
Commission decision no. IV/28748 AEG-Telefunken, of 6 January 1982
Commission decision no. IV/28775 UNIDI, of 17 July 1975
Commission decision no. IV/28796 Beecham/Parke, Davis, of 17 January 1979
Commission decision no. IV/28812 Theal/Watts, of 21 December 1976
Commission decision no. IV/28824 Maize seed, of 21 September 1978
Commission decision no. IV/28852 IV/29127 IV/29149 Fedetab, of 20 July 1978
Commission decision no. IV/28859 Wm. Teacher and Sons Ltd-conditions of sale, of 28 July 1978
Commission decision no. IV/28930 Milchförderungsfonds, of 7 December 1984
Commission decision no. IV/28948 Cauliflowers, of 2 December 1977

Commission decision no. IV/28959 VIFKA, of 30 September 1986
Commission decision no. IV/28967 Bronbemaling, of 25 July 1975
Commission decision no. IV/28980 Pabst & Richarz/BNIA, of 26 July 1976
Commission decision no. IV/28996 Reuter-BASF, of 26 July 1976
Commission decision no. IV/29011 Rennet, of 5 December 1979
Commission decision no. IV/29018 Miller International, of 1 December 1976
Commission decision no. IV/29021 BP Kemi/DDSF, of 5 September 1979
Commission decision no. IV/29133 WANO Schwarzpulver, of 20 October 1978
Commission decision no. IV/29146 BMW Belgium NV and Belgian BMW dealers, of 23 December 1977
Commission decision no. IV/29151 Video cassette recorders, of 20 December 1977
Commission decision no. IV/29176 Vegetable parchment, of 23 December 1977
Commission decision no. IV/29236 Sopelem/Vickers, of 21 December 1977
Commission decision no. IV/29290 Vaessen/Moris, of 10 January 1979
Commission decision no. IV/29418 Spices, of 21 December 1977
Commission decision no. IV/29420 Grundig's EEC distribution system, of 10 July 1985
Commission decision no. IV/29428 GEC-Weir Sodium Circulators, of 23 November 1977
Commission decision no. IV/29430 Kawasaki, of 12 December 1978
Commission decision no. IV/29440 Arthur Bell and Sons Ltd – conditions of sale, of 28 July 1978
Commission decision no. IV/29453 SNPE-LEL, of 12 June 1978
Commission decision no. IV/29525 and IV/3000 SSI, of 15 July 1982
Commission decision no. IV/29535 White lead, of 12 December 1978
Commission decision no. IV/29595 Pioneer Hi-Fi Equipment, of 14 December 1979
Commission decision no. IV/29598 SABA's EEC distribution system, of 21 December 1983
Commission decision no. IV/29629 Rolled zinc products and zinc alloys, of 14 December 1982
Commission decision no. IV/29672 Floral, of 28 November 1979
Commission decision no. IV/29702 Johnson & Johnson, of 25 November 1980
Commission decision no. IV/29725 Wood pulp, of 19 December 1984
Commission decision no. IV/29869 Italian cast glass, of 17 December 1980
Commission decision no. IV/29883 AROW/BNIC, of 15 December 1982
Commission decision no. IV/29955 Carbon Gas Technologie, of 8 December 1983
Commission decision no. IV/29972 Langenscheidt/Hachette, of 17 November 1981
Commission decision no. IV/29995 ANSEAU-NAVEWA, of 17 December 1981
Commission decision no. IV/30064 Cast iron and steel rolls, of 17 October 1983
Commission decision no. IV/30070 National Panasonic, of 7 December 1982
Commission decision no. IV/30077 Cafeteros de Colombia, of 10 December 1982
Commission decision no. IV/30099 Schlegel/CPIO, of 6 December 1983
Commission decision no. IV/30174 Vimpoltu, of 13 July 1983
Commission decision no. IV/30188 Moet et Chandon (London) Ltd, of 27 November 1981
Commission decision no. IV/30261 Ideal-Standard's distribution system, of 10 December 1984
Commission decision no. IV/30299 Grohe's distribution system, of 10 December 1984
Commission decision no. IV/30307 Fire insurance, of 5 December 1984
Commission decision no. IV/30320 Optical fibres, of 14 July 1986
Commission decision no. IV/30350 Zinc producer group, of 16 August 1984
Commission decision no. IV/3036 D.R.U.-Blondel, of 8 July 1965
Commission decision no. IV/30373 P&I Clubs, of 16 December 1985
Commission decision no. IV/30389 IV/30408 Nutricia-de Rooij Nutricia-Zuid-Hollandse Conservenfabriek, of 12 December 1983
Commission decision no. IV/30437 Rockwell/Iveco, of 13 July 1983
Commission decision no. IV/30517 Amersham Buchler, of 29 October 1982
Commission decision no. IV/30525 International Energy Agency, of 12 December 1983
Commission decision no. IV/30525 International Energy Agency, of 21 February 1994
Commission decision no. IV/30658 Polistil/Arbois, of 16 May 1984

Commission decision no. IV/30696 Distribution system of Ford Werke AG, of 16 November 1983
Commission decision no. IV/30717 Uniform Eurocheques, of 10 December 1984
Commission decision no. IV/30739 Siemens/Fanuc, of 18 December 1985
Commission decision no. IV/30804 Nuovo Cegam, of 10 April 1984
Commission decision no. IV/30809 John Deer, of 14 December 1984
Commission decision no. IV/30810 Synthetic fibres, of 4 July 1984
Commission decision no. IV/30839 Sperry New Holland, of 16 December 1985
Commission decision no. IV/30846 Ivoclar, of 21 November 1985
Commission decision no. IV/30863 BPCL/ICI, of 19 July 1984
Commission decision no. IV/30907 Peroxygen products, of 23 November 1984
Commission decision no. IV/30937 Pronuptia, of 17 December 1986
Commission decision no. IV/30971 BP/Kellogg, of 2 December 1985
Commission decision no. IV/30979 and IV/31394 Decca Navigator System, of 21 December 1988
Commission decision no. IV/30988 Flat-glass in the Benelux, of 23 July 1984
Commission decision no. IV/31017 Fisher-Price/Quaker Oats Ltd-Toyco, of 18 December 1987
Commission decision no. IV/31029 French inland waterway charter traffic-EATE levy, of 10 July 1985
Commission decision no. IV/31043 Tetra Pak I, of 26 July 1988
Commission decision no. IV/31055 ENI/Montedison, of 4 December 1986
Commission decision no. IV/31128 Fatty Acids, of 2 December 1986
Commission decision no. IV/31143 Peugeot, of 25 September 1986
Commission decision no. IV/31149 Polypropylene, of 23 April 1986
Commission decision no. IV/31192 and IV/31507 Tipp-Ex, of 10 July 1987
Commission decision no. IV/312 COBELPA/VNP, of 8 September 1977
Commission decision no. IV/31206 Rich Products/Jus-rol, of 22 December 1987
Commission decision no. IV/31291 Uniform Eurocheques, of 19 December 1988
Commission decision no. IV/31302 Boussois/Interpane, of 15 December 1986
Commission decision no. IV/31340 Mitchell Cotts/Sofiltra, of 17 December 1986
Commission decision no. IV/31356 ABI, of 12 December 1986
Commission decision no. IV/31370 31446 UK Agricultural Tractor Registration Exchange, of 17 February 1992
Commission decision no. IV/31428 IV/31429 IV/31430 IV/31431 IV/31432 Yves Rocher, of 17 December 1986
Commission decision no. IV/31458 X/Open Group, of 15 December 1986
Commission decision no. IV/31498 Delta ChemieDDD, of 13 October 1988
Commission decision no. IV/31499 Dutch Banks, of 19 July 1989
Commission decision no. IV/31533 IV/34072 Langnese-Iglo, of 23 December 1992
Commission decision no. IV/31550 IV/31898 Zera Montedison/Hinkens Stahler, of 22 June 1993
Commission decision no. IV/31553 Welded steel mesh, of 2 August 1989
Commission decision no. IV/31559 Sippa, of 15 February 1991
Commission decision no. IV/31572 IV/32571 Building and construction industry in the Netherlands, of 5 February 1992
Commission decision no. IV/31593 British Dental Trade Association – BDTA, of 11 July 1988
Commission decision no. IV/31697 Charles Jourdan, of 2 December 1988
Commission decision no. IV/31739 Internationale Dentalschau, of 18 September 1987
Commission decision no. IV/31741 Sandoz, of 13 July 1987
Commission decision no. IV/31846 Enichem/ICI, of 22 December 1987
Commission decision no. IV/31865 PVC, of 21 December 1988
Commission decision no. IV/31866 LdPE, of 21 December 1988
Commission decision no. IV/31902 Iveco/Ford, of 20 July 1988
Commission decision no. IV/32006 Alcatel Espace/ANT Nachrichtentechnik, of 12 January 1990

Commission decision no. IV/32026 Bayo-n-ox, of 13 December 1989
Commission decision no. IV/32034 Computerland, of 13 July 1987
Commission decision no. IV/32075 Bayer/BP Chemicals, of 5 May 1988
Commission decision no. IV/32150 EBU/Eurovision System, of 11 June 1993
Commission decision no. IV/32150 Eurovision, of 10 May 2000
Commission decision no. IV/32173 Continental/Michelin, of 11 October 1988
Commission decision no. IV/32265 Concordato Incendio, of 20 December 1989
Commission decision no. IV/32290 Newitt/Dunlop Slazenger International, of 18 March 1992
Commission decision no. IV/32306 Olivetti/Canon, of 22 December 1987
Commission decision no. IV/32358 ServiceMaster, of 14 November 1988
Commission decision no. IV/32363 KSB/Goulds/Lowara/ITT, of 12 December 1990
Commission decision no. IV/32368 BBC Brown Bover, of 11 October 1988
Commission decision no. IV/324 Vereniging van Cementhandelaren, of 16 December 1971
Commission decision no. IV/32448 and IV/32450 Cewal, Cowac and Ukwal, of 23 December 1992
Commission decision no. IV/32450 French-West African ship-owners' committees, of 1 April 1992
Commission decision no. IV/32490 Eurotunnel, of 13 December 1994
Commission decision no. IV/32524 Screensport/EBU members, of 19 February 1991
Commission decision no. IV/32659 IATA Passenger Agency Programme, of 30 July 1991
Commission decision no. IV/32725 Viho/Parker Pen, of 15 July 1992
Commission decision no. IV/32732 Ijsselcentrale, of 16 January 1991
Commission decision no. IV/32736 Moosehead/Whitbread, of 23 March 1990
Commission decision no. IV/32737 Eirpage, of 8 October 1991
Commission decision no. IV/32745 Astra, of 23 December 1992
Commission decision no. IV/32792 IATA agency programs, of 30 July 1991
Commission decision no. IV/32797 IV/32798 Lloyd's Underwriters' Association and The Institute of London Underwriters, of 4 December 1992
Commission decision no. IV/32879 Viho/Toshiba, of 5 June 1991
Commission decision no. IV/32948 and IV/34590 Tretorn, of 21 December 1994
Commission decision no. IV/33016 Ansac, of 19 December 1990
Commission decision no. IV/33031 Fiat/Hitachi, of 21 December 1992
Commission decision no. IV/33100 Assurpol, of 14 January 1992
Commission decision no. IV/33151 IV/33997 Jahrhundertvertrag VIK-GVSt, of 23 December 1992
Commission decision no. IV/33157 Eco System/Peugeot, of 4 December 1991
Commission decision no. IV/33242 Yves Saint Laurent Parfums, of 16 December 1991
Commission decision no. IV/33374 Ladbroke, of 29 July 1993
Commission decision no. IV/33384 IV/33378 Distribution of package tours during the 1990 World Cup, of 27 October 1992
Commission decision no. IV/33407 CNSD, of 13 August 1993
Commission decision no. IV/33473 Scottish Nuclear Energy Agreement, of 30 April 1991
Commission decision no. IV/33542 Parfums Givenchy system of selective distribution, of 24 July 1992
Commission decision no. IV/33585 Distribution of railway tickets by travel agents, of 25 November 1992
Commission decision no. IV/33640 Exxon/Shell, of 18 May 1994
Commission decision no. IV/33686 Coapi, of 30 January 1995
Commission decision no. IV/33814 Ford/VW, of 23 December 1992
Commission decision no. IV/33863 Asahi/Saint-Gobain, of 16 December 1994
Commission decision no. IV/33941 HOV SVZ/MCN, of 29 March 1994
Commission decision no. IV/34018 Far East Trade Tariff and Surcharges Agreement (FETTSCA), of 16 May 2000
Commission decision no. IV/34252 Philips-Osram, of 21 December 1994

Commission decision no. IV/34279 ADALAT, of 10 January 1996
Commission decision no. IV/34410 Olivetti/Digital, of 11 November 1994
Commission decision no. IV/34446 Trans-Atlantic Agreement, of 19 October 1994
Commission decision no. IV/34456 Stichting Baksteen, of 29 April 1994
Commission decision no. IV/34466 Greek ferries, of 9 December 1998
Commission decision no. IV/34494 Tariff structures in the combined transport of goods, of 24 February 1993
Commission decision no. IV/34518 ACI, of 27 July 1994
Commission decision no. IV/34600 Night Services, of 21 September 1994
Commission decision no. IV/34607 Banque Nationale de Paris – Dresdner Bank, of 24 June 1996
Commission decision no. IV/34857 BT/MCI, of 27 July 1994
Commission decision no. IV/34891 Fujitsu AMD Semiconductor, of 12 December 1994
Commission decision no. IV/35079 Whitbread, of 24 February 1999
Commission decision no. IV/35280 Sicasov, of 14 December 1998
Commission decision no. IV/35337 Atlas, of 17 July 1996
Commission decision no. IV/35545 LH/SAS, of 16 January 1996
Commission decision no. IV/35612 Tuborg/Pripps, of 18 June 1998
Commission decision no. IV/35617 Phoenix/GlobalOne, of 17 July 1996
Commission decision no IV/35679 Novalliance/Systemform, of 4 December 1996
Commission decision no. IV/35733 VW, of 28 January 1998
Commission decision no. IV/35738 Uniworld, of 29 October 1997
Commission decision no. IV/35814 Alloy surcharge, of 21 January 1998
Commission decision no. IV/35830 Unisource, of 29 October 1997
Commission decision no. IV/35855 Scandairy, of 28 July 1997
Commission decision no. IV/35860B 39041 Seamless steel tube, of 8 December 1999
Commission decision no. IV/36147 EPI code of conduct, of 7 April 1999
Commission decision no. IV/36212 Carbonless paper, of 20 December 2001
Commission decision no. IV/36213 GEAE/P&W, of 14 September 1999
Commission decision no. IV/36237 TPS, of 3 March 1999
Commission decision no. IV/36253 P&O Stena Line, of 26 January 1999
Commission decision no. IV/36490 Graphite electrodes, of 18 July 2001
Commission decision no. IV/36494 EACEM, of 15 April 1998
Commission decision no. IV/36539 British Interactive Broadcasting, of 15 September 1999
Commission decision no. IV/36592 Cégétel, of 20 May 1999
Commission decision no. IV/36718 CECED, of 24 January 1999
Commission decision no. IV/36748 REIMS II, of 15 September 1999
Commission decision no. IV/36836 Yoplait/Valio, of 23 June 1999
Commission decision no. IV/36849 MPEG-2, of 18 December 1998
Commission decision no. IV/36851 Mouscron, of 3 December 1999
Commission decision no. IV/36957 IV/36997 IV/37121 IV/37138 IV/37380 Glaxo Wellcome, of 8 May 2001
Commission decision no. IV/37124 FIFA rules on players' agents, of 16 April 2002
Commission decision no. IV/37231 ACEA, of 11 September 1998
Commission decision no. IV/37396 Revised Trans-Atlantic Conference Agreement, of 14 November 2002
Commission decision no. IV/37398 Joint selling of the commercial rights of the UEFA Champions League, of 23 July 2003
Commission decision no. IV/37506 DVD Patent Licensing Programme, of 9 October 2000
Commission decision no. IV/37533 Choline chloride, of 9 December 2004
Commission decision no. IV/37634 JAMA, of 1 December 1999
Commission decision no. IV/37730 AuA/LH, of 5 July 2002
Commission decision no. IV/37732 Synergen, of 31 May 2002
Commission decision no. IV/37750 French beer market, of 29 September 2004

Commission decision no. IV/37802 Precision Blasting, of 8 May 2000
Commission decision no. IV/37812 Bmi British Midland/Lufthansa/SAS, of 13 June 2001
Commission decision no. IV/37889 GM/Fiat, of 16 August 2000
Commission decision no. IV/37978 Methylglucamine, of 27 November 2002
Commission decision no. IV/37980 Souris, of 26 May 2004
Commission decision no. IV/38121 Fittings, of 20 September 2006
Commission decision no. IV/38170 REIMS II renotification, of 23 October 2003
Commission decision no. IV/38240 Industrial tubes, of 16 December 2003
Commission decision no. IV/38287 Telenor/Canal+/Canal Digital, of 29 December 2003
Commission decision no. IV/38337 Thread, of 14 September 2005
Commission decision no. IV/38354 Industrial bags, of 30 November 2005
Commission decision no. IV/38369 Network Sharing Rahmenvertrag, of 16 July 2003
Commission decision no. IV/38370 UK Network Sharing Agreement, of 30 April 2003
Commission decision no. IV/38427 Pay Television Film Output Agreements, of 26 October 2004
Commission decision no. IV/38456 Bitumen Nederland, of 12 September 2006
Commission decision no. IV/38477 British Airways/SN Brussels Airlines, of 10 March 2003
Commission decision no. IV/38479 British Airways and Iberia, of 10 December 2003
Commission decision no. IV/38620 Hydrogen peroxide, of 3 May 2006
Commission decision no. IV/38645 Methacrylates, of 31 May 2006
Commission decision no. IV/38767 FIPCOM/Koninklijke Philips Electronics N.V., of 9 February 2006
Commission decision no. IV/39125 Carglass, of 12 November 2008
Commission decision no. IV/39142 Toyota Motor Europe, of 13 September 2007
Commission decision no. IV/39177 Which?/DFB + Mastercard + FIFA, of 2 May 2013
Commission decision no. IV/39181 Candle waxes, of 1 October 2008
Commission decision no. IV/39437 TV and computer monitor tubes, of 5 December 2012
Commission decision no. IV/39452 Mountings for windows and window-doors, of 28 March 2012
Commission decision no. IV/39462 Freight Forwarding, of 28 March 2012
Commission decision no. IV/39574 Smart card chips, of 3 September 2014
Commission decision no. IV/39596 BA/AA/IB, of 14 July 2010
Commission decision no. IV/39600 Refrigeration compressors, of 7 December 2011
Commission decision no. IV/39610 Power cables, of 2 April 2014
Commission decision no. IV/39636 Rights Agency Ltd/SCAPR a.o., of 11 March 2011
Commission decision no. IV/39736 SIEMENS/AREVA, of 18 June 2012
Commission decision no. IV/39745 CDS Information Market, of 20 July 2016
Commission decision no. IV/39780 Envelopes, of 10 December 2014
Commission decision no. IV/39824 Trucks, of 19 July 2016
Commission decision no. IV/39850 Container Shipping, of 7 July 2016
Commission decision no. IV/39861 Yen Interest Rate Derivatives (YIRD), of 4 December 2013
Commission decision no. IV/39876 EPC online payments, of 13 June 2013
Commission decision no. IV/39914 Euro Interest Rate Derivatives, of 4 December 2013
Commission decision no. IV/39943 E5 – Cooperation among large telecom operators, of 7 March 2013
Commission decision no. IV/39960 Thermal Systems, of 8 March 2017
Commission decision no. IV/39964 Air France/KLM/Alitalia/Delta, of 12 May 2015
Commission decision no. IV/399904 Rechargeable battery, of 12 December 2016
Commission decision no. IV/4 and IV/3344 Grundig/Consten, of 20 October 1964
Commission decision no. IV/400 Agreements between manufacturers of glass containers, of 15 May 1974
Commission decision no. IV/40013 Lighting Systems, of 21 June 2017
Commission decision no. IV/40018 Car battery recycling, of 8 February 2017
Commission decision no. IV/40028 Alternators and Starters, of 27 January 2016

Commission decision no. IV/40055 Parking heaters, of 17 June 2015
Commission decision no. IV/40360 production and distribution of audiobooks, of 19 January 2017
Commission decision no. IV/417 BPICA, of 30 April 1982
Commission decision no. IV/417 BPICA, of 7 November 1977
Commission decision no. IV/4204 Velcro/Aplix, of 12 July 1985
Commission decision no. IV/426 Papiers peints de Belgique, of 23 July 1974
Commission decision no. IV/428 VBVB/VBBB, of 25 November 1981
Commission decision no. IV/5715 Junghans, of 21 December 1976
Commission decision no. IV/581 Cementregeling voor Nederland, of 18 December 1972
Commission decision no. IV/597 V.V.V.F, of 25 June 1969
Commission decision no. IV/642 Papier mince, of 26 June 1972
Commission decision no. IV/712 Stoves and Heaters, of 3 June 1975
Commission decision no. IV/791 IV/1373 IV/1374 IV/1498 IV/1499 and IV/1500 SCPA, of 11 May 1973
Commission decision no. IV/795 Kali und Salz/Kali Chemie, of 21 December 1973
Commission decision no. IV/847 Saba, of 15 December 1975
Commission decision no. IV/93 EMO, of 7 December 1978
Commission decision no. IV/93 European Machine Tool Exhibition, of 7 December 1978
Commission decision no. IV/93 European Machine Tool Exhibitions, of 13 March 1969
Commission decision no. IV30373 IV/37143 P&I Clubs, of 12 April 1999
Commission decision no. M.8677 Siemens/Alstom, of 6 February 2019
Commission letter rejecting a compliant regarding Asia Motor France III, of 13 October 1994
Commission press release IP-96-1183 regarding Roundwood trade, of 17 December 1996
Commission press release IP/00/297 regarding Gas Natural/Endesa, of 27 March 2000
Commission press release IP/01/1433 IATA, of 19 October 2001
Commission press release IP/01/1690 Bank J.Van Breda & Co, of 14 May 2001
Commission press release IP/01/1845 Scandinavian digital satellite TV broadcasting, of 20 December 2001
Commission press release IP/01/554 SNS, of 11 April 2001
Commission press release IP/01/634 Bayerische Landesbank Girozentrale, of 3 May 2001
Commission press release IP/01/635 Ulster Bank, of 3 May 2001
Commission press release IP/01/650 Dutch and Belgian banks, of 7 May 2001
Commission press release IP/01/82 Broadcasting in Belgium of French horseraces, of 22 January 2001
Commission press release IP/13/82 regarding European Minibulk and Container Feeder cooperatives, of 31 January 2013
Commission press release IP/19/94/345 Interbrew exclusive right, of 28 April 1994
Commission press release IP/95/550 regarding Interconnector, of 1 June 1995
Commission press release IP/96/1183 regarding CECED, of 11 February 2000
Commission press release IP/96/400 Baltic Liner Conference Agreement, of 8 May 1996
Commission press release IP/98/353 regarding Photo-graphic manufacturers, of 15 April 1998
Commission press release IP/98/355 Danish Tennis Federation, of 15 April 1998
Commission press release IV/37811 regarding Algerian gas export contracts, of 11 July 2007
Commission press release IV/38307 regarding PO/Territorial restrictions Germany Gazprom, of 10 June 2005
Commission press release IV/39699 regarding Baltic Max Feeder 2010

Court of Justice

C-1/12 Ordem dos Técnicos Oficiais de Contas, ECLI:EU:C:2013:127
C-107/84 Commission v Germany, ECLI:EU:C:1985:332
C-108/09 Online distribution of contact lenses, ECLI:EU:C:2010:725
C-119/97P Ufex, ECLI:EU:C:1999:116

C-121/16 Salumificio, ECLI:EU:C:2016:543
C-123/83 BNIC, ECLI:EU:C:1985:33
C-125/78 GEMA, ECLI:EU:C:1979:237
C-126/80 SALONIA, ECLI:EU:C:1981:136
C-127/73 SABAM, ECLI:EU:C:1974:6
C-13/61 Bosch, ECLI:EU:C:1962:11
C-13/77 INNO, ECLI:EU:C:1977:185
C-132/19P Cross-border access to pay-TV, ECLI: EU: C: 2020:1007
C-136/12 Consiglio nazionale dei geologi, ECLI:EU:C:2013:489
C-136/86 BINC, ECLI:EU:C:1987:524
C-137/95P Building and Construction Industry in the Netherlands, ECLI:EU:C:1996:130
C-138/11 Compass-Datenbank, ECLI:EU:C:2012:449
C-14/68 Walt Wilhelm, ECLI:EU:C:1969:4
C-140/94 C-141/94 C-142/94 DIP SpA, ECLI:EU:C:1995:330
C-15/74 Centeafarm, ECLI:EU:C:1974:114
C-159/94 Commission v France, ECLI:EU:C:1997:501
C-161/84 Pronuptia, ECLI:EU:C:1986:41
C-167/04P JCB Service, ECLI:EU:C:2006:594
C-17/74 Transocean Marine Paint, ECLI:EU:C:1974:106
C-171/05P FIFA rules on players' agents, EU:C:2006:149
C-172/80 Züchner, ECLI:EU:C:1981:178
C-188/86 Lefèvre, ECLI:EU:C:1987:327
C-189/02 Dansk Rørindustri, ECLI:EU:C:2005:408
C-19/77 Miller International, ECLI:EU:C:1978:19
C-19/92 Yves Saint Laurent Perfumes, ECLI:EU:C:1993:125
C-193/83 Windsurfing surfing International, ECLI:EU:C:1986:75
C-198/01 Consorzio Industrie Fiammiferi (CIF), ECLI:EU:C:2003:430
C-2/91 Meng, ECLI:EU:C:1993:885
C-209/07 Beef Industry, ECLI:EU:C:2008:643
C-210/81 REVOX, ECLI:EU:C:1983:277
C-215/84 Ferey, ECLI:EU:C:1985:369
C-218/00 Cisal di Battistello Venanzio & C. Sas, ECLI:EU:C:2002:36
C-219/00P Cementir, CLI:EU:C:2002:337
C-222/98 Hendrik van der Woude, ECLI:EU:C:2000:475
C-226/11 Expedia, EU:C:2012:795
C-229/83 Leclerc, ECLI:EU:C:1985:1
C-23/99 Pre-Insulated Pipe Cartel, ECLI:EU:C:2000:500
C-230/16 Coty, ECLI:EU:C:2017:941
C-230/96 Cabour, ECLI:EU:C:1998:181
C-231/83 Cullet, CLI:EU:C:1985:29
C-234/89 Delimitis, ECLI:EU:C:1991:91
C-235/92P Polypropylene, ECLI:EU:C:1999:362
C-238/05 Asnef-Equifax, Servicios de Información sobre Solvencia y Crédito, SL v. Asociación de Usuarios de Servicios Bancarios, EU:C:2006:734
C-243/83 Binon, ECLI:EU:C:1985:284
C-245/91 Ohra Schadeverzekeringen, ECLI:EU:C:1993:887
C-248/98P Cartonboard, ECLI:EU:C:2000:625
C-250/03 Giorgio Emanuele Mauri, ECLI:EU:C:2005:96
C-250/92 Gøttrup-Klim Grovvareforening, ECLI:EU:C:1994:413
C-254/87 Syndicat des libraires de Normandie, ECLI:EU:C:1988:413
C-258/78 Maize seed, ECLI:EU:C:1982:211
C-26/76 Metro I, ECLI:EU:C:1977:167
C-262/81 Coditel, ECLI:EU:C:1982:334
C-264/95P Distribution of railway tickets by travel agents, ECLI:EU:C:1997:143

C-266/96 Corsica Ferries France SA, ECLI:EU:C:1998:306
C-27/76 United Brands, ECLI:EU:C:1978:22
C-279/95P Langnese-Iglo, ECLI:EU:C:1998:447
C-28/77 Theal/Watts, ECLI:EU:C:1978:133
C-282/95P Guérin Automobile, ECLI:EU:C:1997
C-299/83 Leclerc, ECLI:EU:C:1985:326
C-30/78 The Distillers Company Ltd, ECLI:EU:C:1980:186
C-30/87 Bodson, ECLI:EU:C:1988:225
C-306/96 Javico International, ECLI:EU:C:1998:173
C-308/04P Graphite electrodes, ECLI:EU:C:2006:433
C-309/99 Wouters, ECLI:EU:C:2002:98
C-31/80 L'Oréal, ECLI:EU:C:1980:289
C-311/85 Vlaamse Reisbureaus, ECLI:EU:C:1987:418
C-32/11 Allianz, ECLI:EU:C:2013:160
C-32/65 Italy v the Commission and Council, EU:C:1966:42
C-327/12 Ministero dello Sviluppo economico, ECLI:EU:C:2013:827
C-332/89 Marchandise, ECLI:EU:C:1991:94
C-338/00P VW, ECLI:EU:C:2003:473
C-343/95 Calì, ECLI:EU:C:1997:160
C-344/98 Masterfoods, ECLI:EU:C:2000:689
C-35/83 Tokecs/Dorcet, ECLI:EU:C:1985:32
C-35/99 Manuele Arduino, ECLI:EU:C:2002:97
C-350/07 Kattner Stahlbau, ECLI:EU:C:2009:127
C-360/92P Net Book Agreements, ECLI:EU:C:1995:6
C-375/09 Tele2Polska, ECLI:EU:C:2011:270
C-38/97 Autotrasporti Librandi Snc di Librandi F. & C., ECLI:EU:C:1998:454
C-382/12P MasterCard Inc., EU:C:2014:2201
C-386/07 Hospital Consulting, ECLI:EU:C:2008:256
C-399/93 H. G. Oude Luttikhuis, ECLI:EU:C:1995:434
C-40/12P Industrial bags, CLI:EU:C:2013:768
C-401/96P Asia Motor France III, ECLI:EU:C:1998:208
C-41/90 Höfner, ECLI:EU:C:1991:161
C-41/96 VAG-Händlerbeirat eV, ECLI:EU:C:1997:283
C-413/13 FNV Kunsten Informatie en Media, ECLI:EU:C:2014:2411
C-42/84 Nutricia-de Rooij and Nutricia-Zuid-Hollandse Conservenfabriek, ECLI:EU:C:1985:327
C-43/85 UINDI, ECLI:EU:C:1987:347
C-437/09 AG2R Prévoyance, ECLI:EU:C:2011:112
C-439/09 Pierre Fabre, ECLI:EU:C:2011:649
C-439/11P Ziegler, ECLI:EU:C:2013:513
C-441/07P Alrosa, ECLI:EU:C:2010:377
C-450/98P IECC, ECLI:EU:C:2001:276
C-46/87 C-227/88 Hoechst, ECLI:EU:C:1989:337
C-461/03 Gaston, ECLI:EU:C:2005:742
C-462/19 Asociación Nacional de Empresas Estibadoras y Consignatarios de Buques (Anesco), ECLI:EU:C:2020:715
C-47/76 De Norre, ECLI:EU:C:1977:11
C-475/99 Ambulanz Glöckner, ECLI:EU:C:2001:577
C-5/69 Völk, ECLI:EU:C:1969:35
C-5/79 Buys, ECLI:EU:C:1979:238
C-515/15P Prestressing steel, ECLI:EU:C:2016:298
C-519/04P Meca-Medina and Majcen/IOC, ECLI:EU:C:2006:492
C-519/15P Prestressing steel, ECLI:EU:C:2016:682
C-52/09 TeliaSonera, ECLI:EU:C:2011:83

C-523/15P Prestressing steel, ECLI:EU:C:2016:541
C-547/16 Gasorba, ECLI:EU:C:2017:891
C-56/65 Société Technique Minière, ECLI:EU:C:1966:38
C-58/12P Industrial bags, ECLI:EU:C:2013:770
C-580/12P Guardian, ECLI:EU:C:2014:2363
C-61/80 Rennet, ECLI:EU:C:1981:75
C-63/75 Fonderies, ECLI:EU:C:1976:15
C-66/86 Flugreisen, ECLI:EU:C:1989:140
C-67/13P Cartes bancaires, ECLI:EU:C:2014:2204
C-67/86 Van Eycke, ECLI:EU:C:1986:187
C-67/96 Albany, ECLI:EU:C:1999:430
C-671/15 Endive, ECLI:EU:C:2017:860
C-681/11 Schenker, ECLI:EU:C:2013:404
C-70/93 BMW, ECLI:EU:C:1995:344
C-71/74 Frubo, ECLI:EU:C:1975:61
C-75/84 SABA, ECLI:EU:C:1986:399
C-8/08 C-96/82 C-97/82 C-98/82 C-99/82 C-100/82 C-101/82 C-102/82 C-103/82 C-104/82 C-105/82 C-108/82 C-110/82 AVEWA-ANSEAU, ECLI:EU:C:1983:310
C-8/08 T-Mobile, ECLI:EU:C:2009:343
C-8/95P UK Agricultural Tractor Registration Exchange, ECLI:EU:C:1998:257
C-94/74 IGAV, ECLI:EU:C:1975:81
C-96/94 Centro Servizi Spediporto Srl, ECLI:EU:C:1995:308
C-364/92 SAT Fluggesellschaft, ECLI:EU:C:1994:7
Joined Cases C-100/80 C-101/80 C-102/80 C-103/80 Pioneer Hi-fi equipment, ECLI:EU:C:1983:158
Joined Cases C-115/97 C-116/97 C-117/97 Brentjens' Handelsonderneming BV, ECLI:EU:C:1999:434
Joined Cases C-159/91 C-160/91 Poucet, ECLI:EU:C:1993:63
Joined Cases C-177/82 C-178/82 Van De Haar, ECLI:EU:C:1984:144
Joined Cases C-180/98 C-181/98 C-182/98 C-183/98 C-184/98 C-185/98 Pavel Pavlov, ECLI:EU:C:2000:428
Joined Cases C-184/13 C-185/13 C-186/13 C-187/13 C-194/13 C-195/13 C-208/13 API, ECLI:EU:C:2013:663
Joined Cases C-186/02P C-188/02P Ramondín, ECLI:EU:C:2004:702
Joined Cases C-209/84 C-210/84 C-211/84 C-212/84 C-213/84 Asjes, ECLI:EU:C:1986:188
Joined Cases C-240/82 C-241/82 C-242/82 C-261/82 C-262/82 C-268/82 C-269/82 SSI, ECLI:EU:C:1985:488
Joined Cases C-25/84 C-26/84 Distribution system of Ford-Werke AG, ECLI:EU:C:1985:340
Joined Cases C-253/78 C-3/79 Procureur de la République, ECLI:EU:C:1980:188
Joined Cases C-264/01 C-306/01 C-354/01 C-355/01 AOK Bundesverband, ECLI:EU:C:2004:150
Joined Cases C-359/95P C-379/95P Ladbroke, ECLI:EU:C:1997:531
Joined Cases C-40/73 C-41/73 to 48/73 C-50/73 C-54/73 to 56/73 C-111/73 C-113/73 C-114/73 European sugar industry, ECLI:EU:C:1975:174
Joined Cases C-403/08 C-429/08 Football Association Premier League Ltd, ECLI:EU:C:2011:631
Joined Cases C-427/16 C-428/16 CHEZ, ECLI:EU:C:2017:890
Joined Cases C-43/82 and C-63/82 VBVB/VBBB, ECLI:EU:C:1984:9
Joined Cases C-501/06P C-513/06P C-515/06P C-519/06P GlaxoSmithKline, EU:C:2009:610
Joined Cases C-56/64 C-58/64 Grundig/Consten, ECLI:EU:C:1966:41
Joined Cases C-8/66 C-9/66 C-10/66 C-11/66 Noordwijks Cement Accoord, ECLI:EU:C:1967:7
Joined Cases C-89/85 C-104/85 C-104/85 C-114/85 C-116/85 C-117/85 C-125/85 C-129/85 Wood pulp, ECLI:EU:C:1988:447

Joined Cases C-89/85 C-104/85 C-114/85 C-116/85 C-117/85 and C-125/85 to C-129/85 Woodpulp, ECLI:EU:C:1993:120
Joined Cases C-94/04 C-202/04 Federico Cipolla, ECLI:EU:C:2006:758

GC

T-106/95 FFSA, ECLI:EU:T:1997:23
T-11/06 Raw tobacco-Italy, ECLI:EU:T:2011:560
T-11/89 Polypropylene, ECLI:EU:T:1992:33
T-111/08 MasterCard, ECLI:EU:T:2012:260
T-112/99 Métropole, ECLI:EU:T:2001:215
T-114/92 BEMIM, ECLI EU:T:1995:11
T-12/06 Raw tobacco-Italy, ECLI:EU:T:2011:441
T-127/04 Industrial tubes ECLI:EU:T:2009:142
T-13/89 Polypropylene, ECLI:EU:T:1992:35
T-131/99 Whitbread, ECLI:EU:T:2002:83
T-14/89 Polypropylene, ECLI:EU:T:1992:36
T-14/93 Distribution of railway tickets by travel agents, ECLI:EU:T:1995:96
T-141/89 Welded steel mesh, ECLI:EU:T:1995:62
T-142/89 Welded steel mesh, ECLI:EU:T:1995:63
T-144/99 EPI code of conduct, ECLI:EU:T:2001:105
T-148/89 Welded steel mesh, ECLI:EU:T:1995:68
T-154/98 Asia Motor France IV, ECLI:EU:T:2000:243
T-168/01 GlaxoSmithKline, EU:T:2006:2969
T-17/02 Fred Olsen, ECLI:EU:T:2005:218
T-17/93 Ford/Volkswagen, ECLI:EU:T:1994:89
T-185/00 Eurovision, ECLI:EU:T:2002:242
T-19/91 Vichy, ECLI:EU:T:1992:28
T-19/92 Yves Saint Laurent Perfumes, ECLI:EU:T:1996:190
T-191/98 Atlantic Container Line, ECLI:EU:T:2003:245
T-193/02 FIFA rules on players' agents, EU:T:2005:22
T-208/13 Telefónica/Portugal Telecom, ECLI:EU:T:2016:368
T-213/00 Far East Trade Tariff Charges and Surcharges Agreement (FETTCSA), ECLI:EU:T:2003:76
T-216/13 Telefónica-Portugal Telecom, ECLI:EU:T:2016:369
T-219/99 British Airways, ECLI:EU:T:2003:343
T-23/99 Pre-Insulated Pipe Cartel, ECLI:EU:T:2002:75
T-231/99 Bass, ECLI:EU:T:2002:84
T-24/90 Automec II, ECLI:EU:T:1992:97
T-25/05 Copper plumbing tubes, CLI:EU:T:2010:206
T-271/03 Deutsche Telekom, ECLI:EU:T:2008:101
T-274/06 Repsol, ECLI:EU:T:2007:323
T-289/01 Der Grüne Punkt – Duales System Deutschland, EU:T:2007:155
T-29/05 Raw tobacco-Spain, CLI:EU:T:2010:355
T-29/92 Building and Construction Industry in the Netherlands, ECLI:EU:T:1995:34
T-30/05 PO/Needles, ECLI:EU:T:2007:267
T-30/89 Hilti, ECLI:EU:T:1991:70
T-309/94 Cartonboard, ECLI:EU:T:1998:91
T-313/02 Meca-Medina and Majcen/IOC, ECLI:EU:T:2004:282
T-325/01 Mercedes-Benz, ECLI:EU:T:2005:322
T-325/16 České dráh, ECLI:EU:T:2018:368
T-328/03 O2, ECLI:EU:T:2006:116
T-34/92 UK Agricultural Tractor Registration Exchange, ECLI:EU:T:1994:258

T-347/94 Cartonboard, ECLI:EU:T:1998:101
T-35/92 UK Agricultural Tractor Registration Exchange, ECLI:EU:T:1994:259
T-352/09 Calcium carbide and magnesium based reagents for the steel, ECLI:EU:T:2012:673
T-353/06 Bitumen, ECLI:EU:T:2012:484
T-355/13 EasyJet, ECLI:EU:T:2015:36
T-357/06 Bitumen, ECLI:EU:T:2012:488
T-357/06 Koninklijke Wegenbouw Stevi, ECLI:EU:T:2012:488
T-360/09 E.ON/GDF, ECLI:EU:T:2012:332
T-362/02 Bitumen, ECLI:EU:T:2006:161
T-370/09 GDF Suez SA, ECLI:EU:T:2012:333
T-387/94 Asia Motor France III, ECLI:EU:T:1996:120
T-39/06 Raw tobacco-Italy, ECLI:EU:T:2011:562
T-392/09 Calcium carbide and magnesium based reagents for the steel and gas industries, CLI: EU:T:2012:674
T-393/10 Prestressing steel, CLI:EU:T:2015:515
T-395/94 Trans-Atlantic Agreement, ECLI:EU:T:2002:49
T-400/09 Calcium carbide and magnesium based reagents for the steel and gas industries, ECLI:EU:T:2012:675
T-406/09 Calcium carbide and magnesium based reagents for the steel and gas industries, ECLI:EU:T:2014:254
T-419/03 Altstoff Recycling Austria AG, EU:T:2010:975
T-427/08 Watch Repair, ECLI:EU:T:2010:517
T-44/00 Seamless steel tubes, ECLI:EU:T:2004:218
T-447/12 Visa MIF, ECLI:EU:T:2014:247
T-451/08 CISAC, CLI:EU:T:2013:189
T-452/05 PO/Thread, ECLI:EU:T:2010:167
T-456/05 T-457/05 PO/Thread, ECLI:EU:T:2010:168
T-456/10 Animal feed phosphates, ECLI:EU:T:2015:296
T-460/13 Lundbeck, ECLI:EU:T:2016:453
T-461/07 Visa, ECLI:EU:T:2011:181
T-467/13 Lundbeck, ECLI:EU:T:2016:450
T-469/13 Lundbeck, ECLI:EU:T:2016:454
T-470/13 Lundbeck, ECLI:EU:T:2016:452
T-471/13 Lundbeck, ECLI:EU:T:2016:460
T-472/13 Lundbeck, ECLI:EU:T:2016:449
T-48/00 Corus, ECLI:EU:T:2004:219
T-480/15 Agria Polska, ECLI:EU:T:2017:339
T-491/07 Cartes bancaires, EU:T:2012:633
T-50/00 Seamless steel tubes, ECLI:EU:T:2004:220
T-51/06 Industrial bags, ECLI:EU:T:2011:666
T-51/89 Tetra Pak, ECLI:EU:T:1990:41
T-513/93 Consiglio Nazionale degli Spedizionieri Doganali (CNSD), ECLI:EU:T:2000:91
T-531/18 LL-Carpenter, ECLI: EU: T: 2020: 91
T-54/14 Shrimp, ECLI:EU:T:2016:455
T-544/08 Candle Waxes, ECLI:EU:T:2014:1075
T-548/93 Ladbroke, ECLI:EU:T:1995:168
T-574/14 EAEPC, ECLI:EU:T:2018:605
T-575/93 Buma, ECLI:EU:T:1996:1
T-58/14 Shrimps, ECLI: EU: T: 2018: 474
T-587/08 Bananas, ECLI:EU:T:2013:129
T-59/99 Greek Ferries, ECLI:EU:T:2003:334
T-6/89 Polypropylene, CLI:EU:T:1991:74
T-65/98 Van den Bergh Foods, CLI:EU:T:2003:281
T-65/99 Greek Ferries, ECLI:EU:T:2003:336

T-655/11 Exotic Fruit (Bananas), ECLI:EU:T:2015:383
T-66/89 Net Book Agreements, ECLI:EU:T:1992:84
T-66/99 Greek Ferries, ECLI:EU:T:2003:337
T-679/14 Teva UK, ECLI:EU:T:2018:919
T-691/14 Servier, ECLI:EU:T:2018:922
T-699/14 Licensing of intellectual property rights for football collectibles, CLI:EU:T:2017:2
T-7/89 Polypropylene, ECLI:EU:T:1991:75
T-7/92 Asia Motor II, ECLI:EU:T:1993:52
T-7/93 Langnese-Iglo, ECLI:EU:T:1995:98
T-70/10 Concrete reinforcing bars, re-adoption, ECLI:EU:T:2014:1031
T-701/14 Niche Generics, ECLI:EU:T:2018:921
T-705/14 Unichem Laboratories, ECLI:EU:T:2018:91
T-712/14 Watch Repair, ECLI:EU:T:2017:748
T-8/89 Polypropylene, CLI:EU:T:1991:76
T-83/91 Tetra Pak International, ECLI:EU:T:1994:246
T-86/95 Far Eastern Freight Conference, ECLI:EU:T:2002:50
T-88/92 Perfumes Givenchy system of selective distribution, ECLI:EU:T:1996:192
T-9/92 Eco System, ECLI:EU:T:1993:38
T-9/93 Langnese-Iglo, ECLI:EU:T:1995:99
T-90/11 Labco/ONP, ECLI:EU:T:2014:1049
T-69/10 Concrete reinforcing bars, re-adoption, ECLI:EU:T:2014:1030
T-85/10 Concrete reinforcing bars, re-adoption, ECLI:EU:T:2014:1037
T-680/14 Lupin, ECLI:EU:T:2018:908
T-682/14 Mylan Laboratories, ECLI:EU:T:2018:907
Joined Cases T-101/05 T-111/05 BASF UCB, ECLI:EU:T:2007:380
Joined Cases T-185/00 T-216/00 T-299/00 T-300/00 Eurovision, ECLI:EU:T:2002:242
Joined Cases T-213/95 T-18/96 Stichting Certificatie Kraanverhuurbedrijf and the Federatie van Nederlandse Kraanverhuurbedrijven, ECLI:EU:T:1997:157
Joined Cases T-217/03 T-245/03 French beef, ECLI:EU:T:2006:391
Joined Cases T-231/01 T-214/01 Österreichische Postsparkasse, ECLI:EU:T:2006:151
Joined Cases T-259/02 T-260/02 T-261/02 T-262/02 T-263/02 T-264/02 T-271/02 Austrian banks – 'Lombard Club', EU T:2006:5169
Joined Cases T-374/94 T-375/94 T-384/94 T-388/94 Night Services, ECLI:EU:T:1998:198
Joined Cases T-39/92 T-40/92 Eurocheque, ECLI:EU:T:1994:20
Joined Cases T-489/09 T-490/09 T-56/10 Concrete reinforcing bars, ECLI:EU:T:2014:1039
Joined Cases T-49/02 T-50/02 T-51/02 Brasserie, ECLI:EU:T:2005:298
Joined Cases T-528/93 T-542/93 T-543/93 T-546/93 EBU/Eurovision System, ECLI:EU:T:1996:99
Joined Cases T-71/03 T-74/03 T-87/03 T-91/03 Speciality Graphite, ECLI:EU:T:2005:220
Joined Cases T-79/95 80/95 Eurotunnel, ECLI:EU:T:1996:155
Joined Cases T-109/02 T-118/02 T-122/02 T-125/02 T-126/02 T-128/02 T-129/02 T-132/02 T-136/02 Carbonless paper, ECLI:EU:T:2007:115
Joined Cases T-458/09 T-171/10 Slovak Telekom, ECLI:EU:T:2012:145

Advocate General Opinions

AG Cosmas opinion in C-359/95P C-379/95P Ladbroke, ECLI:EU:C:1997:234
AG Darmon opinion in C-185/91 Bundesanstalt für den Güterfernverkehr, ECLI:EU:C:1993:309
AG Fennelly opinion in C-140/94 C-141/94 C-142/94 DIP SpA, ECLI:EU:C:1995:226
AG Fennelly opinion in C-266/96 Corsica Ferries France SA, ECLI:EU:C:1998:19
AG Fennelly opinion in C-70/95 Sodemare, EU: C:1997:55
AG Jacobs opinion in C-180/98 C-181/98 C-182/98 C-184/98 C-185/98 Pavel Pavlov, CLI:EU:C:2000:151

AG Jacobs opinion in C-264/01 C-306/01 C-354/01 C-355/01 AOK Bundesverband, ECLI:EU:C:2003:304
AG Jacobs opinion in C-67/96 C-115/97 116/97 C-117/97 C-219/97 Albany, ECLI:EU:C:1999:28
AG Kokott opinion in C-226/11 Expedia, ECLI:EU:C:2012:544
AG Kokott opinion in C-8/08 T-Mobile, ECLI:EU:C:2009:110
AG Léger opinion in C-309/99 Wouters, ECLI:EU:C:2001:390
AG Léger opinion in C-35/99 Manuele Arduino, ECLI:EU:C:2001:389
AG Mazák opinion in C-439/09 Pierre Fabre, ECLI:EU:C:2011:113
AG Poiares Maduro opinion in C-205/03P FENIN, ECLI:EU:C:2005:666
AG Poiares Maduro opinion in C-94/04 C-202/04 Federico Cipolla, ECLI:EU:C:2006:76
AG Saugmandsgaard Øe opinion in C-179/16 Hoffmann-La Roche,ECLI:EU:C:2017:714
AG Tesauro opinion in C-2/91 Meng, ECLI:EU:C:1993:308
AG Tesauro opinion in C-250/92 Gøttrup-Klim, ECLI:EU:C:1994:249
AG Wahl opinion in C-230/16 Coty, ECLI:EU:C:2017:603

FRANCE

Autorité de la concurrence/Conseil de la concurrence

Autorité de la concurrence decision no. 09-D-18 Marseille transportation, of 2 June 2009
Autorité de la concurrence decision no. 09-D-25 Work on railway tracks, of 29 July 2009
Autorité de la concurrence decision no. 09-D-31 Football rights, of 1 October 2009
Autorité de la concurrence decision no. 10-D-01 iPhone marketing, of 12 January 2010
Autorité de la concurrence decision no. 10-D-13 Le Havre Port, of 15 April 2010
Autorité de la concurrence decision no. 10-D-18 Veterinary analyses, of 14 June 2010
Autorité de la concurrence decision no. 10-D-20 Electronic discount coupons, of 25 June 2010
Autorité de la concurrence decision no. 10-D-28 Exchanges Check-Image Fee, of 20 September 2010
Autorité de la concurrence decision no. 10-D-35 Welding electrodes, of 15 December 2010
Autorité de la concurrence decision no. 10-D-39 Road sign, of 22 December 2010
Autorité de la concurrence decision no. 11-D-01 Cargo handling in La Réunion, of 18 January 2011
Autorité de la concurrence decision no. 11-D-02 Restoration of historical monuments, of 26 January 2011
Autorité de la concurrence decision no. 11-D-08 Multi-brand gift card, of 27 April 2011
Autorité de la concurrence decision no. 11-D-11 'CB' payment card, of 7 July 2011
Autorité de la concurrence decision no. 11-D-13 Electrification and electrical installation, of 5 October 2011
Autorité de la concurrence decision no. 11-D-17 Laundry detergents, of 8 December 2011
Autorité de la concurrence decision no. 12-D-02 Géfil, of 13 January 2012
Autorité de la concurrence decision no. 12-D-08 Endives, of 6 March 2012
Autorité de la concurrence decision no. 12-D-09 Flour mills, of 13 March 2012
Autorité de la concurrence decision no. 12-D-17 Non-cash means of payment, of 5 July 2012
Autorité de la concurrence decision no. 12-D-19 Tooth whitening, of 26 September 2012
Autorité de la concurrence decision no. 12-D-26 Fire extinguishers, of 20 December 2012
Autorité de la concurrence decision no. 12-D-29 FFGolf, of 21 December 2012
Autorité de la concurrence decision no. 13-D-02 Towing light vehicles, of 4 February 2013
Autorité de la concurrence decision no. 13-D-03 Pork slaughtering, of 13 February 2013
Autorité de la concurrence decision no. 13-D-09 Miradors Perpignan, of 17 April 2013
Autorité de la concurrence decision no. 13-D-12 Distribution of commodity chemicals, of 28 May 2013
Autorité de la concurrence decision no. 13-D-15 Europe-Antilles Sea Freight, of 25 June 2015
Autorité de la concurrence decision no. 13-D-17 MasterCard, of 20 September 2013

Autorité de la concurrence decision no. 13-D-18 Visa, of 20 September 2013
Autorité de la concurrence decision no. 13-D-23 Publication of companies' legal information, of 30 December 2013
Autorité de la concurrence decision no. 14-D-16 Relocation of military personnel in Martinique, of 18 January 2014
Autorité de la concurrence decision no. 14-D-20 Wallpaper, of 22 December 2014
Autorité de la concurrence decision no. 15-D-03 Fresh dairy products, of 12 March 2015
Autorité de la concurrence decision no. 15-D-04 Bakery flour, of 26 March 2015
Autorité de la concurrence decision no. 15-D-06 Online hotel booking, of 21 April 2015
Autorité de la concurrence decision no. 15-D-08 Sale of poultry meat, of 6 May 2015
Autorité de la concurrence decision no. 15-D-19 Standard and express delivery, of 15 December 2015
Autorité de la concurrence decision no. 16-D-02 School bus transportation in the Lower Rhine, of 27 January 2016
Autorité de la concurrence decision no. 16-D-20 Modelling sector, of 29 September 2016
Autorité de la concurrence decision no. 16-D-28 Property management, of 6 December 2016
Autorité de la concurrence decision no. 17-D-12 Sugar production, of 26 July 2017
Autorité de la concurrence decision no. 9-D-27 MGSR, of 30 July 2009
Autorité de la concurrence opinion no. 09-A-48 Dairy, of 2 October 2009
Autorité de la concurrence opinion no. 09-A-50 Cinema code, of 8 October 2009
Autorité de la concurrence opinion no. 09-A-56 Digital books, of 18 December 2009
Autorité de la concurrence opinion no. 10-A-10 Chartered accountants, of 27 May 2010
Autorité de la concurrence opinion no. 13-A-08 Network sharing and roaming, of 11 March 2013
Autorité de la concurrence opinion no. 15-A-02 Regulated professions, of 9 January 2015
Autorité de la concurrence press release on Professional Association Members' Rent, of 22 April 2020
Autorité de la concurrence press release regarding Adidas, of 18 November 2015
Conseil de la concurrence decision no. 05-D-12 EUROPQN, of 17 March 2005
Conseil de la concurrence decision no. 05-D-32 Dry dog food, of 22 June 2005
Conseil de la concurrence decision no. 05-D-48 Taximeters, of 28 July 2005
Conseil de la concurrence decision no. 05-D-60 Transport to Saint Honorat, of 9 November 2005
Conseil de la concurrence decision no. 06-D-03 Heating, ceramic sanitary and plumbing equipment, of 6 March 2006
Conseil de la concurrence decision no. 06-D-11 Turbo Europe, of 16 May 2006
Conseil de la concurrence decision no. 06-D-24 Bijourama, of 24 July 2006
Conseil de la concurrence decision no. 06-D-28 Home Cinema, of 5 October 2006
Conseil de la concurrence decision no. 06-D-29 Access of local radios to national advertisement, of 6 October 2006
Conseil de la concurrence decision no. 06-D-37 Cycle and cycle products, of 7 December 2006
Conseil de la concurrence decision no. 06-D-40 Association conducting surveys on magazine press, of 20 December 2006
Conseil de la concurrence decision no. 07-D-04 Jeff de Bruges chocolates, of 24 January 2007
Conseil de la concurrence decision no. 07-D-05 UFOP, of 21 February 2007
Conseil de la concurrence decision no. 07-D-07 Sale of cosmetic products on the internet, of 8 March 2007
Conseil de la concurrence decision no. 07-D-16 Cereals, of 9 May 2007
Conseil de la concurrence decision no. 07-D-17 Films, of 10 May 2007
Conseil de la concurrence decision no. 07-D-31 Citroën, of 9 October 2007
Conseil de la concurrence decision no. 07-D-32 Remuneration of press distributors, of 9 October 2007
Conseil de la concurrence decision no. 08-D-06 Specialist Physicians Overcharging Fees, of 2 April 2008

Conseil de la concurrence decision no. 08-D-09 Funeral parlour in Lyon, of 6 May 2008
Conseil de la concurrence decision no. 08-D-26 UAT taxis Abbeilles, of 5 November 2008
Conseil de la concurrence decision no. 08-D-32 Steel trading, of 16 December 2008
Conseil de la concurrence decision no. 08-D-34 Funeral services in Marseille, of 22 December 2008
Conseil de la concurrence decision no. 09-D-01 Pleasure boats, of 12 January 2009
Conseil de la concurrence decision no. 09-D-05 Temporary employment sector, of 2 February 2009
Conseil de la concurrence decision no. 09-D-08 Motorway breakdown services, of 16 February 2009
Conseil de la concurrence opinion no. 04-A-13 Assistance with employment, of 12 July 2004
Conseil de la concurrence opinion no. 05-A-23 Electricity purchases by intensive industrial users, of 5 December 2005
Conseil de la concurrence opinion no. 06-A-07 Fair trade, of 27 March 2006
Conseil de la concurrence opinion no. 08-A-07 Organisation of fruit and vegetable processing industry, of 7 May 2008

Paris Court of Appeal

2005/15784 Dental surgeons in Puy-de-Dôme, of 20 February 2007
2006/07820 Heating, ceramic sanitary and plumbing equipment, of 29 January 2008
2006/18379 Access of local radios to national advertisement, of 6 November 2007
2007/00370 Cycle and cycle products, of 4 March 2008
2007/13915 Distribution of Medicine (I), of 26 November 2008
2008/00508 Distribution of Medicine (II) (2008), of 26 November 2008
2008/01095 Distribution of Medicine (III) (2009), of 26 November 2008
2008/08385 Specialist Physicians Overcharging Fees (2009), of 18 March 2009
2008/12495 Plywood manufactures, of 29 September 2009
2009/00334 Steel trading, of 19 January 2010
2009/03532 Temporary employment sector, of 26 January 2010
2010/20555 Exchanges Check-Image Fee, of 23 February 2012
2012/06498 Endive, of 15 May 2014
2012/06826 Flour mill, of 20 November 2014
2014/22811 Electrification and electrical installation, of 21 January 2016

Cour de cassation

09/13494 09/66021 Specialist Physicians Overcharging Fees, of 7 April 2010
08/70449 Distribution of Medicine (I), of 2 February 2010
08/70450 Distribution of Medicine (II), of 2 February 2010
08/70451 Distribution of Medicine (III), of 2 February 2010
10/12913 10/13686 Temporary employment sector, of March 2011
12/15971 Exchanges Check-Image Fee, of 14 April 2015
14/19589 Endive, of 8 December 2015

Other

03174 Aéroport de Paris, of 18 October 1999 (Tribunal des conflits)

GERMANY

Bundeskartellamt

Bundeskartellamt decision no. B1-116/04 Sand-lime brick, of 9 August 2006
Bundeskartellamt decision no. B1-164/13 B1-167/13 B1-87/14 B1-47/15 Furniture, of 15 December 2016
Bundeskartellamt decision no. B1-25/04 Verta/Danzer, of 17 June 2004
Bundeskartellamt decision no. B1-62/13 Rental of retail space in factory outlet centres, of 26 February 2015
Bundeskartellamt decision no. B1-72/12 Round timber in Baden-Württemberg, of 9 July 2015
Bundeskartellamt decision no. B10-148/05 Lottery, of 23 August 2006
Bundeskartellamt decision no. B10-17/11 Markkleeberg, of 21 November 2011
Bundeskartellamt decision no. B10-44/09 B10-45/09 B10-47/09 B10-48/09 B10-10/10 B10-11/10 B10-13/10 B10-14/10 B10-18/10 B10-19/10 B10-20/10 B10-21/10 B10-22/10 B10-23/10 B10-24/10 B10-25/10 Gas and electricity suppliers resale bans, of 5 July 2010
Bundeskartellamt decision no. B10-6/11 Dinkelsbühl, of 18 October 2011
Bundeskartellamt decision no. B11-13/06 Flour mills, of 25 October 2011
Bundeskartellamt decision no. B11-20/05 Sale of liquefied petroleum gas (LPG), of 9 April 2009
Bundeskartellamt decision no. B12-11/08 Ophthalmic lenses, of 25 March 2009
Bundeskartellamt decision no. B12-14/10 Household porcelain in Germany, of 17 October 2013
Bundeskartellamt decision no. B2-118/10 Procurement of raw milk, of 15 May 2011
Bundeskartellamt decision no. B2-31/17 Edeka/Tengelmann, of 16 November 2017
Bundeskartellamt decision no. B2-90/01-1 Timber, of 17 September 2009
Bundeskartellamt decision no. B2-90/01-2 Timber of 29 January 2009
Bundeskartellamt decision no. B2-90/01-3 Timber, of 3 March 2009
Bundeskartellamt decision no. B2-90/01-4 Timber, of 9 December 2008
Bundeskartellamt decision no. B2-98/11 ASICS, of 26 August 2015
Bundeskartellamt decision no. B3-06/05 OTC medicines – Land pharmacist, of 21 December 2007
Bundeskartellamt decision no. B3-11/13 Ophthalmologists-AÄGB, of 1 July 2013
Bundeskartellamt decision no. B3-11/13 Ophthalmologists-AOK, of 24 June 2013
Bundeskartellamt decision no. B3-123/11 Pharmacists association in Westphalia-Lippe, of 1 October 2014
Bundeskartellamt decision no. B3-130/11 Associations of Ophthalmologists, of 2 May 2012
Bundeskartellamt decision no. B3-134/09 Federal Guild of Hearing Aid Acousticians, of 24 November 2011
Bundeskartellamt decision no. B3-137/12 Adidas, of 27 June 2014
Bundeskartellamt decision no. B3-144/08 Colistin antibiotics, of 25 May 2009
Bundeskartellamt decision no. B3-64/05 Merck and VWR distribution agreement, of 14 July 2009
Bundeskartellamt decision no. B3-93/15 Lighters, of 21 December 2015
Bundeskartellamt decision no. B4-1006/06 Container glass, of 31 May 2007
Bundeskartellamt decision no. B4-13/10 B4-117/15 Fees for ATM withdrawal, of 24 July 2017
Bundeskartellamt decision no. B4-152/07 Coordination of tenders for sales packaging waste collection services by compliance schemes, of 31 March 2011
Bundeskartellamt decision no. B4-31/05 Pecuniary loss liability risks for auditors and chartered accountants, of 13 August 2007
Bundeskartellamt decision no. B4-32/08 Quantity transfer contracts, of 18 August 2008
Bundeskartellamt decision no. B4-71/10 Online banking conditions, of 29 June 2016
Bundeskartellamt decision no. B4-9/11 B4-94/11 Electronic cash card payment system, of 30 April 2014
Bundeskartellamt decision no. B5-100/10 Sanitary fittings, of 12 December 2011

Bundeskartellamt decision no. B5-144/13 GARDENA, of 28 November 2013
Bundeskartellamt decision no. B5-35/14 Lego II, of 18 July 2016
Bundeskartellamt decision no. B6-114/10 Joint selling of media rights, of 11 April 2008
Bundeskartellamt decision no. B6-22/16 Facebook, of 6 February 2019
Bundeskartellamt decision no. B6-32/15 Joint selling of media rights to matches of the German Bundesliga, of 11 April 2016
Bundeskartellamt decision no. B6-46/12 Amazon, of 26 November 2013
Bundeskartellamt decision no. B7-11/13 Bosch Siemens, of 23 December 2013
Bundeskartellamt decision no. B7-17/06 T-Mobile, Vodafone and O2, of 29 October 2007
Bundeskartellamt decision no. B7-22/07 Basic Encryption of TV Programs – Commitments, of 27 December 2012
Bundeskartellamt decision no. B7-30/07-1 Fire detection systems in Düsseldorf, of 27 May 2013
Bundeskartellamt decision no. B7-43/09 Fiber telecommunications networks, of 15 November 2010
Bundeskartellamt decision no. B7-46/13 Telekom and Telefónica, of 6 November 2014
Bundeskartellamt decision no. B8-113/03 Long-term gas supply, of 13 January 2006
Bundeskartellamt decision no. B8-175/11 Titisee-Neustadt, of 28 January 2015
Bundeskartellamt decision no. B9-121/13 Booking.com, of 23 December 2015
Bundeskartellamt decision no. B9-66/10 HRS-Hotel Reservation Service, of 20 December 2013
Bundeskartellamt decision no. B9-96/09 Lufthansa, of 17 December 2011
Bundeskartellamt press release no. B1-232/07 Association of the German construction industry, of 15 June 2009
Bundeskartellamt press release no. B6-81/11 ARD/ZDF online platform ‚Germany's Gold', of 18 February 2014
Bundeskartellamt press release no. B7-1/13-35 Sennheiser, of 15 October 2013
Bundeskartellamt press release regarding Arena and Premiere, of 8 July 2007
Bundeskartellamt press release regarding Audible, of 19 July 2017
Bundeskartellamt press release regarding Crisis management measures in the automotive industry, of 9 June 2020
Bundeskartellamt press release regarding Digital cement trading platform, of 7 December 2017
Bundeskartellamt press release regarding Joint selling of media rights, of 17 July 2008
Bundeskartellamt press release regarding Sanitary sector, of 22 March 2016
Bundeskartellamt press release regarding Tank & Rast, of 24 February 2017
Bundeskartellamt press release regarding Verivox, of 3 June 2015
Bundeskartellamt press release regarding Yomo, of 14 September 2016

OLG Düsseldorf

VI-2 Kart 12/04 (V) Verta/Danzer, of 10 June 2005
VI-2 Kart 1/06 (V) Long-term gas supply, of 4 October 2007
VI-Kart 1/14 (V) HRS, of 9 January 2015
VI-Kart 1/16 (V) Booking, of 4 May 2016
VI-Kart 13/15(V) ASICS, of 5 April 2017
VI-Kart 10/15 (V) Round timber in Baden-Württemberg, of 15 March 2017
VI-Kart 11/07 (V) Pecuniary loss liability risks for auditors and chartered accountants, of 17 September 2008
VI-Kart 5/09 (V) Merck and VWR distribution agreement, of 12 November 2013

BGH Kartellsenat

KVR 34/08 Pecuniary loss liability risks for auditors and chartered accountants, of 23 June 2009
KVR 67/07 Long-term gas supply, of 10 February 2009

KVZ 41/17 ASICS, of 12 December 2017
KVR 38/17 Round timber in Baden-Württemberg, of 12 June 2018

Other

11 U 84/14 Kart Deuter Sport, of 22 December 2015 (Higher Regional Court of Frankfurt)

HUNGARY

GVH

GVH decision no. Vj-1/2008 Hungarian Real Estate Association, of 12 September 2008
GVH decision no. Vj-104/2016 Nemak-Cevher, of 1 August 2017
GVH decision no. Vj-11/2014 Media Service Support and Asset Management Fund, of 29 April 2016
GVH decision no. Vj-115/2010 Dental headpieces, of 20 December 2013
GVH decision no. Vj-120/2004/35 Bio-traditional fruits, of 13 June 2005
GVH decision no. Vj-132/2004/26, Card issuance, of 12 November 2004
GVH decision no. Vj-134/2008 Wheat mill products II, of 19 May 2010
GVH decision no. VJ-138/2004/14 Hungarian Bakers Guild, of 13 December 2004
GVH decision no. Vj-140/2006 newspaper distribution I, of 8 November 2007
GVH decision no. Vj-141/2004 Plant protection products, of 1 June 2005
GVH decision no. Vj-143/16/2008 Chamber Of Plant Protection In Hungary, of 22 April 2010
GVH decision no. Vj-151/2009/260 Model contracts for programme, of 7 August 2013
GVH decision no. Vj-152/2006/86 Budapest Stock Exchange, of 20 March 2008
GVH decision no. Vj-154/2004/16 Distribution of tobacco products, of 1 February 2005
GVH decision no. Vj-156/2004/68 Ice-cream, of 30 March 2006
GVH decision no. Vj-157/2004/73 Frozen food, of 6 July 2006
GVH decision no. Vj-158/2005/148 Hyundai Motors Hungary, of 13 June 2007
GVH decision no. Vj-16/2005 Deontological rules of auditors, of 16 July 2006
GVH decision no. Vj-161/2004/59 Animal Feed Phosphates II, of 21 March 2006
GVH decision no. Vj-162/2004 Universities IT tender, of 15 June 2006
GVH decision no. Vj-166/2006 Car navigation tools, of 19 June 2009
GVH decision no. Vj-169/2003/68 Fertilizers, of 27 May 2004
GVH decision no. Vj-178/2004/5 Vj-178/2004/5 Pont Audio, of 9 May 2005
GVH decision no. Vj-18/2008 Uniform interchange fee levels, of 24 September 2009
GVH decision no. Vj-180/2004 Hungarian Bar Association of attorneys, of 14 June 2006
GVH decision no. Vj-191/2006/10 Euronics, of 12 July 2007
GVH decision no. Vj-195/2007/129 Newspaper distribution II, of 10 February 2010
GVH decision no. Vj-199/2005 Egg cartel, of 30 November 2006
GVH decision no. Vj-2/2010 Car refinishing paints, of 1 August 2014
GVH decision no. Vj-2/2015 Lead-acid batteries, of 26 July 2016
GVH decision no. Vj-200/2004/13 Funeral service in Szolnok, of 5 April 2005
GVH decision no. Vj-201/2005 Hungarian Chamber of Architects, of 11 December 2007
GVH decision no. Vj-207/2004/51 Rába IT agreement, of 9 June 2005
GVH decision no. Vj-23/2005 Rába Group and Integris, of 9 June 2005
GVH decision no. Vj-23/2011 Daily newspapers, of 24 October 2014
GVH decision no. Vj-26/2006 Navigation tools, of 3 December 2007
GVH decision no. Vj-28/2007 Beer supply agreements, of 16 May 2008
GVH decision no. Vj-29/2011-522 Ready-mix concrete, of 30 June 2014
GVH decision no. Vj-3/2008 Rail freight transport services, of 27 April 2012
GVH decision no. Vj-31/2007 Network of Pharmacists, of 4 November 2008

GVH decision no. Vj-36/2008 Association of journalists, of 2 December 2008
GVH decision no. Vj-37/2014 Meat products temporary sales (promotions), of 2 August 2016
GVH decision no. Vj-40/2013 Driving schools in Gy⊠r, of 19 December 2014
GVH decision no. Vj-43/2005/33 waste management, of 24 August 2006
GVH decision no. Vj-45/2008-641 Colour television tubes, or 24 July 2014
GVH decision no. Vj-47/2004 Hungarian Association of Book Publishers and Book Retailers, of 11 April 2006
GVH decision no. Vj-48/2013 Tenders in Nagylóc and Szécsényfelfalu, of 19 December 2014
GVH decision no. Vj-49/2011 Hungarian beer market, of 22 July 2015
GVH decision no. Vj-50/2009 Sugar cartel, of 19 December 2012
GVH decision no. Vj-51/2004 Remittance via mobile phone, of 10 September 2004
GVH decision no. Vj-51/2005 The Hungarian Association of Automobile Dealers, of 21 December 2006
GVH decision no. Vj-51/2008 Professional Guild of Hairdressers, of 15 October 2009
GVH decision no. Vj-57/2008/23 Gyöngy Strategic Association, of 4 December 2008
GVH decision no. Vj-60/2004 Budapest Sports Stadium, of 8 September 2005
GVH decision no. Vj-60/2006/37 Hungarian Chamber of Pharmacists, of 18 May 2007
GVH decision no. Vj-62/2012 Watermelon, of 10 April 2013
GVH decision no. Vj-63/2006/122 Inform Média, of 19 April 2007
GVH decision no. Vj-65/2012 Public procurement in Komló, of 4 February 2015
GVH decision no. Vj-66/2012 Geophysical measuring operations, of 18 May 2014
GVH decision no. Vj-67/2014/59 Waste materials, of 19 February 2015
GVH decision no. Vj-68/2011 Alt Cash Kft, of 16 July 2013
GVH decision no. Vj-69/2008 Wheat mill products I, of 28 October 2010
GVH decision no. Vj-7/2008/178 Motor oils and lubricants, of 19 March 2009
GVH decision no. Vj-71/2005 Sara Lee price restrictions, od 2 April 2007
GVH decision no. Vj-73/2011 Mosquito control, of 29 October 2015
GVH decision no. Vj-74/2003/117 White flour, of 19 October 2004
GVH decision no. Vj-74/2004/58 Public procurement bidding for building a block of flats with respect to bid-rigging, of 13 December 2004
GVH decision no. Vj-74/2011 Mortgage loans, of 19 November 2013
GVH decision no. Vj-78/2013 MasterCard and OTP, of 14 May 2015
GVH decision no. Vj-8/2012 Hungarian Banking Association, of 11 January 2016
GVH decision no. Vj-81/2006/74 Medical equipment, of 18 December 2007
GVH decision no. Vj-91/2004/18 Comix, of 18 July 2005
GVH decision no. Vj-94/2005, British American Tobacco group, of 20 May 2006
GVH decision no. Vj-96/2009-113 Book market, of 23 May 2013
GVH decision no. Vj-96/2009-177 Book market, of 23 May 2013
GVH decision no. Vj-96/2010 Contact lenses, of 23 June 2014
GVH decision no. Vj-97/2013 Driver training ethics code, of 27 October 2015
GVH decision no. Vj-128/2004/23 Tomb construction activities in Túrkeve, of 31 May 2005

Budapest Metropolitan/Metropolitan Administrative and Labour Court

7.K.31.11612007144 The Hungarian Association of Automobile Dealers, of 22 January 2009
7.K.34341/2005/15 Budapest Sports Stadium, of 21 November 2006
11.K.34.958/2006/23 Waste management, of 9 November 2007
11.K.31.445/2008/11 Hungarian Chamber of Architects, of 1 September 2010
3.K.30.051/2009/12 Association of journalists, of 20 January 2010
2.K.31.793/2011/90 Wheat mill products I, of 26 September 2012
5.K.30.278/2014/99 Mortgage loans, of 3 February 2015
7.K.34.976/2009/9 Professional Guild of Hairdressers, of 17 March 2010
2K.30863/2009/8 Hungarian Bar Association of attorneys, of 29 October 2009
38.Kpk.46.218/2014/5 Driver training ethics code, of 27 November 2014

Budapest Appeal/Metropolitan Court of Budapest

2.Kf.27.463/2009/5 Hungarian Chamber of Architects, of 23 March 2010
2.Kf.27.280/2008/7 Hungarian Association of Book Publishers and Retailers, of 14 January 2009
2.Kf.27.027200814 Waste management, of 18 October 2008
2.Kf.27.672/2008/7 Newspaper distribution I, of 22 April 2009
2.Kf.27.217/2010/4 Association of journalists, of 30 June 2010
2.Kf.649.964/2013/20 Wheat mill products I, of 5 March 2014
2.Kf.650.032/2015/28 Mortgage loans, of 24 February 2016
1.Kf.650.154/2016/10 Mosquito control, of 13 December 2017
2.Kf.27.333/2010/6 Professional Guild of Hairdressers, of 29 September 2010

THE NETHERLANDS

Nma/ACM

ACM decision no. 15.0959.29 Ready-mix concrete, of 29 June 2016
ACM decision no. 6538 Houses merchants foreclosure auctions, of 9 July 2014
ACM decision no. 7244/597 Magazine packs, of 7 November 2013
ACM decision no. 7401/106 Demolition firms bid-rigging – Bergambacht & Dilettant, of 24 May 2013
ACM decision no. 7571/40.O1018 Mandatory flood insurance, of 6 June 2013
ACM decision no. ACMDM2015201065_oV Proton therapy, of 3 March 2015
ACM informal opinion no. 12.0256.53 Veterinarian contracts, of 8 November 2013
ACM informal opinion no. 14.1134.15 ATMs in rural areas, of 18 December 2014
ACM informal opinion no. 7512 Geldservice Nederland B.V., of 3 July 2014
ACM informal opinion no. ACM/DM/2013/205913 De Stroomversnelling, of 2 November 2012
ACM informal opinion no. ACM/DM/2014/206028 Chicken for tomorrow, of 26 January 2015
ACM informal opinion regarding Coal power plants, of 26 September 2013
ACM press release regarding Room for collaboration involving the distribution of essential drugs for COVID-19 patients, of 26 May 2020
Nma decision no. 13.0512.53 Mobile operators, of 7 January 2014
Nma decision no. 2501 Assen pharmacies, of 21 June 2004
Nma decision no. 2688 Tilburg pharmacies, of 21 June 2004
Nma decision no. 3031 Temporary employment bureau, of 10 December 2004
Nma decision no. 3371 Branch Associations for Maritime Container Transportation, of 25 March 2005
Nma decision no. 4014 Horticultural Services, of 15 December 2005
Nma decision no. 4108-195 Nozema/Broadcast NT, of 21 November 2005
Nma decision no. 4814-31 Installation, of 22 November 2005
Nma decision no. 5170 VGT (reassessment), of 24 October 2006
Nma decision no. 5170 VGT, of 8 November 2005
Nma decision no. 5210 Metal grilles, of 10 December 2007
Nma decision no. 5211 Nurseries, of 8 May 2009
Nma decision no. 5709 Day-care, of 30 June 2008
Nma decision no. 5851/121 Thuiszorg 't Gooi, of 19 September 2008
Nma decision no. 5998 Insurance pool, of 30 December 2010
Nma decision no. 6091_1/204 Distributors of sodium hypochlorite, of 12 November 2009
Nma decision no. 6108/258 Thuiszorg Kennemerland, of 19 September 2008
Nma decision no. 6109/814 Caraat, of 21 April 2011
Nma decision no. 6274/569 Midden Ijssel, of 21 October 2010
Nma decision no. 6306 Flour, of 12 February 2013
Nma decision no. 6306 Flour, of 16 December 2010

Nma decision no. 6306 Flour, of 4 March 2012
Nma decision no. 6425 Window cleaners, of 20 December 2011
Nma decision no. 6429_1/176 Kazerne I, of 5 June 2009
Nma decision no. 6430_1/131 Meiveld, of 21 August 2009
Nma decision no. 6431_1/172 Kazerne II, of 5 June 2009
Nma decision no. 6442 WMO Friesland (reassessment), of 23 July 2012
Nma decision no. 6492_1/146 De Tongelreep, of 21 August 2009
Nma decision no. 6494 6836 Southern Dutch construction companies, of 29 October 2010
Nma decision no. 6538 Houses merchants foreclosure auctions, of 12 December 2011
Nma decision no. 6601_1/141 Meerhoven, of 29 December 2009
Nma decision no. 6824 Health insurers, of 12 April 2010
Nma decision no. 6888/435 LHV pace of establishment (reassessment), of 3 February 2014
Nma decision no. 6888/435 LHV pace of establishment, of 30 December 2011
Nma decision no. 6895 Amsterdam hospitals, of 31 December 2010
Nma decision no. 6929_1/205 Ship-generated waste collection cartel, of 16 November 2011
Nma decision no. 7036_1/386 Bell peppers, of 15 May 2012
Nma decision no. 7130/216 Taxi transport Ijssel cities, of 20 November 2012
Nma decision no. 7191/138 National Association of General Practitioners, of 4 December 2012
Nma decision no. 7213 NPO, of 27 April 2012
Nma decision no. 7237 7268 Houses merchants foreclosure auctions, of 7 January 2013
Nma decision no. 7377 SGR c.s., of 10 January 2013
Nma decision no. 7533-22 Art auctions, of 15 February 2013
Nma informal opinion no. 4713 Health insurers preferred suppliers policy, of 22 June 2005
Nma informal opinion no. 5194 Over-the-Counter Payment Services Covenant, of 14 November 2005
Nma informal opinion no. 6455 Boars castration, of 27 October 2008
Nma informal opinion no. 7011/23.827 MSC Shrimp Fishery, of 18 April 2011
Nma informal opinion no. Royal Dutch Society for Physical Therapy (KNGF), of 21 October 2010
Nma press release regarding APX and Endex, of 22 December 2006
Nma press release regarding Ballast Nedam, of 19 September 2013
Nma press release regarding Concert organisation and ticket sales, of 20 July 2006
Nma press release regarding Orthobanda industry association, of 3 November 2004
Nma press release regarding press UvA and VU tuition fees, of 13 July 2012
Nma press release regarding Royal Dutch Society for the Advancement of Pharmacology (KNMP), of 5 July 2006
Nma press release regarding VSS, of 19 April 2012

District Court

MEDED 06/4638 STRN VGT, of 5 November 2007
ROT 13/1174 Houses merchants foreclosure auctions, of 18 December 2014
ROT 15/1219 Veterinarian contracts, of 7 April 2016
ROT 15/6209 Magazine packs, of 27 July 2017

CBb

AWB 15/431 WMO Friesland, of 11 January 2017
19/162 Applicant A, of 18 August 2020

Other

C/13/615474/HA ZA 16-959 Nike, of 4 October 2017 (District Court of Amsterdam)

19/00135 State of the Netherlands v. Urgenda Foundation, of 20 December 2019 (Supreme Court of the Netherlands)

UNITED KINGDOM

OFT/CMA and Sector Regulators

Decision of the Civil Aviation Authority no. CA98-001 East Midlands International Airport, of January 2017

Decision of the Competition and Markets Authority no. 50223 Posters and frames, of 12 August 2016

Decision of the Competition and Markets Authority no. 50230 Golf equipment, of 24 August 2017

Decision of the Competition and Markets Authority no. 50235 Residential estate agency services, of 31 May 2017

Decision of the Competition and Markets Authority no. 50283 Cleanroom laundry services, of 14 December 2017

Decision of the Competition and Markets Authority no. 50343 Light fittings, of 3 May 2017

Decision of the Competition and Markets Authority No. 50408 Live online bidding auction platform, of 29 June 2017

Decision of the Competition and Markets Authority no. CE/9531/11 Paroxetine-IVAX/GSK agreement, of 12 February 2016

Decision of the Competition and Markets Authority no. CE/9691/12 Galvanised steel tanks – Main, of 19 December 2016

Decision of the Competition and Markets Authority no. CE/9784-13 Ophthalmology sector, of 20 August 2015

Decision of the Competition and Markets Authority no. CE/9856/14 Refrigeration, of 24 May 2016

Decision of the Competition and Markets Authority No. CE/9857-14 Bathroom fittings & fixtures, of 10 May 2016

Decision of the Competition and Markets Authority no. CE/9859-14 Modelling, of 16 December 2016

Decision of the Gas and Electricity Markets Authority, Energy Trade Association, of 28 June 2013

Decision of the Gas and Electricity Markets Authority, Price comparison websites, of 15 March 2016

Decision of the Office of communications no. CW/00842/06/05 BBC broadcast's provision, of 30 May 2007

Decision of the Office of Fair Trading no. CA98/05/05 MasterCard, of 6 September 2005

Decision of the Office of Fair Trading no. CE/2464-03 UOP/prices for desiccant, of 8 November 2004

Decision of the Office of Fair Trading no. CE/2471-03 Oakley (Case closure summary), of 1 August 2008

Decision of the Office of Fair Trading no. CE/2479/03 London-wide newspaper distribution, of 3 January 2006

Decision of the Office of Fair Trading no. CE/2558-03 TV Eye, of 24 May 2005

Decision of the Office of Fair Trading no. CE/2596-03 Tobacco, of 15 April 2010

Decision of the Office of Fair Trading no. CE/2890-03 Future fees by certain independent fee-paying schools, of 20 November 2006

Decision of the Office of Fair Trading no. CE/3094-03 Dairy retail price initiatives, of 26 July 2011

Decision of the Office of Fair Trading no. CE/4327-04 Bid rigging in the construction industry in England, of 21 September 2009

Decision of the Office of Fair Trading no. CE/7510-06 Construction Recruitment Forum, of 29 September 2009
Decision of the Office of Fair Trading no. CE/7691-06 Airline passenger fuel surcharges for long-haul flights, of 19 April 2012
Decision of the Office of Fair Trading no. CE/8950/08 Loans to large professional services firms, of 20 January 2011
Decision of the Office of Fair Trading no. CE/9161-09 Distribution of Mercedes-Benz commercial vehicles (vans), of 27 March 2013
Decision of the Office of Fair Trading no. CE/9248-10 Access control and alarm systems to retirement properties, of 6 December 2013
Decision of the Office of Fair Trading no. CE/9320-10 Hotel online booking, of 31 January 2014
Decision of the Office of Fair Trading no. CE/9578-12 Mobility scooters, of 27 March 2014
Decision of the Office of Fair Trading no. CE/9627/12 Supply of prescription medicines to care homes in England, of 20 March 2014
Decision of the Office of Fair Trading no. OFT1415 Street furniture advertising, of May 2012
Decision of the Office of Fair Trading no. CA98/03/2005 TV Eye, of 24 May 2005
Decision of the Office of Rail and Road, Provision of Deep Sea Container rail transport services between ports and key inland destinations in Great Britain, of 18 December 2015
Decision of the Office of Rail Regulation no. 213479.02 Supply of grease for use in electric trackside lubricators, of 12 August 2005
Press release of the Competition and Markets Authority regarding BMW car comparison sites, of 24 January 2017
Press release of the Office of Fair Trading regarding CE/9692/12 Amazon's price parity policy, of 29 August 2013
Press release of the Office of Fair Trading regarding Yamaha musical instruments, of 8 September 2006
Short-form Opinion of the Office of Fair Trading regarding Rural broadband wayleave rates, of September 2012

CAT

1035/1/1/04 and 1041/2/1/04, Racecourse Association, [2005] CAT 29
1054/1/1/05 1055/1/1/05 1056/1/1/05 MasterCard, [2006] CAT 14
1067/1/1/06 Price fixing and market sharing in stock check pads, [2006] CAT 24
1071/2/1-06 Cityhook, [2007] CAT 18
1117/1/1/09 1123/1/1/09 1134/1/1/09 1135/1/1/09 1138/1/1/09 1139/1/1/09 Bid rigging in the construction industry in England, [2011] CAT 7
1120/1/1/09 Bid rigging in the construction industry in England, [2011] CAT 11
1125/1/1/09 1128/1/1/09 1130/1/1/09 1131/1/1/09 1136/1/1/09 1137/1/1/09 Bid rigging in the construction industry in England, [2011] CAT 9
1160/1/1/10 1161/1/1/10 1162/1/1/10 1163/1/1/10 1164/1/1/10 1165/1/1/10 Tobacco, [2011] CAT 41
1226/2/12/14 Hotel online booking, [2014] CAT 16

Court of Appeal

C3/2011/1965 Bid rigging in the construction industry in England, [2012] EWCA Civ 1056
CO/7886/2006 Cityhook, [2009] EWHC 57 (Admin)

Bibliography

Abrams, N. (1971). Internal policy: guiding the exercise of prosecutorial discretion, *UCLA Law Review*, **19**, 1–58.

Akpinar, M. (2017). The exercise of power in inter-organisational relationships in response to changes in the institutional environment: cases from the European automotive industry, *International Journal of Automotive Technology*, **17**(1), 51–71.

Aleinikoff, T. A. (1986). Constitutional law in the age of balancing, *The Yale Law Journal*, 96 (5), 943–1005.

Algemene Rekenkamer (2006–2007). *Toezicht op mededinging door de NMa* (Official Publication No. Tweede Kamer, vergaderjaar 2006–2007, 31055, nrs 1–2).

Almunia, J. (2010). *Competition v regulation: Where Do the Roles of Sector Specific and Competition Regulators Begin and End?* Brussels: Speech in Center on Regulation in Europe (CERRE), 23 March 2010.

Almunia, J. (2013). *Remedies, Commitments and Settlements in Antitrust*. Brussels: Speech in SV Kartellrecht, 8 March 2013.

Anderman, S. D. and Kallaugher, J. (2006). *Technology Transfer and the New EU Competition Rules: intellectual Property Licensing after Modernisation*. Oxford University Press.

Andriychuk, O. (2010). Dialectical antitrust: an alternative insight into the methodology of the EC competition law analysis, *European Competition Law Review*, **31**(4), 155–165.

Andriychuk, O. (2012). The dialectics of competition law: sketching the Ordo-Austrian approach to antitrust, *World Competition*, **35**(2), 355–384.

Ashurst (2005). *Modernisation of German Competition Law: the 7th Amendment of the GWB, Competition Law Update*. Available at: www.ashurst.com/doc.aspx?id_Content=1926.

Baarsma, B. and Rosenboom, N. (2015). A veritable tower of Babel: on the confusion between the legal and economic interpretations of Article 101(3) of the treaty on the functioning of the European Union, *European Competition Journal*, **11**(2–3), 402–425.

Bacon, K. (1997). State regulation of the market and EC competition rules: articles 85 and 86 compared, *European Competition Law Review*, **18**, 283–291.

Bailey, D. (2004). Scope of judicial review under Article 81 EC, *Common Market Law Review*, **41**(5), 274–275.

Bailey, D. (2014). United Kingdom. In P. Kellezi, B. Kilpatrick and P. Kobel, eds., *Antitrust for Small and Middle Size Undertakings and Image Protection from Non-Competitors*. Springer, pp. 235–256.

Bailey, D. (2016). Reinvigorating the role of Article 101(3) under regulation 1/2003, *Antitrust Law Journal*, 81(1), 111–144.
Bailey, D. and Whish, R. (2015). *Competition Law*. Oxford University Press.
Baquero Cruz, J. (2007). The state action doctrine. In G. Amato and C.-D. Ehlermann, eds., *EC Competition Law: a Critical Assessment*. Hart, pp. 551–590.
Baxter, W. F. (1982). Separation of powers, prosecutorial discretion, and the common law nature of antitrust law, *Texas Law Review*, 60, 661–703.
Bellamy, C. and Child, G. D. (2013). *Bellamy & Child European Union Law of Competition*. Oxford University Press.
Berthol-Balladur, L. and Anselin, Y. (2014). The Paris court of appeal partially annuls the competition authoritys decision in the packaged flour case due to the lack of by object infringement in its national component, *Concurrences*, (72338).
Bishop, S. (2001). Modernisation of the rules implementing Articles 81 and 82. In C.-D. Ehlermann and I. Atansiu, eds., *European Competition Law Annual 2000: the Modernisation of EC Antitrust Policy*. Bloomsbury Publishing, pp. 55–65.
Bishop, S. and Walker, M. (2010). *The Economics of EC Competition Law*. Sweet & Maxwell.
Black, J. (2001). Managing discretion. *Paper Presented at the Australian Law Reform Conference Penalties: Policy, Principles and Practice in Government Regulation*, Sydney, June.
Black, O. (1997). Per se rules and rules of reason: what are they?, *European Competition Law Review*, 18, 145–161.
Blake, H. M. and Jones, W. K. (1965). In defense of antitrust, *Columbia Law Review*, 65(3), 377–400.
Blanco, L. O. (2006). *EC Competition Procedure*. Oxford University Press.
Blanco, L. O. and De Pablo, A. L. (2012). EU competition law enforcement elements for a discussion on effectiveness and uniformity, *Annual Proceedings of the Fordham Corporate Law Institute*, **2012**, 45–104.
Blockx, J. (2018). The impact of EU antitrust procedure on the role of the EU courts (1997–2016), *Journal of European Competition Law & Practice*, 9(2), 92–103.
Blomme, E. (2007). State action as a defense against 81 and 82 EC, *World Competition*, 30(2), 243–261.
Boeger, N. (2007). Solidarity and EC competition law, *European Law Review*, 32(3), 319.
Böge, U. (2001). The discussion on the modernisation of EC antitrust policy: an update on the Bundeskartellamts point of view. In C.-D. Ehlermann and I. Atanasiu eds., *European Competition Law Annual 2000: the Modernisation of EC Antitrust Policy*. Bloomsbury Publishing, pp. 67–73.
Bork, R. H. (1978). *The Antitrust Paradox: a Policy at War with Itself*, 1st ed., Bork Publishing LLC.
Bork, R. H. (1993). *The Antitrust Paradox: a Policy at War with Itself*, 2nd ed., The Free Press.
Bork, R. H. and Bowman, W. S. (1965). The Crisis in Antitrust. *Columbia Law Review*, 65(3), 363–376.
Boronkay, M. and Molnár, B. (2009). Current developments in member states: Hungary, *European Competition Journal*, 5(3), 872–874.
Botta, M., Svetlicinii, A. and Bernatt, M. (2015). The assessment of the effect on trade by the national competition authorities of the 'new' member states: another legal partition of the internal market?, *Common Market Law Review*, 52(5), 1247–1275.
Boudou, M. et al. (2014). France. In P. Këllezi, B. Kilpatrick and P. Kobel, eds., *Antitrust for Small and Middle Size Undertakings and Image Protection from Non-Competitors*. Springer, pp. 103–127.

Bradshaw, S. (2016). Is a trade union an undertaking under EU competition law? *European Competition Journal*, **12**(2–3), 320–340.

Brodley, J. F. (1987). The economic goals of antitrust: efficiency, consumer welfare, and technological progress, *NYU Law Review*, **62**, 1020–1053.

Brook, O. (2019). Struggling with Article 101(3) TFEU: diverging approaches of the commission, EU courts, and five competition authorities. *Common Market Law Review*, **56**(1), 121–156.

Brook, O. (2020). Priority setting as a double-edged sword: how modernization strengthened the role of public policy. *Journal of Competition Law & Economics*, **16**(4), 435–487.

Brownsword, R. and Goodwin, M. (2012). *Law and Technologies of the Twenty-First Century*. Cambridge University Press.

Brownsword, R. and Somsen, H. (2009). Law, innovation and technology: before we fast forward—a forum for debate. *Law, Innovation and Technology*, **1**(1), 1–73.

Buch-Hansen, H. and Wigger, A. (2010). Revisiting 50 years of market-making: the neoliberal transformation of European competition policy. *Review of International Political Economy*, **17**(1), 20–44.

Budzinski, O. (2003). Pluralism of competition policy paradigms and the call for regulatory diversity, *Philipps-University of Marburg Volkswirtschaftliche Beiträge*, **14**.

Burnley, R. (2002). Interstate trade revisited-the jurisdictional criterion for Articles 81 and 82 EC. *European Competition Law Review*, **23**(5), 217–226.

Butenko, A. and Larouche, P. (2015). Regulation for innovativeness or regulation of innovation? *Law, Innovation and Technology*, **7**(1), 52–82.

Buttigieg, E. (2009). *Competition Law: Safeguarding the Consumer Interest*. Wolters Kluwer Law & Business.

Byers, S. (2000). Letter from the Rt Hon Stephen Byers, MP, Secretary of State for Trade and Industry. Available at: http://www.publications.parliament.uk/pa/ld199900/ldselect/ldeucom/94/9419.htm.

Carpenter, D. and Moss, D. A. Eds. (2013). *Preventing Regulatory Capture: special Interest Influence and how to Limit it*. Cambridge University Press.

Carree, M., Günster, A. and Schinkel, M. P. (2010). European antitrust policy 1957–2004: an analysis of commission decisions. *Review of Industrial Organization*, **36**(2), 97–131.

Castillo de la Torre, F. (2005). State action defence in EC competition law. *World Competition*, **28**(4), 407–416.

Cengiz, F. (2010a). Alrosa v. Commission and Commission v. Alrosa: rule of Law in Post-Modernisation EU Competition Law Regime. Available at: https://papers.ssrn.com/sol3/papers.cfm?abstract_id=1674345.

Cengiz, F. (2010b). Multi-level governance in competition policy- the European competition network. *European Law Review*, **35**(5), 660-677.

Chung, C. (1995). The relationship between state regulation and EC competition law: two proposals for a coherent approach. *European Competition Law Review*, **16**(2), 87–97.

Cicala, A., Haegeman, K. and Cuff, R. (2018). From Metro to Coty - a story to be continued? the CJEUs judgment in Coty Germany GMBH. *Italian Antitrust Review*, **4**(2), 99–111.

Claassen, R. and Gerbrandy, A. (2016). Rethinking European competition law: from a consumer welfare to a capability approach. *Utrecht Law Review*, **12**(1), 1–15.

Clark, J. M. (1940). Toward a concept of workable competition. *American Economic Review*, **30**(2), 241–56.

Clark, J. M. (1961). *Competition as a Dynamic Process*. Brookings Institution.

Cleynenbreugel, P. (2014). Article 101 TFEU and the EU Courts: Adapting legal form to the realities of modernization? *Common Market Law Review*, **51**, 1381–1436.

Colangelo, M. (2016). Parity clauses and competition law in digital marketplaces: the case of online hotel booking. *Journal of European Competition Law & Practice*, 8(1), 3–14.

Colino, S. M. (2010). Recent changes in the regulation of motor vehicle distribution in Europe–Questioning the logic of sector-specific rules for the car industry. *Competition Law Review*, 6(2), 203–224.

Combe, E., Monnier, C. and Legal, R. (2008). Cartels: the probability of getting caught in the European Union. *Bruges European Economic Research (BEER) Papers 12*.

Costa-Cabral, F. (2020). *Future-Mapping the Three Dimensions of EU Competition Law: modernisation Now and After COVID-19*. Available at: https://papers.ssrn.com/sol3/papers.cfm?abstract_id=3581535.

Costa-Cabral, F. and Lynskey, O. (2017). Family ties: the intersection between data protection and competition in EU law. *Common Market Law Review*, 54(1), 11–50.

CPI. (2019). EU: 19 countries call for new antitrust rules to create 'European champions'. *Competition Law International*, of 18 December 2019. Available at: https://www.competitionpolicyinternational.com/eu-19-countries-call-for-new-antitrust-rules-to-create-european-champions/.

da Cruz, V. J. L. (2018). The intensity of judicial review in complex economic matters—recent competition law judgments of the court of justice of the EU. *Journal of Antitrust Enforcement*, 6(2), 173–188.

Csépai, B. (2015). The ceasefire is over. *European Competition Law Review*, 36(9), 404–405.

Cseres, K. (2005). *Competition Law and Consumer Protection*. Kluwer Law International.

Cseres, K. (2007a). Multi-jurisdictional competition law enforcement: the interface between European competition law and the competition laws of the new member states. *European Competition Journal*, 3(2), 465–502.

Cseres, K. (2007b). The controversies of the consumer welfare standard. *Competition Law Review*, 3(2), 121–173.

Cseres, K. (2013). Integrate or separate – institutional design for the enforcement of competition law and consumer law. *SSRN Electronic Journal*. doi: 10.2139/ssrn.2200908.

Cseres, K. (2014). Accession to the EUs competition law regime: a law and governance approach *Yearbook of Antitrust and Regulatory Studies*, 7(9), 31–65.

Cseres, K. (2020). 'Acceptable' cartels at the crossroads of EU competition law and the common agricultural policy: a legal inquiry into the political, economic, and social dimensions of (strengthening farmers) bargaining power, *The Antitrust Bulletin*, 2020, 1–22.

Cseres, K. and Mendes, J. (2014). Consumers access to EU competition law procedures: outer and inner limits. *Common Market Law Review*, 51(2), 483–521.

Cseres, K. and Outhuijse, A. (2017). Parallel enforcement and accountability: the case of EU competition law. In S. Miroslava and M. Luchtman, eds., *Law Enforcement by EU Authorities: Implications for Political and Judicial Accountability*. Edward Elgar Publishing, pp. 82–114.

Daskalova, V. (2015). Consumer welfare in EU competition law: what is it (not) about? *Competition Law Review*, 11(1), 133–162.

Davies, S. and Ormosi, P. (2013). *The Impact of Competition Policy: what are the Known Unknowns?* Available at: http://competitionpolicy.ac.uk/documents/107435/107587/13-7+complete.pdf.

Davies, S. W. and Ormosi, P. (2010). Assessing competition policy: methodologies, gaps and agenda for future research. CCP Working Paper 10-19.

De Brauw, W. B. (2011). Dutch De minimis exemption for hardcore infringements in line with EU law, *Competition Newsletter*. Available at: http://documents.lexology.com/b0af9024–75a2–4034-9d1a-f3b8eb55e7af.pdf.

Deiberova, K. and Nyssens, H. (2009). The new general block exemption eegulation (GBER): what changed? *European State Aid Law Quarterly*, 8(1), 27–38.
Diaz, F. E. G. (1996). The notion of ancillary restraints under EC competition law. *Fordham International Law Journal*, **19**(3), 951–998.
Don, H. (2010). Public interests! What public interests? And how to deal with them? In L. Amicorum and P. Kalbfleisch, eds., *The Art of Supervision, Liber Amicorum Pieter Kalbfleisch*. Netherlands Competition Authority.
Doren, G. B. and Wilks, S. (1996). *Comparative Competition Policy: national Institutions in a Global Market*. Oxford: Clarendon Press.
Drahos, M. (2001). Convergence of competition laws and policies. In M. Drahos, ed., *The European Community: Germany, Austria, and the Netherlands*, 26 vols. Kluwer Law International.
Dreher, M. (2009). *Germany Report to the LIDC Conference 2009*.
Dreher, M. and Korner, I. (2014). Geremany. In P. Këllezi, B. Kilpatrick and P. Kobel, eds., *Antitrust for Small and Middle Size Undertakings and Image Protection from Non-Competitors*. Springer, pp. 129–140.
Drexl, J. (2008). *Research Handbook on Intellectual Property and Competition Law*. Edward Elgar.
Drexl, J. (2010). Competition law as part of the European constitution. In A. Von Bogdandy and J. Bast, eds., *Principles of European Constitutional Law*, 2nd Rev. ed. Hart Publishing, pp. 633–674.
Dunne, N. (2014a). Between competition law and regulation: hybridized approaches to market control. *Journal of Antitrust Enforcement*, **2**(2), 225–269.
Dunne, N. (2014b). Commitment decisions in EU competition law. *Journal of Competition Law and Economics*, **10**(2), 399–444.
Dunne, N. (2014c). Recasting competition concurrency under the enterprise and regulatory reform act 2013. *The Modern Law Review*, **77**(2), 254–276.
Dunne, N. (2016). Convergence in competition fining practices in the EU. *Common Market Law Review*, **53**(2), 453–492.
Dunne, N. (2020). Public interest and EU competition law. *The Antitrust Bulletin*, 1–26.
Easterbrook, F. H. (1986). Workable antitrust policy. *Michigan Law Review*, **84**(8), 1696–1713.
Eckert, S. (2018). Two spheres of regulation: balancing social and economic goals, *Regulation & Governance*, **12**, 117–131.
Ehlermann, C.-D. (1996). Implementation of EC competition law by national anti-trust authorities. *European Competition Law Review*, **17**(2), 88–95.
Ehlermann, C.-D. (2000). The modernization of EC antitrust policy a legal and cultural revolution. *Common Market Law Review*, **37**(2000), 537–590.
Ehlermann, C.-D. and Atanasiu, I. (2001). *European Competition Law Annual 2000: the Modernisation of EC Antitrust Policy*. Hart publishing.
Elzinga, K. G. (1977). The goals of antitrust: other than competition and efficiency, what else counts? *University of Pennsylvania Law Review*, **125**(6), 1191–1213.
Enchelmaier, S. (2012). Mandatory requirements under Art 101(3) TFEU: the complementary relationship between EU competition and free movement law. *Competition Law Journal*, **11**(3), 182–199.
Essens, O., Gerbrandy, A. and Lavrijssen, S. (2009). *National Courts and the Standard of Review in Competition Law and Economic Regulation*. Europa Law Publishing.
Evans, A. (1981). European competition law and consumers: The Article 85 (3) exemption. *European Competition Law Review*, **2**, 425–437.
Evans, A. (1985). Article 85(3) exemption: the notion of allowing consumers a fair share of the resulting benefits. In M. Goyens, ed., *EC Competition Policy and the Consumer Interest:*

proceedings of the Third European Workshop on Consumer Law, held in Louvain-la-Neuve, on May 10 and 11, 1984. Bruylant, Brussels, pp. 99–119.
Ezrachi, A. (2015). The competitive effects of parity clauses on online commerce. *European Competition Journal*, **11**(2–3), 488–519.
Ezrachi, A. (2016). Sponge. *Journal of Antitrust Enforcement*. The University of Oxford Centre for Competition Law and Policy Working Paper CCLP (L), 42. Chicago, 5(1), pp. 49–75.
Ezrachi, A. (2017). The ripple effects of online marketplace bans. *World Competition*, **40**(1), 1–18.
Fair Trade Foundation, (2019). *Competition Law and Sustainability – A Study of Industry Attitudes Towards Multi-Stakeholder Collaboration in the UK Grocery Sector*. Available at: https://www.fairtrade.org.uk/resources-library/researching/policy-resources/competition-law-and-sustainability/.
Farrell, J. and Katz, M. L. (2006). The economics of welfare standards in antitrust. *Competition Policy International*, **2**, 3–28.
Faull, J. and Nikpay, A. (2014). *The EC Law of Competition*. Oxford University Press.
Faure and, M. and Bergh, R. Van den (1995). Restrictions of competition on insurance markets and the applicability of EC antitrust law, *Kyklos*, 48(1), 65–85.
Felsö, F., Baarsma, B. and Mulder, J. D. W. E. (2007). Cooperation for tenders: is it a threat to competition? Advancing public procurement, 71-96. In K. V. Thai and G. Piga, eds., *Advancing Public Procurement: Practices, Innovation, and Knowledge Sharing*. Boca Raton, pp. 71–96.
Fingleton, J. *et al.* (2017). The implications of Brexit for UK competition law and policy. *Journal of Competition Law & Economics*, **13**(3), 389–422.
Fletcher, A. (2020). Market investigations for digital platforms: panacea or complement? *Journal of European Competition Law & Practice*, **12**(1), 44–55.
Foer, A. A. (2006). The goals of antitrust: thoughts on consumer welfare in the US. In P. Marsden, ed., *Handbook of Research in Trans-Atlantic Antitrust*. Edward Elgar Publishing, pp. 266–593.
Foer, A. A. and Durst, A. (2018). The multiple goals of antitrust. *The Antitrust Bulletin*, **63**(4), 494–508.
Forrester, I. (1994). Competition structures for the 21st century. In B. E. Hawk, ed., *Annual Proceedings of the Fordham Corporate Law Institute*. Kluwer Law International, pp. 445–503.
Forrester, I. (2001). The modernisation of EC antitrust policy: compatibility, efficiency, legal security. In C.-D. Ehlermann, and I. Atansiu, eds., *European Competition Law Annual 2000: The Modernisation of EC Antitrust Policy*, pp. 75–110.
Forrester, I. (2006). Where law meets competition: is wouters like a cassis de Dijon or a Platypus. In C.-D. Ehlermann, and I. Atanasiu, eds., *European Competition Law Annual 2004: the Relationship between Competition Law and the (Liberal) Professions*. Hart Publishing, pp. 271–294.
Forrester, I. (2008). Creating new rules or closing easy cases: policy consequences for public enforcement of settlements under Article 9 of regulation 1/2003. In C.-D. Ehlermann, and M. Marquis, eds., *European Competition Law Annual*, pp. 637–661.
Forrester, I. (2011). A challenge for Europe's judges: the review of fines in competition cases, *European Law Review*, **36**(2), 185–207.
Forrester, I. and Norall, C. (1984). Laicization of community law: self-help and the rule of reason: how competition law is and could be applied. *Common Market Law Review*, **21**(1), 11–51.
Fox, E. M. (2013). Against goals, *Fordham Law Review*, 81(5), 2157–2162.

Franck, J.-U. (2017). Defining the leeway for business cooperation- remaining peculiarities under German competition law after its Europeanisation. *Paper Presented at the Fifth International Conference 'Business Networks and Competition Law', University of Valencia, 20–21 Octo.*

Frazer, T. (1990). Competition policy after 1992: the next step. *The Modern Law Review*, **53** (5), 609–623.

Freeman, P. (2008). Is Competition Everything? Talk at the Law Society on 21 July 2008. Available at: http://www.docstoc.com/docs/28498545/Peter-Freeman-Speech-at-the-Law-Society-European-Group—Is.

Frese, M. (2014). *Sanctions in EU Competition Law: principles and Practice*. Bloomsbury Publishing.

Friederiszick, H. W. and Maier-Rigaud, F. P. (2008). Triggering inspections ex officio: moving beyond a passive EU cartel policy, *Journal of Competition Law and Economics*, 4 (1), 89–113.

Galligan, D. J. (1990). *Discretionary Powers – A Legal Study of Official Discretion*. Oxford University Press.

GCLC Annual Conference (2010). *Towards an Optimal Enforcement of Competition Rules in Europe: time for a Review of Regulation 1/2003?* Edited by M. Merola and D. F. Waelbroeck. Groupe de Boeck.

Geradin, D. (2000). Introduction. In D. Geradin, ed., *The Liberalization of State Monopolies in the European Union and Beyond*. Kluwer Law International, pp. ix–xii.

Geradin, D. (2006). Efficiency claims in EC competition law and sector-specific regulation the evolution of European competition law: whose regulation, which competition? In H. Ullrich, ed., *The Evolution of European Competition Law: Whose Regulation, Which Competition?* Edward Elgar Publishing.

Geradin, D. and Henry, D. (2004). Competition law in the new member states – where do we come from? Where do we go? In *Modernisation and Enlargement: Two Major Challenges for EC Competition Law*. Intersentia nv, pp. 273–310.

Geradin, D. and Henry, D. (2005). The EC fining policy for violations of competition law: an empirical review of the commission decisional practice and the community courts' judgments. *European Competition Journal*, 1(2), 401–473.

Geradin, D. and Petit, N. (2005). Judicial remedies under EC competition law: complex issues arising from the modernization process. In B. E. Hawk, ed., *Annual Proceedings of the Fordham Corporate Law Institute*. Juris Publishing, pp. 393–439.

Geradin, D. and Petit, N. (2012). Judicial review in European Union competition law: a quantitative and qualitative assessment. In M. Merola and J. Derenne, eds., *The Role of the Court of Justice of the European Union in Competition Law Cases*. Bruylant, pp. 21–72.

Gerard, D. (2010). EU competition policy after Lisbon: time to review the 'state action doctrine'? *Journal of European Competition Law & Practice*, 1(3), 202–210.

Gerard, D. (2011). Breaking the EU antitrust enforcement deadlock: re-empowering the courts? *European Law Review*, **36**(4), 457–479.

Gerard, D. (2012). The effects-based approach under Article 101 TFEU and its paradoxes: modernisation at war with itself? In J. Bourgeois and D. Waelbroeck, eds., *Ten Years of Effects-Based Approach in EU Competition Law Enforcement*. Brussels: Bruylant, pp. 17–41.

Gerard, D. (2013). Negotiated remedies in the modernization era: the limits of effectiveness. In P. Lowe, M. Marquis and G. Monti, eds., *European Competition Law Annual*. Hart Publishing, pp. 139–183.

Gerber, D. J. (1994a). Constitutionalizing the economy: German neo-liberalism, competition law and the 'new' Europe. *The American Journal of Comparative Law*, **42**(1), 25–84.

Gerber, D. J. (1994b). The transformation of European community competition law. *Harvard International Law Journal*, **35**, 97–147.
Gerber, D. J. (1998). *Law and Competition in Twentieth Century Europe: protecting Prometheus*. Oxford University Press.
Gerber, D. J. (2008). Two forms of modernization in European competition law, *Fordham International Law Journal*, **31**(5), 1235–1265.
Gerber, D. J. (2009). Competition law and the institutional embeddedness of economics. In J. Drexl, L. Idot and J. Moneger, eds., *Economic Theory and Competition Law*. Edward Elgar Publishing.
Gerber, D. J. (2012). The goals of European competition law: some distortions in the literature - comment on Parret. In D. Zimmer, ed., *The Goals of Competition Law*. Edward Elgar Publishing, pp. 85–94.
Gerbrandy, A. (2015). Addressing the legitimacy problem for competition authorities taking into account non-economic values: the position of the Dutch competition authority, *European Law Review*, **5**, 769–781.
Gerbrandy, A. (2017). Solving a sustainability-deficit in European competition law. *World Competition*, **40**(4), 539–562.
Gerbrandy, A., Janssen, W. and Thomsin, L. (2019). Shaping the social market economy after the Lisbon treaty: how social is public economic law. *Utrecht Law Review*, **15**(2), 32–46.
Gerbrandy, A. and Lachnit, E. (2013). Bid-rigging with gingerbread candy: adventures in the land of the Dutch construction cartel. In B. Rodger, ed., *Landmark Cases in Competition Law Around the World in Fourteen Stories*. Kluwer Law International, pp. 203–231.
German Commercial Law Firms, J. (2017). DEAL DES MONATS 11/17: Auf Kurs gebracht, Allen & Overy und Blomstein steuern Kieler Werft in ein Korvetten-Konsortium. Available at: https://www.juve.de/rechtsmarkt/rechtsmarkt-ausgaben-2017/deal-des-monats-1117.
German Monopolies Commission (2000). Cartel policy change in the European Union? On the European commission's white paper of 28th April 1999. *Special report by the German Monopolies Commission pursuant to Sec. 44, para. 1 of the Act Against Restraints of Competition (GWB)*. Baden-Baden: Nomos-Verl.-Ges.
Gerse, J. E. (2010). Designing agencies. In D. A. Farber and J. OConnell, eds., *Handbook on Public Choice and Public Law*. Edward Elgar Publishing, p. 333.
Ginsburg, D. and Haar, D. (2014). Resolving conflicts between competition and other values: the roles of courts and other institutions in the US and the EU. In P. Lowe and M. Marquis, eds., *European Competition Law Annual*. Hart Publishing, pp. 417–435.
Gippini-Fournier, E. (2008). *The Modernisation of European Competition Law: First Experiences with Regulation 1/2003. Community Report to the FIDE Congress 2008*.
Goyder, D. G. (2009). *Goyderss EC Competition Law*. Oxford University Press.
Graham, C. (2009). Judicial review of the decisions of the competition authorities and the economic regulators in the UK, In O. Essens, A. Gerbrandy and S. Lavrijssen, eds., *National Courts and the Standard of Review in Competition Law and Economic Regulation*. Europa Law Publishing.
Graupner, F. (2007). The battle over the role of European competition policy: now you see it, now you don't, *Competition Law Journal*, **6**(2), 89.
Graupner, R. (1965). German antitrust law. English translation. *The Rules of Competition in the European Economic Community*. Martinus Nijhoff.
Graupner, R. (2012). *The Rules of Competition in the European Economic Community: a study of the Substantive Law on a Comparative Law Basis with Special Reference to Patent Licence Agreements and Sole Distributorship Agreemen*. Springer Science & Business Media.

Greaves, R. (1991). *Transport Law of the European Community*. Atlantic Highlands.
Greaves, R. (1994). *EC Block Exemption Regulations*. Chancery Law Publications.
Green, N. (1988). Article 85 in perspective: stretching jurisdiction, narrowing the concept of a restriction and plugging a few gaps. *European Competition Law Review*, 9(2), 190–206.
Von der Groeben, H. (1961). 'Policy on competition in the European Economic Community. Supplement to the Bulletin of the European Economic Community 7-8/61'.
Von der Groeben, H. (1987). *The European Community, The formative years. The struggle to establish the Common Market and the Political Union (1958-66)*. Office for Official Publications of the European Communities.
Groves, P. J. (1995). What ever she brings we sing: DG IV Rebukes the car industry. *European Competition Law Review* 1, 16(2), 98–103.
Guidi, M. (2016). *Competition Policy Enforcement in EU Member States*. Springer.
Gyselen, L. (1984). Vertical restraints in the distribution process: strength and weakness of the free rider rationale under EEC competition law. *Common Market Law Review*, 21(4), 647–668.
Gyselen, L. (1989). State action and the effectiveness of the EEC Treaty's competition provisions. *Common Market Law Review*, 26(1), 33–60.
Gyselen, L. (1993). Anti-competitive state measures under the EC Treaty: towards a substantive legality standard. *European Law Review Competition*, Supp Comp, 55–89.
Gyselen, L. (1994). The emerging interface between competition policy and environmental policy in the EC. In J. Cameron, P. Demaret and D. Geradin, eds., *Trade and the Environment: The Search for Balance*. Cameron May.
Gyselen, L. (2000). Case C-67/96, Albany v. Stichting Bedrijfspensioenfonds textielindustrie; joined cases C-115-117/97, Brentjens' Handelsonderneming v. Stichting Bedrijfspensioenfonds voor de handel in bouwmaterialen; and case C-219/97, Drijvende Bokken v. Stichting Pensio. *Common Market Law Review*, 37(2), 425–448.
Gyselen, L. (2002). The substantive legality test under Article 81-3 EC treaty—revisited in light of the commission's modernization initiative. In A. von Bogdanady, P. C. Mavroidis and Y. Mény, eds., *European Integration and International Co-ordination: Studies in Transnational Economic Law in Honour of Claus-Dieter Ehlermann*. Kluwer Law International, pp. 181–197.
Haas, P. M. (1992). Introduction: epistemic communities and international policy coordination. *International Organization*, 46(1), 1–35.
Hall, M. (2011). *Coding Case Law for Public Health Law Evaluation*. Public Health Law Research: Theory and Methods.
Hall, M. and Wright, R. (2008). Systematic content analysis of judicial opinions. *California Law Review*, 96(1), 63–122.
Harrington, J. E. (2011). When is an antitrust authority not aggressive enough in fighting cartels. *International Journal of Economic Theory*, 7(1), 39–50.
Hauteclocque, A. de (2009). Legal uncertainty and competition policy in European deregulated electricity markets: the case of long-term exclusive supply contracts. *World Competition*, 32(1), 91–112.
Hawk, B. E. (1972). Antitrust in the EEC - the first decade. *Fordham Law Review*, 41(2), 229–292.
Hawk, B. E. (1988). The American (anti-trust) revolution: lessons for the EEC. *European Competition Law Review*, 9(1), 53–87.
Hawk, B. E. (1995). System failure: vertical restraints and EC competition law, *Common Market Law Review*, 32(4), 973–989.
Hegymegi-Barakonyi, Z. et al. (2009). Hungary Report to the LIDC Conference 2009. Available at: http://www.ligue.org/index.php?page=vienna-september-2009.

Heide-Jorgensen, C. (2013). The relationship between Articles 101(1) TFEU and 101(3) TFEU. In C. Heide-Jorgensen, ed., *Aims and Values in Competition Law*. Copenhagen: Djøf Publishing, pp. 91–114.

Heinz, S. (2016). Online booking platforms and EU competition law in the wake of the German Bundeskartellamts booking.com infringement decision. *Journal of European Competition Law & Practice*, 7(8), 530–536.

Heitzer, B. (2008). Consumer welfare as a standard of competition policy. Speech in the European Competition Day.

Hengeler Mueller Weitzel Wirtz Law Firm (2000). German Antitrust Law. English Translation. Available at: http://www.iuscomp.org/gla/statutes/GWB.htm.

Holmes, M. and Davey, L. (2007). *A Practical Guide to National Competition Rules Across Europe*, 2nd ed. Kluwer Law International.

Holmes, S. (2020). Climate change, sustainability, and competition law. *Journal of Antitrust Enforcement*, 8, 354–405.

Hornsby, S. B. (1987). Competition policy in the 80s: more policy less competition. *European Law Review*, **12**(2), 79–101.

Horváth, B. and Tóth, T. (2016). *Antitrust Cases in the Financial Services Sector – An Overview of Seminal Hungarian and EU Cases. Nr. 2016/6.*

House of Lords Select Committee on Regulators. (2007). *UK Economic Regulators. 1st Report of Session 2006–07. Available at:*http://www.publications.parliament.uk/pa/ld200607/ldselect/ldrgltrs/189/189i.pdf.

Van Houtte, B. (1982). Standard of reason in EEC antitrust law: some comments on the application of parts 1 and 3 of Article 85. *Northwestern Journal of International Law & Business*, **4**(2), 497–516.

Hovenkamp, H. (1982). Distributive justice and the antitrust laws. *George Washington Law Review*, **51**(1), 1–31.

Hovenkamp, H. (1985). Antitrust policy after Chicago. *Michigan Law Review*, **84**(2), 213–284.

Hunold, M. (2016). Best price clauses: what policy as regards online platforms? *Journal of European Competition Law & Practice*, 8(2), 119–125.

Hyman, D. A. and Kovacic, W. E. (2013). Competition agencies with complex policy portfolios: divide or conquer? *Concurrences*, 9(9).

Ibáñez Colomo, P. (2010). On the application of competition law as regulation: elements for a theory. *Yearbook of European Law*, **29**(1), 261–306.

Ibáñez Colomo, P. (2012). Market failure, transaction costs and Article 101 (1) TFUE case law, *European Law Review*, **5**, 541–562.

Ibáñez Colomo, P. (2013). Three shifts in EU competition policy: towards standards, decentralization, settlements. *Maastricht Journal of European and Comparative Law*, **20**(3), 363–384.

Ibáñez Colomo, P. (2018). *The Shaping of EU Competition Law*. Cambridge University Press.

Ibáñez Colomo, P. and Kalintiri, A. (2020). The evolution of EU antitrust policy: 1966–2017. *The Modern Law Review*, **83**(2), 321–372.

Ibáñez Colomo, P. and De Pablo, A. L. (2017). On the notion of restriction of competition: what we know and what we don't know we know. In D. Gerard, M. Merola and B. Meyring, eds., *The Notion of Restriction of Competition: revisiting the Foundations of Antitrust Enforcement in Europe*. Bruylant.

Ibrahim, A. (2015). A re-evaluation of the concept of economic activity for the purpose of EU competition rules: the need for modernisation. *European Competition Journal*, **11**(1), 265–286.

Idot, L. (2015). Reform of regulation 1/2003: power to set priorities. *Concurrences*, **3–2015**, 51–58.

Israel, A. and Jakobs, M (2015). Germany: challenges from new online practices to established competition law principles, *Journal of European Competition Law & Practice*, **6**(8), 588–594.

Jacquemin, A. (1999). Theories of industrial organization and competition policy. In *Competition, Efficiency, and Welfare*. Boston, MA: Springer, pp. 199–222.

Janssen, C. and Kloosterhuis, E. (2016). The Wouters case law, special for a different reason? *European Competition Law Review*, **37**(8), 335–339.

Jennings, H. (2015). Prioritisation in antitrust enforcement – a finger in many pies. *Competition Law International*, **1**, 29.

Jenny, F. (1990). French competition policy in perspective. In K. George et al. eds., *Competition Policy in Europe and North America: Economic Issues and Institutions*. Harwood Academic Publishers, pp. 146–188.

Jenny, F. (2015). Worst decision of the EU court of justice: the Alrosa judgment in context and the future of commitment decisions. *Fordham International Law Journal*, **38**(3), 701–770.

Jenny, F. (2016). The institutional design of competition authorities: debates and trends. In F. Jenny and Y. Katsoulacos, eds., *Competition Law Enforcement in the BRICS and in Developing Countries*. Springer, Cham, pp. 1–57.

Joliet, R. (1967). *The Rule of Reason in Antitrust Law; American, German and Common Market Laws in Comparative Perspective*. Springer.

Joliet, R. (1988). National anti-competitive legislation and community law. *Fordham International Law Journal*, **12**(2), 163–188.

Jones, A. (2010). The journey toward an effects-based approach under Article 101 TFEU—the case of hardcore restraints. *The Antitrust Bulletin*, **55**(4), 783–818.

Jones, A. (2017). *Brexit: Implications for UK Competition Law*. Available at: https://papers.ssrn.com/sol3/papers.cfm?abstract_id=2923725.

Jones, A. and Sufrin, B. E. (2008). *EC Competition Law: text, Cases, and Materials*, 2nd ed. Oxford University Press.

Kalbfleisch, P. (2011). Aiming for alliance: competition law and consumer welfare. *Journal of European Competition Law & Practice*, **2**(2), 108–116.

Kalintiri, A. (2016). What's in a name? The marginal standard of review of 'complex economic assessments' in EU competition enforcement. *Common Market Law Review*, **53**(5), 1283–1316.

Kassim, H. and Wright, K. (2009). Bringing regulatory processes back in: the reform of EU antitrust and merger control. *West European Politics*, **32**(4), 738–755.

Kauper, T. E. (1987). The Sullivan approach to horizontal restraints. *California Law Review*, **75**(3), 893–916.

Keyte, J. (2017). Interview with professors eleanor fox and William Kovacic. *Antitrust*, **31**(2), 18–27.

Kieran, F. (2013). A separation of powers approach to non-efficiency goals in EU competition law. *European Public Law*, **19**(1), 189–208.

Kingston, S. (2001). A 'new division of responsibilities' in the proposed regulation to modernise the rules implementing Articles 81 and 82 EC? A warning call. *European Competition Law Review*, **22**(8), 340–350.

Kingston, S. (2010). Integrating environmental protection and EU competition law: why competition isn't special. *European Law Journal*, **16**(6), 780–805.

Kingston, S. (2011). *Greening EU Competition Law and Policy*. Cambridge University Press.

Kjolbye, L. (2004). The new commission guidelines on the application of Article 81 (3): an economic approach to Article 81. *European Competition Law Review*, **81**(3), 1–13.

Klees, A. (2006). Breaking the habits: the German competition law after the 7th amendment to the act against restraints of competition (GWB). *German Law Journal*, **7**(4), 399–420.

Kleine, M. and Rübel, C. (2015). Germany. In M. Thill-Tayara, ed., *Pharmaceutical Antitrust in 29 Jurisdictions Worldwide*. Globel Competition Review, pp. 68–74.

Kloosterhuis, E. (2017). Defining non-economic activities in competition law. *European Competition Journal*, **13**(1), 117–149.

Komninos, A. (2005). *Non-competition Concerns: resolution of Conflicts in the Integrated Article 81 EC. University of Oxford, Working Paper (L) 8.05.*

Korah, V. (1981a). Comfort letters-reflections on the perfume cases. *European Law Review*, **6**, 14–39.

Korah, V. (1981b). The rise and fall of provisional validity-the need for a rule of reason in EEC antitrust. *Northwestern Journal of International Law and Business*, **3**, 320–357.

Korah, V. (1982). *Competition Law of Britain and the Common Market*. BRILL.

Korah, V. (2001). The interface between intellectual property and antitrust: the European experience. *Antitrust Law Journal*, **69**(3), 801–839.

Korah, V. (2004). *An Introductory Guide to EC Competition Law and Practice*. Hart Publishing.

Kort, F. (1963). Content analysis of judicial opinions and rules of law. In G. A. Schubert and V. Aubert, eds., *Judicial Decision Making*. Free Press of Glencoe, pp. 133–197.

Kovacic, W. E. (2003). The modern evolution of US competition policy enforcement norms. *Antitrust Law Journal*, **71**, 377–478.

Kovacic, W. E. (2015a). A case for capping the dosage: leniency and competition authority governance. In C. Beaton-Welles and C. Tran, eds., *Anti-Cartel Enforcement in a Contemporary Age: leniency Religion*. Bloomsbury Publishing, pp. 123–135.

Kovacic, W. E. (2015b). Creating a respected brand: how regulatory agencies signal quality. *George Mason Law Review*, **22**(2), 237–259.

Kovacic, W. E. (2020). Market structure and market studies. In J. P. Choi, W. Lim and S.-H. Lee, eds., *Competition Law and Economics Developments, Policies and Enforcement Trends in the US and Korea*. Edward Elgar Publishing, pp. 30–50.

Kovacic, W. E., Hollman, H. M. and Grant, P. (2011). How does your competition agency measure up? *European Competition Journal*, **7**(1), 25–45.

Kovacs, A., Tóth, T. and Forgacs, A. (2016). Effects of European soft law at national administrative courts. *Loyola University Chicago International Law Review*, **14**(1), 1.

Kovács, C. and Reindl, A. P. (2013). he evolution of the Hungarian competition regime: 2 decades of dynamic change and continuity. In D. Lewis, ed., *Building New Competition Law Regimes: Selected Essays*. Edward Elgar Publishing, pp. 26–80.

Kroes, N. (2005). European competition policy – delivering better markets and better choices. Speech in the European Consumer and Competition Day London, 15 September 2005.

Kroes, N. (2007). Fact-based competition policy – the contribution of sector inquiries to better regulation, priority setting and detection. Speech in the 13th International Conference on Competition and the 14th European Competition Day SPEECH/07/186. Available at: http://europa.eu/rapid/press-release_SPEECH-07-186_en.pdf.

Kroes, N. (2009). Many achievements, more to do. Opening speech at international bar association conference: 'private and public enforcement of EU competition law – 5 years on'. SPEECH/09/106 given at the International Bar Association conference, Brussels.

Kuenzler, A. and Warlouzet, L. (2013). National traditions of competition law: a belated Europeanization through convergence?. In K. K. P. and H. Schweitzer, ed., *The Historical Foundations of EU Competition Law*. Oxford University Press.

Kuhn, K. U. (1997). Germany. In E. M. Graham and J. D. Richardson, eds., *Global Competition Policy*. Peterson Institute.

Lachnit, E. (2016). *Alternative Enforcement of Competition Law*. Dissertation.

Laffont, J.-J. and Tirole, J. (1991). The politics of government decision-making: a theory of regulatory capture. *The Quarterly Journal of Economics*, 106(4), 1089–1127.

Landes, W. M. and Posner, R. A. (1975). The private enforcement of law. *Journal of Legal Studies*, 4, 1–46.

Lanza, E. (2015). Mixed bodies and competition: balancing public measures and private interests. A snapshot of the API's judgment. *Italian Antitrust Review*, 2(1), 193–197.

Larouche, P. (2013). Legal emulation between regulatory competition and comparative law. In P. Larouche and P. Cserne, eds., *National Legal Systems and Globalization*. TMC Asser Press, pp. 247–287.

Lasserre, B. (2009). The new French competition law enforcement regime. *Competition Law International*, 5, 15–20.

Lavrijssen, S. (2009). More intensive judicial review in competition law and economic regulation in the Netherlands. In O. Essens, A. Gerbrandy and S. Lavrijssen, eds., *National Courts and the Standard of Review*. Europa Law Publishing.

Lavrijssen, S. (2010). What role for national competition authorities in protecting non-competition interests after Lisbon? *European Law Review*, 35(5), 636–659.

Lawlor, R. C. (1968). Fact content analysis of judicial opinions *Jurimetrics Journal*, 8(4), 107–130.

Lester, M. (2009). *UK Report to the LIDC Conference 2009*. Available at: http://www.ligue.org/index.php?page=vienna-september-2009.

Levitt, M. and Ziegler, C. (2014). The European commission's extension of the liner shipping consortia block exemption regulation until April 2020. *Journal of European Competition Law & Practice*, 5(10), 696–670.

Lianos, I. (2013). Some reflections on the question of the goals of EU competition law. In I. Lianos and D. Geradin, eds., *Handbook on European Competition Law*. Edward Elgar Publishing, pp. 1–84.

Lianos, I. *et al.* (2014). An optimal and just financial penalties system for infringements of competition law: a comparative analysis. Available at: https://papers.ssrn.com/sol3/papers.cfm?abstract_id=2542991.

Lianos, I. *et al.* (2017). *Brexit and Competition Law*. Available at: https://papers.ssrn.com/sol3/papers.cfm?abstract_id=3077221.

Lianos, I. (2018). Polycentric competition law. *Current Legal Problems*, 71(1), 161–213.

Lianos, I. (2019). The future of competition policy in Europe-some reflections on the interaction between industrial policy and competition law. *CLES Policy Paper Series*.

Lianos, I. and Genakos, C. (2013). Econometric evidence in EU competition law: an empirical and theoretical analysis. In I. Lianos and D. Geradin, eds., *Handbook on European Competition Law: enforcement and Procedure*. Edward Elgar Publishing.

Lianos, I. and Geradin, D. (2013). *Handbook on European Competition Law: enforcement and Procedure*. Edward Elgar Publishing.

Liefmann, R. (1932). *Cartels, Concerns and Trusts, History of Economic Thought Books*. Methuen.

Lista, A. (2013). *EU Competition Law and the Financial Services Sector*. Taylor & Francis.

Loozen, E. (2019). Strict competition enforcement and welfare: a constitutional perspective based on Article 101 TFEU and sustainability. *Common Market Law Review*, 56(5), 1265–1302.

Lowe, P. (2008). The design of competition policy institutions for the 21st century – the experience of the European commission and DG competition. *Competition Policy Newsletter*, 3, 1–11.

Mackenrodt, M. O. (2019). Price and condition parity clauses in contracts between hotel booking platforms and hotels IIC – international review of intellectual property and competition law. *IIC-International Review of Intellectual Property and Competition Law*, 50(9), 1131–1143.

Maher, I. (2002). Networking competition authorities in the European Union: diversity and change. In C. D. E. and I. A. eds., *European Competition Law Annual*. Bloomsbury Publishing, pp. 223–236.

Maier-Rigaud, F. (2012). On the normative foundations of competition law: efficiency, political freedom and the freedom to compete. In D. Zimmer, ed., *The Goals of Competition Law*. ASCOLA Com. Edward Elgar Publishing, pp. 132–168.

de la Mano, M. and Jones, A. (2018). Vertical agreements under EU competition law: proposals for pushing Article 101 analysis, and the modernization process, to a logical conclusion. In D. Healey and M. Jacbos, eds., *Handbook of Research Methods of Competition Law*. Edward Elgar Publishing.

Manzini, P. (2002). The European rule of reason-crossing the sea of doubt. *European Competition Law Review*, **23**(8), 392–399.

Marcos, F. and Sanchez-Graells, A. (2010). A missing step in the modernisation stairway of EU competition law–any role for block exemption regulations in the realm of regulation 1/2003? *The Competition Law Review*, 6(2), 183–201.

Markham, J. W. (1950). An alternative approach to the concept of workable competition. *The American Economic Review*, 40(3), 349–361.

Massadeh, A. (2015). Empirical Assessment of Public Enforcement of Competition Law: Criteria and Three Case Studies (EU, UK and France). Dissertation.

Maziarz, A. (2014). Do non-economic goals count in interpreting Article 101(3) TFEU? *European Competition Journal*, 10(2), 341–359.

Mehta, P. (2006). Competition regimes in the world: a civil society report, in. Available at: https://scholar.google.nl/scholar?hl=en&q=competition+regimes+in+the+world+-+a+civil+society+report&btnG=&as_sdt=1%2C5&as_sdtp=#0.

Meij, A. (2009). Judicial review in the EC courts: Tetra Laval and beyond. In O. Essens, A. Gerbrandy and S. Lavrijssen, eds., *National Courts and the Standard of Review in Competition Law and Economic Regulation*. Europa Law Publishing.

Melamed, A. D. and Petit, N. (2019). The misguided assault on the consumer welfare standard in the age of platform markets. *Review of Industrial Organization*, **54**, 741–774.

Mendes, J. (2014). Law, public interest and interpretation: prolegomena of a normative framework on administrative discretion in the EU. *Yale Law & Economics Research Paper*.

Merkin, R. and Williams, K. (1980). Competition act 1980. *The Modern Law Review*, **43**(4), 429–440.

Mestmäcker, E. J. (2000). The EC commissions modernization of competition policy: a challenge to the community's constitutional order. *European Business Organization Law Review*, 1(3), 401–444.

van Miert, K. (1993). Competition policy in the 1990s. Speech for the Royal Institute of International Affairs (Chatham House, London), 11 May 1993.

Monti, G. (2002). Article 81 EC and public policy. *Common Market Law Review*, **37**, 1057–1099.

Monti, G. (2007). *EC Competition Law*. Cambridge University Press.

Monti, G. (2008). Managing the intersection of utilities regulation and EC competition law. *Competition Law Review*, 4(2), 123–145.

Monti, G. (2013). Restraints on selective distribution agreements. *World Competition*, **36**, 489–511.

Monti, G. (2014a). Independence, interdependence and legitimacy: The EU commission, national competition authorities, and the European competition network, *SSRN Electronic Journal*. Available at: http://awards.concurrences.com/IMG/pdf/ssrn-id2379320.pdf.

Monti, G. (2014b). Legislative and executive competences in competition law. In L. Azoulai, ed., *The Question of Competence in the European Union*. Oxford University Press, pp. 101–124.

Monti, G. (2017). The United Kingdom's contribution to European Union competition law. *Fordham International Law Journal*, 40(5), 1443–1474.

Monti, G. and Mulder, J. (2017). Escaping the clutches of EU competition law. *European Law Review*, **42**(2), 635–656.

Monti, M. (2000a). Competition in a Social Market Economy, Speech at the Conference of the European Parliament and the European Commission on 'Reform of European Competition law' in Freiburg on 9/10 November 2000.

Monti, M. (2000b). Guest editorial: a European competition policy for today and tomorrow. *World Competition. Kluwer Law International*, **23**(2), 1–4.

Monti, M. (2000c). The application of Article 81(3) by ntional courts. Speech in Trier, 27 November 2000.

Monti, M. (2003). European competition policy: Quo Vadis? XX. International Forum on European Competition Policy.

Monti, M. (2004). Convergence in EU-US antitrust policy regarding mergers and acquisitions: an EU perspective. Speech in the UCLA Law First Annual Institute on US an EU Antitrust Aspects of Mergers and Acquisitions (Los Angeles, 28.2.2004).

Morgan, B. and Yeung, K. (2007). *An Introduction to Law and Regulation: Text and Materials*. Cambridge University Press.

Morgan, E. and McGuire, S. (2004). Transatlantic divergence: GE–Honeywell and the EUs merger policy. *Journal of European Public Policy*, **11**(1), 39–56.

Mortelmans, K. (2001). Towards convergence in the application of the rules on free movement and on competition? *Common Market Law Review*, **38**(3), 613–649.

Moses, L. B. (2013). How to think about law, regulation and technology: problems with 'technology' as a regulatory target. *Law, Innovation and Technology*, **5**(1), 1–20.

Motta, M. (2004). *Competition Policy: theory and Practice*. Cambridge University Press.

Mueller, R., Heidenhain, M. and Schneider, H. (1991). *German Antitrust Law: An Introduction to the German Antitrust Law with German Text and Synoptic*. Juris Puc Inc. Fritz Knapp Verlag.

Mundt, A. (2020). The Bundeskartellamt in times of COVID-19: adaption of workflows and implications for our enforcement practice. *Journal of Antitrust Enforcement*, 8(2), 253–255.

Muris, T. (2003). *State Intervention/State Action-A US Perspective. Fordham Corporate Law Institute New York, Law and Economics Working Paper Series*. Available at: https://papers.ssrn.com/sol3/papers.cfm?abstract_id=545163.

Nagy, C. I. (2017). The concept of anti-competitive object under EU competition law: comparative perspectives and European realities. In A. Almăşan and P. Whelan, eds., *The Consistent Application of EU Competition Law: substantive and Procedural Challenges*. Springer, pp. 55–70.

National Audit Office, T. (2010). *Review of the UKs Competition Landscape*. Available at: https://www.nao.org.uk/wp-content/uploads/2010/03/0910_competition_landscape.pdf.

National Audit Office, T. (2016). *The UK Competition Regime*. Available at: https://www.nao.org.uk/report/the-uk-competition-regime/.

Nazzini, R. (2006). Article 81 EC between time present and time past: a normative critique of 'restriction of competition' in EU law. *Common Market Law Review*, **81**(1), 497–536.

Nazzini, R. (2011). *The Foundations of European Union Competition Law: the Objective and Principles of Article 102*. Oxford University Press.

Neuendorf, K. A. (2017). *The Content Analysis Guidebook*, 2nd ed. SAGE Publications.

Nicolaides, P. (2005). The balancing myth: the economics of Article 81 (1) & (3). *Legal Issues of Economic Integration*, **32**(2), 123–145.

Norberg, S. (2007). Making a virtue out of necessity and at the same time Strengthening European competition law enforcement. How the white paper on the modernisation reform came about. In P. N. Liechtenstein of et al. eds., *Economic Law and Justice in Times of Globalisation*. Nomos Verlagsgesellschaft mbH & Co. KG, pp. 523–542.

Nowag, J. (2015). Wouters, when the condemned live longer: a comment on OTOC and CNG. *European Competition Law Review*, **36**(1), 39–44.

Nowag, J. (2016). *Environmental Integration in Competition and Free-Movement Laws*. Oxford University Press.

OLoughlin, R. (2003). EC competition rules and free movement rules: an examination of the parallels and their furtherance by the ECJ Wouters decision. *European Competition Law Review*, **24**(2), 62–69.

Odudu, O. (2005). The meaning of undertaking within 81 EC. *Cambridge Yearbook of European Legal Studies*, **7**, 209–239.

Odudu, O. (2006). *The Boundaries of EC Competition Law: The Scope of Article 81*. Oxford University Press.

Odudu, O. (2008). Developing private enforcement in the EU: lessons from the Roberts court. *Antitrust Bulletin*, **53**, 873–902.

Odudu, O. (2020). Feeding the nation in times of crisis: the relaxation of competition law in the United Kingdom. *Competition Law Journal*, **19**(2), 68–78.

Ogus, A. (1995). Rethinking self-regulation. *Oxford Journal of Legal Studies*, **15**(1), 97–108.

Olsen, G. and Roy, B. (2006). The new world of proactive EC antitrust enforcement - sector inquiries by the European commission. *Antitrust*, **21**(3), 82–88.

Orbach, B. Y. (2011). The antitrust consumer welfare paradox. *Journal of Competition Law and EconomicsEconomics*, **7**(1), 133–164.

Ottow, A. (2015). *Market and Competition Authorities: good Agency Principles*. Oxford Scholarship Online.

De Pablo, A. L. (2011). The slow death of Article 101(3). *Chillin' Competition* blog, 28.10.2011. Available at: https://chillingcompetition.com/2011/10/28/the-slow-death-of-article-1013/.

De Pablo, A. L. (2015). In no man's land- case T-355/13, easyJet. *Chilling Competition* Blog. Available at: https://chillingcompetition.com/2015/01/27/in-no-mans-land-case-t-35513-easyjet/.

Pace, L. (2007). *European Antitrust Law-Prohibitions, Merger Control and Procedures*. Edward Elgar Publishing.

Papp, M. (2017). Application of EU competition law by the Hungarian judiciary: cooperation with the ECJ and relying on the case law of the ECtHR. In A. Almăşan and P. Whelan, eds., *The Consistent Application of EU Competition Law*. Springer, pp. 255–270.

Parret, L. (2009). Do we (still) know what we are protecting? The discussion on the objectives of competition law from different perspectives. *TILEC Discussion paper 2009–10*.

Parret, L. (2012). The multiple personalities of EU competition law: time for a comprehensive debate on its objectives. In D. Zimmer, ed., *The Goals of Competition Law*. Edward Elgar Publishing, pp. 61–84.

Patel, K. and Schweitzer, H. (2013). *The Historical Foundations of EU Competition Law*. Oxford University Press.

de Paz, J. (2014). Understanding the limits of judicial review in European competition law. *Journal of Antitrust Enforcement*, **2**(1), 203–224.

Peeperkorn, L. (2003). IP licences and competition rules: striking the right balance. *World Competition*, **26**(4), 527–539.

Peeperkorn, L. (2016). Coherence in the application of Articles 101 and 102: a realistic prospect or an elusive goal? *World Competition*, **39**(3), 389–411.

Pera, A. (2008). Changing views of competition, economic analysis and EC antitrust law, *European Competition Journal*, 4(1), 127–168.

Pérez, S. M. R. and van de Scheur, S. (2013). The evolution of the law on Articles 85 and 86 EEC [Articles 101 and 102 TFEU] ordoliberalism and its Keynesian challenge. In K. K. Patel and H. Schweitzer, eds., *The Historical Foundations of EU Competition Law*. Oxford University Press, pp. 19–53.

Perroud, T. (2013). Administrative law and competition: how administrative law protects the market? Leviathan as an ordinary market player in Europe? *Jean Monnet Working Paper Series*.

Petit, N. (2009). The guidelines on the application of Article 81(3) EC: a critical review. Working Paper 4/1009 *Institut détudes juridiques Européennes, Liège*.

Petit, N. (2010). How much discretion do, and should, competition authorities enjoy in the course of their enforcement activities? A multi-jurisdictional assessment. *Concurrences: revue des Droits de la Concurrence*, 1, 44–62.

Petit, N. (2011). The Perverse Effects of the Courts Ruling in Tele2 Polska. Available at: http://chillingcompetition.com/2011/06/17/the-perverse-effects-of-the-courts-ruling-in-tele2-polska/.

Petit, N. and Rabeux, L. (2009). Judicial review in French competition law and economic regulation. In O. Essens, A. Gerbrandy and S. Lavrijssen, eds., *National Courts and the Standard of Review in Competition Law and Economic Regulation*. Europa Law Publishing.

Petit, N. and Rato, M. (2008). From hard to soft enforcement of EC competition law – a bestiary of 'sunshine' enforcement systems. In C. Gheur and N. Petit, eds., *Alternative Enforcement Techniques in EC Competition Law: settlements, Commitments and Other Novel Instruments*. Bruylant, pp. 183–220.

Piergiovanni, M. and DElia, P. (2008). Self-assessment of agreements under Article 81 EC: is there a need for more commission guidance. *Global Competition Policy*, OCT-08 (2)(2).

Pina, Á. (2014). *Enhancing Competition and the Business Environment in Hungary*. Available at: http://www.oecd-ilibrary.org/economics/enhancing-competition-and-the-business-environment-in-hungary_5jz2pwfronzq-en.

Pitofsky, R. (1979). Political content of antitrust. *University of Pennsylvania Law Review*, **127** (4), 1051–1075.

Pittman, R. (2004). Competition agencies and the restructuring of formally planned economics: lessons form the experience of central and eastern Europe. In D. Geradin, ed., *Modernisation and Enlargement: Two Major Challenges for EC Competition Law*. Intersentia nv.

Polański, J. (2014). *Informant Reward Schemes in Competition Enforcement*. Available at: https://papers.ssrn.com/sol3/papers.cfm?abstract_id=2457450.

Policy Studies Institute (1989). Government measures in the United Kingdom from 1945 to 1980. In *Appendix D to Innovation and Industrial Strength In the UK, West Germany, United States and Japan*. Available at: http://www.psi.org.uk/publications/archivepdfs/Innovation and Indust/APPD pdf.

Porrini, D. (2016). Which consequences in the insurance market for the end of the block exemption. *Italian Antitrust Review*, **2**, 160–173.

Posner, R. (2009). *Antitrust Law* University of Chicago Press.

Potter, W. J. and Levine-Donnerstein, D. (1999). Rethinking validity and reliability in content analysis. *Journal of Applied Communication Research*, **27**(3), 258–284.

de Pree, J. and Molin, S. (2013). Netherlands. In *Cartel Regulation: the Application of Competition Regulation in 48 Jurisdictions Worldwide*. Global Competition Review.

Prek, M. and Lefèvre, S. (2016). Competition litigation before the general court: quality if not quantity? *Common Market Law Review*, **53**(1), 65–90.

Prosser, T. (2010). EU competition law and public services. In E. Mossialos, ed., *Health Systems Governance in Europe: the Role of European Union Law and Policy*. Cambridge University Press.

Raban, O. (2010). The fallacy of legal certainty: why vague legal standards may be better for capitalism and liberalism. *Public International Law Journal*, **19**.

Rabinovici, I. (2016). Public exchange of information after container shipping. *Journal of European Competition Law & Practice*, 8(3), 149–156.

Refworld (1990). Constitution of the Republic of Hungary (repealed 1989), English Translation. Available at: http://www.refworld.org/docid/3ae6b4e714.html.

Reynolds, M., Macrory, S. and Chowdhury, M. (2009). EU competition policy in the financial crisis: extraordinary measures. *Fordham International Law Journal*, **33**(1), 1670–1731.

Riesenfeld, S. (1960). The legal protection of competition in France. *California Law Review*, 48(4), 574–595.

Riley, A. (2003a). EC antitrust modernisation: the commission does very nicely—thank you! Part one: regulation 1 and the notification Burden. *European Competition Law Review*, **24** (11), 604–615.

Riley, A. (2003b). EC antitrust modernisation: the commission does very nicely—thank you! Part two: between the idea and the reality: decentralisation under regulation. *European Competition Law Review*, **24**(12), 657–672.

Riley, A. (2007). The EU reform treaty and the competition protocol: undermining EC competition law. *European Competition Law Review*, **12**, 703.

Ritchie, J. *et al.* (2013). *Qualitative Research Practice: a Guide for Social Science Students and Researchers*. SAGE.

Rivas, J. (2015). Editors interview with commissioner vestager. *World Competition*, **38**(2), 183–187.

Rodger, B. ed. (2008). *Article 234 and Competition Law: an Analysis*. Wolters Kluwer.

Van Rompuy, B. (2011). CPI antitrust chronicle the impact of the Lisbon treaty on EU competition law: a review of recent case law of the EU courts. *Antitrust Chronicle*, **12**, 1–9.

Van Rompuy, B. (2012). *Economic Efficiency: the Sole Concern of Modern Antitrust Policy?: Non-efficiency Considerations Under Article 101 TFEU*. Kluwer Law International.

Ross, M. (2000). Article 16 EC and services of general interest: from derogation to obligation? *European Law Review*, **25**(1), 22–38.

Rousseva, E. (2013). Reflections on the relevance and proof of efficiency defences in modern EU antitrust law. In J. Bourgeois and D. Waelbroeck, eds., *Ten Years of Effects-Based Approach in EU Competition Law*. Bruylant, pp. 239–291.

Russe, W. A. and Griffiths., R. (1998). Paradise lost or paradise regained? Cartel policy and cartel legislation in the Netherlands. In S. Martin, ed., *Competition Policies in Europe*. Elsevier, pp. 15–39.

Sabbatini, P. (2008). *Funding the Budget of a Competition Authority with the Fines it Imposes*. Available at: http://acle.uva.nl/binaries/content/assets/subsites/amsterdam-center-for-law–economics/cr-meetings/2009/paper_sabbatini.pdf.

Sanchez-Graells, A. (2014). *Monitor and the Competition and Markets Authority, University of Leicester School of Law Research paper* No. 14-32. Available at: http://papers.ssrn.com/sol3/papers.cfm?abstract_id=2528569.

Sárai, J. (2016). New instrument introduced into the Hungarian competition act- the warning. *OECD-GVH RCC Newsletter*, 6, 27–28.
Sauter, W. (1997). Competition law and industrial policy in the EU. *OUP Catalogue*.
Sauter, W. (2010). *The Role of Competition Rules in the Context of Healthcare Reform in the Netherlands*. Available at: https://papers.ssrn.com/sol3/papers.cfm?abstract_id=1546445.
Sauter, W. (2014). Proportionality in EU competition law. *European Competition Law Review*, **35**, 327–332.
Sauter, W. (2015). Containing corporatism: EU competition law and private interest government. *European Competition Law Review*, **36**(5), 187–193.
Sauter, W. (2016). *Coherence in EU Competition Law*. Oxford University Press.
Schepel, H. (2002). Delegation of regulatory powers to private parties under EC competition law: towards a procedural public interest test. *Common Market Law Review*, **39**(2), 31–51.
Schiek, D. and Gideon, A. (2018). Outsmarting the gig-economy through collective bargaining – EU competition law as a barrier to smart cities. *International Review of Law, Computers & Technology*, **32**(2–3), 275–294.
Schinkel, M. and Spiegel, Y. (2016). Can collusion promote sustainable consumption and production? *International Journal of Industrial Organization*, **53**, 371–398.
Schmidt, A. (2001). Non-competition factors in the European competition policy: the necessity of institutional reforms. *CeGE Discussion Paper, No.* 13.
Schwartz, L. B. (1979). Justice and other non-economic goals of antitrust. *University of Pennsylvania Law Review*, **127**(4), 1076–1081.
Schweitzer, H. (2007). Competition law and public policy: reconsidering an uneasy relationship. The example of Article 81 *Working Paper No.* 30. *European University Institute (EUI), Department of Law*.
Schweitzer, H. (2008). Commitment decisions under Article 9 of regulation 1/2003: the developing EC practice and case law. Available at: https://papers.ssrn.com/sol3/papers.cfm?abstract_id=1306245.
Schweitzer, H. (2011). Services of general economic interest: European law's impact on the role of markets and of member states. In M. Cremona, ed., *Market Integration and Public Services in the European Union*. Oxford University Press, pp. 11–62.
Schweitzer, H. (2012). *Commitment Decisions in the EU and in the Member States: Functions and Risks of a New Instrument of Competition Law Enforcement within a Federal Enforcement*. Available at: https://papers.ssrn.com/sol3/papers.cfm?abstract_id=2101630.
Schweitzer, H. (2013). Judicial review in EU competition law. In I. Lianos and D. Geradin, eds., *Handbook on European Competition Law*. Edward Elgar Publishing, pp. 491–538.
Scott, A. (2012). The evolution of competition law and policy in the UK. In P. S. Mehta, ed., *Evolution of Competition Laws and their Enforcement, A Political Economy Perspective*. Routledge.
Seidel, K. and Federico Pace, L. (2013). The drafting and the role of regulation 17: a hard-fought compromise. In K. Klaus Patel and H. Schweitzer, eds., *The Historical Foundations of EU Competition Law*. Oxford University Press, pp. 54–88.
Semmelmann, C. (2008a). *Social Policy Goals in the Interpretation of Article 81 EC*. Nomos Verlagsgesellschaft mbH & Co. KG.
Semmelmann, C. (2008b). The future role of the non-competition goals in the interpretation of Article 81 EC. *Global Antitrust Review*, **1**(1), 15–47.
SER (2003). *Report on the Review and Amendment of the Dutch Competition Act. Available at:* https://www.ser.nl/en/~/media/files/internet/talen/engels/2003/2003_06.ashx.
de Silva, I. (2019). The future of competition law: time to change or time to adapt? Speech in the Fordham Universitys Annual Conference 12 September 2019.

Simonsson, I. (2010). *Legitimacy in EU Cartel Control, Modern Studies in European Law*. Hart Publishing.

Sinclair, A. (2017). Proposal for a directive to empower national competition authorities to be more effective enforcers (ECN+). *Journal of European Competition Law & Practice*, 8(10), 625–633.

Smith, A. (1937). The wealth of nations. modern library. *New York*, **423**.

Snoep, M. (2020a). Competition enforcement in times of crisis – a perspective from the ACM. *Journal of Antitrust Enforcement*, 8(2), 267–269.

Snoep, M. (2020b). Sustainability goals and antitrust: finding the common ground. Speech in the Concurrences Webinar, of 14 September 2020. Available at: https://events.concurrences.com/en/sustainability.

Sosnick, S. H. (1958). A critique of concepts of workable competition. *The Quarterly Journal of Economics*, **72**(3), 380–423.

Souam, S. (1998). French competition policy. In Z. Griliches and V. Ringstad, eds., *Contributions to Economic Analysis*. North-Holland Publishing Company.

Stefan, O. (2008). European competition soft law in European courts: a matter of hard principles? *European Law Journal*, **14**(6), 753–772.

Steindorff, E. (1984). Article 85 and the rule of reason *Common Market Law Review*, **21**(1), 639–646.

Stephan, A. (2013). Cartels. In I. Lianos and D. Geradin, eds., *Handbook on European Competition Law: substantive Aspects*. Edward Elgar Publishing, pp. 217–240.

Stern, J. (2015). Sectoral regulation and competition policy: the UKs concurrency arrangements - an economic perspective. *Journal of Competition Law & Economics*, **11**(4), 881–915.

Steuer, R. M. (2017). The horizons of antitrust. *St. Johns Law Review*, **91**(1), 177–210.

Stewart, J. H. (1951). *A Documentary Survey of the French Revolution*. Macmillan.

Stigler, G. J. (1971). The theory of economic regulation. *Bell Journal of Economics and Management Science*, **2**(1), 3–21.

Stocking, G. W. (1956). On the concept of workable competition as an antitrust guide. *Antitrust Bulletin*, **2**, 3–39.

Streeck, W. and Schmitter, P. C. (1985). *Private Interest Government: beyond Market and State*. SAGE Publications.

Stucke, M. E. (2012). Reconsidering antitrust's goals. *Boston College Law Review*, **53**(2), 551–629.

Stucke, M. E. (2015). Leniency, whistle-blowing and the individual: should we create another race to the competition agency? In C. Beaton-Wells and C. Tran, eds., *Anti-Cartel Enforcement in a Contemporary Age: leniency Religion*. Bloomsbury Publishing, p. 209.

Sufrin, B. (2006). The evolution of Article 81(3) of the EC treaty. *The Antitrust Bulletin*, **51**(4), 915–981.

Svetlicinii, A., Bernatt, M. and Botta, M. (2018). The dark matter in EU competition law: non-infringement decisions in the new EU member states before and after Tele2 Polska. *European Law Review*, **43**(3), 422–443.

Szilágyi (2013). Amendment to the act CXXVIII of 2012 on inter-branch organizations, english translation. In Szilágyi, ed., *Some Aspects of Liability in Hungarian Competition Law Enforcement*. Available at: https://jak.ppke.hu/uploads/articles/12417/file/liability_2013_plain.pdf.

Szilagyi, P. (2012). Hungarian competition law & policy: the watermelon Omen. *Antitrust Chronicle*, **10**.

Szyszczak, E. (2004). Public services in the new economy. In C. Graham and F. Smith, eds., *Competition, Regulation and the New Economy*. Hart Publishing, pp. 185–206.

Talbot, C. (2016). Ordoliberalism and balancing competition goals in the development of the European Union. *The Antitrust Bulletin*, 6(2), 264–289.
Temple Lang, J. (1989). European community competition law and member state action. *Northwestern Journal of International Law and Business*, 10(1), 114–132.
Temple Lang, J. (1994). European community constitutional law and the enforcement of community antitrust law. In H. Berry and J. S. Venit, eds., *Annual Proceedings. Fordham Corporate Law Institute*. Transnational Juris Publications, pp. 525–604.
Temple Lang, J. (1998). *FIDE Congress 1998: general Report on the Application of Community Competition Law on Enterprises by National Courts and National Authorities*.
Temple Lang, J. (2006). Commitment decisions and settlements with antitrust authorities and private parties under European antitrust law. In B. E. Hawk, ed., *Annual Proceedings of the Fordham Corporate Law Institute*. Kluwer Law International, pp. 265–324.
Temple Lang, J. (2014). *After Fifty Years – What I Needed for a Unified European Competition Policy?* Available at: https://papers.ssrn.com/sol3/papers.cfm?abstract_id=2519713.
The Attorney Generals National Committee to Study the Antitrust Laws, U.S. G.P.O. (1955).
Toader, C. (2017). The national judge and preliminary rulings: recent CJEU case law on Articles 101 and 102 TFEU. In A. Almăşan and P. Whelan, eds., *The Consistent Application of EU Competition Law*. Springer, pp. 165–175.
Torre, F. (2010). The 2006 guidelines on fines: reflections on the commission's practice. *World Competition*, **33**(3), 359–416.
Tóth, T. (2004). EU enlargement and modernisation of competition law: some national experiences. In D. Geradin, ed., *Modernisation and Enlargement: two Major Challenges for EC Competition Law*. Intersentia nv.
Tóth, T. (2013). *The Fall of Agricultural Cartel Enforcement in Hungary*. Available at: https://papers.ssrn.com/sol3/papers.cfm?abstract_id=2515967.
Townley, C. (2004). The liner shipping block exemptions in European law - has the tide turned. *World Competition*, **27**(1), 107–153.
Townley, C. (2009). *Article 81 EC and Public Policy*. Bloomsbury Publishing.
Townley, C. (2010). The goals of chapter I of the UKs competition act 1998. *Yearbook of European Law*, **29**(1), 307–360.
Townley, C. (2011). Which goals count in article 101 TFEU? Public policy and its discontents by Article 101 TFEU?, *European Competition Law Review*, **9**, 441–448.
Townley, C. (2018). *A Framework for European Competition Law: co-ordinated Diversity*. Hart Publishing.
Turner, D. F. (1990). The virtues and problems of antitrust law. *Antitrust Bulletin*, **35**, 297–310.
Turner, J. D. C. (2010). *Intellectual Property and EU Competition Law*. Oxford University Press.
Tyree, A. L. (1981). Fact content analysis of case law: methods and limitations. *Jurimetrics*, **22** (1), 1–33.
UAIPIT (2000). Act LVII on the Prohibition of Unfair and Restrictive Market Practices following the 2000 Amendment. English translation. Available in: http://www.uaipit.com/files/documentos/0000005992_Hungarian_Competition_Act_1996.pdf.
Van Bael, I. (1986). The antitrust settlement practice of the EEC commission. *Common Market Law Review*, **23**, 61–90.
Van Bael, I. (1993). Insufficient judicial control of EC competition law enforcement. In B. E. Hawk, ed., *Annual Proceedings of the Fordham Corporate Law Institute*. Fordham Corporate Law Institute, pp. 733–744.

Vane, H. (2015). 'Unprecedented' collaboration leaves Germany isolated on price parity clauses. *Global Competition Review*.

Várady, T. (1999). The emergence of competition law in (former) socialist countries. *The American Journal of Comparative Law*, **47**(2), 229–275.

Varju, M. and Papp, M. (2016). The crisis, national economic particularism and EU law: what can we learn from the Hungarian case? *Common Market Law Review*, **53**(6), 1647–1674.

Vedder, H. (2009). Of jurisdiction and justification; why competition is good for 'non-economic' goals, but may need to be restricted. *Competition Law Review*, **6**, 51–75.

Veljanovski, C. (2007). Cartel fines in Europe-law, practice and deterrence. *World Competition*, **30**(1), 65–86.

Venit, J. S. (1985). The commissions opposition procedure-between the Scylla of ultra vires and the Charybdis of perfume: legal consequences and tactical considerations. *Common Market Law Review*, **22**, 167–202.

Venit, J. S. (2003). Brave new world: the modernization and decentralization of enforcement under Articles 81 and 82 of the EC treaty. *Common Market Law Review*, 545–580.

Verstrynge, J.-F. (1989). The obligations of member states as regards competition in the EEC treaty. In B. E. Hawk, ed., *Annual Proceedings of the Fordham Corporate Law Institute*. Matthew Bender, pp. 1–43.

Vestager, M. (2016). Setting priorities in antitrust, Speech in GCLC, Brussels, 1 February 2016. Available at: http://ec.europa.eu/commission/2014-2019/vestager/announcements/setting-priorities-antitrust_en.pdf.

Vickers, J. (2017). Consequences of Brexit for competition law and policy. *Oxford Review of Economic Policy*, **33**, 70–78.

van der Vijver, T. (2012). Objective justification and Article 102 TFEU. *World Competition*, **35**(1), 55–76.

Vogel, L. (2012). *Global Competition Law, A Practitioners Guide*. LawLex.

Vogel, L. (2016). The recent application of EU and national competition law to distribution agreements: does competition law promote efficient distribution networks? *Journal of European Competition Law & Practice*, **7**(9), 628–640.

Vogelaar, F., Stuyck, J. and van Reeken, B. (2000). *Competition Law in the EU, its Member States and Switzerland.-Vol. 1: EC, France, Spain, Portugal, Italy, The Netherlands, Belgium and Switzerland*. Kluwer Law International.

Waarden, F. van and Drahos, M. (2002). Courts and (epistemic) communities in the convergence of competition policies. *Journal of European Public Policy*, **9**(6), 913–934.

Waelbroeck, D. (1986). New forms of settlement of antitrust cases and procedural safeguards: is regulation 17 falling into abeyance? *European Law Review*, **11**(4), 268–280.

Waelbroeck, D. and Davies, Z. (2018). Coty, clarifying competition law in the wake of Pierre Fabre. *Journal of European Competition Law & Practice*, **9**(7), 431–442.

Waelbroeck, M. (1988). Antitrust analysis under Articles 85 (1) and 85 (3). In B. Hawk, ed., *North American and Common Market Antitrust and Trade Laws 1987, Annual Proceedings of the Fordham Corporate Law Institute*. M. Bender, pp. 693–724.

Wagner-von Papp, F. (2012). Best and even better practices in commitment procedures after Alrosa: the dangers of abandoning the 'struggle for competition law'. *Common Market Law Review*, **49**(3), 929–970.

Wagner-von Papp, F. (2015). Preface: De Minimis. *Bulletin e-Competitions De minimis*, Article N° 72.

Wathelet, M. (2015). Commitment decisions and the paucity of precedent. *Journal of European Competition Law & Practice*, **6**(8), 553–555.

Webley, L. (2010). Qualitative approaches to empirical legal research. In P. Cane and H. Kritzer, eds., *The Oxford Handbook of Empirical Legal Research*. Oxford University Press, pp. 926–950.

Wendt, I. E. (2012). *EU Competition Law and Liberal Professions: an Uneasy Relationship?* Martinus Nijhoff Publishers.

Wesseling, R. (1999). The commission white paper on modernisation of EC antitrust law: unspoken consequences and incomplete treatment of alternative options. *European Competition Law Review*, **20**(8), 420–433.

Wesseling, R. (2000). *The Modernisation of EC Competition Law*. Hart Publishing.

Wessman, P. (1991). Competition law in Hungary – Act LXXXVI of 1990 on the prohibition of unfair market practices. *World Competition*, **15**(4), 17–25.

Whish, R. (2000). Regulation 2790/99: the commission's 'new style' Block Exemption for Vertical Agreements. *Common Market Law Review*, **37**(4), 887–924.

Whish, R. and Sufrin, B. (1987). Article 85 and the rule of reason. *Yearbook of European Law*, 7(1), 1–38.

Wijckmans, F. (2018). Coty Germany GmbH v Parfümerie Akzente GmbH: possibility in selective distribution system to Ban Sales via third-party platforms. *Journal of European Competition Law & Practice*, **9**(6), 373–375.

Wijckmans, F. and Tuytschaever, F. (2011). *Vertical Agreements in EU Competition Law*. Oxford University Press.

Wilks, S. (1993). *The metamorphosis of European competition policy*. In F. G. Snyder, ed., *European Community Law I*. New York University Press, pp. 270–293.

Wilks, S. (2005). Agency escape: decentralization or dominance of the European commission in the modernization of competition policy? *Governance*, 18(3), 431–452.

Wilks, S. and Bartle, I. (2002). The unanticipated consequences of creating independent competition agencies. *West European Politics*, **25**(1), 148–172.

Wils, W. P. J. (2004a). Regulation 1/2003: a reminder of the main issues. In D. Geradin, ed., *Modernisation and Enlargement: Two Major Challenges for EC Competition Law*. Intersentia, pp. 9–83.

Wils, W. P. J. (2004b). The combination of the investigative and prosecutorial funcion and the adjudicative function in EC antitrust enforcement: a legal and economic analysis. *World Competition*, **27**(2), 201–224.

Wils, W. P. J. (2005). *Principles of European Antitrust Enforcement*. Bloomsbury Publishing.

Wils, W. P. J. (2006a). Optimal antitrust fines: theory and practice. *World Competition*, **29**(2), 183–208.

Wils, W. P. J. (2006b). Settlements of EU antitrust investigations: commitment decisions under Article 9 of regulation No. 1/2003. *World Competition*, **29**(3), 345–366.

Wils, W. P. J. (2007). Leniency in antitrust enforcement: theory and practice. *Conferences on New Political Economy*, **24**(1), 203–248.

Wils, W. P. J. (2009). The relationship between public antitrust enforcement and private actions for damages. *World Competition*, **32**(1), 3–26.

Wils, W. P. J. (2011). Discretion and prioritisation in public antitrust enforcement, in particular EU antitrust enforcement. *World Competition*, **34**(3), 353–382.

Wils, W. P. J. (2013). Ten years of regulation 1/2003 – a retrospective. *Journal of European Competition Law & Practice*, 4(4), 293–301.

Wils, W. P. J. (2016). The use of leniency in EU cartel enforcement: an assessment after twenty years. *World Competition*, **39**(3), 327–388.

Wils, W. P. J. (2017). Competition authorities: towards more independence and prioritisation? *Romanian Review of European Law*, **2017**(2), 56–92.

WIPO (1990). Law No. LXXXVI of 1990 on the Prohibition of Unfair Market Practice. English translation. Available at: http://www.wipo.int/wipolex/en/details.jsp?id=2195.

WIPO (2006a). Act LVII on the Prohibition of Unfair and Restrictive Market Practices following the 2005 Amendment, English translation. Available at: http://www.wipo.int/edocs/lexdocs/laws/en/hu/hu085en.pdf.

WIPO (2006b). Commercial Code, English translation. Available at: http://www.wipo.int/wipolex/en/text.jsp?file_id=180801.

Witt, A. C. (2012). Public policy goals under EU competition law—now is the time to set the house in order. *European Competition Journal*, 8(3), 443–471.

Witt, A. C. (2016a). Restrictions on the use of third-party platforms in selective distribution agreements for luxury goods. *European Competition Journal*, **12**(2–3), 435–461.

Witt, A. C. (2016b). *The More Economic Approach to EU Antitrust Law*. Hart Publishing.

Witt, A. C. (2018). The enforcement of Article 101 TFEU–what has happened to the effects analysis? *Common Market Law Review*, **55**(2), 417–448.

Wolf, E. (1962). Cartel and monopoly legislation; Its application in the European economic community. *The American Journal of Comparative Law*, 1, 539–559.

Wolf, E. (1963). The role of the court of the European communities in the antitrust structure of the common market. *Fordham Law Review*, **31**(4), 621–638.

Wright, K. (2008). European commission opinions to national courts in antitrust cases: consistent application and the judicial-administrative relationship. PhD dissertation.

Wu, T. (2018). After consumer welfare, now what? The "protection of competition. *Competition Policy International*; Columbia Public Law Research Paper No. 14-608, available https://papers.ssrn.com/sol3/papers.cfm?abstract_id=3249173.

van der Zee, E. (2020). Quantifying benefits of sustainability agreements under Article 101 TFEU. *World Competition*, **43**(2), 189–208.

Ziegler, D. T. and Horváthy, B. (2017). Europeanization of the Hungarian legal order: from convergence to cancellation? In T. Hashimoto and M. Rhimes, eds., *Reviewing European Union Accession: unexpected Results, Spillover Effects, and Externalities*. Brill.

Zweigert, K. and Kötz, H. (1992). *Introduction to Comparative Law*. Oxford University Press.

Index

For EU product safety concerns, contact us at Calle de José Abascal, 56–1°, 28003 Madrid, Spain or eugpsr@cambridge.org.

www.ingramcontent.com/pod-product-compliance
Lightning Source LLC
LaVergne TN
LVHW011533200926
848484LV00001B/253

* 9 7 8 1 1 0 8 8 3 7 6 0 6 *